HOSPITALITY INDUSTRY
PURCHASING

HOSPITALITY INDUSTRY PURCHASING

Michael M. Coltman

VNR VAN NOSTRAND REINHOLD
New York

Library of Congress Catalog Card Number 89-21472
ISBN 0-442-00132-0

Printed in the United States of America

Van Nostrand Reinhold
115 Fifth Avenue
New York, New York 10003

Van Nostrand Reinhold International Company Limited
11 New Fetter Lane
London EC4P 4EE, England

Van Nostrand Reinhold
480 La Trobe Street
Melbourne, Victoria 3000, Australia

Nelson Canada
1120 Birchmount Road
Scarborough, Ontario M1K 5G4, Canada

16   15   14   13   12   11   10   9   8   7   6   5   4   3   2   1

Library of Congress Cataloging-in-Publication Data

Coltman, Michael M., 1930–
    Hospitality industry purchasing/Michael M. Coltman.
      p. cm.
    ISBN 0-442-00132-0
    1. Food—Purchasing. 2. Beverages—Purchasing. 3. Food service—Management. 4. Hospitality industry—Management. I. Title.
HD9000.5.C625 1990
647.94′068′7—dc20

89-21472
CIP

Contents

Preface

Many hospitality industry managers perceive purchasing as simply a matter of placing orders and assume they have little to gain by spending money on establishing a purchasing system. This view is probably more typical of small enterprises than large ones. Both small and large operations, however, can benefit from knowing the value that a coordinated purchasing system can offer and knowing what techniques are available to manage the purchasing function more effectively. A good purchasing system minimizes costs, eliminates poor-quality products, and guards against the unavailability of products when they are needed.

In earlier days, purchasing was often considered primarily as a quantity-, cost-, and quality-control function, even in large chain operations. Today, because some chain operations in both the accommodation and foodservice sectors of the hospitality industry are huge conglomerates, effective purchasing is often regarded as a part of their overall organizational and financial strategy. The reason is that, by reducing purchasing costs, net profit is increased. This increase, in turn, improves return on investment.

Of course, large organizations are able to implement economies of scale in their purchasing. Through their dollar volume, they can negotiate more effectively for lower prices and influence suppliers to guarantee supply and be more reliable in their delivery schedules. These large companies are also able to negotiate multiyear contracts and exclusive agreements.

In its broadest sense, purchasing includes knowing what products are needed, understanding distribution systems and the intermediaries who can provide needed products, being familiar with which suppliers can provide the highest-quality products required at the most favorable prices, negotiating with suppliers and receiving appropriate services from them, placing orders, receiving products, controlling inventory and production, and paying for products received.

Effective purchasing also includes knowing whether the purchasing system is effectively doing the job. This part is done through an ongoing process of evaluation by establishing measurable purchasing objectives (such as establishing prices the operation is prepared to pay, defining the quality of products needed for guest satisfaction, identifying quantities required, and purchasing from the best sources), determining whether those objectives have been met, and improving the purchasing system to make it even more effective.

Of necessity, this book is primarily concerned with the purchase of food and alcoholic beverages because they are, apart from labor, the major purchase costs that hospitality operations have. However, other costs, such as those for equipment, services, and supplies, are also addressed in this book.

1

The Basics of Purchasing

OBJECTIVES

- Define *purchasing*, and explain the impact of effective purchasing on cash flow.
- Explain the term *purchasing authority*, and differentiate between geographic and product responsibility in purchasing.
- List and briefly explain five purchasing department activities.
- Discuss purchasing department market research methods such as ABC analysis, product price and supply analysis, value analysis, and make-or-buy analysis.
- List major potential purchasing department objectives and the problems sometimes encountered in meeting these objectives.
- Define terms used in the distribution channel such as *breaker, wholesaler, manufacturer's agent, manufacturer's representative, commissary,* and *house account.*
- List and briefly explain the four economic values added in the distribution channel.

COST INCURRENCE

Powers and Powers (1984, p. 77) define *purchasing* as "the determination of your needs and the placement of orders with those suppliers who offer the lowest price for items of stated qualities." Thus, when goods are ordered or services contracted for, a cost is incurred. To minimize costs, therefore, more attention should be paid to the purchasing function than is probably the case in most hospitality enterprises. Perhaps one of the reasons for this lack of attention is that to have a part-time or full-time person responsible for purchasing on the payroll is an added cost that erodes profits. However, many large operations have on their payroll entire purchasing departments with several employees. These companies do not consider a purchasing department a cost center but rather a department that contributes to profits through effective purchasing. In other words, effective purchasing is generally considered to control and reduce overall company costs. Cost control is defined by Dittmer and Griffin (1984, p. 22) as "the process whereby managers attempt to regulate costs and guard against excessive costs."

Effect on Cash Flow

The major reason for establishing the most effective purchasing system possible in any operation concerns the effect of purchasing on cash flow. Products cost money, so obviously the lower the cost of products (while still maintaining a desired quality standard), the less cash is required, thus reducing the operation's cash outflow. This cash flow, however, can be affected by other matters negotiated by the purchasing department. If an astute purchaser can convince a supplier to extend credit terms from the normal 30 days to 60 days (without increasing the cost of the product), for example, the establishment has the use of these funds for a further month. These funds can then be used for other purposes or left in the bank in an interest-bearing account, thus increasing the operation's cash flow and net profit.

The quantity of products purchased and the timing of deliveries can also be used wisely to improve cash flow. For example, deferring purchases or buying in smaller quantities each time conserves cash. Note, however, that both of these tactics may create situations where not enough inventory is on hand for users. Also, in some cases increasing the quantity purchased above normal requirements can pay. For example, the higher the quantity purchased, the larger may be a price discount offered by the supplier. The cost saving (decreased cash outflow) in such a situation may have to be weighed against the extra costs of storage and/or interest paid on money borrowed to make the purchase.

Improving cash flow through more effective purchasing is very important to any organization. Assume that effective purchasing can reduce direct purchase costs by $1,000 a month. This $1,000 passes directly through to the bottom line of the income statement and increases profits by $1,000. If, in contrast, more effective marketing to generate sales produced a 10 percent profit on those sales, sales would have to be increased by $10,000 to generate an added profit equal to that saved on purchase costs.

THE PURCHASING DEPARTMENT

The purchasing department's role in the cost-control process is to make sure that supplies, equipment, and services are available to the operation in quantities appropriate to predetermined standards, at the right price, and at a minimum cost to meet desired standards. According to Kotschevar (1975, p. 1),

The buyer must know not only a lot about the items he procures, but he must know thoroughly his market, buying procedures, market trends, and how the materials he purchases are produced, processed, and moved to market. Buying is not order giving. It involves planning, forecasting, organizing, controlling, and other management-level functions. The market in which the buyer functions is involved, frequently international in scope, and so complex that one can spend a lifetime studying only a small part of it.

Note that for the sake of simplicity from this point on the term *product* will be used to cover both physical products (such as food, supplies, and equipment) as well as services (such as janitorial or grounds maintenance).

Purchasing Authority

Generally, those responsible for purchasing have the authority to commit the establishment's funds to buy required products. Sometimes a maximum dollar amount for any individual purchase may be established, beyond which a higher level of authority is required before proceeding with the purchase. In the case of a small operation in which the owner/manager does the purchasing, the buying authority limit is whatever that owner/manager decides. If the owner/manager delegates that authority (for example, to a department head), then the limits of that authority must be clearly spelled out, including a maximum value that is allowed for any single purchase. If the delegated authority is likely to be exceeded for a particular purchase, then a higher level of managerial or supervisory approval is required. As Kelly (1976, p. 15) states it,

> Without clearly defined buying authority assigned to each person handling the purchasing responsibility, and without established approval lines indicated before the purchase, there is always the unpleasant possibility of a buyer overstepping not only his authority but also his competency in making commitments which will be legally binding on his employer.

Those responsible for purchasing may have authority to question individual purchase requests with reference to such matters as the product's use or its specifications. They may also be required to prepare reports for management, design necessary control forms, ensure smooth cooperation with operating departments, and establish fair practices with suppliers.

Defining Responsibility and Authority

Regardless of an establishment's size and organization, it must therefore define the responsibility and authority for purchasing, keep the number of people with that responsibility to a minimum, and ensure that those without authority do not assume a purchaser's role. This last possibility is particularly a problem in large organizations, where suppliers may try to bypass authorized purchasers to influence others in the organization to be involved in the purchasing decision.

Even though a small enterprise may not need or be able to afford a separate purchasing department, the person responsible for purchasing—whether the chef (in the case of some food purchases), the storekeeper (in the case of other food purchases and general supplies), or the general manager (in the case of capital items such as furniture and equipment)—can benefit from applying some of the purchasing practices and procedures discussed in this and other chapters.

Geographic or Product Responsibility

In large organizations in which a purchasing department may have several buyers authorized to make purchases, a decision needs to be made about whether to assign buyers a geographic territory (such as local, regional, or national) or assign them responsibility for a specific product group or groups. With geographic responsibility, the purchaser, for example, may be assigned to make all purchases (regardless of product) that can be made locally, and another buyer is assigned all products that cannot be purchased locally. With a product responsibility, each purchaser is assigned products of a similar type (such as paper and cleaning supplies or meat and poultry items) to be responsible for purchasing regardless of geographic source.

According to Kelly (1976, p. 17) "a company that organizes its purchasing responsibility along commodity lines tends to develop the most efficient procurement methods." The justification for this statement is that a purchaser who specializes in a particular product or group of similar products becomes more proficient in purchasing them, knows more about these products, can more readily anticipate market trends, knows where to seek alternative sources of supply, and should be able to find substitute products (where they are suitable and still provide value for the money).

Obviously, product responsibility purchasing is just not practical in small firms because only one or two persons may be involved in purchasing. Nevertheless, by following established purchasing procedures, any size of operation can avoid purchasing pitfalls such as panic buying, over- or short-purchasing, buying by price rather than by a combination of quality and price, pressure buying, or—probably quite common—satisfied buying, in which the purchaser operates under the assumption that no improvements in either quality or price can be achieved.

Management Function

According to Virts (1987, p. 6), purchasing or procurement is "a broad series of management activities that are designed to maximize value for the company and its guests." Riegel and Reid (1988, p. 25) state further that "purchasing is now generally recognized as an integral part of corporate strategy, since it affects not only profit margins but also asset turnover, and through this, return on investment." In other words, the purchasing function is one that covers all those activities involved in the management of products before they are received and as they are received, and how they are stored, issued, and used after they are received.

PURCHASING ACTIVITIES

The purchasing management function involves a variety of different activities. Although the size of organization dictates whether or not purchasing department personnel will be fully responsible for all these activities, they will be at least partly responsible for some, while fully responsible for others. Some of these activities are introduced briefly at this point to provide a broad overview of what purchasing involves. These activities are discussed in more depth in later chapters.

Purchase Requisitioning

This activity covers the processing of purchase requisition forms completed by authorized employees in an organization's various departments to advise purchasing department personnel that additional and/or new products are required.

Maintaining Sufficient Inventory

Inventory management is required to ensure that sufficient inventory is on hand so that a stock-out (running out of inventory) does not occur. This concern must be balanced against the need to minimize what is carried in inventory to reduce the cost of money tied up this way. This balancing requirement is easy to state but often difficult to do. Nevertheless, it is part of the purchasing management function to try to maintain an appropriate balance for each item in inventory.

Establishing Quantity Needs

This activity requires knowing what is presently available in inventory and forecasting future requirements to determine present quantities to be purchased. Decisions concerning product requirement quantities are usually made in consultation with product-use managers or department heads.

Establishing Quality Required

The quality of most products required (such as food, beverages, and guest supplies) is dictated primarily by customer needs. These needs have to be assessed and evaluated against the budget available for product purchases to determine the product quality standards to be used in purchasing.

Preparing Specifications

Specifications are detailed descriptions of the products needed. Preparing specifications sometimes requires a considerable amount of time (generally by purchasing department employees and product users) to make sure those specifications properly describe the product quality standards required.

Negotiating with Suppliers

Negotiating with suppliers requires a knowledge of the tactics and strategies that can be used in supplier negotiations to maximize the quality and minimize the cost of products purchased. Negotiation can also include discussions and mutual agreement about supplier services such as frequency of delivery and payment terms.

Selecting Suppliers

In selecting suppliers, information must be available about them. This information covers such matters as prices, quality of products, and quality of supplier services, such as delivery dependability and frequency.

Purchase Order Processing

Purchase orders are written documents provided to suppliers detailing such matters as descriptions of products wanted, in what quantities, at what prices, from which supplier, and on what date.

Order Expediting

Order expediting covers the action of following up on orders placed with suppliers to ensure that needed products are received on-site as they are required.

Receiving Products

At the point of receiving products, ownership of them normally (but not always) passes from supplier to purchaser. Some careful checks are required at this point to ensure that quality, quantity, and prices of products received are as specified. In some small operations the purchaser may also be the receiver, but in large operations the receiving functions are separated (with the receiver reporting to the comptroller) to make fraud more difficult. In the latter situation, the purchasing department may still have some receiving responsibility (for example, product quality checks).

Storing Products and Controlling Inventory

In order to control usage costs, as soon as receiving inspections have been made, products need to be stored under the right conditions to eliminate or minimize loss from deterioration, spoilage, pilferage, and theft. Inventory control procedures and forms have to be established. In small operations the purchasing, receiving, and storing functions may all be handled by one person. In large operations receiving and storekeeping may be separated from purchasing, with the accounting office having authority over the receiving and storekeeping employee(s). In very large establishments separate employees may be involved in receiving and in storekeeping. Nevertheless, just as the purchaser continues to have an interest in receiving controls (without having full responsibility for them), he or she also continues to have an interest in the storekeeping function (for example, in maintaining appropriate inventory levels).

Dispensing with Surplus Products

Sometimes items in inventory are surplus to requirements. For example, a menu item may be discontinued, meaning that items in inventory previously used to produce that menu item are no longer required. In other situations, a new item of equipment is purchased to replace an old one, meaning the organization needs to dispose of the old one. In these situations, purchasing employees are normally responsible for arranging for the sale of these surplus products, a reversal of their usual role.

Maintaining Adequate Records

Appropriate purchasing department records must be maintained. These records include such things as information about past purchase orders and orders in process, about past, present, and prospective suppliers, and about other similar purchasing function information items.

Maintaining Good Supplier Relations

For public relations and other reasons, good supplier-purchaser relationships are essential. This activity involves maintaining a professional and ethical relationship and being aware of appropriate legal considerations related to the purchasing function. Keeping every supplier happy is impossible, but some purchasers try to do it by spending at least some money with each reliable supplier. Fostering good public relations can also be done by keeping potential suppliers informed of the purchaser's changing needs.

Administering the Purchasing Department

In small operations the owner or manager handles the purchasing role as well as other management responsibilities. In other cases, this responsibility is delegated by the owner or manager to individual department heads (such as the chef for food purchasing and food cost control), and the need for purchasing administration is minimized. Most large establishments, however, have a separate purchasing department and thus a need for purchasing department organization and administration. In other words, proper administration must be in effect to control all the various activities for which the purchasing department is responsible.

MARKET RESEARCH

A major aspect of the purchasing department's activities requires market research. This market research involves such matters as gathering information about presently purchased products, investigating new products, and evaluating changing market conditions. Some of the more important market research areas are discussed in the following sections.

The ABC Analysis

Analysis of many organizations' purchases has shown that as few as 20 percent of items purchased represent as much as 80 percent of the total dollar value of all items purchased. This analysis suggests that most of the purchaser's attention should be focused on those items that constitute the 20 percent of all items purchased, and less time and energy should be spent on the remaining 80 percent. Products should be divided into A, B, and C categories—with the A category representing the 20 percent of products that are 80 percent of total dollar volume.

To use this method, a list of all products in inventory along with their costs and annual usage quantities must be prepared. Quantities are then multiplied by costs to arrive at total dollar usage value product by product. Usage values are then categorized as A, B, or C. For example, consider the partial inventory list in Table 1-1.

Note that items 3 and 4 are categorized as class A because the combination of the quantity used and their cost gives a large total value. These A products are generally high-cost and high-usage items that can be easily identified and monitored in most establishments. These items deserve the most attention because a change in either use or cost can have a substantial effect on inventory. Ordering fewer of these items at a time may also be a good idea because less money is then tied up in inventory at any one time. Purchasing research can then be concentrated on finding out more about those items, comparing supplier prices, determining price and avail-

Table 1-1. Partial Inventory List for ABC Analysis

Item	Item Cost	Annual Usage	Total Value	Class
1	$ 2.00	500	$ 1,000	B
2	0.50	1,000	500	C
3	30.00	700	21,000	A
4	15.00	400	6,000	A
5	0.10	2,200	220	C

ability trends, and seeking new substitute products that represent better value for the money.

In Table 1-1 items 2 and 5 constitute only a small part of total inventory value and are categorized as C products. Time and money spent controlling these items may not be worth the effort, and purchasing a year's supply of these items at a time would have little impact on total inventory value. Item 1 is categorized as B, and the amount of effort to be made in controlling B products is a matter of judgment.

Price and Product Supply Analysis

Price and product supply analysis is primarily concerned with forecasting the trends of these two factors. In other words, the purchasing department has a responsibility to research and predict what products will be available and what their prices are likely to be for several months into the future. Unsophisticated research can be used by questioning suppliers about what they know of such trends. More sophisticated research involves projecting past trends into the future on a graph. At a more advanced level, computers can be programmed to do this kind of research, which can be limited to the items of most importance as determined by ABC analysis.

Value Analysis

According to Gee (1975, p. 53), *value analysis* is an "organized, systematic study of the function of a material, part, component, or system, to identify areas of unnecessary cost that can be eliminated without impairing the capacity of the item to satisfy its objective." In other words, the objective of value analysis is to see if the purchase value of a product can be increased. Because the value of a product is a combination of its cost and quality (including the quality of supplier services), value can be affected in a number of ways. If the cost of a product declines, for example, its "value" increases. If the product cost remains the same and supplier service increases (for example, a longer period of cost-free maintenance on an equipment purchase), value again increases. The intent of value analysis is to manipulate the variables to see if value can be improved.

Value analysis also attempts to eliminate unnecessary material or parts of a product that would incur an additional cost. If a high-quality product is not required, then the product is costing more than it should. Even though every product in an establishment can be analyzed for value, generally only those on which larger amounts of money are spent are worth analyzing. Again, ABC analysis can be useful in pinpointing these products. However, even an individual food purchase item can be analyzed critically. For example, does a restaurant need the same quality of tomato for a soup, stew, casserole, or similar dish compared to the standardized size and quality required for a grilled tomato to accompany a steak? Obviously, uniformity of size and appearance are considerably less important in the former, and therefore a lower-quality tomato should be purchased at a lower cost.

Another example might be the purchase of new calculators for the accounting office. The purchaser needs to analyze the exact features required on the calculators. Do they need floating decimals and square root functions? If yes, do they all need them, or are those optional features only necessary at one or two work stations? Do they need both electronic display and tape printout? Is the equipment really required or only desirable? What alternative models might be available? Would more sophisticated models allow a reduction in labor costs? These questions are only some of those that might be asked in that particular instance of value analysis.

The purchaser should not, however, make substantive changes to the purchase of an item in order to increase value without first consulting the product's user about these changes and the effect they may have on work performance. Good reasons may exist why the proposed changes should not be made. Note also that value is a subjective matter that is often in the eyes of the beholder, or the hands of the user.

Another aspect of value analysis with particular reference to food products is packaging. The cost of the packages of some products can be as high as the value of the ingredients in that package. For example, on a comparative basis per pound, the cost of the actual product in basic rather than fancy containers and in large rather than small containers is normally less.

Make-or-Buy Analysis

Another type of research is a make-or-buy analysis. For example, should a restaurant buy a whole beef carcass and do its own in-house butchering (assuming it has the labor resources to do so) to obtain the meat cuts it wants (the "make" decision) or purchase prefabricated, preportioned meat cut to specifications by the supplier? In this type of analysis, all the costs of each alternative must be calculated and other factors considered before the decision is made. For example, can the supplier provide the operation with exactly what it wants in prefabricated, preportioned meat products? Will the size be consistent? Can regular delivery be guaranteed?

PURCHASING OBJECTIVES

Each establishment's purchasing department should have purchasing objectives. These objectives may be determined by the general manager or developed by the purchasing department before they are discussed with and approved by the general manager. According to Stefanelli (1985, p. 45) there are five major potential purchasing department objectives.

1. Maintain an adequate inventory so that products are not out of stock between deliveries.
2. Minimize investment in inventory by not carrying too much and losing the interest on money that could otherwise be left in a savings account. (Although this objective appears to be in conflict with the first, the purchaser's task is to find the right balance, sometimes referred to as *optimizing*, between the two objectives.)
3. Maintain quality standards (within limits) of products purchased to meet quality standards desired by the organization. This objective is not always easy to achieve because, for example, the quality of some fresh food products can vary considerably from day to day.
4. Obtain the lowest possible prices, given the quality standards desired. Remember, again, that "price" should be related to total value received and not just out-of-pocket costs.
5. Maintain the organization's competitive position by obtaining at least the same value (if not more value) from suppliers than the organization's competitors have received. This objective may also not be easy to achieve. Suppliers can change the services (as well as their prices within certain legal limits) from one purchaser to another, and discovering this difference may not be easy. Obviously, if a competitor receives a better value for its purchase dollars, it has a competitive advantage.

Problems in Meeting Objectives

Problems frequently arise that make achieving objectives difficult and sometimes impossible for a purchaser. Some of these problems are:

- Purchasers are given responsibility but insufficient authority to act to achieve objectives. Alternatively, purchasers may have authority but insufficient time to achieve objectives. This lack of time often happens in small establishments when the purchasing job is combined with some other.
- Communication difficulties occur with users in coordinating their conflicting needs, with users who make unreasonable demands, or with users who do not understand the purchasing department's role. Note, for example, the earlier dis-

cussion concerning purchase cost savings adding directly to bottom-line net profits. User department heads often have a greater interest in increasing sales at the
expense of costs.

- Suppliers' sales representatives require too much of a purchaser's time, thus reducing the time that a purchaser has to do market research. Time must be spent
with salespeople in order to obtain product information, but this time should not
be excessive.
- Suppliers' sales representatives use backdoor selling by contacting a product's
user (for example, a department head) to influence that user to convince the
purchaser to order that product rather than some other one providing better value.
- Management-approved suppliers may not deliver when promised, try to deliver
products that are not up to quality standards required, or substitute products.

DISTRIBUTION SYSTEMS

Traditionally, a general lack of knowledge about distribution systems has caused
hospitality industry purchasers to pay higher prices than is necessary. Frequently,
the short-run needs of day-to-day operations take precedence over the long-run cost
savings that knowledge of different distribution systems would allow. Because organizations in the distribution system have varying products and distribution capabilities, those suppliers who suit the requirements of an individual hospitality
operation should be sought out. Knowledgeable purchasers identify ways to optimize the value of the products purchased from the current distribution network; for
example, they negotiate longer-term contracts (rather than short-term ones that suit
only immediate needs) and identify suppliers who offer the best value for purchase
dollars spent. The objective should be to maximize quality, service, and price—all
of which translate into value.

Most products purchased by hospitality businesses have a relatively standard
pattern of distribution. Generally, the channel of distribution is from a source,
through one or more intermediaries, to the hospitality establishment.

Sources of Products

Three sources of product supply can be identified: growers (farmers or ranchers),
manufacturers, and fabricators.

The growers provide raw food items such as fruit, vegetables, and animal products. Supply and demand have an important effect on product prices at this level,
and these price fluctuations are passed on to the manufacturers and fabricators. As
a general rule, small hospitality businesses seldom deal with source growers unless
they buy directly from a farmers' market.

Manufacturers (or processors) are those who take raw food and/or other raw
materials and process them further (for example, a meat packer who takes slaugh-

tered sides of beef and butchers them into more practical, smaller cuts). The term *breaker* is used to describe a company that buys carload lots of raw meat carcasses and breaks them into wholesale cuts that are then sold to wholesalers. Other manufacturers take nonfood raw materials (such as steel or wood) and convert them to equipment and furniture.

Fabricators are differentiated from manufacturers in that they take the products from growers and/or manufacturers and process them further. For example, a fabricator might take produce from a farmer, process it, and then seal it in a can produced by a manufacturer.

Intermediaries

Within the channel of distribution (from sources to users) for most products, several major intermediaries can be identified. Sometimes the functions of these various intermediaries can overlap. Some of these intermediaries are discussed.

Wholesalers

Wholesalers are also known as *dealers, purveyors,* or *distributors.* A *wholesaler* is a firm that purchases items from growers, manufacturers, or fabricators and sells them to hospitality enterprises or to retailers (such as supermarkets) who then sell the items to the hospitality firm as well as to individual consumers. Sometimes a wholesaler buys a product and then processes it in some way before selling it to the hospitality enterprise. For example, a wholesaler may buy truckloads of a particular product and then repackage it in smaller containers to sell it to individual hotels or restaurants. To many hospitality firms, wholesalers are often the most important link in the distribution chain because they are the intermediaries purchasers usually deal with more than any other. They buy, store, sell, and deliver products to the hospitality industry end-user. Moreover, hospitality purchasers receive most of their information about new product availability and changing market conditions from the wholesaler.

Full-service wholesalers carry a wide variety of products. Some provide the purchaser with the convenience of one-stop shopping by selling a broad range of items such as frozen foods, staple grocery items, china, glassware, and silverware, cleaning and paper materials, and even kitchen equipment, office equipment, and guest room furnishings. These large firms are usually regional or national ones that serve a wide variety of hospitality enterprise customers.

Limited-function wholesalers carry a much reduced variety of products. Some of these limited-function wholesalers are local; others may be regional or national. The trend today is that local independent wholesalers are being absorbed by the regional and national organizations.

Some wholesalers are owned by large hospitality chains that established them or took them over to reduce the cost of products distributed to individual operations within their chain. Some of these hospitality industry-owned wholesalers also sell the products they handle to hospitality organizations not part of that chain.

Brokers

A *broker* is a sales company that represents and promotes the products from one or more sources. A broker does not actually buy products from sources or directly sell them to other intermediaries or end-users. In other words, brokers do not have title to the goods at any time. Their function is to put buyers in contact with sellers. They often work closely with sales representatives of wholesalers who sell their products to end-users. They also do not normally represent manufacturers or fabricators with similar product lines that might create a conflict of interest. The broker's territory is usually geographically defined, and he or she normally receives a commission varying from 3 to 5 percent of sales. Brokers are typical of both the food and nonfood supplies side of the distribution channel to the hospitality industry.

A special type of broker is the *field broker,* who generally represents growers of fresh produce and provides a consolidation and distribution service between grower and purchaser. According to Kotschevar (1975, p. 11):

> Many institutions still must purchase from wholesalers or brokers where the markup may be 25 percent of the sale price. Because of this, a buyer may see produce, chickens, meat, or other items advertised by retailers at prices lower than he can buy from his broker. This is possible because a chain may purchase a number of carloads of chickens and sell them at cost or below cost as leaders, whereas the small institution may purchase only several cases from a broker who similarly buys a small supply.

Manufacturer's Representatives

A manufacturer's representative, sometimes known as a *commission house,* goes a step beyond a broker. The representative generally carries products in inventory and delivers them to buyers or end-users. Such a representative takes title to the products carried in inventory and can control the prices for which those products are sold. These representatives often work closely with the sales representatives of the manufacturer and/or fabricator, particularly when introducing new products. The representative's job is to seek out markets and satisfy the needs of the customers in that market. These representatives are typical of the equipment and furniture side of the distribution channel, as well as of both perishable and nonperishable food products.

Manufacturer's Agents

A manufacturer's agent differs from a manufacturer's representative in that he or she generally works for only one manufacturer or fabricator and, as an employee, represents that source in a limited geographic area. Agents do not take title to the goods or establish their selling prices. They function as account representatives (salespersons) for their company. Some large source companies may produce a wide range of products, but their agents often specialize in only a few and can thus concentrate their expertise on those limited products. They generally work on a commission that can range from 2 to 20 percent.

Sales Agents

Sales agents or representatives are the same as manufacturer's agents in many ways, but they are generally differentiated by representing a manufacturer's, fabricator's, or wholesaler's entire inventory of products. They normally work on a commission basis. Sales agents who represent manufacturers or fabricators may sell to wholesalers who then sell to hospitality industry purchasers. Most hospitality purchasers deal with sales agents (primarily representing wholesalers) on a day-to-day basis.

Distribution Flows

Products can flow from sources to users in many ways, either directly or through one or more intermediaries. For example, Figure 1-1 illustrates the many possible distribution flows for food products.

House Accounts

The term *house accounts* is used to describe a hospitality operation that purchases from a wholesaler without the wholesaler having a sales agent regularly calling on that operation. A house account situation is most likely to occur when a particular wholesaler carries an inventory of standard products that can be ordered easily by telephone. This practice is common in the hospitality industry with items purchased daily such as bakery goods, dairy products, and fresh fruits and vegetables.

Purchasing Alternatives

Generally, small hospitality operations do most (if not all) of their purchasing from wholesalers and rarely deal with brokers and manufacturer's representatives. Large organizations, because of their purchasing volume, frequently deal with all types of

Possible Food Product Distribution Channels

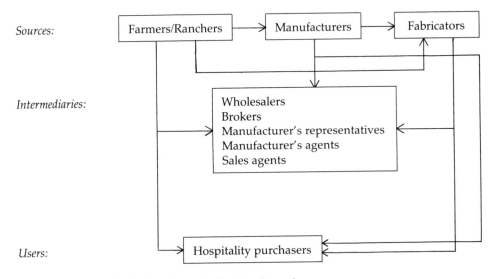

Figure 1-1.   Possible food product distribution channels.

intermediaries, even source growers. They can thus achieve economies of scale in their purchasing.

Self-Distribution

Some large hospitality organizations (particularly chain operations) own their own distribution facilities to help reduce the costs of transportation of products to their individual units. In some cases, they also partly or fully own manufacturing and fabricator companies that produce products they need and may even sell these products to competitor hospitality operations. Some large restaurant chains have also been known to own farms and ranches to guarantee a continuous supply of high-quality fresh produce, beef, and poultry.

Commissaries

Some large restaurant chain organizations operate a commissary to partly or fully process food items (such as soups, sauces, hamburgers, salad ingredients, and bakery items) from a raw to a fabricated state, which they then distribute to their individual operations. This practice allows individual units in the chain to reduce the purchase cost of food and also to reduce their need to produce food on-site and thus lower labor costs. Some commissaries also sell these processed food products to competitive operations. According to Virts (1987, p. 21), the growth of hospitality industry commissaries slowed dramatically when fast-food restaurants appeared because "a commissary requires a regional concentration of retail stores, all of which use similar menus. It became economically impractical to expand the commissary system nationally to compete with the cost-efficient distribution systems used by the fast-food chains."

Alcoholic Beverage Distribution

A special situation exists with alcoholic beverage distribution. Distributors of these products operate under legal requirements that are carefully controlled by one or more levels of government. In most states, the manufacturers (distillers, vintners, and brewers) are not allowed to sell their products directly to the hospitality industry or to other retailers or consumers. They must sell to specially licensed distributors or wholesalers who sell to the hospitality market. As a result, the purchaser frequently has little control over and discretion in the purchasing function for these products.

Suppliers

Because of the variety of potential distribution channel members that a hospitality industry purchaser can contact (depending on the circumstances) for needed products, these various members will be referred to generally from this point on as *suppliers*.

VALUES ADDED IN THE DISTRIBUTION CHANNEL

As products move from sources to end-users, they take on more value. Value adds a cost to the product. For example, if a supplier buys food from a source and processes and packages it, time is required for this to occur before the finished item is sold. During this time the supplier's money is tied up in inventory, which has to be financed, and as a result that money is not earning interest as it would if left in a bank. This cost is obviously built into the supplier's product selling price. Economists identify four utilities or values that are added as products travel through the channel of distribution.

Time Value

Time value allows a purchaser to buy a product from a supplier (such as a wholesaler) at the time it is desired. Consider the time needed if purchasers had to visit the original source (such as a farm) to buy products as they are needed. Product availability, however, adds a cost for processing, transportation, and storage. Storage costs increase if the product must be refrigerated or frozen. Storage always involves the risk of spoilage and the possibility that potential purchasers will not buy everything that is available. These costs are again built into selling prices. Large hospitality chain operations may take over part of the storage function themselves if they operate their own commissaries and thus reduce costs without necessarily reducing value.

Form Value

Form value allows a product to be purchased in the desired form (for example, peeled potatoes rather than unprocessed ones). Packaging is also a form value. Because purchasers like to buy products in various types and sizes of containers, depending on their operation's needs, producers must carry a variety of different packages for the same basic product. This value costs money that the eventual purchaser must pay.

Place Value

Place value allows most products to be delivered to the receiving dock of a hospitality business. In other words, the value is added by the cost (and convenience) of transportation provided by the supplier. The cost of this value increases when products must be moved in refrigerated or frozen vehicles. Transportation costs can be reduced in some cases. For example, a restaurant owner might use his or her own vehicle to pick up supplies from a wholesaler and thus receive a price discount. However, the restaurant operator must consider the compensating costs of owning and operating his or her own vehicle. Also, should a restaurant be in the transportation business? Would the time used be better spent managing the restaurant? Many large chain operations are, nevertheless, in the distribution and transportation business because they consider they can make money (and achieve a higher value) by doing this work. For example, they buy directly from the source, deliver to their own distribution center or commissary, process the products further in some cases, and then distribute them to the chain's member hotels or restaurants with their own delivery vehicles.

Information Value

Information value helps a purchaser make decisions when comparing similar products. Federal government regulations concerning information apply to any food products packaged in closed containers. However, the purchaser must know the law regarding this information. If, for example, the label states that a product is "fancy," then the purchaser can assume that the product meets the requirements of

FOODSERVICE MANAGEMENT MERCHANDISING

You want to serve the best foods available. That includes Washington State apples. These apples are regarded as the highest quality and consistency available. And, they're not just a fall fruit either—they're available virtually year round. Here are some spectacular ways to include Washington apples on your menu:

🍎 Serve a new version of a favorite, deep-fried sandwich—a Monte Apple Cristo! Simply alternate layers of sliced turkey, Washington Golden Delicious apples, cheese (Monterey Jack or Swiss) and ham, then dip in your favorite batter and deep-fry or grill. The apple adds a sweet and tender crunch to this popular sandwich.

🍎 Add thin slices of Golden Delicious apples in place of pineapple to a favorite Canadian-style bacon or ham pizza.

🍎 Try a new twist on apple pie—pile a sheet pan high with Golden Delicious apple slices topped with a mixture of flour, sugar and cinnamon to make a crunchy topping. Serve warm or cold with whipped cream, ice cream or a cheddar cheese slice.

🍎 Try an elegant fresh apple tart. Prepare a standard pie crust or sponge cake in a tart pan, fill with a mapley cream cheese/sour cream mixture, then top with alternating thin slices of Red and Golden Delicious apples arranged in circles. Glaze immediately (to prevent apple browning) with melted apple jelly or orange marmalade and chill until serving.

🍎 Add grated Golden Delicious apples to your favorite spicy cupcake mixture. Apples add texture, flavor and freshness to the cupcakes.

🍎 Add bacon bits and grated Golden Delicious apples to the house cheddar cheese soup just before serving. The apples complement the cheese flavor, and along with bacon, provide body and richness to the soup. Your customers will be pleased with the extra ingredients, too.

🍎 Add Red and Golden Delicious apple chunks to your fresh fruit salads, chicken or turkey salads, curried rice salad or cold pasta salad. Washington State apples are adaptable to most salads, and add crunch and flavor your customers will appreciate.

Information value can be provided by producer associations (Courtesy: Washington State Apple Commission).

the U.S. Fancy federal grade. However, a label that simply states "highest quality" is not illegal, even though this descriptive term has no regulatory meaning.

As Hinich and Staelin state (1980, p. 22), "Information only has value if consumers use the information in making decisions. This view is in contrast to the view that information has value . . . in and of itself." For example, if a California wine bottle label specifies that the wine is made from a particular grape variety (such as Chardonnay), then California wine law specifies that at least 50 percent of the grapes used must be Chardonnay. Thus, the value of this California law is useful only if the purchaser knows the law and uses the label information to decide whether or not to buy that type of varietal wine.

Cost of Values

These values add a surprising amount to the price of the end-product for some products. For example, the price a farmer might receive for the amount of wheat that goes into a loaf of bread might be only a few cents out of the perhaps two dollars the purchaser eventually pays. Because of the extreme cost of these added values, some small operators believe they should take over some of the distribution functions themselves and thus save money. Two arguments can be made against this. First, they only consider and use the costs that support their decision to justify this approach. Second, distribution intermediaries are experts in their field and can usually provide services (added values) that the independent entrepreneur cannot.

DISCUSSION QUESTIONS

1. In your own words, define *purchasing*.
2. Explain the impact of effective purchasing on an operation's cash flow.
3. Explain what is meant by the term *purchasing authority*.
4. Differentiate between geographic and product responsibility in purchasing.
5. List, and briefly explain, five activities for which a purchasing department normally has responsibility.
6. Discuss ABC analysis as part of a purchasing department's market research. Explain the major benefit.
7. Explain price and product supply analysis as part of a purchasing department's market research.
8. Describe what value analysis is as part of a purchasing department's market research.
9. Give an example (other than that described in the chapter) of make-or-buy analysis as part of a purchasing department's market research.
10. List three major potential objectives of a purchasing department.
11. Briefly list and discuss two problems that a purchasing department sometimes has in meeting objectives.

12. In the food distribution channel, what is a *breaker?*
13. Differentiate between a full-service and a limited-function wholesaler.
14. How does a manufacturer's agent differ from a manufacturer's representative?
15. From a supplier's perspective, define the term *house account.*
16. Explain how a commissary fits into the product distribution channel.
17. List, and briefly explain, the four economic values added in the distribution channel.

PROBLEMS

1. Visit the purchasing department of a hotel, large restaurant, or institution (for example, a hospital or college) and discuss with the purchasing manager his or her perception of the role and objectives of the purchasing department in that organization. Ask questions such as the following: Do buyers have a job description? What spending authority do they have? Is purchasing responsibility by product or by geography? Can buyers question department heads about their stated needs? What forms are used? (Obtain blank samples if possible.) What market research does the organization do? What reports does the purchasing manager prepare?

    Write a one-page report of your findings, including comments about how effective that purchasing department is in carrying out its role. (Do not comment about any forms you obtain, but retain them for possible use in problems in later chapters.)

2. Visit a local wholesale supplier to the hospitality industry. Discuss with the sales manager or other responsible individual the role that he or she perceives that supplier plays in the distribution channel to the hospitality industry. What services does the wholesaler provide (in addition to supplying products) to hospitality industry purchasers? Discuss what added economic values (such as repackaging of products, providing information, and so forth) that wholesaler provides in the distribution chain. Write a one-page report of your findings.

3. Visit a large hotel or chain operation commissary that provides some of its own economic values. If no such commissary is in your area, find a hospitality operation that provides some of its own economic values (such as providing its own transportation or butchering its own meat on site). Discuss with a person such as the general manager or purchasing manager in that organization how they rationalize providing that particular economic value themselves. Write a short report of your findings, add your own comments, and explain why you agree or disagree with the organization providing this economic value for itself.

REFERENCES AND SUGGESTED READINGS

Dittmer, Paul R., and Gerald G. Griffin. 1984. *Principles of Food, Beverage & Labor Cost Controls for Hotels and Restaurants.* New York: Van Nostrand Reinhold.

Gee, Chuck Y. 1975. Effective Purchasing Management. *Cornell Hotel and Restaurant Administration Quarterly* 16(3):52–55, 69.

Hinich, Melvin J., and Richard Staelin. 1980. *Consumer Protection Legislation and the U.S. Food Industry.* New York: Pergamon, pp. 22–26.

Kelly, Hugh J. 1976. *Food Service Purchasing: Principles and Practices.* New York: Lebhar-Friedman, pp. 1–7, 9–17, 183–88, 207–11.

Kotschevar, Lendal H. 1975. *Quantity Food Purchasing.* New York: John Wiley.

———, and Charles Levinson. 1988. *Quantity Food Purchasing.* New York: Macmillan, pp. 1–12.

Powers, Thomas F., and Jo Marie Powers. 1984. *Food Service Operations: Planning and Control.* New York: John Wiley.

Riegel, Carl D., and R. Dan Reid. 1988. Food-Service Purchasing: Corporate Practices. *Cornell Hotel and Restaurant Administration Quarterly* 29(1): 25–29.

Stefanelli, John M. 1985. *Purchasing: Selection and Procurement for the Hospitality Industry.* New York: John Wiley, pp. 3–7, 11–20, 39–48.

Virts, William B. 1987. *Purchasing for Hospitality Operations.* East Lansing, Mich.: The Educational Institute of the American Hotel & Motel Association, pp. 3–11, 13–22.

Warfel, M. C., and Frank H. Waskey. 1979. *The Professional Food Buyer.* Berkeley, Calif.: McCutchan, pp. 1–13, 15–31, 47–57, 59–69.

2

Legal and Other Forces

OBJECTIVES

- Discuss how supply and demand affect product prices.
- Discuss how political, ethical, and technological changes can affect product availability and prices.
- Discuss various aspects of contract law.
- Define the acronyms FOB, FAS, and CIF with reference to title to goods.
- Explain agency law and how it affects an organization's purchasing department.
- Differentiate between implied and expressed warranties.
- Discuss purchasing rebates and kickbacks.
- Explain antitrust laws, discuss the major ones, explain the role of the Federal Trade Commission, and define the acronyms FDS and USDA.

Numerous forces affect the availability and price of products in the distribution channel. Five such forces are economic, political, ethical, technological, and legal.

ECONOMIC IMPACTS

One of the most influential elements affecting price is supply and demand. The basic economic law of supply and demand states that when the two are in balance prices remain stable; when supply exceeds demand, prices go down; when demand exceeds supply, prices go up. For example, if a supplier has an excess of a product on hand, then prices will be reduced to sell more of that product. Hotels, of course, do the same thing when they reduce room rates in low occupancy periods in order to sell more rooms.

Those at the beginning of the supply chain (such as growers, farmers, ranchers, and producers of other raw materials) are particularly subject to price fluctuations due to changes in supply and demand. Source suppliers in the food distribution chain often try to stabilize prices (for example, by stockpiling produce during peak production periods and then gradually releasing it to the market) in order to avoid the volatile prices that might otherwise prevail during a year. What they are doing, in effect, is balancing supply with demand.

At the start of the supply chain, products of the same type are undifferentiated (for example, rice is rice) and no economic values (such as those discussed in chapter 1) have been added. Product prices at this point in the distribution channel are often established by a bidding procedure. If an excess of raw product is on the market, bidders offer a lower price, and vice versa. Producers can do little to make their products unique and gain an economic advantage over their competitors.

Product Differentiation

Only later in the distribution system can products be differentiated (for example, by packaging) to make them unique (and therefore more desirable) to the next purchaser. Indeed, by the time source products of the same original type reach the point of being sold by suppliers to the hospitality industry, they may have marked differences, not just in form but in other ways. For example, a supplier may be willing to

- Inventory the product and deliver it when wanted
- Sell it to the purchaser with favorable credit terms
- Offer a price incentive such as a discount
- Offer some special type of service that the supplier's competitors do not
- Provide a better delivery schedule
- Employ more knowledgeable and courteous sales representatives

By convincing hospitality industry purchasers that their products are unique, suppliers can minimize the effects of competition. In other words, through product differentiation the end-supplier (unlike the source producer) generally has some control over the price of the product and is not subject solely to the forces of supply and demand.

Restaurants and other hospitality industry organizations do the same thing. For example, the raw quality of a roast half-chicken in a family-style restaurant is no different than the same chicken in a gourmet restaurant. However, most customers are quite prepared to pay a higher price in the gourmet restaurant because it has differentiated the chicken not only in the way it prepares it but also in the more elegant decor, atmosphere, and service provided.

Suppliers, however, cannot totally ignore the effects of supply and demand, particularly with perishable goods that cannot be stored until an undesirable supply and demand situation reverses itself. If a supplier has an excess of perishable goods subject to spoilage, for example, the price may have to be reduced to generate additional demand. Similarly, the supplier cannot ignore its competitors and their pricing and product-differentiation policies.

POLITICAL IMPACTS

Political forces also play a role in pricing. For example, consider the situation of U.S. cattle ranchers who lobby the federal government to reduce or restrict the quotas of foreign meat products that are allowed into the country. In this way the ranchers can control the amount of meat produced domestically and to a certain degree keep the forces of supply and demand tilted in their favor and so control prices. Those who have the most influence in encouraging legislators to pass laws or create regulations in their favor are those at the source level, who are often fewer in number than members of other distribution groups (such as wholesalers or retailers) and therefore better able to coordinate and unify their lobbying efforts.

Is lobbying politicians to pass laws controlling supply and demand ethical for a powerful group? Although lobbying for legislative changes is commonly accepted and is therefore considered ethical, many other supplier practices are not.

ETHICAL IMPACTS

Many things occur in the distribution channel that may be considered unethical (and thus affect prices), particularly in the fiercely competitive food supplier business where so many products are highly perishable. If they are not sold when fresh, they deteriorate and have to be sold for a reduced price or discarded. For example, is it ethical for a supplier to

- Restrict the supply of nonperishable products in a monopolistic situation so that prices increase?
- Refrain from providing negative information about a product (for example, the lack of freshness of produce) to a potential purchaser who does not specifically ask for this information?
- Offer a kickback (an under-the-table payment) to product purchasers in exchange for that establishment's exclusive business? A purchaser who takes a kickback has no choice but to accept whatever quality of goods are then shipped to the operation. This practice is, in fact, a form of theft.
- Allow a purchaser to buy products for personal use at a price discount or offer him or her "free" gifts? This type of practice encourages the purchaser to favor that supplier, who may then raise selling prices to the operation.
- Donate requested products "free of charge" to the purchaser's annual company picnic or similar event? Often such donations are made with the understanding

that the purchasing company will continue to do substantial business with that supplier. Obviously, the cost of these "donations" is passed on by the supplier in its selling prices.

- Act in collusion with other suppliers of similar products to set a minimum price at which they will all sell products? Generally speaking, this type of price-fixing is not only unethical but also illegal.
- Act in collusion with other suppliers to establish territories, with each one selling exclusively within a separate territory? This type of supplier agreement may not be illegal but does preclude the purchaser from shopping around and buying products at the most favorable prices.

Hinich and Staelin (1980, p. 3) state that some food suppliers have developed techniques of using less expensive ingredients without affecting a product's apparent quality. They cite, for example, that "the development of a fat-encapsulation process permitted raising the fat content of frankfurter to 50 percent in a manner that makes it difficult . . . to detect."

Reciprocity

Kotschevar (1975, p. 24) also discusses reciprocity as an ethical matter, defining it as "a procedure in which a company may purchase from someone because it is advantageous for the company to do so. For instance, if a seller is given orders, he may be able to influence sales for the company or in some other way contribute to the company's well-being." For example, a supplier may allow its sales representatives to eat in the purchasing company's restaurant and charge their meals to the supplier's business on condition that the purchasing company reciprocate by buying most or all of its needed products from that supplier. This practice limits the purchaser's ability to shop around because the reciprocating supplier is automatically given the business. Where management condones this type of arrangement, it must understand what it is giving up in exchange and must not agree to it if it would be in violation of any laws.

Unethical practices invariably result at some point in higher purchasing costs. The Association of Purchasing Agents has developed a code of ethics for its members, and hospitality industry purchasers should make sure they are familiar with this code.

TECHNOLOGICAL IMPACTS

In the past few years, many technological improvements in the distribution channel have affected both product pricing and availability. One is computerized ordering. Many suppliers have computerized their inventory records, and some have computerized their ordering procedures to the extent that a hospitality industry purchaser with a compatible computer linked by telephone line to the supplier's can duplicate purchase orders directly in the supplier's premises without having to send the purchase order by mail. This practice can reduce purchasing costs.

Product Processing and Packaging

Advances in food preservation allow foods to be delivered today in a variety of different forms and with a much reduced possibility of spoilage. For example, processing technology has improved to the point that meat packers can flash-freeze individually preportioned cuts of meat (such as steaks) with minimal loss of quality.

Similar advances have also occurred in the quality of frozen convenience foods. Suppliers who offer these products are able to add this value to the prices of their products because this form of convenience gives them a competitive advantage. One of the disadvantages, however, of many frozen convenience products is that the industry has not yet achieved standardization in packaging, making difficult the comparison of the cost of comparable products in two different supplier package sizes. (The topic of convenience foods is discussed in more depth in chapter 15.)

Product Transportation and Preservation

Faster methods of transportation (for example, overnight shipment between coasts) ensure greater dependability of quality and delivery. Because shipments can also be made in larger quantities than in earlier days, the number of purchase orders that need to be prepared and processed is reduced.

According to Gisslen (1983, p. 5), "Modern refrigeration and rapid transportation caused revolutionary changes in eating habits. For the first time, fresh foods of all kinds . . . became available all year." Even though transportation costs for these products have increased their prices, these price increases are compensated by other values the purchasers receive.

LEGAL IMPACTS

Many legal forces affect supply and demand (and thus prices) in the channel of distribution. Many of these legal forces stem from political impacts, such as lobbying, that result in legislation.

In most hospitality operations, however, purchasers carry out their jobs and are never directly involved in legal difficulties. The purchaser is typically dealing exclusively with local suppliers who deliver on a day-to-day basis to the hospitality business's receiving area using their own vehicles. Nevertheless, regardless of size of operation, the purchaser must be familiar with certain elements of business law. Some aspects of general business law are discussed in the following sections.

Contract Law

A *contract* is a legally enforceable agreement between two or more persons (such as a buyer and seller), whether that agreement is implied or specific. For a contract to be enforceable, it must always involve an offer (a supplier offers a product), consideration (a quoted price for that product, a promise that the supplier will deliver, or a promise that payment will be made subsequent to delivery), and acceptance (the purchaser agrees to buy the product at an agreed price).

Both parties to a contract must be aware of and agree to all its conditions and be legally able to fulfill all contract terms. A contract would not be legal if a supplier and purchaser agree to trade in stolen goods. If a purchaser agrees to buy products from a seller, subsequently discovers the products were stolen, and refuses to accept or pay for them, payment is not enforceable because the contract was illegal. A contract can become invalid if an error was made and one party knew of the error but did not advise the other party.

Generally, an offer may be withdrawn before it is accepted. It becomes binding only at the time of acceptance. Note that a supplier's bid does not constitute a contract. It is only an offer that does not become a contract until it is accepted. Also, an acceptance must conform to the terms of the offer. For example, if a supplier offers a product at $5.00 per pound, and the potential purchaser counters with a reduced price of only $4.90 a pound, that counteroffer itself becomes an offer that in turn becomes a contract only if the supplier accepts the lower price. An offer must be accepted within a reasonable time unless a deadline has been established. Usually, that reasonable time is determined by the normal trading practices of the buyers and sellers in that business.

Contracts can be oral. For example, a purchaser telephones a supplier and agrees to purchase goods at a stated price—a common method of ordering food and other supplies in small hospitality businesses. This method of ordering creates a contract and in most jurisdictions is legally just as binding as a written one, as long as it is made in good faith as if it were a written contract. However, a written contract is often easier to enforce than an oral one. Moreover, a contract for the sale of goods for a price exceeding $500 is enforceable only if it is in writing. Most purchase contracts in large hospitality organizations are written ones. One type of written contract is a purchase order provided by the hospitality purchaser to a supplier in which the purchaser agrees to buy stipulated products at stated prices. (Purchase orders are discussed in chapter 6.)

- A contract may not be binding if some condition of the contract (such as time, price, or amount) is difficult or impossible to determine at the time of agreement. However, a contract may contain an approximate, minimum, or maximum condition (for example, concerning quantities or prices) if actual figures are unknown at the time of agreement. Also, if this condition is decided by only one party, the contract is not binding because of lack of mutual agreement.

- A contract that contains an indefinite condition (such as time) may be canceled by either party with appropriate notice.
- Prices in a contract may be assumed. For example, buyer and seller assume that they are the same as in previous purchases with the understanding that only in the case of an unanticipated price change must the supplier notify the purchaser.
- If a price (or a quantity) condition is subject to confirmation, acceptance of that condition or even the placing of a partial order by the purchaser can be considered acceptance of that condition.
- An escalator clause in a contract is one in which a condition (such as price or quantity) can be changed if other factors or conditions change.
- Cancellation clauses to protect either or both parties from loss are sometimes included in contracts. Such a clause cancels the contract if certain conditions occur.
- Contracts usually have a specified time limit, but this time limit can be canceled if both parties agree. Such agreements (or agreements to cancel for any other reason) should be in writing.
- An agreement to change a contract condition cancels the contract unless both parties agree that all other conditions of that contract remain in force.
- Some contracts contain conditional sale clauses that give the seller product-re-possession rights if the purchaser fails to honor a contract condition. In other words, the seller retains title to the goods until the purchaser meets all contract conditions (such as payment for the products).
- Failure to perform on a contract condition (such as failing to meet a delivery date) is a breach of contract. When a contract is breached or violated, the injured party can sue for damages. For example, if a seller failed to deliver goods as contracted, the purchaser can make the purchase elsewhere and sue the seller for costs incurred (such as having to pay a higher price for required products) above and beyond those that would have occurred if the original contract had not been breached. The clause "time is of the essence" in a contract gives the purchaser the right to refuse deliveries not made by a contracted date. Nevertheless, if the purchaser accepts a late delivery with protest, no contract breach has occurred.

One aspect of purchasing that hospitality purchasers need to guard against is a "lowball" bid, in which the seller purposely bids low on a product to obtain the business and receive a contract, with the intent of later raising prices. To prevent this, purchasers can include in the contract a clause stating that the purchaser may buy from another supplier any product that the seller fails to deliver at the contracted price. The difference between the lowball price and the alternative supplier's price can then be charged to the original seller.

A greater likelihood of contract dispute with purchases occurs when products have to travel some distance between buyer and seller, when a common or third-party carrier is used, when public storage has to be used, when the contract covers a lengthy period of time, or when for one reason or another one of the parties involved cannot carry out the terms of the contract.

Title to Goods

Sales law (among other things) covers the matter of title to goods or products. Title to goods can pass from buyer to seller at many points in the distribution channel, even before the purchaser has received or seen the products. When title passes, so does the risk from such things as spoilage and theft, and the purchaser has the responsibility to insure for those risks from this point on.

Some terms used to describe when title to goods passes from seller to buyer are important to know. For example, FOB (free on board) is used in a phrase such as "FOB purchaser's premises," which means that title remains with the seller until the goods are delivered to the purchaser's receiving dock. If FOB is the seller's premises, then the purchaser assumes title to the goods at the time the seller places them in a third-party carrier's hands. (If the carrier is part of the seller's operation, then its vehicles are part of the seller's "premises," and title does not pass until the goods are delivered to the purchaser's receiving dock and the goods are inspected and signed for.) In the case of goods ordered from a distant location, the phrase "FOB purchaser's local carrier" may appear in a contract. It means that title passes from seller to buyer when goods are delivered to a carrier in the purchaser's city.

"Free alongside ship" (FAS) means basically the same thing as FOB, except that it is used for products moved by ship. With FAS, making sure that the product is insured from this point on, either by the purchaser's organization or by the ship and/or other transportation companies involved, becomes the purchaser's responsibility.

"Cost, insurance, and freight" (CIF) is sometimes also used for waterborne shipments. For example, "CIF destination" means that the seller arranges and pays for costs of water and ground transportation and insurance to the point of delivery at dockside, at which point the purchaser takes possession and arranges for pickup and delivery.

Although many of the transportation terms of sale are traditional ones, they can be amended in a contract. For example, the purchaser can agree that the products will be FOB the seller's premises but nevertheless have the contract specify that the seller is responsible to have the products delivered to the purchaser's premises in a specified condition by a particular date.

Agency Law

In many small hospitality operations, the owner does all purchasing, and the law of agency does not apply. In larger operations, the owner delegates the responsibility to a manager, who becomes the owner's agent. In even larger operations, the manager delegates the purchasing authority to one or more purchasing department employees, in which case, according to agency law, the purchasers may be representing the owner(s) and not the manager.

If purchasing department employees are acting as agents, they generally have the power to obligate the establishment within the limits of the financial authority delegated to them. Purchasers are often formally advised of this authority as part of their documented job description.

Suppliers must know what legal authority purchasers have as agents of their company to bind that company to purchase contracts. Sometimes that authority is limited by management to a certain dollar limit on any individual purchase before a higher authority must approve the contract. In such a situation, the purchasing company has the responsibility to notify sellers of this limit; otherwise, suppliers have the right to assume that purchasers have unlimited spending authority. Suppliers may also assume that purchasers have this authority as a result of having been allowed in the past to act and commit the establishment.

Even though a purchaser as agent may obligate his or her organization with commitments resulting from purchasing decisions, in some instances the purchasers themselves can be held accountable. This could occur if a purchaser agrees to a contract without proper authority. Recognize also that an agent's status can change. For example, in some operations the chef is allowed to act as an agent in the purchase of some food products but not in the purchase of other products.

Although generally purchasers may legally act as agents of a property's owners by arranging contracts, supplier sales representatives frequently do not have an equivalent authority to make binding agreements other than in a broad way. In other words, a purchaser with authority to negotiate and bind his or her organization can negotiate only with a person with similar authority, that is, for example, with a sales manager rather than with a sales representative. Thus, giving an order to a sales representative does not create a contract until that salesperson's manager has agreed.

The law of agency can also affect who is responsible for transportation. For example, assume products are purchased and the contract specifies FOB destination, with the purchaser having the right to select carriers. If the purchaser then requests the seller to ship the best way, the purchaser has, in effect, asked the seller to be the purchaser's agent in arranging transportation and, depending on the circumstances, title to goods can then pass FOB the seller's location.

Warranties

A product sold "as is" has no warranty, and the purchaser assumes all risks. As Peddersen (1981, p. 16) states, "When the merchant inspects the goods and notices an obvious defect, such as a large crack in a table, and accepts the table anyway, the express warranty by description and model does not apply." If a warranty is expressed, what is covered by the warranty is spelled out in writing or by spoken word (orally) by seller to purchaser. An expressed warranty—or a later warranty for the same products—cancels any earlier warranty. A salesperson's statement overly praising ("trade puffing") a product is not a warranty unless it is confirmed by the sales manager indicating the supplier is bound by the sales representative's claims. However, if that salesperson's earlier trade puffing has been accepted by her or his company, authority to make those claims is implied and, even if those claims are fraudulent, a warranty nevertheless exists.

Warranties can also be implied, which means that they are inferred by the seller or are imposed by law on the sale unless the seller specifically negates them or limits them to the extent allowed by law. For example, the law generally states that a contract for sale implies that merchantable goods are fit for a particular purpose and that no particular wording or action is required to evidence such implied warranties as long as the sale is a legal one and the goods are sold with the understanding that they are suitable for the intended purpose. If they are not, and the seller is aware of that fact, the seller is guilty of warranty breach. For this reason purchasers must make sellers aware of the intended use of products unless that use is a commonly understood one (as it would be for food products).

Law of Fraud

Any deliberate act or statement made by one party that is intended to deceive the other party prior to agreeing to a contract is fraud. For example, if a seller deceives a purchaser into believing that a product is of a higher quality than it actually is and knows that it is not, fraud exists. Trade puffing, however, is not considered by itself to be fraud; therefore, purchasers must exercise caution and judgment in making purchases based on it. Purchasers must carefully inspect products on receipt for quality and value. If fraud exists, no contract exists. If fraud is discovered, immediate action must be taken by the purchaser. If action is delayed or if the purchaser's company retains and pays for the products, there may be no case for fraud. Unfortunately, fraud must be proven to be deceptive, which is often not easy to do.

Rebates

After a purchase is made, suppliers sometimes give the purchasing company a rebate in the form of cash or additional free products. Such rebates are not illegal (except in the case of alcoholic beverage purchases) as long as all purchasers are offered the same rebate conditions by a supplier. Rebates are illegal when they take the form of kickbacks. Kickbacks occur when purchasers and sellers conspire to inflate product prices, with the purchaser accepting a rebate after purchase.

Supplier Relationships

A hospitality industry purchaser has the legal right to choose its suppliers. However, the decision to buy from a particular supplier cannot be based on the purchaser limiting that supplier's right to establish the prices at which it will sell products to other purchasers. Further, a purchaser should not require a supplier to sell exclusively to that purchaser or exclusively to it in a particular geographic area, unless the terminology of any such contract is first submitted for legal review to ensure that it does not violate any statutes.

SPECIFIC ACTS

In addition to general business law, a hospitality industry purchaser should be familiar with some specific legal statutes. Most of these statutes are known generally as antitrust laws, and they can sometimes be inadvertently violated by a purchaser unfamiliar with them. The general objective of these laws is to regulate business conduct to prevent economic coercion and to ensure that competition prevails and that purchasers receive fair prices. The statutes achieve this by limiting such practices as collusion between buyer and seller or between two or more suppliers or two or more purchasers.

Most of the antitrust statutes are federal and apply to interstate and foreign commerce. Interstate commerce means business conducted between two or more states. Some states have their own statutes covering commerce within the state. Some states have legislation for which no parallel federal legislation exists. For example, the federal government has no legislation concerning fish plant inspections (even for interstate commerce), but some state laws do cover this area. Most states also have extensive liquor distribution laws, whereas the federal government's legislation in this regard is quite limited.

Robinson-Patman Act

The Robinson-Patman Act makes illegal selling the same products to competing purchasers at different prices if each purchaser's requirements are basically identical. In addition, a purchaser may not try to influence a supplier to provide a lower price than that offered to its competitors. Note, however, that this law does not mean that the purchaser has a right to know what price a competitor purchaser is paying. Also, two purchasers can each pay a different price for the same product because they receive a different level of service; for example, one pays cash on delivery (COD) and the other pays 30 days after receiving the goods. Sellers may not normally sell at a discount unless that discount is offered to all purchasers. Offering purchasers a price discount for purchase of a large quantity of a product is not illegal for suppliers, but setting this quantity so high that only one or two large purchasers can hope to attain it is illegal. In other words, the quantity necessary to earn the discount must be reasonable. Suppliers may also reduce their prices on short notice if they do so to meet a competitive supplier's price reductions.

Sherman Act

The Sherman Act states that every contract, combination in the form of trust or otherwise, or conspiracy, in restraint of trade or commerce among the several states, or with foreign nations, is illegal. Restraint in this context has been interpreted by the courts to be unreasonable restraint, and a contract does not have to be a written one for this act to be enforced. For example, the act prohibits two or more suppliers from agreeing on the prices they will charge hospitality industry purchasers for like products, from agreeing to carve up the market geographically between themselves, and from conditioning the purchase of one product on the purchase of another (for example, a dishwasher equipment supplier cannot make the sale of the equipment contingent upon the purchaser buying dishwasher detergent from that same supplier). Unfortunately, as Stefanelli (1986, p. 30) states, "The language of this law is so general that just about anything relating to unfair competition could be covered under the Sherman Act."

Clayton Act

The Clayton Act goes a step beyond the Sherman Act in that it more precisely outlines the types of business activities that are illegal. For example, it prohibits "tying agreements" to prevent sellers obliging purchasers to buy a particular product only from that seller. It also prohibits "exclusive dealing," for example, a supplier requiring a purchaser to buy only that supplier's branded products and no other branded products from other suppliers. Exclusive dealing, however, does not preclude exclusive selling.

Exclusive selling could occur when a restaurant franchisor develops a particular food product that it will sell only to its franchisees. A restaurant consumer who wants that particular product can obtain it only from one of the franchised restaurants. Note further, however, that a franchisor cannot oblige a franchisee to purchase all products from the franchisor, particularly if they are more expensive and provide the franchisor with excessive profits. For products other than those unique to and available only from the franchisor, franchisees are free to purchase in the marketplace as long as they adhere to franchisor-established quality standards.

Federal Trade Commission

The Federal Trade Commission (FTC) Act empowers the FTC to pursue anticompetitive practices in the courts. This pursuit usually centers on deceptive advertising or promotion, monopolistic situations, and other conduct in the marketplace that it judges to be deceptive to the purchaser. As Hinich and Staelin (1980, p. 92) explain,

> Since the formation of the FTC, the agency has been concerned with preventing unfair and deceptive acts or practices. Until recently, the major vehicle for protecting consumers from this deception was cease and desist orders. However, even though the deception could be forced to stop, there was no way to impose on the firm any money damages attributable to the deception. This deficiency was remedied in part when the FTC instituted its corrective advertising program requiring some firms to devote a portion of their future advertising to expressing retraction of the challenged claim.

Food Industry Regulations

Present food industry regulations cover three broad areas. The first is to ensure that food sold is safe and not hazardous to health. The second concerns the contamination or adulteration of food from ingredients not considered hazardous. The third deals with information (or lack of it) provided about the food on container labels or in advertising.

One of the major acts to aid in this area is the Food and Drug Act of 1906 that established the Food and Drug Administration (FDA). The FDA establishes product-labeling requirements and inspects nonmeat processing plants. The FDA is also empowered to create standards of identity, quality, and container-fill measures. Standards of identity define ingredients and state the amount of them allowed to be used in products with well-known generic names, such as orange juice. Through the years, the powers of the FDA have been enhanced, and no other government agency today can force a manufacturer to remove its product from sale as quickly as can the FDA.

The Meat Inspection Act was also introduced in 1906, with enforcement power given to the U.S. Department of Agriculture (USDA). The USDA is primarily concerned with inspecting plants that manufacture and process fresh meat and products. A USDA inspector, however, also has the right to check restauran the quality of food products stored there to ensure they meet minimum standards for wholesomeness.

DISHONEST PRACTICES

Most suppliers to the hospitality industry are scrupulously honest. E are selling most products to ensure that purchasers receive competit honest suppliers are strict in their sales practices and train their sales representatives to resist purchasers who might try to request favors (such as kickbacks) to obtain the purchaser's business.

Nevertheless, unethical suppliers practice whatever deceit they can to make a sale. For example, they will happily pay a "commission" of as much as 10 percent to a purchaser, even if doing so means they increase their prices to cover the commission cost.

Obviously, unethical purchasers also exist. Sometimes suppliers who try to obtain business honestly are advised by purchasers that their success rate would be improved if they provided the purchaser with free tickets to sporting events, paid for a membership in a social club, or even paid for a vacation trip.

When a potentially dishonest supplier does not gain business through honest means from an honest purchaser, the supplier's next move is often to try to influence the purchaser's supervisor with bribes that the honest purchaser resisted. Sometimes the chain of bribes rises to the property's manager or owner. In one situation the supplier arranged a loan for an owner who was having personal financial difficulties. The loan was repaid by the owner by providing the supplier with purchase orders at prices that were higher than normal. Other practices that can occur are:

- An accounting office employee obtains a personal loan from a supplier in return for approving "padded" invoices. (An invoice is *padded* if the prices billed are higher than they should be for the quality delivered.) In other situations, padded invoice payoffs to accounting office employees take the form of cash and/or merchandise delivered directly to the employee's residence.
- A supplier forges a receiving employee's signature on invoices for products not delivered.
- A supplier resubmits an invoice that has already been paid and thus receives a double payment for the same products.
- A receiver works in collusion with a supplier to receive inferior products while approving payment for high-quality products. The supplier and receiver split the additional "profit" proceeds.
- A supplier short-ships products with an invoice for full shipment and promises the shortfall will be made up the next day. The short shipment is never made whole, but the receiving establishment's system (or lack of it) allows the full invoice to be paid anyway.

Protecting against Dishonesty

Any hospitality establishment must have a security plan in operation to protect against dishonesty. Many aspects of this security plan are covered in later chapters. In addition,

- Management must set the example. If management is dishonest or displays an attitude that it does not care about dishonesty, then why should employees, including purchasing personnel, be honest?
- Management must demonstrate that dishonesty is not tolerated by releasing employees who have been caught being dishonest or, in more serious cases, by prosecuting them.
- Management supervision is a requirement of any security plan. Effective managers make the time to supervise properly. Supervision, control, and security are synonymous. Although supervision does not guarantee honesty in employees, lack of supervision tempts employees to be dishonest. Be alert to purchasing and/or receiving department employees who appear to be overly friendly with suppliers, sales representatives, or delivery drivers; observe if these salespeople or delivery drivers are seen in unauthorized areas. Another area of supervision is to determine if relatives of any purchasing or receiving personnel are employees of suppliers, or if relatives of suppliers are key employees of the hospitality establishment.
- Management should compare prices on supplier invoices with prices quoted from competitive suppliers. Prices paid that are out of line might indicate the possibility of kickbacks from suppliers to purchasers.
- Management needs to maintain good employee relations, which includes paying adequate wages and benefits. Although adequate compensation does not guarantee honesty, it does reduce the temptation to be dishonest. Good employee relations may also include management participation in employee group activities such as sports and social events.
- Management should take responsibility for the final decision of approving the organization's suppliers. Management (accompanied by purchasing department personnel, if appropriate) has the responsibility to familiarize itself with suppliers by visiting their premises and then advising purchasing department personnel as to which suppliers the establishment approves.
- Management should approve new specifications, review old specifications from time to time, and involve itself on test committees to approve new products. Suppliers should be provided with copies of these specifications and be advised that they cannot be altered without management approval.
- Management should prepare or have someone produce a purchasing department operations manual that includes checklists to ensure that internal control procedures for purchasing, receiving, storing, issuing, and preparing goods are properly followed. Many establishments produce such manuals and checklists, but management often fails to ensure that they are properly used.

DISCUSSION QUESTIONS

1. State the basic economic law of supply and demand and its effect on prices.
2. Explain why those at the beginning of the supply distribution channel are particularly subject to price changes.
3. Define the term *product differentiation*.
4. Those who have the most influence to create legislation that affects prices are those at the product source level. Explain why and give an example of how a political force can affect prices.
5. Do you think it is ethical for a purchaser to place an order with a supplier and then cancel it on discovering that the product can be purchased at a lower price from another supplier? Explain your answer.
6. Give an example of a technological change that has affected product availability and price.
7. What three basic conditions must be in place for a contract to be enforceable?
8. An acceptance must conform to the terms of an offer in order for a contract to be in place. Explain what this means.
9. In some contracts the clause "time is of the essence" appears. What does this imply?
10. Some contracts contain conditional-sale clauses. From the seller's perspective, what does such a clause mean?
11. To obtain a contract, some suppliers make lowball bids. What can result if they receive a lowball contract?
12. Explain the acronyms FOB, FAS, and CIF with reference to title to goods.
13. Discuss financial authority given to purchasers with reference to agency law.
14. Differentiate between implied and expressed warranties.
15. Explain what a rebate is and under what condition(s) it becomes illegal.
16. Many of the acts that affect product distribution are antitrust laws. What is the general objective of these laws?
17. State the three main antitrust laws discussed in the text.
18. Explain the role of the Federal Trade Commission.
19. With reference to food regulations, define the acronyms FDA and USDA.

PROBLEMS

1. Discuss with the storekeeper or food department manager of a hotel or restaurant some of the ways in which some standard food products that the organization purchases are differentiated from one supplier to another. See if you can discover why the organization purchases the product in the form it does, rather than in another form from a different supplier. Write a short report of your findings.
2. Discuss with the chef of a hotel or restaurant any technological changes that

have occurred in the last few years that have changed the way the organization purchases and processes any of its food products. See if you can discover how these changes have affected product prices. Write a short report of your findings.

3. Visit the purchasing department of a local hotel or restaurant. Discuss with the purchasing manager what he or she considers to be unethical practices encountered with suppliers (without naming any names) and what was done about each situation. Write a short report of your findings.

REFERENCES AND SUGGESTED READINGS

Gisslen, Wayne. 1983. *Professional Cooking.* New York: John Wiley.

Hinich, Melvin J., and Richard Staelin. 1980. *Consumer Protection Legislation and the U.S. Food Industry.* New York: Pergamon, pp. 5–33, 108–14.

Kotschevar, Lendal H. 1975. *Quantity Food Purchasing.* New York: John Wiley.

———, and Charles Levinson. 1988. *Quantity Food Purchasing.* New York: Macmillan, pp. 12–24, 26–27.

Peddersen, Raymond B. 1981. *Foodservice and Hotel Purchasing.* Boston: CBI, pp. 11–23.

Stefanelli, John M. 1985. *Purchasing: Selection and Procurement for the Hospitality Industry.* New York: John Wiley, pp. 25–35.

Virts, William B. 1987. *Purchasing for Hospitality Operations.* East Lansing, Mich.: The Educational Institute of the American Hotel & Motel Association, pp. 37–39, 43–50.

Warfel, M. C., and Frank H. Waskey. 1979. *The Professional Food Buyer.* Berkeley, Calif.: McCutchan, pp. 33–46, 100–104.

3

Product Prices

OBJECTIVES

- Discuss the concept of "best" price, and explain why the lowest price is not always the best.
- Explain why a business's customers and/or budgets often dictate the price that can be paid for products.
- Discuss different philosophies that purchasers have regarding what to pay for products and how a supplier's services can offset higher product prices.
- Explain how hedging works and how a hospitality purchaser can take advantage of it.
- Discuss bartering, blanket orders, and supplier promotional discounts.
- Discuss the pros and cons of volume discounts in quantity purchasing, and list the questions that should be asked before a quantity purchase is made.

INTRODUCTION TO PRICES

Even though the various forces discussed in the previous chapter all affect the prices paid by hospitality industry purchasers, suppliers to the industry still have some flexibility in setting prices. The amount of price-setting flexibility they have often depends on where they are in the distribution channel. Kotschevar (1975, p. 12) states,

Commodity prices are apt to fluctuate the most at the producer or farm level, next at the wholesale level, and least at the retail level because marketing margins are much less flexible than commodity prices. In a period of rising prices middlemen take less of the consumer's dollar; in a period of falling ones, they take more.

How Suppliers Establish Prices

Suppliers generally establish their prices in the same way that many hospitality industry operators do. For example, a restaurant operator knows what menu products cost, knows the markup that is needed to cover labor, other variable costs, and overhead, and uses a multiplication factor to arrive at a selling price. Thus, a restaurant operator who knows that an overall food cost of 40 percent will cover all costs and yield an acceptable profit will multiply menu cost by 100/40 or 2.5 to establish menu selling prices.

Suppliers basically take the same approach. Typically suppliers of food products to the restaurant industry add a 15 percent markup to their purchase costs to arrive at their selling prices. Others use a factor or rule to achieve the same results. For example, a particular product may traditionally have a rule of 2, which means that the supplier's purchase cost is doubled to arrive at a selling price.

Suppliers, however, are similar to restaurants in that a cost multiplication factor or percentage markup cannot be used indiscriminately for every product. Other considerations (such as those discussed in the previous chapter) affect individual product selling prices. In addition, the competition's price for the same product and what the purchaser is prepared to pay influence selling prices. If circumstances necessitate, the price may be lowered, additional services may be provided to justify the higher price, or the supplier may remove that item from its offerings.

In some cases prices are also controlled directly or indirectly. This control can be by a state (for example, with liquor distribution) or by the association representing the suppliers of particular products.

What Is the "Best" Price?

The best price that a purchaser should pay for a product is the one that provides the best value, in terms of not only product cost but also product quality and supplier service. This best price is the lowest available that is compatible with the quality and service desired. The product cost may have to be converted to make comparisons. For example, consider Table 3-1 with reference to the cost of a certain cut of meat for which butchering (trim) tests indicate that the supplier with the lowest price is not offering the lowest usable cost per pound.

Comparison of the figures shows that supplier A's price appears lower but that,

Table 3-1. Best Price Comparison for a Cut of Meat

	Purchase Weight	Price per lb	Weight after Trim	Net Price per lb
Supplier A	10 lb	$2.00	8 lb	$2.50
Supplier B	10 lb	2.05	8.25 lb	2.48

after trimming, supplier B's net price is lower and thus provides more value, assuming that B's quality and service are acceptable.

In many cases purchasers buy only on the basis of price, and this practice is quite acceptable if all other purchase factors (quality and supplier service) are equal and allow a simple price comparison. This way to buy is easy because the purchaser is comparing only two numbers, and subjective factors such as quality and service can be ignored. In contrast, other purchasers consider only quality and supplier service in their comparisons and ignore prices. Most purchasers probably use one method for some products and the other method for others. As long as they know which method is relevant given the circumstances, this works well. Purchaser experience generally dictates which method to use at which time. According to Bell (1984, p. 70),

> Price is one of the most important purchasing criteria, but it is far from the most important one, at least to professional industrial buyers. A study of patronage motives of some four hundred industrial buyers found the following to be the most important factors (ranked in order of importance):
> 1. Reliability of seller
> 2. Continuous supply under all conditions
> 3. Accessibility of seller
> 4. Low prices
> 5. Quick, reliable delivery

Generally, product cost plays a more important role when the volume of a particular item purchased is high relative to other products. For most food operations, for example, meat, poultry, and seafood constitute about 50 percent of all food purchases, and most operators carefully control the prices paid for these relatively high-cost products (the A products in ABC analysis).

Price versus Quality

Price and quality are normally closely linked: the higher the quality, the higher the price, and vice versa. With some products, however, the price beyond a certain point will continue to increase without any parallel increase in quality. This kind of increase can occur when a supplier is the sole distributor for an item or when the purchaser must purchase that product regardless of price.

Price-quality comparisons are also sometimes difficult to make, particularly when suppliers introduce new products and evaluating them is difficult in this early stage of their use.

Customers Dictate Product Demand and Price

The demand for specific products that a hospitality operation must purchase (and often therefore the level of prices that it must pay) is generally dictated by its customers. Astute suppliers and supplier representatives determine who these hospitality industry customers are and offer compatible products at appropriate prices. A supplier's analysis of an establishment's customers may show that they are not at all price sensitive. For example, suppliers to a high-priced gourmet restaurant may be able to suggest to the restaurant purchaser unusual food products at high prices because they know that the customers will accept them and pay an appropriate menu price. In other words, price is irrelevant, and successful suppliers to that operation stress other factors, such as quality, service, and uniqueness of the product, in their sales presentations. At the other extreme, suppliers to a budget motel would be unlikely to sell high-priced percale bed linens to that operator. They would instead be obliged to suggest low-cost linens and make their sales presentations appropriate to the fact that cost is probably more important than quality.

Product Prices and Budgets

In operations with carefully controlled budgets (for example, institutions such as hospitals), those budgets often dictate the prices that must be paid for products. The more restrictive the budget, the more conscious purchasers are of prices paid for products, and other factors such as product quality and supplier service are relegated to a secondary role. This operating philosophy may also be true of some noninstitutional establishments toward the end of the budget year.

METHODS OF REDUCING PRICES AND/OR INCREASING VALUE

An astute purchaser can reduce costs and/or increase value for products purchased in a variety of ways. One obvious way is to reduce the price paid for products while maintaining product quality and supplier services. This method is directly reflected in increased profits. For that reason it is often the approach selected by some purchasers because their job performance can easily be evaluated by the savings they are able to achieve over previous purchase costs. Improving product quality and/or supplier services while maintaining current purchase prices at the same level is not so obvious or so easy for a purchaser's supervisor to evaluate.

However, the reduction-in-purchase-price approach, if not used judiciously, can also result in a reduced-quality product that does not perform up to desired standards. This problem not only causes a loss of money from products that may have to be discarded but also may create user dissatisfaction and potential supplier public relations problems if the product has to be returned. In other words, a lower product price combined with a reduced product value out of proportion to cost savings is not normally a viable objective in most circumstances. Further, many suppliers do not carry more than one or two levels of quality for most products. Therefore, making substantial reductions in quality to save money is just not feasible. Nevertheless, some suppliers today carry generic brands of commonly used products; the quality is somewhat reduced, but the cost savings can be quite dramatic.

Value Analysis

Value analysis is often a good approach to reducing product costs, particularly for products that have a high purchase cost relative to other items purchased. Value analysis was discussed in chapter 1.

Favorable Credit Terms

Suppliers seldom reduce prices through negotiation on products purchased on a daily basis. However, negotiated price reductions can occur, particularly if an organization is large enough (such as a chain operation) with a central purchasing office and the potential for quantity purchasing. Such firms may also be able to negotiate lower prices by offering long-term contracts to buy products.

A small operation might be able to receive through negotiation more favorable payment terms such as an extension in the time during which invoices have to be paid. Although this time extension does not directly reduce purchase costs or increase product value, it does indirectly add value because the money not paid out until a later date can be left in the bank to earn interest or be used to make more pressing payments.

Offering Cash Payments

An alternative to extending credit terms may be to offer a supplier immediate payment to achieve a reduction in cost prices. In order to negotiate on this basis, a purchaser must have assurance from the accounting office that cash is available for such purchases. In the case of a small, owner-operated establishment whose owner controls both cash and purchasing, this approach may be feasible. In large establishments with more complex channels of organizational communication, it may be more difficult.

If substantial cost reductions can be achieved for cash-on-delivery (COD) purchases, borrowing the funds to make payments may be profitable. The risk with COD deliveries is that, because payment is made at the time of delivery, if the quality of the product is later discovered to be not up to standard, it may be difficult to return the product for credit.

Product Substitution

Another alternative to save on purchase costs or to increase value is to seek out substitute products. Sometimes new products are developed that can take the place of traditional ones. Food establishments can also offer substitutes by taking high-cost items off their menus and replacing them with lower-cost menu items that are nevertheless acceptable to their customers. However, the cost of an item is not always what is important in deciding menu offerings, but rather the relationship of that cost to the menu item's selling price, that is, its gross profit. Gross profit is selling price less cost price. Consider, for example, the menu items in Table 3-2. All other things being equal, selling item 1 would be better than selling item 2. Item 1 has a higher food cost percent, but it also has a higher gross profit (and therefore contribution to net profit) than item 2. For each item 1 sold with a 50 percent food cost, the gross profit is four dollars versus only three dollars for item 2, even though item 2 has only a 25 percent food cost.

Hedging

Large organizations also have the opportunity to practice hedging. Hedging (also known as *forward contracting*) is a method of avoiding potential losses in purchasing a product whose cost price is forecast to increase by investing in the futures market for that product.

Suppose a large restaurant chain wished to protect its price on the purchase of a particular product over the next three months and cannot get a firm price contract from its supplier for more than the next thirty days. It could, however, contract with a supplier to purchase from it a specified amount of that product at market prices during that three-month period. At the same time, the chain buys a futures contract for the same quantity of product due three months from now at today's futures contract price. A futures contract is simply a document attesting to ownership of a quantity of a product (without having to take physical possession of it), much as a stock certificate attests to ownership of a share in a corporation.

As the three months go by, the supplier's price for that product may increase as forecast, and the purchaser will be paying higher prices to the supplier for quantities delivered. However, as market prices rise, the value of the futures contract for that product also increases, and at the end of three months the contract can be sold at a higher price to realize a profit that compensates for the higher prices being paid for the supplier's product. The objective of hedging is to ensure that product cost prices are stabilized (or rather that higher market prices are offset by futures contract profits) during the contract period.

Table 3-2. Gross Profit Calculations

Item	Cost Price	Selling Price	Cost Percent	Gross Profit
1	$4.00	$8.00	50%	$4.00
2	1.00	4.00	25%	3.00

If the product price in the market declines during the hedging period, the chain is able to buy products at a lower price than the original estimate. At the same time, the futures contract value also declines and is sold at a loss at the end of three months. That loss, however, is compensated by the savings resulting from supplier product price savings. Either way, the chain is protected. Hedging, however, is not without its pitfalls.

- Studying futures markets takes time and effort.
- Only large firms can participate because the minimum amount of any single futures contract for a product is quite large. Thus a large amount of cash is required to buy a contract, or else the cash has to be borrowed and interest paid.
- Futures contracts can be purchased only for certain products, such as orange concentrate, eggs, coffee, sugar, cocoa, and certain meat products.
- Transaction costs are involved with buying and selling futures contracts, and these costs reduce any profit (or increase any loss) when a contract is sold.
- When the time arrives to sell a futures contract, it may not be easy to sell at the desired price.

Therefore, hedging should only be used by operations who have knowledgeable purchasers who are very familiar with the futures market. As Kelly (1976, p. 74) states,

> The key point to remember when considering a hedging transaction as a purchasing tool is that it is a protective device designed to guard against the erosion of known profit margins. At no time should it be considered as a potential profit-making opportunity. Furthermore, hedging is a very sophisticated procurement technique and should not be attempted unless qualified commodity experts are handling the transaction.

Nevertheless, even small operations can use product price information from futures market quotations (found in newspapers such as the *Wall Street Journal*) because these prices reflect what those who deal in the market think will happen to prices in the future. This information can be useful in price negotiations with suppliers (even if the purchaser has no intention of assuming the risks inherent in hedging) because of the direct relationship between product futures prices and the actual cash cost of those products on the open market. By recognizing this relationship, the astute purchaser can often forecast market price changes before competitors (and thus gain a competitive advantage) and even in some cases before the supplier.

Bartering

Bartering occurs when an establishment exchanges its products for other needed products without any cash changing hands. A common method of doing this in the hospitality industry is in contra advertising. With contra advertising, a restaurant, for example, might "buy" a certain amount of advertising time on a local radio or television station and then allow authorized employees of that station to "buy" an equivalent amount of meals in its restaurant.

New Product Offers

Price reductions can frequently occur when new products are introduced on the market. These new products are often offered with a price advantage, particularly in the early stage, so that suppliers can penetrate the market. Suppliers reduce the price in order to sell the product to make sure purchasers and users become familiar with it before raising the price as demand increases. Because these new-product prices are generally short-lived, a purchaser seeking them out may be constantly shifting from one product to another and causing inconvenience to both users and suppliers.

Blanket Orders

Blanket orders are used in purchasing many frequently used, low-priced items at one time. By buying all these items at the same time, the total order value may encourage a supplier to provide a price discount. Blanket order items (with reference to the ABC discussion in chapter 1) would be the category C products (and perhaps even some B products) for which shopping around product by product for the supplier with the lowest price on each may not be worthwhile. When blanket orders are used, ordering several months' supply at a time, rather than placing more frequent small orders, may also pay. In other words, the inventory carried of these items is established to take care of several months' needs. The reasoning again is that the supplier's order each time amounts to a larger sum, and price concessions may be gained. Infrequent orders also reduce ordering and receiving costs, although these reduced costs are partially offset by higher storage costs.

Promotion Discounts

For food products, suppliers sometimes offer discounts that can be taken advantage of as long as the purchaser uses the discount to promote the product. This discount is not as common as it once was. It is not usually in the form of a cost price reduction but rather in the form of such things as free menu clip-ons, table tents, or place mats advertising the product being promoted. The supplier-provided promotional pieces are intended to increase the sale of the product and thus benefit both seller and purchaser. The decision to use a promotional discount, however, should consider factors other than increased sales generated. For example, does the operation wish to have that kind of advertising placed at the customer's table?

Volume Discounts

Volume discounts (also known as *opportunity buys*) occur when a purchaser agrees to buy a large quantity of a specific product. The purchaser may also have to agree to pay for the goods in advance or on a COD basis. A volume discount may also occcur when a supplier wishes to introduce a new product and is prepared to reduce the price to increase initial market acceptance. Suppliers may also make these volume discounts available under any, or a combination of, the following circumstances:

- In the normal course of business, a supplier may present the purchaser the opportunity to receive a healthy discount if a large enough quantity is ordered.
- If a supplier has a product that is to be discontinued, that is of poor quality, or that must be sold due to pending spoilage, a volume discount might be offered. In the last case, the purchaser should ensure that spoilage is not so imminent that making the purchase provides no value.
- The supplier has been able to purchase in large quantities to effect a cost saving and is prepared to pass this saving along.
- The supplier is short of cash and needs to make volume sales at a discount to improve his or her own cash flow.

When opportunity buys are presented, certain factors need to be evaluated. These factors may be both quantitative and qualitative. For example, consider the situation of a restaurant that normally uses and orders two hundred cases of paper napkins per month at a current cost of ten dollars per case. Its total cost per month is two thousand dollars. Over a three-month period, the cost would add up to six thousand dollars.

Suppose the supplier offered the restaurant the opportunity of purchasing six hundred cases at a time (a three-month supply) for a price of $9.50 per case. Total cost will be $5,700 (600 × $9.50).

This offer represents an apparent saving of three hundred dollars ($6,000 − $5,700) over the three-month period. However, interest on money must also be considered. Assume the interest cost is 12 percent a year (1 percent a month) on money tied up in inventory that is not earning income elsewhere (for example, as it would be if the money were left in the bank). The comparative situation over the three months (assuming for the sake of simplicity that interest is calculated on the amount of money tied up in inventory at the beginning of each month) is shown in Table 3-3.

The figures in Table 3-3 show that the initial purchase cost saving is now reduced by the extra interest cost of $54.00 ($114.00 − $60.00). Again, this still represents an overall saving of $246.00 ($300.00 − $54.00). However, storage costs (such as insurance, possible product spoilage, space required) of carrying a larger than nor-

Table 3-3. Evaluating Volume Purchases

Interest Calculation	Normal Purchase	Volume Purchase
Month 1 inventory	$2,000.00	$5,700.00
Interest 1 percent	20.00	57.00
Month 2 inventory	$2,000.00	$3,800.00 (⅔ × $5,700)
Interest 1 percent	20.00	38.00
Month 3 inventory	$2,000.00	$1,900.00 (⅓ × $5,700)
Interest 1 percent	20.00	19.00
Total interest	$ 60.00	$ 114.00

mal inventory and the cost of placing an order have still not been considered in the calculations. Another consideration is the demand that this size of purchase places on existing storage facilities. Is sufficient storage space available on-site, or will external storage space have to be arranged at additional cost? To allow a purchaser to consider all these other costs, a method known as the *economic order quantity* (EOQ) can be used. It is illustrated and discussed in chapter 6.

The quantitative aspects of volume purchases are relatively easy to make. However, even if the numbers in a quantity purchase comparison seem positive, certain other questions need to be asked.

- If it is a new or substitute product, how does the quality compare with the quality of the product normally purchased?
- What effect will a long storage period have on quality?
- What is the likelihood that the use of this item will decrease or even be discontinued before the inventory is used up?
- Might the product's price decrease anyway after the large purchase is made?
- Does this purchase require a change of supplier and thus create poor public relations with an existing supplier?
- What effect will this purchase have on supplier services? Will they increase, decrease, or stay the same?
- Is the supplier a legitimate one? Might the supplier have obtained this product from unethical sources or unlicensed distributors? If so, and especially if any required government inspections have not been undertaken, how might this affect the product's quality? It is not unknown for entire truckloads of food and other products to be stolen, and the products sold to unsuspecting purchasers.

Some of the qualitative aspects of large purchase opportunities are often difficult to assess. Therefore, purchasers should be very careful before committing an establishment to such a purchase, even if the numbers seem to indicate the purchase should be made. As Kelly (1976, p. 49) states, "Once a buyer decides to commit on an opportunity to buy, he must recognize that he is locking in that price for the duration of the contract, and that if further price weaknesses develop, he will not be able to take advantage of them." Bell (1984, p. 74) summarizes the situation as follows: "There are no savings unless and until the products are *used.*"

DISCUSSION QUESTIONS

1. Discuss the concept of the "best" price to pay for a product.
2. With some products (such as meat), why is the supplier with the lowest quoted price per pound not necessarily the one from whom to purchase?
3. Explain why the customers who use a hospitality operation's facilities often dictate to a degree the price that will be paid by purchasers for needed products.
4. Explain why, in some operations, budgets dictate prices paid for required products.
5. Why do some purchasers seek the lowest prices available for products while paying less attention to the product's quality and supplier services? What are some of the problems that this purchasing philosophy can create?
6. In the purchasing process, how can a supplier's favorable credit terms add value to products?
7. Some purchasers are prepared to pay cash on delivery to obtain lower product prices. What is the risk with this practice?
8. Explain how hedging works and what its risks are.
9. Even though a small hospitality operation may not practice hedging, how can it use futures contract pricing information to advantage?
10. Explain how bartering can be used and its advantages.
11. What is a blanket order, and under what circumstances can it be used?
12. Explain how a purchaser can use a supplier's promotion discount to advantage.
13. Explain three reasons why a supplier might offer a volume discount on large purchases.
14. List five questions that should be asked and answered prior to making a volume-discount purchase.

PROBLEMS

1. Butcher A's cost price on prime rib roasts weighing twenty-five pounds each is $4.55 per pound. After trimming and cooking this roast, its yield is 70 percent. Butcher B's cost price on similar sizes of roasts is $4.65 per pound; after trimming and cooking this roast, its yield is 80 percent. Which butcher offers the best purchase based on net price per pound?
2. You are the manager of a hotel with fifty guest rooms, a ninety-seat dining room, and a banquet room capable of handling lunches or dinners for up to

two hundred persons. The sales representative of your local coffee supplier has approached you today with an offer. Coffee that you have been buying at $3.75 per pound is due to increase next week by 15 percent, according to the supplier. However, he says he can let you have all he presently has in stock, about five hundred pounds, for the current $3.75 price. He must have your answer today; otherwise, he will make the offer to a competitive hotel. List all the factors that you would consider both for and against the offer. How would you decide? Justify your decision.

3. Assume that you have decided to serve a new steak entree item in your hotel dining room. Cost of the steak in twenty-pound unbutchered cuts is $2.20 per pound from your present supplier, and it yields 75 percent trimmed meat. You plan to serve steaks that weigh six ounces before cooking and estimate that forty per day will be sold. Block Butchers has approached you with a suggestion that you buy preprepared ready-to-cook individual six-ounce steaks from them at a price of $1.40 per steak. Assuming that your restaurant is open seven days a week, what is the additional weekly cost of buying from Block Butchers? Would you make the change to this new supplier? Why? What are other factors that you might consider before making the decision?

4. Assume that you normally purchase and use 120 cases of bourbon whiskey per month at a price of fifteen dollars per case. The supplier has offered you a price of fourteen dollars per case if you buy and pay in advance for a six-month supply. Assume that interest cost on money tied up in inventory is 12 percent a year. Based purely on a quantitative comparison, would you contract for the six-month supply? What other factors might you want to consider before making the decision?

REFERENCES AND SUGGESTED READINGS

Bell, Donald A. 1984. *Food and Beverage Cost Control.* Berkeley, Calif.: McCutchan.

Kelly, Hugh J. 1976. *Food Service Purchasing: Principles and Practices.* New York: Lebhar-Friedman, pp. 33–42, 47–52, 72–78.

Kotschevar, Lendal H. 1975. *Quantity Food Purchasing.* New York: John Wiley.

Stefanelli, John M. 1985. *Purchasing: Selection and Procurement for the Hospitality Industry.* New York: John Wiley, pp. 121–40.

4

Specifications and Quality Standards

OBJECTIVES

- List and briefly discuss the items that can appear on a specification, and detail the important factors to consider prior to preparing a specification.
- Define a *public domain* specification, and discuss the pros and cons of working with a supplier to prepare a specification.
- List and briefly discuss guidelines for writing a good specification.
- List the advantages of specifications.
- Define the term *quality standard,* and discuss how it is related to customer demand.
- Discuss the problems that government grading of products for quality can create, and list the pros and cons of using brand-name products as a quality measure.
- List the guidelines for a food taste-test evaluation committee.

SPECIFICATIONS

Effective purchasing requires that purchasing specifications be completed for major expenditure items. Obviously, specifications may not be practical or necessary for many items purchased in a hospitality operation, including items required on an everyday basis, such as dairy or bakery goods. However, specifications should be used for major food purchases such as meat, fish, and poultry that can account for as much as fifty cents out of each food purchase dollar. They are also recommended for other major purchases such as housekeeping linens or kitchen equipment. These items are generally the A category items discussed in ABC analysis in chapter 1.

Depending on the circumstances, a specification can be quite short and informal and may include only the brand name and quantity desired of a needed product. In the case of other purchases (for example, equipment), a specification can be several pages long.

Who Prepares Them?

In a small operation, specifications may be prepared by the operation's manager or by a department head who has the authority to purchase the item. In other cases, specifications may need to be prepared jointly by two or more people, such as the user in conjunction with an employee of the purchasing department who has purchasing experience in that area. The buyer does not usually prepare specifications alone.

What Can They Include?

Depending on the circumstances, specifications can include any or all of the following items:

- Name or description of the product required and, where appropriate, the geographic origin, variety, style, product or portion size, container size, grade, yield, trim, brand, weight, amount, edible yield or trim, or number of items required. For canned products, the packing medium and density are also required.
- Desired product quality information. For head lettuce, this might be: "Heads to be firm and compact (but not hard), and trimmed with no more than six wrapper leaves. Color should be a good green. Lettuce to be without signs of spoilage or damage, and free of excessive dirt."
- Intended use of the product (for example, olives to be used in cocktails). Suppliers are specialists in their field and may be able to suggest alternative products at a lower cost if they know what it is being used for or what performance is required from it.
- Where appropriate, the government or trade association standards.
- Inspections or test procedures to be used in veryifying the quality and/or performance requirements of delivered products. For example, items to be delivered by weight can be weighed, and products that are required to be delivered in a refrigerated state can be tested for temperature with a thermometer.
- Frequency with which the item is required. If suppliers know the frequency, they can arrange their own purchasing accordingly.
- Quantity and/or cost limitations. For example, the specification could include the maximum and minimum quantity of the product that might be ordered at any

one time or the maximum price the purchaser is prepared to pay during a specified time period.

- Where important, the form that the items should take (for example, fresh, frozen, or canned).
- For refrigerated and frozen items, the temperature at which they must be delivered.
- Packaging requirements, delivery procedures, and/or other supplier services desired or required.
- In the case of purchasing by bid, a specification needs to advise suppliers about bid procedures, seller qualifications required, criteria for supplier selection, how suppliers will be advised about their bids, and when payment will be made subsequent to purchase.

Not all the above information appears on every specification. Only those items relevant to that particular product should be included. Specifications should not be cluttered with irrelevant information such as information about delivery hours or who is designated to receive products.

Factors to Consider before Preparing Specifications

What actually appears on a specification can be influenced by any or all of the following:

- The organization's objectives with particular reference to quality standards. For example, is it a high-quality resort or an economy-priced motor hotel?
- In some cases the budget available can be a constraint, particularly for major capital items such as equipment. In other cases, competition from other hospitality operations may force sales prices to be reduced, which, in turn, reduces the funds available for purchasing products.
- Time and resources (personnel) available for preparing detailed specifications.
- Distance to the supplier's sources of supply (because this can affect delivery schedules).
- The organization's operating system. This factor might be particularly important in food purchases where the storage facilities, kitchen equipment available, and/ or menu requirements may dictate the form in which a product is purchased. For example, if freezer space is restricted, fresh rather than frozen produce may have to be specified. Also, sufficient dry storage may be required for quantity purchases of canned goods.
- Credit rating that the supplier gives to the purchasing establishment. For example, large-quantity purchasers are usually accorded a better credit rating than casual purchasers.

- Where employees do not have high skill levels, a restaurant may have to purchase more convenience foods requiring less on-site preparation. For example, does the operation have on-site butchers or skilled baking and pastry employees?

Public Domain Specifications

The preparation of comprehensive specifications requires qualified employees with the necessary skills to write them. These skills are not always available in small operations. For many standard products, however, specifications can be found in government publications, trade association publications, and similar sources. They may not exactly suit the requirements of any individual establishment, but they can often be easily adapted and simplify the process of having to start from scratch.

In addition, the Agricultural Marketing Service of the United States Department of Agriculture (USDA) produces a great deal of information useful to food purchasers. The USDA also provides a specification preparation service. For a fee, a USDA inspector will write specifications tailored to that particular business's requirements. The additional cost may be considerably less than the cost of writing specifications from scratch. The inspector can also verify at the supplier's location that the products conform to those specifications and mark the products with a USDA acceptance stamp.

An alternative, although more expensive, method would be to employ an outside consultant to write the specifications or at least adapt them from public domain specifications for a particular establishment.

Working with Suppliers to Produce Specifications

In other cases, purchaser and supplier might appropriately work together to prepare specifications. This arrangement is often necessary for small hospitality businesses whose time and resources for writing specifications are limited. Indeed, this method might be quite cost-effective. The problem with this arrangement, however, is that the specifications might be biased toward that supplier and even preclude any other suppliers from bidding or quoting on those products. Whenever practical, specifications should be written so that they apply to products offered from more than one supplier.

Even though suppliers may not work directly with hospitality industry purchasers to develop specifications, they can, according to Virts (1987, p. 61), aid in the following ways:

- Inform properties about available products.
- Offer advice on activities and attitudes of other properties toward various products.

- Counsel buyers regarding new products about to be introduced. Supplier representatives usually learn about new products before operators and purchasers do.
- Review and critique proposed specifications and evaluate whether a product defined by the specification is the most useful one to purchase.

How Many Copies?

Sufficient copies of specifications should be prepared so that one copy may be sent to each potential supplier and copies distributed to appropriate personnel such as the purchasing manager, the department head involved, and the person responsible for receiving the products.

Guidelines for Writing Specifications

The language of the specifications must be sufficiently precise to prevent misunderstanding between supplier and establishment. This precision does not mean, however, that once prepared the specifications cannot be changed. Indeed, as market conditions or the needs of the establishment change, new sets of specifications should be prepared.

Those who prepare specifications need to be aware of potential pitfalls.

- Avoid instructions that are too restrictive. For example, an instruction that limits suppliers to delivering items only between 9 A.M. and 10 A.M. may be too rigid and preclude some suppliers who can offer better value for money from bidding on such a specification.
- Exclude narrow requirements for costs, quantities, or quality tolerances. If tolerance limitations placed on potential suppliers are too strict, none of them may be able to provide the products. For example, if eight-ounce tenderloin steaks are specified with no tolerance stated such as "average 8-ounce but varying between 7.5 and 8.5 ounces," those suppliers who are interested might just charge a higher price for having to select and deliver only steaks that weigh exactly eight ounces.
- Avoid excessive detail and use clear and simple language, but also do not write specifications that are so vague that they allow many marginal potential suppliers to provide a quotation. Each of them may be able to meet vaguely stated quality and cost requirements, but when the decision is made to select among many suppliers, the potential for selecting an unreliable one is much greater. This problem frequently arises when the quality of available products (such as fresh produce) changes frequently or when several different qualities of the same item each meet the minimum quality specified.
- Avoid vague descriptive words. Terms such as "best quality" and "lowest price" have little meaning to suppliers.

- Use terms commonly accepted in the trade. The names of some items, in particular, meat cuts, can differ in different parts of the country. For example, a "hotel-style lamb rack" might be appropriate terminology in one part of the country, but in another area that item may be commonly described as a "lamb bracelet."
- Avoid a specification that limits all but one supplier if bids from several sources are desired. In this case, time and effort have been wasted, and if the supplier is aware that he or she is the sole supplier prices can be raised. This situation may allow a good working relationship to develop with that sole supplier but eliminates the flexibility the establishment has when selection can be made among several suppliers. In situations that require precise quality standards and/or low cost and only one supplier can meet the requirements, a single-bidder specification may be necessary.
- Do not waste time sending out specifications to several suppliers for a bid and then rejecting all the bids except the one from the usual supplier of these items. This type of favoritism creates ill will among other potential suppliers. This situation often comes up when the purchasing department is required by management policy to prepare specifications and seek bids, only to find the general manager makes the decision to buy from the usual supplier even though others could provide the products at competitive prices.
- Do not require a quality that is so high that no supplier can meet it without adding unnecessarily to purchase costs.
- Be careful to review specifications from time to time to ensure that the required geographic origin of products still provides the quality and cost desired. For example, California flame seedless grapes might be stated as a requirement, but at certain times of the year this type of grape originating in Chile might provide better quality and value.
- Be aware of specifications that encourage a supplier, in order to obtain the business, to provide the quality desired but only by reducing the price and normal profit. This practice is known as *lowball* bidding. After winning the purchaser's confidence, prices are gradually increased, quality is lowered, and/or services are reduced.
- Be aware of suppliers who make bids on specifications only because they are in a slow business period. They may quote prices that are lower than normal but nevertheless still provide them with some profit. These suppliers then decline to bid during other times of the year, and purchasers may find themselves constantly switching suppliers and creating ill will among suppliers who would otherwise provide good year-round service. Another problem develops in that each supplier has a fairly regular delivery time, and with frequently changing suppliers those in receiving find that they are constantly having to change their schedules and, with new suppliers, do not even know when deliveries will be made. This situation is more of a problem with small operations in which the receiver's job is often

combined with one or more other jobs. It is less of a problem in large organizations in which a receiver is always on duty during regular delivery hours.

- Finally, specifications must be used. Specifications are of absolutely no value if purchasers do not use them.

Advantages of Specifications

The main advantages of specifications are that they

- Require those who prepare them to think carefully and document exactly what their product requirements are
- Serve as a standard for quality
- Leave no doubt in suppliers' minds about what they are quoting on, thus reducing or eliminating misunderstandings between supplier and establishment
- Eliminate, for frequently purchased items, the time that would otherwise have to be spent repeating descriptions over the telephone or directly to salespersons each time the product is needed
- May reduce the number of products to be purchased; for example, a restaurant might be able to do this by consolidating products needed and using a single product in two or more different menu items
- May reduce purchasing costs as a result of the purchaser not paying for a higher quality than is needed
- Permit competitive bidding where this method of purchasing is used and may increase competitive bidding if generic products are specified
- Make completing purchase orders much easier (Specifications define the products required; purchase orders are contractual obligations to make a purchase and are discussed in chapter 6.)
- Allow the person responsible for receiving to check the quality of delivered goods against a written specification of the quality standard desired
- Serve as a basis for training new purchasing department employees
- In the event that a purchaser is absent, allow someone else to take care of that aspect of purchasing with minimum difficulty

Mutkoski and Schurer (1981, p. 202) make the following point about using specifications:

> Many operators also state that if they write well-defined specifications for their needs, the price on the merchandise purchased generally goes up. Although this often does happen, it is better to pay a slightly higher price in order to receive items of consistent quality and price over the long run than to pay a few pennies less per pound and purchase items that are unsuitable or inefficient for the operation.

QUALITY STANDARDS

Quality is a subjective matter that nevertheless must be stated on most specifications. According to Thorner and Manning (1983, p. 3), food quality from a scientific viewpoint is defined as

> An orderly classification of a product's chemical and physical characteristics. Flavor, texture, appearance, consistency, palatability, nutritional values, safety, ease of handling, convenience, storage stability, and packaging are the essential elements that must be evaluated in establishing a product's quality.

Powers and Powers (1984, p. 81) state that the word *quality* in common usage denotes a degree of excellence but that the use of the product is its principal quality determinant. Therefore, characteristics (such as size, weight, and market form) other than product excellence must be part of its quality measurement.

Quality can be determined if a quality standard is first established. Dittmer and Griffin (1984, p. 25) state that "standards may be defined as rules or measures established for making comparisons and judgments" and that "quality standards refer to the degree of excellence of raw materials, finished products, and by extension, work." Once quality standards are stated, the quality of products can then be readily compared to this standard.

In well-managed hospitality operations, a person such as the general manager or a committee of knowledgeable people establishes the standards desired. For each product, the standard is determined by relating it to what the customers expect because customers judge an operation by the quality of the products (including service) that they receive from it. Customer-desired standards are often determined by conducting market research among customers and potential customers and then translating those standards into specified qualities. In other words, the customer, rather than management, has the final say (albeit indirectly) in the quality standards offered by most hospitality operations. To quote again from Thorner and Manning (1983, p. 3):

> In addition . . . management relates quality to profits. Management equates quality with certain economic factors, such as the cost of the product, profits generated, and consumer acceptance within the intended selling price range. These economic factors are carefully weighed, so that a successful operation will not only produce an adequate return on its investment, but will also ensure healthy long-range growth.

Measuring Quality

Once customer-based quality standards have been determined, they can be measured against products available on the market. One method used by some purchasers to measure quality is by price. Although quality and price frequently are compatible, at some point price usually increases without a parallel increase in quality. Generally speaking, higher-priced operations purchase more expensive products, and lower-priced operations seek out low-cost products. Some establishments buy the highest-quality products available regardless of their cost, even when a lower-cost product would serve equally well.

Regardless of purchasing philosophy, if the quality of a product increases as price stays the same, or if product quality remains consistent as price is reduced, value to the purchaser increases, and vice versa. In all decisions in this regard, perceived value from the perspective of the hospitality operation's customers must be considered.

Government Quality Standards for Food

Another method of measuring quality for food products is to use USDA grade standards that are publicly available for about three hundred different food products, such as

- Fresh fruit, vegetables, and nuts
- Butter, cheese, nonfat dry milk, and certain other dairy products
- Rice, dry beans, peas, and similar products
- Poultry and eggs
- Beef, veal, calf, lamb, and mutton carcasses
- Canned, frozen, and dried fruit and vegetables and similar products such as jams and jellies

Standards are also available for various grains but not for food products made from them such as flour.

The USDA standards identify different degrees of quality (grades) for each product and thus allow the hospitality operator to select the quality that meets the organization's standards. For some items that are quality graded, the product must first have been produced under government inspection. Some products are inspected periodically; others, such as meat, are inspected continuously. However, note that although various federal government branches inspect many food distribution packers, processors, wholesalers, and others, their main task is to check the sanitation of the plants and the wholesomeness of food products produced rather than their quality. Inspection does not rate quality; only grading does that.

In grading, the maximum potential score is 100 points based on various grading factors. To earn the highest grade, the product must achieve a score of more than 85 or in some cases more than 90. Scoring is based on a sample of the product being graded.

If products are inspected and then graded, using these government standards as the only determinant of quality may be unwise. For example, one of the difficulties is that government graders place a great deal of importance on appearance of products, whereas the ultimate restaurant consumers may rely more on factors such as taste, texture, and tenderness in evaluating an operation's food quality.

The purchaser should also know that grading procedures are not without their problems. Stefanelli (1985, p. 94) identifies some of these problems. For example, graders are allowed to use their discretion in grading. Also, a product such as meat can be graded as U.S. Prime (the top grade), but within this grade a tolerance can be allowed from low-Prime to high-Prime. Further, grading based primarily on appearance can be deceiving because appearance and taste are not synonymous and may not even be important in purchasing some products. For example, vegetables to be used in a stew or soup do not need as high an appearance level as those used to accompany a main course entree. Finally, grading products at the source ignores possible deterioration of the product if it is improperly transported to its destination.

Despite these problems, government grades are used by many hospitality industry purchasers as the prime measure of quality. When they are used, they should be modified to suit the circumstances of the individual operation. Unfortunately, they are frequently used by purchasers without modification and as the only quality measure.

Other Sources of Quality Standards

Trade associations and other organizations (such as the National Live Stock and Meat Board) also establish quality standards that can be used by purchasers to help establish their own quality standards and measures.

Brand names are another method of measuring quality. They are particularly useful for food products that do not have government grades. Indeed, brand, trade, or packers' names often are the specification as far as quality is concerned. These brand-name products have usually stood the test of time and obtained purchaser acceptance for quality reliability. Also, brand names usually ensure a quality that goes beyond just appearance to include such things as consistency of size of asparagus packed in a can and density of syrup in which a particular fruit is canned.

Brand-name products from reliable suppliers are also often thought by some purchasers to provide a consistency that government grades do not and, in the case of canned items, a consistent yield of usable product that is the true measure of the cost of the item. Sellers of brands, of course, try to stress the quality of their brands over their competitors' in their sales presentations.

A disadvantage of brand-name products is that they may be available from only a limited number of suppliers, which may mean that they are not competitively priced. In that case, the purchaser might be wise to select a number of similar brands and force suppliers into a competitive pricing situation.

With brand-name products, the processor may use the brand name along with a federal government designation. For example, a box of fresh tomatoes bearing the designation "'U.S. No. 1" will have been government inspected and graded. If the box states only "No. 1," however, then it has not been government graded but in the packer's opinion meets the U.S. No. 1 quality standards.

Combining Quality Measures

The more measures of quality that can be used in preparing specifications, the more likely it is the operation will meet the quality expectations of its customers. Unfortunately, many establishments continue to prepare specifications using only one quality measure rather than a combination of two or more. In other cases, with particular reference to food products, decisions about product qualities are made by a single individual. As Thorner and Manning (1983, p. 17) state,

> It is not unusual to find one person with the responsibility of selecting brands of food using his own personal likes or dislikes as the sole indicator. This system may once have been feasible for small restaurants or where a chef, by tradition, had the full authority to direct purchasing and preparation functions. . . . Regardless of the size of restaurant, a taste panel consisting of three or more people should have the authority to make the necessary selections.

SPECIFICATION TESTS

In many large hospitality businesses, product qualities are determined by testing them. These tests should be conducted by a committee whose members are the key decision makers, such as those who will be using the product. A separate testing committee can be organized, depending on the product being tested. These committees can be particularly useful to taste-test food products and to monitor their quality, costs, and presentation, but they can also be used to test the quality of nonfood products. In a small property the chairperson of the committee is the general manager, with key employees (such as the chef, catering manager, housekeeper, and purchasing manager) as committee members. In a large property, the general manager may delegate the chairperson's role to an assistant manager or department head.

Committee Guidelines

Some guidelines for testing committees, with particular reference to food products, are

- Testing should be done in a suitable environment and in a dedicated test kitchen if one can be set aside. Otherwise, a banquet kitchen or employee cafeteria (when not in normal use) can be reserved for testing.
- Committee members should meet regularly and also hold special meetings when required.
- Specific testing procedures should be established and followed to judge taste quality. When making a taste evaluation, primary factors to consider are flavor (taste and aroma), nutritional attributes, texture, appearance, and consistency of product. Secondary factors to be evaluated might include storage life, packaging convenience, and price.
- When products are tested, two or three samples of competitive products should be used so that quality comparisons can be made. These samples should be as similar to each other as possible (for example, size and trim of a portion of meat or size of can for a processed vegetable), and cooking procedures should be consistent for each sample.
- Suppliers should not be advised that tests of their products are being made. In this way they will not be tempted to deliver "special" test samples.
- Cost of the product and the supplier's name should not be known by committee members until after quality decisions have been made. Each supplier's sample should be labeled only with a code (to identify that supplier) known only by one person such as the purchasing manager or committee chairperson.
- When a major decision is being made (for example, to use a new product or switch from one product to another), a series of tests should be made to ensure the decisions arrived at are not biased.
- Taste test scoring sheets (such as that illustrated in Figure 4-1) should be used to rank products.
- Written records (minutes) of each meeting should be maintained.
- Findings and decisions must be accepted by all committee members.
- Implementing decisions is management's responsibility.

Because taste-test committees recommend the qualities or brands of products that the operation should use, to a large degree they remove the quality decision-making burden from purchasers, as well as the pressure to buy specific products that some suppliers impose on purchasers. In other words, committee decisions can protect purchasers from unreasonable supplier influence.

Revealing Results

Taste tests sometimes reveal interesting results. For example, Warfel and Waskey (1979, p. 124) ran a series of fifty tests on various food items and discovered the following:

	Flavor	Color	Aroma	Tenderness	Appearance	Total
Supplier A						
Supplier B						
Supplier C						
Supplier D						

Product _____   Date _____

Score a maximum of 5 points for each of the following items:

Additional remarks _____

_____

_____

Signature _____

Figure 4-1.   Taste-test score sheet.

1. Only two times out of fifty was the highest-priced item judged to be of the best quality.
2. In eighteen times out of fifty, the lowest-priced item in the test was judged to be of the best quality.
3. At no time was the lowest-priced item judged to be last in quality.
4. At no time was accepting as an alternate a nearly equal item impossible, and thirty-five times out of fifty a third alternate item was acceptable as being of nearly equal quality.
5. At no time did any one product receive all first-place votes.
6. The average saving in purchase price between the product selected and the highest-priced item in each category was 28 percent.

DISCUSSION QUESTIONS

1. List five items that could appear on a specification.
2. When purchasing is done by bid, what information for a supplier should be included on the specification?

3. Prior to preparing a specification, list four important factors to consider.
4. What is a public domain specification?
5. Discuss the pros and cons of a hospitality operator working with a supplier to prepare a specification.
6. How many copies of a specification should be prepared and who receives these copies?
7. Give an example of why narrow requirements for costs, quantities, or quality tolerances should be avoided on a specification.
8. Why should a specification not be prepared that limits bidding to only one supplier? What might be some of the advantages of doing business with only one supplier?
9. Explain the term *lowball bidding*.
10. List five advantages of specifications.
11. What is a quality standard? In your own words, provide a definition of *quality*.
12. Some purchasers believe that a hospitality operation can establish quality standards for products without considering its customers' views. Discuss this.
13. Discuss the problems that government grading of products for quality creates.
14. Discuss the pros and cons of brand-name products as a measure of quality.
15. List five guidelines that a taste-test committee should follow to perform an evaluation of food product quality.

PROBLEMS

1. Assume that you are the new manager of a restaurant that has been profitable for many years. It presently purchases all products without using specifications. The restaurant owner has heard that profitability might be increased by preparing and using specifications and has asked you to produce a one-page report about this. In your report, among other matters you deem important, discuss the time and effort (and thus the cost) that would be involved and whom you would recommend to write the specifications or how they could otherwise be obtained. Also discuss the value of using packers' brands as the specification for some food products.
2. Visit or telephone two hospitality operations (restaurants, hotels, or institutions such as colleges or hospitals). Obtain from each of them a voided copy of a previously used specification form. Compare these two forms for what they include and do not include, using the guidelines listed at the beginning of this chapter for what could be included. Write a short summary of your findings and any recommendations you would make for redesigning these forms.
3. Discuss with the manager or purchasing manager of a large hotel or restaurant how the quality standards for major purchases they make are established. Try to obtain the answers to questions such as: Who determines these standards? How are they determined? How is the purchaser involved in setting those

standards? What is the purchasing manager's function in conforming to standards once they have been established? Write a summary of your findings, including any recommendations you would make if you were the general manager of that operation responsible for product quality standards.

REFERENCES AND SUGGESTED READINGS

Dittmer, Paul R., and Gerald G. Griffin. 1984. *Principles of Food, Beverage & Labor Cost Controls for Hotels and Restaurants.* New York: Van Nostrand Reinhold.

Kotschevar, Lendal H., and Charles Levinson. 1988. *Quantity Food Purchasing.* New York: Macmillan, pp. 50–54.

Mutkoski, Stephen A., and Marcia L. Schurer. 1981. *Meat and Fish Management.* North Scituate, Mass.: Breton.

Powers, Thomas F., and Jo Marie Powers. 1984. *Food Service Operations: Planning and Control.* New York: John Wiley.

Stefanelli, John M. 1985. *Purchasing: Selection and Procurement for the Hospitality Industry.* New York: John Wiley, pp. 81–97.

Thorner, Marvin E., and Peter B. Manning. 1983. *Quality Control in Foodservice.* Westport, Conn.: AVI.

Virts, William B. 1987. *Purchasing for Hospitality Operations.* East Lansing, Mich.: The Educational Institute of the American Hotel & Motel Association, pp. 57–62.

Warfel, M. C., and Frank H. Waskey. 1979. *The Professional Food Buyer.* Berkeley, Calif.: McCutchan, pp. 105–24.

5

Purchasing Methods and Dealing with Suppliers

OBJECTIVES

- Briefly discuss various purchasing methods such as competitive buying, contract buying, cost-plus buying, one-step buying, cooperative buying, and volume buying and warehousing.
- Define purchasing terms such as *cash and carry* and *drop shipments*.
- Explain the problem that purchasing from national suppliers can create with local suppliers.
- Discuss centralized purchasing.
- List the six steps in the negotiation process and the guidelines for concessions.
- List the important factors to consider before making final supplier selection, and discuss the pros and cons of using as few suppliers as possible.
- Discuss suppliers' buyer profiles, and differentiate between a seller's push and pull selling strategies.
- Discuss how suppliers can be evaluated.

To many small hospitality operators, purchasing is simply a matter of telephoning known suppliers who can provide needed products, placing an order, and having it delivered as soon as possible. In other situations, a supplier's representative may arrive at the premises and write up an order without the hospitality operation having any record of products and quantities ordered or their prices. With these often disorganized methods of placing orders (rather than effective purchasing), no attempt is made to contact alternative suppliers or to compare product qualities and prices. In fact, some purchasers do not even ask about prices!

As a result of these "informal" purchasing methods, the supplier is acting primarily as a warehouse for the purchaser and is retained as the supplier because it will make emergency deliveries—a service that is offered because it knows it is the sole or main supplier and charges prices accordingly. Unfortunately, this and similar purchasing practices that focus only on the short-run situation can cost from 10 to 20 percent more than following systematic procedures. A purchaser who is dependent on and loyal to only one supplier may be overlooking quality and price advantages available from alternate suppliers. Before considering suppliers, however, an operator should first be familiar with all possible purchasing methods.

PURCHASING METHODS

Many different purchasing methods are available, and selecting the right supplier cannot be done without first considering the type of purchasing method that is best for the operation and the products that it needs. Many purchasers select only one of the many arrangements to be discussed in the following sections and stick with it without considering other methods. Again, this approach can unnecessarily add to purchase costs. In other words, rarely (other than perhaps in the very smallest hospitality operations) is a single purchasing method best. Purchasers need to select the most appropriate one for each type of product and change that method when necessary to meet market conditions.

Competitive Buying

Competitive buying is also known as *open market buying, quotation buying, market quote buying, call sheet buying,* or *riding the market.* This method entails waiting until the goods are needed and then taking bids from suppliers to fulfill those needs. Probably the majority of food purchases made by the typical hospitality operation are made through competitive buying.

Under competitive buying, quotations are received by telephone, in person directly from a salesperson, or in writing through the mail from suppliers who are aware of the products' specifications and are on the approved-supplier list. Quotations are often recorded on an in-house duplicate quotation sheet such as that illustrated in Figure 8-1. After it is complete and the supplier(s) selected, the original copy of the quotation sheet is retained by the purchaser and the duplicate is sent to the receiver to check prices on invoices received when goods are delivered.

Traditionally, purchasers in small hospitality operations use competitive buying and purchase products from the supplier who offers the lowest price for each product. Large volume purchasers know that this is not the most viable method of purchasing because it means that a supplier would frequently be required to deliver only one or two items of perhaps twenty that were quoted on. The cost is no less for a supplier to deliver one case of a product than ten cases. If the cost of a delivery is fifty dollars, and ten cases are delivered, the delivery cost is only five dollars per case. If one case is delivered, delivery cost is fifty dollars per case. Either way, the purchaser ends up paying this delivery cost in the price of the product.

Further, when suppliers make bids in this type of competitive buying situation, they have no way of knowing if they will receive an order or how many items will be ordered from the list they are quoting on. In this uncertainty and because of the cost of delivery, doubtless all suppliers tend to bid higher than they would if they knew they would receive the complete order as long as their total overall price for all items in a list was lower.

Therefore, if a purchaser needs a variety of products, the best strategy is to buy from the supplier who offers the lowest overall cost (even though the cost on some individual items might be higher than from other suppliers), and advise all suppliers that this policy is in effect. This practice should result in lower overall prices in the long run.

Competitive buying works fairly well as long as purchasers understand that all suppliers are not equal in the services they offer. For example, the supplier with the lowest overall prices may not offer the best delivery schedule.

In some situations, because of the time and cost involved in competitive buying, a hospitality operator selects only one or two suppliers and sticks with them without requesting quotations from others. This situation is most likely to prevail in small, independent enterprises. The important consideration is that these suppliers must be carefully selected on the basis of their reputation for reasonable prices and dependable service.

Competitive buying is not popular with suppliers whose product prices appear higher but whose services (such as extending a longer credit period) make the total value a better purchase. Also, because suppliers offering better services do generally have higher prices, suppliers without comparable services may raise their prices to just under those from "better" suppliers because they know that the purchaser bases the buying decision on price alone.

Stefanelli (1985, p. 157) comments about competitive buying that "many suppliers try to circumvent your desire to bid buy by offering various discounts, other opportunity buys, introductory offers, and so forth. In addition, they try to become the exclusive distributor for some items which, if you want to purchase them, you have no choice then in supplier selection."

Warfel and Waskey (1979, p. 82) list the following as disadvantages of the competitive buying method:

- The purchaser is limited to the stock available on the market.
- Because the purchasing procedure is often used for daily purchases, it does not permit the purchaser to negotiate or take advantage of seasonal trends.

- If the purchaser is not familiar with the best market buys, items may be ordered that are out of season and thus more expensive.
- Suppliers on the approved list may collude to set high prices and agree how the purchaser's business will be shared out among them. (This possibility can be overcome by the purchaser rotating suppliers from time to time and adding new ones who are not part of the cartel.)

Single-Source Buying

In some situations single-source buying is necessary. The product required may be unique, with only one manufacturer or supplier. In such cases, the purchaser may have little control over the cost of the item.

Contract Buying

Contract buying might be useful for a product or products that must be purchased in relatively large quantities over a fairly long period (for example, from three months to a year), and the price can be guaranteed by the supplier during this period. In some cases, contracts might be written allowing for price changes during that period within a specified range.

Government and institutional operations frequently purchase on a contract basis. Chain operations might also use this method for certain products. According to a study on corporate purchasing practices, Riegel and Reid (1988, p. 28) discovered that "prices and guarantee of supply were the items most frequently negotiated in these contracts, and these items were strictly monitored to ensure adherence to the contract."

Sealed-Bid Buying

Sealed-bid buying is generally used only by large organizations, institutions, and government units and is basically a formalized method of competitive buying. Bid forms are not standardized and vary with circumstances. Generally, however, they contain bid conditions, quantity of and specifications for products required, any conditions concerning delivery, and deadline date for bid submissions.

A bid may be written so that the purchaser pays for all products at the time of purchase, even though they may be delivered over several months, or it may be written so that payment is made only as products are periodically received.

Sometimes bids are for a quantity of products to be delivered over a stipulated period at prices that can fluctuate with market prices. If this supplier flexibility were not part of the bid procedure, then potential suppliers are likely to protect themselves by quoting prices that are higher in total over the period than they would be if prices were allowed to fluctuate.

Sealed-bid buying is often used for quantity purchases of processed foods such as canned and frozen items and for staple (nonperishable) foods, as well as for paper and cleaning supplies used in dining and housekeeping areas. This method eliminates the problem of frequent pricing and purchasing. It may also have the advantages of reducing prices of products and eliminating supplier pressure on an individual establishment.

A disadvantage of this purchasing method is that it requires a great deal of paperwork in preparing and sending out bid forms to selected suppliers and in scrutinizing bids received to ensure they meet requirements. Bids received are often reviewed by a committee to relieve the decision-making pressure that might otherwise be placed on an individual purchaser. Suppliers' names should not be disclosed to committee members as bids are reviewed.

Another disadvantage of sealed-bid buying (particularly if long periods of time are involved) may be that the individual establishment may not be able to benefit from subsequent local price advantages as they occur because sealed-bid buying generally requires that a contract be signed between the purchasing organization and the successful bidder for a stipulated quantity of product.

Stefanelli (1985, p. 91) warns of the difficulty in bid buying: "For some items, like equipment, bids may be economically beneficial to the hospitality operator. But on the whole, the buyer who uses this buying plan had better know as much or more about the items as the supplier. Only the large operations consistently approach this requirement."

Cost-Plus Buying

With cost-plus buying, the hospitality purchaser arranges with a supplier to purchase all of its requirements for a product or products at a specific percentage markup over the supplier's cost for a future fixed time period that can vary from thirty days to six months. The advantage to the purchaser is that this markup is generally smaller than would otherwise be the case. Time that would be spent dealing with a variety of suppliers is also reduced. An alternative to using cost-plus on a percentage basis might be to contract for cost plus a fixed fee per delivery.

The problem with this buying method is that verifying the supplier's cost may be difficult, if not impossible. What is "cost" and does the purchaser have the right to inspect or audit the supplier's records (or invoices from suppliers from which it purchases) to determine it? Most likely only a major or chain operation could impose a demand for an audit. For example, a motel chain that decided to purchase all guest room furniture and/or linen requirements from a single supplier might be able to insist on an audit.

Cost-plus buying is not normally used by the typical individual hospitality enterprise. Where it is used, however, the markup is usually 10 to 15 percent over cost compared to a normal 15 to 25 percent markup over cost. The actual percentage is usually negotiated. Suppliers are prepared to take a smaller markup because they consider a guaranteed small markup on volume sales better than a higher markup on sales they are not guaranteed. As Warfel and Waskey (1979, p. 87) state: "Records of companies using the cost-plus system prove that they save, on a yearly basis, 10 percent to 12 percent on the purchase prices of commodities bought in this manner as against open market buying."

Cost-plus buying could also be used when a fixed-price contract is not possible but the purchaser wants a contracted guaranteed delivery and is willing to pay whatever the prevailing price is at the time of delivery. For example, a restaurant that wants to feature an unusual special item on its menu may obtain a guarantee from the supplier that supply will be available and in return agrees to pay the prevailing price; it adjusts the menu selling price from time to time as necessary.

Cost-plus buying involves more risk than long-term contracts because prices can rise sharply during the cost-plus term and the supplier is committed to making those purchases rather than seeking alternatives. Obviously, a thirty-day cost-plus contract is less risky than a six-month one. Keister (1977, p. 212) comments about cost-plus as follows:

> In theory, this sounds fine. In practice it may or may not work. Some purveyors find it difficult to operate in this manner. They, or their employees, may get lax or careless. They may deliver goods that are not quite up to the standards you called for in your specifications. The idea is good in theory, but in reality there is usually nothing like competing for your orders to keep your suppliers at their most efficient.

One-Stop Buying

One-stop buying is also sometimes referred to as *prime-vendor purchasing*. It involves the purchase of all items of a particular type (for example, paper and cleaning supplies) from one supplier. Keister (1977, p. 213) suggests that the name *one-stop shopping* is incorrect and that it should be called *fewer-purveyor shopping* or something similar because "there aren't many purveyors, if any, who can really get you all the items you need."

Whatever it is called, the method eliminates or reduces the constant need to compare suppliers and prices, eliminates constant negotiations, and builds up the selected supplier's trust. Fewer orders are required, fewer deliveries have to be received, and fewer invoices must be processed and paid. Theoretically, this method reduces purchasing costs. Because no competitive bidding takes place, however, the financial advantages of one-stop buying must be carefully weighed before using this purchasing method.

The one-stop purchasing concept developed because suppliers were willing, because of a guaranteed quantity, to reduce their markup from the normal 15 to 25 percent over cost to 10 to 12 percent, thus reducing the purchaser's costs by 3 to 15 percent.

One-stop buying may provide an overall cost advantage to the purchaser, even though the costs on some items may be higher than they would be if purchased elsewhere. Products with higher costs are theoretically compensated for by reduced costs on others and/or the supplier's willingness to offer a volume discount on the total purchase cost of all items. Large suppliers offering one-stop buying may also have product specialists on their payroll who can give the purchaser detailed information on both existing and new product availability. The important ingredients in one-stop buying are careful selection of the supplier and periodic price comparisons to ensure that the supplier's prices are still in line.

The big risk with one-stop buying is that the purchaser becomes too dependent on the supplier and fails to stay alert to prices that are out of line or to newer products or additional services that have been introduced by the supplier's competitors. Another disadvantage is that the one-stop supplier may become a generalist rather than a specialist and thereby decrease the availability of a variety of quality levels within any one product line. For example, a generalist supplier might carry three or four thousand different product lines, many of which are competitively priced high-quality products. Along with those, however, are other products that are priced higher than a specialist supplier might charge because the one-stop supplier applies a higher than normal markup on these items (in the same way that a restaurant operator offers a variety of menu items, some of which have a higher markup than others).

Peddersen (1981, p. 10) comments about one-stop buying of food as follows:

> It is my opinion that one-stop shopping will be the accepted and prevailing mode of purchasing before the end of the twentieth century. One-stop companies are likely to develop from the merger of several small purveyors. This trend can be seen in the merger of fresh produce with frozen produce houses who then pick up distribution of frozen entrees, baked goods, and meat lines, and then merge with a general groceries and canned goods purveyor.

According to Eames and Norkus (1988, p. 31), "Although the amount may vary from area to area and supplier to supplier, $2,000 to $2,500 is usually the floor above which a one-stop supplier will consider an organization as a program account" because the supplier is guaranteed that the purchaser (program account) will buy a certain amount of products and thus reduce supplier costs, such as those for delivery. A risk is that other suppliers will cut their prices, make them known to the one-stop purchaser, and try to convince him or her to revert to competitive bidding, at which point those suppliers begin to raise their prices again. This sequence is an example of lowballing because those suppliers cannot maintain their profits over the long run at the offered low prices.

Combined Competitive and One-Stop Buying

In some situations (particularly for large-volume purchasers), a system that combines competitive pricing with one-stop buying within a particular group of products might be feasible. For example, a beverage purchaser might have five licensed suppliers from whom to buy alcoholic beverages. Over time, the purchaser has found that suppliers A, B, and E consistently offer the best prices for distilled products, so they will be asked to bid competitively each time a purchase is to be made. These three suppliers know that they are in a good position to receive a certain amount of the purchaser's business and thus stay competitive in price, service, and quality. Supplier C can compete only on imported beers (because it specializes in them) but always offers the best overall prices and is given all imported beer orders without competitive bidding. Meanwhile, supplier D is consistently best in variety of wines offered and in wine prices and is given all wine orders without competitive buying. Suppliers C and D must be made aware of the fact that, if their prices, service, or quality and availability of product slip in any way, they may lose the business to their competitors.

Cooperative Buying

Cooperative buying occurs when a group of operators join together to purchase products. The operators benefit from quantity-discount prices as the result of bulk buying. Although not common in the hospitality industry for purchase of food, beverages, and other operating supplies, it could occur, for example, if a group of hotels joined together to contract for the purchase of the same quality of bed linen from a supplier.

An advantage of cooperative buying is that standardized quality as well as lower prices should result because of the group's volume purchasing. Also, individual group members may have to spend less time with supplier sales representatives, and thus they have more time for other day-to-day operations.

Cooperative buying has some disadvantages because the purchasing decision is usually turned over to a committee. Committees are notorious for slowing down any process and sometimes find a decision consensus difficult. Further, individual members of the group may lose some control over supplier selection, loyalty, and product variety and quality because that task must be delegated to the committee.

Where cooperative purchasing is used, members have to agree on the quality standards and specifications for required products so that advantage can be taken of volume purchasing of identical products. This task is time-consuming because, without agreement, the method cannot succeed. Compromise by some participants in the cooperative is often required. Note that cooperative buying does not require that all products for all participants be purchased through the cooperative. Participants should be free to purchase some products independently (particularly those unique to their operation), although this flexibility does decrease the ability of the cooperative to negotiate lower prices on all products.

A cooperative buying arrangement, according to Virts (1987, p. 61), "should be established and operated under the guidance of legal counsel to ensure that federal and state antitrust laws are not violated." For example, the cooperative group could be liable for pressuring suppliers to offer discounts that are unfair to those purchasers who are not members of the group.

Stefanelli (1985, p. 162) comments, "Independent, commercial hospitality properties have experienced mixed success with co-op purchasing.... Each buyer or owner-manager has to make his or her own decision concerning the potential costs and benefits of co-op buying."

Volume Buying and Warehousing

Volume buying and warehousing is also known as *stockless purchasing*. In some situations, a purchaser may be able to buy in large quantity and obtain a major discount. In such cases, the supplier may agree to store or warehouse the product for an additional cost. Alternatively, the purchaser may be responsible for making storage arrangements off the premises (if on-site space is inadequate) and paying the costs. In the case of volume buying of certain food items, additional refrigerator or freezer space may be required.

Volume buying and warehousing usually entails the purchaser paying in advance for products purchased and either paying in advance for storage or paying the storage fee monthly. In all these situations, the purchaser must balance the purchase cost savings against the costs incurred for storage and the loss of interest on money tied up in inventory.

A variation of volume buying and warehousing is an agreement between purchaser and supplier by which the supplier agrees to deliver a contracted amount of a product over time and absorb all warehouse and storage costs until the goods are delivered to the purchaser's establishment. This arrangement is sometimes used for items such as paper products, cleaning supplies, and linens. Wines are also frequently purchased this way because certain vintages will not be available in the future if they are not purchased now and warehoused. It can also be used where personalized chinaware and similar items need fairly large manufacturing runs to make their purchase cost-effective.

Volume buying and warehousing is often a good method to use if price increases are forecast. The added cost of warehousing may still make the products cheaper than if they were purchased later at higher prices. This situation often happens with meat because twice a year meat prices are traditionally low (in January and February and again in November). By buying during those periods and then freezing supplies, meat will be available to the purchaser at lower cost when price is otherwise high. Obviously, the risk exists that the price will decrease rather than increase.

Farmers' Markets and Supermarkets

Farmers' markets (also sometimes known as *public markets)* are a useful source of fresh produce for small foodservice operations. They are seldom used by large operations who have to buy in relatively large quantities. Markets offer fresh fruit and vegetables, fish, eggs, poultry, meat, smoked meat, and dairy products. They are sometimes open seven days a week, often for extended hours, and some operate around the clock in the peak harvest period. These markets are government inspected, particularly for sanitary practices. Prices may be lower and products fresher than from other sources, but to be sure the purchaser must be familiar with local prices and qualities from these other sources. Prices can be lower because the individual producers and sellers bypass wholesale distributors.

As an alternative where there is no farmers' market, the small operator might use the local supermarket for food and other supplies. The main advantage of this source is that virtually all products used by most small hospitality operations are available in one location (a sort of one-stop shopping). Supermarkets also offer the convenience of seven-day-a-week opening, which means products required can be purchased daily, thus reducing the need to carry an inventory on-site, reducing spoilage loss, and allowing better cost control. In some cases, twenty-four-hour service is offered, which can be useful in an emergency. Sometimes supermarkets provide lower pricing than local suppliers can offer because they have tremendous buying power, have their own distribution systems, and thus bypass other intermediaries. They also tend to have excellent and reliable quality-control systems.

Another advantage of both farmers' markets and supermarkets is that the purchaser has to pay cash, thus reducing the problems that can occur when a purchaser receives credit from a supplier, fails to pay bills on time, and then begins to have cash flow problems.

Despite lower prices and/or better quality, even a very small operation may find disadvantages in purchasing from farmers' markets or supermarkets. To the cost of the product must be added the value of the purchaser providing his or her own transportation. This added transportation cost comprises both the cost of operating the vehicle and the cost of the person's time to pick up the needed products. For example, if the chef does farmers' market or supermarket purchasing for a small restaurant, would the time not be better spent supervising today's kitchen production rather than "shopping"? For this reason large operations, other than perhaps in an emergency situation, seldom use this method of buying. Note, however, that many conscientious chefs will put in extra time very early in the morning to be at fresh produce distribution centers in large cities to ensure that they have first selection of the best and freshest produce.

Cash and Carry

To encourage business from small operators who are in the habit of buying from their local farmers' market and/or supermarket, some regular hospitality industry suppliers offer a cash-and-carry service in which the supplier reduces product prices because the purchaser is willing to provide the transportation. However, as Stefanelli states (1985, p. 160), "Most suppliers resist cash and carry (sometimes referred to as "will call") mainly because they have already invested heavily in their trucks and other elements of their delivery function." Cash and carry also has the same disadvantages to the purchaser (cost of transportation and time) as is the case with farmers' market and supermarket buying.

Auctions

Auctions are a purchasing method used by some large operations who need to buy food and other items in large quantities. Auctions are common in big cities where they are held daily to sell truckloads or carloads of fresh fruit, vegetables, and other products such as convenience foods.

Normally the bidding is open only to accredited sellers and to bidding members who use this system on a regular basis. In other words, a restaurant operator could not suddenly decide one day to visit an auction and begin bidding. The operator could arrange to have a regular bidder do this or employ an accredited agent to bid on his or her behalf for an agreed-upon fee. This representative then makes the purchase at the lowest price, inspects the merchandise before it leaves the auction premises, and arranges transportation to the purchaser's receiving dock.

The fee can be either a fixed amount for each container (for example, carton or case) purchased or a percentage of the dollar value of products purchased. This fee may or may not cover the transportation costs of moving the product from the auction area to the purchaser's premises; in some situations the agent's fee includes transportation, and in other cases the commission may be lower and the purchaser pays for transportation separately. Other than for very large purchasers, little cost advantage may be gained by buying at auctions. As Warfel and Waskey state (1979, p. 92), "This type of buying generally produces a net savings to the buyer almost equal to the commission per package paid to the auction member acting as agent."

Meat Carcass Buying

Traditionally, when a restaurant or hotel foodservice operation buys meat in bulk, the chef regularly visits the local meat supplier's premises, selects carcasses or wholesale cuts from those offered, and then uses the operation's personal stamp to mark carcasses and/or cuts to ensure that those selected are the ones delivered for further on-premise butchering. Few small operations buy this way anymore (preferring to buy processed preportioned individual meat products), but this practice is still recommended for those who continue to do their own on-site butchering.

A major reason for inspecting meat at the supplier's premises is that three high-quality grades of the best beef and five separate yield grades within each quality grade (meaning a choice of fifteen different qualities and yields) are available, and the best meat goes to the purchaser who is on the spot to make the selection.

The same practice is also recommended for fruit and vegetables if they are purchased in large quantities. By visiting the supplier's premises, the purchaser can again select the products that offer the best quality and price combination, and again mark cases or containers with the operation's individual stamp to ensure that what is purchased is actually delivered.

Government Acceptance

Because of the difficulty in purchasing meat, some purchasers use the government acceptance service. For a fee, a U.S. Department of Agriculture inspector at a meat processing plant will ensure that meat is processed and packaged according to the purchaser's specifications. Inspectors can also help in preparing specifications. Unfortunately, many purchasers do not take advantage of this service. Keister (1977, p. 214) notes two reasons for this:

1. Managers don't know it exists.
2. Managers are aware of the method but say, "I know so much about meat, I don't need to pay for government inspectors."

Hedging

Hedging is a method of purchasing that entails considerable risks. It was discussed in chapter 3 as a method of protection against possible price increases.

Drop Shipments

For certain nationally produced brands of canned fruits and vegetables, oils and fats, olives and pickles, and other processed foods, the prices of which are relatively stable, drop shipments can be made by large-quantity purchasers. This system does not work well for meats, poultry, and other perishable items because of their day-to-day price instability. A drop shipper places an order (on behalf of the purchaser) directly with a manufacturer who delivers the products at the purchaser's receiving dock. The larger the shipment, the lower the price. According to Warfel and Waskey (1979, p. 86), prices can be 10 to 15 percent lower than the price paid to a local supplier, and in some cases as much as 25 percent.

Local Suppliers versus National Suppliers

In using purchasing methods such as drop shipments and auctions, the question arises (apart from the cost savings) whether a purchaser should bypass a local supplier in favor of a distant national supplier. This question is particularly debatable if the purchaser has to provide and/or pay for transportation from a distant source.

Generally speaking, most small operators do not buy in large quantities and therefore are unable to use auctions and drop shipments. They must deal with local suppliers, despite the higher costs. The advantages, however, are that the local supplier can be much more cognizant of the purchaser's needs, is often helpful in emergency situations, and can be a friend as much as a supplier. Purchasers who bypass local suppliers alienate them, are unlikely to engender sympathy in an emergency, and may generate general community ill will. A solution to this problem is to buy from a national source but have the distribution handled by a local supplier. Slightly higher costs are offset by the added services the local supplier is willing to provide.

Options Available

From the foregoing, obviously each individual purchaser has many purchasing arrangements available, each one with advantages and disadvantages. Which method or methods should be selected often depends on the purchaser's volume requirements. Large operations often have more choice of methods, and (because of their buying power) more opportunities to make cost savings. Whether or not a purchaser enters into a specific type of arrangement with any one supplier also depends on the supplier's willingness to cooperate.

OTHER CONSIDERATIONS

A number of other factors ought to be considered before a final selection of suppliers is made. Some of them are discussed in this section.

Lowest Overall Cost

The real goal in purchasing is to purchase products at the lowest possible total cost, not at the lowest price per se. This goal has implications in the purchase of carcasses or large cuts of meat, for which the restaurant's on-site butchering labor can add considerably to total costs. Few restaurants do their own butchering today. Instead, they purchase preportioned, preprepared individual cuts of meat (convenience or prefabricated foods) that require little or no butchering and thus eliminate a significant labor cost. The total cost of purchasing such foods is lower, and the approach also provides better inventory control (again creating a reduction in costs). Consequently, in contracting for purchases, all possible costs should be considered and not just the quoted price of the products.

Cost of Money

Another consideration is the cost of money. Assuming money costs 12 percent a year (or 1 percent a month), a purchaser who can effect a saving of 10 percent by purchasing a six-month supply of a product would be unwise not to consider that. The 10 percent cost saving is reduced by the 6 percent (6 months × 1 percent) cost of the money, but the net saving is still 4 percent, less the cost of any additional storage. Another consideration is that the cost of money is usually fixed in the short run, but the cost of products is not. In other words, the 4 percent net saving in the above example (less any storage costs) may turn out to be even higher if, during the six-month period, the price of the inventoried product is still rising in the market.

Centralized Purchasing

Large firms can often take advantage of their size through centralized purchasing. Some large firms, however, do not use centralized buying because they feel that the costs of centralization outweigh the benefits. Where centralized purchasing does occur, the degree of centralization can vary. The most highly centralized type of operation is a commissary-based system in which all items (including perishable foods that need to be kept frozen or refrigerated) are purchased. In some commissaries, the food may even undergo further processing before distribution to individual outlets.

Less centralized is a distribution center that purchases and distributes to individual units all nonfood items and nonperishable and/or frozen food items, but lets individual units do their own direct purchasing of perishable foods.

Even more decentralized would be, for example, individual units of a chain or franchised operation that buy whatever they need from local suppliers as long as the local supplier has central purchasing office approval for quality and price of products.

Some centralized buying can also occur when a contract for products at a reduced price is arranged between the central office and a national manufacturer. The central office contracts that all its units will use the product in return for a volume discount, but the units do their purchasing directly from local suppliers, who have had the manufacturer's discount passed on to them. Chain operations can frequently benefit from this type of arrangement for most items, except, perhaps, perishable foods that have to be purchased daily and locally by each unit.

Other advantages of centralized purchasing are that the central purchasing office may be able to contact a greater number of suppliers and that larger overall inventories of certain items can be maintained, thus reducing costs and ensuring a constant supply to individual units in the chain. Centralized purchasing may mean, however, that the individual unit must accept the quality standard dictated by the central purchasing office. It may also preclude individual units from taking advantage of local supplies at a low or "special" price.

NEGOTIATIONS

Negotiated buying occurs when seller and buyer agree on the price to be paid for a product through a bargaining process. The purchaser hopes, through negotiation, to obtain concessions or additional services that would not otherwise be obtained without bargaining. Such negotiations normally occur only with large hospitality enterprises or institutional establishments.

Those involved in negotiations must be highly skilled in the negotiation process. Negotiations involve the use of persuasive communication and information to change the other party's views or positions. Through negotiation, purchaser and seller can reach mutually beneficial agreements about products to be sold and purchased. The six steps in this negotiation process (from the perspective of the purchaser) are as follows:

1. Gather preliminary information about its needs, its purchasing strengths and weaknesses, and the potential supplier's strengths and weaknesses.
2. Assess this information to answer the following questions:

> How soon is the product needed?
> How much time can be devoted to this particular negotiation?
> What has been the seller's past delivery performance?
> How urgent is the seller's need to sell?
> How soon can the product be delivered?
> What concessions can we make during negotiations, who has authority to make them, and what are the concession limitations, if any?
> In past negotiations, what has been the supplier's strategy? In other words, what concessions have been made and have they been made cooperatively?

3. Prepare a negotiation action plan. The answers to the questions in step 2 often point the purchaser in the right direction for this plan. This plan must consider the resources that the purchaser has, the resources that the supplier has, and the supplier's likely negotiation strategy. In this plan deciding who will do the purchaser's negotiating is important. Sometimes an individual purchaser may do this; at other times a team approach (for example, the purchaser and his or her supervisor) may be better.
4. Prepare a negotiation strategy. The negotiation strategy is basically a matter of

the purchaser selecting the time and/or place for negotiations and the communication method (such as telephone, face to face, or special meeting) so that the purchaser has the optimum advantage. For example, using the telephone means an absence of visual feedback. Face-to-face communication generally reduces the risk of misunderstandings but has the disadvantage of not allowing the purchaser to return a telephone call to the seller at the most convenient time after additional necessary information has been gathered.

For nontelephone negotiating, the location does not have to be the hospitality operation's premises. It could be the supplier's, which may allow the purchaser to find out more about how the supplier does business, obtain more information, meet other members of the supplier's organization, view first hand the supplier's premises, and assess aspects of it such as sanitary conditions.

5. Conduct negotiations. The two main approaches to conducting negotiations are cooperative and competitive. Cooperative negotiation assumes that both parties realize that some concessions are necessary in order to prevent potential conflicts that may preclude any negotiated agreement. In other words, it requires a two-party commitment. Competitive negotiation means that one or both parties have taken inflexible positions that the other party sees as unreasonable. Sometimes competitive negotiation can lead to an agreed solution that satisfies both parties. Often, however, a solution is reached that means one or both parties are unhappy, and future negotiations on other contracts are much more difficult. Obviously, cooperative negotiation is normally the preferred method because it usually results in a "win-win" situation (both parties win) rather than the "win-lose" outcome of competitive negotiation in which one party is satisfied and the other is not. Further, in some win-lose situations, the winner receives only a temporary advantage. For example, a purchaser may gradually negotiate down a supplier's price, knowing that the supplier needs the business, only to find that the disgruntled supplier does not provide delivery services as promised. Note also that a cooperative negotiation can sometimes be switched to a competitive one during negotiations if it appears to be advantageous.

6. Closed negotiations. Negotiations are closed when both parties agree that a deal can be made and that no conflicts have been left unresolved. Oral contracts are legally binding, but if major product quantities and/or dollars are involved the agreement should be in writing. A contract spells out matters agreed to (quantities, prices, commitments, and responsibilities) by both purchaser and seller.

Concession Guidelines

The obvious objective of both parties in negotiation is to maximize concessions received and minimize concessions given. Normally, the best approach by a purchaser is to agree on the supplier's base or starting price and then discuss adjustments to this by way of concessions. Concessions usually take the form of negotiating discounts or rebates for quantity purchases, limiting price increases to a specified percentage for a future fixed period of time, adjusting price increases to price indicators or indexes, or improving supplier invoicing and credit terms. Some guidelines for minimizing purchaser concessions are:

- Establish the most desirable result (that is, the one that yields the least in the way of concessions). In other words, have a negotiation goal even though it will not necessarily be achieved.
- List (or at least be aware of) the economic and quality consequences of each concession likely to be given to the supplier.
- Try to have the supplier yield the first concession.
- Do not yield a concession without receiving something in return from the supplier.
- Do not agree to a concession without first trying to reduce it by making a counteroffer to the supplier.
- Make all concessions yielded tentative until the negotiation goal is achieved or the agreement is as close to that goal as is possible even with further negotiation.
- When the seller will not budge from a stated price, provide some face-saving way of reducing it, for example, by changing delivery or other service terms.

SELECTION OF SUPPLIER

According to Riegel and Reid (1988, p. 28), "Once a decision of relatively insignificant consequence, the supplier-selection decision has, in recent years, become increasingly important" because "selecting the right supplier can have significant impact on bottom-line performance." In other words, cooperative and reliable supplier(s) must be found and used.

The many types of suppliers include the manufacturer, wholesaler, retailer, and local producer or farmer. Depending on the product to be purchased, a different type of supplier may be contacted. For example, in the case of an item of capital equipment, it might be the manufacturer or its wholesaler representative. In the case of a food product, it might be the meat packer or even the local farmer.

Factors Involved

The following factors may be involved in the selection of suppliers:

- Finding out who some of the supplier's present customers are to check with them about the supplier's competence, reputation, reliability, consistency of product quality, promptness and frequency of deliveries, and similar matters.
- Testing the quality of the products offered. The "top" quality is not always the "best" in a particular situation. Consider, for example, the requirement for a vegetable to be used in a soup. Here, appearance might not be an important factor

requiring the purchase of a top-quality item; if the same vegetable were to be served as an accompaniment to an entree item, however, quality of appearance would be important.

- Checking product prices. Again, the lowest price may not be the "best" price to pay, depending on the quality actually needed. Are a supplier's prices comparable to its competitors?
- Evaluating the degree to which it provides information about new products on the market. Most hospitality industry purchasers rely to a great degree on suppliers' sales representatives to provide product information. These representatives must therefore be both knowledgeable and willing to provide this information. If they are not, then the purchaser must turn to the supplier's sales manager or other competent person for advice and accurate information. Large suppliers often provide monthly or more frequent printed market information sheets that are automatically distributed to their purchasers and potential purchasers.
- Visiting the supplier's premises and reviewing its sanitation standards, if important. For example, this factor could be critical at the premises of a supplier of perishable food items. Such visits may also indicate if a supplier is experiencing labor difficulties and similar matters that may lead to unreliable service. In the same regard, particularly where food products are concerned, suppliers' vehicles may need to be inspected to ensure they are sanitary and have adequate refrigerator or freezer equipment.
- Determining the lead time a supplier requires. Local suppliers of frequently required products normally accept orders a day ahead of delivery. Others may require two or more days lead time. For some products, some suppliers require even more lead time.
- Checking supplier's delivery frequency and time of deliveries. Delivery costs are often a major expense to a supplier and therefore an area where price negotiation may be possible if the purchaser agrees to have deliveries made at the convenience of the supplier. For example, instead of having daily deliveries from a regular supplier, can deliveries be reduced to two or three times a week with the supplier providing price concessions? Also, most suppliers have delivery schedules that peak in the morning. Can price concessions be negotiated for afternoon deliveries?

According to Stefanelli (1985, p. 154), the most important consideration in supplier selection is performance, that is, "prompt deliveries, the number of rejected deliveries, how adjustments on rejected deliveries are handled, how well the supplier takes care of one or two trial orders, the capacity of a middleman's plant, and his or her technological know-how."

How Many Suppliers?

According to Virts (1987, p. 32), "most moderately sized lodging operations will have over 50 separate suppliers." Any hospitality purchaser faces the question of how many suppliers to use. A property in a remote location may have only a handful of suppliers to choose from for all products, but even in a large city some products may have only one supplier. This situation could occur, for example, if the supplier has the sole distributorship or is the only one who carries a particular brand-name product. Similarly, purchasers who buy only in small volumes may find their choices among suppliers limited because large suppliers are not interested in accepting their business. For most products, however, purchasers will have a choice among several competitive suppliers. Bell (1984, p. 77) makes the following comment about keeping the number of suppliers to a minimum:

> Fewer suppliers means larger orders, and this means that the fixed delivery cost, as a percent of the order, declines. The result can and should be lower prices. Most distributors have flexible pricing with the prices tied to the order size, either in dollars, weight, or cases.

Another advantage to the purchaser is that, by using as few suppliers as possible, the purchaser becomes a more important customer to each supplier and can use this status as a form of price leverage to lower prices. Nevertheless, in other cases only one or two suppliers may exist for specific products, and these suppliers can maintain a monopoly or near-monopoly and refuse to reduce prices. This situation can occur in government-operated liquor distribution, where the government is the sole supplier. It also prevails where a supplier has the sole distributorship for a particular popular product that an operator must have because of customer demand.

Where a product has many suppliers, the purchaser has more ability to shop around and may be able to lower prices by playing one supplier against another. This tactic would probably work, given a large quality and price variance among suppliers for a particular product. In this situation market quotations play an important role. Most food suppliers are in this very competitive situation, as are some liquor suppliers.

PURCHASER-SUPPLIER RELATIONSHIPS

Once suppliers have been selected, the stage is set for establishing relationships between purchasers and sellers. For these relationships to be successful, purchasers must be familiar with the legal aspects of purchasing, know how to deal with suppliers, and conform to both professional and ethical standards that are fair to their organization, to other employees in that organization that the purchasers have contact with, and to suppliers. Purchasers must realize that they represent their organization to suppliers and that the operation can suffer both financially and from a public relations point of view if purchasers put their personal interests ahead of the organization's.

Code of Ethics

Any hospitality business can benefit from establishing its own code of ethics for the guidance of purchasers and other employees of the organization, and the purchaser's relationship with suppliers should reinforce the organization's ethical standards. As stated by Virts (1987, pp. 37–38), the purchaser should

- Adhere to all company policies and procedures in order to maximize goals and objectives
- Seek optimal value for purchasing dollars spent
- Protect the legal rights of the company
- Ensure that the company enjoys a reputation for fair and honest dealings with suppliers

Virts further states that operating guidelines should be provided to each supplier. These guidelines should include the following information:

- Potential volume of product (or level of service) needed and reasonable estimates of usage rates
- Preferred appointment and delivery times, allowing ample lead time to develop price quotations
- Prompt notification of bids accepted or rejected
- Changes or modifications in purchase specifications
- Rush or emergency orders, with consideration given to extenuating circumstances

Some additional suggestions are that

- Purchasers should not provide a supplier's price information, discount levels, and other pricing information to competitive suppliers.
- A supplier's trade secrets should be kept confidential by purchasers.
- Contracts should be given to suppliers who offer the lowest prices within bid specifications.
- Purchasers should not make nonbusiness purchases from suppliers, that is, purchases of products that are for personal use.
- Purchasers should not have any financial interest in any supplier their organization deals with.
- Purchasers should not use or borrow the organization's products (for example, equipment) for personal purposes.
- The organization should prepare and distribute to all its employees (including those in purchasing) policies regarding the receipt of cash, gifts, goods, loans, or other services from suppliers. Some organizations place maximum limits on such items; others state they can be of nominal value or else have a blanket veto on

any such items to avoid any possibility of placing supplier and employees in conflict-of-interest situations.

Supplier Sales Representative Ground Rules

The purchasing department needs to establish ground rules and communicate them to suppliers and their sales representatives so that proper business relationships can be established. Some suggested ground rules are

- Establish hours when sales representatives can make an appointment to see a purchaser.
- Limit visits to a stipulated maximum length, such as thirty minutes.
- All legitimate sales representatives should be accorded the courtesy of sales visits. The purchaser's job is to minimize costs and maximize quality (sometimes a difficult thing to do), and suppliers (both new and old) are always introducing new products that might meet this goal. If purchasers shut the door to potential new suppliers, they may be ignoring new opportunities.

Managers who are also often the purchasers in small operations do not always have the time to meet with all sales representatives. In some situations, they decline to meet with any of them by selecting the one-stop shopping method with a sole supplier. To that supplier, the establishment is known as a *house account,* that is, one that it does not have to fight very hard with to retain its business. Unfortunately, in house account situations, the purchaser-manager may eventually find prices creeping up (because comparison shopping is not done), service declining, or a combination of both problems. In addition to these potential problems, dealing with only one supplier because it minimizes purchasing paperwork and time loss from meeting other suppliers' sales representatives may be alienating other potential suppliers who could provide good (if not better) products, information, and services. Ongoing discussion with all (within reason) potential suppliers' sales representatives is also a good public relations gesture.

Buyer Profiles

Successful suppliers maintain files on purchasers with whom they deal or with whom they hope to deal. These files are known as *buyer profiles.* They contain information such as:

- The purchaser's job responsibilities. Is the purchaser only doing purchasing, or is he or she also an operating department head (such as a chef), that is, both a purchaser and user?
- The purchaser's attitude to and views about the supplier. Does the purchaser have

a favorable impression of the supplier's reputation, ethics, and products that would make getting a sale easier for a sales representative? Does the purchaser treat sales representatives courteously and give them appropriate time to discuss products the supplier wishes to sell?

- The purchaser's attitude toward quality control. Is this attitude flexible or rigid? Can a lower or higher quality be substituted with an adjustment in price?
- The purchaser's philosophy about prices. Is he or she price-conscious, or are quality and supplier services more important than price?
- The purchaser's skill at the job. Is the purchaser a good negotiator or a person who accepts a stated price without trying to reduce it or obtain a quantity discount?
- The purchaser's level of spending authority. For example, does the purchaser have a maximum purchase dollar limit beyond which a higher level of approval is needed?
- The purchaser's attitude to new products. Will the purchaser readily accept the concept of new products, or is he or she stubborn about seeing their benefits? Is a purchaser allowed to recommend new products to users within the operation?
- The purchaser's payment history. Are invoices paid on time? Are discounts for prompt payment used? Are requests for extension of credit made in advance of need? Are these requests frequent?

In other words, buyer profile files contain commonsense information that any self-respecting sales department ought to have available about its customers and potential customers, in the same way that a hotel's marketing department (for example, its banquet sales force) should maintain files about the businesses, associations, and other organizations that are customers or potential customers.

Supplier Strategies and Tactics

A purchaser needs to be familiar with some of the strategies and tactics used by suppliers to obtain business. According to Stefanelli (1985, p. 168), suppliers set the tone of the way they operate their businesses

> By setting the quality standards of the items they carry, by determining the types of economic values and supplier services they provide, and by planning their advertising and promotion campaigns. While considering these aspects of the business, moreover, suppliers seek a balance between what they want to do and what their customers, the hospitality operations buyers, need.

Stefanelli suggests that to achieve their goals, suppliers use two basic sales strategies or a combination of them, depending on the particular products they sell. These two strategies are "push" and "pull."

In a push strategy, suppliers encourage their sales representatives to do whatever is ethically necessary to have the buyer purchase the product. The product can be pushed, for example, by offering a larger and larger discount until the purchaser agrees to buy it.

A pull strategy requires sales representatives to influence those who use the items so that they, in turn, can convince the buyer to purchase them. The users could be consumers who are urged by advertising to demand that their favorite restaurant carry a particular product (for example, a brand of ketchup) or an employee within the operation such as a department head who is convinced by a salesperson that a particular product will do a better job than any competitive product (that is, back-door selling). The pull strategy can be expensive for the supplier to put into practice, and it also entails risks. If it is successful, however, the rewards can be high. This method is also often used by a supplier to take business away from its competitors.

A supplier trying to obtain a purchaser's business for the first time often offers free samples and, if appropriate, promotional literature about the product. These samples and/or literature are a way of justifying the visit, and nothing is wrong with them as long as the sample is used in the operation to test the product (and not by the purchaser as a gift). If the sample is given to a user (backdoor selling) in the purchaser's operation, again nothing is wrong as long as the purchaser is made aware of the situation and the user legitimately tests the product and does not take it home, in which case it could be construed as a bribe to influence the user to convince the purchaser to direct business to that supplier.

A first-time supplier sometimes tries to convince a purchaser to transfer business away from a supplier's competitors. Again, this practice is quite acceptable as long as the supplier has a product that is competitive in both price and quality.

At the very least, the sales representatives tries to obtain a minimum order, regardless of how few dollars are involved. This practice is again acceptable because it provides the supplier with a justifiable reason to return on a later visit and attempt to obtain larger orders. The sales representative's superiors recognize that this tactic is normal, even if they make no money on the sale. Even if over the long run no large orders are received, a sales representative may continue sales visits; both the salesperson and the sales manager know that purchasers move on to other jobs, and a new purchaser may look more kindly on that supplier who has been unsuccessful to date.

Evaluating Suppliers and Sales Representatives

From time to time suppliers and/or salespersons must be evaluated. With some purchasers this process is ongoing. Suppliers who continue to perform well are rewarded with repeat business or additional business; those who are not performing are disciplined in some way. A mild form of discipline might be letting the supplier know that it has competition by placing an order with another supplier for a week or two and then returning to the original supplier to see if a lesson has been learned. This approach often has to be used with suppliers for whom the operation has become a house account, with the supplier allowing product quality or service to slip or prices to creep up higher than those of other suppliers.

A "bonus" to a high-performing supplier may be for the operation to become a house account with that supplier, as long as the purchaser makes known that periodic evaluations will be part of the arrangement. Some sales representatives are not always keen to have organizations they sell to become house accounts because from that point on the sales representative does not have to do anything to earn the business and therefore may no longer receive a commission on sales. In some cases, suppliers then give the sales representative a bonus for having created a house account.

For new suppliers a good idea is to allow them a trial period of a month or two to assess their level of performance with measuring criteria such as number of occasions products were short-shipped, adherence to delivery schedules, and consistency of product quality and services.

Rotating Suppliers

Astute purchasers add new suppliers to approved-supplier lists and discontinue those who are not performing. Some purchasers also regularly drop the bottom performers from the approved list, replace them with the top suppliers in the "also ran" list, and leave the dropped suppliers on that inactive list until they work their way to the top again. As Eames and Norkus (1988, p. 33) state, "This is not a capricious activity. The point of this procedure is to keep vendors who do a good job in business, while those who don't meet your criteria for any reason lose business."

Kelly (1976, p. 25) summarizes the situation as follows:

> Supplier selection should be an ongoing process of continually upgrading the vendors from whom you purchase. Companies are constantly coming into or leaving the market place. With the many new developments in the restaurant industry . . . you simply cannot afford to have a static inventory of suppliers. You must be constantly on the lookout for new and improved sources of supply at the same time as you work with those suppliers who have shown a desire to grow with you.

DISCUSSION QUESTIONS

1. Define *competitive buying,* and explain its pros and cons.
2. Explain contract buying, and state which type of hospitality organization is most likely to use it.

3. Describe cost-plus buying, and state the advantage to the seller and to the buyer of using this method.
4. Explain one-stop buying, and state the major risk to the purchaser in using this method.
5. Define *cooperative buying,* and explain its pros and cons.
6. Describe how volume buying and warehousing works.
7. Explain the role that farmers' markets and supermarkets can play as a purchasing method for some hospitality operations and what their major disadvantage is.
8. What does the term *cash-and-carry buying* mean?
9. Define the term *drop shipment.*
10. Explain why purchasing from national suppliers can alienate local suppliers and why purchasing from national suppliers may not be a good buying method.
11. Discuss the concept of centralized purchasing, and state which hospitality suppliers are most likely to use it.
12. List the six steps in the negotiation process.
13. List three guidelines for minimizing purchaser concessions during negotiation.
14. List five factors that must be considered about suppliers before making the final selection.
15. Discuss the pros and cons of using as few suppliers as possible.
16. From the seller's point of view, what is a *buyer profile?* Give four examples of the type of information it contains.
17. From a seller's point of view, differentiate between push and pull strategies.
18. Discuss how suppliers can be evaluated.

PROBLEMS

1. Discuss with the purchasing manager of a hospitality operation such matters as the operation's purchasing philosophy, which methods it uses to purchase, why it uses them, how many suppliers it deals with for various types of needed products, how it selects suppliers, and how it evaluates them. Write a one-page report summarizing your findings.
2. Visit the sales manager of a supplier who deals with the hospitality industry. In discussing selling with him or her, see if you can discover what sort of selling philosophy the supplier has, how it learns about new potential hospitality operations that it could do business with, what its policy is in such matters as minimum dollar volume of business it will accept before making a delivery, its frequency of deliveries, whether it maintains buyer profiles, and how it thinks it is periodically evaluated by purchasers. Write a one-page report summarizing your findings.
3. Assume you are the owner-operator of a family restaurant in a large city. This restaurant is quite profitable, and you have decided to open three more similar

restaurants in the same city—one a year for the next three years. Each of the new restaurants will be designed in the same way as the present one, operate with the same type of clientele, serve basically the same menu, and have the same operating philosophy. Because the present restaurant has been successful and you opened it without considering what type of purchasing philosophy you should have, you simply selected a supplier for each major product type (paper supplies, cleaning supplies, groceries, fresh produce, meat, and so on), arranged all purchasing yourself, and stayed with that supplier as long as its services and prices were consistent. You realize, however, that with four restaurants to administer three years from now you will have to hire a manager for each and will no longer be able to handle the purchasing yourself. You must therefore plan now to organize the purchasing function differently and start implementing it next year. How would you suggest this be done? What purchasing policies should you detail that differ from the present ones? What type or types of purchasing methods do you suggest be used? Would centralized purchasing for all four restaurants be feasible? Write a report answering these questions and discussing any other matters that you consider important so that each of the four new managers will have a document detailing how purchasing is to be done.

REFERENCES AND SUGGESTED READINGS

Bell, Donald A. 1984. *Food and Beverage Cost Control.* Berkeley, Calif.: Mc-Cutchan.

Eames, Donald, and Gregory X. Norkus. 1988. Developing Your Procurement Strategy. *Cornell Hotel and Restaurant Administration Quarterly* 29(1): 25–29.

Keister, Douglas C. 1977. *Food and Beverage Control.* Englewood Cliffs, N.J.: Prentice-Hall, pp. 207–14.

Kelly, Hugh J. 1976. *Food Service Purchasing: Principles and Practices.* New York: Lebhar-Friedman, pp. 17–21, 29–31, 43–46, 52–55, 201–5.

Kotschevar, Lendal H., and Charles Levinson. 1988. *Quantity Food Purchasing.* New York: Macmillan, pp. 24–25.

Pedderson, Raymond B. 1977. *SPECS: The Comprehensive Foodservice Purchasing and Specification Manual.* Boston: Cahners, pp. 9–48.

Peddersen, Raymond B. 1981. *Foodservice and Hotel Purchasing.* Boston: CBI, pp. 2–11, 23–29.

Powers, Thomas F., and Jo Marie Powers. 1984. *Food Service Operations: Planning and Control.* New York: John Wiley, pp. 84–98.

Riegel, Carl D., and R. Dan Reid. 1988. Food Service Purchasing: Corporate Practices. *Cornell Hotel and Restaurant Administration Quarterly* 29(1): 30–33.

Stefanelli, John M. 1985. *Purchasing: Selection and Procurement for the Hospitality Industry*. New York: John Wiley, pp. 153–71.

Virts, William B. 1987. *Purchasing for Hospitality Operations*. East Lansing, Mich.: The Educational Institute of the American Hotel & Motel Association, pp. 11–12, 27–35, 39–42.

Warfel, M. C., and Frank H. Waskey, 1979. *The Professional Food Buyer*. Berkeley, Calif.: McCutchan, pp. 71–94.

6

Ordering and Inventory Control

OBJECTIVES

- Explain the use of a purchase requisition, and list its pros and cons.
- Discuss the use of purchase orders and the type of information that a purchase order can contain.
- Define the term *expediting*.
- Discuss standing orders and purchase order drafts.
- Explain how par stock ordering works, and list its advantages and disadvantages.
- Give the economic order quantity equation, and use it to solve problems.
- Explain how perpetual inventory cards and requisitions are used in storeroom control.
- Discuss and use four methods of costing storeroom items and requisitions.

ORDERING

Generally, the authority to request a needed item is vested in those responsible for running specific departments. For example, the chef (because he or she is generally responsible for establishing daily menus) usually has the authority to request needed food supplies. The bar manager has the authority to request alcoholic beverages and other supplies to replenish bar stock. The housekeeper is in the best position to recognize the need to replenish housekeeping items such as linen and guest supplies. In small properties, these same individuals may be responsible for actually ordering these items. In large properties, however, where purchasing is centralized in one individual or in the purchasing department, these individuals must communicate their needs to purchasing department personnel, which is generally done by way of purchase requisitions. Purchase requisitions may take many different forms, but a basic format that would cover the needs of most establishments is illustrated in Figure 6-1.

According to Stefanelli (1985, p. 182), the purchase requisition tends to dilute the purchasing function because it assumes that all department heads are aware of matters such as optimum order sizes and prices. It also invites backdoor selling. Backdoor selling can occur, however, without the use of purchase requisitions because department heads can make oral rather than written requests to buyers. Stefanelli also points out that the use of purchase requisitions does have some advantages. For example, they can relieve buyers of responsibility for ordering mistakes, reduce the amount of paperwork they have to do, and control the use of

		#4964

Date _____   Requested by _____

Department _____   Department head checked _____

Date required _____ Purchasing manager approved _____

Note: Please use a separate purchase requisition for each item or group of related items.

Description	Quantity	Purchase order number	Suggested supplier

Figure 6-1.   Purchase requisition (*Source:* Coltman, Michael M. 1989. *Cost Control for the Hospitality Industry,* p. 58. New York: Van Nostrand Reinhold).

products in the departments that requested them. Control of use is achieved by having additional columns printed on the form that indicate how many of the product wanted are on hand and how many were used since the last time the product was ordered.

Although a formal purchase requisition may not be used in small establishments, it is still used by many large organizations, even if only for items that do not have a regular usage as for new products that the user department would like to try.

Purchase Orders

If an organization is large enough to warrant a system of purchase requisitions and specifications, the ordering procedure should be formalized with the use of purchase orders. Three copies of the purchase order are required—one for the supplier, one for the person responsible for receiving, and one for the accounting office to be attached to the invoice when it is received for payment. A sample purchase order is illustrated in Figure 6.2. Note that, for control purposes, this purchase order number should be cross-referenced to the purchase requisition number, and vice versa.

To protect both buyer and seller from misunderstandings, the completed purchase order should contain the following information when appropriate:

- Quantity of product to be delivered.
- Product specifications. The purchaser must ensure on receipt that the products are those specified. This is an important step in receiving procedures in the event of contract dispute.
- Required delivery date. If the seller agrees to ship by a certain date, this implies acceptance of the order. If the seller fails to deliver on time, the purchaser has a basis for damages on condition that damages were suffered because the products were not delivered as agreed.
- Method and timing of payment.
- Who is responsible for insurance.
- Transportation responsibilities and method of delivery.
- Delivery location. If it is not stated, it is generally assumed to be the seller's business premises.
- When title to goods passes from seller to buyer. If the goods are lost or damaged during transportation, one needs to know who is the legal owner at that time.

Note that, if receipt of a purchase order is acknowledged by a seller, no contract exists until it is accepted. For this reason Kotschevar (1975, p. 27) recommends that purchase orders be signed by the seller under a statement such as "We acknowledge

Franklyn Hotel 1260 South St., Manchester Telephone: (261) 434-5734			
PURCHASE ORDER #653			
(The purchase order number must appear on all invoices, bills of lading, or correspondence relating to this purchase. Invoice must accompany shipment.)			
Department_____ Purchase requisition #_____			
Purchase order date _____ Delivery date _____			
To supplier:			
Description		Quantity	Price
Purchasing manager's signature_____			

Figure 6-2.   Sample purchase order (*Source:* Coltman, Michael M. 1989. *Cost Control for the Hospitality Industry*, p. 67. New York: Van Nostrand Reinhold).

and accept the above order and its conditions." Shipment of any part of an order implies that it has been accepted.

After a purchase order is placed, even though it is a valid legal contract, changing it may be necessary. Most suppliers, particularly local ones, will cooperate in such changes, especially if purchaser-seller relationships are on an amicable basis.

In many cases in the hospitality industry, particularly in day-to-day food and supplies ordering, a system of purchase orders is just not practical because most orders are placed at short notice and by telephone. In such cases, special procedures and forms will prevail, as discussed and illustrated in chapter 8 (on food purchasing) and chapter 16 (on beverage purchasing).

Expediting

Expediting is a term used to monitor placed purchase orders to ensure that products arrive at the receiving dock on the day they are required. Expediting is not required for most products (such as fresh food items) purchased regularly, which local suppliers deliver daily as a matter of routine. Expediting is sometimes necessary when large intermittent purchase orders are placed for products that need to be transported from a distant source, and the day of delivery is critical. For example, when kitchen equipment is ordered for a new restaurant and the opening day has been announced, that the equipment be received, installed, and tested in advance of opening day is important.

How Much to Order?

A question that arises in the ordering process is the quantity to order. It is often left to the discretion of the department head involved, because he or she either has authority to order directly what is needed or is in the best position to advise the purchasing department of required quantities. In the case of items purchased only occasionally, the quantity required is not too difficult to determine from past experience. In some cases, for example, equipment purchases, a purchase might occur only once in ten years.

For nonperishable products used regularly, however, daily purchasing should not be used. Generally, buying more cases of an item and having them in stock for usage over several weeks is preferable to buying one case every couple of days. One reason is that a better supplier price should be available for larger purchases. As Kelly (1976, p. 5) states, "The operator who fails to maximize the quantity which he can accept on each delivery is forcing his supplier to charge him the higher price which almost always accompanies the small volume order." Another reason is that it reduces ordering, receiving, and handling costs when purchase quantities are maximized each time.

Many items are purchased by hospitality enterprises that are required very frequently, and often tens or hundreds of these different items may be required each day for restocking depleted inventories. One method for dealing with this problem is standing orders.

Standing Orders

A *standing order* is an arrangement with a supplier to provide a predetermined quantity of a particular product or products on a daily or other periodic basis without contacting the supplier each time. One type of standing order is for a supplier to deliver, at an agreed price, a fixed quantity of a specific item each day.

For example, a daily supplier might be asked to deliver each day a specified number of dozens of eggs. This quantity would remain fixed until a change is needed.

Another type of standing order requires the supplier each day to replenish the stock of a certain product up to a predetermined or par level. The par stock level is established for each item handled this way, according to the needs of the establishment. To prevent replenishing beyond the par level (leading to possible spoilage or pilferage), a par stock form is recommended. This form requires a designated employee to take stock each day of each product covered by this system in order to calculate the quantity required and so advise the supplier. A form that could be used for this purpose is illustrated in Figure 6-3.

Although these two standing order methods are most commonly used for perishable food supplies, they could be used for other items (for example, cleaning or paper supplies) that are used in large quantities and need replenishing on a daily or at least weekly basis. For example, the paper supplies used in a fast-food restaurant might well be handled this way.

As well as being a form of inventory control, standing orders simplify the ordering process because they eliminate the need to produce purchase orders for these products.

Item	Par stock	On hand	Required
Apples, cooking			
Apples, baking			
Apples, crab			
Apples, table			
Apricots			
Bananas			

Figure 6-3.   Par stock form (*Source:* Coltman, Michael M. 1989. *Cost Control for the Hospitality Industry,* p. 68. New York: Van Nostrand Reinhold).

Blanket Orders

Blanket orders could be used for items of nominal cost that in total can represent a worthwhile order to a supplier. Blanket orders can streamline the ordering process as well as reduce purchase costs. Blanket orders were discussed in chapter 3.

Purchase Order Drafts

Purchase order drafts are sometimes used for infrequently purchased items whose cost is nominal. A draft has a check attached so that payment is made to the supplier at the time the order is placed. Management might allow drafts to be used up to a maximum stipulated amount such as twenty-five dollars. Drafts are useful for prompting suppliers (because they receive cash in advance) to supply small quantities of products they might otherwise not be interested in delivering. This system also reduces the need for later paperwork in that the accounting office does not have to match invoices to products received and then prepare a check to cover the invoice. The system requires confidence that the supplier will quickly process the order, even though the amount is nominal. The disadvantage of this system occurs when goods received are inferior to the quality of those ordered, and trying to return to a supplier merchandise that has already been paid for may present difficulties.

PAR STOCK ORDERING

The main objective in effective ordering of products is inventory management and control, that is, having enough of each product in inventory at all times so that the establishment does not run out of products and fail to satisfy guests; at the same time, the quantity of products in storage must be minimized to prevent spoilage, other losses, and the costs of carrying unnecessary inventory.

The best way to achieve this objective is to order the right amount of each product at the right time. This goal is not always easy to achieve because of supplier limitations. For example, in most cases suppliers dictate delivery schedules (the days when they are prepared to deliver, the time of day when they will deliver, and the minimum quantities of products or value of products they will deliver before they will accept an order). They also often dictate when an order will be accepted prior to being delivered (for example, by 3 P.M. the day before delivery). Obviously, the larger the establishment and the higher its purchasing requirements, the more flexible the supplier is likely to be in delivery schedules and similar matters.

Therefore, to have some knowledge of which products are needed, when they are needed, and in what quantities to suit supplier limitations, a system of par stock ordering has to be set up.

Par stock is also known as *maximum stock* because it is the maximum amount of inventory that is allowed to be carried for each product at any one time. As par stock is reduced through usage to a defined minimum level (also known as the *reorder point*), sufficient of that product is then ordered to increase inventory back to par (or maximum) stock. A new operation needs time to set maximum and minimum inventory levels. When initially establishing par stock levels, arriving at the optimum amount for each product is a matter of trial and error. When a par stock method of ordering is used, the quantity normally ordered may have to be adjusted in an establishment that has a large volume of banquet business. The easiest way to control this variable is to add to each day's normal requirements the additional amounts necessary for the banquet business.

Consumption Rate

When par stock and reorder levels are being established, the consumption rate of the item and the time lag between ordering and delivery must be considered. For example, suppose the housekeeping department normally uses twenty-one gallons of bleach a week (or three a day) and reorders every two weeks. Normally, therefore, forty-two gallons would be ordered each time. However, a safety or minimum level of six gallons for that item has been established. Therefore, par or maximum stock is forty-eight gallons, and minimum stock is six. If, on a particular day, nine gallons are in stock and two days are required for delivery, then forty-five gallons should be ordered because that amount will bring the par stock up to forty-eight gallons two days hence.

Par stock levels also need to be evaluated from time to time. Although customer demand for most products used in the hospitality industry remains fairly stable or can be predicted with some certainty, changes in demand may occur (for example, with a change in season). Also, if suppliers are changed, a new supplier's different ordering and delivery schedules may change par stock requirements.

Advantages and Disadvantages

The advantages of the par stock method are that

- No more will be carried in inventory (using up costly storage space) than is necessary
- Investment in total inventory at any one time is at an optimal level
- The likelihood of stockouts is reduced

Possible disadvantages of this method are that

- Maximum and minimum inventory levels are based on various assumptions (such as usage rates and lead time required for deliveries) that may be incorrect

- To use par stock effectively for a large number of different products carried in inventory can be a major task unless perpetual inventory cards (to be discussed later) are used, or the operation has a computerized inventory system
- When suppliers make frequent offers of quantity buys, par stock inventory management is invalidated

Another major disadvantage of the par stock method of ordering and inventory management is that it can ignore some broader aspects of inventory management. As stated earlier, the main objective of effective ordering is to ensure that products are on hand as needed and that no more of a product than is necessary is carried in inventory. However, total inventory management must also consider matters such as the cost of ordering products more frequently compared to less frequently and the total costs of carrying inventory (costs of storage space, finance, insurance, and spoilage).

Sometimes purchasers are unfamiliar with this overall picture. For example, if an opportunity arises to buy a large amount of a product at a considerable discount, the decision might be made on the discount criterion alone, without considering the additional burden this purchase would place on storage requirements and costs. In most situations, where day-to-day ordering is done, the difference between actual costs and optimal costs of carrying total inventory are probably minimal. However, for large purchases a method of evaluating costs, such as the economic order quantity equation, can help make the purchasing decision.

ECONOMIC ORDER QUANTITY

Costs are involved in carrying an inventory of products. These costs include the cost of money that is either borrowed to carry the inventory or that is tied up in inventory and thus not available for other purposes. Costs are also associated with having to store the inventory, such as the necessity to include storage areas in the building (thus increasing the building costs), inventory insurance, labor costs (storekeepers and other personnel), and the cost of control forms (for example, perpetual inventory cards and requisitions). These costs could vary from 10 to 30 percent of the inventory value.

Equation

The economic order quantity equation can be used, where appropriate, to minimize the costs associated with purchasing and carrying inventories. The equation is

$$EOQ = \sqrt{\frac{2FS}{CP}}$$

where

EOQ = Economic order quantity
  F = Fixed cost of placing an order (paperwork, telephoning, purchasing employee salaries, receiving costs, and other costs)
  S = Annual sales or usage in units
  C = Carrying costs (insurance, interest, storage) as a percent of the dollar amount of the inventory
  P = Purchase price per unit

An Example

Assume the head office purchases case lots of hamburger bags for all its fast-food restaurants in the city. Normal annual sales of hamburgers require one thousand cases of bags per year. Carrying cost of the inventory is 15 percent of inventory value. The purchase cost per case or unit is twelve dollars, and the fixed cost of placing an order is eight dollars. Substituting these values in the equation, provides

$$EOQ = \sqrt{\frac{2 \times \$8.00 \times 1,000}{15\% \times \$12.00}}$$

$$= \sqrt{\frac{\$16,000.00}{\$1.80}}$$

$$= \sqrt{8,888}$$

$$= 94 \text{ cases (to the nearest whole number)}$$

Therefore, to minimize purchasing and carrying costs, ninety-four cases should be ordered each time. To determine how many orders a year this is, divide annual usage by the EOQ.

$$1,000 \div 94 = 10.6$$

or approximately every thirty-four days (365 divided by 10.6). If usage of hamburger bags were consistent throughout the year (for example, not affected by seasonal variations), then orders should be spaced at this interval. The average inventory of this item can be calculated by dividing the order quantity by 2:

$$94 \div 2 = 47$$

To carry a safety margin for this item in inventory, add the desired safety margin to the average inventory figure. Multiplying the average inventory figure (plus the safety margin, if desired) by the purchase price per unit gives the average dollar amount tied up in inventory for this item.

This example assumed that because 94 was the EOQ that is the quantity to be ordered. If the supplier delivers only in multiples of five, our order would be increased to ninety-five; if in multiples of ten, then our order would be ninety or one hundred. In these cases, costs are increased slightly over the EOQ cost level.

Supplier Discount

If the supplier offered a discount for larger orders, we might wish to consider this arrangement. Suppose that, with the above facts, we calculate ninety-four to be our economic order quantity but the supplier offers 2 percent off the purchase price if we buy in batches of 150. If this offer is accepted, the saving will be:

$$2\% \times \$12.00 = \$0.24 \text{ per case}$$

or

$$1,000 \text{ cases} \times \$0.24 = \$240.00 \text{ a year}$$

However, an additional carrying cost results because we shall, on average, have more items in inventory at any one time. In fact, seventy-five (150 ÷ 2) units will be in inventory on average, rather than the previous forty-seven. The difference of twenty-eight units means that the additional carrying cost will be

$$15\% \times 28 \times (\$12.00 - \$0.24) = \$49.39$$

A saving on ordering costs offsets the additional carrying cost because fewer orders will now be placed. Previously, 10.6 orders a year were placed. The new number of orders will be 1,000 ÷ 150 = 6.7, a reduction in number of orders of approximately three (10.6 − 6.7). The saving on ordering costs will therefore be

$$3 \times \$8.00 = \$24.00$$

The saving on ordering costs ($24.00) is less than the increase in carrying costs ($49.39). The net increase in costs is about twenty-five dollars. However, in this case the offer should be accepted because the saving of $240 on the purchase price more than covers the net increase in costs.

PERPETUAL INVENTORY CARDS AND REQUISITIONS

For items carried in storerooms that are under the control of an authorized person, a system of perpetual inventory cards is recommended. A separate set of individual perpetual inventory cards should be maintained for each separate storage location. For example, a hotel housekeeper would have a set of cards for linens and other supplies required in the rooms department, and the food storekeeper would have a set of cards for the items under lock and key in the food storeroom.

A card is required for each type and size of item carried in stock. A sample card is illustrated in Figure 6-4. The In column figures are taken from the invoices delivered with the goods; the figures in the Out column are recorded from the requisitions (to be discussed later) prepared and signed by persons in the department served by that particular storage location. Obviously, if all In and Out figures are properly recorded on the cards by the person in charge of the storeroom, the Balance column figure should agree with the actual count of the item on the shelf. Thus the cards aid in inventory control.

| Item _____ Supplier _____ Tel. # _____ |
| Minimum _____ Supplier _____ Tel. # _____ |
| Maximum _____ Supplier _____ Tel. # _____ |

Date	In	Out	Balance	Requisition cost information

Figure 6-4. Perpetual inventory card for a single item (*Source:* Coltman, Michael M. 1989. *Cost Control for the Hospitality Industry,* p. 69. New York: Van Nostrand Reinhold).

Other Uses of Cards

These cards are also useful for accounting purposes because they carry the purchase prices of the items and allow requisitions to be costed out; this procedure ensures that each department is correctly charged with its share of costs. The cards are also useful for maintaining par stock for ordering purposes and help to ensure items are not overstocked or understocked because they can show the maximum stock for each individual item and the minimum point to which that stock level can fall before the item needs to be reordered. Without having to count quantities of items on the shelves, the person responsible has only to go through each of the cards once a week or however frequently reordering is practical. At that time, all items for which the balance figure is at or close to the minimum point are listed, and the quantity required to bring the inventory up to par stock is ordered, allowing for possible delivery delays. Note that the cards can also be designed to carry the names and telephone numbers of suggested suppliers.

Alternative Method

In some establishments, management prefers a single form to summarize all perpetual inventory records, as in Figure 6-5. On this form, a series of columns are dated across the top, with each column representing a day of the month. Each item in stock is represented on a single line. The boxes for each item are divided by a diagonal line. Quantities are entered above, below, or actually on the diagonal line. The figure above the line identifies the balance of that item on hand. A figure

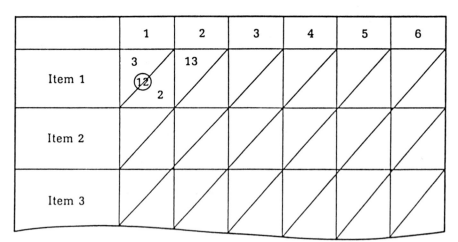

Figure 6-5.   Perpetual inventory card for multiple items (*Source:* Coltman, Michael M. 1989. *Cost Control for the Hospitality Industry*, p. 71. New York: Van Nostrand Reinhold).

straddling the line shows the quantity of an item received, according to purchase records. The figure below the diagonal line shows the quantity of the item issued.

At the end of each day on which a delivery and/or an issue is made, the balance is recalculated and carried forward to the upper left of the diagonal line in the next large square. For example, on day 1 three of Item 1 were on hand as indicated above the diagonal line. During the day, twelve were received (the circled figure on the line) and two were issued (the figure below the diagonal line). A balance on hand of thirteen was carried forward to the left of the diagonal on day 2.

This simplified system of perpetual inventory control can be reserved in a restaurant for high-cost items such as steak or lobster. It also provides a quick daily overview of what needs to be purchased of these items. With this form, a box for each item controlled is needed for each day of the month, even if none of that item has been received or issued that day.

The advantages of perpetual inventory cards for inventory control and saving time in reordering are obvious. The major disadvantages are the time and cost to keep the cards up to date. Each establishment must weigh the costs against the benefits for its own operation.

Requisitions

Whether or not perpetual inventory cards are used to control items in stock and aid in ordering, requisitions should be used to allow authorized people to receive items from the storeroom and to ensure that the various departments are correctly charged with their share of costs. A sample requisition is illustrated in Figure 6-6.

Blank requisitions should be made available, preferably in duplicate, only to those authorized to sign them. The original, listing items and quantities required, is delivered to the storekeeper. Duplicates are kept by the person ordering so that quantities received from the storeroom can be checked.

If perpetual inventory cards are used, they should indicate the current price of the item in stock. Perpetual inventory card Out column figures can be recorded from the requisitions (and the Balance column figure adjusted) and the price of the item can be taken from the card and recorded on the requisition in the Item Cost column. Frequently, the same item in stock may have been received with a different delivery date and price. In this case, several different methods are available for keeping track of the various prices on the perpetual inventory cards.

Most Recent Price

The simplest method is to use the most recent price paid for an item in stock as the price for all of that item in stock. In other words, if five items were in stock at $1.00 each and twelve new items were purchased at $1.10 each, then $1.10 would be recorded on requisitions as the cost for any of those seventeen items subsequently

Department		Date	#6329
Quantity	Item description	Item cost	Total
Authorized signature			

Figure 6-6.   Sample requisition (*Source:* Coltman, Michael M. 1989. *Cost Control for the Hospitality Industry*, p. 72. New York: Van Nostrand Reinhold).

requisitioned. If, before the seventeen were issued, a new order of that item were received, the new order price would again prevail. For example, suppose stock on hand dropped to two, and eighteen were received at $1.05 each; the twenty items in stock are now assumed to each have a price of $1.05. This method is simple to use, but, in times of wildly fluctuating purchase prices, it can be inaccurate. The other methods to be discussed take more time but are also more accurate.

First-in/First-out Price

With first-in/first-out (FIFO) pricing, proper stock rotation is assumed to be in effect (this should be the case regardless of the requisition costing method); as the items purchased earliest are issued first, they are issued at the price that was paid for them. Using the figures from the most recent price method already discussed, recall that we originally had five items on hand at $1.00, and twelve more were purchased at $1.10. If six items were then requisitioned, five would be costed on the requisition at $1.00 and one at $1.10 (for a total of $6.10). Because we have now used all the first group of items at $1.00, the $1.10 price will prevail on requisitions until that stock is used up, and so on. The related perpetual inventory card must have recorded on it, in the Requisition Cost Information column, how many of that balance are on hand at each price. Alternatively, as items are received, the price can be hand-written or recorded in some other way on the case or carton or, if necessary, onto each separate can, bottle, or package.

Last-in/First-out Price

Another method of perpetual inventory card and requisition costing is last-in/first-out (LIFO). With LIFO the last items received are considered to be the ones first issued, even if the items are actually issued on a first-in/first-out basis. In other words, with reference to the earlier figures used to illustrate FIFO, the six items issued would all be issued at the $1.10 price, and the total requisition cost would be $6.60.

Weighted Average Price

The weighted average requires some simple calculations as each new delivery is received. Let us again use the quantities and prices we are familiar with:

$$
\begin{array}{ll}
5 \text{ items on hand at } \$1.00 = & \$\ 5.00 \\
+\ 12 \text{ received at } \$1.10 \quad\ = & 13.20 \\
\hline
17 \text{ items total} \qquad\qquad = & \$18.20
\end{array}
$$

The weighted average price is $18.20 ÷ 17 = $1.07 (rounded to the nearest cent), and that is the cost recorded on all requisitions until another shipment is received. Assume that, just prior to the next shipment, we still have two items on hand at $1.07 and that 18 new items are received at $1.05:

$$
\begin{array}{ll}
2 \text{ items on hand at } \$1.07 = & \$\ 2.14 \\
+\ 18 \text{ received at } \$1.05 \quad\ = & 18.90 \\
\hline
20 \text{ items total} \qquad\qquad = & \$21.04
\end{array}
$$

The new weighted average price will drop from $1.07 to $1.05 ($21.04 ÷ 20).

Dispensing with Perpetual Inventory Cards

If perpetual inventory cards are not used, the easiest method of recording item costs on the requisitions is to write the price of the item, taken from the invoice at the time of delivery, on the container, case, can, bottle, or package. Alternatively, pricing machines (such as those used in supermarkets) could be used. Recording the item price on the cases or items makes transferring this price to the requisition easy to do as the requisition is completed. This price-recording method also has a psychological control advantage in that each person handling the items is made aware of their cost.

Requisitions, once costed out, can be later extended and totaled so that at the end of each accounting period each department can be charged with its proper share of expenses. Issuing to each department blank requisitions of a different color will aid in departmental identification. If necessary for control purposes, requisitions could also be numbered.

Of course, in establishments large enough to support computerized inventory records, much of the paperwork that would otherwise be required with perpetual inventory cards and requisitions can be handled directly by the computer, including, for example, a daily printout of all items whose level has dropped to the reorder point and cost information for inventory on hand.

DISCUSSION QUESTIONS

1. Explain the use of a purchase requisition and list its pros and cons.
2. What is a purchase order? Why are purchase orders sometimes not practical in the hospitality industry?
3. On a purchase order, why should the time when title to goods passes from seller to buyer be stated?
4. What does the term *expediting* mean?
5. What is a standing order? Briefly describe two types of standing orders.
6. What is a purchase order draft? When and why might one be used?
7. Explain how par stock ordering works, and list two advantages and two disadvantages of it.
8. Give the equation for economic order quantity purchasing.
9. Explain how a perpetual inventory card is used, and list the purposes it serves.
10. Explain how requisitions are used in conjunction with perpetual inventory cards.
11. List four methods for costing storeroom items and requisitions.
12. Explain how each of the four methods of costing storeroom items and requisitions works.

PROBLEMS

1. For each of the following three items, calculate the quantity of each item to be ordered:

	Item 1	Item 2	Item 3
Consumption rate	14 a week	7 a week	10 cases a month
Ordering frequency	every 2 weeks	weekly	monthly
Safety level	3	1	1 case
Present stock	6	1	3 cases
Delivery time	2 days	1 day	1 week

Note that item 3 can be ordered only in full cases.

2. Obtain a blank sample purchase order from a hotel or restaurant (or use the one you obtained while doing problem 1 in chapter 1). Compare the information that this purchase order contains with purchase order information discussed in this chapter and with reference to Figure 6-2. Comment about your findings.

3. A catering company uses three thousand cases of paper napkins per year. Fixed costs of placing an order are ten dollars per order. Cost per case is ten dollars, and carrying costs are 12 percent.

   a. Calculate the economic order quantity to the nearest case.
   b. Suppose the supplier offered a discount of 0.5 percent off the purchase price if deliveries were made in five-hundred-case lots. Should this offer be accepted?

4. On 31 January, the perpetual inventory card for a particular item showed twenty-five on hand at a cost of $1.48 each. Purchases of this item were made as follows during February:

   February 8: 3 cases at $9.12 per case
   February 12: 2 cases at $9.24 per case
   February 19: 4 cases at $9.48 per case
   February 25: 1 case at $9.12 per case

Note that six items are in each case. The following quantities of that item were requisitioned during February:

   February 2:12
   February 4:3
   February 7:5
   February 11:10
   February 16:8
   February 18:12
   February 21:8

February 24:3
February 26:6
February 28:5

   a. Prepare a blank perpetual inventory card and record in the In and Out columns the purchases and issued quantity information. Calculate and record the Balance amount after each purchase and/or issue.

   b. Using the most recent pricing method (rounding figures where necessary to the nearest cent), record on the card after each purchase the cost information required for requisitions.

   c. For each date a requisition was made, calculate the total cost figure that would have appeared on the requisition for that date.

   d. Calculate the February month-end total value of that item still in inventory.

5. With reference to the information in problem 4, repeat parts b, c, and d using the FIFO pricing method.
6. With reference to the information in problem 4, repeat parts b, c, and d using the LIFO pricing method.
7. With reference to the information in problem 4, repeat parts b, c, and d using the weighted average pricing method.

REFERENCES AND SUGGESTED READINGS

Kelly, Hugh, J. 1976. *Food Service Purchasing: Principles and Practices.* New York: Lebhar-Friedman

Kotschevar, Lendal H. 1975. *Quantity Food Purchasing.* New York: John Wiley.

———, and Charles Levinson. 1988. *Quantity Food Purchasing.* New York: Macmillan, pp. 54–62.

Stefanelli, John M. 1985. *Purchasing: Selection and Procurement for the Hospitality Industry.* New York: John Wiley, pp. 101–6, 181–90.

Virts, William B. 1987. *Purchasing for Hospitality Operations.* East Lansing, Mich.: The Educational Institute of the American Hotel & Motel Association, pp. 63–66.

Warfel, M. C., and Frank H. Waskey. 1979. *The Professional Food Buyer.* Berkeley, Calif.: McCutchan, pp. 143–66.

7

Receiving and Paying for Products

OBJECTIVES

- Discuss the problem of establishing receiving hours, explain the term *night drop,* and list the receiving checks for delivered products.
- Explain the use of a receiving stamp, a dummy invoice, a notice of invoice error form, and a credit memorandum.
- Discuss blind receiving.
- Explain the role of the purchasing department in the receiving process.
- Discuss the term *credit rating,* and explain the difference between paying from invoices and paying from statements.
- Explain how a petty cash fund works and how control is established when paying by check.
- Explain the term *opportunity cost,* discuss and solve problems about supplier discounts, and differentiate a discount from a rebate.

RECEIVING

Receiving is one of the most important steps in the process of purchasing products. As Keister (1977, p. 225) states,

> Usually it is not the times of delivery (whether you can choose times or not) that create the real receiving problems. Receiving problems are frequently caused by improper planning. . . . You could probably do a lot to improve your situation by designing an effective

receiving system and designating a reliable, trained employee to take charge of receiving deliveries whenever they arrive.

Receiving Hours

Hours for receiving must be established. Hospitality operators in large cities often begin the receiving function as early as 6 A.M. because that is when supplier delivery trucks are able to move most easily through city streets. In smaller towns traffic is less of a problem, and receiving may not begin until later in the morning. In major cities, night deliveries are often made as the only way to avoid traffic congestion delays and minimize supplier delivery costs. Obviously, to accommodate night deliveries the hospitality establishment must be large enough to justify having a receiver on duty at night. An alternative is a night drop, which allows a delivery driver to use a key to enter the establishment, leave the products, and lock the door on leaving. Night drops require the establishment's management to have a high degree of trust in suppliers and their drivers.

Receiving hours and days of the week when deliveries are made for each operation should be coordinated with suppliers to ensure that a person responsible for receiving is at the receiving dock when deliveries are made (except for night drops). By working out a schedule that is convenient to the supplier, the supplier's delivery costs and thus the prices of products delivered may be reduced. Normally, Saturdays and Sundays are not days when most suppliers make deliveries. If a supplier must make deliveries when the receiver is not available, some other on-site person should be delegated to act in this capacity and receive instructions on how to check and approve deliveries.

Staggered Deliveries

Deliveries should be staggered if possible so that the receiver is not under pressure and fails to carry out necessary checks. One of the main advantages of one-stop buying is that limited receiving is required and thus the time when most deliveries are made can be predicted and losses from backdoor pilferage and theft reduced.

Receiving Office

The receiving clerk's office should be adjacent to the receiving dock. The office should be glass-walled as much as possible so that the receiver can observe all activity at the receiving area. Sufficient dock space is necessary so that the receiving area does not become cluttered and make new deliveries difficult to check.

Weighing Scales

Appropriate weighing scales are required. Scales can be balance-arm platform floor models, built-in scales, tabletop or countertop scales, or scales that automatically calculate weight and print the result on a tape that can be stapled to the invoice to show that weight has been verified. Scales can range in capacity from as little as one gram to as much as several tons. Regardless of capacity, good scales are expensive. Cheap ones should be avoided because of their potential inaccuracies in weighing and their maintenance problems.

Scales should be located where they can be used as part of the orderly flow of products from receiving to storage. For a medium-sized operation, Thorner and Manning (1983, p. 21) recommend:

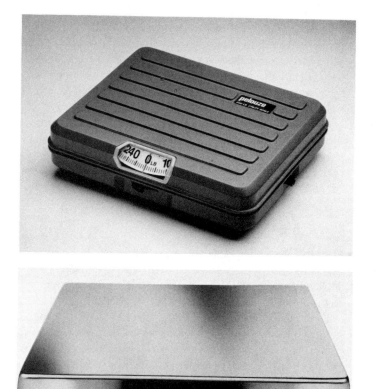

Weighing scales are available in a variety of styles and capacities (Courtesy: Pelouze Scale Co.).

- In the receiving area, one platform scale with a capacity of five hundred to one thousand pounds and one counter scale with a fifty-pound capacity
- In the receiving office and/or quality control section, three portion-control scales of two-, five-, and ten-pound capacity
- In the storage area, one counter scale of twenty-five-pound capacity and one platform scale of five-hundred-pound capacity

Knowledgeable Receiver

The person designated for receiving must be knowledgeable about the products being delivered. In small establishments, the receiver might be the same person who ordered the products (for example, the housekeeper for housekeeping supplies or the chef for meat deliveries). In a large establishment, a separate receiving department is typically responsible for checking all deliveries before distributing the items to the individual departments or storerooms.

According to Stefanelli (1985, p. 196), "Additional control is exerted in the receiving function by placing receiving personnel under the direction of the accounting department. Thus, management minimizes the possibility of any fraudulent relationship between buyer and receiver. Small firms cannot afford this luxury." In other words, in small firms the purchaser and receiver are often the same person.

Receiving Checks

In most hospitality industry operations, invoice receiving is practiced. Suppliers are asked to send a priced invoice with goods delivered so that the receiver can verify such matters as quantities received against those invoiced and check invoice prices to purchase orders (see Figure 6-2).

If purchase orders have been prepared, a copy of the purchase order should be on hand while receiving so that the receiver knows what is to be received. If specifications have been prepared, they too should be available so that delivered goods can be checked in detail against the specifications to ensure that the supplier has not made substitutions. If specifications call for receiving tests, then these tests should be carried out. For example, random sampling of refrigerated food items may be required. In this case thermometers must be available to receiving personnel. According to Keister (1977, p. 228),

Substitutions or errors will call for judgment on the part of receiving clerks. Occasionally they may make mistakes and accept items that you do not want. . . . your purveyors should promptly correct any mistakes they make. If they do not, or if there are more mistakes than you think reasonable, it is probably time to consider changing purveyors. If your receiving clerks make more errors or bad decisions than you feel are acceptable, you may need to re-train them or consider replacing them.

Quantities received should be checked against quantities ordered and invoiced. Wherever items are purchased by weight (as is the case with certain food products), then weights should be verified against those invoiced.

Finally, prices on invoices should be checked against the purchase order. In some cases, a department head may be asked to verify the quality of an item if the receiver is in doubt. Not uncommonly, the chef checks the quality of all meat, fish, and poultry items as they are delivered.

Moving Products to Storage Areas

As soon after receiving as is practical, products received should be moved to their proper storage areas. Hand trucks must be made available to permit products to be easily moved. (Specific storeroom requirements for food are discussed in chapter 8 and for alcoholic beverages in chapter 16.)

Receiving Reports

Receiving reports are recommended for summarizing information about products received. Receiving reports are particularly useful for cost control of food and alcoholic beverages. Specialized types of receiving reports that have been developed by the industry for these two major cost items are discussed in chapter 8 (for food) and chapter 16 (for alcoholic beverages), and more specific receiving control procedures for these product categories are detailed.

Receiving Stamp

All invoices, whether they are recorded on a receiving report or not, should be stamped, and the stamp should be initialed in the appropriate spots to indicate that the checking has been completed. A typical receiving stamp is illustrated in Figure 7-1. By insisting that employees responsible for checking deliveries stamp each invoice and initial where necessary, a form of psychological control is implemented.

```
┌─────────────────────────────────────────┐
│ Date received _____   │
│ Quantity checked by _____   │
│ Quality checked by _____   │
│ Prices checked by _____   │
│ Listed on receiving report by _____  │
└─────────────────────────────────────────┘
```

Figure 7-1.   Typical receiving stamp (*Source:* Coltman, Michael M. 1989. *Cost Control for the Hospitality Industry*, p. 75. New York: Van Nostrand Reinhold).

Dummy or Memorandum Invoices

Sometimes suppliers fail to provide invoices, or copies of them, with each shipment of items. Without an invoice, making all proper receiving checks is difficult for a receiver. If an invoice is not received, then the receiver should prepare a dummy or memorandum invoice from other records (the purchase order or other type of order record) so that it can be later matched with the actual invoice sent in the mail by the supplier to the accounting office. The dummy or memorandum invoice is sometimes referred to as a "products received without invoice" form. A sample of such a form is illustrated in Figure 7-2.

Notice of Invoice Error

As the receiver carries out the receiving function, errors on invoices may be noticed. For example, invoice quantities or prices may be wrong. To take care of such errors, correction on the invoice should be made, and the receiver should complete a notice of error correction form such as that illustrated in Figure 7-3. One copy of this document is sent back to the supplier (either with the driver or by mail), and the other copy is attached to the related invoice to alert the accounting office.

Products Received Without Invoice Form			
Supplier _____ Date _____			
Products received without invoice:			
Quantity	Description	Unit Price	Total
Signature _____			

Figure 7-2.   Products received without invoice form.

	Notice of Error Correction Form				

Franklyn Hotel
1260 South St.
Manchester
Telephone: (261) 434-5734

Supplier _____   Date _____

Corrections have been made as follows on your invoice:

Invoice number _____   Date _____

Item	Reason for correction	Item Price	Your Invoice Amount	Corrected Invoice Amount	Difference

Total corrections _____

Your invoice total _____

Correct invoice total _____

Figure 7-3.   Notice of error correction form.

Credit Memorandum or Invoice

In some cases, goods are invoiced but not received. In other words, they are short-shipped or back ordered. On other occasions, they are delivered and then returned to the supplier because they were not of acceptable quality or for some other reason. In these situations, a credit memorandum or credit invoice should be prepared in duplicate by the establishment. This memorandum should carry necessary details, including an explanation of why the credit memorandum has been prepared. It should be signed by the delivery driver so the establishment has proof that the goods were either not received or else returned. One copy should go to the supplier. The other copy remains with the establishment to ensure that proper credit is received from the supplier. Figure 7-4 is a sample credit memorandum.

In some situations suppliers' delivery drivers carry their own stock of credit forms to be used instead of the hospitality operation having to provide them. Also, some operations use a request for credit form (Figure 7-5) that the delivery driver signs and takes back to the supplier's accounting office so a formal credit invoice can be issued by the supplier and sent to the hospitality operation's accounting office.

Regardless of the system, a credit document should be initiated in the receiving area when products are delivered and the need for credit is apparent. Proper credit documentation should not be substituted with a written note on the invoice about the shortage or return of products or by a driver's oral "promise" that the situation will be corrected with the next delivery. In all cases, the credit document should be cross-referenced to the invoice number and vice versa if the credit document is numbered. Credit documents should be treated as money.

Quality Standards

Restraint should be exercised in shipping goods back that are not completely up to the quality specified. Receivers who are overly cautious with quality standards and focus on minor details or who ship back substituted products that nevertheless are of an equal quality may alienate suppliers who then refuse to do business with that

Supplier _____ Date _____			
Please issue a credit memorandum for the following:			
Quantity	Item description	Unit cost	Total
Reason for request for credit:			
Delivery driver's signature_____			

Figure 7-4.   Sample credit memorandum (*Source:* Coltman, Michael M. 1989. *Cost Control for the Hospitality Industry,* p. 76. New York: Van Nostrand Reinhold).

Request for Credit Form					
Franklyn Hotel 1260 South St. Manchester Telephone: (261) 434-5734					
Supplier _____ Date _____					
Please credit our account as follows:					
Invoice number _____ Date _____					
Item	Reason for credit request	Item Price	Your Invoice Amount	Corrected Invoice Amount
		Total corrections	
		Your invoice total	
		Correct invoice total	

Figure 7-5.   Request for credit form.

operation. In addition, if goods are constantly returned, the operation may be frequently short of needed products. Maizel (1978, p. 208) comments about returned goods as follows:

> Management must be aware that receiving clerks would prefer to accept merchandise than to reject it entirely or accept it with qualification. It is far easier for the receiving clerk . . . to accept the merchandise than to argue with the deliveryman and to do the paper work caused by the problem. An incentive program based on the money that the receiving department saves the operation by spotting undesirable or short-weighted merchandise is often the best way to stimulate vigilance and create a willingness to take on the problem of rejecting deliveries.

Delivery Driver Observations

Delivery drivers are sometimes instructed by their suppliers to report back what they see and hear. If they notice that proper receiving checks are not carried out or that credit forms are not initiated for products short-shipped, they can take advantage of this, either for their own personal benefit or for the joint benefit of themselves and the supplier. Sometimes drivers try to rush the person responsible for receiving, hoping that errors and/or shortages will be overlooked.

Standing Order Receiving

Standing orders should be received with the same care as is exercised with receiving other products, and invoices should be provided by the delivery driver at the time of delivery. Unfortunately, some establishments tend to relax the procedures for standing orders, and drivers are encouraged to be dishonest when they know that proper checks are not made.

Blind Receiving

Some establishments practice blind receiving. In this situation, the supplier is advised not to send an invoice with the goods but to send it through the mail to the accounting office. Instead of the invoice, a shipping, delivery, or packing slip accompanies the products. This slip shows no weights or counts but simply describes the products delivered. As a result, the receiver is forced to count or weigh each item and record the weight or count on the slip, which ensures that this important aspect of receiving is carried out.

Blind receiving is used to prevent a dishonest receiver from removing part of a delivery for personal use and then altering the invoice to cover the fraud. It also reduces the possibility of collusion between delivery driver and receiver. Blind receiving is seldom used today in the hospitality industry because an accounting department verification of all purchasing and receiving documents, as well as invoices, will generally indicate dishonest practices.

Cash on Delivery

If deliveries are made on a cash-on-delivery (COD) basis and the receiver is provided with a cash fund large enough to cover the invoice amount, that fund should be used to pay for the delivery. If no fund exists or the fund is not large enough, the receiver should accompany the delivery driver to the main cashier's office to authenticate delivery so that the invoice can be paid.

Purchasing Department Role

The purchaser may be the receiver in small establishments. In large establishments, the receiver may be a delegated individual who reports to the purchasing department manager or to the accounting department. In either of the latter two cases, the purchasing department's role does not terminate after the purchasing commitment has been made. The purchasing department should continue to have an interest in what happens to products as they are received and processed further.

For this reason, delivery invoices with related credit documents, receiving reports (if used), and copies of purchase orders should be routed through the purchasing department before moving on to the accounting office. The purchasing department should verify all these documents, follow up on any concerns (such as short-shipped products), and carry out any further required checks. In particular, purchasers should watch for frequent credit documents relating to an individual supplier, which can be a form of supplier evaluation for nonperformance. Once the purchasing department is satisfied, documents can be sent on to the accounting department so that suppliers can be paid.

PURCHASES AND PAYMENTS

Although those in the purchasing department do not have any direct influence on the payment of accounts (other than in small establishments where the owner or manager handles both purchases and payments), nevertheless, links exist between those who purchase and those who pay invoices for purchases made because:

- Supplier services (such as quantity discounts) are negotiable with suppliers, meaning that purchasers must have some authority to negotiate matters such as discounts and payment terms with them.
- Discounts offered for prompt payment must be considered by purchasers in product value analysis.
- Contracting for the purchase of large quantities of products requires that sufficient cash be on hand to make payment when it is due.
- If the accounting department is not prompt in paying invoices, suppliers may be reluctant to continue doing business with the purchaser, or may discontinue certain services offered.
- Suppliers sometimes charge an interest penalty (such as 1.5 percent a month, equivalent to 18 percent a year) if invoices are not paid when due; although the credit period allowed is extended, this use of the supplier's money comes at a high cost, and this additional purchase cost reduces the value of the products purchased.

Credit Rating

A valuable tool for a purchasing department is its operation's credit rating. When an operation has a poor credit rating, it may find dealing or negotiating with suppliers difficult and may even find that only COD deliveries will be made.

If a purchaser has an acceptable credit rating, in most cases suppliers expect invoices to be paid within thirty days of receipt or, alternatively, thirty days after the end of the month in which invoices are received. An operation with an excellent credit rating may be able to negotiate an extension of credit terms beyond the normal thirty-day limit, such as for a further ten, twenty, or even thirty days.

When a hospitality operation extends the credit period beyond what the supplier expects, the supplier has to find other sources of cash to pay the businesses from which it purchases and receives credit. In some cases, the supplier may have to factor the accounts. *Factoring* means that the supplier turns over the accounts receivable for cash to a third party who may charge as much as 30 percent interest a year. This added supplier cost must be included in the prices of the products sold to hospitality industry establishments, so the hospitality purchaser ends up paying for being delinquent in the first place!

Invoice Control

Most suppliers are paid once a month, with checks generally mailed to them so that they arrive on the last day for which credit has been agreed. The first step in the invoice-paying process is to check invoice extensions (quantities of goods times purchase price) and then make sure invoice totals are correct. Depending on the situation, invoices may be paid from the invoice or by statement. Payment is made from the invoice(s) when only one or two invoices for purchases come from that supplier during a month. When invoices are paid by statement, the normal situation when an establishment makes frequent purchases from a supplier, at the end of each month the supplier sends a summary form (statement) listing each invoice total for that month. With statements, accounting offfice personnel should ensure that the total of each invoice previously received and checked for extensions and total is properly recorded on the supplier's statement and that the statement adds up correctly. In this situation, a single check is prepared to cover the statement total.

Cash Disbursements

For minor purchases that have to be paid by cash, a petty cash fund should be established. Enough cash should be put into this fund to take care of about one month's transactions. The fund should be the responsibility of one person only. Payments out of it must be supported by a receipt, voucher, or memorandum explaining the purpose of the payment. When the cash fund is almost used up, the supporting receipts, vouchers, and memoranda can be turned in and it will be the head cashier's responsibility to replenish the fund with cash up to the original amount. Receipts, vouchers, or memoranda turned in should be stamped paid or canceled in some other similar way so that they cannot be reused.

All other purchase payments should be made by check and supported by an approved invoice. All checks should be numbered sequentially. The person who prepares checks in payment of invoices should not be the person who has authority to sign checks. Preferably two authorized signatures should be required on checks, and invoices should be canceled when paid so that they cannot be paid twice. Any checks spoiled in preparation should be voided so they cannot be reused.

Opportunity Cost

The objective in making payments for purchases should be to pay invoices when the most benefit will be received. To do this, the opportunity cost of money must be considered. An *opportunity cost* is the cost of doing something else with that money. For example, a business can invest its surplus cash in marketable securities at 10 percent or leave it in the bank at 6 percent. If it invests in marketable securities, its opportunity cost is 6 percent. In other words, it is making 10 percent on the investment, less the opportunity cost of 6 percent; therefore, the net gain is 4 percent. Applying this concept to purchasing, if an establishment pays its invoices ten days before it must, the opportunity of earning interest on this money for a further ten days has been lost.

As far as paying for purchases is concerned, the purchasing and accounting departments must compare the opportunity costs of paying invoices on time versus after the end of the credit term with the negative public relations that will generate, along with a reputation as a slow payer and the possibility that future deliveries will be COD.

Some argue that if an establishment is short of cash and must make a decision between paying off a bank loan or paying suppliers, paying the loan is preferable because suppliers will be more patient than the bank, as they need to retain the establishment's business. Despite the truth in this advice, such a situation cannot continue indefinitely.

Businesses that find themselves in a cash-short situation are likely to receive more support from their suppliers if they advise them in advance that they need an extended credit period. Suppliers, of course, have to pay their own bills from the businesses from which they buy products, and when they are under pressure to make their own payments, they are less likely to want to extend lengthy credit to their hospitality industry customers. In many cases, therefore, suppliers will deliver only on a COD basis or offer only a short credit period, such as seven to ten days.

In some situations, for example, in states where the government dictates credit periods for liquor purchases, purchasers have little room for negotiating supplier credit terms, and the accounting office has little flexibility about when invoices must be paid.

Discounts

When a discount is offered, purchasers who do not pay by the discount date are in fact paying an extra cost for a product. For example, if a discount is 2 percent on all food purchases and a restaurant's normal food cost is 40 percent of sales, failure to take the discount raises the food cost (and reduces profit) by 0.8 percent of sales. In an establishment doing a million dollars a year in sales, that lost discount represents a reduction in profit of eight thousand dollars a year. Indeed, some suppliers to the restaurant industry say that they can predict when an establishment is running into cash problems by noticing whether or not it can meet a discount date.

Some argue that a discount is not a saving on a product's cost but that the discounted price is simply the lowest price available from a supplier for a product. However, today suppliers to the hospitality industry rarely automatically offer a discount. Discounts are normally negotiated on an individual basis by the purchaser, and generally large establishments have more negotiating power than small ones. Where they are offered, discounts can also raise some problems.

- By deciding to stay with suppliers who offer a discount, a purchaser may ignore other suppliers who offer other services and, in effect, provide more product value. For example, a supplier offering a discount may gradually reduce the quality of products delivered to compensate for offering a discount.
- Separating invoices offering a discount from other invoices creates extra work and means establishing two or more separate payment schedules or systems.
- The discount period may need to be renegotiated if goods are returned to the supplier for replacement after receipt and are not replaced for several days.
- In order to make the payment on time to receive the discount, borrowing the cash may be necessary. For example, suppose on a thousand-dollar purchase the terms are 2/10, net 60, which means a 2 percent discount if the invoice is paid within 10 days and otherwise payable within 60 days without a discount. On a one-thousand-dollar purchase paid within ten days, these terms would save twenty dollars, which may not seem to be a lot of money. Multiplied many times over on all similar purchases made during a year, however, it could amount to a large sum. In the example cited, the purchaser may have to borrow the money ($980) in order to make the payment within ten days. Let us assume the money is borrowed for 50 days (60 days less 10 days) at an 8 percent interest rate. The interest expense on this borrowed money is

$$\frac{\$980 \times 50 \text{ days} \times 8\%}{365 \text{ days}} = \$10.74$$

In this case, borrowing the money would be advantageous because the difference between the discount saving of $20.00 and the interest expense of $10.74 is $9.26.

Timing

Whenever possible, an establishment should take advantage of a supplier's invoicing practices, particularly those of frequently used suppliers. Suppose a hotel buys a month's supply of products from a supplier at the beginning of each month and uses the products as required during the month, and that the terms of the supplier's month-end statement are 2/10, net 30, that is, a 2 percent discount off the total month's purchases if the statement is paid within ten days of the month end; otherwise, the statement is payable within thirty days without discount. The hotel thus has the use of the supplier's credit for forty days if it takes advantage of the discount and otherwise for sixty days. The hotel can then use this "free" money to advantage. Even if all it does is collect bank interest on it, it is benefiting from the opportunity cost.

In contrast, suppose the hotel purchases from the same supplier but habitually buys at the end of each month sufficient items to carry it through until the end of the next month. In this case, it will have use of the "free" money for only ten days, if it takes advantage of the discount, and otherwise for only thirty days.

These two cases are extreme, but they do point out that a wise purchaser can take advantage of a supplier's billing practices in order to increase profits.

Rebates

A rebate should be differentiated from a discount. With a rebate, the purchaser pays the full invoice amount but has some cash returned at a later date. The amount of the rebate may vary depending on the volume of purchases made during a period of time (for example, a month or a quarter); the invoice is not discounted at the time of payment because the percentage rebate (discount) is not known until the end of the period.

Rebates are really just a special form of discount that allows the supplier greater flexibility. They are quite legal (except in jurisdictions that do not allow them to be offered in connection with the purchase of alcoholic beverages) as long as the rebate is given to the purchasing organization, is fully documented, and is not paid to an individual within that organization for favoring that supplier. If rebates are given directly to an individual (for example, a purchaser) without any documentation, they are termed *kickbacks* and are illegal.

Another form of kickback occurs when a supplier bills an establishment a higher price than is equitable for a product, and the difference between that higher price and the real price is paid to the person approving the invoice. This practice can occur in small establishments in which the purchaser, receiver, and invoice-approving employee are the same person and in operations without management supervision. It is unlikely to happen in large establishments where several people are involved in the purchasing, receiving, and invoice-approval system because then collusion (and sharing of the kickback "profits") would have to occur.

A more subtle form of kickback occurs when noncash payments are given by suppliers to those involved in purchasing. This type of kickback takes the form of free products or other gifts given to the employee, even to the extent of their being delivered directly to the employee's home. The line between what is an ethical token of gratitude or esteem and what may be a bribe from a supplier is thin, and for this reason many establishments maintain a policy disallowing any gifts—or any gifts above a nominal value—from suppliers.

DISCUSSION QUESTIONS

1. Discuss the problem of establishing receiving hours in a hospitality operation, and explain the term *night drop*.
2. List the receiving checks that should be carried out for delivered products.
3. Explain the use of a receiving stamp.
4. What is a dummy or memorandum invoice, and when is it used?
5. Explain the use of a notice of invoice error form.
6. What is a credit memorandum, and when is it used?
7. Explain what is meant by the term *blind receiving*, and state why it is not commonly used in hospitality receiving.
8. Even though in large hospitality operations the purchasing department is not directly involved in receiving products, it still is indirectly responsible for part of the process. Explain how.
9. Discuss the term *credit rating* with reference to a hospitality operation's purchasing.
10. Explain the difference between paying from invoices and paying from a supplier statement.
11. Explain how a petty cash fund works for COD deliveries.
12. In paying invoices by check, how is control established?
13. Explain the term *opportunity cost* and how it must be considered when invoices are paid.
14. What are two problems that can occur when suppliers offer discounts on purchase invoices?
15. Differentiate a discount from a rebate, and discuss the problem of kickbacks.

PROBLEMS

1. Arrange to spend half a day in the receiving area of a hospitality operation so that you can observe and evaluate its receiving procedures. Find out what forms

it uses (obtain blank voided samples if possible) in controlling the receipt of products, what checks are carried out, and what processes each piece of paperwork goes through. Write a one-page report describing and commenting about your findings, and recommend improvements to that operation's receiving system.

2. Arrange to visit the accounting department of a hotel or large restaurant and discuss with the accountant what the policies are on paying invoices, taking advantage of discounts, and ensuring the business maintains a good credit rating. What is the operation's policy in allowing employees to receive gifts from suppliers? Prepare a one-page report of your findings.

3. You have made a purchase costing five hundred dollars. The supplier's terms are 2/10, net 60. Assume that, to take advantage of the discount, you borrowed money from the bank at 10 percent on the day the invoice was to be paid. The bank will be repaid by you thirty days later. Would you take advantage of the discount?

4. On June 5, a restaurant purchased a new item of equipment costing $3,200. A 1 percent purchase discount is offered by the supplier if the invoice is paid by June 15; otherwise, the invoice is payable in full by July 31. Should the restaurant borrow the money from the bank at 12 percent interest on June 15 (to be repaid July 31) to take advantage of the purchase discount? Would your decision change if the amount to be borrowed were only $1,500, the balance coming from the restaurant's current bank account?

REFERENCES AND SUGGESTED READINGS

Keister, Douglas C. 1977. *Food and Beverage Control.* Englewood Cliffs, N.J.: Prentice-Hall

Maizel, Bruno. 1978. *Food and Beverage Purchasing.* Indianapolis: Bobbs-Merrill.

Peddersen, Raymond B. 1981. *Foodservice and Hotel Purchasing.* Boston: CBI, pp. 107–9.

Stefanelli, John M. 1985. *Purchasing: Selection and Procurement for the Hospitality Industry.* New York: John Wiley, pp. 145–50, 195–212.

Thorner, Marvin E., and Peter B. Manning. 1983. *Quality Control in Foodservice.* Westport, Conn.: AVI.

Virts, William B. 1987. *Purchasing for Hospitality Operations.* East Lansing, Mich.: The Educational Institute of the American Hotel & Motel Association, pp. 74–79.

Warfel, M. C., and Frank H. Waskey. 1979. *The Professional Food Buyer.* Berkeley, Calif.: McCutchan, pp. 125–41.

Food Purchasing, Receiving, and Inventory Control

OBJECTIVES

- Distinguish between perishable and nonperishable food items and their purchasing, and discuss the use of standing orders for purchasing perishables.
- Describe and explain the use of a market quotation sheet and an order form.
- Explain the value of food tests.
- Explain why suppliers should deliver priced invoices with products delivered, and list at least five common methods by which suppliers and/or delivery drivers can profit from an operation's poor receiving practices.
- List at least six standard practices for effective receiving.
- Discuss the use of a daily food receiving report, complete a report from given information, and explain the value of analyzing food purchases by category.
- List in two or three sentences the main points about storeroom location and layout and the requirements for storing food.
- Explain how a food storeroom can be controlled without the use of perpetual inventory cards and requisitions.
- Define a dead stock report, explain inventory-taking procedures, and reconcile actual inventory with book inventory.
- Explain and calculate open stock inventory and inventory turnover.

PURCHASING

In food purchasing, those involved have to tread a fine line between buying products that are of a high enough quality to meet the requirements of the establishment's customers and controlling the amount of money spent on food products. As Maizel (1978, p. 1) puts it:

> Sound food and beverage purchasing is the cornerstone of a quality hospitality operation's reputation and financial success. Its reputation depends on good food, and good food begins with high quality purchases. Its financial success depends on food sales at a profit, and food sales at a profit begin with wise and careful buying.

Knowledgeable Purchaser

The first step in effective food purchasing is to have a knowledgeable person or persons responsible for this function. As is the case with most products purchased, any food product can have wide extremes in quality. Food purchasers must, there-fore, know what quality they need. Effective purchasing does not always mean buying the highest quality if a lower quality at a lower price will suit the needs. Food purchasers must also be very familiar with the availability and seasonality of products. They must be aware of weather and transportation problems that can affect product supply and cost and must be alert to new products that are introduced in the market.

Product Grading

The main task of the food purchaser in most hospitality food operations is to obtain good quality products because low grades or qualities are just not acceptable. Even though government standards for many food products guarantee that they will be wholesome and properly labeled and measured, the purchaser still has the task and responsibility to identify products for freshness and potential yield (because that determines the cost per portion). Many food products (such as meat, poultry, fresh produce, and groceries) are graded for quality. This grading is voluntary on the part of the processor, and many products are on the market without grades. The food purchaser should not necessarily buy only products that are graded because many suitable ungraded products can be found that represent excellent value for money.

Some processors forgo voluntary government grading so they can sell their products labeled under their own brand names. For large processors, the product's brand names are an indication of quality level. A processor labels one quality of a product with one brand name and another quality with a different brand name. The purchaser's role is to find out what quality level is indicated by each brand name.

However, the purchaser needs to be alert, because processors can also label a product as "top quality" or "excellent" even though it is below average in quality.

Standards of Identity

For many food products, the government has also established standards of identity that define what minimum amounts of ingredients must be in a product for it to be so named and without a list of ingredients having to appear on the label. By knowing the standards of identity for products, the wise food purchaser can make comparisons and seek out substitutes or alternatives (such as buying the product as is or making it from scratch on-site).

More information on grading of products, standards of identity, and similar matters are provided in later chapters where specific food products are discussed.

Perishable and Nonperishable Items

Generally, food products can be classified into either perishable or nonperishable items. Perishable items are those that have a relatively short storage life, such as dairy and bakery goods, fresh fruit and vegetables, and fresh meat, poultry, and seafood products. Perishable food products are generally put into production and consumed within a day or so of purchase. Nonperishable items, in contrast, have a much longer shelf life that could conceivably run into years (although investing money in food inventory for several years ahead may not be wise from an opportunity-cost point of view).

Nonperishable items are frequently also called *groceries* or *staples* and are received in sealed cans, packages, or other types of containers. Even certain frozen products could be classified as nonperishable. Because most nonperishables are not usually put immediately into production, they can be stored in a separate, lockable storeroom and controlled with a system of perpetual inventory cards and requisitions (see chapter 6).

Who Orders?

In a small establishment one person, the manager or the chef, might be responsible for all food ordering. In large establishments, the ordering might be split between two or more individuals. For example, the chef might be responsible for some or all of the perishable items, because he or she is usually most knowledgeable about freshness and other important qualities, and the storekeeper might order nonperishable items that he or she is responsible for controlling in the storeroom. Alternatively, the chef might delegate the ordering of certain perishables, such as dairy and bakery goods, to the storekeeper or another qualified assistant. In a fairly large establishment, the chef might be too busy with other tasks to spend time ordering and checking perishables. In such cases, all perishable ordering has to be delegated to an assistant. In a very large organization, with a separate purchasing department, the responsibility for all food purchasing and ordering might be centralized in that department, along with all other products needed by the organization.

Purchasing Perishables

Because purchasing perishables is usually done daily, most establishments are advised to use a system of standing orders for bakery, dairy, and fresh fruit and vegetable products. (Two methods of using standing orders were discussed in chapter 6.) Large fluctuations in the daily volume of business or banquets and similar functions will probably necessitate adjustments to the daily standing orders. One way to do this is to establish a minimum par stock or standing order for each item and add to it each day the additional quantity required for that day's business. Good internal communication is necessary. For example, the person doing the ordering must know what special functions are being held each day and be familiar with daily fluctuations in normal volume caused by the day of the week, special events, holidays, or the weather. Sales forecasts based on historical records are useful for this purpose.

For perishable items not purchased on a standing order or par stock basis, or in establishments where standing orders and/or par stocks are not used, the chef may prepare a daily list of perishables required. In other cases, this list is prepared by the storekeeper in discussion with the chef. As another alternative, the storekeeper ensures that a sufficient supply is on hand of bakery and dairy items as well as fresh fruits and vegetables; then a daily perishables list is needed only for meat, poultry, and fish items.

Purchasing Nonperishables

Purchasing nonperishables is simpler than purchasing perishables. Because nonperishables do not have to be ordered daily, the ordering process can be limited to once a week or once every two weeks. Whenever the frequency of purchasing is reduced, however, more of each item must be ordered each time and carried in inventory. The added costs of carrying a larger inventory must be considered.

When an establishment has a storekeeper, even if only part-time, to receive nonperishable items into the storeroom and later issue them by requisition, perpetual inventory cards (discussed in chapter 6) are recommended. As discussed later, these cards are very useful for food inventory control, but they are also extremely valuable because they considerably reduce the time required to determine how much of each item to order. Without them, each item on the storeroom shelves would have to be counted on each order day and compared with a par stock list to find out how much to reorder.

Market Quotation Sheet

Regardless of the method of ordering and who actually does the ordering, a market quotation sheet is a good idea. Market quotation sheets can be individually designed, or, alternatively, standard quotation sheets are available at stationers who deal with the hotel and foodservice business. Standard forms usually have space on them to list the special requirements that an individual establishment may have. Specialty operations that purchase a lot of unusual food products may have to design their own form.

Wherever possible, obtaining a minimum of three quotations for each item desired is recommended. In small operations, the common industry practice is to circle, on the market quotation sheet, the quoted price from the supplier from whom the product is ordered, as illustrated in Figure 8-1.

		Date _____ February 2 _____			
Item	Quantity required	Suppliers			
		Jang	Tobin	Louie	
CHEESE American	25 lb.	(2.10)	2.30	2.28	
Bel Paese					
Camembert	2 lb.		(4.20)	4.30	
Cheddar, Mild	10 lb.	2.22	(2.22)	2.15	
Cheddar, Medium					
Cheddar, Strong	5 lb.	2.50	(2.50)	2.60	
Cottage					

Figure 8-1.   Market quotation sheet (*Source:* Coltman, Michael M. 1989. *Cost Control for the Hospitality Industry,* p. 90. New York: Van Nostrand Reinhold).

With all ordering, whether for perishables or nonperishables, one should purchase from the supplier who can meet the specifications (if they have been drawn up for that product) and provide the quality desired at the lowest price. However, one may not always buy at the lowest price. Reliability of the supplier and frequency of shipping can be a consideration. Also, the supplier whose quotation is the lowest for only one or two items may not be willing to pay the shipping cost if the order totals only a few dollars. (See the discussion of this topic in chapter 5 in the section on competitive buying.)

Order Form

Because the person receiving the food items ordered may not be the same as the one doing the ordering, summarizing all items ordered each day on a food order form is often useful. A sample order form is illustrated in Figure 8-2. Even if all ordering and receiving are carried out by the same person, an order form can still be a useful control because it can show whether or not the products were actually received. If not, a note or explanation should be placed in the Comment column for later reference or for reordering the products the next day. If the receiving function is separate from the ordering function, the receiver must be given a copy of this form each day so that he or she knows what should be delivered, at what prices, and in what quantities.

Food Deliveries

If hours when shipments can be received must be restricted (for example, if the receiving function is combined with some other job), these limited delivery hours

Order Date _____ February 2 _____			Delivery Date _____ February 3 _____			
Item	Supplier	Quantity ordered	Price	Total	Received	Comment
American	Jang	25 lb.	2.10	52.50	✔	
Camembert	Tobin	2 lb.	4.20	8.40	✔	
Cheddar, Mild	Tobin	10 lb.	2.22	22.20	✔	
Cheddar, Strong	Jang	5 lb.	2.50	12.50	✔	

Figure 8-2.   Sample order form (*Source:* Coltman, Michael M. 1989. *Cost Control for the Hospitality Industry,* p. 92. New York: Van Nostrand Reinhold).

should be made known to suppliers to see if some mutually acceptable time can be determined. In a large establishment with one or more full-time receivers, limited hours would not be a problem. Suppliers should also be advised to provide fully priced invoices with the goods because, as shown in the next section, these invoices are necessary for preparing a daily food receiving report. Blind receiving is not a common practice in food purchasing.

Food Tests

Tests can be carried out on food products to ensure that they provide value for money. For example, canned food tests should ensure that the best net weight yield is obtained after draining the liquid in which the food is packed. The count, uniformity, and quality of canned food contents should also be evaluated. If the liquid is to be used, its quality might also be important. Similar tests can be made on packaged products that are not packed in liquids. Fruit and vegetable tests ensure that the best weight or count of product is received for money spent. Another important area is the butchering and cooking test carried out on meat, poultry, and seafood items. This area of control is covered in the chapters in which these products are discussed.

According to Thorner and Manning (1983, p. 63), the following list of quality control procedures can be used (where applicable) in evaluating products to determine their suitability:

1. Proper sampling techniques
2. Sensory evaluation

    a. Appearance of product (uniformity of size and color)
    b. Texture
    c. Flavor (taste and aroma) characteristics
    d. Evaluation of results with purchase specifications

3. Visual observation of defects
4. Determination of syrup density
5. Determination of sugar content
6. Determination of container fill and headspace for items in can or glass containers (note that the fill of a container is part of a product's standard of identity)
7. Determination of drained weight
8. Determination of percentage breading
9. Determination of percentage fat in chopped meat
10. Determination of presence of insect filth by visual methods
11. Determination of container condition

RECEIVING

Adequate food receiving space must be provided. According to Scriven and Stevens (1989, p. 2), a restaurant serving two hundred to three hundred meals per day needs fifty to sixty square feet of receiving space, one serving three hundred to five hundred needs sixty to ninety square feet, and one serving five hundred to a thousand needs ninety to one hundred thirty square feet. These space requirements vary, depending on frequency of deliveries and menu variations.

Skilled Receivers

With reference to food receiving, Eames and Norkus (1988, p. 32) state, "Without a skilled receiving staff, all other purchasing efforts break down. Proper specifications are critical, but without a trained and equipped receiving staff, they are useless." For example, if porterhouse steaks are specified from the top end of the USDA Choice grade with moderate marbling, does the person receiving this product have the ability to determine whether the delivered goods are average Choice or top Choice? Some suppliers, knowing that the receiver does not have the skills, might substitute a lower grade, a practice known as *upgrading.*

Upgrading quality is always difficult to prove because with some food products quality is often a matter of opinion and the supplier can always claim that the correct quality grade was delivered as specified. This problem is particularly common with fresh produce (such as fruit and vegetables) but also occurs with brand-name items such as bacon, sausages, and canned or frozen products. Some suppliers have also been known to upgrade canned products by removing the label from a cheap brand and replacing the label with a better brand label, even though this practice is illegal.

Methods of Fraud

Apart from upgrading, suppliers or delivery drivers can use various methods to defraud a hotel or restaurant when they observe that control procedures for receiving are not being used.

Failing to Meet Specifications

Suppliers sometimes fail to meet required specifications in order to increase their own profit or to compensate for having deliberately underbid in order to obtain the business (in which case they can now make a normal profit only by doing such things as failing to meet size or trim specifications). For example, a supplier could deliberately leave more fat on a roast than the specifications require, charge for boneless cuts and deliver cuts still containing the bone, include preportioned cuts that are short weight, or send a shipment that is incomplete (short weight or count). To control these problems, qualified and trained receiving employees must be on hand to verify quality against specifications and against purchase order quantities and to prepare credit memoranda for short-count or short-weight shipments.

With size specifications, some tolerance may be allowed. For example, if specifications call for ten-ounce prime rib, bone-in steaks, individual steaks may be allowed to vary from 9.5 to 10.5 ounces, as long as the overall average is 10 ounces. If these items are shipped by weight and by count, they should be taken out of their cases to be counted and weighed. For example,

$$100 \text{ 10-ounce steaks} = 1{,}000 \text{ oz} \div 16 \text{ oz} = 62.5 \text{ lb}$$

This delivery should contain both one hundred items and 62.5 pounds of steaks.

Portioned meats must also be spot-checked for their weights. For example, suppose portioned hamburgers are specified in two-ounce weights and are charged for by the supplier by the pound. If 2.25-ounce hamburgers are regularly delivered, the invoiced total weight is 12.5 percent more than required, and the food cost on this item also increases by 12.5 percent.

Watering and Icing Products Shipped by Weight or Adding Excess Packaging

Another fraudulent method suppliers may employ is to water moisture-retaining vegetables (for example, head lettuce) excessively or to use excessive packing ice for items (such as poultry) that are shipped in crushed ice. Receiving personnel must examine goods for excessive watering (a water-stained container may signal this) and weigh items after taking them out of their ice packing. If items are shipped by weight, verifying the weight should be a matter of routine after removing items from their packaging materials.

Invoicing High-Quality Products for Low-Quality Products Delivered

A supplier may invoice at a quoted price but deliver products of a lower quality than called for by the price. Again, a qualified receiver will be able to catch this type of fraud. Some suppliers, however, have been known to pack a case with correct quality on the top to cover up lower-quality items underneath. Spot-checking the entire case is necessary to control this practice. Alternatively, one or more cases could be opened and inspected from the bottom! Quality, as well as count and weight, of packed products should always be verified against the actual products, not against what is printed or stamped on the outside of the case. Suppliers have been known to repack containers with lower-quality products or products of short weight or count when they notice that only the case-printed information is verified by the receiver. A supplier might also open containers or cases prior to delivery, remove some of the items, reseal and deliver the partially full boxes or cases, and charge for full containers.

Shipping Overweight or Over Count

A supplier may also ship more products than were ordered to add to its sales and profits. Accepting more products than were actually desired can lead to excessive inventories and eventual spoilage of goods. Products not ordered should be returned to the supplier, accompanied by a supporting credit memorandum.

Invoice Overcharging

Normally, food suppliers are requested to send a priced invoice with delivered goods. In this way the priced invoice can be compared with prices on market quotation sheets and/or purchase orders or order forms. Any overpricing should immediately be corrected on the invoice by the receiver and a credit memorandum prepared. If suppliers only mail an invoice sometime later, particular care should be taken to verify prices at that time to ensure that a supplier is not deliberately attempting to overcharge; if any invoice prices have been changed, these changes should also be carefully checked. Such suppliers should be instructed to send a priced invoice with the goods in the future.

Bulk Weighing

A supplier noticing that certain deliveries are bulk-weighed (for instance, a meat order with various cuts that are delivered and weighed in total rather than by individual cut) may be tempted to defraud by substitution. For example, a delivery may call for a hundred pounds of meat broken down into fifty pounds of hamburger at two dollars per pound (total one hundred dollars) and fifty pounds of sirloin at four dollars per pound (total two hundred dollars) for a total invoice cost of three hundred dollars. If these two items are not separately weighed, the supplier could actually ship fifty-five pounds of hamburger (total $110) and only forty-five pounds of sirloin (total $180), for a total value of $290 ($110 + $180), while still invoicing for three hundred dollars and thus making an extra ten-dollar profit. Bulk weighing by a receiver should never be allowed, particularly with expensive items such as meat and seafood.

Putting Products Directly into Storage Areas

The basic rule should be that no products are to be put into storage areas by delivery drivers, either before or after the goods have been inspected by the receiver. If direct storage is allowed, a driver may eventually bypass the inspection and fail to deliver the proper quantity or quality of merchandise.

Delivering Products Outside Normal Receiving Hours

A delivery driver who is allowed to deliver outside the hours when the qualified receiver is available may simply obtain the signature of another employee acknowledging that the products have been received, without any count, weight, or quality checks. Indeed, the driver may simply leave the goods without having anybody check them at all. In both these cases, fraud is encouraged.

Honest Suppliers

Other dishonest practices can occur with specific products in food receiving. The necessary receiving practices to catch these situations are covered in later chapters where those particular products are discussed.

The comments in the preceding sections are not meant to imply that all suppliers are dishonest. Most of them are quite honest. Nevertheless, any operation ought to follow carefully the recommended receiving practices at all times, not only to ensure that fraud does not occur but also to catch honest errors. Also, even though the supplier might be honest, the delivery driver may be dishonest and doing things that cost the hospitality operation money without the supplier's knowledge.

Standard Practices

To eliminate possible causes of losses, a set of standard receiving practices should be prepared in writing so that all employees involved in receiving food products are aware of them. A set of standard receiving practices could include the following:

1. Count each product that can be counted (number of cases or number of individual items).
2. Weigh each product that is delivered by weight (such as meat). Appropriate weighing scales must be provided for this purpose. Scales are available that print a tape showing the weight of each item. Tapes should be attached to the related invoices to indicate that this important aspect of receiving has been properly carried out.
3. Check the count or weight figure against the count or weight figure on the invoice accompanying the delivery. If purchase orders are used, the invoice information should also be verified against the purchase orders.
4. Confirm that the products are of the quality desired; if specifications were prepared and sent to the supplier, check the quality against these specifications. Specifications should also state acceptable production dates or quality expira-

tion dates on perishable goods. These dates should be checked by the receiver to ensure that they are not being breached by a supplier. In this regard, wherever possible, all products received should be dated with the date of receipt. New stock must be put behind old stock. Dating allows this process to be verified and ensures proper stock rotation. For perishable produce that is sensitive to temperature, receipt at the proper temperature should be verified. For example, items to be received frozen should be completely frozen, not partially thawed.

5. Spot-check case goods to ensure that cases are full and that all items in the case are of the same quality. If two or more cases of a particular product are delivered, do not remove all items to be sampled from the same case. If, for example, three samples are needed, they should be taken from separate cases.

6. Check prices on invoices against prices quoted on the market quotation sheet or against the purchase order, if purchase orders are used.

7. If products are delivered without an invoice, prepare a memorandum invoice listing name of supplier, date of delivery, count or weight of items, and, from the market quotation sheet, the price of the items.

8. If goods are short-shipped or if quality is not acceptable, prepare a credit memorandum listing the products returned, and obtain the delivery driver's signature acknowledging that the items have been taken back or that they were short-shipped. Staple this credit memorandum to the original invoice. Do not accept a short shipment without the necessary credit memorandum on the strength of a driver's promise to deliver the balance "tomorrow," because tomorrow may never happen, the matter is forgotten, and food costs increase as a result of products invoiced and paid for but never received.

9. Store all products in proper storage locations as soon after delivery as possible.

10. Send all invoices and credit memoranda to the accounting office so that extensions and totals can be checked and then recorded.

In addition to requiring these practices, control office spot checks should be carried out to ensure that the receiver is performing all required duties. Complete checking of all deliveries cannot be overemphasized. A delivery driver who notices that weighing scales are not used or that quantities are not counted may be tempted to short-ship deliveries. If quality is not checked, a lower quality can be substituted.

Other Potential Losses

Even with all these safeguards in effect, losses can also occur from employees in and around receiving and storage areas.

1. The receiver working with a delivery driver and approving invoices for deliveries not actually made to the establishment

2. The receiver working with a supplier and approving invoices for high-quality products while a low quality is actually delivered
3. The storekeeper removing products from a controlled storeroom and changing perpetual inventory card balance figures to hide the removal
4. Employees pocketing the items from storage areas or smuggling them out the back door in garbage cans

The necessity for constant management supervision and observation to prevent such abuses is thus obvious.

Distribution of Food

Once food items have been properly received and checked, they must be quickly moved to storage areas. Generally, perishable products are put into storage rooms, refrigerators, or freezers as close to the kitchen production areas as possible. In some cases, some products might be delivered directly to sales areas; for example, luncheon rolls might be delivered directly to the dining room each day. Nonperishable products are usually sent immediately to the storeroom. Wherever possible, this storeroom should also be close to the kitchen area to reduce time spent in movement of goods.

Products that are put directly into production (either in the kitchen or in a sales area) are usually referred to as *direct purchases*. Items that are put into a controlled storeroom are referred to as *storeroom purchases*. To simplify the next step in the food cost-control process, the receiver should be instructed to note on each invoice, when it is not obvious, that an item is either a direct or a storeroom product. This information is useful for compiling the daily food receiving report.

Daily Food Receiving Report

A daily food receiving report summarizes each day's invoices as shown in Figure 8-3. Listing each individual item from each invoice on the receiving report is not necessary, because this information, if it is needed later, can also be obtained by referring to that invoice.

According to Stefanelli (1985, p. 205), the use of a detailed receiving report is somewhat redundant because it contains information already on the invoice and/or other documents. He contends that operations that have discontinued using it have not lost any measure of control. That is probably true. However, it has validity if, as is shown on Figure 8-3, only invoice totals are listed (with their breakdown into storeroom or direct items) because this allows a daily food cost to be calculated; the storeroom column can be used to maintain a running balance of the value of goods in the storeroom, which can provide a check when an actual physical inventory of storeroom items is taken at the end of the month.

Supplier	Items	Direct purchases	Storeroom purchases	Other purchases	Invoice total
				Date	February 3
Jang	Cheese	65.00			65.00
Charlton	Groceries		113.20	13.28	126.48
Atlantic	Fresh fish	48.16			48.16
Atlantic	Fresh fish	(12.39)			(12.39)
J.G. Packing	Groceries		25.19		25.19
Totals		216.20	157.92	13.28	387.40

Figure 8-3.   Sample daily food receiving report (*Source:* Coltman, Michael M. 1989. *Cost Control for the Hospitality Industry,* p. 99. New York: Van Nostrand Reinhold).

The important point in completing the receiving report is to allocate the purchase-cost figures from each invoice to either the Direct Purchases column or the Storeroom Purchases column. (For this reason, the virtue of the suggestion about noting the distribution area on the invoice should now be apparent.) In some cases, an invoice may have on it nonfood items. In that case, the dollar amount of those items is entered in the Other Purchases column. In other cases, food items may be received that are not intended for the food department. An example of this might be fruit (such as limes) purchased specifically for the cocktail lounge. Because one of the main reasons for having a daily food receiving report is to aid in calculation of a daily food cost, the food cost should not be charged with purchases for the bar. In such cases, the cost of those items should also be entered in the Other Purchases column. All invoices for each day should be entered on the receiving report. Note, with reference to Figure 8-3, how the credit memorandum from Atlantic has been recorded as a deduction. Once all invoices have been entered, the columns should be totaled and cross-footed to ensure a balance.

$$\$216.20 + \$157.92 + \$13.28 = \$387.40$$

At the end of each day, the person completing the receiving report should forward it to the accounting office together with the related invoices and purchase orders (if they are in use). The accounting office should then verify that

1. All invoices have been extended and totaled properly by the supplier. If any errors are discovered, the invoice and the receiving report figures should be corrected and the supplier notified.
2. Invoice amounts have been properly entered on the daily food receiving report.
3. Invoices have been matched with purchase orders (if they are used), and prices on invoices have been checked against purchase order prices.

Later in this chapter, we shall see how the daily food receiving report figures can be used for storeroom inventory control.

Purchase Analysis by Category

Large organizations sometimes design the receiving report so that it not only breaks down food purchases into either direct use or storeroom but further breaks down direct food purchases into several different categories. One of the reasons for doing this is that, by totaling up the dollars spent on each separate category over a period of time (such as a week or a month), comparisons can be made with dollars spent on those same categories in previous periods. The dollars spent on each category are divided by the dollars spent on all categories for that period so that the breakdown of the purchase dollar can be expressed as a ratio or percent. In this way, relative changes can be more readily observed. By comparing these percentages over time, trends may become evident that might be useful for indicating such things as changing customer preferences resulting in a higher or lower food cost or the need for changes in menus. Figure 8-4 illustrates a type of receiving report that permits this type of purchase cost analysis by category.

STORAGE AREAS

It goes without saying that nonperishable food products placed into a lockable storeroom should be kept under ideal conditions to reduce spoilage, waste, or other nonrecoverable costs. Temperature, ventilation, and sanitation must be a consideration in storeroom location and design. Ninemeier (1982, p. 78) states:

> Actually, the storeroom should be thought of as a bank vault. Products in storage are money. Instead of having $5,000 worth of food in the storeroom, think of it as 5,000 one dollar bills in storage. The same procedures for controlling stored cash should be used for controlling stored foods and beverages. They represent money in terms of their initial cost and the cost to replace them if they are stolen, spoiled, or damaged because of improper storage practices.

Unfortunately, in many hospitality operations those responsible for food storage frequently do not show the same concern about nonperishable products as they do

HOTEL _____

DEPT.							DATE				19____ DAY OF WEEK _____

PURCHASES			STOCK TO STOREROOM				BAR				
1	2	3	4	5	6	7	8	9	10	11	12
NAME OF FIRM	AMOUNT OF INVOICE	DIRECT ISSUES TO KITCHEN	MEAT FISH AND POULTRY	STAPLES	FRUITS & VEGETABLES	DAIRY PRODUCTS	LIQUOR	BEER	WINE	MIXES STORES	CARTAGE

A   TODAY'S PURCHASES
B   BALANCE FORWARD from Yesterday
C   TOTAL TO DATE THIS MONTH

13	14	15	16	17	18	19	20	21	22	23	24	25
	DIRECT ISSUES											FOOD COST 14 TO 24
	MEAT	FISH	POULTRY	FRUITS	VEGET.	DAIRY PRODUCTS	BAKERY PRODUCTS	STAPLES	COFFEE	BUTTER	EGGS	

DIRECT ISS
STORES ISS
TOTAL ISS
FWD. BAL
TOTAL M.D

I	BEGINNING INVENTORY LAST MONTH END											
J	STOCK TO STORE ROOM C4 to 7							5 c				
K	STORE ROOM ISSUES E 14 to 24							21 to 25				
L	I + J K BALANCE ON HAND											
M	PHYSICAL INVENTORY											
N	L + OR M ADJUSTMENT	$										
O	IN% to M ADJUSTMENT	%										
P	SALES M INVENTORY TURNOVER											

EXHIBIT 4.4.   Receiving Report Permitting Cost Analysis by Category

Figure 8-4.   Receiving report permitting cost analysis by category (*Source:* Coltman, Michael M. 1989. *Cost Control for the Hospitality Industry*, p. 101. New York: Van Nostrand Reinhold).

about those requiring refrigeration or freezing. This attitude probably stems from a false sense that deterioration of nonperishable products does not occur. This viewpoint is unfortunate because no food products last indefinitely. Even canned products deteriorate over time, although the rate of deterioration may be slower than for perishable products.

Storeroom Location and Layout

The storeroom should be on the same level as the receiving area and as close to it as possible to reduce movement of heavy goods. For the same reason, proximity to the kitchen would be ideal.

Food products should be placed in sectionalized compartments that can be labeled for easy identification. Heavy items that are issued in bulk (sacks of flour or sugar, for example) and products that are frequently used should be closest to the door. Once items have been placed in specific locations, those locations should be changed as infrequently as possible. Permanent locations mean increased efficiency in placing items in their locations and issuing them when needed. It also means that month-end inventory sheets can be preprinted in the same order as the items are located on the shelves, thus speeding up stocktaking and minimizing the possibility of overlooking items. As products are received and put in their right location on the shelf, they can be date-stamped to ensure proper stock rotation.

Shelving

Food storeroom shelves should be about twenty inches deep and about eighteen inches in height. The bottom shelf should be raised a few inches off the floor to allow better air circulation and facilitate keeping the floor clean. In some locations, local sanitation codes may have to be referred to with reference to shelving materials allowed. Stainless steel is the best material but is usually the most expensive. Wood shelving may be used for nonfood items, but sanitary codes normally do not allow it in food storage areas. In dry storage areas, chrome-plated wire shelving provides both strength and light weight. It should not, however, be used in refrigerated or freezer areas because it is not rust resistant. In refrigerated areas, galvanized, perforated (for better air circulation), slotted metal shelving is often used. All shelving should be of modular design that allows it to be easily rearranged. In refrigerated areas, for sanitary reasons, all food should be in covered containers.

A good rule of thumb is to have shelving limited to about 50 percent of the total storage area so that cases and/or bulk storage containers can be stored on pallets or racks on the floor. Nothing should be stored directly on the floor; again, most sanitary codes prohibit this practice.

Dutch Door

The storeroom door should be a Dutch door so the lower half can be locked in place from inside with the top half left open. The bottom half should have a shelf built onto its top. This arrangement allows the storekeeper to hand requisitioned products to people standing outside the storeroom and ensures that they do not enter it.

Equipment

Two major items of storeroom equipment are required: a hand truck, so that goods can be moved from storage areas to production areas, and two types of scales. A large floor-model scale is needed for weighing large quantities of bulk items (for example, flour and rice), and a smaller table model is required for weighing smaller quantities. Also needed is a stainless-steel work table where merchandise can be inspected and cases of goods unpacked or broken down into small quantities for production area use. The storekeeper also needs office equipment (desk, chair, filing cabinet) in order to process necessary paperwork.

Space Requirement

The size of storeroom required is related in many ways to the type of operation (such as hotel, independent restaurant, club). According to Scriven and Stevens (1989, p. 7), for restaurants and clubs the following guidelines can be used for dry storage area requirements:

    100–200 meals per day: 120–200 square feet
    200–350 meals per day: 200–250 square feet
    350–500 meals per day: 250–400 square feet
    500–1,000 meals per day: 300–650 square feet

Stefanelli (1985, p. 219) states, "Generally speaking, the space needed for all storage is between 5 square feet per dining room seat and 15 square feet per hotel room, depending on the amount of sales, types of items sold, and the quantity of nonfood items carried in storage."

Note, however, that these guidelines are very broad and need to be adjusted depending on the circumstances. For example, a resort hotel with infrequent deliveries may require more than twice the amount of storage space (both dry and refrigerated) as a city restaurant with daily deliveries.

Warfel and Waskey (1979, p. 155) state, "Space requirements should be based on the type of food service, purchasing and inventory policies, the menu, the avail-

Heavy-duty moving equipment may be needed in large storerooms such as a commissary (Courtesy: Clark Equipment Co., Battle Creek, MI).

ability of production and service personnel, and the location of the establishment and the effectiveness of distribution systems.''

Frozen Food Storage

The length of time that frozen food can be safely stored depends on the type of item, the way it is packaged, and the maintenance of a constant storage temperature. A fluctuating temperature reduces the shelf life of these items, and smaller packages are more likely to become dehydrated or suffer freezer burn than large packages

Storeroom portion scales for weighing small quantities of products (Courtesy: Pelouze Scale Co.).

that are better packaged. Also, items such as ham and bacon do not freeze well. Once frozen goods have been thawed, they will generally deteriorate in quality if refrozen and, under any circumstances, should never be kept refrozen more than thirty days.

INVENTORY CONTROL

A system of perpetual inventory cards and requisitions (as discussed in chapter 6) should be used for controlling the inflow and outflow of goods in the food storeroom. The cards are useful for keeping track of what is—or should be—in the storeroom and for charging each department with the cost of food it requisitions from the storeroom.

Dispensing with Perpetual Inventory Cards and Requisitions

Because not all food products purchased can be controlled under a supervised storeroom situation, some suggest that an organization wastes time and money to pay someone to control the storeroom, complete perpetual inventory cards, and cost out requisitions. In addition, manually maintained records have too many errors in them. These claims may be true, except that, generally speaking, the benefits of paying a storekeeper to carry out these functions (even if only during limited hours each day so that the storekeeping tasks can be combined with some other job) would probably outweigh the costs. Controlling say, 50 percent of purchases that are eventually put into production through a storeroom is better than having virtually no control of 100 percent of purchases (both direct and storeroom items). When a storeroom is left unlocked with no supervision, employees can very easily pocket expensive small items (for example, cans of caviar).

Unless inventory records are computerized, however, quite small establishments have just no practical way to supervise a storeroom completely. In such cases, perpetual inventory cards have to be dispensed with, and only one person (such as the chef) should have a key to the storeroom so that other employees are not tempted to remove items for personal use.

In small establishments, requisitions may also be impractical, but knowing what has been taken out of the storeroom may still be desirable. This can be done by having the person with the key record on a sheet each day a list of items issued and their unit costs. The unit cost would have to be recorded on the case, carton, package, can, or bottle at the time the products were received and put into the storeroom. At the end of each day, this master requisition can be extended (quantity of each item times its cost) and totaled, and this figure can then be added to the direct purchases for the day (from the daily food receiving report) to arrive at total food cost for the day.

Other Inventory Control Techniques

Some establishments have a small, controlled food storage area adjacent to the main food production area. In this room a par stock of the most frequently used items is kept and controlled by the chef. This eliminates many frequent trips to the main storeroom.

Proper storeroom management requires a system of stock rotation to reduce losses from spoilage, shrinkage, and quality deterioration. To aid in this objective, all containers (or in some cases individual products) should be stamped with their date of receipt.

One other useful control is a dead-stock report. It should be prepared monthly and list items that have been on hand and unused in the storeroom for a minimum specified period (for example, ninety days). This report should alert management to the need to create special menu items, use the products for employee meals, or to dispose of them in some other way (such as selling them at cost to employees).

Another useful technique is to label each shelf with the item located there and to indicate the minimum level to which inventory can be reduced. When that level is reached, the storekeeper knows that new stock must be ordered to bring the inventory back up to its maximum level.

If standard recipes are used in conjunction with daily production forecasts, ingredients in the correct amount for each day's requirements can be issued from the storeroom for each production area. This system is particularly appropriate if computers can be used to calculate daily production requirements.

Taking Inventory

Inventory in foodservice operations is normally taken monthly, although it can be taken more frequently if desired. This type of inventory is known as an *actual, periodic,* or *physical* inventory. A person other than the storekeeper should take inventory. In large establishments, this task is easier and faster if two people (preferably from the accounting office) perform it. One person counts the quantity of each item on the shelves, and the second person verifies that this count agrees with the perpetual inventory card balance. If the figures do not agree, a recount should be made. If they still do not agree, then the figures recorded from invoices and requisitions on the cards should be traced back to their invoices and requisitions, and the arithmetical accuracy of the card balance checked. However, this checking of items whose count does not agree should not be done during the actual inventory taking because it slows down the process. If discrepancies between actual counts and card counts cannot be resolved, then the card balance figure should be changed to the actual figure so that the card is correct from that point on.

Discrepancies between actual count and card balance can also occur if deliveries have been made to the storeroom on that day but have not yet been recorded on cards, or if the invoice information has been recorded on the cards but the products have not yet been put into the storeroom. Similar situations can arise with items requisitioned on stocktaking day. These possibilities should preferably be checked and corrected before inventory is taken.

To speed the inventory-taking process, perpetual inventory cards and the listing of the items on the inventory sheets should be in the same order as items on the shelves. This practice reduces the possibility of missing items and is, obviously, more efficient. Figure 8-5 illustrates a partial inventory sheet.

If the storekeeper is also the same person who completes the perpetual inventory cards from invoices and requisitions, then he or she could purposely fail to record

Month of ____July____			
Item	Quantity	Unit cost	Total
Balance forward			$3,164.38
Carrots, #10	25	$1.43	35.75
Carrots, baby, 24 oz.	12	0.85	10.20
Corn, creamed, #10	4	1.12	4.48
Corn, kernel, #10	8	1.05	8.40
Total			$4,218.76

Figure 8-5.   Inventory sheet (*Source:* Coltman, Michael M. 1989. *Cost Control for the Hospitality Industry,* p. 103. New York: Van Nostrand Reinhold).

certain information on the cards, remove items from the shelves for personal use, and still have the card balance figure and the actual count agree. Cards should be spot-checked against invoices and requisitions by control office personnel to eliminate this possibility.

If perpetual inventory cards are not used, then stocktaking is simply a matter of recording the actual count of items directly on the inventory sheets. The process is faster and easier, but an element of control is lost.

Once all items are listed on the inventory sheets, each item must be extended (item quantity times item cost) and the total inventory added up.

Book Inventory versus Actual Inventory

With a daily food receiving report and an accurate system of costing requisitions, one can at the end of each month (or more frequently if desired) check the reliability of the food storeroom inventory control. To do this, a food storeroom inventory control form is needed (see Figure 8-6). At the beginning of the month, the Opening Inventory figure of $2,242.16 is the same as the actual inventory figure from the previous month end.

Each day, the Storeroom Purchases figure can be copied from the daily food receiving report. For example, the amount of $157.92 on February 3 is copied from

Month __ February __			
Date	Opening inventory	Storeroom purchases	Storeroom issues	Closing inventory
1	2,242.16	163.19	58.17	2,347.18
2	2,347.18		112.24	2,234.94
3	2,234.94	157.92	182.01	2,210.85
4	2,210.85	42.12	107.60	2,145.37
30	2,406.19	118.70	42.16	2,482.73
31	2,482.73	90.16	116.04	2,456.85
Totals		3,612.40	3,397.71	
Actual month-end inventory				2,443.20
Difference				13.65

Figure 8-6.   Food storeroom inventory contol form (*Source:* Coltman, Michael M. 1989. *Cost Control for the Hospitality Industry,* p. 104. New York: Van Nostrand Reinhold).

the Storeroom Purchases column of that day's daily food receiving report (see Figure 8-3). The Storeroom Issues figure is simply the total of all requisitions—costed, extended, and totaled—each day. A running balance of the closing or book value of storeroom inventory can thus be calculated each day.

Opening Inventory + Storeroom Purchases − Storeroom Issues
= Closing Inventory

The term *book inventory* is used for this figure because it may not be accurate. In fact, accuracy would be surprising because the pricing of products in the storeroom is rounded to the nearest cent, and the requisition costing system used frequently creates inaccuracies, as do storekeeping errors in costing requisitions.

At any time, the closing or book value figure from the food storeroom inventory control form can be compared to the actual inventory figure. Normally, this comparison would be done at month end, but weekly checks could be done.

At the month end, a quick reconciliation to ensure the arithmetical accuracy of the last day's closing or book inventory figure is possible. First, add the Storeroom Purchases and Storeroom Issues columns. Then the first day's Opening Inventory plus Storeroom Purchases column total minus Storeroom Issues column total should equal the last day's Closing Inventory figure. In our case:

$$\$2,242.16 + \$3,612.40 - \$3,397.71 = \$2,456.85$$

The difference between the book inventory and actual inventory figures should normally be no more than 1 percent of total issues for the month. In other words, in our illustration (see Figure 8-6), the difference should be no more than 1 percent of $3,397.71 or about $34. Our difference of $13.65 is thus acceptable. Differences greater than 1 percent of issues would likely be for reasons such as issuing items without requisitions, employees helping themselves to items without requisitions, or outright theft. Possible causes should be investigated so that they can be prevented in the future.

Taking an actual inventory each month end is an integral part of ensuring that accurate income statements are produced for the food operation. In addition, comparison of this figure with the book figure is a check on the effectiveness of the food purchasing, receiving, storing, and issuing procedures for all items controlled through the storeroom.

Open Stock Inventory

The storeroom inventory is not, however, the only food inventory to be considered to ensure that income statements are as accurate as possible. Any food operation has direct purchases and storeroom issues in kitchens and other areas that have not yet been used up, as well as stocks, soups, sauces, and other menu items that are in a state of preparation. This situation is true at month end as well as on any other day. Unused food products such as condiments, sauces, nonalcoholic beverages, and many other items may be in dining room, coffee shop, and banquet areas. All of these items are part of inventory, and their value must be calculated each month end. This part of the inventory is usually referred to as *open stock*.

To obtain an accurate open stock inventory, each item should be physically counted, listed on an inventory sheet, and costed out. In some cases, a cost is difficult to determine for products that have been combined into other items (soups, sauces). In these cases, an estimate must be made (preferably with the help of the chef) to value them.

Repeating this work every month may not be necessary. It can be done quarterly. In the interim months, an estimate could be made as to how much the current month's open stock is above or below the base period. In most cases, the bulk of open stock items can be safely assumed not to fluctuate from month end to month end in total dollar value. What might fluctuate are key items such as meat, poultry, and seafood that constitute the major part of the food-purchase dollar. Therefore, why not use only these items? Taking an inventory of them is relatively easy, and that amount can be used for adjusting total open stock for each interim month.

As an example, assume that an accurate physical inventory of all open stock is taken in month one and the total is $5,400. Of this total, $2,500 is for meat, poultry, and seafood items, and $2,900 is for all other items. In month two, an accurate inventory of the meat, poultry, and seafood items gives a new total of $2,750. This is $250, or 10 percent ($250 divided by $2,500 and multiplied by 100), more than in month one.

At this point, two alternatives exist. With alternative one, we assume that the entire open stock value has increased from month one to month two by 10 percent:

$$10\% \times \$5,400 = \$540$$

and $\qquad \$5,400 + \$540 = \$5,940$ open stock month two

With alternative two, we assume that the value of open stock items other than meat, poultry, and seafood has remained the same as in month one, or $2,900, and that the 10 percent increase applies only to the meat, poultry, and seafood part of our open stock. In this case, the total open stock value is

$$\$2,900 + \$2,750 = \$5,650 \text{ for month two}$$

The difference between the two alternatives is $290. Whether or not this is a large difference must be decided on the basis of how it might affect the food cost percentage. Perhaps the dilemma can be resolved by suggesting that if the 10 percent increase in meat, poultry, and seafood items were the result of overall market price increases, then we can logically assume that all market prices have gone up and therefore we should use alternative one. If the meat, poultry, and seafood open stock increase were the result of carrying more of these items in stock than might normally be the case, however, then alternative two might be more realistic.

One final consideration is that open stock is normally higher if the month end falls on a Friday because additional purchases would have been made to carry the operation through the weekend. If the month end falls at the end of a long weekend or holiday period, the reverse is generally true. Under normal circumstances, with daily delivery of most food items, the value of open stock equals about one-and-a-half day's normal food cost. In other words, if an operation's food cost for a typical month were $30,000 or about $1,000 a day, then open stock would probably be about $1,500.

Inventory Turnover

Finally, we come to the matter of inventory turnover. As already mentioned, to avoid tying up too much investment in inventory and thus losing interest that could otherwise be earned on these funds, do not carry too much in inventory. Conversely, the establishment cannot have too few items and risk running out. This matter can be controlled by recording maximum and minimum quantities on perpetual inventory cards, adjusting them from time to time as the need arises, and ensuring with control office spot checks that the storekeeper is keeping within these limits. Without drastically increasing the total value of items carried in inventory, products of individual small value can normally be ordered in large quantities, thus increasing maximum levels while reducing the frequency of ordering. These products generally also take up little storage space. The reverse is generally the case with higher-value items.

A useful control over the entire food inventory is to calculate the monthly food inventory turnover rate.

$$\frac{\text{Food cost for the month}}{\text{Average inventory}}$$

Food cost is calculated using the following formula:

Beginning of the month inventory + Purchases during month − End of the month inventory = Food cost for the month

Average inventory is calculated as follows:

$$\frac{\text{Beginning of the month inventory} + \text{End of the month inventory}}{2}$$

Assuming that the beginning of the month inventory is $7,000, the end of the month inventory is $8,000, and purchases during the month are $24,500, our calculation of the inventory turnover rate is

$$\frac{\$7,000 + \$24,500 - \$8,000}{(\$7,000 + \$8,000)/2} = \frac{\$23,500}{\$7,500} = 3.1 \text{ times}$$

Traditionally, the food industry food inventory turnover ranges between two and four times a month. At this level, the danger of running out of food items is minimal, but an overinvestment in inventory is not tying up money that could otherwise be put to use earning interest and adding to profits. However, despite this suggested range, there may be exceptions. Perhaps of more importance to an organization is not what its actual turnover rate is, but whether or not this rate changes over time and what the cause of the change is. For example, assume that the figures $23,500 for food cost and $7,500 a month for average inventory (giving a turnover rate of 3.1) were typical of the monthly figures for this operation. If management noticed that the figure for turnover changed to 2, this change could mean that more money was tied up in inventory and not producing a return:

$$\frac{\$23,500}{\$11,750} = 2 \text{ times}$$

Alternatively, a change in the turnover rate to 4 could mean that too little was invested in inventory and that some customers may not be able to order some items listed on the menu.

$$\frac{\$23,500}{\$5,875} = 4 \text{ times}$$

In some establishments, the turnover rate may be extremely low (less than 2). For example, a resort property in a remote location may be able to receive deliveries only once a month and thus be forced to carry a large inventory. In contrast, a fast-food restaurant that receives daily delivery of its food items from a central commissary and carries little or no stock overnight could conceivably have a turnover rate as high as 30. Each organization should establish its own standards for turnover and then watch for deviations from them.

DISCUSSION QUESTIONS

1. Differentiate between perishable and nonperishable food items.
2. Discuss whether or not an establishment with a daily fluctuation in volume can use a system of standing orders for purchasing perishables.
3. Describe how a market quotation sheet is used.
4. Of what value is an order form?
5. Explain the value of food tests.
6. Why should suppliers be instructed to have invoices accompany deliveries?
7. List as many ways as you can think of by which suppliers and/or delivery drivers can defraud an establishment that does not have good receiving procedures.
8. List as many standard practices as you can think of to help ensure good receiving procedures.
9. What are the column headings on a daily food receiving report?

10. Of what value is analyzing food purchases in detail by category?
11. List the main points about storeroom location, layout, and shelving.
12. Discuss the requirement for frozen food storage.
13. Explain how, in a small establishment where storeroom requisitions are not used, a control procedure can be implemented to know the total cost of what has been taken each day out of the storeroom.
14. What is a dead-stock report and of what value is it?
15. Explain the procedure for taking actual or physical inventory in a food storeroom.
16. Explain why having some difference between the book and actual inventory figures is normal.
17. What is open stock inventory?
18. Give the equation for inventory turnover.

PROBLEMS

1. Prepare a blank daily food receiving report and then complete it from the following invoice information:

County Products: $34.68 for fresh dairy products. On this invoice $4.25 was for cream for the cocktail bar.

Hubbard Bakery: $68.20 for fresh bakery products.

Atlantic Fish: $124.52 for seafood products. Of this amount $83.51 was for fresh fish and the balance for canned seafood items put into the storeroom.

Miller Flour: $72.12 for bulk flour put into the storeroom.

Pacific Packers: $148.20 for fresh meat items.

City Suppliers: $46.80. Of this amount $24.10 was for canned items put into the storeroom and the balance for items put directly into production.

Greenland: $32.15 for fresh fruit and vegetables. However, the quality of some of these items was not acceptable. A credit memorandum in the amount of $8.20 was prepared and the goods returned to the supplier.

2. Past records indicate that the purchase-dollar breakdown for a restaurant was as follows:

Meat	16.9%
Fish	6.1
Poultry	5.8
Produce	10.2

Groceries	19.3
Frozen Food	2.7
Bakery products	12.1
Dairy products	15.0
Butter and eggs	9.8
All other items	2.1

For the current period, purchases were as follows:

Meat	$904
Fish	204
Poultry	327
Produce	449
Groceries	747
Frozen food	107
Bakery products	539
Dairy products	771
Butter and eggs	348
All other items	30

Compare the current period's purchase-dollar breakdown with that of the past, and comment about any significant difference.

3. Items in a food storeroom are controlled with perpetual inventory cards. There is one card for each item in the storeroom. Purchase entries from invoices and requisition entries on the cards are made by the storekeeper, who also calculates the running or perpetual balance of items. At the end of each month, a person from the accounting office takes each card in turn, calls out the name of the item, asks the storekeeper to count the quantity of the item on the shelf, and then compares the storekeeper's count with the figure on the card. In this way, inventory is taken and checked. Comment about this situation from a control point of view.

4. For a food storeroom, the opening inventory figure on 1 January was $1,642. For the months of January, February, and March you have the following information:

Month	Storeroom purchases	Storeroom issues	Actual month-end inventory
January	$2,321	$2,211	$1,827
February	2,598	2,619	1,831
March	2,518	2,506	1,943

For each of the three months, compare the book and actual inventories, and state which sets of figures would not normally be acceptable. Why? Explain what you could do to correct unacceptable situations in any month or months.

5. The open stock inventory of a restaurant was estimated to be $1,620 on 30 November. Included in this amount were meat, poultry, and seafood items valued at $520. On 31 December, the meat, poultry, and seafood items had a value of $572.

   a. On the assumption that the increase in meat, poultry, and seafood items was the result of general market price increases for all food items, calculate the open stock inventory at 31 December.
   b. On the assumption that the increase in meat, poultry, and seafood items was solely the result of carrying more of these items in stock at the end of December, calculate the open stock inventory at 31 December.

6. You have the following information: 1 January total food inventory, $3,050; purchases during January, $9,475; 31 January total food inventory, $2,750. Calculate the inventory turnover rate to one decimal place.

7. A restaurant provides you with the following information: opening food inventory, $22,600; food purchases for month, $67,200; closing food inventory, $21,400.

   a. Calculate the food inventory turnover for the month.
   b. Assume that management allowed the food inventory turnover rate to vary between 2.5 and 3.5 times per month. Calculate the minimum and maximum levels of average inventory that would have been permitted for this month.

8. You have been appointed food and beverage comptroller of a restaurant with a sales volume of approximately one million dollars a year. No one has had this job before you, and you find no control system presently in effect for purchasing, ordering, and receiving food. Until now the chef has been purchasing some food items. The storekeeper has been purchasing others and has been responsible for all receiving. No forms or records are used. The manager, to whom you report, has explained that the operation has been running at a higher food cost than it should.

   Write a two-page report describing what purchasing procedures and forms could be used to aid in reducing and controlling food cost. Do not include samples of the forms, as this report is only a preliminary, but briefly describe the use of any forms and why they would help in reducing food cost. State also who will be responsible for form completion and for carrying out the proposed procedures.

The number of forms should be limited to as few as possible. The procedures should be as simple as possible.

REFERENCES AND SUGGESTED READINGS

Bell, Donald A. 1984. *Food and Beverage Cost Control.* Berkeley, Calif.: McCutchan, pp. 67–110.

Dittmer, Paul R., and Gerald G. Griffin. 1984. *Principles of Food, Beverage & Labor Cost Controls for Hotels and Restaurants.* New York: Van Nostrand Reinhold, pp. 77–119.

Eames, Donald, and Gregory X. Norkus. 1988. Developing Your Procurement Strategy. *Cornell Hotel and Restaurant Administration Quarterly* 29(1):30–33.

Izzola, Al. 1984. Factors Buyers Consider When Selecting Suppliers. *Hospitality Education and Research Journal* 8(2):51–54.

Keister, Douglas C. 1977. *Food and Beverage Control.* Englewood Cliffs, N.J.: Prentice-Hall, pp. 201–7, 215–16, 221–35, 237–52.

Kelly, Hugh J. 1976. *Food Service Purchasing: Principles and Practices.* New York: Lebhar-Friedman, pp. 81–99, 147–59, 169–74.

Khan, Mahmood A. 1987. *Foodservice Operations.* Westport, Conn.: AVI, pp. 208–23.

Kotschevar, Lendal H., and Charles Levinson. 1988. *Quantity Food Purchasing.* New York: Macmillan, pp. 3–50.

Maizel, Bruno. 1978. *Food and Beverage Purchasing.* Indianapolis: Bobbs-Merrill, pp. 199–233.

Minor, Lewis J., and Ronald F. Cichy. 1984. *Foodservice Systems Management.* Westport, Conn.: AVI, pp. 98–126.

Ninemeier, Jack D. 1982. *Planning and Control for Food and Beverage Operations.* East Lansing, Mich.: Educational Institute of the American Hotel and Motel Association, pp. 60–94.

Peddersen, Raymond B. 1981. *Foodservice and Hotel Purchasing.* Boston: CBI, pp. 103–7, 110–18.

Powers, Thomas F., and Jo Marie Powers. 1984. *Food Service Operations: Planning and Control.* New York: John Wiley, pp. 98–104, 133–51, 269–72.

Riegel, Carl D., and K. M. Haywood. 1984. Purchasing Attitudes and Behavior in Canadian Food Service Firms. *Hospitality Education and Research Journal* 9(1):72–82.

Riegel, Carl D., and R. Dan Reid. 1988. Food Service Purchasing: Corporate Practices. *Cornell Hotel and Restaurant Administration Quarterly* 29(1):25–29.

Scriven, Carl, and James Stevens. 1989. *Food Equipment Facts.* New York: Van Nostrand Reinhold.

Stefanelli, John M. 1985. *Purchasing: Selection and Procurement for the Hospitality Industry*. New York: John Wiley, pp. 181–90, 195–212, 217–34.

Thorner, Marvin E., and Peter B. Manning. 1983. *Quality Control in Foodservice*. Westport, Conn.: AVI, pp. 35–44, 57–75, 77–94.

Virts, William B. 1987. *Purchasing for Hospitality Operations*. East Lansing, Mich.: The Educational Institute of the American Hotel & Motel Association, pp. 67–79.

Warfel, M. C., and Frank H. Waskey. 1979. *The Professional Food Buyer*. Berkeley, Calif.: McCutchan, pp. 71–94, 125–41, 143–66.

Meat

OBJECTIVES

- Discuss some of the factors that influence meat prices.
- Discuss the federal government's meat inspection program and quality grading of meat.
- Define the term *no-roll* and discuss the yield grading of meat.
- List the various animals that produce beef, and state the primal cuts from a beef side.
- State why veal and calf are not yield graded, and list the primal cuts in a veal carcass.
- Differentiate lamb from mutton, define the term *conformation*, and list the primal cuts in a lamb carcass.
- Explain why most pork is not graded for quality, and list the primal cuts in a pork carcass.
- Discuss the common methods of purchasing meat.
- Define the terms *green meat, dry aging, IMPS numbers*, and *USDA acceptance service*.
- Discuss the pros and cons of an operation buying preportioned meat products.
- List the quality checks that should be made in meat receiving, and explain how meat tags are used to control meat usage.
- Solve problems concerning meat yields and use cost factors.

IMPORTANCE OF MEAT PURCHASING

In hospitality industry food purchasing, meat can represent as much as 50 percent of the purchase dollar. For this reason, most operators pay strict attention to its selection, purchasing, receiving, and other aspects of control.

Meat Quality

United States beef is noted for its extremely high-quality flavor and tenderness. The animals are fed primarily grain and are raised for beef production. In most other meat-producing countries (for example, Argentina and Australia), cattle are primarily grass fed and are raised for both meat and milk. The meat from these cattle is generally of a lower quality than grain-fed beef.

Despite the fact that U.S. beef is produced in large quantity and has such high customer acceptance, the United States still imports more meat (not only beef but also lamb from countries such as New Zealand) than it exports. A great deal of the imported beef ends up in products such as ground beef, luncheon meats, and sausages. Most imported pork is from Europe in the form of canned ham. The U.S. government establishes quotas each year stating how much meat of various kinds can be imported. Any imported meat must meet rigid sanitation standards equal to those imposed for domestically produced meat.

Meat Consumption and Price

The amount of meat product consumption per capita increases relative to its price. Meat prices in the United States are heavily influenced by government grain support prices, subsidies and loans to farmers who produce grain, and by regulations (often imposed for both international and domestic political reasons) on grain export quantities and prices. These regulations affect the price of feed grain, which then affects meat prices. However, meat prices are also heavily affected by the laws of supply and demand. Demand can be influenced by consumer concerns over chemicals used in meat production, health concerns over the amount of fat in certain meats, and meat imports from abroad. The volume of supply is also cyclical. When more meat is produced than consumers are demanding, the price declines, and animal herds are reduced by ranchers and farmers to decrease supply. Prices then increase, and ranchers and farmers begin increasing their herds again to benefit from these higher prices, supply begins to exceed demand, the price falls, and the cycle begins again.

Transportation Costs

Meat prices are also affected by transportation. Cattle are mostly raised and slaughtered away from the cities where most meat is consumed. The product after slaughter must be transported, sometimes to very distant locations, and the transportation costs have a big impact on the end-product prices. To reduce this cost, few whole carcasses are shipped today from packers' plants. Most of them are butchered, processed, and shipped in box form.

Large hospitality chains sometimes purchase directly from meat processors and provide their own transportation and distribution to their individual operations. In some cases, bulk meat is delivered to a hospitality industry chain's commissary for further processing before distribution. In other cases, hospitality purchasers will contract with a local supplier to provide further processing and distribution. Most small operations rely on local suppliers to transport, process, and deliver their required meat products.

REGULATIONS

Inspection of meat for wholesomeness has been required since the 1906 Federal Meat Inspection Act gave the federal government the authority and responsibility for sanitary plant conditions and accurate labeling of all raw meat and meat products (such as sausages and canned meats) transported domestically between states or imported from abroad. Because this act did not cover meat processed and transported solely within a state, states developed their own standards for intrastate transportation that basically paralleled the federal ones.

In 1967 the Wholesome Meat Act was introduced. This act tightened up the standards for imported meat and also established joint federal-state meat inspection standards that required states to achieve the same level as federal standards, even if the meat did not move outside the state.

Inspections of meat plants are handled by the U.S. Department of Agriculture (USDA). Where states do not have their own inspection programs, all meat-processing plants must be USDA inspected. Any meat carcasses or meat products transported across state borders or exported must also be inspected by the USDA.

Inspections

Inspection of meat is done both before and after slaughtering. The cost of this inspection is assumed by the USDA. Before slaughtering, all animals are examined by USDA inspectors for any sign of disease. Any suspicious animal undergoes a special examination. Dead or dying animals are not allowed into abattoirs (slaughtering plants). Once animals have been slaughtered, inspectors examine each carcass and its internal organs for further signs of disease or contamination that would make them unfit for human consumption. Wholesome carcasses are then stamped by a USDA inspector. A sample of this circular stamp appears in Figure 9-1.

If the carcass is designated to be cut up into trimmed or untrimmed wholesale, primal, or "hotel" cuts (such as round, rump, or sirloin), the stamp is placed on

Figure 9-1.   Meat carcass inspection stamp (*Source:* USDA).

Figure 9-2.   Meat grading stamp (*Source:* USDA).

each of the wholesale areas of the carcass so that the stamp is still visible after butchering. Note that the number appearing in this circular stamp is the number assigned to that packer's plant. This stamp must appear on all meat transported by interstate commerce. Where states do their own inspection, they generally use their own inspection stamps. Note that USDA or state inspection is for wholesomeness and not for meat quality. Quality designation is covered under grading.

Quality Grading

After meat has been inspected and approved for human consumption, it may be graded for quality under the authority of the USDA's Agricultural Marketing Service (AMS). Quality grading is not mandatory. The quality grading stamp is in the form of a shield, as indicated in Figure 9-2. Either meat slaughterers (packers) or other meat intermediaries pay for grading. According to Hinich and Staelin (1980, p. 105),

> The stated purpose of grading is to predict the expected palatability characteristics of the lean meat and the expected yield of trimmed, boneless retail cuts from a particular carcass. Grading has nothing to do with health.

Hospitality industry meat purchasers often use federal grading standards as criteria for quality in their purchase specifications. Although hospitality purchasers today may not rely as much on federal quality grading as they once did, their specifications generally make some reference to federal grades, supplemented by further quality specifications.

For beef, veal, and lamb, quality grading considers such factors as the

- Quality and color of the lean meat
- Firmness and texture of the flesh and fat
- Marbling (streaks of fat) in the meat (marbling is probably the most important aspect of quality grading, because that is where the meat flavor is, and more marbling equals more flavor)
- Color of the fat
- Color of carcass bones
- Age of the animal (the older the animal, the lower the grade is likely to be)

All of these factors must be considered together. For example, a well-marbled piece of meat might still receive a low grade because of its toughness. However, not everyone is always happy with voluntary grading. Some purchasers feel the grading service is inconsistent because in some situations inspectors are allowed to use their own discretion.

Three Top Grades

For beef, veal, and lamb, the three top-quality grades are USDA Prime, USDA Choice, and USDA Select. Prime is the highest quality and highest priced but limited in supply. Choice is also high in quality, tender and juicy, and in abundant supply. It is probably the most widely used quality of meat in the hospitality industry. Select is a lower-quality grade than choice. Quality can also vary among grades because of tolerances used in grading. For example, the best choice beef can be close to a prime grade.

There is also an unofficial quality grading with prime and choice qualities: top half and bottom half. A purchaser wishing to buy the top quality within either of these grades must specify "top prime" or "top choice"; otherwise, the bottom range of that quality is likely to be delivered. According to Norkus (1988, p. 15), the grade distribution of the top three grades of beef in 1986 was 3.1 percent for prime, 94.1 percent for choice, and 2.7 percent for good (now known as *select*).

Although there are other quality grades below prime, choice, and select, only a small amount of grain-fed beef ends up being graded at these lower levels. The lower grades of meat are usually leaner and not as tender, although they can be made more tender and flavorful if carefully cooked. They are lower priced and are used in some institutional foodservice operations, but most of this lower-graded meat is used by meat processors because most of these grades are from old animals not intended to be eaten for fresh meat. These animals are used for milk production and breeding, and usually end up in such items as cold cuts, frankfurters, or processed canned products.

Packers' Grades and Brands

Some fresh-meat processors choose not to have their products graded for quality by the USDA. They market it ungraded (in the trade, *no-roll*) or do the grading themselves and package the products with their own labels indicating the product's quality level. These products are known in the trade as *packers' grades* or *packers' brands*. The grades of these products generally parallel the grade qualities of the USDA, but some question the objectivity of a packer that does its own grading. Nevertheless, many processed meat items that are not frozen or preprepared in individual portions (for example, cured pork products) are normally purchased by brand name, and the brand name is the only quality indication the purchaser has.

According to Norkus (1988, p. 15), "Only 56.7 percent of all inspected beef was graded in 1986."

Processed Meat Products

The USDA is responsible for approving the labels for processed meat products, whereas the Food and Drug Administration (FDA) is responsible for general food products. As a result, in processed meat (including poultry) products, the jurisdiction of the USDA and the FDA can overlap because processors who produce meat products often use nonmeat products (such as spices in sausages) in their products. Even though these nonmeat items may have been inspected by the FDA prior to use, the USDA also inspects them in the final product, which then bears the "Inspected and Passed" stamp of the USDA (illustrated in Figure 9-3). Note that if the meat that bears the inspection stamp is shipped from an inspected plant, it leaves the

Figure 9-3.   "Inspected and passed" stamp for processed meat products (*Source:* USDA).

direct control of the USDA at that point and jurisdiction passes to local and state control and to the FDA for interstate commerce.

Yield Grading

Quality grading is not the same as yield grading. When a quality grade is assigned to a carcass, a yield grade must also be assigned. Yield grading is designed to identify inspected carcasses for their cutability or yield of boneless, closely trimmed cuts from certain primary areas of the animal, that is, the quantity of meat they produce. In other words, the yield grades indicate the amount of usable meat compared to the amount of product (for example, bones and fat) eventually trimmed and removed.

The yield grade scale runs from 1 to 5 within each quality grade. The yield grade stamp is in the form of a shield, as illustrated in Figure 9-4. Yield grade 1 has the highest degree of cutability, and grade 5 has the lowest. In other words, yield grade 1 produces more usable product than higher-number yield grades. Note, however, the limiting regulations concerning yield numbers. For example, USDA Prime beef cannot be given a 1 or 2 yield grade because it has more fat (and thus more flavor) and as a result also has less usable lean meat. For the same reason, USDA Choice cannot receive a yield grade of 1. The implication is that quality and yield grades are closely related.

According to Maizel (1978, p. 144) the usable yield difference in grades is about 6.4 percent. In other words, in order to obtain three thousand pounds of usable meat, the purchaser would have to buy 3,659 pounds of yield grade 1; 3,876 pounds

Figure 9-4.   Meat yield grading stamp (*Source:* USDA).

of yield grade 2; 4,121 pounds of yield grade 3; 4,384 pounds of yield grade 4; and 4,717 pounds of yield grade 5.

Generally, yield grades are not particularly helpful to meat purchasers unless they desire whole carcasses, half carcasses (sides), or wholesale cuts that need some further butchering. Many establishments today buy their meat without having the facilities or the desire to do on-site butchering. They buy fully processed individual portions of the cuts desired, such as steaks. In such cases, in specifications they are more concerned with the quality grade and fat amount rather than with yield grade.

Note also that yield grades were originally intended to identify retail cuts of meat for the individual consumer (who prefers not to buy meat with a thick fat layer) rather than for hospitality industry purchasers. An establishment's interest in yield grades depends on its requirements for meat. Hospitality purchasers may choose to buy higher-quality grades of meat (because more fat generally means more flavor and tenderness even though the actual meat yield is lower), particularly if the price differential is favorable and restaurant customers end up more satisfied.

BEEF

Beef can be identified by the animal from which it is processed. These animals are

- Steer: a male animal with its male hormones removed while it is still young
- Bull: a mature male animal with intact male hormones
- Stag: a male animal heavier and fatter than a bull
- Bullock: a young bull
- Heifer: a female animal that has never borne a calf
- Cow: a female animal that has borne one or more calves

Quality Grades

Quality grades for steers, heifers, and bullocks are

- Prime
- Choice
- Select
- Standard
- Commercial
- Utility
- Cutter
- Canner

Cows, bulls, and stags may be graded for the same qualities, but they are not eligible for prime grade.

Yield Grades

The yield grades for beef are based on the following:

- Amount of external fat
- Size of the rib eye muscle and thickness of fat over it
- Quantity of kidney, pelvic, and heart fat
- Carcass weight

Primal Cuts

When a beef side (half the carcass) is cut up, it is initially divided into a forequarter and a hindquarter. Within each of these the following are the major primal (wholesale) cuts:

Forequarter
- Rib
- Chuck, square cut
- Shortplate
- Brisket
- Foreshank

Hindquarter
- Round
- Sirloin
- Short loin
- Flank

Figure 9-5 illustrates where these cuts are located on a beef side as well as the "retail" cuts that each wholesale cut produces. According to Maizel (1978, p. 144), "Most of the purchases of primal cuts of beef are limited to the rib and loin, which represent the most expensive cuts and often the most expensive menu items."

VEAL AND CALF

Veal is a bovine up to three months of age. Veal lean meat is light pink-gray and extremely tender. Calf is a bovine older than three months whose lean meat is reddish pink and not as tender as veal but not nearly as firm as lean beef.

Quality Grades

The quality grades for veal and calf are

- Prime
- Choice
- Select
- Standard

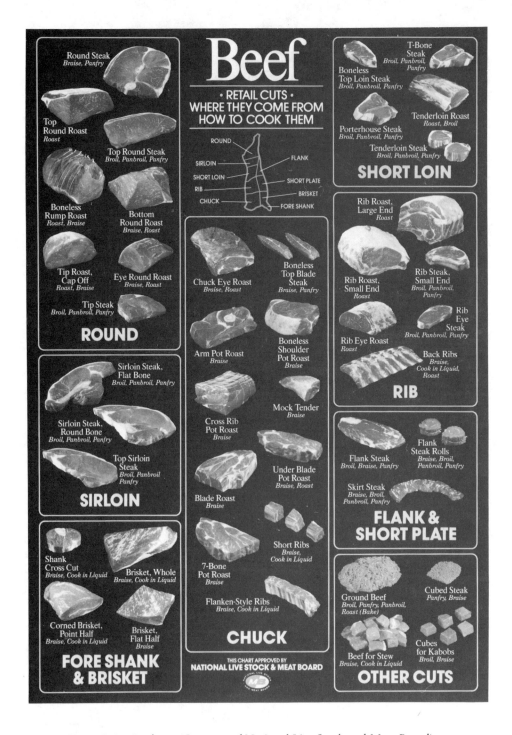

Figure 9-5. Beef cuts (Courtesy of National Live Stock and Meat Board).

- Utility
- Cull

With veal and calf, marbling is not a major consideration in quality grading because veal and calf have virtually no fat. Veal and calf are not yield graded.

Primal Cuts

The primal (wholesale) cuts of veal and calf are leg (round), sirloin, loin, rib, shoulder, and foreshank and breast. These cuts are illustrated in Figure 9-6, which also shows the retail cuts that each primal cut produces.

LAMB AND MUTTON

The meat of sheep can be broadly categorized into young animals (lamb) and mature animals (mutton), but within each of these two categories are some important subcategories based on age. Very young lamb (less than two months old) is sometimes known as *hothouse lamb* or *genuine spring lamb*. Its meat is both delicate and expensive. Lamb between two and five months of age is known as *spring lamb, milk lamb,* or *milk-fed lamb*. At the age of one year, lamb becomes mutton. Mutton meat is tougher than lamb meat, and little of it is used in better restaurants other than in the form of mutton chops.

Quality Grades

The quality grades for lamb are

- Prime
- Choice
- Select
- Utility
- Cull

With lamb, marbling is not a major consideration in quality grading. The quality grades for mutton are the same as those for lamb except that there is no prime grade.

Yield Grades

Yield grades for lamb and mutton are based on

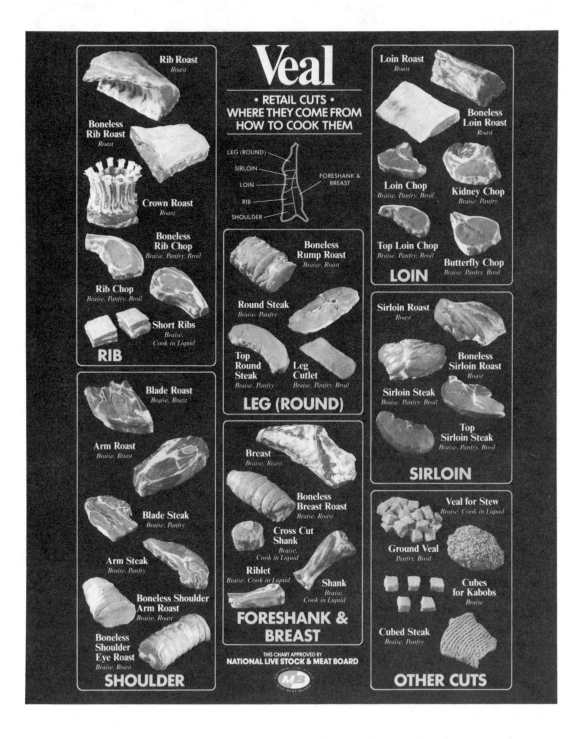

Figure 9-6. Veal and calf cuts (Courtesy of National Live Stock and Meat Board).

174

- Amount of external fat
- Amount of kidney and pelvic fat
- Conformation grade of the leg

Yield grades for lamb are judged primarily by "conformation," that is, the animal's shape and a determination by the grader that the meat is in the right areas, such as the loin and leg.

Primal Cuts

The primal (wholesale) cuts for lamb are leg, rib, shoulder, loin, and foreshank and breast, as illustrated in Figure 9-7, along with the retail cuts that each primal cut produces.

PORK

The quality grades for pork are

- U.S. No. 1
- U.S. No. 2
- U.S. No. 3
- U.S. No. 4
- Utility

With pork, marbling is not a major consideration in quality grading. Although some pork does receive a quality grade, most of it is not graded because it ends up in the form of bacon (the cured belly) and ham. This process gives the products a distinctive flavor making normal grading inappropriate.

Yield Grades

Yield grades for pork are judged primarily by "conformation," that is the animal's shape and a determination by the grader that the meat is in the right areas, such as the loin and ham areas. If pork is yield graded, the grades are on a scale from 1 to 4 (rather than 1 to 5 as for beef, veal, and lamb), but most pork is sold already trimmed and cut up.

Primal Cuts

The primal cuts for pork are leg, loin, blade shoulder, side, and arm shoulder, as illustrated in Figure 9-8, along with the retail cuts that each primal cut produces.

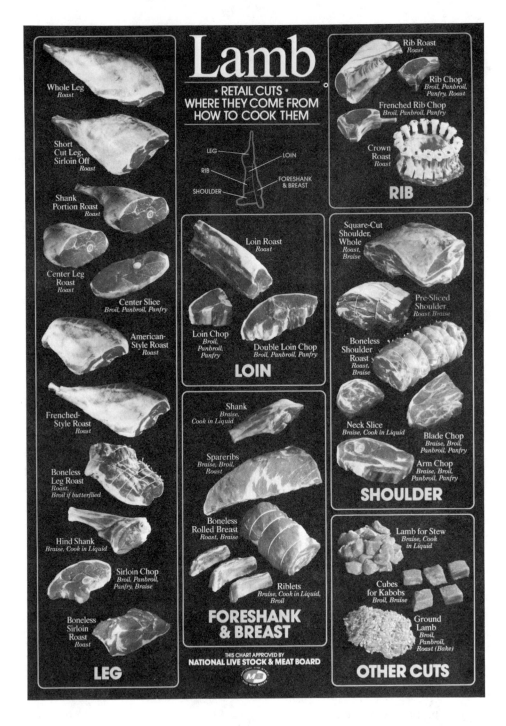

Figure 9-7. Lamb cuts (Courtesy of National Live Stock and Meat Board).

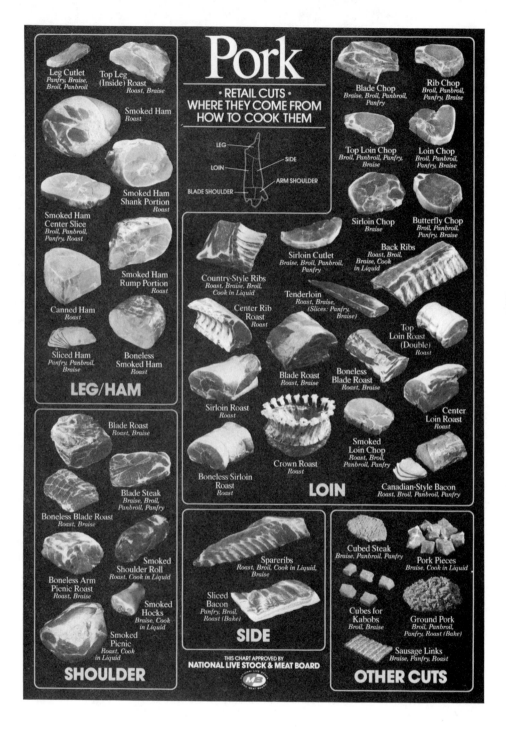

Figure 9-8.   Pork cuts (Courtesy of National Live Stock and Meat Board).

VARIETY MEATS AND SAUSAGES

Variety meats are the internal organs and extremities of meat animals such as kidneys, liver, tripe (the stomach), sweetbreads (the thymus gland), tongue, and brains. These products are not graded.

Sausages are primarily processed mixtures of various meats (including fat) and nonmeat ingredients (including seasonings). Many different sausages are available, many of them uncured pork or beef based. Some of them are ready to eat (such as bologna) and others require cooking (such as fresh pork sausage). Some are smoked but require cooking before using, and others are both cooked and smoked.

PURCHASING MEAT

A number of common methods are used by hospitality industry purchasers to buy meat: competitive bids (ride the market), cost-plus, buy and inventory, long-term contracts, and hedging (using futures). Various combinations of these methods can be used. However, purchasing meat is a tricky business. The quality desired, particularly if it is the top grade, is not always available. By the same token, if low-quality meat products are acceptable, they too can be in short supply. As a result, many hospitality operators stay with a single meat supplier (if the price is competitive) in order to ensure a continuity of supply and switch to a different supplier only when prices are out of line or the supplier falls short in other ways.

Often purchasing frozen meat is necessary when fresh is desired, particularly when large quantities of meat are needed. If the product is thawed and cooked properly, normally little difference can be tasted between fresh and frozen, even if the product is cooked directly from the frozen state. Most restaurant customers probably do not notice any difference.

Price Information

In addition to price information available from local meat suppliers, information is also available from publications such as *The National Provisioner Daily Market Service* (commonly known as the *yellow sheet* and published five times a week by The National Provisioner, Chicago), on which about 90 percent of U.S. wholesale meat sales are based. A sample of the yellow sheet is illustrated in Figure 9-9. Prices quoted are at stated FOB points. Therefore, freight costs to the purchaser's destination must be added. The National Provisioner also publishes the weekly *Hotel, Restaurant, Institution Meat Price Report* (commonly referred to as the *green sheet*). A sample of the green sheet is illustrated in Figure 9-10.

THE NATIONAL   15 West Huron Street, Chicago IL 60610

PROVISIONER DAILY MARKET & NEWS SERVICE

"The Yellow Sheet"   Phone: 312/944-3380   Fax: 312/944-3632   Telex: 255176

Published 5 days weekly. By mail $375, The National Provisioner, a year; 13 weeks, $99. Back issues $2 each. Service available by Fax, computer and Telex. This copyrighted report is for exclusive use by subscribers. Do not reproduce in whole or part. Weekly HRI Meat Price Report also available by mail, Fax and computer.

U.S.D.A. LIVE HOG MARKET QUOTATIONS   ****Not enough in the yards to make a market.**

CODE	WEIGHTS	OMAHA	SIOUX CITY	INT. IOWA	ST. PAUL	ST. LOUIS	INT. ILLINOIS	IND'PLS
	220-230	48.00-48.50	48.00-48.25	47.00-49.00	47.00-47.50	48.00-48.00	47.50-49.00	**
	230-240	48.50-48.50	48.00-48.25	47.00-49.00	47.00-47.50	48.50-48.50	47.50-49.00	**
	240-250	48.50-48.50	48.00-48.25	47.00-49.00	47.00-47.50	48.50-48.50	47.00-49.00	49.00
	220-240	48.00-48.50	47.50-48.00	46.50-49.00	47.00-47.00	48.00-48.00	47.50-48.50	**
	230-240	48.00-48.50	47.50-48.00	46.50-49.00	47.00-47.00	48.50-48.50	47.50-48.50	**
	240-250	48.50-48.50	47.50-48.00	46.50-49.00	47.00-47.00	48.50-48.50	47.50-48.50	48.75-49.00
	250-270	48.50-48.50	47.00-47.50	45.00-48.50	46.50-47.00	48.25-48.50	46.50-47.50	**
	270-300	**	**	42.50-47.50	**	**	**	**
	220-230	**	**	46.50-48.50	47.00-47.00	48.00-48.00	47.50-48.25	**
	230-240	48.00-48.50	**	46.50-48.50	47.00-47.00	48.50-48.50	47.50-48.25	48.50-48.75
	240-270	48.00-48.00	**	45.00-48.00	47.00-47.00	48.25-48.50	46.50-47.50	48.00-48.50
	270-300	45.50-46.50	44.50-47.00	42.50-47.00	46.00-47.00	46.25-48.25	**	**
	220-240	**	**	46.00-48.00	**	**	**	**
	240-270	**	**	45.00-47.50	46.00-47.00	**	**	**
	270-300	**	**	42.50-46.50	**	46.25-48.25	**	**
	300-350	**	43.50-44.00	**	**	**	**	**
	300-400	35.00-35.50	35.00-36.00	28.00-35.00	34.50	34.50-35.50	32.00-34.00	**
	400-500	34.50-35.00	35.00-36.00	28.00-35.00	34.50	34.50-35.00	32.00-34.00	32.00
	500-600	35.50-36.00	35.00-35.50	28.00-35.00	33.00-33.00	35.00-37.00	32.00-35.00	**
	600-700	35.50-36.00	35.00-35.50	28.00-35.00	33.00-33.00	38.00	32.00	**

PEORIA HOG MARKET (USDA) Top Price $49.50 at 150 Head, Receipts 1,200 for July 5, 1989. Peoria for July 3, 1989 Avg. Price Barrows & Gilts $48.48, Avg. Weight 240#. Avg. Price All Hogs $44.24, Avg. Weight 282#. Avg. Price Sows $35.77, Avg. Weight 438# with 18 Percent.

HAMS: Fresh skinned hams 17/20 sold 59 R basis. Fresh 20/26 skinned hams sold early 60 later sold 59 River basis.

PICNICS: Fresh 4/8 and 8/up picnics trading reported.

BELLIES: Fresh 12/14 a early 33 to 34 Rive sis.

LARD 14½ tra

ard sold steady iet. No early

e sold d Cow

Figure 9-9.   The Yellow Sheet (Courtesy of The National Provisioner, 15 W. Huron, Chicago, IL 60610).

Competitive Bids

Most small hospitality operations who do not stick with a single supplier probably use competitive bids. This buying method involves having two or more local suppliers quote prices FOB the purchaser's receiving dock. These quotations are normally taken weekly, and the day of the week can be a factor because midweek prices

HOTEL · RESTAURANT · INSTITUTION

MEAT PRICE REPORT

A GUIDE TO CURRENT MEAT PRICES BEING PAID TO WHOLESALERS AND PURVEYORS BY COMMERCIAL FEEDERS

PUBLISHED BY NATIONAL PROVISIONER, INC. · *"SINCE 1891"* · 15 W. HURON ST. · CHICAGO, IL 60610 · 312/944-3380
PUBLISHED THURSDAYS · SUBSCRIPTION RATES: ANNUAL $125.00–SEMI-ANNUAL $75.00

(+) and (−) Denotes prices up or down from previous week.

IMPS	BEEF CUTS	IMPS	PRIME	CHOICE	UTILITY
103	Rib, Primal	103	255@265	200@210	120@125
107	Rib, Oven Prepared	107	325@335	255@265	... ---
109	Rib, Roast Ready 18/down	109	385@395	275@285–	... ---
109	Rib, Roast Ready, 18/up	109	385@395	275@285–	... ---
112	Ribeye Roll-Lip Off	112	735@745	600@610	370@380
112A	Ribeye Roll, Lip On	112A	625@635	415@425	... ---
113	Square-Cut Chuck	113	... ---	105@115	100@105+
114	Shoulder Clod	114	... ---	180@190	165@170+
115	Square-Cut Chuck, Boneless	115	... ---	135@145	160@165+
116A	Chuck Roll	116A	... ---	175@185	165@170+
120	Brisket, Boneless, Deckle Off	120	... ---	140@150–	... ---
123	Short Ribs-Regular	123	... ---	255@265–	... ---
123A	Short Ribs, Short Plate	123A	... ---	315@325–	... ---
134	Beef Bones	134	... ---	45@55	... ---
135	Diced Beef	135	... ---	200@210	... ---
135A	Beef For Stewing-lean	135A	... ---	240@250	... ---
---	Stroganoff Strips	---	... ---	320@330	... ---
136	Ground Beef, Regular 75% lean	136	... ---	134@144	... ---
1136	Ground Beef Patties, Regular 75% lean	1136	... ---	142@148	... ---
137	Ground Beef, Special 80% lean	137	... ---	149@158	... ---
1137	Ground Beef Patties, Special 80% lean	1137	... ---	152@161	... ---
136A	Ground Beef, Regular, TVP Added	136A	... ---	136@143	... ---
1136A	Ground Beef Patties, Regular, TVP Added	1136A	... ---	141@148	... ---
158	Round, Primal	158	155@165	146@156–	132@137
164	Round, Rump and Shank Off	164	205@215	195@205–	... ---
165	Round, Rump and Shank Off, Boneless	165	230@240	215@225–	192@197
167	Knuckle	167	... ---	185@195	... ---
167A	Knuckle, Special	167A	... ---	205@215–	182@187–
168	Top (Inside) Round	168	225@235	205@215–	193@198–
170	Bottom (Gooseneck) Round	170	... ---	165@175–	... ---
170A	Bottom (Gooseneck) Round, Heel Out, Trimmed	170A	... ---	205@215–	... ---
171B	Outside Round	171B	... ---	220@230–	191@196+
172	Full Loin, Trimmed		315@325	265@275	...
173	Short Loin				

Figure 9-10. The Green Sheet (Courtesy of The National Provisioner, 15 W. Huron, Chicago, IL 60610).

tend to be more stable. For example, assuming the hospitality operator is placing an order for delivery the following week, if the local supplier purchases on a Wednesday, then so should the hospitality purchaser for next week's supply.

Cost-Plus

In many ways, hospitality purchasers use informal cost-plus purchasing (without realizing it) when they purchase from a local meat supplier. The supplier knows what its meat purchase costs are and simply adds to that a markup (cost-plus) to cover all operating costs and obtain a selling price yielding a desired profit. The purchaser unfamiliar with national meat market prices is simply not aware of what the supplier's markup is.

A formal cost-plus method based on the local supplier's buying costs is not commonly used by most independent hospitality purchasers. It is, however, sometimes used by chain operations or other large meat purchasers who are familiar with national meat prices and can negotiate with a large meat supplier an agreed markup that is less than "normal." Such a system, in which the quantities involved are also agreed to, allows the supplier to plan its purchasing, processing, and deliveries. As a result, its operation may be more effective, and it may be willing to pass on some of these savings or provide other cost-free services to the purchaser.

Buy and Inventory

A purchaser might use buy and inventory if meat shortages are anticipated and/or price increases are forecast. Purchasers must calculate whether large-quantity purchases are worthwhile. A supplier price reduction over present prices may be available for buying in large quantities, but to this must be added an additional storage cost. Also, because the purchaser assumes the risk, the cost of this purchasing method can be very high if the market price declines. Other questions that need to be answered are

- What effect will the use of frozen rather than fresh meat have on the operation's quality standards?
- Will customers accept a frozen product?
- Will more cooking shrinkage occur with a frozen product?
- Does the operation have the cash to pay for a large purchase quantity?
- For a large purchase order, what concessions is the supplier willing to grant (for example, extended credit terms or free storage)?

Long-Term Contracts

A long-term contract is one signed with a meat supplier for anywhere from three to six months to buy a stipulated amount of a product from that supplier at a firm price. According to Virts (1987, p. 106), products involved are usually processed items such as hams or hot dogs.

Hedging

Hedging (discussed in chapter 3) is used only by large-volume purchasers with experience and with knowledgeable buyers who are familiar with the risks involved.

Meat Tenderization

Soon after an animal is slaughtered, its muscles stiffen as a result of chemical changes in the meat. After a few days, however, the flesh begins to soften. Meat that has not had enough time to soften is known as *green meat.* Green meat is seldom a problem (unless it is frozen while still green) for hospitality industry purchasers because under normal conditions several days are required for meat to be moved from the slaughterhouse through other levels in the distribution system to the purchaser's receiving dock.

Meat needs to have a certain amount of tenderness for most cooking methods. If it is to be broiled or fried (for example, steaks and chops), then more tenderness is desirable. In the case of beef and lamb, the meat becomes naturally tender through an aging process; pork needs no aging to make it tender, and veal is not usually aged because it does not have enough fat covering on it to protect it from bacteria and excessive drying.

Most aging is done by meat distributors. One method of aging is to hang the meat for up to a month in a humidity- and temperature-controlled storage room. This method is known as *dry aging,* and it adds both tenderness and flavor. Note, however, that if a carcass is very tough (as it would be in an old animal), aging is not going to tenderize it. Dry aging is an expensive process because of the time involved and the fact that the distributor has money tied up in meat being aged. Also, as meat is dry aged, it loses moisture, and thus weight. Aging time and carcass weight loss costs are passed on to the purchaser.

To lower aging costs, some meat is fast aged by holding it at a higher temperature and humidity for a shorter period of time than for dry aging. Most fast-aged meat is sold in retail food shops rather than to hospitality industry purchasers.

Today, many meat products are aged rapidly by cutting carcasses into smaller cuts, wrapping them in tightly-sealed air- and moisture-proof heavy plastic, and then refrigerating them under controlled conditions for about ten days to two weeks. Part of this rapid aging can be done while the meat is transported in controlled-condition refrigerated trucks. This method does not result in any weight loss. Because of the shorter time involved and elimination of weight loss, these products are less expensive than dry-aged ones. The disadvantage of this method is that the product does not become more flavorful as it does with dry aging. It also cooks more rapidly than dry-aged meat, and, according to Stefanelli (1985, p. 417), can become quite dry if cooked beyond the medium state.

For large wholesale cuts of meat (for example, a prime rib roast), aging can be simulated by cooking at a relatively low temperature such as 200 to 225°F (104–107°C).

Institutional Meat Purchase Specifications

Although quality and yield grades are helpful to some degree in meat purchase specifications, more specific purchase specification standards are also needed. To aid in this area, the USDA has established institutional meat purchase specifications (IMPS). These IMPS are numbers that are assigned to identify specific cuts of meat. The numbers run from the 100 series to the 1000 series as follows:

100—fresh beef
200—fresh lamb and mutton
300—veal and calf
400—fresh pork
500—processed pork
600—processed beef
700—variety meat
800—sausage meat
1000—preportioned meats

The first digit of the IMPS refers to the type of product, and the remaining digits to a specified cut. Tables 9-1, 9-2, 9-3, and 9-4 list the IMPS for fresh beef, fresh lamb

Table 9-1. IMPS for Fresh Beef Products

Item No.	Product
100	Carcass
101	Side
102	Forequarter
102A	Forequarter, boneless
103	Rib, primal
107	Rib, oven-prepared
109	Rib, roast-ready
109A	Rib, roast-ready, special
109B	Blade meat
110	Rib, roast-ready, boneless, tied
111	Spencer roll
112	Ribeye roll

Table 9-1. IMPS for Fresh Beef Products *(continued)*

Item No.	Product
112A	Ribeye roll, lip-on
113	Square-cut chuck
114	Shoulder clod
114A	Shoulder clod roast
115	Square-cut chuck, boneless
116	Square-cut chuck, boneless, clod out
116A	Chuck roll
117	Foreshank
118	Brisket
119	Brisket, boneless, deckle on
120	Brisket, boneless, deckle off
121	Short plate
121A	Short plate, boneless
122	Full plate
122A	Full plate, boneless
123	Short ribs
123A	Short ribs, short plate
123B	Short ribs, special
125	Armbone chuck
126	Armbone chuck, boneless, clod out
127	Cross-cut chuck
128	Cross-cut chuck, boneless
132	Triangle
133	Triangle, boneless
134	Beef bones
135	Diced beef
135A	Beef for stewing
136	Ground beef, regular
136A	Ground beef, regular, TVP added
137	Ground beef, special
155	Hindquarter
155A	Hindquarter, boneless
158	Round, primal
159	Round, boneless
160	Round, shank off, partially boneless
161	Round, shank off, boneless
163	Round, shank off, 3-way boneless
164	Round, rump and shank off
165	Round, rump and shank off, boneless
165A	Round, rump and shank off, boneless, special
165B	Round, rump and shank off, boneless, tied, special
166	Round, rump and shank off, boneless, tied

Table 9-1. *(continued)*

Item No.	Product
166A	Round, rump partially removed, shank off
167	Knuckle
167A	Knuckle, trimmed
168	Top (inside) round
170	Bottom (gooseneck) round
170A	Bottom (gooseneck) round, heel out
171	Bottom (gooseneck) round, untrimmed
171A	Bottom (gooseneck) round, untrimmed, heel out
171B	Outside round
171C	Eye of round
172	Full loin, trimmed
173	Short loin
174	Short loin, short cut
175	Strip loin
176	Strip loin, boneless
177	Strip loin, intermediate
178	Strip loin, intermediate, boneless
179	Strip loin, short cut
180	Strip loin, short cut, boneless
181	Sirloin
182	Sirloin butt, boneless
183	Sirloin butt, trimmed
184	Top sirloin butt
185	Bottom sirloin butt
185A	Botton sirloin, flap
185B	Bottom sirloin, ball tip
185C	Bottom sirloin, triangle
185D	Bottom sirloin butt, trimmed
186	Bottom sirloin butt, triangle
189	Full tenderloin
189A	Full tenderloin, defatted
190	Full tenderloin, special
190A	Full tenderloin, skinned
191	Butt tenderloin
192	Short tenderloin
193	Flank steak

Source: USDA

Table 9-2. IMPS for Fresh Lamb and Mutton Products

Item No.	Product
200	Carcass
202	Foresaddle
203	Bracelet (double)
204	Rib rack (double)
205	Chucks and plates (double)
206	Chucks (double)
207	Square-cut shoulders (double)
208	Square-cut shoulder, boneless
209	Breast, flank on
209A	Breast, flank off
210	Foreshank
230	Hindsaddle
231	Loin (double)
232	Loin, trimmed (double)
233	Leg (double)
233A	Leg, lower shank off (single)
233B	Leg, lower shank off, boneless
233C	Leg, shank off (single)
233D	Leg, shank off, boneless
233E	Hindshank, heel attached
234	Leg, oven-prepared
234A	Leg, oven-prepared, boneless and tied
235	Back
236	Back, trimmed
237	Hindsaddle, long cut
238	Hindsaddle, long cut, trimmed
1204	Rib chops
1204A	Rib chops, frenched
1207	Shoulder chops
1232	Loin chops
1295	Lamb for stewing
1296	Ground lamb
1296A	Ground lamb patties

Source: USDA

Table 9-3. IMPS for Fresh Veal and Calf Products

Item No.	Product
300	Carcass
303	Side
303A	Side, 2-rib hindquarter
303B	Side, 1-rib hindquarter
303C	Side, boneless
304	Foresaddle, 11 ribs
304A	Foresaddle, 12 ribs
305	Bracelet, 7 ribs (double)
306	Hotel rack, 7 ribs (double)
308	Chucks, 4 ribs (double)
308A	Chucks, 5 ribs (double)
309	Square cut chucks, 4 ribs (double)
309A	Square cut chucks, 5 ribs (double)
309B	Square cut chuck, 4 ribs, boneless
309C	Square cut chuck, 5 ribs, boneless
309D	Square cut chuck, neck off, 4 ribs, boneless and tied
309E	Square cut chuck, neck off, 5 ribs, boneless and tied
310	Shoulder clod
310A	Shoulder clod, special
310B	Shoulder clod roast
311	Square cut chuck, 4 ribs, clod out, boneless
311A	Square cut chuck, 5 ribs, clod out, boneless
311B	Square cut chuck, 4 ribs, clod out, boneless and tied
311C	Square cut chuck, 5 ribs, clod out, boneless and tied
312	Foreshank
313	Breast
330	Hindsaddle, 2 ribs
330A	Hindsaddle, 1 rib
331	Loin, 2 ribs (double)
331A	Loin, 1 rib (double)
332	Loin, 2 ribs, trimmed (double)
332A	Loin, 1 rib, trimmed (double)
333	Full loin, trimmed
334	Legs (double)
335	Leg, oven-prepared, boneless
336	Leg, shank off, oven-prepared, boneless
337	Hindshank
339	Leg, short cut
340	Back, 9 ribs
340A	Back, 8 ribs
341	Back, 9 ribs, trimmed
341A	Back, 8 ribs, trimmed

Table 9-3. IMPS for Fresh Veal and Calf Products *(continued)*

Item No.	Product
342	Hindsaddle, 9 ribs, long cut
342A	Hindsaddle, 8 ribs, long cut
343	Hindsaddle, 9 ribs, long cut, trimmed
343A	Hindsaddle, 8 ribs, long cut, trimmed
1300	Cubed steaks
1301	Cubed steaks, special
1306	Rib chops
1309	Shoulder chops
1332	Loin chops
1336	Cutlets
1395	Veal for stewing
1396	Ground veal
1396A	Ground veal patties

Source: USDA

Table 9-4. IMPS for Fresh and Processed Pork Products

Item No.	Product
400	Carcass
401	Ham, regular
401A	Ham, regular, short shank
402	Ham, skinned
402A	Ham, skinned, short shank
402B	Ham, boned and tied
403	Shoulder
404	Shoulder, skinned
405	Shoulder, picnic
406	Boston butt
406A	Boston butt, boned and tied
407	Shoulder butt, boneless
408	Belly
409	Belly, skinless
410	Loin
411	Loin, bladeless
412	Loin, center cut
413	Loin, boneless
413A	Loin, boned and tied
414	Canadian back
415	Tenderloin
416	Spareribs

Table 9-4. *(continued)*

Item No.	Product
416A	Spareribs, breast off
417	Shoulder hock
418	Trimmings (90% lean)
419	Trimmings (80% lean)
420	Front feet
421	Neck bones
422	Back ribs
423	Country style ribs
500	Ham, short shank (cured)
501	Ham, short shank (cured and smoked)
502	Ham, skinned (cured)
503	Ham, skinned (cured and smoked)
504	Ham, skinless (cured and smoked), partially boned
505	Ham, skinless (cured and smoked), completely boneless
505A	Ham, skinless boned, rolled, and tied (cured and smoked)
506	Ham, skinned (cured and smoked), fully-cooked, dry heat
507	Ham, boneless, skinless (cured and smoked), fully-cooked, dry heat
508	Ham, boneless, skinless (cured), pressed, fully-cooked, moist heat
509	Ham, boneless, skinless (cured and smoked), pressed, fully-cooked, moist heat
515	Shoulder (cured)
516	Shoulder (cured and smoked)
517	Shoulder, skinned (cured)
518	Shoulder, skinned (cured and smoked)
525	Shoulder, picnic (cured)
526	Shoulder, picnic (cured and smoked)
527	Shoulder, picnic (cured and smoked), boneless, skinless, rolled and tied
530	Shoulder butt, boneless (cured and smoked)
535	Belly, skin-on (cured)
536	Bacon, slab (cured and smoked), skin-on
537	Bacon, slab (cured and smoked), skinless, formed
539	Bacon, sliced (cured and smoked), skinless
541	Bacon, sliced (cured and smoked), ends and pieces
545	Loin (cured and smoked)
546	Loin, bladeless (cured and smoked)
550	Canadian back (cured and smoked), unsliced
551	Canadian style bacon (cured and smoked), sliced
555	Jowl butts, cellar trim (cured)
556	Jowl squares (cured and smoked)
558	Spareribs (cured)
559	Spareribs (cured and smoked)
560	Hocks, shoulder (cured)

Table 9-4. IMPS for Fresh and Processed Pork Products *(continued)*

Item No.	Product
561	Hocks, shoulder (cured and smoked)
562	Fatback (cured)
563	Feet, front (cured)
1400	Fillets
1406	Boston butt steaks, bone-in
1407	Shoulder butt steaks, boneless
1410	Chops, regular
1410A	Chops, with pocket
1410B	Rib chops, with pocket
1411	Chops, bladeless
1412	Chops, center cut
1412A	Chops, center cut, special
1412B	Chops, center cut, boneless
1413	Chops, boneless
1495	Pork for chop suey
1496	Ground pork
1496A	Ground pork patties

Source: USDA

and mutton, fresh veal and calf, and fresh and processed pork, respectively. Obviously, these numbers, popular with both sellers and purchasers, are convenient to use on specifications because the guesswork for a supplier about the trim and cutting desired by the purchaser is eliminated.

Other Specification Information

However, even with these numbers the purchaser may need to provide more information in specifications. A complete meat specification might include the following:

• A requirement for mandatory meat inspection
• Animal's age or type (if appropriate)
• Quality grading desired, including the upper or lower half of the grade
• IMPS number, including modification in trim desired beyond the IMPS standard
• Fat limitations (such as three-quarters to one inch maximum at any point except for seam fat)
• Weight tolerances on wholesale cuts (such as a prime rib roast from twenty to twenty-five pounds) and retail cuts (such as New York strip steaks from nine to ten ounces)
• Intended use of item

- Its form, if appropriate, such as bacon sliced twelve to fourteen strips to the pound
- Packer's brand if the item is to be purchased by brand
- State of refrigeration (chilled, refrigerated, or frozen)
- Packaging desired (for processed, prepared items)
- Delivery procedure (such as date or day of week and time of day)
- Inspection (testing) procedures to be used
- Other requirements, for example, "Meat must be of good color for the grade and free of objectionable odors and bruises or other mutilations. There must be no evidence of freezing and defrosting."

Any product wording used in specifications should also conform to the terminology used in the IMPS number system.

USDA Acceptance Service

The USDA offers an acceptance service to hospitality operators by preparing meat specifications for a fee. The writer prepares specifications appropriate to the operation and ensures that the specified items and quality grade are what is delivered. This acceptance service is sometimes referred to as *certified buying* or *certification*.

Another service offered by the USDA is known as the *product examination service*. With this service an inspector examines graded meat that has been in transit and ensures that the quality as the product reaches the destination is the same as when it leaves the packer or processor.

Preportioned Meat Products

The purchaser of meat products has the choice of buying whole carcasses of meat, wholesale (or primal) cuts, or preportioned fabricated (or retail) cuts. As long as a purchaser has on-site butchering personnel, according to Gisslen (1983, p. 188), the following four factors dictate in which form meat is purchased:

- The butchering employees' meat cutting skills
- The amount of storage and work space available
- The dictates of the establishment's menu
- The form that provides the most advantageous cost per portion (including labor cost)

Few hospitality operations do their own butchering today. Most meat packers and distributors can cut meat more efficiently than the hospitality operation's employees because of the volume they deal in. Even though whole carcasses and wholesale cuts cost less per pound than retail cuts, there is more waste from fat and bone. Nevertheless, those operations that still do their own butchering probably feel that they have better control over quality.

However, buying portion-controlled meat may have some disadvantages.

- Even though each pork chop, for example, in a purchase may be the same weight, all chops may not have the same shape, thickness, or quality. This lack of uniformity can be a problem to inexperienced cooks.
- To be processed into portion-controlled cuts, products have had to be handled a great deal more, and bacterial contamination problems may have been increased.
- Individual cuts of meat cannot be stored as long as larger wholesale cuts. Indeed, their storage life can be reduced from weeks to days.
- Some suppliers do not do a good job of wrapping or packaging individual items for longer storage or do not wrap them individually at all.
- If they are packaged in a carton, the supplier may decide on the quantity of individual items to be packaged in each carton, providing the purchaser with less flexibility in the quantity to be ordered.
- Individual portion-controlled meats are more prone to pilferage.

RECEIVING MEAT

In meat receiving, many establishments rely on the chef (or someone else in the organization who is knowledgeable about meat) to verify its quality. The regular receiver often does not have the qualifications to do this. For example, can the receiver differentiate cow tenderloins from steer tenderloins? Although less-expensive cow tenderloins may be acceptable for the standards of some operations, they may not suit others because they are smaller, darker in color, lack the marbling, and have a spongier texture than steer tenderloins. Even though steer tenderloins may have been specified, unscrupulous suppliers could substitute cow tenderloins if they know the receiver is not qualified to distinguish one from another.

Other supplier upgrading practices can occur if a receiver is not alert.

- Substituting choice-grade meat for prime grade, or a packer's grade for a USDA grade.
- Substituting defrosted frozen meat for fresh. This practice is not wrong if fresh has not been specified or if the purchaser has agreed to accept frozen in order to obtain needed products. However, previously frozen products should not otherwise be accepted, particularly for those items that do not freeze well, such as pork and veal.
- Using poor-quality meat (such as necks, flanks, and brisket) or low-quality imported carcasses in ground beef.

Specific meat quality checks to be made in receiving are

- *Color.* Fresh meat should be a bright, cherry red, known as *bloom* in the trade. If it is not the right color, it could be old meat or have been packaged so tightly (such as in air- and moisture-proof plastic packaging) that it did not have sufficient exposure to oxygen, which provides the bright red color.
- *Odor.* If the odor is unpleasant, the meat should not be accepted. Note, however, that fresh pork deteriorates from the center rather than from the outside, and the odor may not indicate off meat.
- *Touch.* A slimy feel to the meat is another indication that it is not acceptable.
- *Trim.* Trim should not be excessive. A supplier can easily generate additional profits by "padding" on trim, such as leaving excess fat on prime ribs or at the end of the eye on a strip loin. These items are expensive per pound to begin with, and to pay a high price per pound for excess fat does not make sense. Also, if trim is excessive enough to provide the supplier with added profits, it also significantly increases the purchaser's food costs.
- *Temperature.* For fresh meat the receiving temperature should be about 40° F (4° C), and for frozen meat no higher than 0° F. (−18° C). Frozen processed items preserved with chemicals (such as sausages) can be less frozen than frozen meat, but these frozen processed items should not be accepted if they are too warm. Spoilage is not easy to detect in frozen meats.
- *Quantities.* Specification weight, count, or size should be verified against the purchase order and specifications. If different types of meat are all delivered in a single container, empty the container and check the weight, count, or size of each item against the purchase order. If a carton containing a single product is weighed in the container, deduct the carton weight and any packaging to arrive at the net weight. Do not rely on weight, count, and sizes printed on a carton. Dishonest suppliers have been known to repack items from one carton to another that shows a higher printed weight. Weights, counts, or sizes should also be checked against invoices delivered with the goods.
- *Prices.* Prices should be checked against purchase order prices and against prices on invoices delivered with the goods.

Storage

Store fresh meat in a separate meat refrigerator if possible. Temperature should be 35 to 40°F (2–4°C). In storage, fresh meat should not be wrapped or stacked too tightly because cold air circulation around the products is reduced. Avoid storing cooked meat items in the same area, but if they must be cooked items should be placed on higher shelves so that any dripping from raw meat will not contaminate the cooked items. Recommended maximum storage periods for some meat products are

Beef (vacuum packaged): 2 months
Beef (fresh): 10 days
Lamb and veal (fresh): 1 week
Pork (fresh): 5 days
Ground meat: 2 days
Variety meats: 2 days
Sliced cold cuts: 6 days
Smoked meat and sausage: 10 days
Bacon: 1 month
Ham (cured): 6 weeks
Processed meats (after package is open): 7 days

Frozen meat should be kept well frozen in the freezer. The hospitality operator should not try to freeze fresh or cooked meat in this freezer because it is designed to hold already-frozen meat and not to actually freeze it. Recommended maximum storage times for some frozen meat products are

Beef, lamb, and veal (uncooked): 9 months
Beef, lamb, and veal (cooked): 3 months
Pork (uncooked): 6 months
Pork (cooked or smoked): 1 month
Ground meat and sausages: 3 months
Smoked sausages: 1 month

Issuing

In issuing meat, the most important consideration is stock rotation so that items received first are issued first. This practice reduces the spoilage possibility. Any meat that is issued one day and not used by the end of that day should be returned to the refrigerators or freezers. Again, this practice reduces spoilage possibilities. Meat items in the production process in kitchens at any one time should be kept to a minimum to encourage the reduction of waste, pilferage, and spoilage.

An operation that still does its own on-premise butchering often uses a system of meat tags (Figure 9-11) to control meat. Each meat tag is sequentially prenumbered and has two sections (separated by a perforation) that contain identical information. When meat is received, a meat tag for each separate large cut is prepared by the receiver. The relevant information is copied from the invoice. The meat tag is then separated along the perforation; the top half is attached to the meat, and the bottom half to the invoice.

With this system, even though meat is put into refrigerators or freezers rather than in the storeroom, the receiver, insofar as the daily food receiving report (see chapter 8) is concerned, treats the invoice as if the meat were in a locked storeroom.

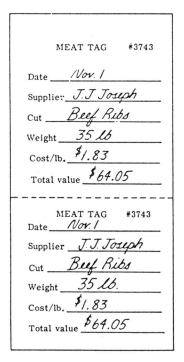

Figure 9-11.   Meat tag (Courtesy of M C Media Corp.).

In other words, the amount of the invoice is recorded in the Storeroom column of the daily food receiving report.

In the accounting office, the bottom half of each meat tag should be checked against the invoice for correctness of information. This part of the tag can then be filed away in numerical sequence.

As meat is removed by the kitchen preparation staff to be put into production, the top half of the tag still attached to the meat is removed and forwarded at the end of the day to the accounting office. These tags are treated as if they were requisitions. In other words, the total dollar amount on these tags each day becomes part of that day's total food cost. The corresponding bottom halves of the tags are then removed from the accounting office file where they were previously placed. At any time top halves of tags still attached to meat in the refrigerators or freezers should match up with the bottom halves still filed in the accounting office.

Stefanelli (1985, p. 207) summarizes the use of meat tags.

The meat tag control is, however, cumbersome, and, like the receiving sheet, it tends to be redundant as well. If used, they tend to be used for only high-cost products. Nevertheless, both meat tags and receiving sheets are used in operations that desire close control over stock.

MEAT YIELDS

Rarely does an individual hospitality enterprise buy whole meat carcasses or meat sides and do its own butchering. Today, most operations buy their meat in prepared preproportioned cuts to suit their individual menu requirements. The higher purchase cost is offset by a reduction in labor cost because an on-premise butcher is no longer required.

Nevertheless, many places still do purchase wholesale or large cuts of meat (such as a prime rib of beef) and may do some butchering on-site, such as bone and fat trimming before cooking. In such cases some yield testing should be done to determine what is left in the way of usable product. In addition, today most establishments use standard recipes that include preparation methods to ensure a consistent end-product for customer satisfaction. These recipes generally contain the cooking temperature, which can affect the yield of cooked meat. For example, a medium-done beef roast cooked at 230°F (110°C) can have a weight loss up to 15 percent. The same medium-done roast cooked at 360°F (182°C) can have a weight loss of well over 20 percent.

Butchering and Cooking Test Form

If meat is purchased unbutchered and is subject to trim loss (bones, fat) and/or weight loss in cooking, a butchering and cooking test form like that shown in Figure 9.12 will be useful. Trim and cooking loss tests should be carried out on a number of items of the same type and weight from various suppliers so that any variations in loss can then be averaged out. The illustration shows that the butchering and cooking test on this particular prime rib gives us a cost of $0.138 per ounce before cooking, and $0.165 per ounce after cooking. Depending on whether a particular recipe called for a portion size to be costed out before or after cooking, one or the other of these two unit cost prices would be used. By doing a number of tests such as this, the operation can determine which supplier's product produces the lowest yield cost.

Tests can also be carried out on processed meat items such as canned hams. For example, even though the weight of two separate packers' brand hams are the same, tests may show that one may be better trimmed and/or have less gelatin than the other. What is important in such a situation is a comparison of the net yield so that the purchase can be made from the supplier whose brand yields the most (as long as quality is still acceptable).

Cost Factors

Calculating and recording the cost factor(s) on the butchering and cooking test form is useful. The advantage is that if the selected supplier's price per pound changes,

NAME OF ITEM _Prime Rib_ _____ GRADE _Choice_ _____
PIECES _1_ WEIGHING _13_ LBS. _4_ OZ. AT _$2.00_ TOTAL _$26.50_
DATE _Oct. 15/19 –_ _____ DEALER _Meats Unlimited_

| ITEM | WEIGHT | | RATIO | COST | | |
	LB.	OZ.		TOTAL	LB.	OZ.
RAW YIELD:						
INITIAL RAW WEIGHT	13	4	100.0%			
LESS BONES FAT & TRIM	1	4	9.4			
SALEABLE RAW WEIGHT	12	0	90.6	26	50	2	21	0.138¢
BREAKDOWN						
TOTAL				26	50	
COOKED YIELD:						
SALEABLE RAW WEIGHT	12	0	90.6%			
SHRINKAGE	2	0	15.1			
SALEABLE COOKED WEIGHT	10	0	75.5	26	50	2	65	0.165¢
TOTAL				26	50	

Figure 9-12.   Butchering and cooking test form (Courtesy of M C Media Corp.).

the operation does not have to retest and recalculate to obtain a new cost for menu-costing purposes. The general equation for developing a cost factor is

$$\frac{\text{Our calculated cooked yield cost per pound}}{\text{Supplier's price per pound}} = \text{Cost factor}$$

Using information from Figure 9-12, our calculated yield cost per pound of prime rib is \$2.65 (\$26.50 total cost divided by ten pounds of usable product), and the supplier's price per pound of raw meat was \$2.00. Cost factor is therefore

$$\frac{\$2.65}{\$2.00} = 1.325$$

If the supplier now changes the price, this cost factor of 1.325 can quickly be used to calculate the new yield cost per pound after butchering, trimming, and cooking.

Suppose the supplier's price increased from $2.00 to $2.15. The new yield cost will be

$$\$2.15 \times 1.325 = \$2.85 \text{ per pound}$$

A cost factor can be calculated for a stipulated portion of prime rib. The formula, however, will be slightly different than the one given above.

$$\frac{\text{Our calculated cost per portion}}{\text{Supplier's price per pound}} = \text{Cost factor per portion}$$

Assuming a ten-ounce portion, our portion cost is $10 \times \$0.165$ (the cost of one ounce of cooked meat), or $1.65, and the portion cost factor is

$$\frac{\$1.65}{\$2.00} = 0.825$$

If the supplier's price goes up from $2.00 to $2.15, the new cost per ten-ounce portion of prime rib will be

$$\$2.15 \times 0.825 = \$1.77 \text{ per portion}$$

Lowest Yield Cost

Butchering (trim) tests may even indicate that the supplier with the lowest price may not be offering the lowest *net* cost per pound. Comparison of the figures in Table 9-5 shows that Supplier A's price appears lower ($2 versus $2.10), but after trimming, the net cost per pound is lower from Supplier B ($2.36 versus $2.41).

By-Products

Butchering done on-site often yields usable by-products in addition to fat and bones. For example, Figure 9-13 shows a prime rib that has two by-products: short rib and hamburger.

Table 9-5. Trim Test Comparison of Suppliers

	Purchase Weight	Price per lb	Total Cost	Weight after Cooking	Net Cost per lb
Supplier A	13.25 lb	$2.00	$26.50	11 lb	$2.41
Supplier B	13.5 lb	2.10	28.35	12 lb	2.36

NAME OF ITEM _Prime Rib_				GRADE _Choice_		
PIECES _1_ WEIGHING _30_ LBS. _8_ OZ. AT _$1.70_ Total _$51.85_						
DATE _Oct. 21/19—_ DEALER _Mid West_						

ITEM	WEIGHT		RATIO	COST		
	LB.	OZ.		TOTAL	LB.	OZ.
RAW YIELD:						
INITIAL RAW WEIGHT	30	8	100.0%			
LESS BONES FAT & TRIM	7	4	23.8			
SALEABLE RAW WEIGHT	23	4	76.2			
BREAKDOWN						
Prime Rib	18	8	60.7	46 01	2 49	0.156¢
Short Rib	3	8	11.5	4 69 ᵐᵃʳᵏᵉᵗ	1 34	0.084¢
Hamburger	1	4	4.0	1 15 ᵐᵃʳᵏᵉᵗ	0 92	0.058¢
TOTAL				51 85		
COOKED YIELD:						
SALEABLE RAW WEIGHT	18	8	60.7			
SHRINKAGE	3	4	10.7			
SALEABLE COOKED WEIGHT	15	4	50.0	46 01	3 02	0.189¢
TOTAL				46 01		

Figure 9-13.   Butchering and cooking test form (Courtesy of M C Media Corp.).

Total cost of the purchase was $51.85, and the problem is to distribute that cost among the three separate items yielded. They cannot all be costed out at the overall cost per pound purchase price of $1.70, for that would mean that prime rib would have an unusually low cost for menu pricing, and hamburger would have too high a cost. The by-products should be costed out at the price that would have been paid if they had been purchased separately at the market price. This information will be readily available from the supplier. Multiplying these costs by the weights of the items gives the following

$$
\begin{array}{ll}
\quad 3.5 \text{ lb short rib at } \$1.34 \text{ (market price)} & = \$4.69 \\
+ \ 1.25 \text{ lb hamburger at } \$0.92 \text{ (market price)} & = \ \ 1.15 \\
\hline
\quad \text{Total} & \quad \$5.84
\end{array}
$$

Deducting $5.84 from the total cost of the initial purchase, $51.85, gives the value to be assigned to prime rib, $46.01. (Note, on the top part of Figure 9-13, that figures have been worked upward from the total cost of $51.85 to arrive at the $46.01 to be assigned to prime rib before cooking.) Finally, $46.01 divided by the amount of prime rib before cooking (18.5 pounds) provides the precooked cost per pound of $2.49.

The cost per ounce figures can then be calculated for each separate item. In the case of prime rib, the calculations on the bottom half of the figure show the cooked cost per pound ($3.02) and per ounce ($0.189). The portion cost factor for prime rib is

$$\frac{\$3.02}{\$1.70} \times 1.776$$

If the supplier's price goes up from $1.70 to $1.80, the new cost per pound (cooked) for prime rib is $1.80 × 1.776, which is $3.20 (instead of $3.02). If the supplier's price goes down to $1.60, the new cooked cost per pound for prime rib is $1.60 × 1.776, which is $2.84.

Cost Factors for By-Products

Cost factors can also be developed for the by-products. Although not shown on the butchering and cooking test form in Figure 9-13, they can be calculated as follows

$$\frac{\text{Market price of by-product per pound}}{\text{Supplier's price (including by-products) per pound}} = \text{Cost factor for by-products}$$

$$\text{Short rib } \frac{\$1.34}{\$1.70} = 0.788$$

$$\text{Hamburger } \frac{\$0.92}{\$1.70} = 0.541$$

If the supplier's price goes up to $1.80, the following would be the new cost prices for by-products:

$$\text{Short rib } \$1.80 \times 0.788 = \$1.42$$

$$\text{Hamburger } \$1.80 \times 0.541 = \$0.97$$

If the supplier's price goes down to $1.60, then

$$\text{Short rib } \$1.60 \times 0.788 = \$1.26$$

$$\text{Hamburger } \$1.60 \times 0.541 = \$0.87$$

Alternative Costing Method

An alternative method can be used for costing the prime ingredient and the by-products when purchasing wholesale cuts of meat and doing on-site butchering. To illustrate, assume that forty pounds of unbutchered meat at one dollar per pound have been purchased. Total cost is forty dollars. After butchering, the purchase yields twenty pounds of roasting meat, ten pounds of braising meat, and ten pounds of hamburger meat, with no bones or other wastage.

The supplier advises that, if each of these three cuts had been purchased separately already butchered at market prices, those prices per pound would have been $1.75 for roast, $1.00 for braising meat, and $0.50 for hamburger.

Therefore, if separate, already-butchered cuts were purchased, total cost would not have been $40 but

20 pounds roast at $1.75	$35.00
+ 10 pounds braising meat at $1.00	10.00
+ 10 pounds hamburger at $0.50	5.00
Total	50.00

By doing on-site butchering, the cost is $40/$50 (⅘) or 80 percent of what it would otherwise be. If this 80 percent ratio is applied to the supplier's already-butchered cost figures, the following results:

Roast	$1.75 × 80% = $1.40
Braising meat	$1.00 × 80% = $0.80
Hamburger	$0.50 × 80% = $0.40

These costs—$1.40, $0.80, and $0.40 for roast, braising meat, and hamburger, respectively—can thus be assumed to be the costs that result from purchasing the wholesale cut and doing on-premise butchering. This can be easily proved by multiplying these costs by the quantities purchased as follows

Roast	20 pounds × $1.40 = $28
+ Braising meat	10 pounds × $0.80 = $ 8

+ Hamburger	10 pounds × $0.40 = $ 4
Total	$40

Cost factors can then be calculated with the equation

$$\frac{\text{Our calculated cost per pound}}{\text{Supplier's price per pound}} = \text{Cost factor}$$

to yield

$$\text{Roast } \frac{\$1.40}{\$1.00} = 1.4$$

$$\text{Braising meat } \frac{\$0.80}{\$1.00} = 0.8$$

$$\text{Hamburger } \frac{\$0.40}{\$1.00} = 0.4$$

If the supplier raises the price of the unbutchered wholesale cut to $1.20, the new cost per pound for each of the three cuts, using the already calculated cost factors, is

Roast	$1.20 × 1.4 = $1.68
Braising meat	$1.20 × 0.8 = $0.96
Hamburger	$1.20 × 0.4 = $0.48

Although the method outlined in this section to calculate cost per pound of various cuts purchased in wholesale form and butchered on-site might give costs that differ somewhat from the approach detailed in an earlier section, it is arithmetically just as accurate and in some ways more logical.

DISCUSSION QUESTIONS

1. Discuss some of the factors that influence meat prices.
2. Briefly discuss the federal government's inspection requirements and practices for the wholesomeness of meat.

3. State the federal government's requirement for quality grading of meat, and explain why purchasers are sometimes dissatisfied with the procedure used.
4. List the three top-quality grades for beef, veal, and lamb.
5. Define the term *no-roll* with reference to meat.
6. Under what conditions must yield grading of meat be carried out. Explain why these yield grades are not particularly useful to hospitality industry purchasers.
7. Define *steer, bull, stag, bullock, heifer,* and *cow.*
8. List the four primal cuts in a forequarter and the five primal cuts in a hindquarter of beef.
9. Why are veal and calf not yield graded?
10. List the primal cuts in a veal carcass.
11. List the primal cuts in a lamb carcass.
12. At what point does lamb become mutton?
13. Yield grades for lamb are judged primarily by conformation. What does that mean?
14. List the primal cuts in a pork carcass.
15. Why is most pork not quality graded?
16. In purchasing meat, why do many hospitality purchasers stay with a sole supplier?
17. Define the terms *green meat* and *dry aging.*
18. What are IMPS numbers, and how are they used?
19. What is the USDA's acceptance service?
20. Why do many hospitality operations today buy preportioned meat products? List three disadvantages of doing this.
21. List four quality checks that should be made in meat receiving.
22. Explain how meat tags work in controlling meat storing and issuing.
23. State the general equation for calculating a cost factor.

PROBLEMS

1. Assume you are the manager of a steak restaurant whose annual sales are two million dollars a year. The restaurant operates at a 40 percent food cost, and steak purchases represent 60 percent of all money spent on food purchases. You have dealt with the same meat supplier for several years now because he provides quality meat at competitive prices, is reliable, offers good credit terms, and helps out in emergencies. A new meat supplier wishes to obtain your steak business and has proposed a six-month contract with you at a price 5 percent below the present supplier's price with a comparable quality meat and similar services. What factors should you consider in deciding to make the switch or stay with your present supplier? How would you decide? Explain why you would decide this way.

2. Your present meat supplier is providing you with lean hamburger at $1.80 per pound. In cooking, this meat shrinks 10 percent. Your supplier suggests that you buy as an alternative a less-lean hamburger at $1.20 per pound. This hamburger will have a 25 percent shrinkage in cooking.
   a. Which product is the better buy from a net yield point of view?
   b. At what price must the supplier sell you the lean hamburger in order to make it equal in value to the less-lean product from a purely price-yield point of view?
   c. In making the decision between the two products (assuming they were equivalent in cost price when compared to yield), what other factors might you consider other than price?

3. You have purchased a forty-pound rolled rib roast at $1.65 per pound. Cooking loss is 50 percent.
   a. How many four-ounce (cooked weight) portions can be served?
   b. What is the cost per portion?
   c. What is the cost factor per portion.
   d. If the supplier's price goes up to $1.70 per pound, calculate your new cost per portion using the cost factor.

4. You purchase a certain wholesale cut of meat in average forty-three-pound weights. Present cost is $1.35 per pound. When butchered, it yields twenty-eight pounds of roast, five pounds of hamburger, two pounds of stew, and 8 pounds of bones and waste. If the hamburger and stew had been purchased separately at market prices, their costs per pound would have been sixty-five cents and eighty-five cents per pound, respectively. The roast is subject to 30 percent shrinkage in cooking and is to be served in five-ounce cooked weight portions.
   a. Calculate the butchered cost per pound of roast.
   b. Calculate the cost per pound of the roast after cooking.
   c. Calculate the cost per portion.
   d. Calculate the cost factor per pound before cooking, per pound after cooking, and per portion.
   e. Using these cost factors, and assuming the supplier's cost to you of the unbutchered cut is decreased from $1.35 to $1.30, recalculate the roast cost per pound before cooking, cost per pound after cooking, and cost per five-ounce cooked-weight portion.

5. You have purchased unbutchered meat weighing eighty pounds at a cost of $1.25 per pound. When butchered, it yields thirty pounds of roast, twenty-five

pounds of braising meat, fifteen pounds of stewing meat, five pounds of hamburger, and five pounds of wastage. If you had purchased the four usable cuts already butchered from your supplier, you would have paid $2.25 per pound for roast, $1.60 per pound for braising meat, $1.00 per pound for stewing meat, and fifty cents per pound for hamburger.

   a. Using the above information, calculate your butchered cost per pound for each of the four cuts.
   b. Prove the accuracy of your answer to *a*.
   c. The thirty-pound roast is to be served in six-ounce cooked-weight portions and is subject to a 40 percent weight loss in cooking. How many portions can be served?
   d. What is the cost to you per portion?

6. You purchase a certain type of unbutchered meat at one dollar per pound in forty-five-pound quantities. After butchering, it gives average yields of eight pounds of rump roast, fourteen pounds of sirloin roast, three pounds of filet, nine pounds of stewing meat, and eleven pounds of bones and trim. If you had purchased the four usable cuts separately (already butchered) from your supplier, you would have paid 80¢ per pound for rump roast, $2.50 per pound for sirloin roast, $3.00 per pound for filet, and 70¢ per pound for stewing meat.

   a. Using the above information, calculate your butchered cost per pound for each of the four cuts.
   b. Prove the correctness of your answer to *a*.
   c. Calculate the cost factors for each of the four cuts of meat.
   d. Using these cost factors, recalculate your butchered cost per pound for each of the four cuts of meat, assuming the supplier's price of the unbutchered meat goes down from one dollar to ninety cents.
   e. The rump roast is subject to a 35 percent shrinkage loss in cooking. It is served in four-ounce cooked-weight portions. At the unbutchered price of ninety cents per pound, what is your cost of a portion of rump roast?
   f. Calculate the cooked-weight portion cost factor for rump roast.
   g. Using this cooked-weight portion cost factor, recalculate your portion cost for rump roast if the supplier's price increases from 90¢ to $1.10 for unbutchered meat.

REFERENCES AND SUGGESTED READINGS

Gisslen, Wayne, 1983. *Professional Cooking.* New York: John Wiley.

Hinich, Melvin J., and Richard Staelin. 1980. *Consumer Protection Legislation and the U.S. Food Industry*. New York: Pergamon, pp. 97–107.

Khan, Mahmood A. 1987. *Foodservice Operations*. Westport, Conn.: AVI, pp. 186–96.

Kotschevar, Lendal H., and Charles Levinson. 1988. *Quantity Food Purchasing*. New York: Mcmillan, pp. 393–473, 476–81, 647–61.

Levie, A. 1979. *Meat Handbook*. Westport, Conn.: AVI.

Maizel, Bruno. 1978. *Food and Beverage Purchasing*. Indianapolis: Bobbs-Merrill, pp. 137–64.

Morgan, William J. Jr. 1988. *Supervision and Management of Quantity Food Preparation*. Berkeley, Calif.: McCutchan, pp. 305–39.

Mutkoski, Stephen A., and Marcia L. Schurer. 1981. *Meat and Fish Management*. North Scituate, Mass.: Breton, pp. 1–5, 20–113, 175–81, 200–210, 220–49.

National Association of Meat Purveyors. 1976. *Meat Buyer's Guide to Portion Control Meat Cuts*. Tucson, Ariz.: National Association of Meat Purveyors.

National Association of Meat Purveyors. 1976. *Meat Buyer's Guide to Standardized Meat Cuts*. Tucson, Ariz.: National Asssociation of Meat Purveyors.

National Association of Meat Purveyors. 1978. *The N.A.M.P. Guide to Quality Assurance*. Tucson, Ariz.: National Association of Meat Purveyors.

National Live Stock and Meat Board. 1975. *Meat in the Food Service Industry*. Chicago: The National Live Stock and Meat Board.

Norkus, Gregory X., 1988. Goodbye, Good—Hello, Select. *Cornell Hotel and Restaurant Administration Quarterly* 29(2):14–17.

Peddersen, Raymond B. 1977. *SPECS: The Comprehensive Foodservice Purchasing and Specification Manual*. Boston: Cahners, pp. 69–238.

Peddersen, Raymond B. 1981. *Foodservice and Hotel Purchasing*. Boston: CBI, pp. 78–86, 425–96.

Powers, Jo Marie. 1979. *Basics of Quantity Food Production*. New York: Wiley, pp. 86–108, 175–82.

Powers, Thomas F., and Jo Marie Powers. 1984. *Food Service Operations: Planning and Control*. New York: John Wiley, pp. 109–17.

Stefanelli, John M. 1985. *Purchasing: Selection and Procurement for the Hospitality Industry*. New York: John Wiley, pp. 393–424.

U.S. Department of Agriculture. 1976. *Institutional Meat Purchase Specifications for Sausage Products Approved by USDA*. Washington, D.C.: USDA's Agricultural Marketing Service, Livestock Division.

U.S. Department of Agriculture, 1981. *Labels on Meat and Poultry Products, Information Bulletin #443*. Washington, D.C.: USDA Food Safety and Quality Service.

U.S. Department of Agriculture, 1981. *Meat and Poultry Inspection, Fact Sheet #18*. Washington, D.C.: USDA Food and Safety Quality Service.

U.S. Department of Agriculture. 1970 *USDA's Acceptance Service for Meat and Meat Products, Marketing Bulletin No. 47.* Washington, D.C.: USDA.

U.S. Department of Agriculture. 1974. *USDA Yield Grades for Beef, Marketing Bulletin No. 45.* Washington, D.C.: USDA.

U.S. Department of Agriculture. 1970. *USDA Yield Grades for Lamb.* Washington, D.C.: USDA.

Virts, William B. 1987. *Purchasing for Hospitality Operations.* East Lansing, Mich.: The Educational Institute of the American Hotel & Motel Association, pp. 93–107, 109–29.

10

Poultry and Eggs

OBJECTIVES

- Differentiate between the various types of poultry.
- Discuss the federal government inspection requirements for and the grading of poultry.
- List and briefly discuss the items that might appear on poultry specifications.
- Describe the USDA's acceptance service for poultry purchasing.
- List the procedures to be used when receiving fresh and frozen poultry.
- Discuss the storage requirements for fresh and frozen poultry, and describe how the frozen product should be defrosted.
- Describe the federal government's inspection and grading requirements for fresh eggs, and define the term *candling*.
- List the six egg sizes, and state the weight per dozen for each size.
- Discuss the purchasing and receiving of fresh eggs.

The general term *poultry* is used for domesticated birds used for their meat and to produce eggs. Poultry includes chickens, turkeys, ducks, geese, and pigeons. The term *game birds* is generally used to define wild birds that are not raised domestically such as ducks, geese, and pheasant. Note, however, that in today's market some so-called game birds are domestically raised.

Poultry has a short production cycle. Three weeks are needed for a chicken egg to become a chick and then another six to nine weeks for the bird to be usable as meat. In contrast, the hog production cycle requires up to ten months and cattle up to three years. For poultry the feed-to-weight ratio is 2:1, for pork it is 3.5:1, and for beef 7:1. These factors explain why the cost of poultry meat per pound of yield is considerably less than for pork or beef and perhaps also why per capita consumption is increasing steadily while that of pork and beef is declining. Increased poultry consumption is evidenced by the growth in number of fast-food restaurants that specialize in chicken. In addition, health concerns contribute to higher poultry consumption as diet-conscious consumers stay away from the relatively high cholesterol and fat content of red meats.

TYPES OF POULTRY

The USDA classifies poultry into various categories based on the birds' maturity. Younger birds generally have more tender meat and may be used for baking, barbecuing, broiling, frying, and roasting. The meat of more mature birds is tougher and requires cooking methods such as braising, simmering, or steaming to tenderize it. Older birds also have more fat, which is not desirable from the customers' point of view, even though fat adds flavor. For that reason, most mature birds are not used as is in hospitality operations but are processed for use in soups, stews, and similar items.

The bird's sex is not particularly important in younger birds. In older birds, however, females tend to be tastier and juicier and also have a higher yield of usable meat. Therefore, purchase specifications must state the sex desired in mature birds. The two broad categories of poultry products are chickens and turkeys.

Chickens

Chickens are subcategorized by the USDA based on such factors as age and sex. Note that the name of a bird generally indicates its age. For example, a Cornish hen is a five- to seven-week-old chicken, and a broiler is generally about eight weeks old. The sex of a bird is also sometimes indicated by its age. A hen is a female chicken; the male is a rooster. The major categories of chickens used in the hospitality industry follow.

Broilers or Fryers

These tender young male or female chickens have smooth-textured skin, tender flesh, and flexible cartilage, and usually are between nine and twelve weeks old. They are available either fresh or frozen in such forms as whole eviscerated (with intestines, spleen, and other organs removed), halved, quartered, or in pieces such as legs or breasts. Broilers generally weigh from 1.5 to 2.5 pounds and fryers from 2.5 to 3.5 pounds.

Roasters

These older male or female chickens are usually between twelve and twenty weeks old, similar in some ways to broilers (but with a less flexible cartilage), except that they weigh from 3.5 to 7 pounds and thus provide more meat. They are available in the same forms as broilers, but if used for roasting are normally purchased in whole eviscerated form.

Capons

These male chickens are normally less than eight months old and weigh between five and nine pounds. They have been castrated to retard muscular development. As a result, their muscle meat is well marbled with fat, and they have a higher ratio of breast to bone than broilers. Flesh is tender and well flavored. They are available primarily in whole eviscerated form because they are usually used for roasting.

Stewing Chickens

These hen or fowl female chickens are at least ten months old and weigh from 3.5 to seven pounds. Because these birds have been egg layers, they tend to have tougher meat and thus generally need to be poached or simmered for use in soups or stews. Because demand for these birds is not high (other than by commercial processors such as soup manufacturers), they are relatively cheap but not always available.

Cocks or Roosters

These mature males (more than ten months old) have a coarse skin and tough, dark meat. They generally weigh from four to six pounds.

Cornish Game Hens

Also known as Rock Cornish, these are a special breed of young immature chicken with a very tender and delicate meat. They are normally only five or six weeks old and weigh between three quarters of a pound and two pounds ready to cook. They are available in the same forms as broilers and are usually roasted whole because of their size.

Turkeys

The major types of turkeys used by hospitality operations are:

Toms

Toms are male turkeys. According to Virts (1987, p. 157) they account for about 90 percent of U.S. turkey production and, like chicken, their prices depend to some extent on the prices of competing beef and pork. The larger they are, the higher the meat-to-bone ratio, except that when they exceed twenty pounds this ratio stays relatively constant. Most toms are bought in frozen or fresh whole form, although they are also available when needed in parts such as legs, thighs, or breasts.

Fryer-roasters

These immature turkeys of either sex are usually less than sixteen weeks old and thus very tender when cooked. Weight is usually four to nine pounds. They are usually available in whole frozen or fresh form and eviscerated with neck and giblets included.

Young Turkeys

A young turkey may be either male or female and is older than a fryer-roaster. Male young turkeys (toms) are usually about thirty weeks old; females (hens) are about twenty weeks old and thus weigh less than toms (about twelve to fifteen pounds compared to twenty pounds or more).

Yearlings

A yearling turkey is a male or female usually less than fifteen months old whose flesh is still reasonably tender. Weight range is from ten to thirty pounds.

Mature

A yearling older than fifteen months is known as a mature turkey. Mature birds have tougher meat than other turkeys and are usually used for soups or turkey pot pies or processed further. Weight range is from ten to thirty pounds.

Processed Turkey

A great deal of turkey meat is in processed forms such as turkey rolls, hams, franks, and bologna.

Other Poultry

Some other forms of poultry, in addition to chickens and turkeys, are also available to the hospitality industry.

Ducks

Most ducks available are the domesticated variety known as Long Island Duckling. Broiler and fryer ducklings are usually less than eight weeks old and weigh two to four pounds. Roasters are generally between eight and sixteen weeks old and weigh between four and seven pounds. Mature ducks are old birds (over six months) with a tough flesh. They weigh between four and ten pounds.

Geese

A young goose (less than six months old) has tender flesh and weighs from six to ten pounds. A mature goose (over six months old) weighing over ten pounds will be tough.

Pigeons

Mature birds of this family are known as *pigeons* and have a tough dark meat; if immature (less than four weeks old and weighing only about a pound), they are known as *squabs*. Squabs have light, tender meat. Pigeons and squabs are both low in fat.

Guineas

Guineas are domestic relatives of wild pheasants. Young guineas (about six months old) are tender and weigh from 0.75 to 1.5 pounds. Mature guineas (from six to twelve months old) are tough and weigh from one to two pounds.

Game Birds

Several varieties of game (wild) birds are sometimes purchased by hospitality operations. They include wild ducks, wild geese, pheasant, quail, swans, and peafowl. Because these birds have lived in the wild, they generally have relatively tough meat except when available during the hunting season, when they have built-up fat that would normally carry them through the winter.

GOVERNMENT INSPECTION

The USDA's federal inspection program for poultry is similar to that for meat. The inspection process involves poultry processing plant sanitation, the wholesomeness of the birds, and the use of additives and labeling. Inspection is not concerned with quality or grade of poultry. The federal government regulates both interstate and foreign poultry commerce and requires that for intrastate (within-state) commerce, state inspection programs be at least equivalent to the federal ones. For states that do not have programs that meet this equivalency test, federal inspections are mandated. Inspection costs are paid by the processing plants, which, in turn, no doubt reflect them in their product prices. The inspection stamp for poultry is a circular one, as illustrated in Figure 10-1.

Since 1980 a voluntary quality control system has been in effect. Under this system, some poultry processing plants are not required to have continuous inspections on-site. Note that plants that slaughter poultry are not eligible for this voluntary program. It is only available to those who receive slaughtered poultry and process it further. The wholesomeness of raw materials is verified on arrival and the processed products are inspected again before being shipped out. Plants using the voluntary system must, however, be able to demonstrate that their in-house inspections are at least equal to those of USDA inspectors, who in turn make periodic inspection visits to those plants.

Quality Grading

Generally, there is little quality difference between poultry from one supplier and those from any other suppliers. The reason is that each type of poultry is raised the same way in every farm or "factory" for the same length of time. All poultry consume a similar diet and are processed through packing plants using the same assembly-line techniques.

Although federal grading of poultry is not required, as long as the product has been inspected for wholesomeness, a poultry producer can elect to purchase the USDA's grading service. However, some states mandate that producers have their products graded after inspection. Also, because most hospitality industry purchase specifications require that the product be quality graded, suppliers wishing to supply to hospitality purchasers generally have to have grading done anyway.

However, some poultry-processing plants do not avail themselves of the USDA grading service but rather sell their products to chain hospitality businesses who have established their own quality specifications and have the birds distributed under their private labels. Sometimes these chain operations (as well as retail food-

Figure 10-1.   Poultry inspection stamp (*Source:* USDA).

stores) have their own inspectors in the plants. By bypassing the USDA inspection, costs are reduced.

Factors used in grading include

- *Conformation:* the shape or form of the bird
- *Fleshing:* how well developed the flesh is
- *Fat covering:* any flesh showing through the skin because of a lack of fat causes the bird to be considered thin skinned and not as desirable
- *Other factors:* lower grades are assigned for presence of pinfeathers, bruises, discoloration, broken bones, and similar items
- *Freezer defects:* these apply if the product is frozen

The three consumer grades (the ones used by most hospitality purchasers) for poultry are A, B, and C. Grade A is the top quality and indicates a full-fleshed bird with an attractive appearance. Grade B may have some dressing defects such as a skin tear. Its appearance may also be less attractive (for example, not as fleshy). Grade C is even less attractive and may have more defects, such as a missing part of the wing. The federal grading stamp is in the shape of a shield, as illustrated in Figure 10-2.

Note that grades assigned do not identify poultry eating qualities but rather appearance; that is, a mature bird can be given a Grade A, while a younger, more tender bird can receive a Grade B or Grade C. Generally speaking, however, if birds do not receive an A grade, they are not graded lower but are sent on for processed products. Most hospitality industry purchasers specify Grade A birds ready to cook, that is, with head and feet removed, dressed, and eviscerated. They are usually purchased whole or in parts (with or without bones), either chilled or frozen.

For the institutional market (very large buyers), the government also has two procurement grades: I and II. Some state and local markets may use three commercial grades: Extra, Standard, and No Grade. These grades are similar to the consumer and institutional grades, but tolerances between grades may be wider.

Figure 10-2.   Poultry grading stamp (*Source:* USDA).

PURCHASING POULTRY

Because for most fresh and frozen poultry products there is little to choose between one supplier's product and the next, most purchasers have little loyalty to particular suppliers. Cost and supplier service are more critical factors. Sometimes more quality variety is found in products such as duck and turkey, and some supplier discrimination may prevail. For this reason, packers' brands are not of great concern for fresh and frozen birds. They are of more concern in the area of processed birds.

Prices

Fresh and frozen poultry prices vary little from one producer to another, although transportation distance from producer or processor to the end-supplier can have an effect on end-user prices. Prices of poultry also tend to be stable, or at least predictable, because the production cycle is relatively short compared to pork or beef.

Poultry price instability is usually the result of increases or decreases in production at a source caused by changes in demand due to consumption area weather.

Poultry prices are also closely related to other meat prices and particularly to the other white meat, pork. Changes in demand (affecting price) are caused by consumers' perceptions of the relative values of competitive meat product prices at any one time.

Two publications are commonly used by purchasers to obtain poultry pricing information. The *Poultry Market News Report* is published three times a week by the USDA's Agricultural Marketing Service and Urner Barry Publications' *Urner Barry's Price-Current* is published five times a week (Figure 10-3).

Specifications

Because of the quality standardization for most poultry products, specifications are easier to prepare than for other meat products. Most purchasers require mandatory plant inspection and use the USDA's grades as a basic specification. Most foodservice buyers purchase Grade A poultry for frying, roasting, broiling, and similar cooking methods. When appearance is less important (such as for chicken salads or turkey pot pie), a lower grade is likely to be purchased. Poultry parts normally have the same grade as the bird before it was cut into parts.

In addition to grade, specifications generally also include the following:

- Kind of bird such as chicken, turkey, duck, or goose.
- Class of bird such as broiler or stewing hen.
- Size (weight) of bird (including weight limitations), such as "birds to weigh 2.5 lbs each plus or minus 3 ounces."

Urner Barry's Price-Current
WEST COAST EDITION
Established 1858

Number 59

TURKEYS
Delivered West Coast
Does Not Include Netting or Timer
READY TO COOK (R.T.C.) FROZEN
Grade A or Comparable Quality

	Truck Loads & Similar Quantities	L.C.L. 25 box min Export Dock
YOUNG HENS		
Heavy Breeds-		
8 to 12 lbs.	.65	.70-.73
12 & up	.65	.70-.73
YOUNG TOMS		
Heavy Breeds-		
14 to 22 lbs.	.70	.75-.78
22 to 24 lbs.	.70	.75-.78
24 to 26 lbs.	.73	.78-.81
26 to 28 lbs.	.75	.80-.83
28 to 30 lbs.	.81	.86-.89
30 to 32 lbs.	.83	.88-.91
32 to 34 lbs.	.88	.93-.96
34 lbs. & up	.89-.96	.94-1.04
BELTSVILLES		
3 to 9 lbs	-	-

FRESH TURKEYS
Delivered West Coast

	Truck Load	L.C.L.
YOUNG HENS -		
8 to 14 lbs.	-	-
14 to 16 lbs.	-	-
YOUNG TOMS -		
16 to 24 lbs.	-	-
24 to 26 lbs.	-	-
26 to 28 lbs.	-	-
28 to 30 lbs.	-	-
30 lbs. & up	-	-

CANNER PACKED TURKEYS
Delivered Midwest Areas
Carlot or Trucklot - no neck/no giblets - deliv. Midwest area.
LINE RUN -
(% A balance may be B's, C's or P.M.'s)

	FROZEN	FRESH
YOUNG TOMS -		
14 to 17 lbs.	-	.68
17 to 20 lbs.	-	.69
20 lbs. and up	-	.71
YOUNG HENS -		
10 to 14 lbs. average	-	-
REGULAR PACK (B's, C's or P.M.'s)		
YOUNG TOMS -		
14 to 17 lbs.	.61	.64
17 to 20 lbs.	.62	.65
20 lbs. and up	.64	.67
BREEDER HENS -		
Under 10 lbs.	-	-
Over 10 lbs.	.38—	.40—
YOUNG HENS -		
10 to 14 lbs. average	-	.56—

Carlot or Trucklot — No neck/No giblets
Delivered West Coast area.
LINE RUN YOUNG TOMS

14 to 17 lbs.	-	-
17 to 20 lbs.	-	-
20 lbs. and up	-	-
REGULAR PACK YOUNG TOMS		
14 to 17 lbs.	-	-
17 to 20 lbs.	-	-
20 lbs & up	-	-

Figure 10-3. *Urner Barry's Poultry Price-Current* (Courtesy of Urner Barry Publications, Inc., Toms River, N.J.).

- Cutting instructions for parts. Although some operations specify whole poultry shells (that is, carcasses without neck or giblets) and do their own on-premise cutting, parts that are purchased are usually specified as halves, quarters, or smaller parts (such as breasts, legs, thighs, or drumsticks). For chicken parts, weight should be stated on specifications; if five-ounce chicken breasts are specified and 5.5-ounce ones are shipped, then food cost will increase by 10 percent. If these parts are to be breaded, the ratio of breading to poultry must be specified.

- Packaging requirements, such as parts to be packed in approximately thirty-pound containers.
- State of refrigeration. If purchased fresh and unfrozen, poultry can be purchased iced, chilled, or vacuum packed. The desired method should be specified. Ice packing is the traditional method of shipping in crushed ice. Chilled birds are shipped partly frozen in polybags and stored and transported at a temperature slightly below freezing (30° F or −1° C). Today, vacuum packaging is also used. Poultry packages are vacuum sealed and then flushed with carbon dioxide gas to eliminate oxygen. This process retards potential bacterial growth, helps maintain product quality, and extends shelf life. Regardless of shipping method, poultry's internal temperature should be specified to be maintained at 34° F (1° C) or less.
- Some purchasers also specify the delay allowed between processing time and delivery (such as three days).

USDA Acceptance Service

The USDA offers an acceptance service for a fee (in the same way that it does for meat products) to help an operator prepare purchase specifications for poultry. For this fee, the acceptance service employees inspect the supplier's product and accept or reject it according to specifications.

RECEIVING POULTRY

As with meat products, the chef is often present (if the regular receiver does not have the qualifications) to check poultry as it is received. The following procedures should be carried out when receiving poultry:

- Receiving it if possible in a refrigerated inspection area because harmful bacteria can multiply rapidly on poultry held at room temperature.
- Verify that the quality received conforms to specifications and the order form.
- Poultry purchased in fresh form should arrive packed in ice and be held this way until used. It should have smooth, firm, clean flesh. Skin should be dry and without stickiness. No blood should be evident. In particular, check joints for this. Neither skin nor carcass cavity should have any odor.
- For poultry purchased in frozen form, packages should contain no air. There should be no discolored flesh. After it is thawed, quality checks should be made as for fresh poultry.
- With frozen products, check for signs of thawing and then refreezing. Some sup-

pliers have been known to sell defrosted poultry packed in ice as if it were a fresh product.

- Check that the grade conforms to specifications. On frozen poultry this grade shield will be on the carton; on fresh birds it will be on the wing of each bird. Selling ungraded poultry is not illegal, but, if specified, then graded products should be delivered. A trained receiver is necessary to differentiate some Grade B from Grade A poultry, especially when it is ice-packed.
- Check the production date on containers to ensure that it is recent and within the time period specified.
- With birds in cartons, check that the bird quality conforms with the grade shield on the carton. Suppliers have been known to repack high-grade cartons with low-grade birds.
- Check that poultry parts delivered are the right parts! If chicken legs are required, make sure that wings have not been delivered.
- For canned processed poultry products, check cans for leaks, rust, and swollen containers indicating likely spoilage.
- Verify quantities (counts, sizes, weights) against those specified and against the order form and invoice. Because fresh poultry is usually delivered packed in ice, weighing may be difficult. In this case, spot checks of some birds should be made to make sure they conform to the weight range specified. To check that total delivery weight conforms to the weight invoiced, birds have to be removed from packaging and ice before weighing.
- Check invoiced prices against those quoted.

Storing

Fresh poultry should be stored at a temperature of about 30 to 32°F (0°C). If it is received packed in ice, it should be left this way, but package drainage should be provided so that the water from melted ice does not surround the birds. More ice should be added if needed to replace melted ice. Poultry has a shelf life of only three or four days, even when properly stored. Minimize the handling of poultry while it is being stored because excessive handling increases the possibility of contamination.

Poultry received frozen should be kept in the freezer at a temperature of 0°F (−18°C). If properly stored, frozen poultry can be kept frozen for up to a year.

Issuing and Using

As with meat, poultry inventory should be rotated; that is, items received first should be issued first in order to minimize spoilage.

When defrosting frozen poultry for use, defrosting should be done by transferring it to a refrigerator for a day or so. Thaw poultry in original wrapper, and allow one or two days for chickens and two to four days for larger poultry. If poultry must be defrosted in a hurry, it should be kept in its original wrapper and defrosted in the sink in cold, running water. It should never be refrozen once defrosted nor defrosted at room temperature, which encourages bacterial growth. Poultry is particularly susceptible to bacteria such as salmonella. Even if these bacteria are not present in the poultry when it is received, they can be transferred by human handling or by placing the product on a contaminated kitchen surface. Therefore, wash all equipment and cutting surfaces after handling poultry to ensure that no potential contamination is passed on to other foods. These bacteria grow particularly quickly at temperatures of 40 to 120°F (4 to 49°C). Chicken in a cream sauce (for example, chicken à la king) kept in a warm, rather than hot, steam table for several hours can contaminate quickly and cause food poisoning. Similarly, chicken salad held in the kitchen rather than in a refrigerator until needed can cause similar problems. However, poultry dishes cooked and then frozen right away can be kept up to six months.

When poultry is issued, only sufficient for each day (or even meal period) should be issued at any one time. After each meal period, any unused poultry should be returned as soon as possible to refrigeration.

POULTRY YIELDS

Poultry yields should be tested in the same way as for meat. Cost factors can also be used. For a discussion of these topics, see chapter 9.

EGGS

Purchasing fresh eggs is not difficult. Purchasing processed eggs (frozen, dried, and so forth) is more difficult. Today, most eggs sold are in processed form.

Government Inspection

The USDA's Food Safety and Quality Service (FSQS) inspects fresh shell eggs for wholesomeness. This inspection is voluntary. However, most states either require egg producers to use this service or else provide a mandatory state service. Inspectors also control the condition of producer premises, as well as the environment of laying hens and their feed. Plants that process eggs must undergo continuous government inspection because of concern about the risk of contamination. To minimize this risk, federal and state agencies coordinate inspections.

Grading

Egg grading is voluntary. To be graded, eggs must first be inspected. An uninspected egg cannot be graded. The three USDA grades for fresh eggs are Grade AA (or Fresh

Fancy) for the top quality, Grade A for a somewhat lower quality (an AA egg becomes an A egg after ten days), and Grade B for the lowest-quality egg (an A egg that is two or three weeks old becomes a B egg). Within these categories, an egg can further be rated as high, medium, or low, resulting in a total of nine possible grades.

Federal government grading stamps indicate both the grade of the egg and the egg size. (Egg sizes are discussed later in the chapter.) Every egg in a case need not be of the grade shown. Some tolerances are allowed. Generally, however, producers try to meet the minimum USDA standards because, by shipping according to grade standards, they can receive a higher price. Price can vary considerably between grades.

Quality Factors

The following quality factors are used in grading eggs:

- Interior quality—usually judged primarily by freshness. The fresher the egg, the higher the quality, as long as the laying hen is from six to eighteen months old, is eating a nutritious diet, and is laying in a healthy environment. Eggs should have no blood spots or other internal defects.
- Exterior quality—cleanliness, shape, soundness of shell. Older hens lay eggs with rougher and thinner shells. Egg shells are porous and allow air to penetrate the interior of the egg, which weakens the egg white and thins out the yolk. It is more likely to happen with thin shells or when an egg has been exposed to too much air or subjected to high temperatures.

To check quality, the grader "candles" the egg, that is, passes it over a light source to examine yolk centering (a centered yolk implies freshness), interior air space (the older the egg, the larger the air space), and the shell for cracks or impurities. Random checks are sometimes made by breaking open an egg and sampling its white: the firmer the white, the younger the egg.

White versus Brown Eggs

Absolutely no quality difference (either physical or chemical) exists between eggs with white shells and those with brown shells. Shell color merely identifies the hen species. Purchasers need only state the desired color if customer demand is a factor, such as when boiled eggs are served and most of the restaurant's customers prefer one color over the other.

Egg Preservation

Most fresh eggs are preserved under refrigeration below 45°F (7°C) at all times. As eggs get older, they lose quality as internal moisture reduces and whites become thinner. Refrigeration retards this quality loss. Note, however, that no federal legal requirement calls for producers to refrigerate eggs, although some states require it. Therefore, a purchaser's requirement for refrigerated eggs should be stated in the specifications.

Some eggs are sprayed or dipped with oil to reduce moisture loss and help preserve them. The oil excludes any air from penetrating the shell and retards deterioration. Oil spraying or dipping is not as good as refrigeration to preserve eggs. Note also that oil-dipped eggs usually lose more weight than oil-sprayed ones.

Processed Eggs

Another method of preserving eggs is to process them. One form of processed egg is dried. Dried eggs can be processed from whole eggs, or whites and yolks can be dried separately. To be used, dried eggs must be reconstituted with water. For this reason, they are not usually used in egg dishes (such as scrambled eggs) in which fresh eggs produce a better product. They are used in recipes requiring the use of eggs as only one of several ingredients.

Processed eggs can also be frozen. They can be frozen whole, or the whites and yolks can be frozen separately. If frozen yolks or whole eggs have been improperly frozen and have not had some sugar added before freezing, the yolks can be tough and rubbery. Frozen egg products must be defrosted in the same way that poultry is (in the refrigerator) and not at room temperature because of potential bacteria multiplication.

Processed eggs (such as frozen whole eggs and cooked, peeled eggs) have legal standards regarding processing and preservation, but no quality grades can be specified because eggs for processing are not graded. All processed egg products are produced under continuous federal inspection. The inspection stamp for processed eggs is illustrated in Figure 10-4. During inspection, the product is carefully checked for salmonella bacteria. These products may be produced from shell eggs that did not qualify for grading, but are nevertheless perfectly wholesome, as well as from eggs that were produced solely for further processing. Any nonegg ingredients added during processing must be listed on the package label. Total egg-solid content, however, may never be less than 24.7 percent of the total package ingredient weight if the item is made from whole eggs, which is important for purchasers to know when comparing processed egg product costs. Although packers' brands of graded fresh eggs are not normally important to the hospitality industry purchaser (the quality of graded fresh eggs is very consistent), packers' brands can be important in processed-egg products. Indeed, the packer's brand name may be the only indication of quality.

Figure 10-4.   Inspection stamp for liquid, frozen, and dried egg products (*Source:* USDA).

PURCHASING EGGS

The problem with purchasing fresh eggs is not so much one of selecting quality (as long as the eggs have been graded) but rather one of finding a supplier who can be relied on for consistent delivery of quantities required and can provide the freshest eggs. A case marked Grade A is no indicator of freshness. To be called a fresh egg, it must be less than 30 days old. However, most eggs are shipped within a few days of being laid.

Some buyers purchase from local farmers because they feel they obtain the freshest eggs this way. Such eggs may be only a day or so old, whereas an egg normally takes at least a week to move through regular distribution channels. However, are the farmer's eggs refrigerated? A two-day-old unrefrigerated egg may not be as good as a ten-day-old refrigerated one. A further risk in buying from farmers is that these producers may have poor farming practices, may not be producing high-quality eggs, and may not be inspected by government agents. The purchaser also has no guarantee that the farmer has not purchased the eggs from some other source and is simply reselling them as "farm-fresh" eggs.

Specifications

In specifications for fresh eggs, most purchasers specify that they want Grade A eggs because Grade AA are difficult to find and turn into Grade A eggs within six to ten days anyway, and at least this amount of time is usually necessary to move from producer to purchaser.

Some purchasers specify that their eggs not be graded but be produced under the federal government's quality-approved program. As with grading, this program is voluntary, but to obtain a purchaser's business in such circumstances the producer has little choice but to use it if specified. Under this program, a quality-approved stamp shows that the eggs were produced and packaged under continuous government inspection. Quality-conscious buyers require this stamp because federal egg inspection is not required (unless eggs are to be graded) and some states also do not require egg inspection. For example, if ungraded eggs are purchased, the buyer has no guarantee that shells are not cracked. Cracked shells offer a good haven for harmful bacteria.

Although specifying ungraded eggs during cool seasons is acceptable (as long as they are to be used only in mixtures with other ingredients), this practice should not be followed in hot weather because of the bacteria multiplication problems that heat can cause in the eggs.

Purchasers should also state the size and uniformity of fresh eggs in their specifications. The federal government requires that egg size be indicated on the container in which they are shipped. The size indicates the weight per dozen eggs and is not related to the quality of the egg.

Size	Weight per Dozen
Peewee	15 oz per dozen
Small	18 oz per dozen
Medium	21 oz per dozen
Large	24 oz per dozen
Extra large	27 oz per dozen
Jumbo	30 oz per dozen

Egg size is related to age of the hen. For example, peewee eggs (sometimes referred to as *pullet eggs*) are produced by younger hens, and jumbo eggs are produced by older hens near the end of their laying life. Most eggs, however, fall into the four middle classes. Generally, the difference from one weight size to the next is about 15 percent. This difference normally translates into about a 15 percent difference in egg price from one size to the next. If market prices do not follow this spread, then one of the sizes is obviously a better buy from a cost point of view. When eggs are purchased for frying, scrambling, poaching, or for use in omelettes, purchasers usually specify the larger sizes because these eggs have a good plate appearance. Also, most commercial recipes are based on the large size of two-ounce eggs (twenty-four ounces per dozen).

Also included in specifications can be a requirement for constant egg refrigeration prior to delivery, as well as the time delay between inspection and delivery (for example, three days).

Specifications for processed eggs can require that they be packed under continuous USDA inspection. For frozen eggs, the container size must be stated (for example, thirty-pound cans). The purchaser may also require that frozen eggs be pasteurized. For frozen whole eggs and yolks, the color level needs to be specified (such as level four). Generally, the higher the color level, the higher the price. Some frozen egg products are packed with a percentage of sugar and salt (varying from 2 to 12 percent). The desired percent must be specified.

Prices

Fresh egg prices can change rapidly. When prices do change, distributors generally sell any inventory on hand at the new price and make additional profit on that inventory purchased at lower prices. When prices decline, then the reverse occurs; distributors lower the price on existing inventory and take a loss on that. If price increases are forecast, purchasers can buy now in quantity shelf-stable egg products at the still-prevailing lower price.

In large hospitality operations, eggs are purchased using cost-plus to ensure a steady, dependable supply. Small operations will generally purchase them by using a competitive bid situation.

Egg pricing information can be obtained from *Urner Barry's Price-Current* (published five times a week).

RECEIVING EGGS

Receiving checks should be carried out when receiving eggs. Supplier upgrading, that is, substituting a smaller size of egg than that specified, substituting Grade A for Grade AA, or substituting ungraded eggs for graded ones, is not uncommon. Inspected and graded eggs should be delivered to the receiving dock in cartons that show the grade. This procedure provides some protection but does not guarantee that substitutions have not been made. Although verifying the age of fresh eggs is difficult for receiving employees, some quality checks can be conducted.

- Check case dates. The date on the package is the date of packaging and not laying.
- Spot-check eggs by holding them in front of a light source. A fresh egg should have a well-centered yolk. Alternatively, place some of them in water. Old eggs float.
- Inspect eggs for lack of size uniformity, dirt, or shell cracks.
- Check for oiled eggs. Oiled eggs are acceptable if specified, but oiled eggs should not be substituted for nonoiled eggs if that has been specified.
- Count quantities delivered, or, alternatively, weigh the containers. Fresh eggs are normally packed in cases of either fifteen or thirty dozen. Thus, if purchasers know the standard weight of the case in which eggs are delivered, the case including eggs can be weighed and then the weight of the case deducted to determine the weight of the eggs in that case. According to the USDA, the minimum net weight in pounds for a case of thirty dozen eggs is as follows:

Jumbo	56.0
Extra large	50.5
Large	45.0
Medium	39.5
Small	34.0
Peewee	28.0

- For frozen processed-egg products, use a thermometer to ensure they were delivered at the correct temperature.
- Check frozen processed-egg products for crystallization, indicating that the product has been defrosted and then refrozen.
- Verify quantities and prices on invoices against the purchase order and invoice prices.

Storing

Fresh eggs should be refrigerated immediately after they have been received in their original containers. Indeed, carrying out receiving checks in the egg refrigeration area is a good idea. This refrigerated area should preferably be separate from other refrigerated storage because eggs quickly pick up odors through their shells from other products. At the very least, do not store fresh eggs close to products that impart a strong odor, such as peeled onions. Maximum storage time is one week.

Store processed-egg products in the environment stated on the product package. Maximum storage time for frozen egg products is one year.

Issuing and Using

The main cost-control aspect of fresh eggs is to issue them on a first-purchased, first-issued basis to ensure proper stock rotation and minimize the potential for spoilage.

Because fresh eggs and some processed-egg products deteriorate rapidly in a kitchen environment, only sufficient eggs should be issued for each meal period's requirements. Any unused products should immediately be returned to their appropriate storage areas at the end of the meal period.

DISCUSSION QUESTIONS

1. Differentiate between a broiler or fryer chicken and a roaster.
2. Define each of the following:

   Capon
   Cornish game hen

Yearling turkey
Squab
Guinea

3. Discuss the federal government inspection requirements for poultry.
4. State the grades and list three factors used in grading poultry.
5. List the major items that should be specified when purchasing fresh poultry.
6. Differentiate between iced, chilled, and vacuum-packed fresh poultry.
7. What is the USDA acceptance service for poultry purchasing?
8. List six procedures that should be used when receiving fresh poultry.
9. List specific checks that should be made when receiving frozen poultry.
10. Discuss the storage requirements for both fresh and frozen poultry.
11. How should frozen poultry be defrosted?
12. What are the USDA inspection requirements for fresh eggs?
13. What are the grading requirements for fresh eggs, and what grades can be assigned?
14. To check egg quality, inspectors candle them. What does that mean?
15. Processed eggs have no quality grades assigned to them. Why not?
16. Discuss the pros and cons of purchasing fresh eggs from local farmers.
17. Egg sizes are based on weight per dozen. List the six egg sizes, and state the weight per dozen for each size.
18. List five receiving checks that should be carried out for fresh eggs.

PROBLEMS

1. You are conducting turkey yield tests from two different suppliers. Supplier A can provide twenty-pound birds at a price of $1.05 per pound, and after cooking, boning, and trimming the yield of usable meat is 40 percent. Supplier B can provide twenty-five pound birds at a price of $1.10 per pound, and after cooking, boning, and trimming the yield of usable meat is 45 percent.
   a. Based on yield, which supplier's price provides better value?
   b. Before making the decision to buy from one supplier or the other, what other factors might you consider?

2. Assume that you are presently buying broiling chickens from a supplier at a price of ninety-five cents per pound. Average bird size is two pounds, and, when cooked, usable meat yield is 50 percent.
   a. How many cooked-weight four-ounce portions of chicken can be served per bird?
   b. What is the cost per portion?
   c. What is the cost factor per portion?

    d. If the supplier's price goes up to $1.10 per pound, calculate your new cost per portion using the cost factor.

3. You normally buy whole twenty-two pound turkeys at a price of $1.25 per pound. When cut up, they yield ten pounds of breast, six pounds of thighs, four pounds of legs, and two pounds of waste. If the thighs and legs were purchased separately from your supplier at market prices, their costs per pound would be eighty cents and sixty cents, respectively. The breasts are subject to a 25 percent shrinkage in cooking and are served in four-ounce cooked-weight portions.
    a. Calculate the butchered cost per pound of breasts.
    b. Calculate the cost per pound of breasts after cooking.
    c. Calculate the portion cost of breast.
    d. Calculate the cost factor of breast per pound before cooking, per pound after cooking, and per portion.
    e. Using these cost factors, and assuming the supplier's price to you of whole turkeys decreases from $1.25 to $1.15, recalculate the breast cost per pound before cooking, cost per pound after cooking, and cost of a four-ounce cooked-weight portion.

4. Assume that you are the manager of a fast-food chicken restaurant specializing in chicken breasts. Normal usage is five thousand fresh (unfrozen) chicken breasts per week at an average weight before cooking of four ounces each. Present price is four dollars per pound. Your supplier has consistently delivered you a quality product at competitive prices and has offered fair credit terms and reliable service. A poultry-processing plant manager has approached you because the plant is being closed down. He has five thousand pounds of frozen chicken breasts of a five-ounce size that he is prepared to sell you at 25 percent less than your present supplier's price per pound. You have forty-eight hours in which to make your decision. What factors will you consider in making this decision? If you were the restaurant manager, what would your decision be? Explain.

REFERENCES AND SUGGESTED READINGS

Hinich, Melvin J., and Richard Staelin. 1980. *Consumer Protection Legislation and the U.S. Food Industry.* New York: Pergamon, pp. 97–107.

Khan, Mahmood A. 1987. *Foodservice Operations.* Westport, Conn.: AVI, pp. 196–98.

Kotschevar, Lendal H., and Charles Levinson. 1988. *Quantity Food Purchasing.* New York: Macmillan, pp. 282–320.

Maizel, Bruno. 1978. *Food and Beverage Purchasing.* Indianapolis: Bobbs-Merrill, pp. 123–36.

Morgan, William J., Jr. 1988. *Supervision and Management of Quantity Food Preparation*. Berkeley, Calif.: McCutchan, pp. 339–46, 373–76.

Mutkoski, Stephen A., and Marcia L. Schurer. 1981. *Meat and Fish Management*. North Scituate, Mass.: Breton, pp. 114–28.

Peddersen, Raymond B. 1977. *SPECS: The Comprehensive Foodservice Purchasing and Specification Manual*. Boston: Cahners, pp. 239–70.

Peddersen, Raymond B. 1981. *Foodservice and Hotel Purchasing*. Boston: CBI, pp. 89–91, 95–96, 403–22.

Powers, Jo Marie. 1979. *Basics of Quantity Food Production*. New York: Wiley, pp. 108–9.

Powers, Thomas F., and Jo Marie Powers. 1984. *Food Service Operations: Planning and Control*. New York: John Wiley, pp. 118–19.

Stefanelli, John M. 1985. *Purchasing: Selection and Procurement for the Hospitality Industry*. New York: John Wiley, pp. 345–56, 361–73.

U.S. Department of Agriculture. 1971. *Acceptance Service for Poultry and Eggs, Marketing Bulletin No. 46*. Washington, D.C.: USDA.

U.S. Department of Agriculture. 1971. *Regulations Governing the Grading and Inspection of Poultry and Edible Products Thereof and United States Classes, Standards, and Grades with Respect Thereof*. Washington, D.C.: USDA, Agricultural Marketing Service, Poultry Division

U.S. Department of Agriculture. 1978. *Regulations Governing the Grading of Shell Eggs and U.S. Standards, Grades and Weight Classes for Shell Eggs*. 7CFR, Part 56.218 (Table 1). Washington, D.C.: USDA Agricultural Marketing Service, Poultry Division.

U.S. Department of Agriculture. 1978. *Regulations Governing the Voluntary Inspection and Grading of Egg Products*, 7CFR Part 55. Washington, D.C.: USDA, Agricultural Marketing Service, Poultry Division.

U.S. Department of Agriculture. 1978. *Regulations Governing the Grading of Shell Eggs and U.S. Standards, Grades, and Weight Classes for Shell Eggs*, 7CFR Part 56. Washington, D.C.: USDA, Agricultural Marketing Service, Poultry Division.

U.S. Department of Agriculture. 1981. *Labels on Meat and Poultry Products, Information Bulletin #443*. Washington, D.C.: USDA, Food Safety and Quality Service.

U.S. Department of Agriculture, 1981. *Meat and Poultry Inspection, Fact Sheet #18*. Washington, D.C.: USDA, Food Safety and Quality Service.

Virts, William B. 1987. *Purchasing for Hospitality Operations*. East Lansing, MI: The Educational Institute of the American Hotel & Motel Association, pp. 155–75.

11

Fish and Shellfish

OBJECTIVES

- Discuss the difficulty that purchasing fish presents, outline the government inspection services for fishery products, and list the fish grades.
- Differentiate roundfish from flatfish and mollusks from crustaceans, and define the term *shucked*.
- State the grading requirements for processed fish, and explain the acronym PUFI.
- List the items that might appear on a fresh fish specification.
- Explain the terms *round, drawn, dressed, fillet, butterfly fillet, glaze,* and *IQF.*
- Discuss the term *count* with reference to shrimp and other seafood products.
- List the receiving checks that should be carried out for various fishery products.
- Discuss the storage requirements for fresh and frozen fish.

Although canned, frozen, and salted fish are relatively easy to buy, fresh fish is not. Despite the more than a hundred commonly available varieties, seasonal fluctuations in availability and price and the product's perishability make it difficult to purchase. Unlike meat, the quality of fresh fish is not always reliable, suppliers are far fewer, and frequently the choice of products is limited. In other words, restaurants that offer fresh fish on the menu are often in an unpredictable supply situation with regard to both quantity and quality available, unless the operation can use frozen or processed products as a substitute. Traditionally, North Americans (other than in some areas such as New England) have not been big fish eaters. The result has been a general lack of information about fish and shellfish and their suitability as a substitute for meat.

Another complicating factor is that the vast variety of seafood products encourages misleading marketing because the uninformed purchaser has difficulty telling the difference between many fish varieties that seem similar; once fish are skinned and filleted, identification becomes even more difficult. There can be a big difference in price between a cheap variety that can be substituted by an unscrupulous supplier for a more expensive one specified and paid for.

GOVERNMENT INSPECTION

Fish products are not required to be inspected for wholesomeness prior to interstate shipment, as is the case with meat and poultry. Processing plants must produce wholesome and edible products under Food and Drug Administration (FDA) requirements, but inspections are sporadic.

The U.S. Department of Commerce's (USDC) National Marine Fisheries Service (NMFS) does offer an inspection service, but it is voluntary and requires the payment of a fee. As a result, many fishery products are not inspected, although some states and local governments have set up inspection services for fishery items arriving from outside the state. According to the *Wall Street Journal,* the NMFS inspects only about 10 percent of the total seafood produced.

Plants that are inspected for sanitary conditions can be approved and listed in the USDC's biannual publication *Approved List of Sanitary Inspected Fish Establishments,* which is available to interested purchasers. Approved plants are allowed to display on their product packages the NMFS stamp, "Packed under Federal Inspection." This stamp (often referred to as the *PUFI seal)* is illustrated in Figure 11-1.

The U.S. Public Health Service (USPHS) is involved in bivalve fishery products such as clams, mussels, and oysters, along with some other seafood products. These products are often taken from polluted areas. As a result, what they ingest is very susceptible to the growth of pathogenic bacteria. They receive special USPHS attention to ensure that they are not tainted.

Figure 11-1.   Fish "packed under federal inspection" (PUFI) stamp (*Source:* National Marine Fisheries Service).

Quality Grades

The NMFS provides a quality-grading service for fish products in a similar way that the USDA does for other foods. This grading service is voluntary. Grading standards to date are available for only a relatively few types of fish.

Fish that is graded must first be inspected; in other words, if it has not been inspected, the NMFS will not grade it. A grade stamp on a product signifies that it is

- Clean, safe, and wholesome
- Of a specified quality identified by the appropriate U.S. grade designation determined by a federal inspector
- Produced in an acceptable establishment, with proper equipment and in an appropriate processing environment
- Processed under supervision by federal food inspectors and packed by sanitary food handlers
- Truthfully and accurately labeled with its common or usual name

Some purchasers do not realize that fishery items do not undergo the same strict grading service as meat. Where a fishery product is graded, inspectors normally check for appearance, size, color, odor, shell tightness for shellfish, and origin of product. Origin is important because even though a fish may bear the same name, its origin can affect such things as texture and flavor. Many buyers state the product origin they require in specifications.

Three grades are available for federally graded fish products:

Grade A: top or best quality. Products are uniform in size, practically free of blemishes and defects, in excellent condition, and possess good flavor for the species.

Grade B: good quality. Products may not be as uniform in size or as free from blemishes or defects as Grade A.

Grade C: fairly good quality. Products are just as wholesome and nutritious as higher grades. They are good value for money if appearance is not important.

Note that Grade B or C products are usually marketed without any grade designation. Figure 11-2 illustrates the grading stamp in the shape of a shield.

Some fish packers avoid the inspection and grading program because it costs them money that they would then have to pass on in higher costs to intermediaries and then to foodservice purchasers. Other packers establish their own internal grading systems in the same way that some meat processors do. However, the purchaser has to question how objective this type of grading is.

Figure 11-2.   Fish grading stamp (*Source:* National Marine Fisheries Service).

TYPES OF FISHERY PRODUCTS

In broad terms, fishery products can be categorized into fish and shellfish.

Fish

Fish can be generally categorized into either freshwater or saltwater varieties. Most fish purchased by foodservice operations, however, is of the saltwater variety, although some freshwater farm-raised fish (such as trout) are available.

Fish can also be categorized into *roundfish* (such as salmon or haddock) and *flatfish* (such as sole, flounder, halibut, and turbot). Most fish are of the round category. Flatfish are usually found on the bottom of coastal shelves. They are oval in shape with both eyes on the same side of the head. Flatfish have a lean, white flesh and a mild, delicate flavor.

Some fish are also described as lean fish (that is, they are low in fat, such as red snapper) and fat fish (such as salmon).

Most foodservice operations do not offer a wide range of fish products (unless they are specialty seafood restaurants), probably because for most North American consumers it has not traditionally been a popular product, and consumers are familiar with the names of only the most common and expensive products. The astute hospitality purchaser will, of course, seek out unfamiliar fish because many of them have the same taste and other characteristics as more popular varieties, and they can usually be purchased at a lower price because they are not in great demand. Common fish are:

Bluefish	Red snapper
Catfish	Salmon
Cod	Shad
Flounder	Sole

Haddock	Swordfish
Halibut	Trout
Mackerel	Tuna
Perch	Turbot
Pike	Whitefish
Pollock	Whiting (Hake)

Further information about each of these fish can be found in appendix A.

Shellfish

Shellfish are differentiated from finfish by their hard outer shells and by their lack of a backbone or internal skeleton. The term *shellfish* is used to cover two broad categories of sea food: mollusks (true shellfish with hard shells) and crustaceans (animals with segmented shells and jointed legs). Mollusks are animals that live inside a shell. Although some mollusks have no shell (such as squid and octopus), they are not commonly used in restaurants. Mollusks include abalone, clams, oysters, scallops, and snails. Crustaceans include crabs, crayfish, lobsters, and shrimp. Members of these two categories are available in a variety of forms. For example, clams, crabs, lobsters, and oysters are often purchased live in the shell, can be cooked for immediate use, or can be cooked and then chilled or frozen for later use. The meat of crabs, lobsters, and shrimp can also be purchased precooked without the shell. Clams, oysters, and scallops are available in shucked form (the term *shucked* means fresh meat removed from the shell). Finally, crustaceans such as shrimp and lobster are available in headless form, that is, only the tail is purchased.

Further information about shellfish can be found in appendix B.

Processed Fish

Processed fishery products are available in many forms: canned, frozen, dried, smoked, salted, and even portion-controlled such as in fish patties and fish sticks. Fresh fish does not carry a brand name, although most processed fishery products do. Indeed, for processed products the brand name may be the only guide to quality consistency. Although most processed items are not graded, some (such as fish sticks and raw breaded shrimp) do carry the grade A or B designation. Some processed canned and frozen items also bear the PUFI stamp (Figure 11-1) to show they have been inspected and have achieved an acceptable commercial quality level, even if they are not graded. A quality brand name, combined with the PUFI seal, is the purchaser's best guarantee of quality for these items.

Fishery Product Prices

The NMFS, as well as promoting the use of fish products and providing inspection services, also publishes the *Fishery Market News Report,* which provides statistical information relating to catch sizes and prices and also trends in fishery products. Urner Barry Publications produces the *Seafood Price-Current* five times a week. A sample of this publication is illustrated in Figure 11-3.

Knowing the seasonality of various fishery products is important to purchasers. Seasonality affects supply and demand (and thus prices), with prices the lowest during the peak catching season. Purchasers should therefore know when these seasons are for each variety, and adjust their menus as frequently as possible to capitalize on low purchase prices. Adaptability to alternative sizes, forms, sources, and even other varieties when necessary or when high prices prohibit the use of a certain product is essential.

Considering quantity buying of processed products may also be useful because if these are purchased in the peak season of availability, a considerable saving can be made by purchasing, for example, a six- or twelve-month supply and then storing and using it as required. Some frozen fish suppliers provide this service with only a minimum charge for storage at their location.

Unlike processed (for example, canned) fruit and vegetables, often the price spread between one packer's brand and the next is not large. Although quality and price go hand in hand with many other products, this rule is not necessarily true of processed fish products. In other cases, a large difference in price may mean little difference in quality. For example, the price difference between two brands of canned salmon can be quite large, yet the only difference in quality is color. If such products are to be used in sandwiches or salads, most consumers are probably not too concerned about color.

PURCHASING FISH

Compared to meat and poultry products, public domain fishery industry specifications for fish and shellfish provide minimum information. They are not well defined and lack uniformity. Neither consumers generally nor the hospitality industry in particular have pressured the government and suppliers to produce more precise standards. The fishing industry is also very fragmented and made up primarily of many small fishers and other entrepreneurs in the distribution chain. Fishing is also an international industry. A great deal of fish consumed in the United States is imported, and the quality of the fish is often dictated by the traditional practices of fish-exporting countries, although the NMFS is responsible for inspecting imported fish and shellfish.

Specifications

The NMFS produces *Institutional Purchasing Specifications for the Purchasing of Fresh, Frozen, and Canned Fishery Products,* which provides purchasers with guidelines for competitive bidding and some general specifications that can be added to

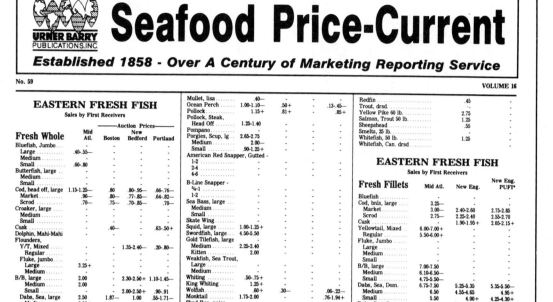

Figure 11-3. *Urner Barry's Seafood Price-Current* (Courtesy of Urner Barry Publications, Inc., Toms River, N.J.).

by individual purchasers to meet their own establishment's requirements. The most important step in purchasing fishery products is to specify the desired quality. Although this step may not be too meaningful for some fresh fish because the purchaser has little choice but to accept or reject the quality available from what may be the only supplier, specifications can still be useful. For example, purchasers can provide their supplier with these specifications and ask that they be advised when a shipment is available that meets them.

In specifications, the purchaser should

- Make sure that the fish packer-supplier is on the NMFS "approved" list of inspected plants.
- Require that the supplier meet at least the minimum NMFS Grade A standards for products that presently have standards.
- State the need for PUFI labeling if appropriate.
- Use fishery industry terminology (discussed below) in specifications. This terminology mainly concerns how fish is prepared.
- State the exact species (for example, "gray sole" or "lemon sole," and not simply "sole").
- State the market form (for example, whole or eviscerated for finfish, alive or shucked for shellfish, or frozen and breaded for fishsticks).
- State the tolerance allowed (for example, fish sticks in two-ounce portions with a 5 percent tolerance; that is, each portion can be 5 percent more or less than two ounces).
- State the country of origin, where appropriate.
- If a choice is possible, state whether the product required is to be wild or fish farmed.
- Use the brand name, if appropriate, for processed products.
- List the size, range of size, or count required for shellfish.
- Where appropriate, state the required percentage of breading or batter.
- State the packaging instructions, such as breaded shrimp to be in three-pound boxes packed in cartons, each containing eight boxes, with each carton to show the date when packed.
- State the shipping method and state of refrigeration required, including temperatures.
- List the freshness conditions required (for flesh, eyes, skin, and so forth).

Fish Terminology

The purchaser should be familiar with certain words and terms used in the fish industry. The more common ones and their meanings are:

- *Round:* a fish as it is taken from the water, sometimes without the head.
- *Drawn:* a whole fish that has been eviscerated (that is, with entrails, gills, and scales removed; as entrails cause rapid spoilage, drawn fish have a longer storage life).
- *Dressed* or *pan-dressed:* completely cleaned (but sometimes with the head still on) and ready to cook.
- *Fillet:* the meaty side of the fish cut parallel to the backbone. Round fish (such as cod) have two fillets. Flat fish (such as sole) have four fillets.
- *Butterfly fillets:* two single fillets held together by a small piece of skin. This form provides a better plate presentation. Shrimp is sometimes described as *butterflied* when it is partially split down the center.
- *Breaded fillets:* fillets with a seasoned crumb coating.
- *Fish sticks:* uniform portions cut from frozen blocks of fish and then covered with a seasoned crumb coating. Sticks may also be made from minced flesh.
- *Breaded portions:* uniform serving portions cut from frozen blocks or fillets and then covered with a seasoned crumb coating.
- *Steaks:* cross-grain cuts (at right angles to the backbone) of large round fish such as halibut and salmon.
- *Individually quick frozen (IQF) portion:* separately frozen, individual pieces of fish or seafood (such as shrimp).
- *Individually quick frozen (IQF) block:* the product is frozen into a solid block (rather than having pieces individually frozen) and sold in blocks, usually with a minimum weight of five pounds ranging up to sixteen pounds. Most headless shrimp are sold in IQF blocks.
- *Glaze:* most frozen products that have had their skin or shell removed are generally lightly ice-glazed. This process protects them from dehydration.
- *Headless shrimp:* sometimes referred to as *shell on*, meaning the head has been removed, leaving the tail. This type of shrimp is known as *green (raw) shrimp*.
- *Count:* the way many products are sold. Count is the number per pound (for example, 16/20 means from sixteen to twenty in a pound). Count means the number of thawed, drained pieces of a product per pound. It can be checked by counting the number of pieces in a pound or by weighing the number of pieces stated in the count. Note, however, that with shrimp, count is used to designate a particular size of shrimp and means the number of green (unpeeled) headless shrimp that would make up a pound, even if the shrimp are peeled and deveined or cooked. Because the weight loss in peeling and deveining shrimp is about 25 percent, a pound of 21/25 shrimp will contain twenty-five to thirty (and not twenty-one to twenty-five). Cooking loss is another 25 percent; thus, a pound of 21/25 peeled, deveined, and cooked (PDC) shrimp contains forty-two to fifty shrimp. With very small sizes (ninety and higher), count refers to the actual number of pieces. Similarly, breaded shrimp counts also refer to the actual number

of shrimp in a pound, and not the original unbreaded size of the shrimp. Sometimes count is expressed as size per item. For example, a 4/6 lobster tail means that each tail is in a range between four and six ounces.

FISHERY PRODUCT YIELDS

As with meat and poultry, boning, trimming, and cooking tests may be useful to determine the net yield of a particular product from two or more suppliers or, alternatively, the net yield from two different species or varieties that can be substituted for each other. The objective of these yield tests is to see which product provides the best value for money.

Fish, like meat, is paid for by the pound and sold by the portion. For example, fish weight yield from fish purchased whole and then converted to fillets can be as low as 30 percent (70 percent wastage) from an item like perch; yield can also be as high as 65 percent (35 percent wastage) from an item like salmon converted to "steaks." Therefore, yield tests on various menu fishery items are necessary in order to calculate cost per portion.

Cost Factors

The calculation of cost factors is also an aid to quick recalculation of portion costs of fishery items when the supplier's selling price increases or decreases. (See chapter 9 for a discussion of yields and cost factors.)

Shellfish Counts

Counts for some types of shellfish (such as shrimp, prawns, and scallops) must also be carefully controlled. These items are generally purchased in counts per pound, such as 18–22 (or 18/22) for scallops, meaning as few as eighteen and as many as twenty-two per pound. On average, the count should be twenty; if portion cost calculations are based on twenty and on average the supplier provides this count per pound, cost per portion will remain as it is supposed to be.

Suppose, for example, that the cost of scallops is $9.20 per pound for 18–22 count. Average cost for each scallop is

$$\frac{\$9.20}{20} = \$0.46$$

If five scallops are served as the portion count in a scallop cocktail appetizer, portion cost is $2.30 (5 × $0.46). If the selling price for this portion is $6.00, food cost is

$$\frac{\$2.30}{\$6.00} \times 100 = 38.3\%$$

and gross profit (selling price less cost) per portion will be $3.70 (less the cost of any other ingredients served with that scallop cocktail).

If the supplier's delivered count is consistently eighteen (rather than an average of twenty), cost per scallop increases to

$$\frac{\$9.60}{18} = \$0.53 \text{ (to the nearest cent)}$$

and food cost climbs to

$$5 \times \$0.53 = \$2.65$$

or

$$\frac{\$2.65}{\$6.00} \times 100 = 44.2\%$$

and gross profit per portion drops to $3.35. This change reduces net profit by thirty-five cents for every scallop cocktail sold, which can amount to a large decline in net profit over a year.

Breaded Products

The government standard on raw breaded portions is 25 percent breading to 75 percent fish; for oven-finished portions it is 35 percent breading for 65 percent fish. Battered portions are 50 percent battering to 50 percent fish. These federal standards also specify the procedure to be used to determine these percentages so that purchasers can make product comparisons. The five steps are

1. Select enough pieces at random from the packages to weigh about one pound. If a significant amount of loose breading is in the packages, include a fair proportion of it with the sample.
2. Weigh the pieces immediately (before moisture condenses on them or they begin to thaw) on a scale accurate to 0.1 ounces.
3. Place the breaded pieces in a tepid water bath until the breading falls off or can be easily removed by hand. The larger the sample, the longer the dip.
4. Remove from water, blot lightly with toweling, scrape off breading, and weigh the debreaded portions.
5. Calculate the percentage of fish

$$\frac{\text{Weight of debreaded fish}}{\text{Weight of breaded fish}} \times 100 = \text{Percentage of fish}$$

For example, if the weight of debreaded fish were 11.8 ounces out of a 15.6-ounce sample, the percentage of fish is

$$\frac{11.8}{15.6} \times 100 = 75.6\%$$

and the amount of breading is therefore 24.4%.

The same procedure can be used for battered products, as well as for breaded shrimp and scallops. With breaded shrimp, the federal standards allow a 5 percentage point tolerance to compensate for the method's inaccuracy. In other words, add 5 percentage points to the calculated amount of shrimp, and deduct 5 percentage points from the calculated amount of breading.

Purchasers also have to calculate the cost of unbreaded (or unbattered) fish to make price comparisons between the net yields of different suppliers' products. A lightly breaded product normally commands a higher price because it has more high-priced fish and less low-priced breading.

For example, assume that a breaded fish product cost is ninety cents per pound, that it contains 30 percent breading, and that the present cost of breading is thirty cents per pound. To determine the price per pound of unbreaded fish, the following six steps can be used:

1. Multiply the cost of one pound of breading by the percent of breading to obtain the cost of breading used in the product.

$$\$0.30 \times 30\% = \$0.09$$

2. Multiply sixteen ounces by the percent of breading to obtain the number of ounces of breading.

$$16 \text{ ounces} \times 30\% = 4.8 \text{ oz}$$

3. Subtract the number of ounces of breading from sixteen ounces to obtain the number of ounces of unbreaded fish.

$$16 \text{ ounces} - 4.8 \text{ ounces} = 11.2 \text{ ounces}$$

4. Subtract the cost of breading (see step 1) from the cost of the product to obtain the cost of unbreaded fish in the product.

$$\$0.90 - \$0.09 = \$0.81$$

5. Divide the cost of unbreaded fish by the number of ounces of unbreaded fish to obtain the cost of one ounce of unbreaded product.

$$\frac{\$0.81}{11.2} = \$0.072$$

6. Multiply the cost of one ounce of unbreaded fish by sixteen ounces to get the cost of one pound of unbreaded fish.

$$\$0.072 \times 16 = \$1.15$$

Glazed Products

Tests should also be carried out on glazed products. If an entire package is deglazed, the net deglazed weight should be as stated on the package. However, if a test is done on only a portion of the package, the following two steps are necessary:

1. Divide the deglazed weight of the portion by the glazed weight of that same portion. For example, if a block of shrimp weighed 6.25 pounds (100 ounces) before deglazing, and the test portion weighed 1.5 pounds (24 ounces) before deglazing and 1.25 pounds (20 ounces) after deglazing, the net weight of the glazed portion would be

$$\frac{20}{24} \times 100 = 83\%$$

of the glazed weight.

2. Multiply that percentage by the glazed weight of the total package to obtain the net deglazed weight of the total package.

$$100 \text{ ounces} \times 83\% = 83 \text{ ounces or 5 pounds, 3 ounces}$$

RECEIVING

Fish and shellfish are delicate and highly perishable products. They must be verified properly on receipt and then quickly stored. In receiving fish, some general factors to check are

• Make sure the product is delivered in a refrigerated truck (for fresh products) or a freezer truck (for frozen products).

- Check for excess ice. Also verify that the case weight printed on the outside is for the weight of the product after it is removed from ice. Some products lose or absorb liquids (moisture migration). This process should be minimal in most fresh products. Net weight should not vary more than 6 percent from the stated weight. Scallops tend to lose more moisture than most fresh seafoods, and the common industry practice is to overpack them so that, even when drained, the net weight is close to the stated weight. Note, however, that fresh-shucked oysters should not be drained before weighing because the liquid in which they are packed is their natural liquid and considered an integral part of the product. This liquid should, nevertheless, not represent more than 8 percent of the weight of the product.
- Count containers or packages and check for leakage damage or spots of dried moisture that could indicate thawing and then refreezing of frozen products.
- Where appropriate or specified, check for brands, federal inspections, and/or PUFI stamps.
- Open each container to ensure that live or fresh products still have ice intact, that frozen products are still frozen solid, and that no offensive odor is detected in any container.
- Randomly unwrap individual fish, fillets, or frozen blocks of product, and check for temperature, quality, weight or count, and correct species.
- Check the case date to ensure that the product is recent.
- Do not accept any undesirable products.
- For items purchased by count, make sure the count is correct.
- Verify that items such as shrimp do not contain an excess of broken pieces.
- For items that are breaded, ensure that the breading-to-product ratio is as specified.

In addition to these general guidelines, further receiving checks should be made for fishery products received in each particular form.

Fresh Fish

The following checks should be made when receiving fresh fishery items:

- *Species.* A major problem with fresh fish is that, if the receiver is not qualified, a cheaper variety could be substituted by a supplier for the item specified. For example, a dishonest supplier could substitute flounder for lemon sole, cod for haddock, or ocean perch for red snapper. For the same reason as in meat receiving, the chef is usually present during the receiving process.
- *Odor.* Odor is the primary check for freshness. Fresh fish should not have a "fishy" smell but should smell fresh and pleasant. If a fishy odor is detectable, the

fish is not fresh. The longer it is out of water, the worse this smell will be. Fresh fish should be received in crushed or shaved ice, which can help the fish retain its freshness. The fishy taste that some fish have after cooking (and that discourages some people from eating it) is actually a sign of decomposition that should have been detected by smell before the fish was cooked.

- *Eyes.* The eyes of fresh fish should be clear, bright, round, and building, with no hint of dullness or sinking.
- *Scales.* They should be tight to the skin and shiny.
- *Gills.* They should be clean, be pink or red, and not sticky. Gray or brown color indicates that the fish is not fresh.
- *Flesh.* Fresh fish should not feel slimy. Flesh should be firm and elastic. Soft or easily dented flesh is a sign that the fish is not fresh. Note, however, that most freshwater fish have more natural surface slime present than their saltwater counterparts.
- *Headed and gutted fish.* They should have the same general quality characteristics that apply to whole fish except that some of the quality indicators (eyes and gills) are missing. Receivers should watch for such things as body cavity cuts, incomplete evisceration, improper heading, and indication of belly burn (caused by gut enzymes softening the bones and meat).
- *Fillets and steaks.* Fresh fish purchased in filleted or steak form should be firm, bright, moist, and without any bruises or brown or blood spots. Fillets should be packed flat with skin side down and have paper layered between each fillet. In addition, fillets and steak should not have cutting and trimming imperfections, should be without bones (if specified), should have complete skin removal (if specified), and should be consistent in size.
- *Dryness.* If the fish appears to be drier than normal, it could be thawed, previously frozen fish being passed off as fresh fish. Previously frozen fish sold as fresh can also be spotted in whole fish by the sunken appearance of the eyes and by the gray gills. Sometimes suppliers sell previously frozen fillets as fresh ones after first soaking them in salt water, which makes the substitution difficult to detect. Previously frozen fillet steaks are more difficult to detect, but an experienced receiver can tell by their feel.
- *Packaging.* Fish purchased fresh should be in airtight containers refrigerated at about 32°F (0°C).
- *Weight.* Weigh acceptable fish to see that it conforms to the purchase order and requisition, and then move it immediately to refrigerator storage. Fresh fish that is not stored under refrigeration deteriorates rapidly.

Fresh Shellfish

Some specific tests for fresh shellfish are

- *Odor.* Odor should not be offensive.
- *Shells.* Shells should be tightly closed for clams, mussels, and oysters. If they are open and do not close tight when tapped, the shellfish is dead and should not be accepted.
- *Movement.* Movement is important for live lobsters and crabs. If they do not move, they are no longer fresh. Shells of lobsters should be hard.
- *Packaging.* Packaging should include a covering of moist seaweed or paper.
- *Fresh shrimp.* Flesh should be firm, with a bright pink or white color.
- *Fresh-shucked products.* Oysters and clams should be completely covered with their own natural juices. Oyster color should be creamy, and clams a light pinkish yellow. Note, however, that oyster color can vary depending on what the oyster has been eating. Color can be tan, brown, green, yellow, or red. Fresh-shucked scallops should be firm, without excess liquid, and a creamy white, light tan, or pinkish color.
- *Temperatures.* Live shellfish should be shipped at between 40 and 45°F (4–7°C).
- *Cooked products.* Crabs, lobsters, and shrimp sold cooked in the shell should be either chilled or frozen, depending on specifications. Shell should be bright red and meat snowy white. The odor should not be off.

Partially Processed Shellfish

Partially processed shellfish include items such as green (raw) headless shrimp. The checks are

- Flesh when depressed with a finger should be resilient and return to its original form.
- Color should be consistent.

Frozen Products

Frozen items account for more of the fish served in most restaurants today than any other form of fishery products. Only in this form can they be made as readily available as they are across the country. Specific checks for frozen fishery products are

- Products should be solidly frozen and not thawed when received.
- Check that frozen items such as shellfish have not been thawed and then refrozen. Packages that contain excessive ice formation at the bottom of the box could indicate that the item was thawed and then refrozen. Again, this practice is sometimes difficult to detect if the defrosted products have been washed in sea-

water and then packed in bags with ice and refrozen by the supplier prior to delivery.

- The product should have little or no odor. A fishy smell indicates that the product should not be accepted.
- Products should be well packaged with no sign of freezer burn. Frozen products, when thawed, should have the same odor and texture characteristics as their fresh counterparts.
- Packaging should be free of air that would cause dehydration and posible freezer burn.
- If products have been glazed to prevent them from drying out, check that the glaze is still present by its shine and that it has not melted off or evaporated. Only the weight without the glaze should be paid for. These items should be randomly sampled by removing the glaze and then weighing, as discussed earlier.
- Specifications for breaded products should state the amount of breading as a percentage of the finished product. This percentage should then be randomly tested, as discussed earlier.
- IQF portion or block packages should list both the gross (with ice) and net (free of ice) weights. These items should be randomly sampled by thawing and checking the net weight.

Smoked Products

Smoked products should have a bright, glossy appearance. The texture should be firm and springy to the touch. The odor should be clean and smoky.

Canned Products

For canned products, check that the cans have no damage. Do not accept swollen cans. In the case of sauced products and seafood cocktails, the seafood content must be percentage labeled.

Sample Tests

When tests are conducted (for example, for the gross versus net weight of frozen or breaded items), these tests can be carried out by the receiver, the chef, or the chef's delegate. Products from new suppliers should be checked regularly until suppliers have established their credibility. Although some deviations (both plus and minus) can be expected, minus deviations that show up in all tests are indicative that the supplier is unreliable and should not continue to be used. If the results from tests show substantial shortfalls, then the cash value of these shortfalls should be deducted from supplier invoices before paying them.

Storage

After receiving and inspecting any fish, those that show any signs of spoilage before storing should be rejected. According to Gisslen (1983, p. 308), the three objectives in storing fresh fish are

1. To keep the fish moist
2. To prevent fish odors and flavors from being transferred to other foods
3. To protect the delicate flesh from being bruised or crushed

To achieve these objectives, whole or drawn fish should not be wrapped but should be rinsed with ice water before storing. Fillets, steaks, or other fish portions should also be rinsed in ice water and then wrapped or left in their original moistureproof wrapping. Fillets and steaks should be stored on ice but without direct contact with it to prevent loss of soluble food elements. All containers holding fresh fish on ice should have openings at the bottom for drainage. If fresh fish is bought in round or whole form, it must be gutted and cleaned before storage. Whole fish should be stored vertically with the head lower than the tail to allow for better drainage.

Wherever possible, store fresh fish in its own refrigerator. Fresh fish refrigerator storage temperature should be about 32°F (0°C), with a humidity of about 65 percent where this can be controlled. Space limitations may preclude a separate fish refrigerator, and products may have to be stored with other produce that may require a refrigerator temperature of about 40°F (4°C). In that case, store the fish in crushed or shaved ice in the refrigerator, particularly if it is to be kept for a day or two before use. Fresh fish should be stored for only one or two days. If it is to be kept longer, then it should be wrapped and frozen on receipt or cooked and then refrigerated for use in recipes requiring cooked fish.

Frozen products need to be stored at 0°F (-18°C) or lower. They should be well wrapped to prevent freezer burn. Never allow frozen fish to stand at room temperature between delivery and storage. Taste and texture of refrozen seafood is noticeably inferior. In the freezer, stack frozen seafood packages away from walls, ceiling, and floor to improve air circulation. Maximum storage time for fat fish is six months and for lean fish twelve months. As with fresh fish, stock rotation should be used.

Thawing frozen fishery products should be done under refrigeration and not at room temperature. In an emergency, fish can be defrosted if kept in its wrapping and thawed under cold running water. Cut fish (steaks and fillets, for example) can be cooked directly from the frozen state; if these items are to be breaded before cooking, breading can be done while they are partially thawed because they are easier to handle this way. Thawed, previously frozen fish should be handled like fresh fish and be used within a day or so. It should never be refrozen.

Some hard shellfish (clams, oysters, and mussels) are sometimes purchased live and packed in barrels that can contain a lot of dirt. In such cases, remove these products from the barrels, clean them, and then store them in different containers filled with the original strained liquid. Do not let these live products come into contact with any fresh water or ice, which will kill them. Fresh shucked oysters, however, should be stored with ice in the container.

Unfrozen smoked fish products should be kept refrigerated at 32°F (0°C). Most of these products today are only lightly smoked because most consumers do not want them heavily smoked. As a result, their maximum storage time is only a few days.

Issuing

The main consideration in issuing fish from storage (as is the case with meat) is proper stock rotation; that is, products received first should be issued first to reduce the possibility of spoilage. When fish is issued, it should again be checked for freshness to ensure that it has not deteriorated during storage. No more than is absolutely necessary for each meal's production should be issued to kitchens because in the heat of production areas fish spoil rapidly. Needless handling of fish also spreads bacteria and speeds up deterioration of fish quality. Remember also that fish are high in water (as much as 80 percent for some shellfish such as shrimp), and they lose a significant amount of this weight if they are extensively handled.

DISCUSSION QUESTIONS

1. Explain why purchasing fresh fish is more difficult than purchasing meat or poultry.
2. Discuss the government inspection services for fishery products.
3. List the grades for fish, and state what these grades imply.
4. Differentiate between roundfish and flatfish, and give an example of each.
5. Differentiate between mollusks and crustaceans, and give an example of each.
6. What is a shucked shellfish?
7. State the grading requirement for processed fish, and explain the acronym PUFI.
8. List five items that should appear on a specification for fresh fish.
9. Explain each of the terms *round, drawn,* and *dressed.*
10. Differentiate between a fillet and a butterfly fillet.
11. Explain the acronym IQF.
12. What is glaze on a fish?
13. Discuss the term *count* with reference to certain fishery products.
14. List five general checks that should be carried out when receiving fish.
15. List five specific checks that should be carried out when receiving fresh fish.

16. List three specific checks that should be carried out when receiving fresh shell-fish.
17. List five specific checks that should be carried out when receiving frozen fish.
18. Discuss the storage requirements for fresh fish.
19. Discuss the storage requirements for frozen fish.

PROBLEMS

1. You are conducting salmon purchasing tests from two different suppliers. Supplier A can provide whole five-pound fish at a price of $3.15 per pound, and after trimming and cooking the yield of usable fish for steaks is 45 percent. Supplier B can provide whole four-pound fish at a price of $3.05 per pound, and after trimming and cooking the yield of usable fish for steaks is 40 percent.
    a. Based on yield, which supplier's price provides better value?
    b. Before making the decision to buy from one supplier or the other, what other factors might you consider?

2. Assume that you are presently buying haddock for a fish and chip menu item. The supplier's price is $2.40 per pound. Average fish size is five pounds, and when trimmed and cooked usable fish yield is 40 percent.
    a. How many cooked-weight four-ounce portions of haddock can be served per fish?
    b. What is the portion cost?
    c. What is the portion-cost factor?
    d. If the supplier's haddock price increases to $2.60 per pound, calculate the new portion cost using the cost factor.

3. You purchase PDC breaded shrimp in package sizes of 26–30 at a price of $5.60 per package. The shrimp is served in a cocktail appetizer using six shrimp per portion at a selling price of $4.95.
    a. Calculate the portion cost, portion cost percent, and gross profit per portion.
    b. Tests reveal that the average content of each package shows a count of only twenty-six. Calculate the effect of this on portion cost, portion cost percent, and gross profit per portion.

4. You presently buy a breaded fish stick at a cost of $1.25 per pound. Breading content is 25 percent, and present cost of breading is 32¢ per pound. Calculate the price per pound of unbreaded fish sticks.

5. A block of glazed shrimp is being tested for glaze. The glazed block weighs 9.5 pounds. The test-piece portion weighs 1.25 pounds with glaze and one pound after deglazing. Calculate the net deglazed weight of the complete block.

REFERENCES AND SUGGESTED READINGS

Dore, Ian. 1982. *Frozen Seafood: The Buyer's Handbook, A Guide to Profitable Buying for Commercial Users*. Huntington, N.Y.: Osprey.

Dougherty, Jack. 1976. *Institutional Purchasing Specification for the Purchasing of Fresh, Frozen and Canned Fishery Products*. Washington, D.C.: U.S. Department of Commerce, National Marine Fisheries Service.

Gisslen, Wayne. 1983. *Professional Cooking*. New York: John Wiley.

Khan, Mahmood A. 1987. *Foodservice Operations*. Westport, Conn.: AVI, pp. 200–201.

Kotschevar, Lendal H., and Charles Levinson. 1988. *Quantity Food Purchasing*. New York: Macmillan, pp. 322–89.

Maizel, Bruno. 1978. *Food and Beverage Purchasing*. Indianapolis: Bobbs-Merrill, pp. 115–22.

Morgan, William J. Jr. 1988. *Supervision and Management of Quantity Food Preparation*. Berkeley, Calif.: McCutchan, pp. 346–56.

Mutkoski, Stephen A., and Marcia L. Schurer. 1981. *Meat and Fish Management*. North Scituate, Mass.: Breton, pp. 129–62.

Peddersen, Raymond B. 1977. *SPECS: The Comprehensive Foodservice Purchasing and Specification Manual*. Boston: Cahners, pp. 311–60.

Peddersen, Raymond B. 1981. *Foodservice and Hotel Purchasing*. Boston: CBI, pp. 86–88, 385–401.

Powers, Jo Marie. 1979. *Basics of Quantity Food Production*. New York: Wiley, pp. 109–17.

Powers, Thomas F., and Jo Marie Powers. 1984. *Food Service Operations: Planning and Control*. New York: John Wiley, pp. 120–22.

Stefanelli, John M. 1985. *Purchasing: Selection and Procurement for the Hospitality Industry*. New York: John Wiley, pp. 377–89.

U.S. Department of Commerce. *Approved List of Sanitary Inspected Fish Establishments*. Washington, D.C.: National Marine Fisheries Service (semiannual).

U.S. Department of Commerce. 1977. *Regulations Governing Processed Fishery Products, Title 50 and U.S. Standards for Grades of Fishery Products*. Washington, D.C.: National Marine Fisheries Service.

Virts, William B. 1987. *Purchasing for Hospitality Operations*. East Lansing, Mich.: The Educational Institute of the American Hotel & Motel Association, pp. 131–54.

Wagenvoord, James, and Woodman Harris. 1983. *The Complete Seafood Book*. New York: Macmillan.

Wall Street Journal. 1989. Digging for Fast Profit: Fishermen Harvest Much Tainted Shellfish. June 8, p. 1.

12

Dairy Products

OBJECTIVES

- Explain how the government attempts to keep dairy products supply and demand in balance, and discuss government milk product standards.
- Define *homogenized whole-fluid milk,* and differentiate between evaporated and condensed milk.
- List the four commonly used types of milk, and state their fat content.
- List the three common fermented-milk products, and briefly describe each.
- List and briefly describe the major categories of cheese, and identify specific types of cheese and their origins.
- Discuss various types of frozen desserts, such as ice cream, sherbet, water ice, and sorbet, and define the term *overrun* with reference to ice cream.
- List the receiving checks that should be made for butter, ice cream, and cheese.

In recent years, technological advances in dairy product processing, refrigeration, and transportation methods have resulted in increased dairy product quality stability, distribution, and availability.

GOVERNMENT REGULATIONS

Milk, which is the basic ingredient of all dairy products, is regulated under the U.S. Public Health Service Milk Ordinance and Code and administered under the U.S. Food and Drug Administation (FDA). Even though each state has its own legislation concerning milk production, all state statutes meet minimum federal requirements. Federal standards apply not only to processing plants but also to dairy herds, interstate shipments, imported products, pasteurization and handling of milk during production, and milk holding temperatures.

Product Pricing

Federal and state dairy product legislation affects product pricing. Even though cows produce more milk in spring and summer than at other times of the year, the demand for milk is relatively stable throughout the entire year. Theoretically, therefore, supply and demand are seldom in balance, and the price should go up and down accordingly. Government price stabilization helps the industry to cope with this imbalance. For example, federal marketing orders (published monthly by the USDA for each separate jurisdiction) set the prices that milk producers are paid for their products. In addition, many states set resale prices and penalize producers if they offer price discounts to increase demand. Finally, the government buys surplus products such as butter, cheese, and powdered milk to ensure a stable supply.

Both federal and state governments also use price supports to equalize prices, increase competition within the industry, and help small local producers to compete with larger producers who may have cost advantages as a result of economies of scale. Despite all this, the government sometimes encounters difficulties in keeping supply and demand in balance. Because the government purchases surplus products, producers are encouraged to overproduce, knowing they will receive an adequate price.

Product Standards

Milk and milk product standards are established by the federal government and revised annually. These standards cover such things as minimum butterfat content, a minimum nonfat milk solids content, and minimum moisture content (for example, in cheese and powdered milk). These standards are listed in Table 12-1. Producers are, nevertheless, free to produce products that exceed minimum standards. For example, the minimum butterfat content of ice cream is 10 percent, but ice cream products are available at much higher butterfat levels than that.

MILK

Whole-fluid milk is fresh milk as it is taken from the cow with nothing removed and only Vitamin D added. Most whole-fluid milk is produced and sold locally, which helps to minimize transportation costs and therefore prices. All whole-fluid milk must meet federal standards that require it to be free of undesirable flavor, contain no less than 8.25 percent nonfat solids, contain 3.25 percent butterfat, and be pure and unmixed (unadulterated with other ingredients).

Whole-fluid milk is pasteurized, that is, heated to about 160°F (71°C) and then

Table 12-1. Minimum Federal Standards for Butterfat and Nonfat Percent Content of Dairy Products

Product	Minimum Butterfat (%)	Minimum Nonfat Milk Solids (%)
Fluid whole milk	3.25	8.25
Homogenized milk	3.25	8.25
Two-percent milk	2.0	10.0
Skimmed milk	0.5	7.75
Buttermilk	0.5	8.25
Evaporated whole milk	7.5	18.0
Evaporated skim milk	0.2	18.0
Condensed milk	8.5	19.5
Whole dry milk	26.0	In the product (5 percent moisture maximum)
Nonfat dry milk	1.5	In the product (5 percent moisture maximum)
Table cream	18.0	8.25
Half-and-half cream	10.5	8.25
Light whipping cream	30.0	8.25
Heavy whipping cream	36.0	8.25
Sour cream	18.0	8.25
Ice cream	10.0	10.0
Frozen custard	10.0	10.0
Fruit sherbet	1.0	2.0
Milk shake	3.25	8.25
Butter	80.0	

Source: USDA.

rapidly cooled to destroy undesirable bacteria. Any bacteria remaining in the milk after this process are harmless. Bacteria counts can vary from state to state but must meet minimum levels for consumer protection.

Most whole-fluid milk is also homogenized, a process that separates milk's fat globules into fine particles that remain suspended in the milk and do not rise to the top as cream.

Fat is partially removed in some milk products (for example, in 2 percent milk) or entirely (as in skim milk). In the defatting process, vitamin A is removed from the milk but is usually then added back. Vitamin D is also often added to milk.

Generally, flavor varies little from one dairy's brand of milk to another because they all use primarily the same milk-production management techniques. However, some differences can result from different quality-control programs, milk-processing methods, or cattle feed used. Taste tests indicate these variances.

Milk, a basic dairy product (Courtesy: The American Dairy Association).

Milk Grading

Although grades do not exist for many dairy products, milk is graded, which means that dairy products in which that milk ends up are also indirectly graded. Most states also have strict health codes covering milk production. Milk producers are free to elect to purchase the federal grading service, although in many states grading is mandatory.

Milk is graded for bacteria count, appearance, odor, and taste. The two basic grades are Grade A (the highest quality) and Manufacturing Grade (sometimes known as *Grade B*). Note that Grade A milk is rated only for fitness for consumer consumption and not for quality, but graded-milk quality is normally adequate to meet the standards of most hospitality operations. More bacteria are allowed in Grade B, and it is generally the quality of milk used for making milk products such as butter, ice cream, and cheese.

Milk Products with Water Removed

Some milk products with water removed are available, including dry milk, evaporated milk, and sweetened condensed milk.

Dry whole milk is whole-fluid milk dried to a powder. Skim milk can be dried into nonfat dry milk. Both products are available in regular and instant form, the latter dissolving more readily when mixed with water. Dry skim milk can have the grades Extra or Standard. The grade depends on how lumpy the product is, how much water it contains, and how it dissolves in water when reconstituted.

Evaporated milk is whole-fluid milk with about 60 percent of its water removed before it is sterilized and canned.

Condensed milk (available canned or in bulk) also has about 60 percent of its water removed and is then heavily sweetened with sugar.

Cream

Cream is available in a number of forms based on its fat content.

Heavy whipping cream: 36 to 40 percent fat
Light whipping cream: 30 to 35 percent fat
Light cream (also known as *table cream* or *coffee cream*): 15 to 20 percent fat
Half-and-half: 10 to 12 percent fat

Note that whipping cream labeled as ultrapasteurized has a longer shelf life than regular whipping cream but will not whip as well.

Fermented Milk Products

The three main fermented milk products are sour cream, yogurt, and buttermilk.

Sour cream is a cultured or fermented cream that is about 18 percent fat. It is thick and has a tangy flavor because of the lactic acid bacteria used to ferment it.

Yogurt is a bacteria-cultured milk with milk solids added. It has the consistency of custard, and some forms of it are flavored and sweetened.

Originally, buttermilk was the liquid left after butter was made from milk. Today, it is generally made from fresh milk (whole or skimmed) that is cultured with bacteria.

Substitute Dairy Products

Available today are imitation or substitute dairy products produced and used because they keep longer and cost less than real dairy products. These imitation

Yogurt, a fermented milk product (Courtesy: The American Dairy Association).

products are made from fats and chemicals (as identified on their labels) and for that reason, and for taste reasons, many operations do not purchase them.

CHEESE

Cheese is made by separating milk solids by curdling (coagulating) milk to separate the curds from the remaining whey. Depending on the milk used, the method of curdling, temperature during curdling, and the way curds are then drained, processed, cured, and matured, many different varieties of cheese can be produced.

Even though often flavor varies only slightly between one dairy's milk and another's, that is not the case with milk-derived products such as cheese. The flavor of cheese tends to be unique to each producer, based on the ripening process and length of cure period used (affecting both texture and taste), even though the end-products look the same. For example, cheddar is generally a firm-textured cheese, but it can be more or less crumbly, vary in color, and taste remarkably different from one cheddar to another, even at the same stage of maturity.

Many different cheeses are available to the purchaser (Courtesy: The American Dairy Association).

Unripened Cheeses

Some cheeses are produced without ripening. Ripening is the process that converts curds into cheese. Unripened cheeses are soft and white. Some of these unripened cheeses are

- *Cottage.* Generally made with defatted cows' milk. It may or may not have cream added. Variations are baker's cheese and pot cheese.
- *Cream.* Smooth, buttery, mild, and with a high fat content. Neufchâtel is a French variety with less fat.
- *Mozzarella.* A soft, mild product made from whole or partly skimmed milk. Its texture is stringy. It is used primarily in pizza and pasta dishes.
- *Ricotta.* A smooth, moist cheese with a sweet flavor. It is also sometimes referred to as *Italian cottage cheese.*
- *Primost.* A soft, light brown, mild-flavored cheese from Norway.

Ripened Cheeses

Cheeses can be differentiated by the method by which they are ripened. Ripening develops through bacteria or molds (added during processing) that ripen the cheese either from the inside or the outside. The specific ripening process gives each type of cheese its individual character. Ripened cheeses can be classified as semisoft, soft ripened, hard ripened, blue veined, or hard grating.

Semisoft Cheeses

Semisoft cheeses are usually bland and creamy when young but more full flavored when aged. Some common semisoft cheeses are Bel Paese (Italy), fontina (Italy), Muenster (Germany), and Port du Salut (France); U.S. varieties are Munster and brick.

Soft-ripened Cheeses

Soft-ripened cheeses ripen from the outer crust toward the center of the cheese. Firm and bland when young, they soften and become quite smooth and even runny when fully aged. Some soft-ripened cheeses are Brie (France), Camembert (France), Limburger (Belgium), and Liederkranz (United States).

Hard-ripened Cheeses

The most commonly purchased cheeses are hard-ripened. They have a firm texture and can vary from a mild taste when young to a sharp taste when fully aged. One of the most popular is cheddar, originally produced in England but now also commonly produced in North America (and referred to as American cheese). The U.S. cheeses similar to cheddar, but somewhat milder, are Colby and Monterey jack.

Swiss-type hard-ripened cheeses rank in popularity with cheddars. Main varieties are Emmenthaler (sometimes referred to as *Swiss cheese*) and Gruyère, both from Switzerland. Emmenthaler is a pliable, nutty-flavored product that has large holes in it created by gases during production. The U.S. variety is usually referred to as *domestic Swiss cheese*. Gruyère has a sharper flavor than Emmenthaler, and can be identified by its smaller holes.

Two Dutch hard-ripened cheeses are Edam and Gouda. Both of these are round cheeses, but Edam has a yellow-wax rind and Gouda a red-wax rind. Both have a mild, somewhat nutty flavor.

A well-known Italian hard-ripened cheese that is quite sharp when aged is provolone. Others are Apple, Asiago, and sapsago (all from Italy).

Blue-veined Cheeses

Blue-veined cheeses (often simply referred to as *blue cheeses)* are distinguished by the blue-green streaks or veins that run through them. The best known is Roquefort (France), and others are Stilton (England) and Gorgonzola (Italy). Other blue cheeses are made in Denmark and the United States. Most blue cheeses are somewhat soft and creamy with a very sharp flavor.

Hard-grating Cheeses

The most widely used hard-grating cheese is Italian Parmesan. The best-known Parmesan is parmigiano, although another Italian Parmesan, Romano, is also widely used. Both are made from sheep's milk. Although many other hard-grating cheeses are made (mostly from cows' milk) in other countries, the two Italian products are considered the best quality. Hard-grating cheeses can be bought whole or already grated. Already-grated cheese is a convenience, but the whole product has far more flavor if it is grated only as needed.

Processed Cheeses

Commercially, the biggest-selling type of cheese is processed American. It is popular because of its consistent color, flavor, and texture, by the fact that it is bacterially more stable than other cheeses (thus lengthening its shelf life), and because it has a quick and even melting quality (explaining why it is popular in such products as cheeseburgers). Processed cheese is manufactured by heating, melting, and blending one or more natural cheeses (with American cheddar a prime ingredient) and then adding emulsifiers and other ingredients before solidifying the cheese into a product that neither ages nor ripens but keeps well. European processed cheeses often contain Swiss cheeses (such as Gruyère) as their main ingredient.

Three Designations

Three designations of cheese are available: natural, processed, and cheese food. To be labeled natural or processed, cheese must meet federal standards for fat, moisture, and certain other criteria. Products labeled "cheese food" or "cheese spread" generally have less fat and more moisture. Nevertheless, they may still be acceptable for cooking purposes in some hospitality operations.

There are also synthetic or imitation cheeses on the market made from dried milk protein, or casein, that is combined with vegetable oil and then flavored and colored. These are very low-cost items compared to natural, processed, or cheese-food products.

Cheese Grades

Cheese producers may for a fee employ USDA inspectors to grade their domestically produced products. The four grades are AA, A, B, or C. Grades are based on appearance, flavor, and odor. For example, AA cheddar standards state that it must meet federal standards for fat and moisture content. It must have a fine, highly pleasing cheddar flavor, smooth compact texture, uniform color, and attractive appearance, and the plant in which it is produced must meet USDA sanitary standards. Grade A cheddar must meet the same standards as AA cheddar, but flavor and texture may vary between packages. All packages carrying the USDA grading shield must also show the cure category.

Mild:	Partly cured (two to three months)
Mellow aged:	Moderately ripened (four to seven months)
Sharp:	Fully ripened (eight to twelve months)
Very sharp:	Aged over twelve months

Some states, in particular, Wisconsin, have developed their own grading standards. The highest grade is Wisconsin State Brand, equivalent to USDA Grade AA.

Cheese Prices

Imported, naturally made cheeses are usually more expensive than competitive domestic types. Cheese made from whole milk is also generally more expensive than that made from skim milk. Price is also affected by cheese moisture content. In comparing prices, tests should be made to see if the price difference is worth the quality difference.

Imitation-cheese products are generally lower in price than naturally produced cheeses and, because of their advertised low-cholesterol content, are more and more in demand by restaurant customers.

BUTTER

Butter is made by treating pasteurized milk with a milk acid. This curdles the milk, which is then churned into butterfat to be processed, colored, and in some cases flavored. Butter is available in large containers (tubs or blocks), one-pound prints or packages, quarter-pound sticks, butter chips (square, individual portions on a cardboard liner), butter reddies (individually wrapped portions), and individual plastic cups with a foil wrap. Chips and reddies usually are either seventy-two or ninety count per pound, and foil-wrapped cups are generally fifty count per pound. Butter is also available in a whipped form that incorporates air in the product. Whipped butter is commonly purchased in seven-pound tubs.

Butter's quality depends on the quality of the milk used to produce it. It is generally salted for flavor but is available unsalted, in which case it is known as *sweet butter*.

Grading

Virtually all butter is processed under USDA supervision, where it is inspected for quality and wholesomeness. Federal standards require butter to contain 80 percent

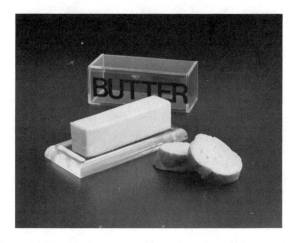

Butter, a major dairy product purchase cost (Courtesy: The American Dairy Association).

butterfat, 17 percent water, 2 percent salt (unless it is sweet butter), and 1 percent coloring and other matter.

Butter is graded by a combination of letters and numbers (score) based upon flavor, body, color, and salt content.

Grade AA (93 score):   Delicate, sweet flavor, with fine, highly pleasing aroma. Made with high-quality, fresh sweet cream. Smooth texture, with salt completely dissolved.

Grade A (92 score):   Pleasing flavor, made from fresh cream. Fairly smooth texture.

Grade B (90 score):   May have slightly acid flavor. Generally made from sour cream.

FROZEN DESSERTS

Gisslen (1983, p. 658) classifies frozen desserts into ice creams, sherbets and ices, and still-frozen desserts.

Ice Cream

Ice cream is a smooth, frozen mixture of milk, cream, sugar, flavorings, and sometimes eggs. According to Peddersen (1981, p. 380),

Manufacturers of ice cream may now use a USDA symbol to indicate that their product lives up to USDA standards for ingredients and composition. . . . The symbol is a rectangular box, containing the words: "Meets USDA Ingredient Standard for Ice Cream."

Ice cream, another dairy product available in a variety of types and qualities (Courtesy: The American Dairy Association).

With ice cream, descriptive terms are sometimes used that do not represent the government grades. For example, it may be labeled "premium" (15 to 18 percent butterfat), "regular" (12 percent butterfat), or "competitive" (10 percent butterfat, the minimum allowed by USDA standards). As the amount of butterfat increases in ice cream (as is true of other dairy products), the price tends to increase. Higher butterfat products also tend to have higher-quality ingredients (such as flavorings and fruits, rather than syrups), again increasing the price. Ice cream labeled "French" indicates that the product is creamier because it has been thickened with egg yolks, and Philadelphia ice cream has no eggs.

The air content is important in the quality of ice cream. This air amount is known as *overrun*. Overrun is the percentage by volume of air whipped into the unfrozen ice cream mix prior to freezing it. A gallon of ice cream with an 80 percent overrun produces 1.8 gallons of frozen product. Note that unfrozen milk shake mix contains no overrun. The air is mixed into this product as it is prepared on-site.

Ice milk is like ice cream, but with a lower butterfat content; frozen yogurt contains yogurt in addition to the usual ingredients for ice cream or ice milk.

Sherbets and Ices

Sherbet is made from fruit juice, water, and sugar. The U.S. sherbets also normally contain milk or cream and sometimes egg whites to increase smoothness and volume.

Ices, sometimes known as *water ices* or (in French) *sorbets,* are like U.S. sherbets, but without milk or cream.

Still-Frozen Desserts

Still-frozen desserts are either ice cream or water ices that are constantly churned while being frozen. Churning incorporates air into the mixture to prevent it from turning into a solid block of ice. Included in this category are frozen soufflés and frozen mousses that contain either whipped cream or beaten egg white to provide a light-bodied product that can be frozen without the need for churning. No production plant inspections or grading standards are available for these products.

Table 12-2 shows the minimum federal standards for some frozen desserts.

PURCHASING DAIRY PRODUCTS

Kotschevar (1975, p. 251) has the following to say about purchasing dairy products:

> Because dairy products are so important as food, are highly perishable, and can be easily adulterated, contaminated, or develop undesirable characteristics, buyers should purchase only the highest quality products and see that they conform to established codes and standards that have been developed to assure quality and wholesomeness.

Most fluid milk products are produced and purchased locally. This practice reduces transportation costs and the possibility of bacteria spoilage. Cheese is a more stable product and is available through normal distribution channels. Because transportation is a major factor in cheese costs, a distributor buying these products in bulk can pass on freight cost savings to end purchasers. Many egg dealers also handle cheese products. Frozen desserts also pose few problems. However, the distributors of these products (some of which can be fragile as far as quality control is concerned) are generally specialists in their distribution.

The quality of dairy products is affected extensively by government regulation

Table 12-2. Minimum Federal Standards for Frozen Desserts

Product	Milkfat (%)	Total Milk Solids (%)	Minimum Weight (lbs/gal)
Plain ice cream	10	20	4.5
Flavored ice cream	8	16	4.5
Frozen custard	10	20	4.5
Milk shake mix	3.25	11.5	
Sherbet (minimum)	1	2	6.0
Sherbet (maximum)	2	4	6.0

Source: USDA

and constraints that differ from most other products. Also, although governments inspect dairy processing methods to ensure wholesomeness, they do not grade flavor quality, which can be particularly important in an item like cheese, whose flavor can vary considerably between two identically labeled and packaged products. Effective purchasing of dairy products therefore requires purchasers to be completely knowledgeable about their operation's quality requirements.

Pricing

For pricing information on dairy products, two publications are available: the USDA's weekly *Dairy Market News* (see Figure 12-1) and Urner Barry Publications' *Urner Barry's Price-Current* (published five times a week), which contains information about egg and dairy products (Figure 12-2).

In purchasing dairy products, many operations (particularly smaller ones) use one-stop shopping for all their requirements. Even if a supplier's prices are higher on some items than another supplier's, the slightly higher total cost paid (because total dairy product cost is only a relatively small percent of overall food costs) may be more than worth the added time and costs of shopping around to achieve the lowest cost on each separate dairy item needed. Sometimes the supplier does not have all the required products, in which case two or more suppliers are needed.

Some establishments purchase their dairy products directly from local farmers. This practice may be appropriate from a price and quality point of view, but generally these products are not covered by strict federal or state control requirements.

Specifications

Extensive specifications are not needed for most dairy products because most purchasers select specific packers' brands and stay with them as long as quality and price are what the operation desires. Brand names are used extensively for products such as butter, cheese, yogurt, sour cream, ice cream, and sherbet. For unbranded products, specifications generally detail butterfat and milk-solid requirements, supplier services desired (for example, delivery schedules), and cost tolerances allowed.

For most milk fluid products (whole milk, 2 percent milk, skim milk, half-and-half, and cream), federal or state standards are normally adequate in purchase specifications. The Grade A rating is also usually used for these products.

For cheese, specifications should list the percentage required for milkfat, nonfat solids, and moisture, in addition to aging time (if appropriate). For processed cheese, packaging requirements might be listed (such as 160 slices per five-pound box).

For butter, the grade and score required would be stated, as well as the size

DAIRY MARKET NEWS   VOLUME NO. 56, REPORT NO. 26

NATIONAL DAIRY MARKET AT A GLANCE

At the Chicago Mercantile Exchange, all grades of bulk butter are unchanged: Grade AA $1.3050, Grade A $1.3000, and Grade B $1.1200. At the National Cheese Exchange in Green Bay, 40# Blocks advanced 5 cents to $1.3525 and Barrels increased 5 1/4 cents to $1.3100. On June 28, Secretary of Agriculture Clayton Yeutter announced that effective July 1, the level of dairy price supports will return to $10.60 per cwt. for milk with an average butterfat content of 3.67%. Converted to a 3.5% basis, the price is $10.35 per cwt. The CCC purchase price for butter will decline 11 1/2 cents to $1.2050 per pound. For Cheddar block and barrel cheese, the CCC purchase prices will be reduced by 4 3/4 cents per pound to $1.1550 and $1.1150 respectively. The nonfat dry milk price will be unchanged at $0.79 per pound. The May Consumer Price Index (CPI) for all food is 124.9, up 6.8% from May 1988. The dairy products index at 113.8 is 6.0% above a year ago. The May to May changes for selected dairy products are as follows: fresh whole milk is 7.1% higher, cheese is up 5.6%, and other dairy products (including butter) are 2.5% higher. May cold storage figures indicate that estimated butter supplies total 438.3 million pounds, 56% more than May 1988, 75% greater than May 1987, and 16% more than last month. The government owned share is 354.7 million pounds, 66% more than last May and 12% more than a month ago. Natural American cheese holdings totaling 305.0 million pounds are 17% less than May 1988, 46% less than May 1987, but 6% more than April of this year. The government owned share of American cheese is 8.3 million pounds, 86% less than May of last year, but 7% more than April 1989. Milk production throughout most areas of the country continues to decline seasonally. Hot-humid weather conditions prevailed in many areas, contributing to the steady downward pattern. Most milk handlers do not anticipate any problems in processing milk volumes over the 4th of July holiday. Dry dairy product markets remain mixed. Nonfat dry milk and buttermilk powder are in short supply and prices continue to rise. The dry whey market is weak and prices are lower. During the week of June 26 - 30, CCC purchased 9.6 million pounds of bulk and print butter, 669,600 pounds of process cheese, 3.1 million pounds of mozzarella, and no nonfat dry milk. The milk equivalent, on a milkfat basis, of these purchases is 236.1 million pounds compared to 159.9 million pounds last week and 60.4 million pounds during the comparable week in 1988.

SPECIAL THIS ISSUE

CONSUMER PRICE INDEX (PAGE 2)
MAY COLD STORAGE (PAGES 7-8)
CCC PRICE SUPPORT INFORMATION (PAGES 9-10)

BUTTER MARKETS

CHICAGO WHOLESALE

Dollars per pound, trucklot, bulk in fiber boxes, delivered metropolitan area, prices include CCC purchase price whenever bulk butter is moving to CCC from the Midwest area.

GRADE :	JUNE 27 :	JUNE 29 :	JUNE 30
AA :	$1.3050-1.3200 :	$1.3050-1.3200 :	$1.3050-1.3200
A :	$1.3000-1.3200 :	$1.3000-1.3200 :	$1.3000-1.3200
( ) Change from previous price.			

BUTTER HIGHLIGHTS: Butter markets across the United States are unsettled and weak. Following the an~~~~~~t of the 11.50 cents decline in the butter su~~~~ sales are reported to be very ligh~ ~~~~~ ~~~~down. Supplies ~~~

CHEESE MARKETS

WISCONSIN ASSEMBLY POINTS

Dollars per pound, standard moisture basis (37.8-39.0%), carlot/trucklot, F.O.B. plants or storage centers, prices include CCC purchase price whenever cheese is moving to CCC from the Midwest area.

CHEDDAR STYLES :	JUNE 26 - 30, 1989
BARRELS* :	$1.2575 - 1.2875 (+ 2 1/4) (+ 2 3/4)
40# BLOCKS :	$1.3325 - 1.3575 (+ 2 3/4) (+ 3 1/4)
( ) Change from previous week.	* If steel, barrel returned.

CHEES~ ~~~~~~~~~~~~~~~~ntinues firm. ~~~~~~~~~~~low a year ~~~~~~~~~~factured ~~~~

Figure 12-1.   Weekly *Daily Market News* (*Source:* USDA).

required (such as one-pound prints, or ninety-count reddies) and the carton size or weight. For whipped butter, the percent overrun should also be stated.

For ice cream, specifications should state the required percentages of butterfat, nonfat dry milk solids, and other ingredients, as well as the level of overrun per

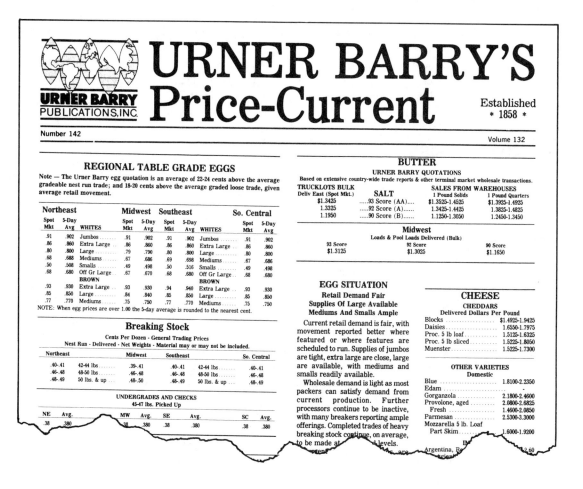

Figure 12-2. *Urner Barry's Dairy Product Price-Current* (Courtesy of Urner Barry Publications, Inc., Toms River, N.J.).

gallon. In addition, weight per gallon (such as 4.5 pounds per gallon) must also be indicated. Often the percentages stated for butterfat and nonfat milk solids, as well as weight per gallon, are the federal standards. Milk shake mix specifications are similar to those for ice cream, except that no overrun or weight per gallon will be stated. For some products (such as chocolate milk and milk shake mixes), several ingredients may have been added in sufficient quantity to change the percentages of solids and fats from government minimum standards. Specifications should therefore be adjusted, and knowledgeable buyers test the products for the quality of these added ingredients.

Specifications for frozen desserts such as cakes, cream pies, and other items containing cream are a challenge for any purchaser. Primary ingredients such as milk have federal standards, but other ingredients do not. In addition, quality (and price) are affected by the use of other ingredients such as sugar, flavorings, and stabilizers.

RECEIVING DAIRY PRODUCTS

Because dairy products are very perishable, they should be moved to their proper storage areas before doing receiving checks. The following are suggested receiving practices for dairy products:

- Examine containers for breakages, dirt, and faulty wrapping (of cheese). Dairy products spoil rapidly, and lack of cleanliness encourages bacteria. If a supplier is suspected of carelessness in sanitary practices, the products can be tested by outside laboratories. Obviously, if the situation is not corrected, the supplier should be replaced with a more quality-conscious one.
- Verify that milk, cream, and ice cream have the stipulated butterfat content. Suppliers have been known to substitute lower-fat products and even deliver products that do not meet minimum federal standards. For example, if light cream is substituted for whipping cream and a stabilizer is added (even though this practice is illegal), it will still whip well and the purchaser will pay a higher price for an upgraded product. Similarly, ice milk (with as little as 2 percent butterfat) can be substituted for ice cream if purchasers and/or receivers are not alert. Again, butterfat content can be tested by an outside laboratory.
- Check all dried milk products for uniformity in color.
- Check for cheese product substitution. For example, if Roquefort cheese has been ordered, has the supplier substituted some other type of blue cheese?
- Check the overrun of ice cream (and any other products that contain overrun) to ensure that it is according to specifications. If overrun is higher than stipulated, the purchaser is paying for air.
- Check that artificially flavored products have not been substituted for fruit-flavored water ices and sherbets.
- Check that a pound of butter does weigh sixteen ounces. A supplier delivering fifteen-ounce "pounds" is making an extra profit, and the purchaser's food cost for this item increases by about 6 percent.
- Check butter chips and reddies for freshness. Butter packaged this way deteriorates rapidly and should never be accepted if not absolutely fresh.
- Conduct random quality-taste tests on all dairy products.
- Verify all product counts or weights to the purchase order and invoice quantities. Verifying dairy product counts can be difficult if they are delivered on standing

orders or on a par stock basis (see chapter 6). The par stock system can be particularly risky if delivery drivers are allowed to stock refrigerators or freezers without supervision.

Storing

Store dairy products in their proper storage area as soon after receiving as possible. Dairy products generally require refrigerated or freezer storage, but some items (such as powdered or dry milk products) can be placed in dry storage as long as this area is cool. Because dairy products, just like eggs, can pick up strong odors from other products, store them in a separate refrigerated area if possible; if not, keep them away from strong-smelling products. Store frozen items at 0°F (−18°C).

Keep cheese products, in particular, in the original packaging (to prevent drying) in refrigerators, and avoid excessive handling that might create breakage or cuts to wrappers that would expose the cheese to air and encourage spoilage. Cut cheeses dry rapidly; when cut, they should be rewrapped in plastic before returning them to refrigerators. Firmer and more mature cheeses keep longer than others. For example, whole Parmesan cheese keeps for a year if properly stored, but cottage cheese may last only a week. Soft-ripened cheeses, however, deteriorate quickly once they are mature. This maturity period may last for only a few days.

Butter, if adequately wrapped, can be stored frozen until it is needed, at which time it should be kept refrigerated until used. Keep butter away from pungent foods (such as onions) because it absorbs odors and flavors. Best storage temperature is 35°F (2°C).

Issuing and Using

Dairy products should be issued only when needed for each meal period. Obviously, as with most other perishable products, proper stock rotation should be practiced, that is, first-in, first-out. Cheese can be issued several hours in advance of need because it is best when served at room temperature, at which it develops its full flavor. However, it should not be issued so far in advance of need that it begins to dry out and change its appearance, flavor, and odor. Cut cheese into serving-size portions just before serving, again to prevent it from drying out.

Dried milk products when opened should be used immediately. Otherwise, they absorb moisture and spoil.

DISCUSSION QUESTIONS

1. Dairy product supply and demand is seldom in balance. In such circumstances, prices would normally fluctuate wildly. How do the federal and state governments help to stabilize prices?

2. Discuss federal government milk and milk product standards.
3. Most whole-fluid milk is homogenized. What does that mean?
4. Differentiate between evaporated and condensed milk.
5. List the four common types of cream, and state the fat content of each.
6. List the three common fermented milk products and briefly describe each.
7. List and briefly describe three unripened cheeses.
8. List three common semisoft cheeses and the country where each originates.
9. For each of the following hard-ripened cheeses, state the country of origin: Apple, Asiago, Edam, Emmenthaler, Gruyère, Gouda.
10. What types of cheeses are parmigiano and Romano, and what are they used for?
11. How is American processed cheese made, and what is it commonly used for?
12. What are the basic ingredients for ice cream? What differentiates French ice cream from other ice creams?
13. Define the term *overrun*.
14. How is sherbet made? Differentiate between a sherbet and a water ice.
15. What is a sorbet?
16. List the receiving checks that should be made for butter.
17. List the receiving checks that should be made for ice cream.
18. List the receiving checks that should be made for cheese.

PROBLEMS

1. One-stop shopping for dairy products is commonly used by small hospitality businesses. Why do you think this is so, and what are its advantages and disadvantages? If you were the manager of a small hospitality business, would you use one-stop shopping for dairy products? Explain your answer.
2. Discuss the purchasing of dairy products with the purchaser for a large hospitality operation. Determine what dairy products that operation commonly uses, which method of purchasing is used for each product, and why this method is used. If one-stop shopping only is used, what reasons does the purchaser have for using this method?
3. Assume that a restaurant purchases chocolate milk at $3.20 per gallon and that on average about fifteen gallons are used per week, with three gallons a day delivered each day from Monday through Friday. The restaurant is considering mixing up a fifteen-gallon batch of chocolate milk each Monday on-site and using it as required during the week. Fifteen gallons of milk would cost $2.40 per gallon, and sufficient chocolate syrup to make one gallon of chocolate milk would cost $0.60. This situation requires a make-or-buy decision. List the advantages and disadvantages of either making or buying chocolate milk. If you were the restaurant manager, what would you decide? State your reasons.
4. Visit three different restaurants and talk with the dining room manager to see why they do or do not offer a cheese selection as a dessert item. Then talk to

five people you know who commonly dine in restaurants. Ask their opinion about whether or not they would like to see a cheese selection as a dessert item and, if so, what cheeses they would like to see included. Summarize your findings, and then make a list of what cheese products you would select for a cheese tray as a dessert item.

REFERENCES AND SUGGESTED READINGS

American Dry Milk Institute. 1970. *Sanitary/Quality Standards Code for Dry Milk.* Chicago: American Dry Milk Institute.

American Dry Milk Institute. 1971. *Standards for Grades of Dry Milk.* Chicago: Dry Milk Institute.

Gisslen, Wayne. 1983. *Professional Cooking.* New York: John Wiley.

Khan, Mahmood A. 1987. *Foodservice Operations.* Westport, Conn.: AVI, pp. 198–200.

Kotschevar, Lendal H. 1975. *Quantity Food Purchasing.* New York: John Wiley.

Kotschevar, Lendal H., and Charles Levinson. 1988. *Quantity Food Purchasing.* New York: Macmillan, pp. 207–33.

Maizel, Bruno. 1978. *Food and Beverage Purchasing.* Indianapolis: Bobbs-Merrill, pp. 95–106.

National Dairy Council. 1980. *New Knowledge of Cheese and Cheese Products.* Rosemont, Ill.: National Dairy Council.

National Dairy Council. 1982. *Newer Knowledge of Milk.* Rosemont, Ill.: National Dairy Council.

Peddersen, Raymond B. 1977. *SPECS: The Comprehensive Foodservice Purchasing and Specification Manual.* Boston: Cahners, pp. 271–310.

Peddersen, Raymond B. 1981. *Foodservice and Hotel Purchasing.* Boston: CBI, pp. 91–95, 363–83.

Stefanelli, John M. 1985. *Purchasing: Selection and Procurement for the Hospitality Industry.* New York: John Wiley, pp. 327–40.

U.S. Department of Agriculture. 1981. *Cheese Alternate Products,* Code of Federal Regulations, Title 7, Part 210. Washington, D.C.: USDA, Food and Nutrition Service.

U.S. Department of Agriculture. 1978. *Cheese Varieties and Descriptions.* Washington, D.C.: USDA, Dairy Division.

U.S. Department of Agriculture. 1980. *Federal and State Standards for the Composition of Milk Products.* Agricultural Handbook No. 51. Washington, D.C.: USDA, Food Safety and Quality Service.

Virts, William B. 1987. *Purchasing for Hospitality Operations.* East Lansing, Mich.: The Educational Institute of the American Hotel & Motel Association, pp. 177–87.

13

Fresh Fruit and Vegetables

OBJECTIVES

- Explain why purchasing fresh produce is difficult, and describe how the government is involved in fresh produce marketing.
- Differentiate between condition and quality in fresh produce grading, and explain the government's acceptance service.
- List and define the four fresh produce wholesale grades.
- Explain the three ways in which most fresh produce is channeled through the market, and define the term *first receiver*.
- Discuss the relationship between price and quality in fresh produce purchasing and the problems it creates in purchasing.
- Discuss the role of fresh produce packers' brands and the pros and cons of buying from local farmers.
- Discuss the importance of size, count, variety, and geographic origin in purchasing some fresh products.
- List and discuss the receiving, storage, and handling procedures for fresh produce.

SEASONAL CHARACTERISTICS

Fresh produce (fresh fruit, vegetables, and nuts) grown in the United States is seasonal. Most crops are harvested only once a year. Harvesting takes only a short time, during which the product is available fresh in abundance. At this time, supply is high and price is low. Depending on the product's storage characteristics, when the harvest is abundant the product may be available year round. Sometimes, the harvest is not good due to poor weather conditions. In such cases, the supply is low, prices are high, and a year-round supply is often not available.

Despite these problems, a large variety of fresh produce is available year round. According to Peddersen (1981, p. 123),

> It is not unusual for 70 or more distinctly different kinds of fresh produce (not counting the several varieties of each) to be on the market at the same time. During the year, more than 100 kinds of fresh produce are on sale, and if only the main varieties are counted, the number rises to 285.

One of the reasons for this variety is the change in packaging of fruits and vegetables that has occurred over the past twenty years, with the elimination of waste and inedible parts (such as carrot and radish tops) prior to packaging. This change was necessitated by the need to reduce weight to save on expensive transportation costs.

Difficult Market

The fresh produce market is a difficult one for purchasers to cope with. According to Kotschevar and Levinson (1988, p. 68), three reasons account for this difficulty. First, it is a highly dynamic and rapidly changing market. Rapid changes can be caused by supply, demand, and weather conditions, as well as the fact that it is highly competitive. Assigning growers quotas and maintaining an orderly flow of produce to the market help to stabilize some of these variables. Second, harvested fresh produce is still a living organism whose quality can deteriorate quickly if it is not properly handled. For example, high temperatures can cause sugar in some products to turn to starch. Nevertheless, automated harvesting and packaging, improved transportation, and vacuum cooling of products have helped in this regard. Third, great variation exists in market practices and grading of products, including the terminology used in grading.

GOVERNMENT INVOLVEMENT

The government is involved in the marketing of fresh produce to encourage fair competition, apply legislation to help balance supply and demand, and establish standard terminology to improve understanding between produce buyers and sellers.

Grading

The USDA's Agricultural Marketing Service (AMS) is the main body involved in establishing standards and grading fresh produce. Standards of appearance, condition, and quality are the factors on which produce is graded and traded. Appearance is the most important criterion.

Virtually every fresh produce item (about 160 in total) now has a U.S. standard, and some also have state standards. For example, Florida (for oranges) and Washington (for apples) have state standards that are generally higher than the federal ones.

Produce shippers are not legally required to have their plants continuously inspected and have products graded. Inspections are carried out, however, in major producing areas.

All inspectors are licensed to inspect and grade any fresh produce item, although some specialize in certain products. In inspecting, random samples are taken from containers. This sample is large enough to ensure that it reasonably reflects the quality of the entire lot. Inspectors score each lot of merchandise for such matters as lack of uniformity and other defects. As a result of the final score, a grade is assigned.

According to Peddersen (1981, p. 52), "A distinction should be noted with regard to the terms *grade, condition,* and *quality.*" Grade is based on the inspector's score at the time of grading and includes both quality and condition. Quality is concerned with more permanent characteristics such as shape, texture, color, size, size uniformity, maturity, and freedom from insect defects. Condition is concerned with factors that may change with time, such as ripeness and firmness. As a result, even though a product is graded in the top-quality category when inspected (meaning that it not only has the quality characteristics of the grade but also is in good condition within the meaning of the grade and not in poor condition), it may after a long journey or careless handling become out of grade due to its condition.

Acceptance Service

The AMS also offers (for a fee) an acceptance inspection in which its agents inspect and pass products to ensure they meet a particular operation's specifications. This service is provided to an establishment that does not have its own qualified inspection employees or is too distant from the source to provide its own inspection. If produce has been so inspected, the container bears a special stamp, as illustrated in Figure 13-1. Upon request, an inspection certificate is provided, again for a fee.

Grading Terminology

Prior to 1976 the grading of fresh produce was very confusing because different products had different grading terminology. Since that time, however, according to Stefanelli (1985, p. 259), the USDA has established a new policy to use common terminology covering four grades for all fresh fruit, vegetables, and nuts. Most products today conform to this new standard.

Figure 13-1.   Fresh produce "accepted as specified" stamp (*Source:* USDA).

Fancy: the top quality
No. 1:   the grade assigned to most products
No. 2:   lower quality than No. 1, but much better than No. 3
No. 3:   the lowest quality, which applies to products that are only just
            suitable for processing

Note that these are wholesale numeric grades. Produce packed in small plastic bags primarily for the consumer market carry two U.S. grades—A and B—to distinguish them from the wholesale market.

No grades other than these four may be used in grading products. Note, however, that all products do not carry all four grades. Whenever one of these grades is used for any particular product, it represents a consistent quality level. A sample of the grade shield is illustrated in Figure 13-2.

Even if a product has not yet been graded with the new terminology, if a purchaser specifies U.S. Grade No. 1, the supplier knows what is required.

The grades used in most hospitality operation specifications are the top ones because these products yield more, have a longer shelf life, and require less labor in trimming and other preparation for food production. Lower grades of product are usually used to produce processed items such as canned vegetables, soups, or jams.

Price Stabilization

Because produce supply and demand fluctuate, as do prices, one government aim is to try to ensure that the entire harvest of a particular product moves through the distribution channel. One way they do this is through grading. By grading more strictly when supply is high, more of the product is graded and priced lower, and demand is stimulated. The reverse occurs when supply is low. Produce graded as U.S. No. 2 at the peak of harvesting may be of higher quality than produce graded as No. 2 during the shoulder-harvest period.

Also, if the grader is grading the product on the West Coast and knows that the

Figure 13-2.   Fresh produce grading stamp (*Source:* USDA).

product is to be shipped to the East Coast, a lower grade may be assigned because the product's quality at the destination is what interests the purchaser. Further, graded products are not always available, either because the supplier does not want it graded, or because it may have been imported. (Imported products, even if they do not carry a grade, must still be inspected before they are allowed to enter the country.)

PURCHASING PRODUCE

Most fresh produce is channeled through the market in one of three ways. One of these is through cooperatives formed to distribute the products for a group of growers. Cooperatives emphasize brand names (packers' brands) in their marketing endeavors. Another way is through large farm corporations who compete head-on with cooperatives. The third method is for individual growers to sell at source through an auction process. Even though few hospitality organizations bid at these auctions, they are generally affected by them anyway, because auction prices are often the ones that dictate general market prices.

Distribution intermediaries (suppliers) can buy their produce from any one of these three sources and generally choose the one that offers the best availability and price to suit their purchasers' specifications. Generally, two types of suppliers can be identified: primary suppliers and secondary ones. Primary suppliers normally specialize in one or two products (for example, potatoes or tomatoes) and try to buy

Red Delicious apples, one of many varieties available (Courtesy: Washington State Apple Commission).

them in large enough quantities (for example, truckloads or carloads) to obtain the best prices and lowest transportation costs. Imported fresh produce (much of it from Mexico) is sold through primary suppliers. Primary suppliers are sometimes referred to as *first receivers*.

Secondary suppliers are smaller firms who may negotiate directly with one of the three sources but may find it just as advantageous to buy from a first receiver. Indeed, in some cases they have no choice but to buy from a first receiver if it is the exclusive distributor for that product. Because of their smaller volumes, secondary suppliers' prices are normally higher.

Wherever possible, hospitality purchasers should deal directly with primary suppliers because prices are generally lower and products fresher. In some cases, large chain operations may be able to purchase from primary suppliers in truck or carloads or even make bids through agents for large quantities at grower auctions. For an agreed fee, agents handle the bids, do the invoicing, and arrange transportation. Obviously, purchasers of large quantities must have adequate storage for warehousing or else have a commissary for prepreparing these products for subsequent distribution to their member hotels or restaurants.

Some large-city suppliers may also do some fresh produce preparation before they sell directly to individual hospitality operations. For example, prepeeled potatoes and carrots, salad ingredients, and fruit segments are often preprepared and purchased this way by foodservice operations directly from suppliers.

Price and Quality

Throughout each product's growing season, produce quality varies. Sometimes all of a particular product may be of poor quality. The wise buyer will know this and not try to pressure a supplier to provide U.S. No. 1 quality when it is just not available. The nearer the harvesting of a crop is to the purchaser's location, the higher the quality generally is. The USDA publishes produce price and quality information in the *Daily Fruit and Vegetable Report*. Other pricing information can be obtained from the USDA's *National Shipping Point Trends* (which provides price estimates FOB produce-growing areas) and from a national weekly industry publication, *The Packer*. Local suppliers may also be a source of both current pricing and pricing trends.

In purchasing, buyers need to be aware of two prices. The first of these is FOB growing area, and the second is local (terminal) market price. Purchasers use FOB pricing when they bypass local suppliers, buy at source through an agent by auction, and pay transportation and other costs for delivery to their premises.

Purchasers buying at terminal market prices may use a bid system and compare bids with FOB growing area prices to ensure the reasonableness of quotations from local suppliers. Alternatively, they can use a cost-plus system and have suppliers

Grapes are a fruit favored by many customers (Courtesy: California Table Grape Commission).

use FOB growing area prices with an agreed markup for transportation and other costs.

Because produce prices are quite volatile due to weather and other conditions, suppliers with produce in stock immediately increase the price of that stock when FOB growing area prices increase. In this case the purchaser pays higher prices, and the supplier makes more profit. Astute purchasers familiar with price trends will, of course, buy in quantity in anticipation of impending FOB growing area price rises. When prices fall, purchasers pay less and suppliers' profits decrease on stock they currently have on hand. Again, astute purchasers do not buy in quantity in anticipation of FOB growing area price declines.

Purchasers who buy produce solely on price are not necessarily astute buyers. Even though price is important in any operation, a purchaser who pays only low prices for fresh produce is going to end up in most cases with low-quality produce and also poor supplier services because this type of purchaser buys some low-priced produce from one supplier and other low-priced produce from other suppliers, providing none of them with sufficient business to generate their full services. In other words, the cheapest price is normally not the best. Low-priced products also may have a very low yield.

Most fresh produce crops are harvested only once a year. Therefore, the maximum time a producer or distributor can warehouse this crop is one year. It has to be moved to make way for the new harvest. By knowing the timing of product harvests, a purchaser should be alerted if, at about that time, a supplier offers considerably reduced prices in an endeavor to move the remainder of last year's inventory; such an offer should not necessarily be turned down if the product quality (for color, flavor, and texture) is still acceptable to the operation and is so stipulated in the specification.

Purchaser Problems

Produce quality is one of the factors that make the purchaser's job so much more difficult than the purchase of other foods. Other problems are

- Lack of acceptable sources of supply. The quantity and quality desired are unavailable.
- Wide pricing swings that accompany quality and quantity availability. Year-round, consistent pricing is just not a factor in produce purchasing.
- Distribution channel storage conditions that affect a product's quality. For example, harvested apples are stored in a controlled environment with gases that preserve quality and retard deterioration. Once removed from these controlled conditions, apples deteriorate rapidly and, when purchased by the hospitality operation, must be used quickly. The wise buyer must therefore know if a product

has been stored under controlled conditions before making a quantity purchase decision that would lead to excessive spoilage costs on-site.

- The large number of varieties of certain products such as apples, tomatoes, and grapes. Each variety is used for a different culinary purpose. The buyer must therefore know these purposes before preparing specifications.
- Terminology can be confusing. For example, there are many different types of lettuce such as Boston bibb, iceberg, and escarole, and sometimes the name of a lettuce in one geographic location differs from the name of the same lettuce in another.

Packers' Brands

Some purchasers specify a particular packer's brand for fresh produce. These brands are desired because the product may be unique (such as in the way it is packed and shipped) or because it is consistently of the same quality. With brands, the usable yield cost (as opposed to the purchased cost) can also be a consideration. For example, many products such as cauliflower and lettuce are sold by the case count (regardless of case weight). If the product is firm and heavy and requires little external trim, its cost per pound can be less than the same product from another packer yielding a great deal more trim loss.

Sometimes packers' brands are produced in two different categories bearing the same brand name but with different qualities. This practice can be confusing to purchasers. To avoid this problem, purchasers can specify both the packers' brand and the U.S. grade in their specifications.

Packers' brand producers are not required to have their products graded, but

Avocados may be used in many different ways (Courtesy: California Avocado Commission).

their premises are regularly inspected by government agents. Ungraded packers' brands, however, constitute only a small percent of total fresh produce available.

Yields and Prices

Yields have a major effect on value received for prices paid. For example, if the price quoted for celery is fifteen dollars per twenty-pound carton and usable yield is 75 percent, then the cost per usable pound is

$$\frac{\$15.00}{75\% \times 20 \text{ pounds}} = \frac{\$15.00}{15} = \$1.00/\text{pound}$$

If a better-quality product can be purchased from another supplier at $15.50, but usable yield increases to 80 percent, cost per usable pound is

$$\frac{\$15.50}{80\% \times 20 \text{ pounds}} = \frac{\$15.50}{16} = \$0.97/\text{pound}$$

In other words, by paying a higher initial price, more value is received because the usable product cost per pound (and thus cost of portions served to customers) is less. This type of yield-to-cost test needs to be carried out from time to time on all fresh produce purchased.

Produce Buying Methods

In some locations, only one or two local suppliers may be able to provide the quantity and quality desired by a purchaser, and bid buying may be impractical. Indeed, in some situations only one supplier can provide the produce. In such cases, the purchaser becomes a *house account*.

Sometimes a purchaser has an opportunity to buy from a local farmer. Often the quality of farmers' products can be quite high because the farmer delivers daily and little quality is lost due to transportation delays. However, the processing facilities of these farmers are unlikely to have been government inspected. Also, some "farmers" have been known to buy produce from local suppliers and pass them off to unsuspecting purchasers as "farm-fresh" products.

Sizes and Counts

When fresh produce products are purchased, the size and counts desired are frequently important. Unfortunately, sizes and counts are often inconsistent from one produce-growing area to another. For example, oranges are normally purchased by the box, but the count (or quantity) per box varies, depending on the size specified. The lower the count, the larger the size, and vice versa. For some products the count is stipulated by layer because of the way the product is packed. For example, tomatoes are packaged in a box in layers, and ordering requirements may specify a count of twenty-five per layer.

In some cases, products are sold in container sizes with no correlation to count. For example, a crate of lettuce could contain anywhere from a dozen to two dozen heads. In other cases (such as a bag of carrots or a flat of strawberries), little correlation may be evident between container size and weight of product purchased if it is shipped from one growing area rather than from another.

Thus, in specifications, weight (if appropriate) is the best specification. For example, a specification stating one hundred pounds of carrots leaves little room for doubt in a supplier's mind. In other cases, however, count is more useful than weight. For example, if 64-count grapefruit are specified, then on receipt sixty-four individual grapefruit should be in the container.

Specifications are often less precise when products are sold by volume (such as spinach sold by the bushel), and weight and count are irrelevant.

Specifications

The following are some considerations in preparing specifications for fresh produce:

- Grade should be specified, even though it alone does not cover all the quality factors that a foodservice operation may require. Specifications should state that the grade required must meet that grade at the time of delivery of the product to the establishment's receiving area.
- Use of the product, where appropriate.
- If brand-name products are available, and a particular brand is known to be of consistently good quality, then specifying that brand name is appropriate.
- Variety can be important with some types of fruit. For example, not all apple varieties are alike in their qualities. Washington State Delicious apples are appropriate for fruit salad, but not for apple pies. Variety is less important for vegetables (other than potatoes). For most vegetables, what some people refer to as a variety is actually only a type designation.
- The quality of produce may be better from one growing area than from another due to climatic and other conditions, particularly for fruit needed for a specific purpose and also for some vegetables (for example, Idaho baking potatoes).
- Freshness is particularly important for vegetables because those not held in proper storage conditions wilt and lose quality quickly.
- The quantity required should be precisely stated relative to the product desired.
- Size invariably needs to be included on specifications. Size is normally indicated by the count (number) of items in a standard container (such as 24s in a lettuce

container), with low number counts meaning the largest sizes. Medium sizes generally are more expensive per container than either small or large sizes because they are more in demand. Nevertheless, for some items (such as fruit to be served whole), the portion cost of large size may be too high, and thus an operation may be better off paying a higher price per pound for medium (rather than large) because portion cost is lower. Size may also be stated in length or diameter (for example, for cucumbers).

- Yield or maximum trim loss allowed can be specified. For example, a specification may state that lettuce yield after trimming must be at least 75 percent.
- In many locations suppliers offer some fresh produce partially prepared (such as prepeeled potatoes and prepeeled and cut-up apples). If they are available and desired in this form, the state of preparation needs to be specified.
- Some vegetable products bought very early or late in their season need special attention when specifications are prepared. The purchaser needs to know each product's season. In shoulder-season periods, a high quality just may not be available (even though the price is high).
- Fruits and vegetables are often available in a variety of different container sizes and with different degrees of protection. In this case, a container size and type should be stated that is appropriate to the needs of the establishment and that provides a desired degree of protection to safeguard the product while it is transported and subsequently stored on-site.
- Where special packaging (for example, film-wrapped cauliflower without its ribs and jacket leaves) is available and desired, it should be specified.

Further information about commonly purchased fruit is shown in appendix C and about commonly purchased vegetables in appendix D.

RECEIVING PRODUCE

Minimum quantities of fresh produce should be received at any one time. In other words, dealing with a supplier who can deliver daily requirements that can be immediately put into production is preferable so that on-site storage and spoilage problems are minimized. Even though daily deliveries add to purchasing, ordering, receiving, and paperwork-processing costs, these added costs are compensated by always having only fresh produce on hand.

Produce has a short shelf life. If proper receiving procedures are not followed, more than an acceptable level of spoiled produce in a delivery can occur, even though specifications state that only unspoiled produce will be accepted. For this reason, many suppliers protect themselves by selling unripe produce (this practice also reduces their warehousing costs because they do not hold the produce until it is ripe). If ripe produce has been specified, however, ripe produce is what should be delivered; otherwise, the restaurant customer may be served an inedible product.

Onions are a necessity in most foodservice operations (Courtesy: South Texas Onion Industry).

Because fresh produce is fragile and subject to deterioration in warm temperatures, it should be moved immediately after receiving to appropriate storage areas before receiving inspections are carried out. For example, after fresh corn is harvested, it loses about 50 percent of its sugar content within twenty-four hours if it is not kept refrigerated.

The following are recommended receiving procedures for fresh produce:

• Inspect cases to ensure that what is printed on the outside with reference to quantity of items in the container is correct. Opening every container and handling every item is not recommended because fresh produce is fragile and handling should be minimized. Nevertheless, some containers should be randomly opened and sampled. These checks should be for weight, count, size, and quality throughout the box. Ensure that a case marked for the desired quality has not been emptied by the supplier and repacked (upgraded) with lower-quality produce.

• Quality should be inspected for freshness specified. After harvesting fresh vegetables continue to live and breathe (using oxygen, giving off heat, and gradually losing water) until they decay. To preserve freshness, they must be stored and shipped at low temperatures (and in most cases with high humidity) to retard decay and conserve moisture. Vegetables that are warm when delivered should be considered suspect (even if no wilting is obvious) because the remaining storage life of most vegetables is greatly reduced if they are held at room temperature for only a few hours. Note, however, that some vegetables (such as white potatoes, sweet potatoes, tomatoes, and some others) can be stored at room temperature. (Freshness quality checks have been included in the alphabetic listings of fruit in appendix C and vegetables in appendix D.)

- If products are layered, counting only the items in the top layer is not sufficient. Lower layers should also be verified. Another method is to check the top layer, and then weigh the entire case to see if the net product weight is correct after deducting the container weight.
- Sizes of certain products, such as lemons, limes, oranges, grapefruit, and melons, should be verified. Suppliers can upgrade by placing 24-count fruit in a 28-count box and charging for the higher count or by removing one or two items from the box, shaking the box, and charging for the full count. Spot counts should be made by receivers to ensure that this type of upgrading is not occurring.
- Invoice prices need to be verified against purchase order prices.

Storing

If fresh produce is not put into food preparation areas for immediate use, it should be placed in refrigerated areas. If possible, this refrigerated space should be separate from other refrigerators.

Even though a number of separate refrigerated storage areas with different temperatures and humidities for different types of fruits and vegetables is desirable, most food establishments have only one storage area, and compromises must be made. Even with only two refrigerated areas (one at a higher temperature, the other at a lower) storage life would considerably increase. Nevertheless, even a single refrigerated area can have a range of temperatures. For example, the area closest to the fan is colder than an area near a constantly opened door. Products can therefore be located where most appropriate for them. Also, if products need high humidity, they can be covered with wet towels, and the most perishable items can be kept on ice.

For most fresh produce, the refrigerator storage temperature should be in the 32 to 35°F (0–2°C) range, and relative humidity should be between 90 and 95 percent. Improper storage temperatures and humidity can reduce the nutritional value of some fresh produce.

Tropical fruits and vegetables do not have to be stored under refrigeration. They can be held in a cool storage area, preferably at about 55°F (13°C).

Fresh produce should not be washed before it is stored. Washing adds moisture to the product, encourages deterioration, and reduces shelf life. It may also remove the exterior protective wax coating that is put on some products (such as apples, green peppers, and cucumbers) to preserve them.

Although some fresh produce can be held for several months (for example, celery and topped carrots), most products can be stored for only two to three weeks, and others (such as broccoli) deteriorate if held for more than two weeks. Suppliers can usually advise how long particular products they have delivered can be safely held before they should be used. Recent improvements in packaging have been designed to lengthen the shelf life of many products as long as they are kept under refrigera-

Melons may be used in many different ways (Courtesy: South Texas Melon Industry).

tion in the packaging in which they are received. Storage time can also be extended by inspecting all produce daily to remove wilted leaves and spoiled stems or other pieces.

Some specific storage guidelines for fruit and vegetables are

- Handle all fruit and vegetables gently and as little as possible. Even so-called hard vegetables such as potatoes and cabbage can be damaged by rough handling.
- Between the time of receiving and storage of fresh produce, do not hold containers near hot areas (such as near stoves or radiators), on wet floors, or on extremely cold or windy receiving docks.
- Date all containers immediately on arrival to help ensure that all produce is issued on a first-in, first-out basis. Do not store new containers on top of older ones.
- Stack containers according to their weight and size, with any pressure from above on the container structure and not on the product. Keep stacks low to reduce any pressure on lower containers. Follow container instructions concerning stacking (some should be stored on their bottoms, some on their sides, some on their ends). Stack also so that air can continue to circulate. Fruit and vegetables continue to "breathe," giving off heat that must be removed through air circulation. Green, leafy vegetables in particular generate a considerable amount of heat.
- Note that some fruit (such as avocados and bananas) should not be exposed to low temperatures (near freezing) for even a short time because the cold adversely affects their quality.
- Some vegetables (such as onions) give off odors that can be absorbed by other products such as butter, cheese, and eggs. Such products should never be stored together.

Issuing and Using

As stated earlier, if deliveries can be made daily to meet that day's production requirements, items can be immediately issued to food preparation areas, and storage and issuing problems are eliminated.

In other cases, only sufficient items for that day's production should be issued from storage. Needless to say, as with any type of food product, storeroom inventory should be properly rotated; that is, the earliest items received should be issued first.

DISCUSSION QUESTIONS

1. Explain why the fresh produce market is a difficult one for purchasers.
2. Explain how the government is involved in marketing fresh produce.
3. Differentiate between condition and quality in the grading of fresh produce.
4. Explain the government's acceptance service with reference to fresh produce.
5. List and define the four wholesale grades used today for fresh produce.
6. Why do most hospitality purchasers buy only the top qualities of fresh produce if they are available?
7. Explain the three ways in which most fresh produce is channeled through the market.
8. In fresh produce distribution, what is a first receiver?
9. Discuss price versus quality in fresh produce purchasing.
10. List and briefly discuss three problems that purchasers have in buying fresh produce.
11. Discuss the role of fresh produce packers' brands.
12. Discuss the pros and cons of buying fresh produce from a local farmer.
13. Discuss the importance of size and counts in purchasing some fresh products.
14. Why is variety and/or geographic origin important in purchasing some fresh products?
15. List and briefly discuss three recommended receiving procedures for fresh produce.
16. Why should fresh produce be moved to proper storage areas immediately after receipt?
17. Why should fresh produce not be washed before it is stored?
18. Why should all fresh produce containers be marked with the date of receipt?

PROBLEMS

1. You presently buy oranges in forty-pound cartons from your citrus supplier at $18.50 per carton. These oranges are used in a fruit cocktail and yield 45 percent fruit after peeling and preparation. A new citrus supplier offers you a

different variety of orange in forty-five-pound cartons at a price of $21.25 per carton. Yield on these oranges is 50 percent. From a cost to yield point of view, which supplier offers the better value? Apart from yield cost, what other factors might you consider in choosing to stay with the present supplier or switching to the new one?

2. Supplier A's tomatoes are layered six by six (total thirty-six tomatoes) in ten-pound boxes and cost five dollars per box. Supplier B's tomatoes are packed six by seven in ten-pound boxes and cost $5.50 per box. From each of Supplier A's tomatoes, six slices can be produced, and from Supplier B's, five slices. On a cost-per-slice basis, which supplier's tomato offers the best value?

3. Your grocery supplier presently supplies you with cauliflower packed twelve heads to a carton at a price of $14.40 per carton. Each head weighs on average 2.25 pounds and trimmed yield of usable product is 55 percent. He offers you a different size of cauliflower packed sixteen heads to a carton at a price of $19.20 per carton. Each head weighs on average two pounds and trimmed yield of usable product is 60 percent. Four ounces of cauliflower (before cooking) are served per portion. Which product offers the best portion value?

4. Supplier X sells head lettuce at $18.25 per 24-count case. Each head of lettuce weighs on average eight ounces before trimming and after trimming yields 75 percent. Supplier Y sells head lettuce at $15.50 per 24-count case. Each head of lettuce weighs on average six ounces before trimming and after trimming yields 80 percent.

    a. Which supplier's product offers the best value for money?

    b. Assume that supplier X delivers only COD and supplier Y extends thirty-day credit. Your restaurant uses one hundred cases of lettuce per week. Which supplier would better suit your needs? Explain your decision.

REFERENCES AND SUGGESTED READINGS

Khan, Mahmood A. 1987. *Foodservice Operations*. Westport, Conn.: AVI, pp. 175–82.

Kotschevar, Lendal H., and Charles Levinson. 1988. *Quantity Food Purchasing*. New York: Macmillan, pp. 68–156.

Maizel, Bruno. 1978. *Food and Beverage Purchasing*. Indianapolis: Bobbs-Merrill, pp. 11–78.

National Restaurant Association. 1973. *Buying, Handling and Using Fresh Fruits*. Chicago: National Restaurant Association.

Peddersen, Raymond B. 1977. *SPECS: The Comprehensive Foodservice Purchasing and Specification Manual*. Boston: Cahners, pp. 469–846.

Peddersen, Raymond B. 1981. *Foodservice and Hotel Purchasing*. Boston: CBI, pp. 49–59, 123–211, 217–99.

Powers, Jo Marie. 1979. *Basics of Quantity Food Production*. New York: Wiley, pp. 249–54, 285–87.

Powers, Thomas F., and Jo Marie Powers. 1984. *Food Service Operations: Planning and Control*. New York: John Wiley, pp. 122–25.

Produce Marketing Association. 1983. *The Foodservice Guide to Fresh Produce*. Newark, Del.: Produce Marketing Association.

Stefanelli, John M. 1985. *Purchasing: Selection and Procurement for the Hospitality Industry*. New York: John Wiley, pp. 253–73.

Virts, William B. 1987. *Purchasing for Hospitality Operations*. East Lansing, Mich.: The Educational Institute of the American Hotel & Motel Association, pp. 189–216.

14

Processed Produce and Groceries

OBJECTIVES

- Differentiate between and discuss various types of processed foods such as canned, frozen, dried, dehydrated, and freeze-dried.
- Define and discuss each of the terms *standard of identity, misbranded, standard of fill,* and *standard of quality.*
- List and discuss the label information that must appear on packaged food.
- Explain the government's grading of processed foods.
- Discuss quantity buying of processed foods and define the term *break point.*
- Detail the information that could appear in a processed food specification, and define the terms *can cutting, solid pack,* and *heavy pack.*
- Define each of the terms *brazil, robusta,* and *mild* with reference to coffee, and explain the various categories of tea.
- Explain the three different ways in which carbonated beverages can be purchased.
- Define *baker's sugar,* differentiate a fat from an oil, and differentiate cured from fresh-pack pickles.
- List the receiving procedures and storage requirements for processed foods.

TYPES OF PROCESSED PRODUCTS

Most processed produce (fruit and vegetables) and grocery items (pastas, fats, spices, and similar items) are forms of convenience foods. With convenience foods, the producer has provided the labor to process these foods. Because of the form in which they are purchased (generally packed in cans or boxes), their quality is relatively stable, and prices do not vary as much as with fresh produce because processors can produce to even out seasonal demand changes. Most processed

288

goods have standardized packaging, longer shelf life, and reduced storage costs (no refrigeration or freezing required). However, processed products do have some shortcomings.

- Many of them, once thawed, opened, or heated, have a very short shelf life.
- Canned goods, in particular vegetables and fruits, have a tinny taste that in no way resembles the taste of the cooked fresh product (for example, compare canned asparagus with the fresh product).
- The quality of fruit and vegetables is often inferior to fresh produce, even though they have been processed at the peak of their flavor and quality when harvested.

Canned Products

Canning is the process of placing food in a sealed container and then applying heat to kill any bacteria present. Standard commercial can sizes are shown in Table 14-1.

Frozen Products

Frozen products are considered to be superior to their canned counterparts because the freezing plants are often located close to the areas where products grow, and

Table 14-1. Common Can Numbers, Sizes, and Uses

Number and Size	Uses
6 fl oz	Frozen concentrated juices and individual servings of single-strength juices
8 oz (7.75 fl oz)	Many fruits, vegetables, and specialty items such as ripe olives
No. 1 (picnic) 10.5 oz (9.5 fl oz)	Condensed soups, some fruits, vegetables, meat and fish products
No. 300 (15.5 oz; 13.5 fl oz)	Specialty items such as beans with pork, spaghetti, macaroni, chili con carne, also a variety of fruits such as cranberry sauce
No. 303 (1 lb; 15 fl oz)	Vegetables, fruits, fruit cocktail, and apple sauce; the most commonly used can
No. 2 (1.25 lb; 1 pt, 2 fl oz)	Vegetables and many fruits and juices
No. 2½ (1 lb, 13 oz; 1 pt, 10 fl oz)	Primarily for fruits and vegetables
46 oz (1 qt, 14 fl oz)	Almost exclusively for juices, but also for whole chicken
No. 10 (6 lb, 9 oz; 3 quarts)	Institutional or restaurant-size can for most fruits and vegetables

they can be frozen immediately after harvesting before quality deterioration sets in. Nevertheless, frozen products have some unique problems. Frozen items do not have as long a shelf life as canned products. Even though frozen products' flavor compares well to the cooked raw product flavor (and some suppliers suggest it is fresher because produce is frozen immediately after harvesting), frozen products can have risks. For example, they can suffer freezer burn or inadvertently thaw. More can be thawed than is needed, and surplus unfrozen products cannot be refrozen without considerable quality loss. Surplus defrosted products can sometimes be used in stocks and soups, but this practice results in the use of expensive ingredients to produce those items. The cost of frozen products also tends to be higher than the same product fresh or canned, and storage costs for freezer space are higher.

Common pack sizes for commercial frozen vegetables generally vary from two pounds up to five pounds, although some sizes are smaller than two pounds and some are as large as twenty pounds for items such as bulk peas and corn.

Common pack sizes for commercial frozen fruit generally vary from six to thirty pounds, although some packages are smaller than six pounds. Frozen fruits are usually packed in sugar or syrup, which helps preserve flavor, color, and texture. High-quality frozen fruits have a fruit to sugar or syrup ratio varying from 4:1 to 5:1. The ratio required should be included in the specifications.

Dried Products

Although canned and frozen products have virtually replaced dried ones as a method of preserving food, some dried products (such as beans, peas, and cereals) are still available because they retain their quality better in this form. These dried products also offer fewer problems of storage and shelf life than fresh or frozen products. They are often cheaper because of reduced (nonrefrigerated) transportation costs. Storage is also less expensive because no refrigeration is required. Unfortunately, not many dried products can be purchased as an alternative to the fresh or canned ones, and those that are available are relatively expensive. Packaging of dried fruit can also be a problem because fruit is usually bulk (slab) packed, meaning that the product near the bottom can be damaged. Another problem with some dried products is the need to reconstitute them.

According to Kotschevar and Levinson (1988, p. 182), "The quality factors for dried foods are empirical and cannot be reduced to writing. Color, uniformity of size and shape, absence of defects, and character (texture, tenderness, and maturity) indicate quality. Flavor and odor are important." Quality can also be judged by the amount of foreign matter included in the dried product and whether products are whole or contain many broken pieces.

Dehydrated Products

Some dehydrated foods (such as potatoes and onions) are also available. Dehydrated products are first dried and then have most of their remaining moisture removed. As a result, they have a long storage life, refrigeration is not necessary, and they are cheaper to transport (because of their light weight). The resulting reduction in transportation cost can be passed on from sellers to purchasers.

Freeze-Dried Products

Some food products are available in freeze-dried form. These products are first frozen and then dried in a partial vacuum that changes their water content from ice crystals to water vapor that is then removed. Included in this category are certain spices, herbs, chicken, shellfish, and some vegetables. As a result of freeze-drying, these products often have a better color and texture than if they were processed frozen or dehydrated.

Convenience of Use

Despite the problems some processed foods create, most operations use them as a matter of convenience, particularly when quality of raw product is not important (such as when using canned tomatoes rather than fresh ones in a soup or sauce). The end-product does not taste much different. Further, raw foods can sometimes be mixed with processed foods without loss of quality from a customer's point of view. For example, a bean salad can be made using cooked fresh green beans mixed with canned garbanzo and other beans. In other cases, such as with brand-name sauces, the operator has no choice but to purchase them in processed form, particularly if customers demand a brand-name product (for example, Heinz ketchup or HP sauce).

GOVERNMENT STANDARDS

The government has established three regulatory standards for processed produce and grocery products: standards of identity, standards of fill, and standards of quality.

Standards of Identity

Although standards of identity for meat, poultry, and egg products are established by the USDA, the FDA establishes them for most processed products. Some three hundred products presently have standards of identity, which establish what a food

Many foodservice operations purchase preportioned processed food products such as salad dressings (Courtesy: Heinz U.S.A.).

product is. For example, for canned goods the minimum product mixture in the can and the ingredients used are stipulated. The label need only state the name of or synonym for that product. The ingredients need not be listed on the label, unless the processor has included ingredients not normally part of the standard, such as extra spices, flavorings, or preservatives. According to Kotschevar (1975, p. 19),

> Standards of identity require that if a word defined by the standards is used, the product must meet the definition of the standard. Thus "ice cream" means that the product has 8 percent or more milkfat. . . . A product is called *misbranded* if it uses the identity name but does not meet the standard.

An individual packer can include more of certain ingredients or add other ingredients to produce its own quality of product. Thus, every product labeled "ice cream" does not taste the same. For this reason, purchasers should not use standards of identity as the sole quality designation in specifications.

Some standards require particular processing procedures (such as cooking) so that consumers can be sure of the item's wholesomeness. If a product falls below its required standard of identity, it cannot carry the name of the product for which the standard is developed. For example, if a drink is orange flavored rather than made only from orange juice, it cannot be labeled as orange juice. Nor can products be given the name of another product, such as naming a blue-veined cheese Roquefort when it is not the authentic French Roquefort, or naming a cola drink Coke or Coca-Cola when it is not. If chemicals are used, words such as *chemical preservative* must appear on the label alongside the ingredient name. Finally, if a product contains simulated color, flavor, or other things, this fact must be stated on the label with a descriptive adjective such as *artificial*.

With reference to meat and poultry products, a processed food containing these items must contain a minimum amount of meat or poultry to meet a standard of identity. For example, ready-to-serve chicken soup must contain at least 2 percent chicken. If it is condensed, that ratio increases to 4 percent because it will reduce to 2 percent when the package contents are diluted with water. The standards for meat are usually based on the fresh weight of the product, whereas for poultry they are based on the cooked and deboned product. As an illustration of a standard of identity for a meat product, Thorner and Manning (1983, p. 329) cite the following for corned beef hash:

> Must contain at least 35 percent beef (cooked basis). Also it must contain potatoes (either fresh, dehydrated, cooked dehydrated, or a mixture of these types), curing agents, and seasonings. It may be made with certain optional ingredients such as onions, garlic, beef broth, or beef fat, but may not contain more than 15 percent fat nor more than 72 percent moisture.

Standards of Fill

Standards of fill specify how full a container must be so that it is not deceptively packaged. In other words, standards of fill prevent a processor selling air or water instead of food. This standard does not mean that the container must be filled to the brim; a normal headspace is allowed (for example, to allow for expansion during a temperature increase). If a standard of fill is not met, the product may still be sold, but only if it is labeled "below standard in fill" or "slack fill" with a reason. In other words, short filling that is deceptive is not allowed. For some products the standard of fill is based on maximum allowable head space (for example, for canned peas this is within 3/16 inch of the top of the can's double seam). In other cases, the standard of fill is based on the minimum percent of water capacity. For example, for tomatoes, corn, and potatoes the fill must be not less than 90 percent of total capacity. In yet other cases (notably for canned fruit), the standards state that the fill must be the maximum quantity of ingredients that can be sealed in the container and processed by heat to prevent spoilage without crushing or breaking the ingredients.

Both standards of identity and standards of fill must be adhered to if the product moves interstate; otherwise, processors can face litigation for criminal action. As a result of this possibility, illegal practices are rare.

Standards of Quality

Standards of quality are established for many processed fruit and vegetable items (as well as a number of other products such as jams, jellies, and peanut butter) to supplement the standards of identity for those products. These quality standards define minimum required quality levels based on factors such as color, tenderness, texture, and absence of blemishes or defects. Note that these are regulatory standards, whereas USDA grade standards (to be discussed later) are voluntary. Note that a product does not have to meet its quality standard. However, if it does not (but still meets its standard of identity), the label must state "below standard in quality . . . " or "good food not high grade . . . " and may be followed by a brief statement explaining why. For example, if a can of mushrooms contains many broken pieces, the label might read: "Below standard in quality: excessive broken pieces." Although such labels are rare, purchasers need to be aware that they exist. Also, a product that is below standard in quality is not unwholesome. For example, cans of mushrooms with many broken pieces might be perfectly acceptable for making a mushroom soup, and astute purchasers seek these out if they offer prices that provide value for purchase dollar.

Other Label Information

In addition to the information already discussed that must appear on a processed food package, other information must also be displayed.

- Legal or common name or names of the product
- Specific names (and not a collective name) for ingredients unless the product is a commonly known food with a U.S. standard of identity (such as mayonnaise); if ingredients are listed, the names of all ingredients are shown with the one of greatest proportion first, and others in descending order
- Name and address of the manufacturer, packer, or distributor
- Net content by count, weight, or measure
- If relevant, the variety, style, and packing medium; for example, canned fruits are packed in water or in syrup that can vary from plain syrup to heavily sugared
- Dietary properties, if important

Finally, all this information must be sufficiently prominent to be easily read and understood and must be printed in English unless the product is imported, has a foreign language label, and is distributed in an area with a predominant language other than English. In any regard, any foreign language words must not circumvent legal labeling requirements.

Government Inspection

Although the FDA and the USDA are both heavily involved in the food processing industry, the FDA is primarily concerned with consumer protection in such areas as product contamination or adulteration, package labeling, and standards of product identity, quality, and fill. The USDA's Agricultural Marketing Service (AMS) is responsible for inspecting processed food items. If these items contain any meat products, the USDA's Food Safety and Quality Service (FSQS) is also involved on a continuous inspection basis, as they are with fresh or frozen meat products. If no meat is included in a processed food, then only periodic inspections are made, primarily for wholesomeness of the product. If product-processing plants are under continuous inspection, packages display a shield stipulating that the product is "packed under continuous inspection of the U.S. Department of Agriculture."

Government Grading

The government's processed food grading service is voluntary and must be requested and paid for by the processor. Federal grades have been established for canned and frozen produce, fruit and vegetable juices, grocery items such as dried fruit and vegetables, and some other processed foods. The U.S. grading shields are more common today than previously because more purchasers are specifying government-graded products even on packers' brands.

Grading for canned goods covers such matters as color, size uniformity, shape, blemishes and defects, and the character (aroma, tenderness, texture) of the product. Sometimes additional criteria are used such as the quality of the liquid (water or syrup) in which the product is packaged. Syrup density is not a factor in grading. Generally, however, the denser the syrup, the higher the grade. Nevertheless, syrup density for the same grade may differ, depending on the type of fruit and the density of syrup appropriate for it. According to Kotschevar and Levinson (1988, p. 176),

A label must state the type of packing medium. But the packing medium is not a grade factor, although very frequently higher-grade fruit has a heavier syrup. The heavier the syrup, the less chance fruit has of breaking up. Packing mediums on fruit may be water, juice, slightly sweetened juice, light syrup, medium syrup, heavy syrup, or extra-heavy syrup.

Grading factors for frozen food cover the product's maturity, size and shape uniformity, color, blemishes and defects, and general quality.

Grading factors for dried foods cover size and shape uniformity, color, blemishes and defects, moisture content, quality of packaging (are products layered with protection between layers, or are they slabbed, leading to possible loss of desired appearance?).

As with fresh produce, tidy standardization of grading levels does not exist. However, for canned and frozen items, the following are a guide:

U.S. Grade A: The top grade with almost perfect quality, good color, appearance, texture, and flavor, and virtually free from defects or blemishes. This quality represents the best of the crop, and fruits are usually packed in heavy (dense) syrup.

U.S. Grade B: Almost as good as Grade A with some imperfections, such as that not all items are of a uniform size. This grade is still a high quality, and fruits are still packed in heavy syrup.

U.S. Grade C: Sometimes referred to as standard quality. Some pieces may be broken, flavor is not as good, and color is not as attractive. Products are less uniform in size and/or color. Fruits are in a light syrup. These products are still completely wholesome and have about the same nutritional value as higher grades.

Items falling below Grade C are sometimes labeled Substandard. However, virtually no products are processed with this grade. They are converted into products such as soups and sauces.

Some difficulties are inherent in this grading system. For example, the best canned tomatoes grown on the West Coast may have the same Grade A identification as the best canned ones grown on the East Coast, but qualities can differ. Also, in poor growing years the best of the crop may still receive a Grade A rating, even though it does not compare well with the quality of the preceding year. In other words, grading standards are not rigid. In addition, the complete grading system is not used with all foods. For example, some foods have only three grades: A, B, and Substandard.

Grade designations may be printed on packages as long as the plant has a government inspection program in effect and the products meet both FDA and USDA requirements. Processing plants with a certified control program can qualify to do their own self-inspections and assign grades. In such cases, processed food packages are marked Grade A (rather than U.S. Grade A). This indicates that the products have not been graded by a federal inspector, but the government allows such labels if the products would have been graded as U.S. Grade A if inspected. Sometimes, in the trade, the word *Fancy* is used instead of U.S. Grade A. The terms *Choice* or

Extra-standard normally refer to a quality slightly below U.S. Grade A or Fancy. A sample of the grading shield is illustrated in Figure 14-1.

Because of the potential grading confusion, purchasers should outline their quality requirements after discussion with potential suppliers who can advise the appropriate terminology to use.

Packers' Brands

For many processed foods, packers' brands are the best indication to a purchaser of the product's quality. The reason (with particular reference to fruits and vegetables) is that the harvest quality can vary from year to year, and the packers of the best brands try to even out seasonal variations. Can sizes are fairly well standardized for processed foods, but frozen and dried products tend to be available in nonstandard packages, particularly for packers' brands. If large quantities of these products are being purchased, the packaging should be inspected to determine if it will continue to protect the product during long storage periods with possible repeated handling. Are packages susceptible to moisture penetration? If large packages of a product are purchased and only a small amount of product is needed at a time, can the package be resealed? This type of packaging may cost more, but if it protects the product from spoilage the extra cost may be worth it.

PURCHASING PROCESSED PRODUCTS

A decision to be made in buying processed foods is the container size. Most products are available in a variety of sizes. Generally, the larger the container, the lower the per portion cost. Consider, on the one hand, the cost of buying individual portions

Figure 14-1. Grading stamp for processed food products (*Source:* USDA).

of ketchup versus purchasing it in a large container. Individual portions cost more than bottles for the same total volume of product. They are also usually more sanitary than bottles, and customers often prefer them. On the other hand, ketchup costs can be reduced considerably by keeping bottles clean, washing them when empty, and refilling them from ketchup bought in bulk in No. 10 cans. Some waste may occur from spoilage of opened and unused large containers, but portion cost is considerably less as long as labor is available to fill the bottles.

Some products should be bought only in small packages. For example, most spices deteriorate quickly after the package is opened. If only a small amount of a particular spice is needed at a time, buying this spice in large containers that cannot be completely resealed will probably not pay (even if the per-weight cost is lower).

Because such a variety of packaging and qualities is available for processed foods, a parallel variety in prices also exists. Sometimes reducing the grade desired by one notch can save on cost. For some recipes, a lower grade is quite acceptable. For example, the grade of a canned vegetable to be used in a purée can generally be reduced without any loss of end-product quality.

Quantity Buying

Quantity discounts are frequently offered by sellers of processed foods, particularly if the purchaser is prepared to buy certain products during the peak-availability season and if prompt payment is offered. If a purchaser is prepared to buy in quantity, bid buying is often used to encourage sellers to offer quantity discounts. Note, however, that a purchaser buying in large quantities needs to be sure that customer demand for the product will stay the same over the six months to a year that the item is in stock. In other words, is the menu likely to change and eliminate a continued need for this product?

Using Local Suppliers

Another consideration in quantity buying of processed food is that a local supplier may not be able to bid on this product for one reason or another, and distant suppliers may have to be contacted. Bypassing local suppliers in this way can alienate them and may discourage them from doing business with the establishment when it needs them for other products, services, or information. For example, if the price of a product is soon going to increase or if a product shortage is anticipated, a good local supplier may warn the purchaser and allow a large purchase to be made at today's prices. A distant supplier may not provide such a warning.

Stockless Buying

Another method of purchasing is to make a commitment to a supplier to buy a certain amount of a product over a period such as six months or a year at a supplier-guaranteed price but not carry the inventory on-site. The supplier then delivers the product only as needed. This method is known as *stockless* purchasing. However, this purchasing method rarely saves as much as regular quantity purchasing.

Break Point

In quantity buying the term *break point* is often used. It is the point at which a discount is offered. For example, on the first forty-nine cases of a supplier's product, no discount may be offered. If fifty or more cases are purchased, a discount is given. Fifty is the break point.

One-Stop Buying

For many small hospitality enterprises, most processed foods can be purchased with one-stop shopping. Most suppliers in large cities offer a broad enough range of products that an establishment's entire needs can be satisfied. For large hospitality enterprises with a broader range of requirements and often a need for specialized products or package sizes, one-stop shopping may not be suitable, particularly if they have facilities and resources to buy and inventory specialized products in bulk.

Specifications

When preparing specifications for processed foods, a broad range of factors need to be considered.

- Grade, such as Grade A.
- Container or package size. For example, a container could be a case holding six No. 10 cans, a case holding twenty-four No. 2 cans, or some other alternative.
- Quantity, that is, the number of containers or cases.
- Count and/or size designations. For example, if the purchaser needs green olives in a gallon jar, the olive size must be specified by stating the count of olives in the jar. The lower the count, the fewer olives in the jar and the larger their size.
- Packing method. For example, is the product in a can to be packed in water or syrup? If syrup, what is the ratio of fruit to syrup and the density of the syrup (ratio of water to sugar)?
- Drained weight of canned products, that is, the yield or quantity of solid product left after excess liquid is removed.

- Variety. For example, for canned apples the purchaser may have a choice among several varieties.
- Origin of product, if important. For example, are California or Florida canned orange segments preferred?
- Time of harvest. It dictates when the items were packed, which in turn influences quality. For example, items picked early in the harvest are of a different quality than those picked at the end of the harvest.
- Special requirements such as size tolerances allowed, variances from federal standards, if the product is to be solid pack (meaning no liquid has been added), any broken pieces allowed, fruit juice sugar to acid ratio, fruit juice pulp ratio, and for frozen items the method of freezing, such as IQF (individually quick frozen).

The recommended approach in preparing processed food specifications is to use federal standards as a guide and modify them as necessary.

Specifications should be developed so that they do not preclude good suppliers. One problem in this area may be consumer demand for nationally advertised brands of products (such as sauces) when they dine in restaurants. Consumer demand for a certain brand reduces possible supplier competition for a hospitality operation.

Yield Sampling

One way of checking canned products to test them against specifications is by sampling them. The term for this sampling is *can cutting*. According to Keister (1977, p. 205), "The time to do can cutting tests is right after your purveyors have received their new supplies for the year—probably in the autumn." The reason for can-cutting tests is to determine the drained weight of the product or its yield net of excess liquid. It is done by draining the product on a specific size sieve for a stipulated length of time (so that fair comparisons can be made among different suppliers' products of the same type) and then weighing the remaining product.

Yield cannot be determined from the can's label because the government requires only that total weight of content, including liquids, be shown. As a result, one brand of an item may have more liquid and less vegetable content, and another have less liquid and more vegetables. Sometimes the amount of liquid can be estimated if the words *solid pack*, meaning no liquid has been added, or *heavy pack*, meaning only a minimum amount of liquid has been added, appear on the label.

If fruit items are packed in syrup, syrup density may be a consideration. The thicker the syrup, the more sugar it contains and the heavier the liquid in the container (meaning the product itself has less weight). Packers must state the syrup density on can labels. Nevertheless, drained weight (or yield) is still the best test because from it portion costs can be calculated and compared from one supplier's product to another. For example, if a particular supplier's No. 10 (132-ounce) can of corn yields 85 percent when drained, net yield is 112 ounces. If drained-weight portion size is four ounces, then twenty-eight (112/4) portions can be served. The can cost divided by 28 gives the portion cost.

Other Tests

When canned goods are being sampled, the opened cans should be checked for odor. Canned products are cooked during the canning process to kill any harmful bacteria and to help ensure that the product does not spoil and stays wholesome. An offensive odor likely indicates the presence of harmful bacteria.

Sampling can also be done with frozen products. Frozen fruit should be thawed and frozen vegetables cooked without first thawing them before they are weighed and yields calculated. With fruit, the texture, which can suffer during the freezing process should also be tested. If dried products (such as dried fruit, vegetables, and soups) are being sampled, they should be reconstituted before weighing.

One problem with sampling is that the purchaser has no assurance that the delivered product will be the same as the sample tested unless the sample was taken from a production lot (or run) with a guarantee that that will be the lot delivered if the sample meets specifications. Production lots are coded on the package. This code identifies the plant that produced the item and the day it was produced. Where necessary, the purchaser should find out from the processor how to interpret the date code.

NONALCOHOLIC BEVERAGES

Three major nonalcoholic beverages are discussed in this section: coffee, tea, and carbonated beverages. Usually each is dispensed by special equipment designed for that purpose. Three factors affect the quality of the end-product: the raw ingredients, water condition and temperature, and equipment condition. Of these, water probably plays the major role because it accounts for more than 95 percent of coffee and tea, and about 85 percent of carbonated beverages. Therefore, to have a quality end-product, water should be filtered to remove chlorine, other chemicals, and any other impurities. Hard water contains calcium that tends to corrode equipment and also affects the taste of the end-product; therefore, soft water is preferable. If soft water is not naturally available, hard water can be converted with a softener. Unfortunately, this conversion does not apply to water for coffee. As Thorner and Manning (1983, p. 280) state,

> The use of an ion exchange system will create unfavorable conditions in a brewing process so a finished brew will be totally unacceptable. The precipitation of sodium salts, such as sodium carbonate or bicarbonate into treated water will form a cohesive gel in a coffee bed. The result is a dramatic increase in the brewing cycle causing undue overextraction

and an extremely bitter beverage. The color of the brew is also affected by the production of a darker coffee.

The correct ratio of water to ingredients must be used. In many cases products (such as coffee) are prepackaged in amounts that can be combined with standard liquid measures (such as quarts or gallons). In other cases, dispensing machines automatically measure the correct amounts of basic ingredient (such as carbonated beverage syrup) with a measured amount of water.

Coffee

The United States produces no coffee (other than small amounts in Hawaii); therefore, virtually all coffee is imported. Weather conditions, economic conditions, and political changes in growing countries can all cause dramatic coffee price increases and decreases.

High-quality coffee can be grown only under certain conditions. For example, better types are grown at higher than two thousand feet above sea level and require the right combination of shade from the sun, rain at the right times, and proper pruning. Because Colombia has regions that meet all these requirements, Colombian coffee is often regarded as the premium type. Colombian coffee is characterized by its fine coffee flavor and aroma, body and sharpness, and mellowness. Excellent coffees are also grown in Africa, Brazil, Mexico, the Middle East, Indonesia, and Venezuela.

Three terms are used to identify the geographic origin of coffee. Note that these terms do not describe flavor or quality.

The term *brazil* defines a coffee grown in Brazil. This term is often used in conjunction with the name of the place grown or the port through which the coffee is shipped. For example most of Brazil's coffee is exported through Santos and thus is "Santos brazil" coffee. Brazil coffee is characterized by its sharp, strong flavor.

The term *robusta* is used to define coffees originating primarily in Africa. Again the term is used in conjunction with the country of origin, such as "Kenya robusta" coffee.

The term *mild* is used to cover all coffee other than brazil and robusta. These coffees are named after the country of origin such as "Colombia mild" coffee. Note that a mild coffee does not mean that it is mild in flavor. A mild coffee can contain just as much bitterness (a desirable characteristic in a quality coffee) as the other two types.

Two other terms describe coffee characteristics: *rio* (river) and *soft*. Rio coffees are from low areas where rivers flow. These coffees are sometimes harsh in flavor. Soft coffees are finer-flavored ones. Note, however, that these are broad terms that do not define any individual coffee's quality.

Other terms used to describe coffee are *body* and *thin*. A coffee with body is one with a heavy aroma and flavor, whereas a thin one has a light aroma and flavor. Some coffees are also described as *sharp*. Sharpness derives from acidity in the coffee and is normally considered a desirable characteristic.

Coffee quality is highly dependent on growing-season weather, and for this reason coffee beans from the same region can vary dramatically in quality from one season to the next. The time the beans are in storage also affects quality because beans can dry out during long storage or become moldy. Therefore, most quality coffee has to be blended from a variety of beans (sometimes from several different sources and of different qualities). Most large companies that sell nationally advertised brands employ expert blenders to ensure the consistency of their product's quality and characteristics. Many blends at different prices and qualities are available. According to Gisslen (1983, p. 513), coffee selection has to be based on four factors: the operation's taste evaluation, needs of the operation, customer preferences, and cost constraints.

Two important specifications for coffee are roasting and grinding. Roasting is the process that releases the coffee beans' volatile oils, caramelizes their carbohydrates, and develops the coffee's flavor. Roasting can be specified as light, medium, heavy, or dark. Although heavy roasting is preferred by coffee drinkers in many other countries, in the United States light to medium roasting generally produces the coffee of choice.

Some hospitality operations grind their coffee beans on-site. Most, however, purchase their coffee ground and packaged by the processor. Specifications thus need to state the grind required, which is usually dependent on the type of equipment used. Three basic grinds are regular, drip, and fine. Regardless of the grind, each contains coffee particles of many sizes. The three grinds differ only in the proportion of particular particle sizes contained in the package.

On the market today are high-extraction or high-yield flaked coffees that manufacturers state yield up to 25 percent more brewed coffee than the regular grind. A special process of roasting and grinding is used. This coffee costs more than regular grinds, but a comparison can be made of the cost per cup (per portion) for high-yield coffee compared to regular. Regular coffee generally produces fifty cups per pound; therefore, high-yield coffee should produce 62.5 cups (25 percent more). Suppose that for the same quality of product regular coffee is $3.00 per pound and high-yield is $3.30. Then cost per cup for each is

$$\text{Regular: } \frac{\$3.00}{50} = \$0.06$$

$$\text{High yield: } \frac{\$3.30}{62.5} = \$0.0528$$

making the high yield a better value.

Purchasers should not be influenced to buy coffee from a supplier who states that coffee quality will be retained for three or four weeks rather than the normal two weeks. Quality of all coffee deteriorates rapidly after two weeks, and accepting less frequent deliveries saves the supplier delivery costs and leaves the operator with stale coffee.

Purchasers should also be wary of bargain prices on coffee. Suppliers have been known to take back old coffee from their larger accounts and sell it at low cost as supposedly fresh coffee to unaware purchasers.

Instant Coffee

Instant coffee is a powdered, soluble extract made from coffee beans. In its manufacture, it loses some of its aroma and flavor and is not often used by foodservice operations as a substitute for fresh coffee. However, decaffeinated instant coffee is used when customers require it. Caffein is naturally present in coffee but can be removed in its processing.

Espresso (Expresso) Coffee

Espresso (or expresso) coffee is made from coffee beans roasted until they are almost black. Beans are then ground to a powder. The result is a strong, dark coffee.

Tea

The United States is the second-largest importer of tea in the world. Main exporters of tea are Africa, Ceylon, India, Indonesia, and Pakistan. Tea quality, just like coffee quality, can vary depending on where grown, weather conditions, and picking and processing practices. It is invariably blended by processors in order to maintain consistency of quality and flavor.

The three broad categories of tea are black (the kind popular in the United States), green (popular in Asian countries), and oolong (primarily used for blending with other teas). Within the three broad categories of tea, two grades can be identified: broken and leaf. Broken grade has leaves that are smaller than leaf grade (broken grade does not mean, however, that the leaves are broken). Broken grade constitutes most of the available tea supply and is usually higher priced than leaf grade.

Although tea can be purchased in bulk containers as large as one hundred pounds, most hospitality operations have little need for such a quantity purchase at any one time. For this reason, most purchase tea in more convenient forms such as tea bags. Tea bags are more costly per pound and per cup served, but most purchasers believe that the added cost provides value through portion control and reduced inventory needs.

Standard cup-size tea bags are packaged two hundred to the pound, and pot-sized bags are 150 to 175 to the pound. Therefore, if the operation serves tea only in cups, buying pot-sized bags would not be economical. For iced tea, larger bags are available because iced tea needs to be double strength.

Tea is also available in instant soluble form. Like instant coffee, this type of tea has less aroma and flavor, but it may be appropriate for making iced tea.

Carbonated and Noncarbonated Beverages

Carbonated and noncarbonated beverages (soft drinks) can be a major source of revenue for many hospitality operations. The soft drink industry is typified by a few large companies. For example, cola drinks represent more than 50 percent of all soft drinks served, and two major companies dominate the cola market.

Purchasers can select three different ways of purchasing nonalcoholic beverages. They can buy nationally advertised brand products (which most hospitality operations do because those are the brands customers ask for), buy regional brands (often demanded by the operation's customers who live in that region), or buy private-label brands produced by a large manufacturer (for example, a chain organization might offer this type of exclusive product that no one else does).

Carbonated-drink dispensers are of either the premix or postmix type. Premix tanks have the syrup, water, and carbonation already mixed in a five-gallon tank. The mix runs from the tank through plastic tubes that are chilled before reaching the dispensing head, where carbon dioxide is added. Premix is not often used today because the tanks are large and take up a lot of space.

Postmix is simply a syrup container. The syrup is propelled by pressure from carbon dioxide through chilled plastic tubes and is mixed with five parts of purified (filtered) chilled water at the dispensing head at the time carbon dioxide is also added. Postmix is most often used today because its cost is considerably less than premix, and far less space is required for syrup containers. One possible problem is that if the syrup is mixed at the time of dispensing with regular tap water, rather than with purified water, some loss of quality may result.

Some operations use neither premix nor postmix but serve carbonated beverages in bottles or cans. They are more expensive than either of the other two systems and take up a lot of space. However, many hospitality industry bars (in particular) like to use them because these containers hold the carbonation better, often have very high-quality water in them, and are demanded by a certain type of clientele.

One important consideration is to ensure that any deposits paid on returnable empty containers are properly accounted for so that money is not lost on empty containers not returned to the supplier for credit.

Dispensing Equipment

In some cases, the soft drink supplier may agree to install and maintain soft drink–dispensing equipment free for as long as the operator uses the supplier's particular brands of soft drinks. Nothing is wrong with this arrangement, as long as the beverage quality satisfies the operator's and the customers' expectations and as long as the price paid for the product is reasonable in view of the fact that "free" equipment is being used.

In some cases, if the equipment is not offered free, an operator may be allowed to purchase the equipment on an installment basis; the cost of the equipment is then added, over a number of years, to the cost of the soft drink products.

Whenever such an arrangement for the use of equipment is made—either free or on an installment basis—the purchaser should ascertain how well the distributor will maintain the equipment and ask for details about the supplier's delivery schedule, ordering procedures, and minimum order requirements (if any).

OTHER GROCERY ITEMS

Hospitality operations purchase many different grocery items. Space does not allow coverage of all of them, but some of the most commonly used ones are discussed.

Sugar

Sugar is used by virtually every foodservice establishment, even though many other processed food products might not be. The classifications for sugar are based on the size of the grain: fine granulated, standard granulated, sanding grade, and coarse grade. Establishments that do their own baking usually also need a finer grain of sugar often referred to as *baker's sugar*. Classifications for it carry an X designation. The range is from 1X to 10X, with 10X the finest grade available. Brown sugar is simply regular sugar with molasses added. It is available in three color classifications: light, medium, and dark.

Jams, Jellies, and Preserves

The USDA grade standards for jams, jellies, and preserves are Grade A (or Fancy) and Grade B (or Choice). To receive a grading, products must meet standards of color, consistency, and flavor and must be at least forty-five parts of fruit or fruit juice to fifty-five parts of sweetener by weight. If the product does not meet these requirements, it must be labeled "imitation." The sweetener may be natural sugar or a noncalory sweetener, and the label must state which sweetener is in the product.

Jams, jellies, and preserves are available in individual portion packs (each containing about a half-ounce), which are usually priced by the hundred or thousand and normally purchased under a brand name. They are also available in a number of larger containers ranging up to a No. 10 size (132 ounces). In comparing costs of these larger containers, the weight of the product excluding the container should be sampled on a cost-per-ounce basis.

Honey

USDA grades for honey are Grade A (or Fancy) and Grade B (or Choice). Most foodservice establishments not using honey in large quantities for baking or similar purposes purchase it in individually preportioned packs as they do with jams, jellies, and preserves.

Wheat Flour

Specifications for wheat flour are important because different types of flour are manufactured for different baking purposes. In broad terms, wheat flour can be described as *hard* or *soft*. Hard flour is high in the protein gluten that is necessary in most bread products. Soft flour is low in gluten and is used for biscuits and cakes, where chewiness is not desired.

Bread and Other Baked Products

Specifications for bread and fancy baked products are more subjective than for most other products because their ingredients are not standard. Federal standards exist for products such as bread shipped in interstate commerce and labeled as "enriched." These products must contain specified amounts per pound of thiamine, riboflavin, niacin, and iron and may contain optional ingredients such as calcium and vitamin D.

Specifications for bakery products are generally restricted to items such as bread slice size and slices per loaf or weight per dozen for hamburger buns. Specifications could also include the packaging method required and how soon after baking the products must be delivered.

Rice

Different types of rice are on the market packaged in many convenient forms. Most foodservice operations use converted rice. This product has been partially cooked under steam pressure, redried, and then milled or polished to produce a rice with a high vitamin and mineral content.

Breakfast Cereals

Most foodservice operations that are open for breakfast need to carry breakfast cereals. Most buy nationally advertised brands because customers ask for them. Some large operations may have their own brands specially manufactured for them and may be able to effect a cost saving by doing this type of volume purchasing.

Fats and Oils

Fats (such as lard) can be differentiated from oils in that fats generally derive from an animal base and are solid at room temperature, whereas oils generally derive from plants and are liquid at room temperature. Major oils are soybean, cottonseed, corn, peanut, and coconut. Included in the category of fats and oils are processed products such as mayonnaise and salad dressings that are made basically from one of the oils (usually soybean, cottonseed, or corn) and margarine, which can be made from a fat, although most of it today is made from an oil. Any fats and oils purchased must be specified for the product for which they are used on-site and must be evaluated with reference to this purpose (by discussing it with users) and their cost. The challenge for purchasers today is often to find a substitute that is inexpensive but still provides the quality desired.

Olives

The two basic types of olives are black (primarily from California but some are imported from Greece) and green (primarily imported from Mediterranean countries). Green olives are available in whole, pitted, or stuffed varieties. The USDA grades are Grade A (or Fancy), Grade B (or Choice), Grade C (or Standard), and Substandard. Olives are usually sold in containers by count. The lower the count per container, the larger the olive.

Pickles

The two broad types of pickles are cured and fresh-pack. Cured pickles are processed by storing them in a flavored brine before packing them. Fresh-pack pickles are packed immediately after harvesting in a brine-flavored solution in the container and are then pasteurized in the sealed container to preserve them. The USDA grades for pickles are Grade A (or Fancy), Grade B (or Extra Standard), and Substandard. As with olives, pickles (whether whole or sliced) are sold in containers by count.

Spices and Related Products

The term *spices* is often used as an umbrella term to categorize a number of different products. True spices are produced from natural plants and include such items as cinnamon, cloves, and peppers. When spices are ground, their volatile oils are released to increase their aroma and taste. With ground spices, however, this fragrance disappears quickly unless packages are purchased vacuum sealed and then resealed between uses. Once packages are opened, their contents should be quickly used.

Herbs are technically not spices. They are produced from plant leaves such as mint and sage. Other products are seeds such as caraway, celery, and mustard. Dehydrated vegetable flakes include celery, onions, and parsley. Flavorings (or extracts) are made from either a natural plant or are created artificially.

The quality of these products is derived from taste and smell. They do not have standards of identity, nor are they graded by the government. According to Maizel (1978, p. 173), "It is extremely difficult to write specifications for them, unless rather precise scientific equipment is available to control purchasing." In other words, purchasers just have to use their own judgment when defining and evaluating quality.

RECEIVING PROCESSED PRODUCTS

The following are recommended receiving checks for processed food items:

- Inspect canned items for potential spoilage indicated by swelling, leaks, rust, dirt, and similar evidence.
- Do not accept cans that leak or bulge at either end. Dents in cans do not harm can contents unless they have pierced the can or sprung a seam.
- Inspect frozen products for container condition and indications of thawing and refreezing (water stains on packages) and freezer burn (because products have not been protected properly by the packaging).
- Verify frozen food packages to ensure that items are solid. Any packages that are limp, wet, stained, or sweating indicate that the products may have been thawed, and they should not be accepted. Some packages today contain thaw indicators that prove thawing at any time prior to receipt. Some states today require that thaw indicators be affixed to containers of certain frozen foods.
- Check frozen products for temperature. Use a thermometer if in doubt. Temperature should be below $0°F$ ($-18°C$).
- Inspect dried products for container condition (such as odd-shaped packaging and/or food mold). Check dry vegetable quality for size uniformity, freshness of color, cleanliness, and freedom from plant debris.
- Test seasonings, herbs, and spices by tasting them. Many of them deteriorate quickly after harvesting. Only an experienced receiver can test them for quality deterioration. Suppliers sometimes adulterate spices with starch or ground shells to expand their weight or volume. This foreign matter can be spotted with a magnifying glass.
- Coffee should be checked for quality. One quality-consistency check is to compare the quality of the current shipment with some of the coffee from the preceding shipment. Some new suppliers initially provide a blend as specified with a high-cost Colombian content and then gradually reduce the ratio (without a noticeable change in aroma and taste) to increase their profits.
- Pound bags of coffee should be tested from time to time for weight to ensure they

contain a full pound and not just fifteen ounces, providing the supplier with an extra 6 percent profit.

- Check dates on all coffee packages to aid in determining freshness.
- Check cases or boxes full of individual items for proper count and to ensure no substitutions have occurred, which can sometimes be indicated if container seals have been broken. If case or box seals are still intact, the receiver can generally assume everything is in order, but some of these containers should nevertheless be opened for spot checks.
- Verify all qualities, brands, and quantities against specifications, order forms, and invoices.
- If any returnable containers (for example, soft drink bottles) have deposits, they should be properly accounted for by ensuring that appropriate credit is received (for example, by using a credit memorandum such as in Figure 7-4) when these items are returned to suppliers.

Storing

In general, no processed food items should be stored on the floor. If bulk items must be stored at this level, place them on a raised platform. For canned food products,

- Store them in a dry area with a constant temperature of about 70°F (21°C). A higher temperature accelerates the reaction of acids present in some foods and produces pinholes in the metal cans and darkens their inside surfaces. High temperatures can also cause texture changes in some foods and create off flavors in citrus-based canned fruit juices.
- Maximum storage time for canned foods is six months under ideal conditions. Because part of this six months may have already expired at the supplier's premises, keep inventory of canned products to a minimum. In other words, in contemplating large-quantity purchases of canned foods, consider the implications of potential spoilage if they have to be stored for a long time. Storage time can be extended if the temperature is reduced below 70°F (21°C). Keep thermometers in storage areas to test the temperature from time to time. Adequate air circulation also helps to maintain a constant temperature.
- Avoid dampness, which causes can rust.

For frozen products,

- Store at 0°F (−18°C) or lower. This temperature allows maximum flavor retention.
- Avoid temperature fluctuations, which can drastically reduce shelf life.
- Avoid damaging packages; otherwise, freezer burn can occur.
- Keep frozen products frozen for no longer than the recommended period printed

on the package. Freezing slows deterioration but does not eliminate it. In general, three months is the recommended maximum storage time.

For dry products:

- If possible, keep these products in a separate, cooler storage area than that for canned items. This practice discourages insects.
- Keep all bulk-container covers tightly closed (for example, large containers of rice or flour); otherwise, shelf life of these products can be reduced.
- When filling these bulk containers with new product, put the new product at the bottom and the old product at the top. Alternatively, use containers in which the old product to be issued is removed at the bottom and the new product can be filled from above.
- Avoid dampness because it encourages mold, which leads to speedy spoilage of these items.
- Coffee inventory should be minimized and rotated rapidly. Regardless of how it is packed, it seldom retains its quality beyond fourteen days, although refrigerating or freezing it can retard quality loss.
- Avoid temperature fluctuations, particularly high heat, which can remove flavor from spices and speed fat oxidation. In hot climates, items such as spices and fats may need to be kept refrigerated.

Recommended Storage Times

The recommended maximum storage time for some grocery items is as follows:

Salad oils	1 year
Bottled and canned condiments, pickles, and relishes	180 days
Jams, jellies, and spreads	180 days
Sugar and pasta products	90 days
Flour	60 days
Cereals, crackers, fats, spices, bottled or dried fruit, and canned salad dressings	30 days

Issuing and Using

Many processed food products are stored in small containers and are often not given the same degree of security of storing, issuing, and using as are products such as meat, fish, and poultry. Nevertheless, processed products can be costly (for example, cans of caviar) and still represent money tied up in inventory. They lend themselves well to perpetual inventory card control or at the very least issuance only by requisitions signed by authorized employees. (See chapter 6 for a discussion of inventory cards and requisitions.)

DISCUSSION QUESTIONS

1. Frozen grocery products are considered to be superior to their canned counterparts. However, detail some of the problems they pose.
2. Differentiate between a dehydrated and a freeze-dried product.
3. Define the term *standard of identity,* and briefly discuss its importance in purchasing grocery items.
4. What does the term *misbranded* mean with reference to a standard of identity?
5. Discuss the term *standard of fill* with reference to canned or bottled grocery products.
6. Discuss the term *standard of quality* with reference to grocery items.
7. List the label information that must appear on packaged food products, and explain the circumstances under which this information does not have to be in English.
8. List the factors that the government uses in grading canned food, frozen food, and dried food products. Why are some purchasers not happy with how grades are assigned?
9. State the three grades that can be assigned to grocery products, and state how the grades differ if a processing plant does its own self-inspections.
10. Some large purchasers bypass local suppliers for grocery items and buy them instead from distant national distributors. What problems can this create for the purchaser?
11. Define the term *break point* with reference to purchasing large quantities of grocery products.
12. List six items that would normally appear on a specification for canned fruit or vegetable products.
13. Define the terms *can cutting, solid pack,* and *heavy pack* with reference to canned food products.
14. Explain each of the terms *brazil, robusta,* and *mild* with reference to coffee.
15. List the three broad categories of tea that are available, and differentiate broken- from leaf-grade tea.
16. Explain the three different ways in which carbonated drinks can be purchased.
17. What is baker's sugar?
18. Differentiate a fat (such as lard) from an oil.
19. Differentiate cured from fresh-pack pickles.
20. List the receiving procedures that you would use for frozen food products and for coffee.
21. State the storage requirements for canned food products and for frozen food products.

PROBLEMS

1. You are investigating two comparable canned food products. Product A costs $24.30 a case of six No. 10 (132-ounce) cans, and can-cutting tests indicate that its drained weight yield is 84 percent. Product B costs $25.72 a case, and can-cutting tests indicate that its drained weight yield is 88 percent.
   a. On the basis of portion cost (assuming a four-ounce drained-weight portion), which product would be the better buy?
   b. Before making the decision to buy, what other factors would you consider?

2. Assume you are the manager of a family-style restaurant that sells a lot of hamburgers and French fries. You buy ketchup in bottles at a cost of seventy-five cents per bottle. Bottles contain twelve ounces, but normally only ten ounces are usable because the rest is not drainable out of the bottle. You currently use about five thousand bottles per year. As an alternative to this method, you are considering using individual one-ounce foil packages of the same brand of ketchup. These packages would cost ninety-seven dollars per thousand.
   a. Based solely on cost, which would be the better purchase?
   b. What other factors might you consider before making the decision?
   c. What other method or methods of purchasing ketchup might you also evaluate?

3. You presently buy sweet pickles in gallon jars, four jars to a case, and use about half a jar of pickles per day in your coffee shop, which is open 365 days per year. Your supplier advises you that pickle prices will be increasing next week by 10 percent, but that he can sell you fifty cases at today's prevailing price if you will pay for them on delivery in forty-eight hours. If you were the coffee shop manager, what would you decide? Explain your answer.

4. Assume you are the purchasing manager for a chain of five local restaurants. You want to place a contract for a year's supply (250 cases, each case containing six No. 10 cans) of canned peach slices, deliverable as required on a weekly basis. You are comparing a brand-name product from a local supplier to a generic brand from a national distributor. The product from the local supplier is of the quality you desire, but the national supplier's product is about 10 percent less with only a slightly reduced quality (each can has some broken pieces). Yield on both products is comparable. List all the factors that you would consider before making the decision. How would you decide? Explain why.

REFERENCES AND SUGGESTED READINGS

Gisslen, Wayne. 1983. *Professional Cooking*. New York: John Wiley.

Hinich, Melvin J., and Richard Staelin. 1980. *Consumer Protection Legislation and the U.S. Food Industry*. New York: Pergamon, pp. 22–26.

Keister, Douglas C. 1977. *Food and Beverage Control*. Englewood Cliffs, N.J.: Prentice-Hall.

Khan, Mahmood A. 1987. *Foodservice Operations*. Westport, Conn.: AVI, pp. 182–86.

Kotschevar, Lendal H. 1975. *Quantity Food Purchasing*. New York: John Wiley,

Kotschevar, Lendal H., and Charles Levinson. 1988. *Quantity Food Purchasing*. New York: Macmillan, pp. 150–204, 235–79, 593–646.

Maizel, Bruno. 1978. *Food and Beverage Purchasing*. Indianapolis: Bobbs-Merrill, pp. 79–93, 107–14, 165–80.

National Frozen Food Association. 1977. *Frozen Food Institutional Encyclopedia*. Hershey, Pa.: National Frozen Food Association.

National Institutional Food Distributors Association. 1985. *Canned Goods Specifications Manual*. West Lafayette, Ind.: Purdue Research Foundation.

National Institutional Food Distributors Association. 1986. *Frozen Food Specifications Manual*. West Lafayette, Ind.: Purdue Research Foundation.

Peddersen, Raymond B. 1977. *SPECS: The Comprehensive Foodservice Purchasing and Specification Manual*. Boston: Cahners, pp. 847–75, 881–994.

Peddersen, Raymond B. 1981. *Foodservice and Hotel Purchasing*. Boston: CBI, pp. 59–78, 343–61, 499–561.

Powers, Thomas F., and Jo Marie Powers. 1984. *Food Service Operations: Planning and Control*. New York: John Wiley, pp. 125–30.

Sivetz, M., and N. W. Desrosier. 1979. *Coffee Technology*. Westport, Conn.: AVI.

Stefanelli, John M. 1985. *Purchasing: Selection and Procurement for the Hospitality Industry*. New York: John Wiley, pp. 295–321, 445–51.

Thorner, Marvin E., and R. J. Herzberg, 1979. *Non-alcoholic Food Service Beverage Handbook*. Westport, Conn.: AVI.

Thorner, Marvin E., and Peter B. Manning. 1983. *Quality Control in Foodservice*. Westport, Conn.: AVI.

U.S. Department of Agriculture. 1971. *How to Buy Canned and Frozen Fruits*, Home and Garden Bulletin No. 191. Washington, D.C.: USDA.

U.S. Department of Agriculture. 1975. *How to Buy Canned and Frozen Vegetables*, Home and Garden Bulletin No. 167. Washington, D.C.: USDA.

U.S Department of Agriculture. 1970. *How to Buy Dry Beans, Peas, and Lentils*, Home and Garden Bulletin No. 177. Washington, D.C.: USDA.

Virts, William B. 1987. *Purchasing for Hospitality Operations*. East Lansing, Mich.: The Educational Institute of the American Hotel & Motel Association, pp. 217–29, 250–57.

15

Convenience Foods

OBJECTIVES

- Give a definition for *convenience foods*; state and give examples of the three broad categories of convenience foods.
- List six questions that should be asked before using a fully processed convenience food.
- List the advantages and disadvantages of convenience foods.
- Describe the various types of kitchen equipment that can be used in reconstituting convenience foods.
- Discuss the labor and food cost implications of using convenience foods.
- List the six steps in the convenience food make-or-buy decision.
- List five guidelines for handling, storing, and using convenience foods.

DEFINING CONVENIENCE FOODS

Some people think that convenience foods are a recent phenomenon. As long ago as the beginning of the nineteenth century, however, the process of hermetically sealing food cooked for future use in a container was developed. That process was canning. Today, foodservice operators use canned and other convenience foods of one type or another for various reasons, one of which is the labor saving that can result from using them. As Peddersen (1977, p. 361) states, "Those in large cities have abundant potential labor, but it tends to be expensive. The small city and rural operator has the opposite problem, a lower wage scale, but a small pool of potential workers."

Definition

Despite the confusion about what is and is not a convenience food, it can, nevertheless, be defined as a food or combination of foods to which some economic value has been added, generally in the form of labor. For example, Gisslen (1983, p. 99) defines it as "any product that has been partially or completely prepared or processed by the manufacturer." In other words, the food has been processed in some way to make it more convenient to use.

Many different terms are used as an alternative to the use of the term *convenience foods*. Some of these are *efficiency foods, ready-to-serve foods, fast foods, prepared foods,* and *frozen foods.* Indeed, many restaurant operators think only of frozen entrees when thinking of convenience foods, even though many convenience foods (and even convenience entrees) are not frozen.

Because of the difficulty in arriving at an acceptable definition, a continuing debate has gone on over their use in the restaurant industry. Even today, when certain convenience foods have been around for decades, what is acceptable by fast-food restaurant customers is often not acceptable if served in a gourmet restaurant. Nevertheless, customers in gourmet restaurants sometimes use a convenience food without perhaps realizing it. For example, if a restaurant makes available nationally advertised bottled tomato ketchup, the customer is using a convenience product because it has not been made on the premises from freshly purchased tomatoes.

Three Categories

Maizel (1978, p. 184) categorizes convenience foods by their degree of processing into three categories: minimally processed items, partially processed items, and completely processed items.

Minimally processed items include products such as peeled potatoes and butter in pats. These items are the easiest to purchase and introduce into a foodservice operation wishing to convert to convenience foods. In most cases, the added cost for buying this category of convenience foods is much less than the cost of processing the item on-site.

Partially processed items include products such as preportioned meat and prebreaded fish fillets that may or may not represent a labor cost saving to the operation.

Completely processed items include products such as completely prepared and frozen entrees (including sauces), desserts, and salad dressings. With these items, "true" convenience is obtained, and the purchase cost includes raw materials, labor, waste elimination, and greater flexibility in menu offerings. Sometimes determining the value of this total convenience is difficult.

Question of Degree

The term *convenience,* is simply one of degree. For example, a restaurant needing bread has various options available. It can buy the raw ingredients and bake the bread from scratch; buy preprepared dry dough mix and process it as needed to make a loaf; buy frozen dough mix and use it as needed to make a loaf; buy baked but unsliced bread; or buy ready-to-serve, presliced bread.

Any decision to use convenience foods must be made on an item-by-item basis by selecting items that reduce operating costs without reducing quality. Many other factors also have to be kept in mind in making the convenience food decision. These factors include cost, space, equipment, and effect on food preparation procedures.

Questions to Ask

Minimally processed food items should be evaluated by the same standards that are used for fresh items prior to purchasing, that is, by relating quality to price. Partially processed foods are evaluated primarily on their suitability to the operation and its standards. In reviewing menu items to consider whether they should be fully processed on site or could be replaced with completely processed convenience foods, the decision can be quite complex. Following are some questions that need answers before any decisions can be made:

- Is the product's taste and appearance of a quality that meets the operation's standards? This question is often answered by having a testing panel evaluate the product.
- Do present food preparation employees have the appropriate skills to do all preparation on-site?
- If convenience foods are to be used, can present equipment handle them or must additional, specialized equipment be purchased? If specialized equipment is to be purchased, is space available for it?
- What are the operational changes (such as training of employees by changing to convenience foods or switching from convenience foods to on-site preparation) that must be considered?
- If a convenience food is to be used, what form will it take? For example, will the product be canned, frozen, boil-in-the-bag, dehydrated, dried, or in some other form, and is this form suitable to the operation?
- Are convenience food products being considered consistently available in the quality and quantity desired, and are the suppliers reliable?
- Are the convenience foods available distinctive enough that they offer product "differentiation"? In other words can production employees add to it in some way to differentiate it from the same product used by competitor restaurants? A

restaurant that serves the same type of product as its competitors is failing to use product differentiation as a competitive tool.

- Will each convenience food used be easy to serve, particularly if it is to be used in volume situations such as banquets? This consideration is particularly important when large volumes have to be prepared and held in steam tables. Some convenience products do not hold up well to prolonged holding periods.
- Does the product, at its proposed menu selling price, offer the customer value for money? Some convenience entree items (so the processor can minimize prices) do not include sufficient meat to satisfy some customers and convince them that they are receiving value for money.
- Can portion costs be readily controlled?

Advantages

Purchasing fully prepared convenience foods has both advantages and disadvantages. Some of the advantages are that they

- Can allow more menu items to be offered because they take less time and labor to prepare.
- Are generally easier to control with reference to portion sizes and costs.
- Can control and reduce costs (such as those for purchasing, receiving, storing, and issuing) because the number of different items required is reduced.
- Generally have a more consistent quality, even though this quality may not be as high as items prepared on the premises. (However, the high quality of items prepared on-site may become low quality the next day if a cook is not up to par.)
- Generally require less preparation equipment and thus free up space for other needs. This equipment reduction also reduces equipment maintenance costs. (This advantage is more apparent when planning a new operation than when converting an existing one to the use of convenience foods.)
- Normally reduce skill levels required by food preparation employees. This, in turn, may also reduce supervisory costs.
- May reduce energy costs because less fuel is needed to reconstitute convenience foods in comparison to those prepared from scratch.
- May reduce raw materials inventory and thus storage costs.
- Allow purchasing in larger quantities because products generally have a longer shelf life than raw ingredients.
- May reduce losses from waste, spoilage, and overproduction.
- Allow management to pay more attention to menu planning and merchandising rather than food preparation.
- Generally make the calculation of recipe (menu item) costs easier.

Disadvantages

Some of the disadvantages of using fully prepared convenience foods are

- Raw ingredients are often more consistently available from a variety of sources, thus ensuring a steady supply of needed items. Suppliers have been known to be out of stock of needed convenience items or to discontinue handling some manufacturer's products (or else the manufacturer discontinues making the product).
- Packaging quality standards vary widely from product to product, and package sizes and weights are not standardized.
- The federal government presently requires certain convenience foods to contain minimum amounts of some ingredients, but each manufacturer has latitude to improve the product with other ingredients. This latitude can make brand comparisons more difficult.
- Menu items prepared on-site are often higher in quality. Note, however, that this problem can often be overcome by using convenience foods as a base for preparing an item and then using creative ways (such as adding flavors or garnishes) to improve that quality.
- Once a convenience food package is opened, the product can sometimes spoil rapidly.
- Food preparation employees often resist using convenience foods because they fear losing their jobs (or else being employed only part-time) and also fear they will no longer be allowed to be creative in producing menu items.
- If equipment and labor are already available on-site and can cope with the demands of nonconvenience items, buying convenience foods may yield no cost advantage.
- Equipment and space costs may not be reduced if they are still required on-site for preparation of nonconvenience foods. Indeed, convenience foods may require additional equipment and space for refrigeration and/or freezing as well as specialized reconstituting equipment.
- Even though portion costs of convenience items are easier to determine, the use of these ready-made products also makes them more easily pilfered.
- From a marketing point of view, advertising on menus that items are made fresh on the premises is often preferable.

EQUIPMENT CONSIDERATIONS

A major issue in the decision to opt for fully prepared convenience foods is the matter of equipment. Most existing food operations that have been using conventional food preparation methods probably have considerably more refrigeration space and equipment than freezer space and equipment. When such an operation considers the use of convenience foods, in particular, frozen entree and dessert products, it finds that this ratio needs reversing. This expenditure is costly.

In addition, many types of new equipment also have to be purchased. As Thorner and Manning (1983, p. 5) state, "Convenience food preparation, reconstituting, and heating involve techniques different from those used for traditional foods." For example, equipment is needed to thaw frozen convenience foods in a rapid and sanitary fashion and then hold those products at an automatic preset temperature above the danger temperature zone that would otherwise encourage bacteria multiplication. Equipment must also be purchased that will heat, cook, or bake frozen products that have not yet been cooked. Often equipment already on the premises

Portion scales are necessary for checking the weight of many convenience foods (Courtesy: Pelouze Scale Co.).

(such as ovens) is still required and, space is severely limited for specialized convenience-food equipment.

Types of Equipment

In some cases, fully prepared convenience items only have to be heated prior to service. This heating can be quickly done if the operation has a convection oven. A convection oven has one or more fans inside that circulate hot air evenly throughout the oven and allow items to be heated both at a lower temperature and in a shorter time than with a regular oven. Peddersen (1981, p. 25) states about convection ovens, "If the product permits, there is no doubt that a properly adjusted, forced-air convection oven does an effective job in terms of load, efficiency, and cost in reheating frozen convenience foods."

Infrared or quartz ovens heat and/or cook even more rapidly than convection ovens. They are also useful for broiling and finishing convenience food dishes.

Microwave ovens also considerably reduce heating and/or cooking time. They are most practical when convenience items are used one at a time and do not need to be bulk-heated or cooked because microwave ovens do not do an efficient job of that. Wilkinson (1981, p. 69) listed the uses of microwave ovens as follows:

1. Reheating single servings of precooked food
2. Complementing existing food heating equipment, especially during slow periods at the beginning and end of meal periods
3. Speedy defrosting (one minute for a frozen steak) that eliminates oven preparation
4. Eliminating bottlenecks in preparation and service
5. Decreasing labor costs through the elimination of extra help during peak periods

Nevertheless, some convenience foods (such as steaks or roasts) do not lend themselves well to microwave ovens. Sometimes, however, these items can be first heated in a microwave and then browned or crisped in an infrared or quartz oven.

A reconstitution oven is a type of all-purpose conventional-food and convenience-food oven useful for frozen, preprepared entree items. This type of oven can broil or roast conventional items or rapidly reconstitute precooked frozen products.

One of the more recent ovens is the convection steamer that can both cook and heat a variety of convenience-food products. This equipment circulates steam around the oven compartment but does not operate under pressure as some steam heating equipment does.

Convenience foods also require portion scales in various locations to check the weight of products as they are received and also as they are assembled and prepared for portion control. Scales are particularly necessary when microwave ovens are used because the oven's time cycle can be properly set only if the product's weight is known. After cooking, the prepared portion sizes should again be weighed to check for consistency.

LABOR COST VERSUS FOOD COST

A consideration in the use of convenience foods is the influence they have on labor and food cost. When convenience foods are used, food preparation labor time is reduced. This saving on labor cost often influences purchasers to buy convenience foods. However, the cost of the convenience item is higher than if each of the ingredients were purchased separately and the item prepared on-site because the manufacturer's processing costs (including labor) are passed on to the purchaser. Theoretically, the increased cost of purchasing convenience foods is compensated by a reduced on-site labor cost.

This theoretical reduction in labor cost is, however, baseless if no actual reduction of dollars spent on labor occurs. Frequently, the preparation time saved by using convenience foods does not allow any reduction in food preparation employee hours because those employees are still needed in the kitchen to produce other products that are not convenience items. Thus, if labor cost does not decrease and food cost increases with the use of convenience foods, profits decline and no cost advantage accrues from using convenience foods.

If labor hours can be reduced (for example, as a result of employees agreeing to work shorter hours) or if employees leave through attrition and are not replaced, labor cost may be reduced when fully processed convenience foods are used. Another alternative is to have employees with free time produce batches of menu items that can then be frozen. In other words, the freed-up labor time can be used so that the operation can produce some of its own convenience foods.

With reference to labor cost, Maizel (1978, p. 184) states,

> The convenience food purchased . . . may save as much as 70 percent of the labor needed to produce the menu. In other words, were the convenience foods not purchased, three times as much manpower would be needed in the kitchen.

This view is reiterated by Peddersen (1981, p. 26).

> The possibilities convenience foods offer for increasing productivity are almost limitless. A kitchen planned for total convenience food use may take perhaps half as much space and capital as a conventional kitchen. Labor requirements may be reduced by as much as 80 percent, although 40 to 60 percent is more common.

Reversing the Trend

In some cases, operations have discovered that costs can be reduced by switching back from convenience foods to conventional methods. As Warfel and Waskey (1979, p. 117) state,

With delivery costs soaring, some operators have decided to reopen pastry shops and bakeshops and to expand their butcher shops . . . whenever controlled tests have been made during the past thirty years food costs have gone up from two to four points as a result of the introduction of prefab, preprepared, or portioned foods.

They also suggest that the average food preparation employee's time is nonproductive in establishments in which convenience items are presently used, and if this time were put to use doing food preparation on-site, the number of convenience items purchased could be reduced, thus reducing food cost.

On the other hand, Pedderson (1981, p. 30) cites the following example for an operation processing its own meat:

Can you afford the butcher's salary? If the butcher's salary . . . is $250 per week (or $13,000 per year), and if the operation saves an average of $0.10 per lb. of meat through self-butchering, then the operation must use *more than* 2,500 lb. of meat per week to break even with buying fabricated or portion controlled meat cuts. Since 20 percent of the butcher's time is spent in set-up and clean up, this means he must be able to butcher almost 70 lb. of meat per hour. If the operation uses a lot of roasts, this will be possible, but if the operation uses mostly steaks, chops, ground meat, and diced meat, this level of productivity may well not be possible. Also, an institution that uses 2,500 lb. of butchered meat per week must feed an average of over 700 people per meal.

THE MAKE-OR-BUY DECISION

Very few establishments use exclusively on-site prepared items or fully processed convenience foods. Most restaurants use a mix of both, depending on such matters as source of supply, price, storage space, equipment, labor, and many similar factors. When a decision is made to introduce new menu items, compare making the item from scratch (the make decision) or using a convenience item (the buy decision). This decision may seem like a simple one, but it is both difficult and time-consuming.

In research for the make-or-buy decision, those in purchasing play a key role in identifying suppliers who can provide the products, obtaining cost information and samples for testing, participating on taste committees, and providing any other pertinent data for comparison between the make decision and the buy decision.

Six-Step Process

Six steps are required in the make-or-buy decision.

1. Identify the Problem

Usually the problem is to decide whether a menu item should be prepared on-site or be purchased as a convenience food from a supplier who has the product available. Usually this problem boils down to which alternative will provide the customer with the best quality at the most favorable cost. For example, if the item is not available from a supplier in the quantity and with the quality desired, then the decision is easy: the product must be prepared on-site or not be offered. Alternatively, if the operation does not have the proper equipment and/or the employees to prepare the item on-site, then it must be purchased as a convenience food; or if it is not available in the right quantity or appropriate quality, again it cannot be offered.

Generally, however, the problem narrows to the fact that the product can be purchased and provide the value desired in convenience form and can also be prepared on-site. In this case the decision maker moves to step 2.

2. Gather Cost Data

The gathering of costs is fairly simple for a convenience food item. Usually that cost is the supplier's price, to which are added other costs such as a garnish or other ingredient, the costs of reheating (reconstituting) the product, and depreciation of convenience-food equipment.

The costs for on-site preparation are sometimes much more difficult to assemble. To the cost of raw food ingredients must be added preparation labor cost (including supervisory labor), supplies, energy, and equipment depreciation costs.

Most foodservice operators probably do not have the time to go through all the necessary calculations to make this type of cost comparison. Nevertheless, some analysis of costs should be possible.

3. Compare Cost Alternatives

Once cost figures are assembled, a comparison can be made on a cost basis, assuming the quality of the two alternatives is comparable. Before making the final decision in favor of lowest cost, however, some other factors must be considered as listed in step 4.

4. Consider Other Factors

Some of the other factors to consider are

- Can suppliers make the convenience products available in the quantity required on a guaranteed continuous basis?
- Is the convenience item fully compatible with the operation's existing equipment, space, and employee skill levels?
- Is the packaging of the convenience product acceptable? For example, will the package size fit into available storage space?

- Is the unit size of the package available in individual portions or only in multiple portions? Are portion sizes consistent in size and weight?
- How will employees react to the introduction of convenience foods? For example, will they react negatively in fear of losing their jobs?

Once satisfactory answers to these questions have been received, the decision can be made.

5. Implement the Decision

Implementation of the decision requires preparing specifications for either the raw ingredients for on-site preparation or for the convenience item, contracting with suitable suppliers, and establishing kitchen and service operating procedures.

6. Evaluate the Decision

Evaluating the decision requires monitoring employees to ensure that they are following established procedures, monitoring guests' reactions to the new product, discussing the product's quality with guests and involved employees, and conducting taste and other tests to consider the appropriateness of continuing to offer the product in that form.

HANDLING CONVENIENCE FOODS

Gisslen (1983, p. 99) gives the following seven guidelines for handling convenience foods:

1. Handle with the same care as fresh, raw ingredients. Many people think that frozen convenience foods are damage-proof, and handling them under this assumption can cause quality loss.
2. Examine products as soon as they are received. Frozen foods should be checked with a thermometer for temperature. Items with thaw indicators can be inspected so that items that have thawed and then been refrozen can be returned to the supplier.
3. Store them properly. Frozen items should be stored at 0°F (−18°C) or lower and refrigerated items at 40°F (4°C) or lower. Shelf-stable products (canned, packaged, and other dry goods) should be stored at 70°F (21°C) or lower. All storage areas should have thermometers so that temperatures can be verified from time to time.
4. Know the shelf life of each product. Even convenience foods do not keep forever and some (such as prepeeled potatoes) have a shelf life much shorter than the same product in nonconvenience form. Do not purchase at any one

time more than can be properly stored, and rotate all stock on a first-in, first-out basis.

5. Defrost frozen foods properly, ideally in a refrigerator at 28 to 30°F (−2 to −1°C). Small items might defrost in a day; larger items may need several days. If time is short, defrost under cold running water in the original container. Never defrost at room temperature or in warm water, which encourages bacterial growth and spoilage. Do not refreeze defrosted foods. Know which foods (such as frozen french fries) can be cooked without thawing.

6. Know how and to what extent the product has been prepared. Partially cooked convenience foods need less heating to prepare them. Without this knowledge, frozen convenience items could be overcooked, be rejected by the customer, and become waste.

7. Use proper cooking methods. Most container packaging provides proper preparation information.

DISCUSSION QUESTIONS

1. Give a definition for *convenience foods*.
2. State the three broad categories of convenience foods, and for each category give an example (other than those mentioned in this chapter).
3. Before using any fully processed convenience foods, list six questions that should be asked.
4. List six advantages of using convenience foods.
5. List six disadvantages of using convenience foods.
6. Discuss the impact that switching to convenience foods may have on conventional kitchen equipment.
7. What is a convection oven?
8. Why is a microwave oven frequently not suitable for reconstituting convenience foods?
9. Discuss the labor and food cost implications of using convenience foods.
10. List the six steps in the convenience food make-or-buy decision.
11. List five guidelines for handling, storing, and using convenience foods.

PROBLEMS

1. Make an appointment to visit the chef of a large hotel or restaurant operation. The purpose of the visit is to discuss that operation's usage of convenience foods. Try to determine what the chef's philosophy is concerning their use. Are any completely processed convenience foods purchased? If so, how is the decision made to use them? Are cost comparisons made using a make-or-buy approach? Are tasting committees used to evaluate convenience products? Write a one-page report of your findings.

2. A restaurant manager is doing a cost analysis to determine whether to make chicken stock for soup from scratch or to buy a preprepared chicken soup base. To produce five gallons of chicken stock from raw ingredients, the ingredients would cost $24.85, and two hours of labor will be required at $12.50 an hour plus fringe benefits of 20 percent. In addition, energy and other production costs will amount to an estimated $3.50. If a preprepared chicken-stock base is purchased in one-gallon cans, each can will cost $7.78. Water will have to be added, but no cost is attached to that. However, twelve minutes of labor time will be required per gallon of finished soup at a cost of $12.50 per hour plus 20 percent fringe benefits. Energy and other costs are estimated at forty cents per gallon. On a cost per five-gallon basis, would making or buying the chicken stock be better? What other factors might you consider before making the decision?

3. A gourmet restaurant features duck as one of its menu items. It purchases on average twenty whole ducks a day and sells each half-duck portion for $15.95. Ducks are purchased almost fully prepared from a local supplier at a cost of $8.95 per duck. The on-site labor cost each day to cut up and finish final duck preparation is estimated at a half hour per day at a labor cost of $12.00 an hour plus 25 percent fringe benefits. Energy and other costs are $4.50 per day for all forty half-duck portions prepared.

    The restaurant's manager is considering buying completely unprepared ducks from a local farm at a cost of $3.50 each. They would be fully prepared on-site. To do this, a new employee would have to be hired for eight hours each day at a cost of six dollars per hour (plus 25 percent fringe benefits). Previous labor cost to do final duck preparation on-site would be eliminated. By preparing ducks on-site, management considers that it can reduce the menu selling price of half-duck portions by $2.00. Which would be the better purchasing method? What other factors might you consider in your decision?

4. A chain restaurant company owns and operates six fast-food restaurants in the same city. Its big-selling item is hamburgers. It presently buys hamburgers preprepared in patties and delivered frozen by the supplier each Monday in sufficient quantity for a week's business to each of the six restaurants. The owner is considering buying beef rounds in wholesale cuts and having them ground up at one of the fast-food restaurants that has sufficient space to do this. Fresh hamburger patties would then be delivered each day to each of the other five restaurants by a restaurant employee who would be paid to use his own car to do this. By purchasing this way, the owner expects a considerable saving on meat purchase costs.

    Before making the final decision, the owner has asked for your advice. List and comment about all the factors that must be considered by the owner in making this purchasing policy change from a convenience food to a nonconvenience one.

REFERENCES AND SUGGESTED READINGS

Copson, D. A. 1975. *Microwave Heating*. Westport, Conn.: AVI.

Gisslen, Wayne, 1983. *Professional Cooking*. New York: John Wiley.

Keister, Douglas C. 1977. *Food and Beverage Control*. Englewood Cliffs. N.J.: Prentice-Hall, pp. 216–19.

Kelly, Hugh J. 1976. *Food Service Purchasing: Principles and Practices*. New York: Lebhar-Friedman, pp. 101–6.

Maizel, Bruno. 1978. *Food and Beverage Purchasing*. Indianapolis: Bobbs-Merrill, pp. 181–87.

Peddersen, Raymond B. 1977. *SPECS: The Comprehensive Foodservice Purchasing and Specification Manual*. Boston: Cahners, pp. 361–402.

Peddersen, Raymond B. 1981. *Foodservice and Hotel Purchasing*. Boston: CBI, pp. 23–31.

Powers, Jo Marie. 1979. *Basics of Quantity Food Production*. New York: Wiley, pp. 443–62.

Stefanelli, John M. 1985. *Purchasing: Selection and Procurement for the Hospitality Industry*. New York: John Wiley, pp. 279–90.

Thorner, Marvin E. 1973. *Convenience and Fast Food Handbook*. Westport, Conn.: AVI.

Thorner, Marvin E., and Peter B. Manning. 1983. *Quality Control in Foodservice*. Westport, Conn.: AVI.

Virts, William B. 1987. *Purchasing for Hospitality Operations*. East Lansing, Mich.: The Educational Institute of the American Hotel & Motel Association, pp. 231–39.

Warfel, M. C., and Frank H. Waskey. 1979. *The Professional Food Buyer*. Berkeley, CA: McCutchan, pp. 223–40.

Wilkinson, Jule. 1981. *The Complete Book of Kitchen Equipment*. Boston: CBI.

16

Alcoholic Beverage Purchasing, Receiving, and Storeroom Control

OBJECTIVES

- Explain the ways in which purchasing beverages is easier than purchasing food.
- Differentiate between monopoly and license situations for the distribution of alcoholic beverages.
- Discuss the pros and cons of having only one or two suppliers versus having many suppliers, and list some of the factors to consider, other than price, in selecting suppliers.
- Explain how kickbacks can occur and be controlled in beverage purchasing, and define the term *post off*.
- Differentiate between well (or house) liquor and premium (or call) liquor, calculate the cost per ounce of liquor, and explain why this figure is of value.
- Discuss the problem of which beverage products to carry and how much to order of each.
- List the procedures to follow when receiving beverages, and explain and complete a beverage receiving report.
- Explain the principles of beverage storeroom control, including par stock control, full-bottle replacement, and bottle coding.
- Complete a beverage storeroom reconciliation, and calculate and discuss beverage inventory turnover.

PURCHASING

For most operations, purchasing alcoholic beverages is less of a problem than purchasing food items for a restaurant. Beverage purchasing and control are simplified because the brands that customers like to drink can be reasonably easily established and become the specifications, these beverages are generally purchased in sealed cases or bottles that are easy to receive and check, the product quality is consistent from one purchase to the next for any particular type or brand of beverage, and most beverages (except keg beer) have a fairly long shelf life, which means that purchases can be made on a periodic basis rather than daily. Finally, all beverages, on receipt, can be delivered to a locked, controlled storeroom prior to being issued. This situation is not the case with food, where the problem of control over direct purchase can be a major one.

Control of Distribution

In most jurisdictions, the government is the sole wholesaler and distributor, and the prices to the purchaser are controlled and fixed, with few opportunities (if any) for "sales" or quantity buys at special prices. In these jurisdictions, the government may specify the liquor-ordering and invoice-paying procedures. In other words, the only supplier offers specific products at noncompetitive prices and requires that specific purchasing procedures be followed.

In the United States, states that have government distribution of liquor are known as *control* or *monopoly* states. The others are known as *license* or *open* states. Bell (1984, p. 206) lists the following as control states:

Alabama	Ohio
Idaho	Oregon
Iowa	Pennsylvania
Maine	Utah
Michigan	Vermont
Mississippi (wholesale only)	Virginia
Montana	Washington
New Hampshire	West Virginia
North Carolina	Wyoming (wholesale only)

All other states are license states.

Monopoly Situations

Monopoly or control states generally have only one price for each product, and the operator cannot shop around for lower prices. As a result, the product cost is usually higher in control states than in license states. These states may also have a limited brand selection because the government monopoly usually carries only products that sell well and because it may be less responsive to purchasers' needs. Nevertheless, some monopoly governments are willing to bring in specialty products for a purchaser if the purchaser is willing to buy them in a specified minimum number of case lots.

In control states, the government normally requires purchasers to pay in cash or by certified check at the time of pickup, as well as to arrange and pay for their own pickup and delivery.

License Situations

In most license or open states, a monthly list of the names of wholesalers is published, including the products each carries and the prices each charges. The alcoholic beverage purchaser may buy from any wholesaler licensed by the state; in some states, the purchaser may also buy from licensed manufacturers and distributors (distillers, brewers, or vintners). However, local laws sometimes override state laws, and the regulations for beer and wine sometimes differ from those for distilled spirits. Some manufacturers—for example, breweries—have their own distribution networks and do not sell through other wholesalers or distributors. Wholesalers and distributors may handle the products of many manufacturers and vintners, and importers may handle products from many different countries.

In license situations, prices may be lower because of competition, but such is not necessarily the case on all items. Some manufacturers grant exclusive distribution rights for some products to a particular supplier, who then has no competition. With some competition, the suppliers may nonetheless be reluctant to compete on the prices of products that a bar must stock. These "must stock" items are the heavily advertised brands that customers demand in any bar. Thus, the customer dictates in most cases what a bar will carry, and to some extent the suppliers can maintain prices even in a competitive situation. Suppliers then compete only on the discretionary products that a bar may wish to carry or through discounts or other inducements not allowed in government-controlled jurisdictions.

In license situations, the reputable operator also has access to supplier credit and is allowed to delay paying invoices until the end of an agreed credit period. In many jurisdictions, if the invoice is not paid by that date, the supplier is required to advise the licensing authorities, who have the discretion to prevent the operator from making further purchases until the bill is paid.

Pricing of Alcoholic Beverages

Supplier pricing of alcoholic beverages does not follow any established pattern, as it often does with food products. Virts (1987, p. 248) has the following comment:

Pricing of alcoholic beverages is subject to a bewildering array of laws and regulations, primarily because of the taxes connected with these products. Some "controlled" states operate distribution and retail outlets with non-negotiable prices. In other "open" states, distribution and retailing are handled by private businesses. There are also states using a combination of suppliers. . . . Other states control the price of liquor at wholesale (distributor) and at retail levels, yet do not perform the selling function themselves.

Most liquor suppliers, regardless of state system, change their prices monthly to reflect their cost changes and any "specials" made available to them by distillers, vintners, and brewers.

Where allowed, purchasers (such as large chain operations) may be able to deal directly with distillers and vintners to obtain their private label on bottles and to negotiate a price for these "house" products, even though these products must still go through normal distribution channels and be taxed and marked up in the usual way. Despite these distribution costs, the lower prices negotiated with distillers or vintners prior to the product entering the system usually produce a price saving.

Familiarity with Local Situation

The purchaser of alcoholic beverages has to be familiar with all the necessary legal requirements and distribution channels in the jurisdiction where the establishment is located; even where the government is the sole supplier, importers, wholesalers, dealers, or their agents or sales representatives may still be trying to influence purchasers to buy their products through the government supplier.

Suppliers are often very useful in advising about local or regional trends in the drinking tastes and habits of customers or potential customers. Of course, suppliers are eager to tell purchasers about any new products they have and (where allowed) about any discounts or other purchase incentives they are offering. However, purchasers must be wary of discounted wines and beers that may have reached the limit of their quality or freshness.

Number of Product Suppliers

In situations with a choice of suppliers, a purchaser has to consider how many different purchase sources the operator should use. Concentrating orders with a limited number of suppliers creates larger-sized orders, and the purchaser thus becomes a more important customer of the supplier. In recognition of this status, lower prices and/or better supplier services can be expected.

If as many suppliers as possible are dealt with, however, each one may be forced to compete harder, although with some products, as mentioned earlier, they may be reluctant to do so. For major-selling products a purchaser could place an order for each separate product with a different supplier simply because that supplier currently has the lowest price for the item and meets the quality standards desired.

The opposite extreme would be to place all product orders with a single supplier that—despite having a higher cost on one or two products—provides the lowest overall cost on all products. Because this decision simplifies the overall purchasing, ordering, receiving, storing, and invoicing problem, it is often the best approach. Unfortunately, it is often rejected by purchasers because they think about their purchasing only on a product-by-product basis.

Virts (1987, p. 249) states,

> It is best to use as few distributors as possible, even if some modification in the list of brands carried must be made. . . . Generally, a primary distributor is used, with others used only as necessary.

Weekly Purchasing

An effective purchaser tries to limit purchasing and completion of purchase orders to once a week in order to lessen the demands on time, reduce the possibility of errors, and simplify the paperwork and bookkeeping.

In a small, independent bar, the owner should handle the purchasing function personally because it is a key element in cost control. However, in certain circumstances the function may have to be delegated, in which case the owner-operator should be alert to the possibility of supplier-purchaser kickbacks or bribes.

Kickbacks

Kickbacks can take the form of cash or merchandise given to the purchaser for favoring a supplier or agent, even in situations where liquor has to be purchased from a government outlet.

In other cases, the kickback can occur when a supplier sells to the purchaser directly but inflates the price of products, includes items on the invoice that were not actually delivered, or substitutes low-quality products while invoicing for higher-quality products. The "savings" to the supplier are then split with the person doing the purchasing.

These kinds of kickbacks can be spotted through effective management supervision. The manager should watch for a supplier whose products seem to be favored by the person doing the purchasing. The best protection is to ensure that the purchasing and receiving functions are separated and that proper receiving controls are implemented and practiced. (Receiving is discussed later in this chapter.)

Dishonest kickbacks should be differentiated from honest discounts. Legal discounts (either in the form of cash or free alcoholic beverage products) should be received by the establishment and not by an employee. Employees should be notified that any violation of this practice will lead to termination, and suppliers should be advised that their services will be discontinued.

Supplier Services

Liquor, wine, and beer producers may be allowed in some jurisdictions to provide useful services such as supplying an operator with blank purchase orders, bin cards, and other control forms (the use of which is discussed later). These "free" forms can save an operator money because they help control the purchase, storage, and use of alcoholic beverages.

In some cases, a wine supplier may be useful in helping create wine menus or lists, training wine service employees, providing sales and promotion suggestions, and other matters.

A beverage operator should not, however, be unnecessarily influenced to favor a particular supplier. Instead, purchasing should serve the purpose of buying the products that, at a reasonable price, satisfy the market, that is, the operation's customers.

Other Considerations

Other questions or considerations in purchasing from a particular supplier include the following:

- What is the frequency of delivery? A supplier that is prepared to deliver daily, even though orders are normally placed less frequently, allows the operator to carry less in inventory and still obtain needed supplies in an emergency.
- How large a variety of products does the supplier offer? A supplier with a large and varied inventory is more useful to an operator than a specialist supplier with a limited inventory.
- For beer supply in particular, does the supplier have a refrigerated warehouse and refrigerated delivery vehicles? Visiting the supplier's warehouse to see how beer and wine are stored may be a good idea (for example, are corked wine bottles stored on their sides?).
- Where is the supplier's location? If the supplier is remote from the operation, how will this distance affect such things as delivery times? Will travel time and weather affect the product's quality?
- Does the supplier offer other bar supplies, such as carbonated drinks and drink mixes?
- What are minimum quantities that must be ordered at any one time?
- What are the supplier's credit terms?
- Is the supplier's representative an order-taker or a salesperson? With the former,

an order is simply processed; with the latter, an operator can obtain advice and counsel about products offered.

- Does the supplier deliver as promised? Undelivered products can translate into lost profits.

Post Offs

In some states, liquor suppliers are allowed to offer a price discount known as a *post off*. According to Virts (1987, p. 249), these discounts usually range from 5 to 10 percent of the product's listed wholesale price, and the offering period lasts for about thirty days. Post offs are generally available for various liquor brands at different times of the year, depending on the jurisdiction.

To obtain a benefit from a post off, a purchaser needs to buy post-off brands in larger quantities. Purchasers can make themselves aware in advance of when a post off is to occur in their jurisdiction and which products will be available at the lowered price and then reduce their inventory of those products prior to purchasing at the discount so that large-quantity purchases can be made. However, according to Keister (1977, p. 353), "If you have to buy much more than a six-month supply to get the discount, you will probably be better off buying smaller quantities more often and not tying up too much money in inventory."

The post off is not always in the form of a price discount. For example, it can take the form of a free bottle of liquor for every full case ordered.

Premium and Nonpremium Liquor

In purchasing liquor, the major decision to be made involves the premium and nonpremium liquor brands to be carried.

Most bars serve a house brand (sometimes known as *well* liquor) to customers who do not specify a particular brand but merely the generic type of drink desired (for example, scotch). On the other hand, premium or "call" liquor refers to specific brand names, such as Chivas Regal scotch.

Well Liquor

Well liquors are usually the largest-selling items of the basic brands of liquor (rye, gin, rum, scotch, vodka, and bourbon) in a typical beverage operation. Because they usually provide the best (lowest) cost to the operator, they are also the cheapest for the customer to buy. Because they are generally served with other ingredients, such as a soft drink or other mixer, little taste discrimination by the consumer is possible.

Despite the fact that a purchaser should seek the best possible price bargain with well liquors, some judgment may be needed because distillers do sometimes produce brands that are unacceptable and because what the customer should be expected to tolerate ought to have limits.

In other words, a purchaser should not buy Rotgut Rum just because it is ten cents less per bottle than better brands. Where the government controls the purchase and distribution of liquor, unacceptable brands are less likely to be available.

A purchaser should select well brands that offer value for money and stay with those brands for drink consistency. By obtaining a slightly higher-quality product at slightly more money, the purchaser will not pay an appreciably higher cost per drink. For example, consider two well liquors, one costing ten dollars, and the other nine dollars per bottle, from each of which an operator can obtain thirty-five drinks per bottle. On the ten-dollar bottle, the cost per drink would be $0.2857, and on the nine-dollar bottle it would be $0.2571. Thus the difference is less than three cents per drink.

Call Liquor

In the case of premium or call liquor, less control over cost is possible because an operator generally has to carry the brands that customers regularly request. Drink selling prices are dictated primarily by what the customer is prepared to pay. Because an operator cannot substitute cheaper brands for call brands, liquor cost cannot be reduced as it can through selection of low-priced well liquor.

A rule of thumb with call liquors, including liqueurs, is that if the product sells it should be carried in inventory; otherwise, it should not. An inventory of unsold call liquors and liqueurs represents money tied up and not earning any income. One good inventory operating method is never to add a new product without deleting an old one.

If a particular type of call liquor is tied up and just not moving, selling it as house or well liquor might be a good idea. At least that way, even if the liquor costs the operator a little more per drink than normal well liquor, money from dead inventory will be freed up.

Because the same selling flexibility is not true of liqueurs, an operator should invest in them as part of inventory only if customers clearly want them.

One bar marketing device is to put strict limits on the number of brands carried and to print a list of those limited brands offered. Most customers then choose from the list, and the problem of customers' having an open-ended choice disappears. What to carry depends on the type of bar, the volume of business, the type of clientele, the cash available for investment in inventory, and the customers' preferences.

Cost per Ounce

The difference in cost price between well and call liquors is not large per drink but could amount to a significant difference in total liquor cost if only premium or call brands were served at all times at the well brand's selling price. Good beverage cost control begins with knowing what drinks cost. This information is most easily established on a cost-per-ounce basis because comparisons are easier between brands and between containers of different sizes. Generally, the larger the container in which liquor is purchased, the lower the cost per ounce. This saving is not always the case, however, providing another reason to convert the entire container (bottle) cost to a per-ounce cost before making the purchasing decision.

Nevertheless, although cost per ounce is important, it may not be the only factor to consider. Other significant factors include volume of business and availability of a container size that is convenient for pouring. Also, the quantity that a purchaser is required to buy to obtain desirable savings might necessitate a considerable investment in inventory that may not be used up for several months or even longer. A purchaser must then consider the resulting loss of interest on money that could otherwise be left in the bank.

Metric Equivalents

Cost per ounce is calculated by dividing the bottle price by its size in ounces. Because alcoholic beverage bottles today are in metric sizes, metric volumes must be converted to an equivalent ounce size. The following table can be used:

Metric size (liters)	Ounce equivalent
4	134.8
3	101.0
1.75	59.2
1.5	50.7
1	33.8
.750	25.4
.375	12.7
.200	6.8
.187	6.3
.100	3.4
.050	1.7

ORDERING

A typical beverage operation orders liquor, beer, and wine once a week. For items used in quantity, about ten days' supply should be on hand after each order is received. These items are usually ordered in case lots. For slow-moving items, quantities may be ordered in multiples of bottles—unless the supplier refuses to break open cases, at which point an operator may have to order a full case of an item that may take a year to sell. Alternatively, the supplier may be willing to sell a split case, or a case of several different brands totaling up to a normal case lot of twelve bottles. For example, a supplier may be willing to sell four bottles of each of three wines at the case-discounted price. This example is an additional service by a supplier that provides value to the purchaser.

How Much to Order?

One of the problems in beverage purchase control is calculating (without having to take a physical inventory of what is on hand) how much of each product to purchase to carry the bar through until the next order date. One of the easiest ways to control this situation is to use storeroom perpetual inventory cards. From each card (one for each type and size of product carried in stock), the purchaser can quickly determine what is on hand at any time.

Because each card can also have recorded on it the maximum quantity normally carried of that product, the order quantity is the amount required to increase the present stock to the maximum level, allowing (if necessary) a safety margin for any time delay between ordering and receiving the goods. (Perpetual inventory cards and their use in inventory control are discussed in detail in chapter 6.)

Developing the ordering system into as precise a function as possible is desirable. Liquor is expensive; when too much has been purchased and is sitting idle on a shelf, that money is not earning a profit elsewhere. Furthermore, a larger inventory requires more space, more paperwork, and more security, and deterioration of quality may be a problem with beer and some wines; in addition, changing customer tastes may leave the operation with inventory that cannot be sold. However, a bar that specializes in fine wines may have to buy quality wines in large quantities when they are available; otherwise, that opportunity will disappear.

Who Orders?

In a small hospitality operation, beverage purchasing and ordering is probably handled by the owner or manager. In a large operation, particularly one associated with a restaurant or hotel, the food and beverage purchasing might be centralized in one person who has full-time responsibility for this work. Regardless of the situation, the person who does the purchasing must be familiar with the different brands and types of alcoholic beverages needed.

Detailed specifications are not generally needed for alcoholic beverages because most of them are purchased by brand, and any particular brand may have only one supplier. However, the purchaser should be aware of any quantity discounts, sale items, or other specials that are in effect.

Order Form

If many different items are ordered, a purchase order form is useful because it helps the person responsible for receiving to know what is to be delivered from each supplier and at what prices. Figure 6-2 illustrates an order form.

RECEIVING

In receiving alcoholic beverages, the common practice is to break down products received into three separate categories: beer, wine, and liquor. Any nonalcoholic beverages received, such as soft drinks, are generally included in the liquor category because the revenue derived from drinks in which these nonalcoholic beverages are used is generally liquor revenue.

Sales Mix

The reason for the three separate categories is that, because the markup for each category is generally quite different, distortions, false assumptions, and erroneous decisions could result if cost analysis were not made by category. Figure 16-1 illustrates this. Notice that, from month one to month two, the overall beverage cost has declined from 36.6 percent to 36.3 percent. This decline might seem desirable. However, analysis of the cost percent by category shows that, in each case, the cost percent has increased, despite the decline in the overall percent.

The decline in the overall percent was caused solely by a change in the sales mix. A major shift has occurred in month two in the amount of beer sold relative to wine (with little change in liquor revenue). Because beer has a lower cost percent than wine, this shift has influenced the overall percent downward, even though the cost percent of all three categories has gone up. Only analysis by category shows the underlying trend. Again, as with food cost percentages, beverage cost percentages by themselves can be misleading. For example, in Figure 16-1, despite the decline in overall cost percent from month one to month two, the gross profit has also gone down from $45,800 to $45,000, which would not normally be a desirable trend.

Receiving Checks

Because alcoholic beverages are prone to "evaporation" or removal by unauthorized persons, the person responsible for receiving and checking absolutely must be there at the moment of delivery. The suppliers may have to be instructed to deliver

Sales Mix Cost Analysis by Category

	Month 1			Month 2		
	Cost	Revenue	Percent	Cost	Revenue	Percent
Beer	$ 2,400	$ 6,100	39.3%	$ 4,800	$12,100	39.7%
Wine	11,800	24,000	49.2	8,200	16,600	49.4
Liquor	12,200	42,100	29.0	12,600	41,900	30.1
Totals	$26,400	$72,200		$25,600	$70,600	
Overall cost	$\dfrac{\$26,400}{\$72,200} \times 100 = 36.6\%$			$\dfrac{\$25,600}{\$70,600} \times 100 = 36.3\%$		
Gross profit	$72,200 – $26,400 = $45,800			$70,600 – $25,600 = $45,000		

Figure 16-1.   Sales mix cost analysis by category (*Source:* Coltman, Michael M. 1989. *Cost Control for the Hospitality Industry*, p. 179. New York: Van Nostrand Reinhold).

only during the hours when the person who combines the beverage-receiving function with some other job is available. The receiver should ensure that

• The quantities received agree with the quantities listed on the order form and with the invoice. This comparison requires counting all bottles or other types of containers or counting the number of cases if items have been delivered in case lots. In the latter event, cases should be opened to ensure no bottles have been removed prior to delivery. Alternatively, if the correct full weight of the case is known, cases should be weighed. If bottles are sealed, then spot checks should be carried out to ensure that seals are not broken.
• Prices on the invoice agree with prices listed on the order form.
• The quality of the product is checked (proof of liquor, vintages of wines, freshness of keg beer) if this type of check is appropriate. As Stefanelli (1985, p. 443) states, "Canned and bottled beer often are delivered in unrefrigerated trucks. Thus, some quality deterioration has already begun, though if you then place it in a refrigerator, you can slow it somewhat."

In the event that bottles have been broken prior to receipt, the wrong product has been delivered, or items have been short-shipped, then a credit memorandum (Figure 7-4) should be prepared by the receiver. If an invoice does not accompany the shipment, then a memorandum invoice (Figure 7-2) should be prepared by the receiver, using actual quantities delivered and obtaining pricing information from the order form. Once all receiving checks have been carried out, each invoice should be stamped with the receiving stamp (Figure 7-1) and initialed in the appropriate places. Finally, the beverages should be immediately moved to the locked storeroom.

Beverage Receiving Report

The final step in the receiving process is the completion, from invoices, of the beverage receiving report. A sample daily beverage receiving report is illustrated in Figure 16-2. This type of daily report is used by a large operation whose sales volume necessitates frequent deliveries. In operations in which both food and beverage receiving are the combined responsibility of one person, the daily food receiving report (Figure 8-4) might appropriately be designed to list daily beverage deliveries. In either case, the daily beverage total would be subsequently transferred to the beverage receiving summary form illustrated in Figure 16-3.

In small operations whose deliveries are not frequent and in some cases might be limited to once or twice a week, both a daily and a summary report would not be necessary. All delivery cost information could be listed directly on the summary form to be later totaled at the end of the control period (a week, ten days, or a month, depending on the policy of the individual establishment).

How this beverage purchase cost information can be used to aid in beverage storeroom control is explained later in this chapter.

STOREROOM CONTROL

In a beverage operation, the storeroom is best located adjacent to the bar. In a food and beverage operation, the beverage storeroom might be part of the food storeroom, although this location is not recommended. A separate beverage storeroom, because of the "perishable" nature of the product, is preferable. In a large hotel

			Date____March 2____	
Supplier	Beer	Wine	Liquor	Invoice total
Pacific Brewers	$114.60			$ 114.60
Vintage Imports		$125.90		125.90
J. & H. Agency		75.40	$275.48	350.88
Total purchases	$315.95	$461.80	$893.21	$1,670.96

Figure 16-2. Sample daily beverage receiving report (*Source:* Coltman, Michael M. 1989. *Cost Control for the Hospitality Industry*, p. 181. New York: Van Nostrand Reinhold).

		Period	March 1-7	
Date	Beer	Wine	Liquor	Total
March 1	$ 72.35		$ 114.10	$ 186.45
2	315.95	$461.80	893.21	1,670.96
Total purchases for period	$1,615.60	$985.46	$2,756.48	$5,357.54

Figure 16-3.   Beverage receiving summary form (*Source:* Coltman, Michael M. 1989. *Cost Control for the Hospitality Industry*, p. 181. New York: Van Nostrand Reinhold).

with a number of different bars, each bar may have its own small storeroom in addition to the main storeroom. In this case, for control purposes all beverage purchases definitely must be processed through the main storeroom before any of the products are distributed to the individual bar storerooms.

In some situations, centralizing beverage storage is not possible. For example, in the case of keg beer that must be kept refrigerated, the storage location may have to be separate from other products. Also, quality wines should be stored at lower than normal temperatures (wine storage is discussed in chapter 17). If properly cooled storage cannot be provided for these wines in the liquor storeroom, then an area elsewhere may have to be set aside for them.

Regardless of the number and type of beverage storage areas, only one person should have access to them. In a small operation, this person might be the owner or manager. In a large operation, the food storekeeper might also handle beverage storeroom responsibilities. In a very large operation, the volume of business might require a separate beverage storekeeper. In order to have control and define responsibility for losses if they occur, only one person should have a storeroom key. For emergency situations, however, the manager on duty's passkey should also open the beverage storeroom door.

Perpetual Inventory Cards and Requisitions

In chapter 6, a system of storeroom control using perpetual inventory cards and requisitions is discussed. This material is very relevant to alcoholic beverages because all beverage purchases should be recorded by item on perpetual inventory cards as the items are placed in storage. Items should be issued only by properly authorized requisitions. First-in, first-out pricing (see chapter 6) should be used on requisitions. Figure 16-4 illustrates a special type of beverage requisition (with column headings describing the size of bottle requisitioned) that could be used to reduce the amount of writing required.

If an operation has a number of bars, each requisitioning its own requirements from storage, a specially designed perpetual inventory card is useful. This card shows, for each requisition recorded, the particular bar to which the items were transferred. Figure 16-5 illustrates such a perpetual inventory card.

Par Stock

To aid in knowing how much of each item to requisition each day, the bar(s) should be provided with a par stock list. The list shows the person responsible for requisitioning how many of each item should be on hand to start each day's business. These par stock lists must be changed when necessary (for example, if the customers' drinking habits change, as is sometimes the case with a change of season). The lists may also have to be adjusted on any particular day because of a special event or for some other reason. Accounting office personnel should verify from time to time that the par stock lists are being followed.

Full-Bottle Replacement

Usually a bar cannot replenish its stock each day exactly to the par stock list because of partly used bottles in the bar. Therefore, a system of full-bottle replacement for

				Size						Unit cost	Total cost
Bin no.	Item	On hand	Ordered	1.75 liters	1.0 liter	0.75 liter	0.5 liter	0.375 liter	0.25 liter	Unit cost	Total cost

Bar _____   Date _____

Ordered by _____   Completed by _____

Figure 16-4. Sample specialized beverage requisition form (*Source:* Coltman, Michael M. 1989. *Cost Control for the Hospitality Industry*, p. 183. New York: Van Nostrand Reinhold).

Date	In	Out				Balance	Requisition cost information
		Main bar	Bar #1	Bar #2	Bar #3		

Item_____   Supplier _____   Tel # _____
Minimum _____   Supplier _____   Tel # _____
Maximum _____   Supplier _____   Tel # _____

Figure 16-5.   Perpetual inventory card for establishment with multiple bars (*Source:* Coltman, Michael M. 1989. *Cost Control for the Hospitality Industry,* p. 185. New York: Van Nostrand Reinhold).

each empty bottle on hand is often used. Empty bottles should be returned to the storerom and destroyed (unless, of course, a refundable deposit is available from the supplier). In this regard, Keister (1977, p. 373) relates the following story:

> A beverage operation stored all its beer bottles, full and empty, together in one area. A beer delivery man wheeled five cases of beer into the beverage operation on his cart. He intentionally took out four cases containing full bottles of beer, with one case of empty bottles on top as camouflage. This is a remote example of what can happen, but it *can* happen. This man was caught, reported, and fired by the company he worked for.

Bottle Coding

Some establishments issue full bottles with coding devices that are difficult or impossible to duplicate (such as an ink-stamped logo or symbol) or with marks readable only with an infrared light. These coding devices identify bottles before they are issued. If an operation has only one bar, all bottles can be coded as they are received and put into storage. An operation with two or more bars is advised to code bottles just prior to issuing so that each bar can receive a separate and unique code identifying that bar. Obviously, empty bottles returned for replacement should still have this code on them. This control does not prevent a bartender from bringing in his or her own privately purchased bottles, selling the contents, not recording the sale, and pocketing the cash. It does reduce the possibility, however, because spot checks by management will show whether or not all bottles at the bar are properly coded. In that case, management must be alert to a bartender transferring the contents of a privately purchased bottle to an empty, coded one before selling the liquor and pocketing the cash.

Ninemeier (1982, p. 93) gives two other important reasons for coding bottles.

First, if the cost, from the receiving clerk's daily report or delivery invoice, is recorded on the bottle, it is easier to complete the issue requisition. Second, if the date of issue is recorded on the bottle, it is easier to keep track of rotation of bottles behind the bar.

Storeroom Inventory Reconciliation

Each day the accounting office should verify that the invoices for beverage purchases have been properly recorded on the daily beverage receiving report (Figure 16-2). At the end of each beverage storeroom control period (a week, ten days, or month, depending on each operation's policy), an actual count of each item in inventory should be taken. The procedures for taking food inventory were described in chapter 8. These procedures apply equally well to beverage inventory, particularly with regard to reconciling differences between the perpetual inventory card and actual count figures.

Once inventory has been taken, the final figures for the period can be recorded on the beverage storeroom inventory reconciliation form (Figure 16-6). On this form, the opening inventory figure is the actual inventory from the previous period. The purchases for period amount is transferred from the beverage receiving summary report for that period (see Figure 16-3). The requisitions for period figure is simply the total cost information from all relevant requisitions completed for that period. Opening inventory plus purchases for period less requisitions for period provides the closing inventory amount, which can be compared with the actual inventory for the end of the period. Minor differences between the two sets of figures can be expected because the item cost figures taken from invoiced amounts are

			Period	March 1-7
	Beer	Wine	Liquor	Total
Opening inventory	$ 482.80	$ 611.58	$1,319.20	$2,413.58
Add: Purchases for period	1,615.60	985.46	2,756.48	5,357.54
Deduct: Requisitions for period	1,432.20	1,032.10	2,576.36	5,040.66
Closing inventory	$ 666.20	$564.94	$1,499.32	$2,730.46
Actual inventory	665.14	566.70	1,496.50	2,728.34
Difference	($ 1.06)	$ 1.76	($ 2.82)	($ 2.12)

Figure 16-6. Beverage storeroom inventory reconciliation form (*Source:* Coltman, Michael M. 1989. *Cost Control for the Hospitality Industry,* p. 187. New York: Van Nostrand Reinhold).

rounded to the nearest cent on the perpetual inventory cards and requisitions. Differences of more than a few dollars should be investigated to try to determine the cause.

Bar Inventory

As far as beverage inventory is concerned up to this point, only the storeroom inventory has been discussed. At the end of each accounting period, we must include in total inventory the value of all items in each of the bars in the establishment. At each bar is an inventory of items previously requisitioned from the storeroom that have not yet been used up. Those items should be inventoried and costed. Once all inventory (both in the storeroom and at each bar) has been costed, the inventory turnover for the period can be calculated. The equation for this is the same as that illustrated in chapter 8 for food inventory turnover, except that we substitute beverage inventory figures for food inventory figures. The turnover rate in a typical beverage operation normally ranges from one half to one time a month, or from six to twelve times a year. Each beverage operation should establish its own standard and then compare the actual turnover with this standard to discern any major deviations.

DISCUSSION QUESTIONS

1. In what ways is beverage purchasing easier than food purchasing?
2. Discuss the difference between a control or monopoly situation and a license or open situation for the distribution of alcoholic beverages.
3. Why, in an open situation with several suppliers for the same products, may pricing competition not exist for some of those products?
4. Discuss the pros and cons of having only one or two suppliers for alcoholic beverage purchases versus having many suppliers.
5. Explain how kickbacks can occur in liquor purchasing and how they can be controlled.
6. List five factors to consider (other than price) when deciding whether or not to use a particular supplier.
7. Define the term *post off*.
8. Differentiate between well (or house) liquor and premium (or call) liquor.
9. Why is pricing liquor products on a cost-per-ounce basis useful? How is cost per ounce calculated?
10. List two factors that you might consider, other than cost, in deciding whether or not to buy a particular alcoholic beverage product.
11. In beverage purchasing, what items should be checked when goods are received?
12. Explain how the beverage receiving report is completed.

13. What is par stock in a bar operation?
14. Explain the system of full-bottle replacement. Why are full bottles sometimes coded before being issued from the storeroom to the bar?
15. In reconciling the storeroom inventory at the end of a period, how is the closing inventory calculated?
16. What is the inventory turnover rate in a typical bar operation, and how is it calculated?

PROBLEMS

1. A cocktail lounge has the following revenue and cost percent figures for two successive months:

	Month 1 Revenue	Month 1 Cost	Month 2 Revenue	Month 2 Cost
Beer	$10,212	45%	$12,815	50%
Wine	8,405	60	8,214	65
Liquor	48,622	30	51,675	29

   a. Calculate, for each month, the overall beverage cost percent, and comment about the changes that have occurred from one month to the next.
   b. Calculate the gross profit for each month and comment.

2. After beverages are received by the receiver, they are transferred to the store-keeper, who records the quantities received on the respective perpetual inventory cards. As items are requisitioned, the storekeeper records the issues on the related cards. At the end of each month, the storekeeper lists, from the cards, the balance on hand for each type or brand, along with the cost price. The accounting office subsequently uses this inventory list as a check against the closing inventory figure of its beverage storeroom inventory reconciliation form. Discuss the weaknesses of this system. How would you change the system to improve control?

3. For a weekly control period for a bar, you have the following information:

   Purchases: liquor $825.08, beer $309.18, and wine $585.80
   Issues: liquor $909.48, beer $53.90, and wine $378.65
   Opening inventory: liquor $2,032.48, beer $205.06, and wine $803.56
   Actual inventory: liquor $1,937.44, beer $461.20, and wine $1,010.68

   Reconcile the beverage storeroom inventory, and state whether or not you would be satisfied with the results.

4. A hotel has a weekly cycle for control of its bar storeroom inventory. On 1 July, the opening inventory was liquor $4,822.95, beer $1,233.18, and wine $787.50. For the period 1 to 6 July, purchases were: liquor $1,016.80, beer $412.10, and wine $349.02. On 7 July, a purchase was received broken down as follows: liquor $328.02, beer $31.12, and wine $303.99. For the first six days of the same week, issues were: liquor $862.12, beer $361.04, and wine $703.88. On 7 July, additional requisitions were processed: liquor $296.42, beer $121.15, and wine $187.46. The actual closing inventory on 7 July was: liquor $5,027.70, beer $1,190.55, and wine $531.87. Prepare the storeroom inventory reconciliation by category and in total for that week. Would you be satisfied with the results?

5. A hotel's cocktail bar had an opening total beverage inventory on 1 June of $2,008.10; on 30 June, total inventory was $1,908.46. June beverage revenue totalled $8,214.40, and the bar that month operated at a cost of sales of 30.4 percent.
   a. Calculate the bar's inventory turnover for June.
   b. Would you consider this acceptable under normal circumstances? Explain.

6. A restaurant owner cannot afford the services of a storekeeper. He has made the chef responsible for reception and storage of food. The dining room manager receives and stores alcoholic beverages, as well as issuing daily requirements to the dining room's service bar and managing the dining room operation. The dining room is generally quite busy. Food revenue is quite satisfactory, but beverage revenue compared to food revenue seems lower than industry figures indicate it should be for that type of dining room. However, the beverage cost percent seems to be in line with industry figures. The owner cannot be at the dining room during all the meal periods because he has to visit other restaurants he owns. His office is at one of the other restaurants, and he does his paperwork there. Explain to the owner what you think might be the cause of the apparent shortage of beverage revenue. What would you suggest he do (without hiring extra labor) to correct this situation?

REFERENCES AND SUGGESTED READINGS

Bell, Donald A. 1984. *Food and Beverage Cost Control.* Berkeley, Calif.: McCutchan, pp. 153–61, 199–225.

Dittmer, Paul R., and Gerald G. Griffin. 1984. *Principles of Food, Beverage & Labor Cost Controls for Hotels and Restaurants.* New York: Van Nostrand Reinhold, pp. 233–50.

Katisgris, Gus, and Mary Porter. 1982. *Pouring for Profit: Profitable Bar Management.* New York: Wiley.

Kelly, Hugh J. 1976. *Food Service Purchasing: Principles and Practices.* New York: Lebhar-Friedman, pp. 109–17.

Keister, Douglas C. 1977. *Food and Beverage Control.* Englewood Cliffs, N.J.: Prentice-Hall.

Ninemeier, Jack. D. 1982. *Planning and Control for Food and Beverage Operations.* East Lansing, Mich.: The Educational Institute of the American Hotel and Motel Association, pp. 60–94.

Powers, Thomas F., and Jo Marie Powers. 1984. *Food Service Operations: Planning and Control.* New York: John Wiley, pp. 289–95.

Stefanelli, John M. 1985. *Purchasing: Selection and Procurement for the Hospitality Industry.* New York: John Wiley, pp. 431–45.

Virts, William B. 1987. *Purchasing for Hospitality Operations.* East Lansing, Mich.: The Educational Institute of the American Hotel & Motel Association, pp. 248–50.

17

Wine

OBJECTIVES

- List and briefly discuss each of the three basic types of wine, and discuss wine vintages.
- Define the four types of French wine, state the major regions where wines are produced, interpret the terminology used with French wine, and identify where better-known wines are produced.
- Discuss German wines, identifying how high-quality wines are labeled and defining the terminology used with those wines.
- Discuss Italian wines and their legal categories, and identify the geographic origins of some of the better-known wines.
- Discuss U.S. wines, how they are named, the common grapes used for California wines, and the terminology used on bottle labels.
- Discuss fortified wines, and identify various types and their geographic origins.
- Discuss champagne, other sparkling wines, and the terminology used on bottle labels.
- Discuss wine storage and handling.

TYPES OF WINE

The three basic types of wine are still, sparkling, and fortified.

Still Wine

Most wine that is produced is still wine. Still wine is also sometimes known as *dinner* or *table wine*. It can be produced in various shades of red, rosé, and white and has an alcohol content generally ranging from 9 to 14 percent by volume.

Red wine is often more full bodied than rosé and white. It is often heartier, tarter, and drier. (The word *dry* when used with wine refers to an absence of sweetness.) Rosé wine color can vary from pale pink to red. It may be slightly sweet and often has a fruity flavor. Rosé wines tend to be more like white wines than like red ones. White wine color can range from a pale straw to a deep gold. Whites are lighter bodied and more delicate wines than reds and have a much less pronounced flavor. They range from extremely dry to extremely sweet.

Sparkling Wine

Sparkling wines contain carbon dioxide bubbles that provide the effervescence in these wines. Red, rosé, and white wines can all be made into sparkling wines. As with still wines, sparkling wines range from 9 to 14 percent alcohol by volume.

Fortified Wine

Fortified wines are still wines that have a distilled grape spirit such as brandy added to them. This fortification increases the wine's alcohol content to between 15 and 24 percent by volume. Fortified wines can vary from very dry to very sweet.

Vintage wine

Many people, particularly those new to wine, like to know if the date on a wine bottle's label represents a "good" year. They refer to these good years as *vintage years*. However, every year for wine production is a vintage year because the word *vintage* means a grape harvesting and, strictly speaking, has no particular meaning other than that.

Many different variables make one vintage better than another. For example, as grapes ripen, their sugar content increases and acidity decreases, and a good wine develops when the sugar and acid levels are at their best balance. The correct amount of sugar ensures that the wine has enough alcohol, will be a more stable product, and has enough acidity to enhance its flavor. In poorer years the wines are alcoholically weaker and more acidic (tarter).

Significant Vintages

Note also that a good year in France for grapes may not be a good year in Italy, and a bad year in Germany may be a good year in the United States. Even within a country, a good year for French Bordeaux may be a bad year for French Burgundy, and within the Bordeaux region one wine village may have a good year while the

Rhône Valley vineyard scene (Courtesy: Food and Wines from France, Inc.).

village down the road does not. Indeed, a specific vine in a particular vineyard may produce a good vintage year while its next-door neighbor's wine from a different type of grape compares poorly. Even red and white wines produced from the same vineyard may not both be good vintages.

Vintage Charts

Vintage charts, with a numerical scale of quality, are often produced by wine suppliers. These charts can be only a rough guide, however, because they cannot go into great detail vineyard by vineyard and are often produced to serve the needs of the distributor and/or importer. They should be used with caution, and they should not be used as the only determinant of a quality wine. Lipinski and Lipinski (1989, p. 477) state,

Vintage charts are actually "generalizations" of a specific wine-growing region, and most charts don't take into consideration the region, when the grapes were harvested, climate (the combination of sunshine, temperature, and precipitation), various microclimates, or the expertise of the individual winemaker. Therefore, the numbers used on a vintage chart represent broad-range averages or estimations. Some mediocre wines have been made in great years and excellent wines produced in moderate to poor years.

Remember also that a high-quality wine listed on a vintage chart cannot be assumed to be a high-quality wine forever. Like any product, wines have life cycles. Some high-quality wines mature in a couple of years and then decline in quality, whereas others need several years to reach their peak and then hold that high quality for many more years before starting to decline.

Unfortunately, some purchasers buy high-quality wines because of their vintage date and then consume them too soon before they reach maturity. In other words, a date on the bottle is not a guarantee of quality at the time the wine is consumed.

Finally, remember that by far the majority of wines in the world are blended and are meant to be consumed within a year of grape harvesting. Freshness and youth are the important attributes of these wines, rather than the vintage date on the label.

WINES OF FRANCE

The wine laws of France are known as *appellation contrôlée* (meaning *controlled name*) laws and are designed to control the authenticity of high-quality French wines.

The highest-quality French wines are known as *appellation d'origine contrôlée* (or controlled origin name), often shortened to AOC. The AOC designation appears on the bottle's label and is used for outstanding-quality wines.

One level down from AOC wines are the *vins délimités de qualité supérieur* (superior-quality wines), and those words or VDQS must appear on the label. The quality of these wines is not quite as high or as consistent as that of the AOC wines.

Two other qualities of wine are also available: *vins de pays* (country or regional wines) and *vins de table* (table wines).

Bottle Labels

Generally, for French wines imported into North America, seven categories of information are required on the label in addition to the wine's name.

1. A statement that the wine is a product of France
2. The region where the wine was produced
3. The appellation of the wine (AOC, VDQS, *vin de pays,* or *vin de table*)
4. The name and address of the shipper

5. The name and address of the importer
6. The percent alcohol by volume
7. The net content of the bottle

A sample label might appear as in Figure 17-1.

Illustrations and special words may—and frequently do—appear on French wine labels. However, certain designated words such as *château* (strictly meaning a castle, but commonly meaning a wine estate or vineyard, and a word usually used on the labels of the very best Bordeaux wines) may be used only for products having the right to an *appellation contrôlée* designation and originating from wine estates that actually do exist.

French words that sometimes appear on wine bottle labels are useful to know. Some of the more common ones are

Château: Estate, usually owned by a single vintner or wine producer

Cru: Growth or place of origin

Domaine: Estate, usually owned by a single vintner or wine producer

Mis(e) en bouteille(s) au château or *mis(e) en bouteille(s) à la propriété:* Estate bottled, meaning that 100 percent of the grapes come from that vineyard; these terms may appear on any label

Mis(e) au château or *mis(e) au domaine:* Also meaning estate bottled, but these two terms may be used only for wines entitled to an *appellation con-trôlée*

Mis(e) en bouteille(s) dans la région de production: Bottled where produced, a term that may be used only with *appellation contrôlée* wines

---

DOMAINE DE LA SALLE

Chusclan
Côtes-du-Rhône
APPELLATION CÔTES DU RHÔNE VILLAGES CONTRÔLÉE

SHIPPED BY:	IMPORTED BY:
M. Roussilie Viticulteur à Chusclan (Gard) embouteillé et distribué par S.A. Sofip, 3, rue du Chais, Paris 6°	Novum Wholesale Wines New York, NY

750 ml   **Product of France**   **12.5% alc./vol.**

Figure 17-1.   Label information on imported French wine bottles (*Source:* Coltman, Michael M. 1989. *Beverage Management,* p. 23. New York: Van Nostrand Reinhold).

French Wine Regions

The several major French wine-producing regions have many different districts within each region. The major regions are Bordeaux, Burgundy, Côtes-du-Rhône, Loire Valley, and Alsace. Other regions are Jura, Provence, Languedoc-Roussillon, Savoy, the Southwest, and Champagne. The general location of these French regions is illustrated in Figure 17-2. Wines from the various French regions can often be identified by the shape of the bottle, with each region generally using a distinctive shape. These shapes are illustrated in Figure 17-3.

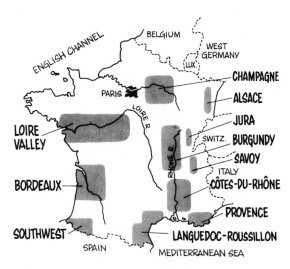

Figure 17-2.   Map of French wine-producing regions (*Source:* Coltman, Michael M. 1989. *Beverage Management*, p. 24. New York: Van Nostrand Reinhold).

Figure 17-3.   French regional wine bottle shapes (*Source:* Coltman, Michael M. 1989. *Beverage Management*, p. 24. New York: Van Nostrand Reinhold).

Bordeaux

Bordeaux red wines are generally delicate, light bodied, and dry, but full-bodied red wines are also produced. Bordeaux whites are sometimes sweet but not invariably. Bordeaux also produces some rosé wines. The quality of Bordeaux wines varies from ordinary to some of the best-known high-quality wines in the world. The price range is also just as extreme.

Any wine grown in the Bordeaux area, as long as it conforms to the related *appellation contrôlée* may be labeled Bordeaux. To understand Bordeaux wines, however, breaking them down into three main categories is best: the regional wines (mostly blended), the district wines (from a more precise geographical area), and the *château* wines (from a specific vineyard).

Bordeaux Regional Wines

Regional wines are most frequently labeled Bordeaux Rouge (red), Bordeaux Blanc (white), Bordeaux Rosé, Bordeaux Mousseux (sparkling), or Bordeaux Supérieur (superior, red or white).

Wines labeled simply Bordeaux Rouge (or one of the other categories in the preceding paragraph), with no further description, are normally not of high quality, although still agreeable to drink. Such wines are generally blended by a wine dealer or shipper who has selected them from different vineyards and bottled them under his or her own name. If the shipper is reliable, the wine is good but not outstanding.

A shipper's label bears the word *négociant* (meaning shipper or bottler), followed by the shipper's name. Alternatively the label may bear the word *monopole* (literally meaning a vineyard in single ownership but also meaning shipper or bottler), followed by the shipper's particular brand name for that wine.

Bordeaux District Wines

Of the more than thirty-five legally defined Bordeaux wine districts, most of them produce adequately good wine. Only five of those districts are noted for quality wines: Médoc, Pomerol, St. Emilion (all three producing mainly red wines), Graves (producing both red and white wines), and Sauternes, noted particularly for its mostly sweet white wines.

A wine from Bordeaux labeled simply Appellation Contrôlée Bordeaux may be from anywhere within the Bordeaux region, but a wine labeled Appellation Contrôlée Sauternes is from a vineyard within the Sauternes district and is generally a better-quality wine.

Bordeaux Château Wines

If the wine is further labeled with the name of a commune or vineyard within a specific district, it is usually one step higher in quality. Traditionally, an individual vineyard in Bordeaux is referred to as a *château*. Normally, if the word *château* appears on the label you can generally be sure that the wine is a Bordeaux. However, sometimes the word *château* may be replaced with the words *domaine* or *clos*. Generally the *chateau*-labeled wines of Bordeaux are among the finest that region has to offer.

Médoc Wines

The best wines of Bordeaux's Médoc district are categorized by a system known as *crus classés*. The grading system within the *crus classés* is a numerical one. Top-quality wines are given the name *premier cru* (literally, "first growth" or, more loosely, "top quality"). Only five Bordeaux wines fit into the *premier cru* category, and four of these are from Médoc: Château Lafite-Rothschild, Château Latour, Château Margaux, and Château Mouton-Rothschild. The fifth *premier cru* wine, Haut Brion, is from the Graves district, discussed later in this chapter. Following *premier cru* wines are the *deuxième cru* (second growth), down to the fifth. However, even a fifth-growth Médoc wine is far from a low-quality wine. It just is not ranked as high as those in higher (lower-numbered) growths. The wines in these various growths are listed in Table 17-1.

Table 17-1. The *Crus Classés* Wines of Médoc

	Commune Appellation
Deuxième Cru—Second Growth	
Château Brane-Cantenac	Margaux
Château Cos d'Estournel	St. Estèphe
Château Ducru-Beaucaillou	St. Julien
Château Durfort-Vivens	Margaux
Château Gruaud-Larose	St. Julien
Château Lascombes	Margaux
Château Léoville-Barton	St. Julien
Château Léoville-Las-Cases	St. Julien
Château Léoville-Poyferré	St. Julien
Château Montrose	St. Estèphe
Château Pichon-Longueville	Pauillac
Château Pichon-Longueville-Lalande	Pauillac
Château Rauzan-Gassies	Margaux
Château Rauzan-Ségla	Margaux

Table 17-1. The *Crus Classés* Wines of Médoc
(*continued*)

	Commune Appellation
Troisième Cru—Third Growth	
Château Boyd-Cantenac	Margaux
Château Calon-Ségur	St. Estèphe
Château Cantenac-Brown	Margaux
Château Desmirail	Margaux
Château Ferrière	Margaux
Château Giscours	Margaux
Château d'Issan	Margaux
Château Kirwan	Margaux
Château Lagrange	St. Julien
Château La Lagune	Haut Médoc
Château Langoa	St. Julien
Château Malescot-Saint-Exupéry	Margaux
Château Marquis d'Alesme-Becker	Margaux
Château Palmer	Margaux
Quatrième Cru—Fourth Growth	
Château Beychevelle	St. Julien
Château Branaire-Ducru	St. Julien
Château Duhart-Milon	Pauillac
Château La Tour–Carnet	Haut Médoc
Château Marquis-de-Terme	Margaux
Château Pouget	Margaux
Château Prieuré-Lichine	Margaux
Château Rochet	St. Estèphe
Château Saint-Pierre	St. Julien
Château Talbot	St. Julien
Cinquième Cru—Fifth Growth	
Château Batailley	Pauillac
Château Belgrave	Haut Médoc
Château Camensac	Haut Médoc
Château Cantemerle	Haut Médoc
Château Clerc-Milon	Pauillac
Château Cos-Labory	St. Estèphe
Château Croizet-Bages	Pauillac

Table 17-1. (*continued*)

	Commune Appellation
Château Dauzac	Margaux
Château Grand-Puy-Ducasse	Pauillac
Château Grand-Puy-Lacoste	Pauillac
Château Haut-Bages-Libéral	Pauillac
Château Haut-Batailley	Pauillac
Château Lynch-Bages	Pauillac
Château Lynch-Moussas	Pauillac
Château Mouton-Baron-Philippe	Pauillac
Château Pédesclaux	Pauillac
Château Pontet-Canet	Pauillac
Château du-Tertre	Margaux

Source: Coltman, Michael M. 1989. *Beverage Management,* pp. 29–30. New York: Van Nostrand Reinhold.

Crus Bourgeois Wines

Situated between the classified growths and the "common" growths of Médoc are wines known as *crus bourgeois*. These wines come from excellent estates in the region that were originally owned by the bourgeois class of merchants and shippers. These *crus bourgeois* constitute a logical extension of the *crus classés,* without being as expensive. For these wines, the words *cru bourgeois* appear on the label. Some of the more common of these wines are Château Bel-Air-Marquis d'Aligre, Château Chasse-Spleen, Château Fourcas-Dupré, Château Fourcas-Hosten, Château Phélan Ségur, and Château Siran.

Graves Wines

Although the Graves district is noted for its *premier cru* Château Haut Brion (mentioned earlier as one of only five Bordeaux wines given this prestigious classification), its other red wines are also noted for their quality. These wines are fuller than those of Médoc but without as much finesse. Red Graves *crus classés* (classified growths) are

Château Bouscaut
Château Carbonnieux
Château de Fieuzal
Château Haut-Bailly
Château La Mission-Haut Brion

Château La Tour-Haut Brion
Château La Tour-Martillac
Château Malartic-Lagravière
Château Oliver
Château Pape-Clément
Château Smith-Haut-Lafite
Château de Chevalier

White *crus classés* are

Château Bouscaut
Château Carbonnieux
Château Couhins
Château Haut-Brion
Château La Tour-Martillac
Château Laville-Haut Brion
Château Malartic-Lagravière
Château Olivier
Domaine de Chevalier

Pomerol Wines

Pomerol is a relatively small Bordeaux district producing primarily red wines. It has no official *crus classés* wines. However, one of the best-known quality wines is Château Pétrus. Other well-known wines are

Château Gazin
Château La Conseillante
Château l'Evangile
Château Lafleur
Château La Fleur-Pétrus
Château Latour Pomerol
Château Petit-Village
Château Trotanoy
Vieux-Château Certan

St. Emilion Wines

St. Emilion has both *premiers grands crus* (first great growths) and *grand crus* (great growths). These wines are listed in Table 17-2.

Table 17-2. The *Premiers Grands Crus* and *Grand Crus* Wines of St. Emilion

Premiers Grands Crus	Grand Crus
Château Ausone	Château L'Angélus
Château Beauséjour	Château Balestard-la-Tonnelle
Château Belair	Château Cadet-Piola
Château Berliquet	Château Canon-La-Gaffelière
Château Canon	Château Cap de Mourlin
Château Cheval Blanc	Château Corbin
Château Figeac	Château Corbin-Michotte
Château La Gaffelière	Château Curé-Bon
Château Magdelaine	Château Dassault
Château Pavie	Château Fonroque
Château Trottevieille	Château Grand-Barrail-Lamarzelle-Figeac
Clos Fourtet	Château Grand-Corbin
	Château La Clotte
	Château La Dominique
	Château Lamarzelle
	Château Larcis-Ducasse
	Château La Tour-Figeac
	Château Pavie-Macquin
	Château Ripeau
	Château Soutard
	Château Tertre-Daugey
	Château Trimoulet
	Château Troplong Mondot
	Château Villemaurine
	Château Yon-Figeac
	Clos des Jacobins

Source: Coltman, Michael M. 1989. *Beverage Management,* p. 33. New York: Van Nostrand Reinhold.

Sauternes Wines

The fifth well-known Bordeaux district is Sauternes, most famous for its white wines. The most outstanding of these wines is Château d'Yquem. Indeed Château d'Yquem is classified as the only *premier grand cru* (first great growth) wine of Sauternes.

Within Sauternes is the commune of Barsac. Barsac wines are in fact Sauternes wines that are allowed to be labeled Appellation Contrôlée Barsac, although some of them also use both words: *Sauternes* and *Barsac*

The wines of Sauternes and Barsac (in addition to the *premier grand cru* Château d'Yquem) are classified as *premier cru* (first growth) and *deuxième cru* (second growth) wines. They are listed in Table 17-3.

Burgundy

Burgundy (*Bourgogne* in French) red wines challenge the wines of Bordeaux in color and alcoholic strength, but they differ from them in bouquet, flavor, and style or personality. This difference is not so much one of quality as of character. Although the white wines of Burgundy cannot compare as favorably to the rich whites of the Sauternes district of Bordeaux, some of the drier whites still have a reputation as some of the finest in the world (for example, Chablis). Because fewer wines are produced, they are scarcer and usually more expensive than the wines of Bordeaux.

Burgundy Wine Identification

In Burgundy the words *domaine* or *clos* usually indicate that the wine is estate bottled. However, a vineyard in Burgundy may be shared among dozens of different owners, each of whom may use an individual label with the vineyard's name on it. As a result two bottles with the same vineyard name may contain two completely different qualities of wine.

To select a quality Burgundy wine, you need to know the names of the major villages and the names of the *grand cru* wines from them, as well as pay strong attention to the name of the grower or shipper that appears on the label. This

Table 17-3. The *Premier Crus* and *Deuxième Crus* Wines of Sauternes

Premier Cru	Deuxième Cru
Château Coutet	Château d'Arche
Château Climens	Château Broustet
Château Guiraud	Château Caillou
Château La Tour–Blanche	Château Doisy-Daëne
Château Lafaurie-Peyraguey	Château Doisy-Védrines
Château Rabaud-Promis	Château Filhot
Château de Rayne-Vigneau	Château Lamothe
Château Rieussec	Château de Malle
Château Sigalas-Rabaud	Château de Myrat
Château Suduiraut	Château Nairac
Clos Haut-Peyraguey	Château Romer
	Château Suau

Source: Coltman, Michael M. 1989. *Beverage Management*, p. 34. New York: Van Nostrand Reinhold.

knowledge is particularly important in the case of blended wines (which the majority of those from Burgundy are) because the growers who produce specific wines generally sell them to big shipping firms who do the blending in order to produce a wine of consistent, dependable quality. In such cases the wine label will usually state *mis en bouteilles dans nos caves* ("bottled in our cellars"), a statement that has little meaning because all the wines in Burgundy are bottled in cellars. Further, if the bottler is not the vineyard owner, this statement is likely made to imply to the purchaser that the bottler is the estate owner, even though the wine is not estate (or *domaine*) bottled.

Burgundy wines fall into three separate classifications. *Grands crus* wines are outstanding and may have on the label only the name of the vineyard. Only about thirty wines qualify as *grand crus* wines. Next in line are the *premiers crus*, which are usually labeled with the name of the village followed by the name of the vineyard, for example, Pommard–Le Clos Blanc. Finally, the village wines have been made from any vineyard within that village, such as Pommard or Volnay.

With a knowledge of the geography of Burgundy, you can identify the major village names and know that a given village-labeled wine is good. If another name follows the name of the village, the wine is likely to be better. If you can learn which are the thirty or so *grands crus* wines, then you can identify the best.

The five Burgundy region wine districts are Côte d'Or, Chalonnais, Mâconnais, Beaujolais, and Chablis.

Côte d'Or Wines

The supreme Burgundy wines are generally agreed to be those produced in the Côtes d'Or district. The Côte d'Or is divided into two parts: the Côte de Nuits (immediately south of Dijon) and the Côte de Beaune (somewhat farther south).

The Côte de Nuits is where some of the great and famous red wine vineyards are found. The Côte de Nuits village names, along with their *grands crus* and *premiers crus* red wines, are listed in Table 17-4.

In the Côte de Beaune are found some great white wines and many impressive red wines. The village names in the Côte de Beaune, along with their *grand crus* red and white wines, are listed in Table 17-5, and the *premiers crus* red and white wines of the Côte de Beaune are listed in Table 17-6.

Chalonnais Wines

The wines of Chalonnais (sometimes refered to as the Côte Chalonnaise) are not well known outside France but are, nevertheless, very good. Some names are Givry, Mercurey, and Rully (for reds and whites) and Bouzeron and Montagny (for whites).

Table 17-4. The *Grand Crus* and *Premiers Crus* Wines of Côte de Nuits

Village	Grands Crus	Premiers Crus
Fixin		Clos de la Perrière
		Clos du Chapitre
		Les Arvelets
		Les Hervelets
Gevrey-Chambertin	Chambertin	Clos St. Jacques
	Chambertin–Clos de Bèze	Combe-au-Moine
	Chapelle-Chambertin	Les Cazetiers
	Charmes-Chambertin	Varoilles
	Griotte-Chambertin	
	Latricières-Chambertin	
	Mazis-Chambertin	
	Mazoyères-Chambertin	
	Ruchottes-Chambertin	
Morey-Saint-Denis	Bonnes Mares	Clos Bussière
	Clos de la Roche	Clos des Lambrays
	Clos de Tart	
	Clos Saint-Denis	
Chambolle-Musigny	Bonnes Mares	Les Amoureuses
	Clos de Tart	Les Charmes
	Musigny	
Vougeot	Clos de Vougeot	
Flagey-Echézeaux	Echézeaux	
	Grands-Echézeaux	
Vosne-Romanée	La Romanée	Aux Brûlées
	La Tâche	Les Beaumonts
	Richebourg	Clos des Réas
	Romanée-Conti	La Grande Rue
	Romanée-Saint-Vivant	Les Gaudichots
		Les Malconsots
		Les Suchots
Nuits-Saint-Georges		Aux Boudots
		Aux Perdrix
		Aux Thorey
		Clos de la Marée
		Clos des Corvées
		La Richemone
		Les Cailles
		Les Didiers
		Les Porrets
		Les Pruliers
		Les Saint-Georges
		Les Vaucrains

Source: Coltman, Michael M. 1989. *Beverage Management*, p. 37. New York: Van Nostrand Reinhold.

Table 17-5. The *Grands Crus* Red and White Wines of Côte de Beaune

Village Name	Red Wines	White Wines
Aloxe-Corton	Le Corton	Charlemagne
		Corton-Charlemagne
Puligny-Montrachet		Bâtard Montrachet
		Bienvenue-Bâtard-Montrachet
		Chevalier Montrachet
		Montrachet
Chassagne-Montrachet		Bâtard-Montrachet
		Criots-Bâtard-Montrachet
		Montrachet

Source: Coltman, Michael M. 1989. *Beverage Management,* p. 38. New York: Van Nostrand Reinhold.

Table 17-6. The *Premiers Crus* Red and White Wines of Côte de Beaune

Village Names	Red Wines	White Wines
Aloxe-Corton	Corton Bressandes	
	Corton Clos du Roi	
	Corton Les Meix	
	Corton Maréchaudes	
	Corton Renardes	
Pernand Vergelesses	Iles des Vergelesses	
Savigny-les-Beaune	La Dominode	
	Les Jarrons	
	Les Lavières	
	Les Marconnets	
	Les Vergelesses	
Beaune	Clos du Roi	Les Clos des Mouches
	Les Avaux	
	Les Bressandes	
	Les Cent Vignes	
	Les Clos des Mouches	
	Les Fèves	
	Les Grèves	
	Les Marconnets	
Pommard	La Platière	
	Le Clos Blanc	
	Les Chaponnières	
	Les Epenots	
	Les Pézerolles	
	Les Rugiens	

Table 17-6. The *Premiers Crus* Red and White Wines of Côte de Beaune (*continued*)

Village Names	Red Wines	White Wines
Volnay	Clos des Ducs	
	Le Clos des Chênes	
	Les Caillerets	
	Les Champans	
	Les Fremiets	
	Santenots	
Monthélie	Les Champs Fuillots	
Auxy-Duresses	Clos du Val	
	Les Duresses	
Meursault		Blagny
		Charmes
		La Goutte d'Or
		Les Genevrières
		Les Perrières
		Poruzot
		Santenots
Puligny-Montrachet		Clovaillon
		Le Champ Canet
		Les Caillerets
		Les Chalumeaux
		Les Combettes
		Les Folatières
		Les Pucelles
		Les Referts
Chassagne-Montrachet	Clos de la Boudriotte	Les Caillerets
	Clos Saint-Jean	Les Chenevottes
	La Maltroie	Les Ruchottes
	Le Caillerets	Morgeot
	Morgeot	
Santenay	Clos Tavannes	
	Gravières	

Source: Coltman, Michael M. 1989. *Beverage Management*, pp. 38–39. New York: Van Nostrand Reinhold.

Mâconnais Wines

Mâconnais is sometimes referred to as the Côte Mâconnaise. The Mâcon district produces red, white, and some rosé wines. Generally, the whites are better and also less expensive than the whites of the Côte de Beaune. Perhaps the best-known wine from Mâconnais is Pouilly-Fuissé, a pale golden wine that can be consumed while still young and is excellent with fish or poultry. A neighbor of Pouilly-Fuissé is Pouilly-Vinzelles. Other names are Pouilly-Loché, Saint Véran, Mâcon, Mâcon Supérieur, and Mâcon-Villages.

Beaujolais Wines

Beaujolais is probably one of the best-known French wine names in North America. One of the reasons for this is the immense publicity that surrounds its name each year in November with the introduction of the Beaujolais Nouveau (sometimes known as Beaujolais Primeur). As a result of this publicity and the related demand for Beaujolais wines, their prices have risen considerably in the last few years. Peddersen (1981, p. 327) has this to say about Beaujolais Nouveau:

> It improves with keeping about as much as fresh lettuce. It is one of the exceedingly rare wines which truly cannot "travel." It is never quite as good in Lyon as in the vineyard where it was born. It is even slightly less good in Paris; decidedly less attractive in New York; and when it reaches Chicago or San Francisco, it is not at all what it was originally intended to be.

Many people think all Beaujolais is alike, but the variation in quality and taste among Beaujolais products is vast. For this reason a Beaujolais wine should be chosen with care and knowledge. The ten red *grands crus* Beaujolais wines are

Brouilly	Juliénas
Chénas	Morgan
Chiroubles	Moulin-à-Vent
Côte de Brouilly	Régnié
Fleurie	St. Amour

Somewhat lower in quality are wines that are labeled Beaujolais-Villages (with the name of a village seldom appearing on the label). Next in line is Beaujolais Supérieur and then ordinary Beaujolais. The only difference between Beaujolais Supérieur and Beaujolais is that the former contains about 1 percent more alcohol without any difference in quality.

Chablis Wines

Although the district of Chablis is geographically a part of the Burgundy wine region, its wines are often thought of as different. The very dry white wine of Chablis is world famous. It is free of both sweetness and acidity.

Chablis is classified under four headings: *grand cru* Chablis (or more simply *grand* Chablis), *premier cru* Chablis, Chablis, and *petit* Chablis (a lighter-bodied

Chablis intended to be consumed very young and preferably within a year). *Grand* Chablis is produced in only seven vineyards: Blanchots, Bougros, Les Clos, Les Grenouilles, Les Preuses, Valmur, and Vaudésir. One can be fairly certain that a *premier cru* Chablis is also excellent, whereas the other two classifications, although still good, are not of such high quality. Some of the best *premier cru* names are Chapelot, Côte de Fontenay, Fourchaume, Mont-de-Milieu, Montée de Tonnerre, Vaucoupin, and Vaulorent. Many countries produce a wine labeled Chablis (and doing so is not illegal for them), but it is far from the same product.

Côtes-du-Rhône

The Côtes-du-Rhône is the Rhône River valley. One of the best known of all Côtes-du-Rhône wines is Châteauneuf-du-Pape. It is made in both red and white varieties but is best known for its red. Although Châteauneuf-du-Pape is seldom an outstanding wine, it can usually be relied upon for its consistent quality from year to year. Other well-known wines are Côte Rôtie (red), Hermitage (red and white), Clairette de Die (white), Condrieu (white), and Château Grillet (white).

The Rhône Valley is also the home of Tavel, France's best rosé. Other better-known Côtes-du-Rhône names are

Coteaux du Tricastin (red and rosé)	Lirac (rosé)
Côtes du Ventoux (red and rosé)	St. Joseph (red and white)
Crozes-Hermitage (red and white)	St. Péray (white)
Cornas (red)	

Loire Valley

One of the best known Loire Valley wines is Anjou. Although it is produced in both white and red and dry and sparkling varieties, the best Anjou wines are the rosés. None of the Anjou rosé wines is dry. Cabernet d'Anjou is a rosé wine that is a little less sweet than the Anjou rosé.

Muscadet is a dry Loire Valley wine that is a popular alternative to Chablis and much less expensive. Another excellent wine is Pouilly-Fumé (not to be confused with Pouilly-Fuissé from the Mâconnais district of Burgundy), sometimes called Blanc Fumé. Other well-known Loire Valley wines are

Bourgueil (red)
Chinon (red)
Gros Plant du Pays Nantais (red or white)
Mountlouis (white, also known for its *vin mousseux* or sparkling wine)
Sancerre (white and rosé)

Rhône Valley wine cellar (Courtesy: Food and Wines from France, Inc.).

Saumur (still and *mousseux* reds, whites, and rosés)
Touraine (red, white, and rosé still and sparkling wines)
Vouvray (white, also *vin mousseux)*

Alsace

Alsace is the only French wine region that names its wines by the name of the grape used. The better wines of Alsace are made from Sylvaner, Riesling, and Gewürztraminer grapes, but other grapes are used, such as Muscat, Pinot, or Traminer. The official appellation of these wines is Alsace or Vin d'Alsace, followed on the label by the grape variety (of which 100 percent must be used) and the producer's name. Sometimes the name of the village of origin will follow the grape name, such as Riesling de Ribeauville.

Jura

Jura wines are not very well known, which is a pity because this region produces a unique wine known as *vin jaune* (yellow wine). This wine results from storing the fermented wine in cool cellars in vats that previously contained other *vin jaune*, whose old yeast cells form a veil of yeast on the surface of the wine. As a result, the wine is protected from excessive oxidation, turns a unique yellow color, and has a flavor unlike any other wine produced in France. The major one is Château Chalon. Three other notable Jura wines are Etoile, Arbois, and Côtes-du-Jura.

Provence

Most of the wines from the region of Provence are labeled Côtes de Provence. One of the better-known ones is Cassis. (Do not confuse Cassis wine with the French Crème de Cassis, a sweet, black currant–flavored syrup.) Other wine names are Palette (red and white) and Bandol (red and rosé).

Languedoc-Roussillon

The region of Languedoc-Roussillon is also known as the Midi. Some wine names from this region are

Blanquette de Limoux (sparkling)	Fitou
Corbières	Minervois
Costières du Gard	Muscat de Frontignan
Coteaux du Languedoc	St. Chinian
Faugères	

Southwest

In the southwest corner of France, some notable wines are also produced, such as Bergerac, Cahors, Gaillac, Madiran, Monbazillac, and Montravel.

Savoy

The Savoy region is located at the foothills of the Alps along rivers and overlooking Lake Geneva (Lac Léman is its French name). One of its best wines is the dry white Crépy. Savoy also produces the sparkling wine Seyssel.

Champagne

One exceptional wine-producing region of France is Champagne. The wines from this region are used to produce the world-famous sparkling wines that go by that name. Because these wines are so special, they are treated separately later in this chapter.

WINES OF GERMANY

The wines of Germany are produced primarily in the valleys of the Rhine (Rhein in German) and Moselle (Mosel in German) rivers, with Belgium, Luxembourg, and France bordering to the west and Switzerland to the south. These two river valleys are the most northerly wine areas in Europe, along with the Alsace and Champagne regions of France.

Some of the best German wines are produced when the grapes are overripe, a condition that concentrates the grape sugar and natural flavor. The degree of ripeness present forms the basis of German wine laws. These laws dictate the three basic categories of German wine not only on geographic origin but also by the natural sugar content of the grapes at the time they are picked.

Wine Types

German wines have three major legal categories: *Qualitätswein mit Prädikat, Qualitätswein bestimmter Anbaugebiete,* and *Deutscher Tafelwein.*

Qualitätswein mit Prädikat (frequently shortened to Q.m.P.) means a quality wine with special attributes; in other words, this is the best German wine. These top-quality German wines are similar in status to the AOC wines of France. This type of wine is usually sublabeled *Kabinett, Spätlese, Auslese, Beerenauslese,* or *Trockenbeerenauslese.* Each of these five words indicates a different degree of wine sweetness, with Kabinett being the driest and Trockenbeerenauslese the sweetest.

Qualitätswein bestimmter Anbaugebiete (frequently shortened to Q.b.A.) means a quality wine from a controlled growing district. This quality is the next level down of German wines. These Q.b.A. wines are good-quality wines whose natural sugar content is not high enough for them to achieve Q.m.P. status.

Deutscher Tafelwein means "German table wine" and is a lower-quality wine. This quality of wine is not often exported.

Legal Regions

Eleven legal (delimited) regions fall within the *Qualitätswein* (quality wine) categories.

Rheingau	Franken (Franconia)
Rheinhessen	Württemberg
Rheinpfalz	Baden
Mittelrhein	Ahr
Nahe	Bergstrasse
Mosel-Saar-Ruwer	

The first six of these, plus perhaps Franken (Franconia), are the most important. These regions are located on the map illustrated in Figure 17-4. For a *Qualitätswein*, the name of one of these regions must appear on the bottle label. Within each region are two or more districts, with thirty-four districts in total. Each district has several villages or parishes forming a geologic and climatic unit, and each village has several vineyards. In total there are about 1,400 wine villages and some 2,600 vineyards whose names may appear on high-quality wine labels. Because German wines are generally identified by the village name where the grapes are grown, the purchaser needs to know the names of the more important villages.

Rhine Wines

Five of the eleven delimited wine-producing regions lie within the Rhine River area. These are the Rheingau, the Rheinhessen, the Rheinpfalz, the Mittelrhein, and the Nahe, of which the first three are the most important.

Rhine wines (as well as other wines of Germany) are generally all made from the same varieties of grape, the Riesling (which is considered to produce the very best

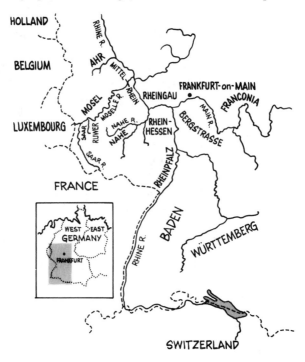

Figure 17-4.   Map of German wine-producing regions (*Source:* Coltman, Michael M. 1989. *Beverage Management*, p. 53. New York: Van Nostrand Reinhold).

of the German wines), the Sylvaner, and the Müller-Thurgau (a cross between the Riesling and Sylvaner). Some of the better known villages in the Rheingau are

Eltville	Johannisberg
Ebach	Oestrich
Geisenheim	Rauenthal
Hattenheim	Rüdesheim
Hochheim	Winkel

Well-known Rheinhessen villages are Alsheim, Bingen, Bodenheim, Nackenheim, Nierstein, and Oppenheim. One of the better-known wines from the Rheinhessen is liebfraumilch. Many purchasers think that liebfraumilch is a wine from a specific village, but it is not. Liebfraumilch is an invented name that does not refer to a specific geographic location. The name can refer to any wine from this region, and it is frequently a blend of lower-quality wines that can vary considerably in both quality and price. The quality of a liebfraumilch can best be judged by the name of a reputable shipper.

The third Rhine wine area is the Rheinpfalz, sometimes referred to as the Palatinate. This area is also on the west bank of the Rhine south of Rheinhessen. Some village names are Deidesheim, Dürkheim, Forst, Ruppertsberg, Speyer, and Wackenheim. In addition to the three main Rhine areas is the less known area of the Nahe River, a tributary of the Rhine. Three important village names of the Nahe are Bad Kreuznach, Niederhausen, and Schloss Böckelheim.

Moselle Wines

Another of the high-quality wine-producing regions is the Mosel-Saar-Ruwer, made up of the Mosel (Moselle in English) River and its two tributaries, the Saar and the Ruwer. Moselle wines are quite low in alcohol, as low as 10 percent. The best-known Moselle villages are Bernkastel, Graach, Piesport, Trittenheim, Urzig, Wehlen, and Zeltingen. Well-known Saar villages are Ayl, Kanzem, Ockfel, and Wiltingen. Some of the Ruwer villages are Eitelsbach, Grünhaus, and Kasel. Note that the wines from any of the three river areas (the Moselle, the Saar, and the Ruwer) all bear the same region label identification: Mosel-Saar-Ruwer.

The Moselle region also has its generic equivalent to the Rhine's liebfraumilch: Moseltaler, a dry, crisp wine quite distinct from the sweeter liebfraumilch. In earlier days the generic wine of the Moselle was named Moselblümchen (meaning little flower of the Moselle) but this name is now replaced in the North American market with the easier to pronounce Moseltaler.

Bottle Colors

The easiest and quickest way to differentiate Moselle wines from Rhine wines is the color of the bottle. Both come in tall, fluted, elegant bottles similar to those for

French wines produced in Alsace, but Rhine wine bottles are brown, whereas Moselle bottles are green (just like those of Alsace).

Franconia (Franken) Wines

One other important wine-producing region in Germany is Franconia (Franken in German). The wines produced here are much drier with a less intense bouquet than those of either Rhine or Moselle. These wines are sometimes referred to as *Steinwein* and are invariably shipped in their flat-sided, gourd-shaped bottle (a sort of stumpy flagon) known as a *Bocksbeutel*. The wines of Franconia are often dry and more similar to French wines than to the sweeter wines from the Rhine and the Moselle. Some village names are Eschendorf, Randersacker, Retzbach, Stetten, and Würzburg.

Bottle Labels

German wine labels at first seem more confusing than labels on wine bottles of other countries. This confusion is simply because the labels carry more information about the wine. This information includes not only the grape's regional origin, the year the wine was made, and the vintner's name but also facts about the grape-growing conditions and the method used to make the wine.

The comments that follow concerning German wine bottle labels pertain specifically to the two top-quality wines: *Qualitätswein mit Prädikat* (Q.m.P.) and *Qualitätswein bestimmter Anbaugebiete* (Q.b.A.).

Name of Region

The first item to appear is the name of one of the eleven delimited or controlled regions (such as Rheingau or Mosel-Saar-Ruwer) established by German wine law.

Year

The next item on the label is the year the wine was made. However, remember that German vineyards are quite far to the north, with less sunny locations than those in France. Reasonably good wines are produced in Germany every year, but weather conditions inevitably influence results, especially with high-quality wines. Really great years are rare.

Village and Vineyard Names

The next label item states the name of the village where the grapes were grown, followed by the name of the vineyard. For example, Niersteiner Schlossberg indicates that the grapes are from the Schlossberg vineyard in the village of Nierstein. (Note that the village name takes on an extra *er* in much the same way that a person from New York becomes a New Yorker.)

However, this village-vineyard rule has exceptions. Some German wines are so outstanding that only the vineyard name appears on the label and no village identification is needed. Some of these vineyard-only names are Maximin Grünhaus and Scharzhofberg in the Mosel-Saar-Ruwer region and Schloss Johannisberg, Schloss Vollrads, and Steinberg in the Rheingau region.

Grape Name

After the village and vineyard names (if they appear) usually follows the name of the grapes used. For the finest wines of Germany, this is Riesling. If the grape name does not appear, it may be one of the highly recognized wines that are assumed to be made with Riesling; otherwise, it is a wine not made from the Riesling grape but from some other (such as Sylvaner), and the winemaker does not wish to draw attention to the fact that Riesling has not been used!

After the grape name may follow one of five words, if the wine is a Q.m.P. one, stating the ripeness or sweetness of the grapes when picked. The meanings of these five words were discussed earlier.

Shipper

The next item to appear on a German wine label is the name of the producer or producers. Most vineyards in Germany (just as in the Burgundy region of France) are owned by several different proprietors, and one proprietor may have a share in several different vineyards. This fact must be considered when reading a German wine label. If a proprietor bottles a wine on his or her own estate, the label will state *Erzeugerabfüllung* (bottled by the producer or grower), *Aus eigenem Lesegut* (from the producer's own harvest), or *Abfüller* (bottler), followed by the producer's or proprietor's name. The astute purchaser must thus have some knowledge of the names of the best producers as well as the best vineyards.

The A.P. Number

One other requirement of German wine law is that on the *Qualitätswein* (either Q.m.P. or Q.b.A.) bottle labels appears the certification, or *Amtliche Prüfungsnummer* (meaning "official test number"), usually abbreviated to A.P. Nr., followed by an actual number. In order for a producer to obtain this number, each lot of wine must have been approved by sample quality control testing and tasting by a regional board who affirm that it is typical of its type's style and quality.

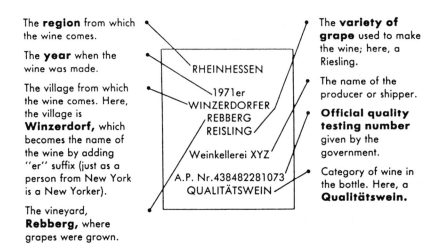

The **region** from which the wine comes.

The **year** when the wine was made.

The village from which the wine comes. Here, the village is **Winzerdorf,** which becomes the name of the wine by adding ''er'' suffix (just as a person from New York is a New Yorker).

The vineyard, **Rebberg,** where grapes were grown.

RHEINHESSEN

1971er
WINZERDORFER
REBBERG
REISLING

Weinkellerei XYZ

A.P. Nr.438482281073
QUALITÄTSWEIN

The **variety of grape** used to make the wine; here, a Riesling.

The name of the producer or shipper.

Official quality testing number given by the government.

Category of wine in the bottle. Here, a **Qualitätswein.**

Figure 17-5.   Typical German wine bottle label (*Source:* Coltman, Michael M. 1989. *Beverage Management,* p. 62. New York: Van Nostrand Reinhold).

Wine Category

Finally on the label will appear the wine category, such as *Qualitätswein mit Prädikat* (followed by one of the harvest descriptive words such as *Kabinett)* or *Qualitätswein bestimmter Anbaugebiete.* Note that the authorities allow Q.b.A. wines to be simply labeled *Qualitätswein.*

Illustration

Figure 17-5 illustrates a typical German high-quality wine bottle label and the sequence in which the items appear. Note that the label lists the wine category as *Qualitätswein,* indicating that it is a Q.b.A. quality wine and not a Q.m.P. one.

Other Terms

Two relatively new types of better-quality *Tafelwein* known as *Landwein* (country wine) are produced in Germany by some of the estates along the Rhine and Moselle. These are *Trocken* (meaning dry) and *Halbtrocken* (meaning half or medium dry). They are wines with less residual sugar than other German wines. These terms are official government designations.

WINES OF ITALY

Vines are grown in each of Italy's twenty provinces to yield a tremendous variety of moderately priced wines as well as some extremely fine quality wines. About 60 percent of the wines in Italy are red, and the remainder white. Italy's red wines have a greater recognition, probably because they have a mature taste as a result of long aging in the cask before bottling.

The wines of Italy are not classified as they are in France and Germany with a clearly structured delineation from region to district, to village, and to vineyard. In fact, very few Italian wines are given individual vineyard names, and Italy has no ranking of classified vineyards as is the case in Bordeaux with its various qualities of *crus* or growths.

Italian wine names can be confusing because some are known by the grape from which they are made (such as Barbera), others by the name of the village or district (such as Barbaresco), and some by both the grape and the village or district name. Some are even labeled with names that do not reflect either the grape or location of origin. Further, some wines are given the same name even though the wine is bottled as a dry one, a sweet one, or even a sparkling one. Therefore, knowing the geography of Italy, unlike France and Germany, is not always too helpful in recognizing a good-quality wine.

Wine Laws

In the mid-1960s, the Italian government started to introduce more stringent wine laws known as *denominazione di origine controllata* (denomination of controlled origin) similar to the *appellation contrôlée* laws of France. These laws provide four classifications for Italian wine.

Denominazione di origine controllata e garantita (the acronym DOCG is often used) means controlled and guaranteed denomination. This category is reserved for outstanding wines that have their quality guaranteed by a committee of experts. These are Italy's most prestigious wines. At present they are Barolo, Barbaresco, Vino Nobile di Montepulciano, Brunello di Montalcino, and Chianti, which are red wines, and Albana di Romagno, a white wine.

Denominazione di origine controllata (or DOC) means a controlled denomination. The DOC designation certifies that the wine is made from grapes grown in a defined production zone and complies with specific quality levels. The DOC laws for many regions also allow a wine made from grapes grown in a special zone within that region to be labeled *Classico* (such as Chianti Classico).

Vino Tipico (meaning "typical wine") is a type of wine that in France would be labeled *vin de table*. These wines are made from an established grape variety but are not yet up to DOC quality standards.

Vino da Tavola (meaning "table wine") includes wines that are excluded from other categories for quality reasons: perhaps an unapproved grape variety was used in their manufacture, or their DOC status has not yet been codified or is pending because they are relatively new types of wine. Some of these wines, although not entitled to DOC labeling, equal or surpass the quality of some DOC wines.

Wine Regions

The following regions are numbered in parentheses and keyed to the map of Italy illustrated in Figure 17-6. Generally the numbers move from west to east and from north to south.

Valle d'Aosta or Aosta Valley (1)

The Aosta Valley region's best-known wines are the full-bodied red Donna and Enfer d'Arvier.

Piedmont (2)

The best and most varied Italian wines are produced in the Piedmont region. The two best known of these wines are the robust reds: Barolo (a DOCG wine and one

Figure 17-6.   Map of Italy (*Source:* Coltman, Michael M. 1989. *Beverage Management,* p. 69. New York: Van Nostrand Reinhold).

of the great red wines of Italy made from Nebbiolo grapes) and Barbaresco (also a DOCG wine and made from Nebbiolo grapes), which is considered somewhat superior to Barolo because it is slightly less robust. A third well-known wine from the Nebbiolo grape is Gattinara. Five other villages around Gattinara produce quality red wines: Ghemme, Boca, Fara, Sizzano, and Lessona. Other Nebbiolo wines named after a village are Carema and Spanna.

The Barbera grape is commonly used in Piedmont. Many wines made from it are named with both the grape and the village, such as Barbera d'Alba and Barbera d'Asti. From the Moscato (Muscat) grape comes the famous delicate and somewhat sweet sparkling white wine Asti Spumante. One other important white Piedmont wine is Cortese di Gavi (made from the Cortese grape). Other red grape varieties are Grignolino, Dolcetto, and Freisa. These grapes are also usually followed by the place name such as Grignolino d'Asti, Dolcetto d'Alba, and Freisa di Chieri.

Liguria (3)

Liguria produces relatively little wine, but two names might be encountered: Cinqueterre (a dry white) and Dolceacqua (a dry red wine sometimes known as Rossese di Dolceaqua).

Lombardy (4)

In Lombardy's Valtellina Alps, Nebbiolo grapes are grown and produce a hardy red wine, Valtellina. In this area is produced a dry wine higher in alcohol than Valtellina: Sfursat or Sforzato. The subdistricts of Sassella, Grumello, Inferno, and Valgella often lend their names to red wines. Other grapes grown in Lombardy are the Pinot and Riesling, which produce such white wines as Franciacorta Pinot. Franciacorta Rosso (red) is made from a variety of other grapes. From the Lombard bank of Lake Garda comes a very pale red wine labeled Riviera del Garda Rosso. If it is labeled Riviera del Garda Chiaretto, it is a rosé. A delicate white from this area is named Lugana.

Trentino-Alto Adige or the Adige Valley (5)

In the Adige Valley, the Teroldego grape gives its name to a full-bodied red wine Teroldego Rotaliano. Other grape-named wines are Merlot (such as Merlot del Trentino), Cabernet (Trentino Cabernet), Pinot, Moscato, and Riesling, as well as the rosé Casteller.

Surprising to many visitors to Italy is that in the upper part of the Trentino Valley, as it narrows toward Bolzano, German is the main language. Until 1919, this region was part of Austria (and indeed the Austrians still refer to it as South Tyrol). Many of the wines are still bottled with labels bearing German terminology and script.

Red wines produced here are Caldaro (Kalterer in German), Lago di Caldaro (Kaltersee in German), and Santa Maddalena (St. Magdalener in German); a white wine is Terlano (Terlaner in German).

Veneto (6)

The Veneto region is best known for its two great red wines, Valpolicella and Bardolino. Recioto della Valpolicella has more alcohol and flavor than Valpolicella and may be slightly sweet with a hint of sparkle, although if it is labeled Recioto della Valpolicella Amarone it will have been fermented out to a dry wine.

Some of the grapes grown in this area that lend themselves to wine names are Cabernet, Merlot, Pinot, and Tocai, with wine names such as Cabernet di Pramaggiore, Merlot del Piave, and Tocai di Lison. The Prosecco grape is used to make both still and sparkling wines. Soave, produced in Veneto, is perhaps Italy's most famous white wine.

Friuli-Venezia Giulia (7)

Another district in northeast Italy is Friuli-Venezia Giulia. Wines are usually labeled with varietal names such as Cabernet, Merlot, Pinot Nero, Riesling, Sylvaner, Sauvignon, Traminer, and Pinot Grigio. However, six wine-producing subregions also lend their names to wines: Colli Orientale di Friuli, Grave del Friuli, Collio Goriziano (or simply Collio), Isonzo, Latisana, and Aquileia. Sometimes these names are combined with a grape name, such as Cabernet di Latisana (red).

Emilia Romagna (8)

The Emilia-Romagna district produces four important wines named after grapes: Lambrusco (a semisparkling, somewhat sweet red; one of the better known ones is Lambrusco di Sorbara), Sangiovese such as Sangiovese di Romagna (a red made from the Sangiovese grape that is also used to make Chianti), Trebbiano (white), and Albana (white), as well as Albana di Romagno, one of the only six DOCG wines.

Tuscany (9)

Tuscany is well known for its Chianti. The Chianti wines from Italy should not be confused with the generic word *chianti* used to describe certain wines from California. Italian Chianti has become one of the best-known Italian red wines simply because so much of it has been produced and because it was traditionally exported in a wicker-covered *fiasco*. This bottle design and straw mantle were a useful marketing device that caught the public's imagination and became symbolic of Italy. Today, most quality Chianti is exported in a standard Bordeaux-type bottle.

Chianti quality can vary greatly. A Chianti that is at least two years old may be labeled *Vecchio* (meaning "old") and *Riserva* if it is at least three years old. Some of the best Chianti is known as Chianti Classico, one of the few wines entitled to the DOCG designation. The word *classico* means that the wine was produced in a restricted zone within a general DOC area. The best of all Chiantis is Chianti Classico Riserva, an excellent Chianti that is aged in oak casks for three to six years before it is bottled.

Although Chianti is the best-known wine of Tuscany, other high-quality wines are Brunello di Montalcino (DOCG red), Vino Nobile di Montepulciano (also a DOCG red), Vernaccia di San Gimignano (white), Vin Santo (white), Tignanello (red), Solaia (red), Galestro (white), and Pomino (white).

Marches (10)

The best-known Marches wine is Verdicchio del Castelli di Jesi, a dry white wine. Another white wine made here is Bianchello del Metauro. Good red wines also made in this area are Rosso Conero and Rosso Piceno (both from Sangiovese grapes).

Umbria (11)

Produced in Umbria is the well-known white wine Orvieto. An Orvieto labeled *Secco* is dry; if labeled *Abboccato,* it is semisweet. Another Umbria wine is the red and white Torgiano. Other wines are Sagrantino and Montefalco.

Latium (12)

In the Latium region, white Frascati is produced in both *secco* (dry) and *abboccato* (semisweet) styles. Other wines from this region are Colli Albani, Colli Lanuvini, and Marino, all white wines.

Est! Est!! Est!!! di Montefiascone is also produced here. It is a white wine similar to Frascati. Its unusual name has a story. The steward of a twelfth-century German bishop was traveling to Rome ahead of his master to mark the inns where good wine could be found. On the doors of those inns, he was to chalk Est (meaning "this is it"). At Montefiascone he was so enthusiastic about the wine he chalked "Est! Est!!Est!!!"

Some grape varieties used in Latium are Trebbiano (white) and Sangiovese and Merlot (reds) that lend themselves to such wine names as Merlot di Aprilia.

Abruzzo (13) and Molise (14)

East of Latium are the two regions of Abruzzo and Molise on the Adriatic coast. Some pleasant wines are produced here, such as Montepulciano d'Abruzzo (red), Trebbiano d'Abruzzo (white), Biferno (red and white), and Pentro (red and white).

Campania (15)

Among the wines for which Campania is famous are the reds and whites of Ischia (an island off the coast) and Lacryma Christi (meaning "tears of Christ"), grown on the slopes of the volcano Vesuvius and with bottle labels distinguished by the added words *del Vesuvio*. Lacryma Christi is made as a red, a white, and a rosé, with the white (both still and sparkling) the best known. Other wines from this district are Greco di Tufo (white), Taurasi (red), and Fiano di Avellino (white).

Apulia (16)

A well-known wine from Apulia is Castel del Monte (white, red, and rosé). The rosé is considered to be one of Italy's most important rosés. Other wines from this district are San Severo (white and red) and Locorotondo (white).

Basilicata (17)

Between the heel and the toe of Italy is Basilicata, with its extinct volcano Vulture on whose slopes grow the unusual Aglianico grapes that produce the dry red Aglianico del Vulture. The white wine of this region is Asprino.

Calabria (18)

Calabria's best-known wine, Ciro (red, white, and rosé), is made from Gaglioppo grapes. Other red wines are Donnici, Pollino, and Savuto.

Sardegna or Sardinia (19)

Sardinia is an island well off the west coast of Italy across the Tyrrhenian Sea. Its unique wine is Vernaccia di Oristano (a dry and bitter aperitif wine). Others are Cannonau di Sardegna (red and rosé) and Monica di Sardegna (red).

Sicily (20)

Finally Sicily, a huge island off the toe of Italy, is most famous for its fortified dessert wine, Marsala, which is often used as a cooking ingredient. Sicily is also famous for Mount Etna, after which Etna wine (red and white) is named. Other wines produced in Sicily are Alcamo, Faro, Corvo, Ragaleali, Faustus, and Cerasuolo di Vittoria.

WINES OF THE UNITED STATES

The United States has two separate major wine regions. The first is in the northeast, centered in the state of New York and spreading out into Ohio, Indiana, Michigan, Wisconsin, and Pennsylvania, and even north across the Canadian border into the Niagara Peninsula.

The other region is centered in California but spreads north into Oregon and Washington and even into British Columbia in Canada. The best of the wines come from the northern part of California close to San Francisco.

Wine Names

In the United States wines are named in three different ways: generic, varietal, and by brand.

Generic Wines

A generically named wine is one that bears the name of a broad general European type of wine such as burgundy, chianti, chablis, or rhine. This terminology has traditionally been used because early United States winemakers tried to imitate European wines, even though the resemblance was slight. According to Virts (1987, p. 246), "There is no variety requirement for California generics. A Burgundy may be made from any red grape in California while a French Burgundy . . . is most likely made from the Pinot Noir grape." Indeed, some California wineries have been known to market the same wine in different bottles with merely a change in generic labeling. A bottle labeled "chablis" might end up being dry or sweet, whereas a Chablis from the Burgundy region of France is always an extremely dry wine.

Similarly, a Sauternes wine from the French Bordeaux region is a naturally sweet wine, whereas a California sauterne probably has grape concentrate added to it as it is bottled in order to sweeten it. (Note also that French Sauternes has an *s* at the end of its spelling, and the U.S. sauterne does not.)

By U.S. law, generically named wines must include the place of origin on the bottle label, such as California chablis. This distinguishes them from their European counterparts.

Generic wines are usually blended to maintain consistency of quality and taste and are often suitable as house or table wines or for use in wine cocktails or coolers. They may not keep well when opened. Red wines should be used within a day or so, and whites within two or three days. Generic wines are often sold in large containers and are sometimes referred to as *jug wines*. Many of them are pasteurized to retard spoilage.

Varietal Wines

A varietal wine is named after the grape from which it is made and is one in which 75 percent or more of a single grape predominates. In comparison, in France a varietally named wine must contain 100 percent of that grape, and in Germany 85 percent. A varietal wine generally is moderately priced, although higher than a generic wine, but a varietal name is no guarantee of quality; even among wines with the same varietal name, the divergence of flavors can be large. However, the best California wines are now found among varietals. Some of the best exceed the 75 percent minimum single grape requirement, and some even have 100 percent of the named grape because that particular grape imparts a unique character to the wine.

Brand-name Wines

Generally, the best-quality U.S. wines carry a specific brand name. These wines are sometimes referred to as *proprietary wines*. Brand-name wines have names that are exclusive to a particular vintner or shipper. Brand-name wines must legally state the class or type of wine; although the brand name is emphasized on a label, it may actually be a varietal wine. For example, wine with a label stating "Chateau Blanc —a California white burgundy wine made entirely from Pinot Blanc grapes" is basically a varietal wine.

The Northeast

The earliest settlers in the northeastern United States discovered native vines growing wild along much of the Atlantic Coast. Attempts to cross them with imported European *Vitis vinifera* varieties in the seventeenth and eighteenth centuries were not successful because of disease and very cold winter temperatures that the *Vitis vinifera* could not cope with. The native vines (notably Catawba and Concord of the *Vitis labrusca* type) were thus generally used in that area. These native vines have a distinctive flavor that gives wines made from them a pungent aroma often described as foxy. These *labrusca* vines are also cultivated in some other states (such as Oregon and Washington) and in other countries such as Canada and Brazil.

However, the northeast is now using some *vinifera* vines (primarily in the Finger Lakes area of New York) because a method was found in the 1950s to help them survive the cold winters. American-French hybrids are also being used.

Most of the northeastern wine production is in New York State, but only a small proportion of all table wine produced in the United States is from New York because most of its grapes are used to produce sherry, port, and sparkling wine.

The four recognized New York state wine regions are Erie-Chautauqua (along the shoreline of Lake Erie), Finger Lakes (in the center of the state), Hudson River, and Long Island.

A wine labeled New York State may contain as much as 25 percent of wine from outside the state. This blending helps to mellow the harsher taste of the *labrusca* vine. If the label says American, rather than New York State, then more than 25 percent of the content is wine from outside the state.

The California Districts

About two thirds of all wines consumed in the United States are now produced in California. Many people still think of California as a single grape-growing district with a climate and conditions that are the same wherever the grapes are grown, but this is not the case. The grape-growing districts are diverse and dissimilar, in the same way that the Bordeaux and Burgundy regions of France, although in the same country, are each unique. Just as in Bordeaux and Burgundy (as well as in many other European grape-growing areas), vintners have discovered that different areas lend themselves better to some grape varieties than to others.

In very broad terms the California wine districts can be categorized geographically as either coastal areas or Central Valley areas. However, within each of these areas several subdistricts can be identified, as illustrated in Figure 17-7.

Coastal Areas

The coastal area embraces the following general regions: north coast counties, San Francisco Bay area, the north central coast, the south central coast, and southern California.

The north coast counties (Mendocino, Sonoma, and Napa) are immediately north of San Francisco. The fine wines of California are grown primarily in this and the San Francisco Bay area.

Mendocino is the most northerly county and has a moderate climate that produces high-quality red and white wines. The counties of Sonoma and Napa are parallel to each other and are separated by the Mayacamas Mountain range. The Sonoma Valley has a moderate climate somewhat similar to that of Burgundy in France. In Sonoma County three other winegrape-producing areas are the Russian River Valley (with a climate cooler than that of the Sonoma Valley) and two areas that have a climate similar to that of France's Bordeaux region, the Dry Creek Valley and the Alexander Valley. Napa County is considered to be California's top-quality wine-producing area. Most of its production is red wine that includes the finest Cabernet Sauvignons in the United States.

To the south of the three north-coast counties is the San Francisco Bay area with its counties of Alameda, Santa Clara and Santa Cruz. Within Alameda County is

Figure 17-7.   Map of California's wine-producing regions (*Source:* Coltman, Michael M. 1989. *Beverage Management*, p. 85. New York: Van Nostrand Reinhold).

the Livermore Valley, noted for its white Sauvignon Blanc wines and its sweeter sauterne-type dessert wines.

The north-central coast embraces the counties of San Benito and Monterey, and the south-central coast includes the counties of San Luis Obispo and Santa Barbara.

Central Valley Region

The other major California area that can be differentiated from the coastal ones is the widespread and hot inland region with its three general viticultural areas: Central Valley, Sacramento Valley, and San Joaquin Valley. This region stretches some two hundred miles north from Bakersfield, and most of California's vineyards planted in the last twenty years are in this inner valley. The wines from this valley, because it is so much hotter, tend to have less individuality and character than the varietals produced in the cooler coastal regions. Grapes are primarily used to produce bulk (jug) wines, as well as sweet dessert and fortified wines.

The Sierra foothills area is a relatively small hilly area (embracing the counties of Amador, El Dorado, and Calaveras) that is at a higher altitude than the Central

Valley. It thus has a cooler climate that allows a wider range of different grape types to be grown.

American Viticultural Areas

Traditionally, California vineyards have been referred to by their county names. Recently, more specific geographic names, American Viticultural Areas (AVAs), have been used. They are similar to the French appellations of origin. The AVAs are administered by the government through the Bureau of Alcohol, Tobacco, and Firearms, and the AVA names can be listed on the label.

California Red Grapes

The best California wines are the dry red ones made from the Cabernet Sauvignon grape (also used in the Bordeaux region of France, as well as in Italy, Argentina, Chile, and Australia for their best wines). Another well-known grape variety is the Pinot Noir, found also in the Burgundy and Champagne districts of France.

Other major red grape varieties used in California are Gamay Beaujolais, Napa Gamay (also known as Gamay Noir), Barbera, Merlot, Zinfandel (a grape native to and grown only in California), and Petite Sirah. Some other less-known varieties are Charbono, Grignolio, Carignane, Carnelia, Carmine, and Centurio.

California White Grapes

For white wines the prime grape used is Chardonnay, famous for its use in the Chablis and Champagne regions of France. On some labels, Chardonnay is named Pinot Chardonnay. Other white wine grapes are Folle Blanche, Chenin Blanc, Sauvignon Blanc, Pinot Blanc, Semillon, Riesling (sometimes labeled Riesling-Sylvaner or Franken Riesling, whereas other varieties are Grey Riesling and Emerald Riesling), Gewurztraminer, French Colombard, Moscato di Canelli, Green Hungaria, and Flora.

California Wine Labels

In many ways California wines are easier to understand than many of their European cousins. Labeling descriptions are minimized but still informative. Although California wine labels do sometimes indicate the wine's specific place of origin (for example, Sonoma Valley Pinot Noir or Napa Valley Chablis), the place of origin is no guarantee of quality. In Europe the soil, grapes, and production methods must meet rigidly controlled government-approved standards for an area to use a place-of-origin name producing wines with a special and distinctive character. In California, less correlation exists between place of origin and the wine's character.

Geographic Origin

On a California wine label an indication of the geographic origin is required. For a wine to be labeled simply California, 100 percent of the grapes must be from the state. If the origin is more specific, such as Sonoma County, at least 75 percent of the grapes must be grown in that county and the rest from elsewhere in California. Sometimes more than one county is shown. As many as three are allowed, as long as corresponding percentages of grape origin are shown by county. If the label shows an inner region, such as Alexander Valley (or other official American Viticultural Area), at least 85 percent of the grapes must be from that area.

Varietal Labeling

If the label has a varietal grape name, then 75 percent of the wine must be from the named grape. If used with a geographic appellation, the minimum required percentage of the named grape (as detailed in the preceding paragraph) must come from the appellation area. A generically labeled wine has no requirements as to grape varieties used, as long as they are all from California.

Estate Bottled

If a label states "Estate bottled," then 100 percent of the grapes must be grown by that winery, and the wine must be bottled there.

Alcohol by Volume

The law allows a 1.5 percent variation on either side of the stated amount of alcohol by volume. A bottle labeled 11.5 percent can range from 10 to 13 percent.

Vintage Dates

Vintage dates are more common on California wine bottle labels than they once were. If the label has a vintage date on it, then 95 percent of the grapes must have been harvested and crushed that year in the region named on the label. The 5 percent tolerance allows for topping up of wines that are aging in containers. Note also that, just as a high-quality French Bordeaux vintage wine does not mean that all French wines produced that year are high-quality vintage wines, so too does a vintage-dated California wine from a particular valley not represent the quality of all California wines of that year.

Other Information

If the label says, "Produced and bottled by . . .," at least 75 percent of that wine was fermented by the winery named, whereas if it says, "Made and bottled by . . .," as little as 10 percent and as much as 74 percent may have been crushed and fermented by that winery, and the rest is blended wine. The terms "Perfected and bottled by . . .," "Cellared and bottled by . . .," or "Vinted and bottled by . . ." do not require the bottler to have fermented any of the wine.

The term *blush* is sometimes used on labels. This generally means the wine is a rosé.

Some California wines are made in a similar fashion to some German wines by using shriveled grapes highly concentrated in sugar. The labels of these bottles state that the wines are "late harvest" or "selected late harvest." The label must also state the sugar content of the grape when harvested and the wine's residual sugar after fermentation. Obviously, the higher the residual sugar, the sweeter the wine.

WINES OF SPAIN

Spanish red wines have four quality classifications. *Gran Reserva* is the top quality and is used for wines aged for a minimum of two years in wood and then for three in the bottle. *Reserva* is aged one year in wood and two years in the bottle. *Crianza* (literally meaning that the wine has been "nursed," or aged) has one year of aging in wood and only a few months in the bottle. If a wine is labeled *Sin crianza*, it has not had any aging. *Garantia de Origen* (meaning "guarantee of its origin") has virtually no aging in either wood or bottle. The corresponding regulations for white and rosé wines require less aging.

The best wines of Spain are from the Rioja region in the north of the country. Wines are generally marketed under brand names or proprietary names of individual shippers. What can be confusing to the purchaser is that some Rioja wine is bottled in Bordeaux-type bottles, whereas others are in Burgundy-type bottles.

The district of La Mancha produces an abundant amount of both red and white wine, with its Valdepeñas one of the better known. The area known as Catalonia also produces red, white, and rosé wines.

If a wine label bears the word *Reserva* or *Reserva Special,* generally the wine has been specially bottled by the shipper and is of a higher quality. The word *cosecha* on a label means vintage, but vintage year has far less meaning than it might on a Bordeaux or Burgundy wine.

Spain is also noted for its fortified wine, sherry, to be discussed later in this chapter.

WINES OF PORTUGAL

The Portuguese have adopted a system of designating wines that is patterned after the French system, with the best wines labeled *Designaçao de Origem* (designation of origin).

About 25 percent of all Portuguese wine is produced in the northern area. These wines are labeled *Vinho Verde,* literally meaning "green wine." However, *green* in this context refers to the youth of the wine and not its color, which can be a pale lemon (for the whites) or a light ruby (for the reds).

The Douro region is famous for its port grapes, but it also produces an abundance of red and white table wine. The Dao region produces the country's best red wines.

Other Portuguese wine regions are Bairrada (mostly reds), Bucelas (mostly whites), Colares (reds and whites), Carcavelos (best known for its fortified sweet wine), Setubal (famous for its dessert wine, Moscatel de Setubal), and Algarve.

Two of the better-known rosé wines are Mateus and Faisca, which is available as a still or a sparkling wine.

Quality Portuguese wines are labeled *garrafeira,* which means that they are specially selected or a wine that a shipper feels is above average. The label bears the vintage date. The word *colheita* on a label means "vintage."

Portugal is also noted for its fortified wines, port and Madeira, to be discussed later in this chapter.

WINES OF OTHER COUNTRIES

Many other countries around the world produce wines and export them to the United States, although not in large volume. Space does not allow a discussion of all these countries.

FORTIFIED WINES

Fortified wines were originally made to prevent the wines from oxydizing (turning to vinegar) when shipped on long sea journeys. Fortification stabilized the wines. Fortified wines are still wines that are made in a normal way and then have extra alcohol added to them. This alcohol is added either to stop further fermentation and produce a sweet fortified wine or after fermentation is complete to produce a dry fortified wine. The alcohol added to produce a fortified wine is usually distilled grape spirit, such as brandy. Fortified wines can be broadly classified into two types: aperitif and dessert.

Aperitif Wines

Aperitif wines are often aromatized with herbs and other ingredients that are either soaked in the wine or added as an extract before bottling.

Probably the best-known aperitif wine is vermouth. Vermouth is classified as either dry or sweet. Dry vermouth is normally made from white wine, and sweet vermouth from red wine. Dry vermouth can be made anywhere, but the best is considered to be made in France, with brand names such as Noilly Prat. Sweet vermouth can also be made anywhere, but the best is considered to be Italian, with brand names such as Martini (not to be confused with the martini cocktail) and Cinzano.

Traditionally, Italian vermouth is considered to be dark (almost red) in color and sweet, whereas French vermouth is pale and dry. In practice, however, both types are made in each country, as well as in many other countries.

Another aperitif is Dubonnet from France. Dubonnet can be made from either sweet red or white wine and is flavored with bitter bark and quinine. Other common aromatic aperitif wines are St. Raphael, Byrrh, and Lillet (all from France).

Dessert Wines

Fortified dessert wines are generally sweet (although dry sherry is an exception) and are often consumed with a dessert or as after-meal drinks. The dessert wines from Spain, Portugal, Madeira, Marsala, and Malaga are the most important.

Sherry

Sherry has many imitations around the world (for example, South Africa, Australia, and the United States all produce good-quality sherries), but few producers make it in the same way as is done in Spain. *Fino* and *oloroso* are the two basic categories of Spanish sherry. Both types are fortified with Spanish brandy. *Finos* are raised to about 15 percent alcohol by volume, and *olorosos* are raised to 18 percent.

Finos

Finos (such as Tio Pepe and amontillado) are generally pale, rich, and very dry. *Finos* are more natural wines because they do not have any sweetener added. Different types of *finos* are made. For example, a Manzanilla is an extremely dry *fino*. Amontillado is a nutty-flavored type that is technically a *fino* with a longer barrel age and thus a fuller body; although consumed dry in Spain, it is sometimes made sweeter for the North American market. Some people classify it as a type of sherry between a *fino* and an *oloroso*.

Olorosos

Olorosos are darker and heavier than *finos*. They can be medium dry (such as Aloroso sherry) or heavy and sweet (such as Brown, Cream, or Golden sherry).

Olorosos are converted to heavier, creamier sherries by adding a special sweet wine in the last stage of blending. The most popular *oloroso* sherry in the United States is Harvey's Bristol Cream, which accounts for about 50 percent of all sherry consumed. Amoroso is a golden-colored sherry that is between an amontillado and a heavy cream sherry in both sweetness and color.

Almacenista Sherry

One other very special sherry is almacenista. Almacenistas are well-matured, unblended sherries that have aged in their casks for decades. In the past, they were frequently sold to big bottling houses when old high-quality sherry was needed for blending to improve their top lines. Today, some almacenista sherries are being exported and sold as a product in their own right as an extremely high-quality sherry.

Sherry Exporters

Some of the better-known Spanish sherry exporters are Croft, Emilio Lustau, Gonzales, Harvey, Hidalgo, Sandeman, and Williams & Humbert.

Port

Just as what is considered to be the best sherry is made in Spain, what is considered to be the best port is made in Portugal. Grapes from the port-making regions in Portugal are rich in sugar at harvesting time. As a result, they would normally ferment quickly in Portugal's hot climate and leave no sugar unfermented. The addition of brandy during fermentation completely stops the fermentation and results in a wine with about 5 percent unfermented sugar and a little less than 20 percent alcohol. The two basic kinds of port are vintage and wood.

Vintage Port

Vintage port is considered to be the superior product. Vintage port may be made only three or four times a decade and may be bottled in as little as eighteen months. However, bottled vintage port may require twenty years to reach its peak. In recent years, vintage port has become quite a popular drink in North America, and demand has forced up prices considerably because very little vintage port is produced. Crusted port is a type of vintage port that is one step down in quality.

Wood Port

Most port produced and sold is wood port. The two types of wood port are ruby and tawny, named after the color they take on as a result of aging in wood. As long as six to eight years may be required for a ruby to develop, and a tawny port may take twelve years. Because a tawny port's added spirit has matured, it is smoother than most other ports. Lower-priced tawny is sold when about five years old, but the wine is at its best after maturing in cask for twenty years or more. Wood ports do not improve in the bottle and should be consumed within a few months after purchase.

Other Ports

The word *vintage* may appear on the labels of some types of port without them being true vintage ports. One of these is Late Bottled Vintage (LBV) port, which is bottled from a single vintage, with the year of bottling appearing on the label. This LBV port has more or less replaced crusted port as a quality product. Port of the Vintage is not a vintage port but rather a tawny wood port from a specific year.

Port Exporters

Some of the major Portuguese port shippers are Burmester, Calem & Filho, Cockburn, Dow, Fonseca, Graham, Sandeman, Taylor, and Warre.

Madeira, Marsala, and Malaga

Another dessert wine is madeira, made on the Atlantic island of Madeira. Light and dry madeira wines are Sercial (with a pale, dry, nutty taste) and Verdelho (not quite so dry). Rich, dark, and heavy madeiras are Bual (or Boal) and Malmsey. Madeira, like sherry, can be consumed as an aperitif or as a dessert wine. Madeira is the longest-lived of any wines. Bottles have been opened after a hundred years and the product has still been excellent.

Two other dessert wines are Marsala and Malaga. Marsala is a fortified wine made in Sicily. It is fermented out until dry and then fortified and sweetened. Malaga, made on the southern coast of Spain, is a sweet, fortified wine.

Other countries have their own varieties of dessert wine, such as Ratafia (made in France's Champagne region) and Commanderia (Cyprus).

CHAMPAGNE AND SPARKLING WINE

French Champagne is made in the province of Champagne in France. Only limited vineyards in this area have the right to the appellation Champagne. Champagne is blended and marketed almost exclusively by brand name of a bottler or shipper and is the only French appellation wine whose label does not need to have the words *appellation contrôlée*.

Champagne is made from a blend of grapes so that its quality can be consistently maintained from year to year. French law allows only three vine varieties to be used: Pinot Noir and Pinot Meunier (both red) and Chardonnay (white). If Champagne is made solely from white grapes, it is entitled to be labeled Blanc de Blancs; if it is made solely from red grapes, it may be labeled Blanc de Noirs.

After regular Champagne wine has been fermented, the wine is placed in bottles and stored in cellars, where a second fermentation occurs as the result of sugar added just before bottling. This second fermentation creates carbon dioxide in the bottles and gives Champagne its traditional fizz when it is poured. To prevent the bottles from exploding due to this second fermentation, Champagne bottles are made of thick glass and specially shaped with an indented bottom that strengthens the glass.

Only Champagne made in France by this traditional process is allowed to use the word *Champagne* by itself on the label. Champagne (sparkling wines) made anywhere else in the world may not use the single word *Champagne* on the label. Instead, the bottles must bear the terms *La méthode champenoise* (meaning "Champagne method"), *Champagne fermented in this bottle,* or *Champagne process.* The labels must also describe the geographic origin, such as California Champagne.

Types of Champagne

The amount of sugar present dictates the type of Champagne. These types are

Brut, Natur, or *Zero:* Bone dry, less than 1 percent sugar

Extra Sec or *Très Sec:* Literally means "extra dry," but actually this type is a bit sweeter than *brut,* with 1 to 2 percent sugar

Sec: Literally means "dry," but this Champagne is actually slightly sweet, with about 3 percent sugar

Demi-sec: Literally means "half-dry" but is actually medium sweet, with about 5 percent sugar

Doux or Rich: Quite sweet

The cheaper Champagnes are the sweeter ones because the sugar is often used to hide a lack of quality.

Champagne Shippers

Because the process of making Champagne is a complicated one, few individual vineyard operators do it themselves. Most sell their grapes to manufacturers or shippers who have the resources to contract with many vineyard operators (as well as owning some of their own vineyards) and can produce a consistent quality from year to year. The largest shipper of Champagne is Moët et Chandon (makers of

Dom Perignon Champagne) who produce twenty-four million bottles annually. The names of other well-known shippers, in alphabetical order, are

Ayala	Mercier
Bollinger	Mumm
Canard-Duchêne	Perrier-Jouët
Charbaut	Piper-Heidsieck
Deutz & Geldermann	Pol Roger
Heidsieck, Charles	Pommery et Greno
Henriot	Roederer, Louis
Krug	Ruinart
Lanson	Taittinger
Laurent-Perrier	Veuve-Clicquot

Vintage Champagne

Nonvintage Champagne makes up about 80 percent of all Champagne made. Although most Champagne is blended, often from the wines of more than one harvest in order to maintain its particular shipper's type, occasionally a vintage Champagne is produced. This production occurs in a particularly good grape-growing year. When that happens, only the grapes from that year are used and the Champagne becomes a vintage one, with the date appearing on the bottle's label and on the cork. These Champagnes are still blends of many wines but generally all from the same year.

The vintage years can also actually differ from one shipper to another because the shippers do not always agree about the quality of the wines in any given year, and even a declared vintage Champagne may have some wine from another year added in order to enhance its personality and maintain that shipper's style of Champagne.

Charmat Process

In most other places in the world other than in the Champagne region of France, the second fermentation is not carried out in the bottle because it is a lengthy and labor-intensive (therefore costly) process. Instead, refermentation occurs in large containers. This method is known as the Charmat, tank, or bulk process. The refermented wine is then bottled under pressure to retain its carbon dioxide fizz. This method allows the product to be produced in a few weeks. This type of champagne is lower cost and considered by some to be lower quality, with a short-life of fizz or effervescence once it is poured.

An alternative method to the Charmat process is to carry out refermentation using the champagne process and then transfer the finished champagne to a new bottle. The label then reads "fermented in bottle." (Note that it does not state "fermented in *this* bottle"!)

German Sekt

German sparkling wine is commonly known as *Sekt*. Three categories of Sekt are available. *Deutscher Sekt bestimmter Anbaugebiete* is often abbreviated to Deutscher Sekt b.A. It means German Sekt made exclusively from grapes from one of the eleven specified growing regions for quality grapes. *Deutscher Sekt* is Sekt made exclusively from the grapes of more than one of the eleven growing regions. *Sekt* (without the word *Deutscher)* is made from imported grapes or wine.

A well-known brand name is Henkell Trocken. Others are Söhnlein Brillant, Rüttgers Club, Faber Krönung, Kupferberg Gold, and Deinhard Kabinett.

Sparkling Wine of Other Countries

The sparkling wines of Italy are labeled Spumante, such as in the well-known Asti Spumante (sparkling wine from the village of Asti in northern Italy). Italian Spumante is invariably made by the Charmat process and usually contains less than 10 percent alcohol and as much as 8 percent sugar.

A dry Italian sparkling wine is labeled *brut, brut riserva,* or *brut nature.* If the wine is bottled fermented, its label says "*Metodo champenois*" or "*Fermentazione naturale in bottiglia.*"

Spain also produces an abundance of sparkling wine. In fact, today Spain is the largest producer of sparkling wines in the world, with the best of them made by the Champagne method. If they are made with this method, they are labeled Cava. One of the best-known producers is Codorniu. In Portugal sparkling wines are labeled Espumante.

The United States produces most of the sparkling wine consumed in North America. In its sparkling wine, the word *champagne* can legally be used to describe the product as long as it is preceded by the name of origin, such as California Champagne. Most U.S. champagne is made by the Charmat bulk process, and this method must be stated on the label.

WINE STORAGE

The best storage area for any wine is a below-ground cellar that is cool. Many restaurants do not have such a cellar and must compromise. In that case, some basic rules should be followed.

Basic Rules

Keep stored wines away from hot pipes, radiators, and cooking stoves. Vibrations should also be avoided, as well as fluctuations in temperature, because continuous changes hasten a wine's maturity and eventual decline. Keep storage areas dark because bright lights and direct exposure to sunlight are not good for wine.

Red wines should be stored at 55°F (13°C) and white wines at 40°F (5°C). If cold storage cannot be provided for white wine, store it with red wine and then cool the white just prior to service.

If wine bottles are cork-stoppered, then they should be stored on their sides to keep the cork moist and prevent air from making contact with the wine through the cork and possibly leading to spoilage. With corked wines, avoid very dry storage, which encourages corks to dry out. In other words, a humid atmosphere is desirable.

Wine Racks

Use proper wine racks that allow correct storage of bottles on their sides. Wine space is often wasted when proper storage racks are not used. Use wine racks that are designed to be stacked and that can be expanded as the wine inventory grows. However, do not store fine red wines in racks so that the neck of the bottle is pointed downward because any sediment present in the bottle is simply going to settle in the neck. Store all bottles with their labels facing up. This practice makes them easy to read and also allows any sediment in a wine bottle to settle on the side opposite the label.

Handling High-Quality Wines

Many high-quality wines improve in the bottle with age, and they should be handled and used accordingly. In some cases the maturing process lasts only so long before the quality begins to deteriorate. The operator needs to know for each type of wine when that deterioration is likely to occur. Red wines generally have a longer life cycle than white. High-quality aged red wines have to be handled carefully because they often develop a sediment that clouds the wine if it is roughly handled.

Pasteurized Wines

Some wine purchased in large glass or plastic containers (jug wine) and used for house wine may have been pasteurized. Pasteurization is a process of heating the wine and then cooling it after it has been bottled and stoppered. Pasteurization kills any living organisms that may have been in the wine and lengthens its shelf life but does not prevent deterioration once containers have been opened.

Keeping Wines

In general, expensive high-quality red wines, once opened, should be consumed that day because they rarely retain their quality for another day. Inexpensive reds—in particular, the so-called jug wines—keep for some days because they have been manufactured to allow them to remain stable. Opened white wines can usually be kept refrigerated for several days. However, keep all partly used bottles tightly stoppered or corked to minimize exposure to air.

DISCUSSION QUESTIONS

1. List and briefly discuss each of the three basic types of wine, and define the term *dry* with reference to wine.
2. Discuss wine vintages.
3. With reference to French wine, define the acronyms AOC and VDQS. Apart from AOC and VDQS wines, what are the other two qualities of French wine?
4. Excluding Champagne, name five major French wine-producing regions.
5. With reference to Bordeaux region wines:
   a. List the five districts that are noted for their high-quality wines.
   b. Define the term *cru classé.*
   c. List the five wines designated as *premiers crus,* and state the districts from which they come.

6. What does the term *crus bourgeois* mean with reference to Médoc wines?
7. Why are Burgundy wines more difficult to identify than, for example, those of Bordeaux?
8. What does the term *mis en bouteilles dans nos caves* mean, and what does it signify on a Burgundy wine label?
9. List the two subdistricts within Burgundy's Côte d'Or district, and, apart from the Côte d'Or, state the other four Burgundy region wine districts.
10. State the Burgundy district in which Pouilly-Fuissé is produced, and name five red *grands crus* Beaujolais wines.
11. In which French wine region is Châteauneuf-du Pape produced, and in which region is Anjou produced?
12. Name the three kinds of grapes from which the best wines of Alsace are made.
13. For German wines, list the three major categories of high-quality wines, list the five words that describe the sweetness of grapes used in the highest-quality wine, and list the five Rhine wine-producing areas.
14. State what liebfraumilch and Moseltaler are and in which German wine region each is produced.
15. How do the bottles for Rhine wines differ from those for Moselle wines?
16. Define each of the following German wine terms: *Amtliche Prüfungsnummer, Trocken,* and *Halbtrocken.*
17. Explain the confusion that can arise from the way Italian wines are named.
18. What do the acronyms DOC and DOCG stand for with reference to Italian wine? List the six DOCG wines.

19. Name the two best-known robust red wines produced from Nebbiolo grapes in Italy's Piedmont district, and name the high-quality sparkling white wine made from Moscato grapes in Piedmont.
20. Why do some of Italy's Adige Valley wine bottle labels contain German words?
21. Although Italy's Tuscany district produces many wines, for what particular one is it well known?
22. Explain how Italy's wine Est! Est!! Est!!! di Montefiascone obtained its name, and state what the wine name Lacryma Christi means.
23. Describe and briefly discuss the three ways of naming U.S. wines.
24. What is the name of the native grapevine usually used in the northeastern United States to make wine, and what are two types of its grapes?
25. A New York wine in a bottle labeled "Made in New York State" must contain what percentage of wine from that state? What does a label that says American rather than New York State mean?
26. What are California's two major wine-producing areas? Explain what the acronym AVA stands for.
27. List five of the most common kinds of grapes used to make red wines and five of the most common grapes used to make white wines in California.
28. Discuss the geographic-origin labeling and varietal labeling requirements for California wines.
29. State what each of the following California wine bottle terms means:
    a. Estate bottled
    b. Produced and bottled by . . .
    c. Made and bottled by . . .
    d. Late harvest or Selected late harvest

30. In what region are Spain's best wines produced? Besides its still wine, Spain is noted for what fortified wine?
31. What does the Portuguese wine term *vinho verde* mean? Besides its still wine, Portugal is noted for what fortified wine?
32. Describe and compare Italian and French vermouth.
33. Differentiate between a *fino* and an *oloroso* sherry.
34. State the two basic types of port, describe how they differ, and define *crusted port.*
35. Differentiate between ruby and tawny port, and state what the acronym LBV means on a port bottle label.
36. State what Sercial, Bual, and Malmsey are and where they are made, and state what Marsala and Malaga are and where they are made.
37. What do *Blanc de Blancs* and *Blanc de Noirs* mean on a label of a French champagne bottle? What is unique about the fermentation of French Champagne?

38. Explain what *brut, extra sec, sec,* and *demi-sec* mean on a bottle of French Champagne, and explain why the least expensive Champagnes are usually also the sweetest ones.
39. List five of the better-known French Champagne shippers.
40. Explain the Charmat, tank, or bulk process of manufacturing sparkling wine.
41. What is Sekt? What is the Italian word for a sparkling wine?
42. Discuss wine storage and handling.

REFERENCES AND SUGGESTED READINGS

Adams, Leon D. 1985. *The Wines of America.* New York: McGraw-Hill.

Ambrosi, Hans. 1976. *Where the Great German Wines Grow.* New York: Hastings House.

Amerine, Maynard A., and Vernon L. Singleton. 1977. *Wine: An Introduction.* Berkeley: University of California Press.

Anderson, Burton. 1980. *Vino, The Wines and Winemakers of Italy.* Boston: Atlantic-Little, Brown.

Baxevanis, John J. 1987. *The Wines of Bordeaux and Western France.* Totowa, N.J.: Rowman & Littlefield.

Broadbent, Michael. 1980. *The Great Vintage Wine Book.* New York: Knopf.

Chidgey, Graham. 1977. *Guide to the Wines of Burgundy.* London: Monarch.

Dallas, Philip. 1983. *Italian Wines.* London: Faber and Faber.

De Blij, Harm Jan. 1985. *Wine Regions of the Southern Hemisphere.* Totowa, N.J.: Rowman & Allanheld.

Evans, Len. 1985. *Complete Book of Australian Wine.* Sydney: Hamlyn.

Flower, Raymond. 1979. *Chianti: The Land, the People and the Wine.* 1979. New York: Universe Books.

Gold, Alec (editor). 1972. *Wines and Spirits of the World.* Coulsdon: Virtue.

Grossman, Harold J. 1977. *Grossman's Guide to Wines, Beers, and Spirits.* New York: Scribner.

Hanson, Anthony. 1982. *Burgundy.* London: Faber and Faber.

Jeffs, Julian. 1982. *Sherry.* London: Faber and Faber.

Johnson, Frank. 1983. *The Professional Wine Reference.* New York: Harper & Row.

Johnson, Hugh, 1988. *Hugh Johnson's Pocket Encyclopedia of Wine.* New York: Simon and Schuster.

Kaufman, William I. 1973. *Champagne.* New York: Viking.

Lichine, Alexis. 1982. *Alexis Lichine's Guide to the Wines and Vineyards of France.* New York: Knopf.

Lichine, Alexis. 1985. *New Encyclopedia of Wines and Spirits.* New York: Knopf.

Lipinski, Robert A., and Kathleen A. Lipinski. 1989. *A Professional Guide to Alcoholic Beverages.* New York: Van Nostrand Reinhold.

Livingstone-Learmonth, John, and Melvyn C. H. Master. 1978. *The Wines of the Rhone.* London: Faber and Faber.

Meinhard, Heinrich. 1980. *The Wines of Germany.* Briarcliff Manor, N.Y.: Stein and Day.

Misch, Robert Jay. 1977. *Quick Guide to the Wines of All the Americas.* New York: Doubleday.

Muscatine, Doris, Maynard A. Amerine, and Bob Thompson (editors). 1984. *Book of California Wine.* Berkeley: University of California Press/Sotheby.

Peddersen, Raymond B. 1981. *Foodservice and Hotel Purchasing.* Boston: CBI.

Penning-Rowsell, E. 1981. *The Wines of Bordeaux.* New York: Scribners.

Price, Pamela. 1978. *Guide to the Wines of Bordeaux.* London: Monarch.

Read, Jan. 1982. *The Wines of Portugal.* London: Faber and Faber.

Read, Jan. 1982. *The Wines of Spain.* London: Faber and Faber.

Robards, Terry. 1976. *The New York Times Book of Wine.* New York: New York Times.

Roncarti, Bruno. 1987. *Viva Vino: 200 + DOC + DOCG Wines & Wine Roads of Italy.* London: Wine and Spirit Publications.

Schoonmaker, Frank, 1975. *Almanac of Wine.* New York: Hastings House.

Schoonmaker, Frank. 1975. *Encyclopedia of Wine.* New York: Hastings House.

Schoonmaker, Frank. 1983. *The Wines of Germany,* revised by Peter Sichel. New York: Hastings House.

Sutcliffe, Serena. 1981. *Andre Simon's Wines of the World.* New York: McGraw-Hill.

Virts, William B. 1987. *Purchasing for Hospitality Operations.* East Lansing, Mich.: The Educational Institute of the American Hotel & Motel Association.

Wasserman, Sheldon. 1977. *The Wines of the Côtes du Rhône.* Briarcliff Manor, N.Y.: Stein and Day.

Wasserman, Sheldon, and Pauline Wasserman. 1983. *Guide to Fortified Wines.* Piscataway, N.J.: Scarborough.

Wasserman, Sheldon, and Pauline Wasserman. 1985. *Italy's Noble Red Wines.* Piscataway, N.J.: New Century.

Wasserman, Sheldon, and Pauline Wasserman. 1984. *Sparkling Wine.* Piscataway, N.J.: New Century.

Wildman, Frederick S., Jr. 1976. *A Wine Tour of France.* New York: Vintage.

Yoxall, Harry W. 1978. *The Wines of Burgundy.* Briarcliff Manor, N.Y.: Stein and Day.

18

Beer and Distilled Spirits

OBJECTIVES

- Differentiate ale from lager, and identify some of the individual types of each.
- Discuss the storage requirements for beer.
- Describe how a distilled spirit is made, and discuss the term *proof*.
- Explain the origin of and identify various types of gin.
- State the main ingredient in rum, and differentiate between the two major types of rum.
- Differentiate between the two main types of Scotch whisky, explain how Scotch differs from Irish whiskey, and discuss the various types of U.S. whiskey.
- Identify and discuss types of spirits such as vodka, akvavit, schnapps, and tequila.
- Explain how cognac differs from brandy, discuss cognac bottle labeling, and list the main French cognac shippers.
- Identify and discuss various brandies such as Armagnac, fruit brandies such as calvados, and other distilled spirits such as Pernod.
- Define a bitters, name some examples, and explain how liqueurs are made and how they differ from fruit brandies.

BEER

Yeast is the factor that most influences the type of beer that is produced. The two types of fermentation with yeast are bottom fermentation and top fermentation. Bottom fermentation produces lager, and top fermentation produces ale.

Lager

With bottom fermentation, the yeast settles to the bottom of the fermenting tank after it has finished its work. Most beer is bottom fermented and is known as *lager*. Lager beer is generally aged for several weeks, and in some cases for months, to clear it of sediment and to make it smoother and more mellow. Lager is generally a lighter-bodied and lower-alcohol drink than ale.

Several lager subtypes, such as pilsner, light, malt, and bock, can be identified.

Pilsner beer (Pilsen-Urquell) originated and is still made in the town of Pilsen, Czechoslovakia, but today the term *pilsner* is used generically to describe a lively, mild, thirst-quenching style of beer. The bottle label may or may not use the descriptive term *pilsner*. By contrast the authentic Pilsen-Urquell beer has more body and flavor than its North American counterpart.

Light lagers are similar to pilsner beers but are lower in alcohol, carbohydrates, and calories. Because they are more expensive to produce (the manufacturing runs are made in only small quantities), they tend to be more expensive.

Malt beers are lagers with a higher alcohol content than pilsners. The malt from which they are made is dark roasted, and the beer has a caramel color and taste.

Bock beers are also made from dark-roasted malt and are dark, rich, and heavy lagers, again with a caramel flavor.

More expensive lagers (the premium or superpremium brands) have more body and taste than regular lagers, as well as a higher price tag. Some of these lagers are made in North America, and European examples are represented by Heineken (Netherlands), Tuborg and Carlsberg (Denmark), Three Crowns (Sweden), and St. Pauli Girl (Germany).

Ale

Ale is top fermented. When the yeast has finished its job, it rises to the top of the liquid rather than settling to the bottom. Ale normally requires less aging than lager and can be sold within days after fermentation is complete. Generally, ale has a more defined taste than lager, as well as a stronger hop flavor. Some ale also has a higher alcohol content.

Two variations of ale are stout and porter. Stout has a high hop content and a strong malt taste. The malt used for stout is first roasted, which gives this beer its very dark color. One of the best known stouts is Guinness, made in Ireland.

Porter is similar to stout but has a milder hop flavor, although it is higher in alcohol content and can be as much as 6 to 7 percent alcohol by volume.

To remember which process of fermentation produces which of the two types of beer, note that *A* for ale is at the top of the alphabet and produces top-fermented beer, whereas *L* for lager is much lower down in the alphabet for bottom fermentation.

Bottled and Canned Beer Storage

Most bottled and canned beer is pasteurized to lengthen its shelf life and does not have to be refrigerated until shortly before it is needed. However, it should always be kept below 70°F (21°C) and preferably in a dark room. Canned beer and bottled beer can be kept without refrigeration for about three months. Under refrigeration, canned beer can be kept four months and bottled beer six months.

Beer should never be frozen because, when thawed, it will precipitate unsightly solids. Also, if beer is refrigerated for too long or is handled roughly, it may gush when poured. Bright light can also cause beer deterioration, which is why beer bottles are dark brown or green. Sunlight can be particularly damaging, and beer served in a glass in bright sunlight will begin to deteriorate in minutes.

Because of its perishability, canned and bottled beer stock should be properly rotated to ensure that the earliest beer purchased is the first sold. Any unpasteurized canned or bottled beer should be handled in the same way as keg beer (discussed in the next section).

Keg (Draft) Beer Storage

According to Virts (1987, p. 242), "Approximately 15 percent of total beer volume is sold in kegs." The reason beverage operations like to sell keg (or draft) beer is explained by Stefanelli (1985, p. 434): "Draft beer is a good merchandising tool, and it can attract considerable business. Also, draft beer can yield a lower pouring cost than bottled beer, even taking into account the additional labor and other costs involved." Keg beer is not pasteurized and must be kept refrigerated (at 36–38°F, or 2–3°C) at all times; otherwise, the active yeasts continue to work and produce more alcohol and carbon dioxide. If this process continues unchecked, the beer sours, and the kegs could explode. Even refrigerated keg beer has only a maximum two-week shelf life; therefore, kegs should be properly rotated so that those purchased first are used first.

Because keg beer needs constant refrigeration, a separate storage area for it may be necessary. This storage area should be close to the bar because keg beer must be opened in storage and travel through lines to the bar, and shorter rather than longer lines are preferable.

The U.S. Beer Brands

There are far fewer breweries today than there used to be. Peddersen (1981, p. 341) explains this situation:

Cans make it relatively easy to ship beer over long distances, a capability that has hastened the consolidation of the industry. In 1910 there were about fifteen hundred breweries in the country, most of them selling not much beyond their own neighborhoods. By 1933 there were only seven hundred fifty, and today we are down to forty-nine. And even that number disguises the real concentration of the industry. Only ten years ago the five biggest brewers in the country accounted for only one-third of the entire market. Today the big five—Anheuser-Busch, Schlitz, Miller, Pabst, and Coors—have about 69 percent of the market.

Further, according to the *Wall Street Journal* (27 September 1989, p. A4), by 1989 the two giants between them had 65 percent of the market—Anheuser-Busch 43 percent and Miller Brewing 22 percent. Despite this concentration a great choice among brands is still available. Lipinski and Lipinski (1989, p. 244) identify the following U.S. beer brands:

Anchor	Hamm's	Ortlieb's
Andeker	Henry Weinhard	Pabst
Augsburger	Hudepohl	Pearl
Ballantine	Iroquois	Piel's
Bergheim	Jax	Primo
Black Horse	Knickerbocker	Porter
Blatz	Koch's	Prior
Blue Fox	L.A.	Rainier
Break Special	Lite Beer	Reading
Budweiser	Lone Star	Red, White & Blue
Bull's Eye	Löwenbrau	Rheingold
Busch	Magnum	Robin Hood
Carling	Matt's	Rolling Rock
Champale	Maximus	Schaefer
Champion	McSorley's	Schlitz
Chesterfield	Meister Brau	Schmidt's
Cold Springs	Michelob	Schoenling
Colt 45	Mickeys	Simon
Coors	Miller	Stegmaier
Coqui 900	Milwaukee	Steinbrau
Erlanger	Naragansett	Sterling
Falls City	Natural Light	Stroh's
Fort Schuyler	New Amsterdam	Tuborg
Fox Head 400	Olde English	Utica Club
Gablinger	Old German	Wiedemann
Genesee	Old Milwaukee	Yuengling
Gibbons	Olympia	

According to *Beverage World* (March 1987, p. 43), the ten most popular brands of American beer in order of popularity are

1. Budweiser
2. Miller Lite
3. Miller High Life
4. Coors
5. Old Milwaukee
6. Coors Light
7. Bud Light
8. Busch
9. Michelob
10. Stroh's

Imported Beer Brands

Many brands of beer sold in North America are imported from other countries. The names of some of these, along with the country of origin, are listed in Table 18-1.

Table 18-1. Beers Sold in North America

Country	Beer Name
Australia	Courage
	Foster
	Swan
Austria	Stefflebrau
Canada	Molson
	Moosehead
China	Tsingtao
Czechoslovakia	Pilsner-Urquell
Denmark	Carlsberg
	Tuborg
England	Bass
	Watney
	Whitbread
Ecuador	Club Cerveza
France	Kronenbourg Alsatian
	33 Export
Holland	Heineken
	Amstel
Hong Kong	Sun Lik
India	Kingfisher
	Khoday
Ireland	Guiness Stout
	Harp
Italy	Moretti
Japan	Kirin
	Sapporo
Korea	OB
Mexico	Carta Blanca
	Corona
	Dos Equis XX

Table 18-1. (*continued*)

Country	Beer Name
New Guinea	South Pacific
New Zealand	Steinlager
Norway	Frydenlunds
Peru	Pilsen
Philippines	San Miguel
	Manila
Poland	Krakus
Scotland	McEwan's
Singapore	Tiger
Sweden	Three Crowns
Tahiti	Hinano
Thailand	Kloster
	Singha
Vietnam	33
West Germany	Beck's
	Dortmunder
	St Pauli Girl

DISTILLED SPIRITS

To obtain distilled spirits, a fermented product is heated to 173°F (78.5°C) in a container known as a *still*. At this temperature, the alcohol in the fermented product is converted into steam, rises, is collected in a separate container, and then cooled to a liquid that is pure alcohol or distilled spirit. The water (along with most other ingredients) in the fermented beverage is left behind, as the temperature would have to be raised to 212°F (100°C) before it would evaporate. This process is illustrated in Figure 18-1.

Proof

Spirit alcohol levels are often quoted in "proof." The proof scale in the United States runs from 0 to 200 (200 on the scale equals 100 percent alcohol by volume). In other words, proof is twice the alcohol by volume or, alternatively, alcohol by volume equals 50 percent of proof. For example, an 80 proof bourbon is half that in alcohol by volume, or 40 percent. Today, on distilled spirit bottle labels in the United States, alcohol by volume must be shown in percent and not just in proof. According to Stefanelli (1985, p. 434), knowing the proof is important because

Some equally well-known brands have different proofs. Some have 80, some 86, some 90,

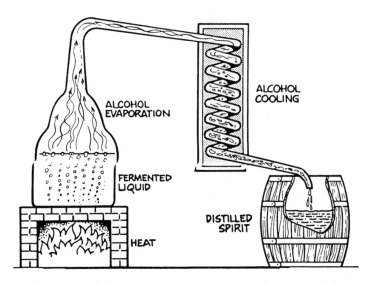

Figure 18-1.   Illustration of distillation process (*Source:* Coltman, Michael M. 1989. *Beverage Management,* p. 152. New York: Van Nostrand Reinhold).

and others have 100 or more. If you decide on a lower proof, you may not be able to dilute it so much in a mixed drink. Thus, the premium brand advocates point out that the . . . cost per serving, sometimes referred to in bars as the "pouring cost," for the lower proof brands may not be significantly less than the pouring cost of a higher proof brand.

SCOTCH WHISKY

The use of grain as a basis for distillation to make whisky originated with the Celts in the British Isles somewhere between the tenth and fifteenth centuries. The early Scottish highlanders used only barley for their grain. From this barley they produced malt. Malt is produced when the grain is heated and begins to sprout. Sprouting creates an enzyme (diastase) that turns the grain's starch into the sugar maltose. The grain by itself cannot be fermented; it needs the maltose to produce fermentation. The sprouted grain is dried over peat fires. Peat is a compacted mass of grass, heather, and other vegetation found on the Scottish moors. It is cut out of the ground in solid blocks and used for fuel. Its pungent smoke is absorbed into the malt as it dries and gives Scotch its particular aroma (known as *peat reek)* and its smokey flavor.

The sprouted malt is next mixed with hot water to create a mash, which then has yeast added to it to start it fermenting. Fermentation turns the remaining starch into sugar and the sugar into alcohol and carbon dioxide. The resulting product (with

Pot still, a type of still used in making scotch whisky (Courtesy: The Scotch Whisky Information Center).

Barley being malted for making scotch whisky (Courtesy: The Scotch Whisky Information Center).

about 6 to 8 percent alcohol) is sometimes referred to as *distiller's beer* because the process of whisky production and beer production is virtually the same up to this point. The distiller's beer is finally distilled in a still to produce Scotch whisky.

Single-Grain Malt Whisky

This process (using only barley) is used today for single-grain malt whisky (often shortened to *malt whisky*). Today Scotland has about a hundred malt distilleries.

Laphroaig is considered by many connoisseurs to be the most outstanding of all malt whiskies. However, the two best known in North America are Glenfiddich and Glenlivet. Glenfiddich is somewhat less peaty than most other malts. Note also that about twenty-five different whiskies use Glenlivet in their name, but only the one produced by the George & J. G. Smith distillery can name its product "The Glenlivet." All the others must use a hyphenated word in their name, such as in Aberlour-Glenlivet. Other well-known malt whiskies are Auchentoshan, Cardhu, Glen Grant, Glenmorangies, Macallan, Mortlach, Rosebank, and Talisker.

Blended Scotch Whisky

Only about 5 percent of total malt whisky produced today is bottled unblended. Most malt whisky distillers sell their product in bulk to other companies for blending with grain whiskies. A grain whisky is a virtually tasteless, neutral spirit. The addition of malt whiskies in the blending process gives it its character and flavor.

Blended whisky was first produced for consumers who did not like the strong flavor of malt scotch. As well as being lighter and smoother, it was also cheaper.

Scotch whisky aging in oak casks (Courtesy: The Scotch Whisky Information Center).

Today's mass-produced, blended whiskies are frequently referred to as grain whiskies, in contrast to the malt whiskies.

From fifteen to fifty different malt whiskies may be used in a blended scotch. Blended whiskies generally have a malt content of between 25 and 50 percent (the remainder being grain whisky), with the cheaper blends having the highest proportion of grain whisky. The more malt whisky in a blend, the smokier and "scotchier" it is inclined to taste. There is no legally required percentage of malt whisky to grain whisky in a blended scotch.

There is also one other difference between a blended grain whisky and a malt whisky. A blended whisky does not deteriorate when the bottle is opened as long as it is properly reclosed, but malt whisky loses its flavor if not all consumed fairly quickly.

Most scotch sold in North America is between 80 and 86 proof (40 to 43 percent alcohol by volume). Some scotch is labeled as light-bodied. The term *light-bodied* does not necessarily mean light colored, nor does it mean low in alcohol. Light-bodied whiskies have generally been distilled at higher proofs to make them lighter in flavor.

A list of popular standard blended scotch brands bottled in Scotland is as follows:

Ballantines	J. & B (the best selling brand in the
Bells (the best selling brand in the U.K.)	United States)
Black & White	John Begg
Claymore	Johnnie Walker Red Label
Crawfords	King's Ransom
Cutty Sark	100 Pipers
Dewars	Queen Anne
Famous Grouse	Something Special
Grand Old Parr	Teachers
Grants	White Horse

Premium, more expensive, brands of scotch are:

Ballantines 17 Year	Haig Pinch
Ballantines 30 Year	Johnnie Walker Black Label
Chivas Regal	Usquebach
Chivas Royal Salute	

Bulk Whisky

A great deal of blended scotch is shipped to North America in bulk in barrels and bottled on arrival. The bulk blends have a very low peat flavor and can also vary in quality from shipment to shipment. Bulk shipping reduces the cost to the purchaser

Typical scotch whisky distillery in a pastoral setting (Courtesy: The Scotch Whisky Information Center).

who is seeking value for money, and these brands are perfectly acceptable for use in mixed drinks. When a scotch is shipped in bulk, its label usually states, "Distilled and blended in Scotland." In other words, the term "Bottled in Scotland" found on nonbulk bottles is missing. Brands of bulk scotch found in North America are Clan MacGregor, Inver House, Old Smuggler, Passport, Ushers Green Stripe, and Vat 69.

IRISH WHISKEY

Irish whiskey has been traditionally made from malted barley in a similar manner to single-grain malt scotch, but the malt is not dried over peat fires so it does not have the smokey flavor characteristic of scotch. Irish whiskey is also triple-distilled, whereas most scotch is only double-distilled. Irish is today blended to create a lighter and smoother drink.

Two well-known Irish whiskeys are Old Bushmill's and Jameson's. Only four other Irish whiskeys are still made: Dunphy's, Murphy's, Paddy's, and Power's.

UNITED STATES WHISKEY

Note that U.S. whiskey (as is the case with Irish whiskey) has an additional *e* in its spelling (unlike scotch whisky). There are several different types of U.S. whiskey.

Bourbon Whiskey

The term *bourbon* by law can be used for any U.S. whiskey with at least a 51 percent corn base that has been aged at least two years in charred new oak barrels (good business for the barrel manufacturers). The charring of the inside of the barrels adds a special flavor. Bourbon is generally sold straight; that is, it is not blended with any other spirit, and it can thus be considered an equivalent to a single-grain malt scotch. Some of the better-known brands of bourbon are

Ancient Age	Maker's Mark
Benchmark	Mattingly & Moore (M & M)
Cabin Still	Old Charter
Early Times	Old Crow
Henry McKenna	Old Fitzgerald
Hiram Walker Ten High	Old Grand Dad
I. W. Harper	Rebel Yell
Jim Beam	Stitzel-Weller

Some very high-proof bourbons are also available, including Eagle Rare, Ezra Brooks, Grand-Dad Barrel Proof, Old Weller, and Wild Turkey.

Rye Whiskey

For a whiskey to be labeled *rye whiskey* in the United States, it must contain at least 51 percent rye grain and be aged in new, charred-oak barrels. Rye whiskey is not as popular as it once was, and not much is produced today. Two brands of rye whiskey still available are Old Overholt and Wild Turkey. Note that the word *rye* is often incorrectly used, primarily in the northeast, as a generic word for a blended whiskey.

Corn Whiskey

Corn whiskey is another type of U.S. whiskey. To be called *corn whiskey*, it must be made from a base of 80 percent corn and be aged for at least two years in new or used uncharred barrels. A great deal of corn whiskey is bottled with less than two years aging. Corn whiskey, sometimes known as *corn likker*, is a clear, pungent, harsh, and strong spirit often described as *white lightning*. It is not seen much outside the southern states, where it is often sold in mason jar "bottles."

Tennessee Whiskey

Tennessee whiskey is not a bourbon. Tennessee distillers make their whiskey with the added step of leaching it slowly through maple charcoal to give it its unique flavor and bouquet. It is generally a smoother and more mellow product than bourbon. Only two distilleries today make Tennessee whiskey: Jack Daniel's and

George Dickel. Indeed, Jack Daniel's is not only the leading brand of Tennessee whiskey but also it outsells most bourbons.

Sour Mash

Sometimes U.S. whiskey is described as either sweet mash or sour mash, the mash being the mixture of hot water, grain, and malt to which yeast is added for fermentation prior to distillation. What differentiates a sour mash from a sweet mash is that a sour mash (sour because it has a slightly acid flavor) uses some mash from an old batch in each new batch. This practice encourages yeast growth, reduces the possibility of bacterial contamination, and provides flavor continuity from one batch to the next. A sour mash does not add a sour flavor to the finished product. Like sourdough bread, it just has an extra tang and depth.

Labeling of U.S. Whiskeys

Labeling of U.S. whiskeys can be confusing. Whiskey can be classified in three ways: straight, blended straight, and blended American.

A straight whiskey may be a mixture of various grains but must contain at least 51 percent of a particular grain. For example, a bourbon whiskey must contain at least 51 percent corn to be a straight bourbon, and a rye must be at least 51 percent rye to be a straight rye. A straight whiskey is not a blended whiskey.

A blended straight whiskey is a blend of several straight whiskeys of the same type. A blended straight whiskey must consist of at least 20 percent 100-proof straight whiskey that is then mixed with other whiskeys or neutral spirits. Most reputable brands have more than 20 percent straight whiskey content. Although blended straight whiskey is often erroneously referred to as *rye*, it can be made from corn, rye, or a combination of these products.

Blended whiskey is a lighter-bodied product requiring no aging. It has no distinctive single characteristic. Scotch and bourbon drinkers consider it too bland, whereas those who like mild Canadian whiskey consider it too harsh. Bottles are labeled "American Whiskey—A Blend," "American Blended Whiskey," or just simply "Blended Whiskey." If the blend contains any grain spirits, the exact percentage must be shown. If the label does not state any components, then the contents of the bottle are only whiskey (with no neutral spirits), of which at least 20 percent must be straight and the rest light, but percentages do not have to be stated. In blended whiskeys, manufacturers are allowed to add up to 2.5 percent sherry to the end-product to give it additional color. The sherry addition does not affect the whiskey's taste. Common brands of blended whiskey are Calvert Extra, Fleischmann Preferred, Kessler, Imperial, Schenley, and Seagram 7 Crown. Two additional products sold in the United States are Canadian whisky and light whiskey. Canadian whisky is a blended, light-bodied, and mellow-flavored whisky generally aged for three years, although some of the better ones are aged a lot longer. Light whiskey is distilled at a higher proof than other U.S. whiskeys to produce a lighter-bodied product to compete more effectively with imported light-bodied scotch and Canadian whiskeys. Light whiskey is a relatively new type that was officially declared a category of whiskey only in 1972. Any type or proportion of grain spirits may be used, although corn generally predominates. This whiskey is often used in blended whiskeys. Common brands are Barton QT Premium, Jacquin Light, and Park & Tilford American Light.

Bottled in Bond Whiskey

The term *bottled in bond* is sometimes seen on U.S. whiskey bottle labels. To use this term, the whiskey must be a straight whiskey (usually bourbon) produced by a single distillery all within the same year. It must be aged at least four years and regularly inspected by federal revenue agents. These controls allow the distillery to pay tax on the whiskey at the time it is bottled and not during aging. A bottled-in-bond whiskey does not guarantee that it is a quality product, although it usually is. Because of changing tastes, very little bottled-in-bond whiskey is produced today.

Government Regulations

Federal regulations require that any whiskey, either domestic or imported, must state on its label if it is aged in wood less than four years. If the aging period is not stated, it has been aged for more than four years.

CANADIAN WHISKY

About 75 percent of all Canadian whisky (without the *e*) produced is exported, primarily to the United States. In Canada, Canadian-produced whisky is invariably referred to as "rye," even though it may have absolutely no rye content. No legal requirements cover the minimum amount of any single grain that must be used in its production. Corn, because it has a high starch content and is easily converted to sugar, is a favored ingredient. Canadian whisky is invariably a blended product that is generally aged for a minimum of two years in charred oak barrels previously used to age U.S. bourbon. Aging in used bourbon barrels gives the product a slight bourbon flavor. The best age for Canadian whisky is six to eight years, although some whiskeys are aged longer.

Canadian whisky is the lightest and smoothest of all the whisky products produced in Scotland, Ireland, or the United States. To be called Canadian in the United States, the whisky must have been produced entirely in Canada, although it is often shipped in bulk and bottled in the United States. Common bulk brands are Black Velvet, Canadian Mist, Lord Calvert, and Windsor Supreme. Two of the best known nonbulk brands are Seagram's V.O. and Canadian Club. These two brands rank among the most popular liquors consumed in the United States. Other popular brands are Crown Royal and Schenley O.F.C.

JAPANESE WHISKY

The Japanese have been making whisky for more than fifty years. Most of it is blended. The major distiller is Suntory, one of the largest distillers in the world.

GIN

One of the earliest distilled spirits was produced in Holland in the seventeenth century. It was a neutral grain spirit flavored with the juniper berry and was named *jeneva, jenever,* or *genever* (a distortion of the French word for "juniper," *genièvre)*.

English soldiers in Holland liked it and brought it back to England, where it was described as "Dutch courage." However, the English decided to manufacture their own variation of genever, without the strong juniper flavor, and they abbreviated its name to *gin*. Until the end of the nineteenth century, virtually all gin consumed in England was strongly sweetened and very acrid or pungent. By the turn of the century dry gin was far more common. Dry, in this sense, means an absence of sweetness.

Normally gin needs no aging. It can be consumed as soon as it is distilled. Usually it is stored after distillation in stainless-steel or glass-lined tanks until it is bottled and for that reason remains a colorless product. However, one gin in North America, Seagram's Golden, is aged and has a golden color. Three types of gin are manufactured today: Dutch, English, and U.S. gin.

Dutch Gin

Dutch gin is distilled at low proof from a variety of grains. It may undergo two or more distillations, the last one with juniper to give it its unique flavor. It is still sometimes named Genever but may also be referred to as Hollands or Schiedam. It has a very strong juniper flavor and is thus not suitable in a mixed drink or cocktail. It is usually drunk by itself either cold or over ice.

English Gin

The only thing that English gin has in common with Dutch gin is the word *gin*. English-type gin is not flavored with juniper but with more mellow botanicals such as fruits, herbs, or spices. It is usually referred to as *dry gin* (because no sugar products are added to it) or *London dry*, even when manufactured in North America, as much of it now is, by British distillers. Some brand names for English gin are

Beefeater, Bombay, Booths, Burnetts, Burroughs, Gilbeys, Gordons, Plymouth, and Tanqueray.

United States Gin

United States gin is made of high-proof neutral spirits redistilled with juniper and/ or other flavors. Most of it is made in the London-dry style. Generally, British gins are fragrant and full flavored, whereas U.S. gins are light and crisp, with less flavor and more of a citrus characteristic. Brands of U.S. gin are Fleischmanns, Gilbeys, Gordons, Hiram Walker, and Seagrams.

Other Gins

A type of gin produced in Germany is known as *Wacholder,* named after the German word for gin. Brands known in the United States are Doornkaat and Jueckemoeller.

Pimm's No. 1 Cup, made using a secret recipe developed in the mid-1800s in England, is a prefabricated gin sling that, in the bottle, is almost the consistency of a cordial or liqueur. In the glass it is mixed with fruit juice, lemonade, or ginger ale and then garnished with fresh fruit or cucumber.

Sloe gin is not a gin, but a liqueur. Liqueurs are discussed later in the chapter.

RUM

To make rum, sugar cane juice is boiled into a concentrated syrup, the sugar is removed, and what is left is molasses (with about a 5 percent sugar content). The molasses is then fermented and finally distilled. Today rum is made in many hot countries around the world where sugar cane is grown. It can also be made from sugar beet grown in colder climates (such as Europe), but the end result is not as good. The two main types of rum are light bodied and heavy bodied, with a handful of medium bodied in between.

Light-bodied rums are generally made in countries that have a Spanish heritage, such as Cuba and Puerto Rico. Light-bodied rums are popular in North America since they lend themselves well to mixing in cocktails because of their lightness and dryness.

Heavier-bodied, more aromatic rums are made in countries such as Barbados, Jamaica, Trinidad, Haiti, and Guyana. These rums are more pungent and are the rums favored in cold weather. They mix well in hot drinks (such as a hot toddy), but can be used in certain cocktails such as the Cuba Libre (rum and cola).

Rum Brands

The world's largest selling alcohol product is Bacardi Rum. It originated in Cuba, where the Bacardi distillery used water from the Dacquiri River in its production.

When Prohibition was introduced in the United States in 1919, Cuba, because of its proximity to the coast of Florida, became a major exporter of illicit rum to the United States. Cuba remained a major exporter after Prohibition was repealed in 1933 until Fidel Castro came to power in 1959. Today, Bacardi rum is produced mainly in Puerto Rico.

Puerto Rico is the world's largest producer of light rums, which have captured about 80 percent of the world's market. Some of the better known Puerto Rican rums (in addition to Bacardi) are Captain Morgan, Don Q., Myers', Ron Castillo, Ron del Barrilito, and Ronrico. One notable sugar-producing area lies along the Demerara River in Guyana. Demerara sugar is considered to be an excellent base for making a full-bodied and heavy rum. A well-known brand is the heavy-bodied Lemon Hart.

Virgin Island rum brands are Cruzan and Ron Carioca, both of which are light bodied. A coconut-flavored rum known as Cocoribe is also produced there.

Haiti rum is medium to full bodied and quite fragrant. One of its best known rums is Rhum Barbancourt, distilled from raw sugar rather than molasses.

Medium rums are found in the islands of Guadeloupe, Trinidad, Réunion, Cuba, and Barbados. Barbados is the home of the well-known medium-bodied Mount Gay's Eclipse.

Jamaica rums are full bodied and aromatic. They are exported primarily to England, where they are shipped in barrels for aging in cool, damp cellars to prevent evaporation. Rum bottled this way is often named London Dock Rum. Other well-known Jamaican brands are Appleton's, Dagger Jamaica, Lemon Hart, and Myers'.

Martinique produces Rhum St. James and Rhum Clement (both heavy bodied), Trinidad produces medium-bodied Caroni, and Indonesia produces light-bodied Batavia Arak.

VODKA

Vodka is basically a diluted pure alcohol or neutral spirit. It can be made from any fermented product such as grain, rice, or potatoes, although the best vodkas are made from grain because those made from other ingredients usually end up with a taste of the base product used. Vodka is distilled at a very high proof and then finely filtered through charcoal to remove any trace elements and to smooth the flavor, with the end result that it has almost no smell and virtually no taste—perhaps the reason why it has become so popular and now has the largest share (about 20 percent) of the distilled spirit market in North America.

European Vodkas

Although most vodka consumed today in North America is made there, four well-known imported (and some say "authentic") vodkas are Stolichnaya and Moskovaya (from Russia) and Zubrowka and Wyborowa (from Poland). No doubt these authentic vodkas, just like authentic scotch, are manufactured especially for the North American palate because vodka traditionally made in Europe is often flavored with strong herbs or spices. For example, Zubrowka in Poland is flavored with the addition of buffalo grass blades, which give it an aromatic bouquet and yellowish color, but the addition of this grass is not allowed for Zubrowka sold in the United States.

Another Polish vodka is Starka. This vodka is aged in oak barrels, has a golden brown color, and is flavored with fruit leaves. Russia also produces the pepper-flavored vodka, Pertzovka, which has a dark brown color, heavy aroma, and burning taste. Other flavored European vodkas are Limonnaya (lemon flavored) and Okhotnichya (meadow grass and heather honey flavored).

United States Vodkas

Only minor differences exist among vodkas produced in the United States because they must all conform to the same legal requirements. They must be made from distilled neutral spirits and be without distinctive character, aroma, taste, or color. The leading brand of U.S. vodka is Smirnoff. Other popular brands are Gilbey's, Gordon's, Kamchatka, Popov, Relska, and Wolfschmidt. Other countries also produce vodka. Some of these brands are

Canada: Silhouette   Finland: Finlandia
China: Great Wall and Tsing Tao   Israel: Anatevka and Carmel
Denmark: Sermeq   Japan: Suntory
England: Burrough's   Sweden: Absolut

Other Vodka-type Products

Akvavit, aquavit, and akevitt are the Scandinavian versions of vodka. *Akvavit* is the spelling in Denmark, *aquavit* in Norway and Sweden, and *akevitt* in Finland. These products are distinguished by their slight caraway or dill flavor, particularly in Denmark. Like vodka, they are usually colorless and consumed straight by Scandinavians, often followed by a beer "chaser."

Schnapps is a type of vodka produced in Germany and Holland. It may or may not be flavored. Like vodka and akvavit, it is colorless. Today, the word *schnapps* is often used to refer to any strong spirit and in Scandinavian countries to refer to aquavit.

TEQUILA

Legally, today, tequila can only be made from a single type of agave plant (which, by the way, is not a type of cactus, as many believe) grown in a specified delimited region in Mexico. The producers of authentic tequila receive a number (known as *Norma Official Mexicana* or NOM) from the Mexican government, and the appearance of this number on the bottle label indicates its authenticity and quality.

Tequila that has been recently distilled and bottled with little or no aging is clear and colorless and is referred to as *white* or *silver tequila*. Tequila stored for a year in oak barrels takes on an amber color and is known as *gold tequila*. If it has been aged for more than a year in wood, it takes on a deeper golden color and is referred to as *añejo*. The best-selling tequila in Mexico is Sauza, and in the United States it is Cuervo. Other brands are Herradura, Montezuma, and Pepe Lopez.

Mezcal

Mezcal (sometimes spelled *mescal*) is also made from the agave plant but not from any particular species. It can sometimes be a rather rough spirit because it is subject to little or no legal regulation. Sometimes a worm is placed in a mezcal bottle as a sign of its authenticity.

COGNAC AND BRANDY

You might wonder why this section heading includes Cognac and brandy as separate topics. Isn't Cognac the same thing as brandy? The answer is that Cognac is a type of brandy allowed to bear the name Cognac, whereas brandy not made in a special region in France is not Cognac, much as Champagne is a sparkling wine, but all sparkling wine is not Champagne.

Cognac

Brandy can be made in any country where wine is available, but the most prestigious is considered to be made in France in the region of Cognac. Cognac is the only brandy in the world entitled to use the word *Cognac*.

Cognac is made from a white wine produced from a certain type of grape grown in the region around the town of Cognac, located north of Bordeaux in France. The wine from these grapes is of poor quality but produces excellent Cognac. Much of the grape crop is sold by growers directly to the big Cognac distilling firms owned by (or under contract to) the well-known Cognac shippers.

Cognac, like all distilled spirits, is colorless when first distilled. It takes on its color during barrel aging. However, this color can vary according to age (and the kind of barrel used) from pale brown to dark brown. In order to ensure a consistent color, some shippers add caramel coloring at the time of bottling, which does no harm to the product. Also, like all distilled products, Cognac ages only while in the barrel, and the time spent in wood dictates its quality.

Bottle Labels

There is no vintage Cognac because it is always a blended product (often from different years and usually from different growing districts), and for this reason the year does not appear on the label. Instead, a system of labeling by symbols is used. Labeling of Cognac is governed by the French appellation laws and is determined by the age of the youngest brandy in each blend. Note that the minimum age at which cognac may be marketed varies from one country to another. For example, in France it is three years, whereas in the United States it is two years.

On Cognac bottle labels acronyms are used made up of the following letters and meanings:

V—very
S—superior or special
O—old
P—pale
E—especial or extra
F—fine
X—extra or extraordinary

For example, the acronym VSOP stands for very superior (or special) old pale. Note that the use of these acronyms may depend on the manufacturer; they are not always indicative of the product's age. Why are these symbols equivalent to English words? When Cognac was first developed, the British market was extremely important to the French producers, and therefore they used symbols that would be meaningful in English.

United States Bottle Labels

Cognacs marketed in the United States fall into two basic categories: those labeled Three Star (or Five Star) and those labeled VSOP (very superior old pale). The stars on a label have no meaning except to place the cognac in the youngest age bracket. Shippers are replacing stars with their proprietary brand names and VS or VSO, which generally means that the minimum age in the blend is two years, but the average age is likely to be three to five years. The acronyms VSOP, VSEP, VSO, and VO mean that the minimum age in the blend is four years, but the average is likely to be ten to fifteen years.

Another age designation is Napoleon, which can be used only for Cognac at least five years old. No Cognac can legally be described as older than five years because the French government no longer issues age certificates to this effect, even though the Cognac is much older.

However, some Cognac labels say Extra, XO (extra old), Royal, Vieux, Grande

Reserve, Vieille Reserve, Cordon Bleu, Triomphe, Extra Anniversaire, or VVSOP. These bottles contain brandies that can be much older than five years, even twenty, forty, or fifty years old.

Cognac Shippers

Presently in France well over three hundred firms produce Cognac. However, four shippers of Cognac produce about 75 percent of all exported Cognac. These four are Courvoisier, Hennessy, Martell, and Remy Martin. Some of the other better-known Cognac shippers are

Bisquit	Hine
Camus	Monnet
Delamain	Otard
Denis-Mounie	Plignac
Gaston de Lagrange	Salignac

Today, many of the major brand-name Cognacs are shipped from France in bulk and bottled in North America. A bottle that is labeled French Brandy contains a lesser-quality product and not a Cognac.

Armagnac

Armagnac is another well-known French brandy (not entitled to the use of the word *Cognac*) made from grapes grown just south of the Bordeaux region. It is generally drier than Cognac, with a less distinct aroma, and it is also less expensive. Today, Armagnac generally uses the same system of acronyms and names on bottle labels as Cognac. If a year appears on the label, it indicates that the Armagnac is made only from grapes harvested that year and has not been blended with Armagnacs from other years. Some of the well-known Armagnac producers are Samalens, De Montal, Larressingle, and Saint-Vivant.

Other Brandies

More brandy is made in Spain than in any other country in the world. Spanish brandy is noted for its heavy, sweet flavor, compared to the finer brandies of France. Spanish brandies, unlike Cognac and Armagnac, are usually distilled from a blend of wines. In Spain, brandy is known as coñac, some think illegally. Domecq and Fundador are well-known brands.

Portuguese brandy is similar to Spanish but a bit drier. Macieira is a Portuguese brandy known in the United States.

German brandy is drier and more delicate than either Spanish or French brandy. In Germany, brandy is often made from wine imported from other countries. The best-known brand is Asbach Uralt.

High-quality Italian brandies have the word *vecchia* or *vecchio* (meaning "old"), *stravecchia* (meaning "very old"), or *riserva* (meaning "reserve") on the label. Three well-known brands are Stock, Vecchia Romagna, and Carpene Malvolti.

The major Greek brandy is Metaxa. In the United States, however, this product cannot be labeled as a brandy because it has a small amount of a secret liqueur in it and is therefore classified as a Greek liqueur.

One well-known South American brandy is Pisco, named after the Peruvian seaport where it is produced. Pisco brandy is now also made in Chile. It is different from many other brandies because it is aged in clay containers.

Finally, Israel has its Carmel brandy, and Mexico its Presidente.

Lees (Pomace) Brandies

Some special distinctive and pungent types of brandy are distilled from the lees, pulp, or pomace (skins and other residue from grapes) left over after grapes have been pressed and their juice used for making wine. Water is added to the lees, it is left to ferment, then it is distilled. The best type of lees brandy produced in France is marc, which comes from the Burgundy district.

In Italy, a similar type of lees brandy is grappa. It is a little rougher (less mellow) and richer than the French marc. Grappa is not usually aged in wood and is left colorless. In Spain lees brandy is known as Aguardiente; in Portugal, Bagaceira; in South Africa, Dopbrandy; and in Germany, Trester Brantwein or Dreimannerwein. *Dreimannerwein* literally means "three-man wine."

California Brandy

Most of the brandy consumed in the United States is American and is made from raisin and table (rather than wine) grapes. It is produced primarily in California's San Joaquin Valley.

In 1976, California brandy was given the right to an official controlled appellation and the right to be labeled California Brandy. If a bottle is so labeled, it must be made from only California wine and be distilled in that state.

Some California brandy is bottled straight, that is, without blending. However, most brandies are blended. These blended brandies are generally smooth and light, with a fruity aroma and flavor. Standard brands of California brandy are

Almaden	Gallo E & J
Aristocrat	Korbel
Ceremony	Lejon

Christian Brothers   Old Mr. Boston
Conti-Royale   Paul Masson
Coronet   Setrakian

Some premium brands of California brandy are Christian Brothers XO, R & S Vineyards California Alambic, and Woodbury.

Fruit Brandies

Although the term *brandy* is generally used to denote a distilled product made from grape wine, brandy can be distilled from many other fruit products. One fruit that lends itself well to this is apples.

Calvados

One of the best-known French apple brandies is calvados, distilled from apple cider. The very best calvados bears the words *Appellation d'origine contrôlée* or AOC on the bottle label. The best AOC calvados is Pays d'Auge. A lesser quality is labeled *Appellation d'origine réglementée* or AOR. If the label states *Appellation eaux-de-vie de cidre* (meaning a "cider brandy"), it may not be called calvados. German apple brandy is known as Apfelschnapps.

Applejack

In the United States, apple brandy is usually referred to as *applejack* and is a traditional New England brandy made from a blend of cider brandy and neutral grain spirits. The early colonists planted apple orchards in the seventeenth century and made a cider from the apples. Today, for all practical commercial purposes, only Laird's of New Jersey, founded in 1780, still produces applejack. No fermenting agents or other agents are used, and the product is made from 35 percent pure apple brandy (the minimum legal requirement is 20 percent) and 65 percent neutral grain spirits. Applejack is lighter than calvados and has less of an apple taste.

Cherry Brandy

Another well-known fruit brandy is made from black cherries. It is produced and is popular in France (Alsace), where it is known as *kirsch*, and in Germany and Switzerland, where it is known as *kirschwasser*. Kirsch is colorless. Sixty pounds of cherries are needed to make five bottles of kirsch. Thus, production is limited and the cost of the product quite high.

Plum Brandy

Plum brandy is popular in Yugoslavia and Czechoslovakia, where it is known as *slivovitz* (named after the sliva plums) or sometimes Rakija. In France, it is known as Mirabelle when it is made from yellow mirabelle plums, Reine-Claude when made from greengage plums, and Quetsch when made from the blue plums of Germany and Alsace. In Germany, plum brandy is known as Zwetschgenwasser. Plum brandies are usually gold colored.

Pear Brandy

Another popular fruit brandy is pear brandy, produced from the Williams pear in France and Switzerland. It is usually labeled as Poire Williams or Pear William. In Germany, this product is known as Williamsbirnenbrand. It is a colorless brandy.

Fruit Brandies versus Liqueurs

Do not confuse fruit brandies with fruit products such as apricot brandy, which are much sweeter and made quite differently. These sweet fruit products, commonly referred to as *liqueurs* or *cordials,* are discussed later in this chapter.

ABSINTHE AND SIMILAR PRODUCTS

The original absinthe was first produced in 1792 as a medicine to treat malaria. However, in the early part of this century an emerald green toxic spirit, distilled from wormwood and other aromatics, known as *absinthe* was commonly consumed in Europe. Genuine absinthe was as high as 70 to 80 percent alcohol and had a licorice flavor. Excessive consumption of it was discovered to affect not only digestive organs but also nerve centers (because it had a narcotic effect), and it may have produced delirium and idiocy. Its manufacture and sale were prohibited in most European countries in the early 1900s.

However, some derivatives, substituting aniseed for wormwood, have survived in a less toxic form. These derivatives are sold today under such names as Pernod (from France, where it is sometimes referred to as *pastis)* and ouzo (from Greece). These colorless, licorice-flavored spirits go cloudy if water is added.

BITTERS

Bitters are usually distillations flavored with bark, fruit, herbs, and/or roots of various kinds. Most bitters have a quinine base and were initially developed in the early 1800s as a medicine for malaria. Today most bitters have a greatly reduced quinine content and are mostly used as minor ingredients in some cocktails.

One of the most common bitters is Angostura, produced in Trinidad. Orange bitters is a similar product also used in certain cocktails. Campari is a low-proof, red-colored bitters made in Italy. Other bitters are Amer Picon and Fernet Branca (France), Unicum (Italy), and Underberg (Germany). Peychaud's bitters is made in New Orleans.

LIQUEURS (CORDIALS)

A *liqueur*, sometimes known as a *cordial*, is defined in the United States as a distilled spirit mixed with a flavoring substance and containing at least 2.5 percent sugar by volume. Most liqueurs on the market today contain as much as 35 to 40 percent sugar or other sweetener. Even liqueurs labeled "dry" may contain as much as 10 percent sugar. Liqueurs that are very heavy in sugar are often referred to as *crèmes*, such as crème de cacao and crème de bananes.

Liqueurs are often confused with *eaux-de-vie* or fruit brandies, discussed earlier in this chapter. The difference is that a fruit brandy is produced by fermenting the fruit and then distilling it; a liqueur is produced by adding the fruit flavor to an already-distilled spirit (often a flavorless neutral spirit produced from a grain or from grapes or other products). In other words, a liqueur is basically a distilled spirit that is steeped in, has macerated in it, or is percolated or redistilled with any number of fruits, flowers, juices, extracts, barks, herbs, seeds, spices, plants, or other natural flavorings. The basic distilled spirit may be brandy, whiskey, rum, vodka, or neutral spirit. Only the manufacturer's imagination limits what may go into a liqueur.

Artificial flavors are regulated in almost every country. In the United States, any domestically made liqueur that contains artificial flavoring higher than one thousand parts per million must be labeled "Artificial" or "Imitation." Extracts, however, may be added to improve flavor. For example, crème de cacao usually has vanilla extract added to heighten its chocolate flavor. Any color present is usually added for effect (for example, in yellow or green Chartreuse, green crème de menthe, blue Curaçao). Some liqueurs are aged before bottling; others are not.

Classifying Liqueurs

Several methods have been used to classify liqueurs, such as by fruit flavors, plant flavors, botanical mixtures, or liquor-based ingredients. However, all these classifications have a great deal of overlap. Nevertheless, liqueurs can be broadly classified into generics or proprietaries. A *generic* is a liqueur that can be made by any manufacturer and be bottled under the producer's name. Examples are crème de cacao, blackberry brandy, and cherry whiskey. *Proprietaries* are made under a registered name that cannot be used by others. Often a secret formula is used. Examples are Drambuie, Benedictine, and Grand Marnier.

List of Liqueurs

Some of the more common liqueurs, with their spirit base and basic flavoring, are listed in Table 18-2.

DISCUSSION QUESTIONS

1. How does the manufacture of ale differ from the manufacture of lager beer?
2. What is a pilsner beer, and where did it originate?
3. Name three well-known European lager beers and their country of origin.
4. What are stout and porter?
5. Discuss the storage requirements for canned or bottled beer.
6. Discuss the storage requirements for keg beer.
7. Describe how a distilled spirit is made from a fermented product and discuss the term *proof*.
8. What is the origin of gin? Differentiate among Dutch gin, English gin, and U.S. gin, and explain what dry gin is.
9. What are Genever, Hollands, and Schiedam?
10. From what is rum made? What are the two main types of rum, and how do they differ?
11. What is the main difference between scotch malt whiskey and blended scotch whisky? What are Glenfiddich and Glenlivet?
12. What are the two main production differences between scotch whiskey and Irish whiskey?
13. What is a sour-mash bourbon?
14. What is the legal requirement for a whiskey to be called a straight rye in the United States?
15. From what ingredient(s) is vodka made?
16. What are Stolichnaya and Zubrowka, and where are they made?
17. What are akvavit, aquavit, and akevitt, and where is each produced? What is schnapps, and where is it generally made?
18. What is tequila, what is its basic ingredient, and where is it generally made?
19. How do Cognac and brandy differ, and where is the Cognac region in France?
20. Why is Cognac never labeled with the vintage year, and what do the letters V, S, O, P, E, F, and X stand for on Cognac bottle labels?
21. List five of the main Cognac shippers.
22. What are Armagnac, marc, and grappa, and where are they made?
23. What is calvados, and where is it made? What is the U.S. equivalent of calvados?
24. What are kirsch and kirschwasser, and where are they made?
25. What are slivovitz, Quetsch, and Mirabelle, and where are they made?
26. What are Pernod and ouzo, and where are they made?

Table 18-2. Common Liqueurs

Name	Spirit Base	Basic Flavor
Advocaat	Brandy	Eggnog
Amaretto	Neutral spirit	Almond/apricot
Anisette	Neutral spirit	Licorice
Apricot brandy	Neutral spirit	Apricot
Benedictine	Neutral spirit	Herbs/spices
B & B	Neutral spirit/Cognac	Herbs/spices
Blackberry brandy	Neutral spirit/brandy	Blackberry
Chartreuse	Neutral spirit/brandy	Herbs/spices
Cherry brandy	Neutral spirit/brandy	Cherry
Cherry whiskey	Whiskey	Cherry
Cointreau	Neutral spirit	Orange
Crème de bananes	Neutral spirit	Banana
Crème de cacao	Neutral spirit	Chocolate/vanilla
Crème de café	Neutral spirit	Coffee
Crème de cassis	Neutral spirit	Black currant
Crème de menthe	Neutral spirit	Mint
Crème de noyaux	Neutral spirit	Almond
Curaçao	Neutral spirit	Orange
Drambuie	Scotch whisky	Scotch/honey
Galliano	Neutral spirit	Licorice/vanilla
Glayva	Scotch whisky	Scotch/honey
Grand Marnier	Cognac	Orange
Irish Cream	Irish whiskey	Chocolate
Irish Mist	Irish whiskey	Honey
Kahlua	Neutral spirit	Coffee
Kirsch liqueur	Kirsch	Cherry
Kümmel	Neutral spirit	Caraway
Maraschino brandy	Neutral spirit	Cherry/almond
Peach brandy	Neutral spirit	Peach
Peppermint	Neutral spirit	Mint
Peter Heering	Neutral spirit/brandy	Cherry
Raspberry brandy	Neutral spirit	Raspberry
Sloe gin	Neutral spirit	Plum
Southern Comfort	Bourbon	Bourbon/peach
Strawberry brandy	Neutral spirit	Strawberry
Strega	Neutral spirit	Herbs/spices
Tia Maria	Rum	Coffee
Triple Sec	Neutral spirit	Orange
Vandermint	Neutral spirit	Chocolate/mint
Yukon Jack	Canadian whisky	Citrus/herbs

27. What is bitters? Name two examples.
28. How are liqueurs or cordials made, and how do they differ from fruit brandies?

REFERENCES AND SUGGESTED READINGS

Allison, Norman, and Sonia Allison. 1978. *Drinks Dictionary*. London: Collins.

Bell, Donald. A. 1976. *The Spirits of Hospitality*. East Lansing, Mich.: Educational Institute of the American Hotel & Motel Association.

Cooper, Derek, and Dione Pattullo. 1980. *Enjoying Scotch*. London: Johnston and Bacon.

Getz, Oscar. 1978. *Whiskey: An American Pictorial History*. New York: David McKay.

Gold, Alec (editor). 1972. *Wines and Spirits of the World*. Coulsdon: Virtue.

Gorman, Marion, and Felipe P. de Alba. 1978. *The Tequila Book*. Chicago: Contemporary.

Greenberg, Emanuel, and Madeline Greenberg. 1983. *The Pocket Guide to Spirits and Liqueurs*. New York: Putnam.

Grossman, Harold J. 1977. *Grossman's Guide to Wines, Beers, and Spirits*. New York: Scribner.

Hallgarten, Peter 1983. *Spirits and Liqueurs*. London: Faber and Faber.

Hannum, Hurst and Robert S. Blumberg. 1976. *Brandies and Liqueurs of the World*. New York: Doubleday.

Henriques, E. Frank. 1979. *The Signet Encyclopedia of Whiskey, Brandy, and All Other Spirits*. New York: Signet.

Jabbonsky, L. Premium Brands Carry the Weight. *Beverage World* 106(1387): 43–44.

Lichine, Alexis. 1985. *New Encyclopedia of Wines and Spirits*. New York: Knopf.

Lipinski, Robert A., and Kathleen A. Lipinski. 1989. *Professional Guide to Alcoholic Beverages*. New York: Van Nostrand Reinhold.

Peddersen, Raymond B. 1981. *Foodservice and Hotel Purchasing*. Boston: CBI.

Ray, Cyril, 1973. *Cognac*. Briarcliff Manor, N.Y.: Stein and Day.

Stefanelli, John M. 1985. *Purchasing: Selection and Procurement for the Hospitality Industry*. New York: John Wiley.

Virts, William B. 1987. *Purchasing for Hospitality Operations*. East Lansing, Mich.: The Educational Institute of the American Hotel & Motel Association.

Wall Street Journal. 1989. Coors Acquisition Plan Challenged by Rival S. & P. 27 September 1989, p. A4.

19

Supplies, Services, and Equipment

OBJECTIVES

- Discuss the role of specifications for the purchase of supplies.
- Define the terms *permanent* ware and *glaze,* and explain why stainless-steel flat-ware is used by most restaurants today.
- Discuss the purchasing of cleaning supplies and cleaning tools.
- Define the term *disposable ware* as it applies to a restaurant.
- Give the formula that can be used to calculate the cost per use of linen.
- Discuss a usage control system that can be implemented for supplies.
- List three guidelines to use in contracting for services.
- Define the terms *capital equipment* and *depreciation,* and list the procedures to be used in the bid process for equipment.
- Define and briefly discuss equipment programs.

SUPPLIES

Supplies are defined as consumable products such as paper goods, cleaning compounds, and similar items but also includes some relatively long-lasting items such as glassware, chinaware, linens, and uniforms. Large hospitality operations may use thousands of different supply items in their operations. Small operations may use fewer, but the variety can easily run into the hundreds.

In most hospitality operations, the department head concerned with the budget for these items is usually given the authority for deciding which products are needed (just as the chef does for food), sometimes in consultation with management. Department heads are also usually responsible for par stocks on hand of these items and for usage rates; that is, the cost of products used is charged to their departments.

Questions to Ask

Some general questions that arise with regard to supplies purchasing are

- What degree of product convenience is required? For example, is a special cleaning compound required for each different function or job, or would having only one compound for a variety of different jobs be more convenient? Some argue that no single cleaning compound can do everything; therefore, the operation should take time to seek out the compound that will do the job properly and cost less in the long run.
- What should be the par stock of these items, and how frequently should they be purchased? These questions can best be answered by reviewing consumption rates and supplier delivery services.
- Should products be personalized? In other words, should the operation's name and logo appear on them? Obviously, in the case of back-of-the-house items, personalization is not necessary, but what about matchbooks, guest-room soap bars, coffee shop placemats, and other such items? The cost of personalization (that is, the additional cost above the cost of the item without personalization) can be considered an advertising cost.
- Should one-stop shopping, bid buying, or some other purchasing method such as blanket orders be used? If a great many standard supply items are frequently purchased, one-stop shopping may be appropriate. Standard products offer a smaller spread in price, quality, and supplier services among suppliers, but this purchasing method is probably the most appropriate for the small operator. Bid buying is probably more appropriate for large operations (and for chain and franchised organizations) who can buy in quantity, receive several bids from competitive suppliers, and take advantage of the wider spread in prices that occurs when personalized items or items with special qualities are required.
- Should reusable or disposable items be purchased? For example, should we purchase reusable plastic coffee shop placemats or use disposable paper ones? In the dining room, should we use linen napkins or paper ones? In some situations such as a fast-food operation, the decision is often clearly in favor of disposables because food is generally consumed away from the premises. Some studies also show that disposables result in considerable savings in the dishwashing area. Other studies, however, suggest that the cost-saving aspects of this decision are not clear and that permanent ware saves money in the long run.

Specifications

Specifications for supplies should be developed with the product's function in mind. Large operations may prepare specifications for their own particular needs and even have supplies manufactured for them (such as a unique design of chinaware bearing the organization's logo and name) if their volume is large enough. Because of cost, however, most small operations draw up specifications for standard products offered by suppliers because, even with standard products, enough different quality levels are usually available to suit the needs of any individual operation.

Permanent Ware

Permanent ware is the name given to items such as china, glass, flatware (knives, forks, and other eating utensils), and other table items such as ashtrays, salt and pepper shakers, creamers, sugar dispensers, and vases.

Most manufacturers produce these items in a standardized range of designs and qualities with published specifications and prices (including discounts for volume purchases) that allow purchasers to readily draw up their own specifications. Generally, these stock items show little spread in price among suppliers. Obviously, price can be reduced by selecting a lower quality. There is also a trade-off between price and durability (the more durable the product, the higher the quality and price). Most establishments select all their permanent ware as a matching set to ensure compatibility and portray a standard image.

The more personalized an establishment wishes to be in its purchase of permanent ware, the more these items cost, the more have to be purchased at any one time (or guaranteed to be purchased) in order to make the order economical for both purchaser and manufacturer, and the fewer the suppliers.

Because large quantities (in dollar volume) of these products are purchased at any one time, purchasers need to consider not only cost but also supplier services such as credit terms offered.

China

No standard sizes exist for china. Each manufacturer produces its own sizes, and even with a single manufacturer these sizes may vary from one pattern to another. Specifications are usually limited to stating a required pattern choice (other than for large purchasers requiring personalized china). Durability is an important selection criterion because breakage can be high if handling, washing, and storage are carried out with incorrect procedures. Most manufacturers produce commercial china that is resistant to breaking, chipping, and scratching.

An important aspect of china quality is its glaze, the surface finish with a type of glass that adds both a shine and toughness to china. Glaze should be even over all surfaces and allow water to run off freely during washing. Glaze should also be able to withstand cutting from sharp knives. Toughness and resistance to impacts are also added to china when it has a thicker body and base as well as rolled or scalloped edges. China should be tested by ensuring that it can take severe temperature changes.

Much of the china used in the hospitality industry today is made in Asia (Korea, Taiwan, China, and Japan). Imported product quality is usually satisfactory, but should be checked for problems such as glaze defects and lack of finished bottoms on cups and saucers that cause scratching. Prices for imported products are usually lower than for domestic ones, but large-quantity ordering is usually required and lead times are long. In some operations, stoneware and earthenware may be an alternative to china. In fast-food restaurants, disposables are often the alternative.

Glassware

Durability is as important in glassware as it is in china. Most glass is machine molded and weakest at its fusion points; therefore, more expensive glassware is often desirable because breakage is reduced. Glassware selected should be compatible with the theme of the chinaware that it accompanies.

Flatware

In earlier days, most flatware was made of solid silver. Only the most exclusive establishments can now afford that. Silverplate is sometimes an alternative. It is produced by electroplating a nickel and copper base with silver. In most restaurants today, however, stainless steel is the flatware of choice. As Peddersen (1981, p. 631) states,

> Due to the skyrocketing prices of silver, stainless steel flatware is used in most restaurants and institutions. Stainless steel flatware may cost as little as 10 to 50 percent as much as silverplate and 3 to 15 percent as much as sterling silver. It is not difficult to understand the wide acceptance of stainless steel on raw cost alone, but it is even easier to understand when one considers the necessity of burnishing and periodic replating of silver.

Most stainless-steel flatware contains an 18-8 formula (18 percent chrome, 8 percent nickel, and 74 percent steel). Although chrome adds luster to flatware's appearance, it can become rusty and pitted if not properly handled. In selecting knives, note that those with hollow handles provide better balance, but handles must be welded to the blade and weld points are thus susceptible to rust. Forks should not have any rough edges.

The countries in Asia that produce china also produce a great deal of the flatware used in the hospitality industry. Kelly (1976, p. 121) comments,

Frequently a buyer can save up to 20 percent on items . . . manufactured and purchased in the Far East. If a buyer decides to follow this course, he should not attempt to carry out these overseas negotiations on a direct basis. Because of the many pitfalls involved in dealing in foreign markets, a vendor experienced in this area should be employed to handle not only the initial negotiations, but also the myriad of details involved in the actual importation of the merchandise at a later date.

Cleaning Supplies

Cleaning supplies include such items as guest supplies (hand and bath soap and shampoos), chemical cleaners, detergents and bleaches, and polishes and waxes.

The United States has hundreds of regional producers of cleaning supplies, but a few large national manufacturers tend to predominate because they produce very broad product lines. Their prices are based on quantities purchased, and even though their prices may be higher than those of regional suppliers, they often offer services that smaller manufacturers cannot offer. These services include twenty-four-hour troubleshooting, employee training in proper product use and quantity control, and inspection of equipment used in conjunction with cleaning supplies. These services are optional, but most purchasers buy them because they are worth the cost.

As a result, most purchasers specify brand-name products from national suppliers, negotiate fixed-term contracts at a fixed price, and change suppliers infrequently. Sometimes purchasers can negotiate for promotional discounts for some guest-room supplies. For example, a national manufacturer may provide individually wrapped guest-room soap bars with the manufacturer's name and logo on the wrapper and reduce the price to the purchaser in return for this free advertising.

Some guidelines for selecting cleaning supplies (other than those used by guests) include the following:

- Use controlled, comparative tests of products long enough to identify the ones that do the best job. In other words, how efficient is the cleaner? Efficiency includes not only the product itself but also the cost of labor required and energy used. Calculations are usually based on the total costs to clean a specified area such as one hundred, five hundred, or one thousand square feet so that comparisons between various products can be made. Cleaning effectiveness can also be evaluated to determine if the supplier has made exaggerated claims about efficiency.
- Verify each product's safety. Will it harm the surface on which it is used? Will it harm the user? Does it have a strong odor offensive to users, other employees, and guests? If a cleaner is toxic, it should not be used; if a poisonous cleaner is needed for a particular purpose, the purchaser should consider hiring a professional external company to handle that job.

- Is each product easy to use, or do employees have to be trained to use it? If training is required, will the supplier pay for this?
- Is the product available only in very large containers? If so, does usage justify this quantity, even though the cost of volume buying may be reduced? Large containers are wasteful if they are inadvertently spilled. They are also harder to handle.
- Determine if cleaners can be used for more than one job. Some argue that there is no such thing as an all-purpose cleaner, and even if there were the total cost of purchase and inventory would not be reduced. Nevertheless, if a multipurpose cleaner can be found that does the job, it saves having to buy and stock a variety of cleaners and may eliminate the high cost of buying seldom-used products limited to only one cleaning task.
- Restrict the use of products to their intended use.
- Store all cleaning supplies well away from food and beverage supplies to eliminate potential contamination. Most local health departments require this separation as a matter of course.

Cleaning Tools

Cleaning tools include buckets, brushes, brooms, mops, squeegees, and similar items. Many of the guidelines for selecting cleaning supplies are also appropriate for cleaning tools. In addition, other considerations are

- Who is going to use them? Usually, low-skilled employees need better and more convenient products.
- Out-of-pocket cost is often not a major consideration in the purchase of these items (it is a much lower cost than the cost of the labor for their use), and usually higher-quality products last longer, take more punishment than cheap products, and thus justify their higher initial cost.
- Sometimes local charity groups offer for sale items such as mops and brooms made by the handicapped. Usually, the quality of these products is not as important as the good public relations generated by buying from this source from time to time.
- An important aspect of cleaning tool life is maintenance. This life can be considerably lengthened if employees are properly trained and supervised in the use of the tools.

Maintenance Supplies

Maintenance supplies include products such as light bulbs, fuses, and minor plumbing parts that small operations keep in inventory to allow on-site personnel to maintain certain items of equipment. Large operations with their own full-time maintenance employees carry a much wider inventory of this type of supply item.

Most of these items can be purchased only as good-quality products because they must pass federal and/or local government safety standards. Where selection among products is available, the replacement life of the item is often the most important criterion. For example, the cost of light bulbs can be evaluated against their average length of life. An interesting maintenance cost exercise often conducted by large properties is to determine when to replace light bulbs. Obviously, in many cases they are individually replaced when they burn out, but consider the case of a banquet room chandelier with dozens of light bulbs that require a special scaffolding to be raised in order to reach them. Should bulbs be replaced one at a time, should replacement be done only when a certain proportion are burned out, or at a regularly scheduled point in time should all bulbs be replaced, even those that are still working?

Disposable Ware

The term *disposable ware* covers paper and/or plastic items such as plates, cups, "glasses," platters, bowls, knives, forks, spoons, and similar items used in food operations. Some of these items can also be purchased packaged together as a set, such as a knife, fork, spoon, individual small salt and pepper shakers, and napkin.

Many disposable products are made from a petroleum base, and for this reason they can be quite expensive. The more they are personalized with the establishment's name and logo, the higher the price is. Several degrees of quality are available for each type of product.

Restaurants buy disposable ware because it reduces (or eliminates) the need for dishwashing, is more sanitary, and must be used when consumers purchase food to be eaten off the premises. The purchasing decision that most operations face is which items to purchase in this form. For many fast-food restaurants, the decision is to opt for nothing but disposable items, whereas most high-priced restaurants purchase few, if any, disposable items. Most operations, however, are in between these two extremes.

Some restaurants use some of these items as a means of food cost control. For example, if 2,500 hamburger boxes were in stock at the beginning of the day and 2,000 at the end of the day, then 500 hamburgers must have been sold, and the equivalent amount of cash must be in the cash drawer.

Linens

Linens include bed linens, tablecloths, napkins, dishcloths, aprons, cooks' uniforms, and similar items. They can be purchased outright and replaced as needed, be leased, or (in some cases) be purchased in disposable form. Disposable "linens" used by some operations include napkins and cooks' aprons and hats.

If linens are purchased or leased, the decision then has to be made either to launder them in-house or to have them laundered by an outside company. Most large hotels operate their own laundries and have employees on staff qualified to handle the repair of such things as torn bed linens. Most small hotels and most restaurants use an outside service.

Linen items purchased by establishments can be personalized with the operation's name and logo. Obviously, this personalization increases their cost.

A consideration in purchasing is whether to buy wash-and-use types of fabrics that need no ironing and thus reduce ongoing costs. The quality of this type of linen today is high enough that appearance is not the problem it once was, although the cost of the better-quality ones can be quite high. They generally also have shorter life spans than regular linens. According to Peddersen (1981, p. 602),

> In selecting the proper linens, the three most important features to look for are durability, laundry costs, and purchase price. From these three features, the true cost of an item can be determined.
>
> The original cost is a minor factor in determining the actual cost of an article during its period of service. The cost per use is obtained by adding the original cost of the article to the total laundry cost during its life expectancy, divided by the life expectancy, or the total number of launderings that might be expected for the item.

The following formula can be used to obtain cost per use:

$$\frac{(\text{Weight} \times \text{Laundry cost/pound} \times \text{Life expectancy}) + \text{Original cost}}{\text{Life expectancy}}$$

For example, if a tablecloth weighs 1.5 lbs and has a life expectancy of 250 launderings, an original cost of fifteen dollars, and a laundry cost of fifty cents per pound, cost per use is

$$\frac{(1.5 \times \$0.50 \times 250) + \$15.00}{250} = \frac{\$202.50}{250} = \$0.81$$

The cost per use of this tablecloth can then be evaluated against the cost per use of comparable tablecloths. These calculations also show that the original cost of the tablecloth ($15.00) is a relatively small part of its total lifetime cost of $202.50. Thus, the number of launderings and their cost are the more important consideration in evaluating linen purchases.

Uniforms

Some establishments purchase uniforms for their employees and let them clean and maintain them themselves, sometimes providing them with an allowance to compensate for this responsibility. In some situations, employees are required to purchase their own uniforms and clean and maintain them. In this case, state laws usually require that the employees be compensated for this cost. The fact that employees may have to clean and maintain their own uniforms is a factor to keep in mind when purchasing them. Suppliers of uniforms can be helpful in steering purchasers to uniforms that fit in with the operation's theme and atmosphere.

CONTROLLING SUPPLIES COST

The supplies cost for most hospitality operations generally represents from 5 to 15 percent of total sales. Through cost control of these items, sizable savings can be made. Unfortunately, these potential cost savings often go unnoticed because of lack of control or lack of attention to cost increases. Similar cost increases, on a percentage-of-sales basis, would probably not go unheeded with food or beverage cost. For example, a hundred-dollar daily saving in supplies cost represents a total annual saving, or increase in profit, of $36,500. One of the main difficulties in attracting management's attention to the cost of supplies is that its relationship (ratio) to sales is assumed to be correct, and no analysis is ever carried out to determine the accuracy of this relationship.

Quantity Control Approach

The system of control to be outlined for supplies control emphasizes quantities that should be used. The system does not suggest control over every single different supply item because many are used in insufficient quantities and have too low a value to warrant control-system expenditures. In fact, most establishments would probably find that about 20 percent of the items represent 80 percent of the total dollar cost of all supply items. One should, therefore, concentrate on those that represent the greatest dollar value. The control system also assumes that the items to be monitored are put into lockable storerooms subsequent to purchase and are controlled through a system of perpetual inventory cards and requisitions.

Historic Usage Rates

After which of the supplies will be controlled is decided, a historic analysis of past consumption is made. This analysis should preferably cover a year to take care of peaks and valleys of usage. Consumption information can be taken from the perpetual inventory cards and should be listed monthly, item by item.

Consumption of each item is then related to some logical standard unit. For example, the usage of guest-room soap bars could be related to the number of guests accommodated during the period. Coffee shop paper placemats could be related to coffee shop guests served during the period. Once tabulations have been made, an average monthly consumption figure related to the standard unit must be made for each separate supply item. For example, if the guest count for a month in a hotel were three thousand and if six hundred postcards were used that month, the average monthly usage is one postcard for each five guests (3,000 divided by 600).

In other cases, consumption may be logically related to dollars of sales rather than to hotel room guest count or restaurant customers served. In some cases, the item in question cannot be easily related to a standard unit. For example, can the number of gallons of floor-cleaning detergent used in the kitchen be related to restaurant guests served? Probably not, because the kitchen floor has to be cleaned regardless of the number of guests. In that case, the standard unit may just be left as a period of time, such as twenty gallons of detergent per month.

If in some months the average consumption of an individual supply item seems disproportionate to other months for that same item, the cause of the distortion should be determined and the usage figure for that month adjusted accordingly. Frequently, such distortions can be explained by the department head concerned.

Average Monthly Usage

Once all figures have been thoroughly checked, an overall average monthly usage figure is calculated, item by item. Figure 19-1 illustrates how this is done for a couple of hypothetical items. At this point, management might want to question how realistic the figures are. For example, an average of 2.25 guest letterheads per

	Item: Bar coasters	Item: Guest letterheads
January	1 for each $200 bar revenue	2 for each room arrival
February	1 for each $180 bar revenue	2¼ for each room arrival
March	1 for each $195 bar revenue	1¾ for each room arrival
Totals	12 for $2,280 of bar revenue	27 for 12 room arrivals
Average	$\dfrac{\$2,280}{12}$ = 1 for each $190 of bar revenue	$\dfrac{27}{12}$ = 2¼ for each arrival

Figure 19-1.   Quantity per standard unit calculation (*Source:* Coltman, Michael M. 1989. *Cost Control for the Hospitality Industry*, p. 296. New York: Van Nostrand Reinhold).

arrival seems reasonable. However, coffee shop placemat figures indicating that two placemats were used on average for each coffee shop customer might seem unreasonably high.

After these calculations have been made, they should be tabulated by department. Note that, if the same item is used by two or more departments, the consumption calculations must be separated by department because the quantity used per standard unit can vary from one department to another. The departmental figures should then be discussed with the department heads concerned so that they can have input. If necessary, after discussion, final amended figures should be prepared, department by department, for all supplies normally used. Copies of departmental lists must be provided to the departments. Copies of all lists must also be filed with the appropriate supplies storekeeper.

Relating Issues to Forecast

The list should be initially put into effect on a trial basis. The monthly budgets or forecasts prepared by the operation provide the basis for determining the quantities of supplies that should be used (requisitioned and issued from the storeroom) each month. If departments have sufficient storage space of their own, they could requisition a month's supply to meet the forecast. For example, if the standard for placemats in the coffee shop is 1.2 for each guest served, and the forecast is for 20,000 guests that month, the coffee shop will need 24,000 placemats (20,000 × 1.2), less any that it still has on hand from last month. If the coffee shop cannot store that quantity, then it must requisition in smaller quantities as required. Needless to say, the storekeeper's responsibility is to monitor the requisitions against the standard lists and against the forecast for each department. Should the storekeeper note that more of an item is requisitioned than the forecast and standard lists indicate, he or she should be instructed to make a note of this as a double-check on the month-end control.

Month-End Control

At each month's end, an analysis report is prepared by the control office for each department. Each departmental report should indicate, for each item controlled, the forecast figures, the actual figures, and variances between the two in quantity, percentage, and dollars. In any calculation of actual usage figures, adjustment must be made for the inventory of each item on hand in the department. The calculation is

Beginning inventory + Quantity requisitioned − Ending inventory

= Quantity used

A completed departmental supplies analysis form is illustrated in Figure 19-2.

Item	Forecast quantity	Actual quantity	Quantity variance	Variance percent	Variance dollars	Comment
Paper napkins	37,800	40,200	+ 2,400	6.3%	$12.00	Rev. 5% over forecast
Coffee filters	500	620	+ 120	24.0%	$ 3.60	New quality used—not durable
Placemats	37,200	39,400	+ 2,200	5.9%	$66.00	Rev. 5% over forecast

Department ___Coffee Shop___   Month___April___

Figure 19-2. Departmental supplies control form (*Source:* Coltman, Michael M. 1989. *Cost Control for the Hospitality Industry,* p. 298. New York: Van Nostrand Reinhold).

Initially, the control system should be put into effect for a trial period of perhaps three months. It should then be reviewed to see how it is working, to check if miscalculations have been made, and to see how closely quantities used per standard unit conform to previous calculations. Adjustments may again be necessary. Once final lists have been prepared, they can be put into effect on a permanent basis. Subsequently, they need amending only as changing conditions are perceived.

Just as the lists for one department may differ (item by item) from a second department, so do usage lists differ (probably to an even greater degree) from one establishment to another, even if they are part of the same chain and using the same product. Factors such as establishment layout, type of equipment used, and the demands of the clientele can all play a part in affecting supplies consumption rates.

Psychological Control

Employees often do not consider supplies to be high-cost items. On an individual supply item, this may be the case. Instituting the control system outlined may bring both direct and indirect benefits. Direct benefits arise from the control system indicating an almost immediate reduction of the percent of supplies cost related to sales. Over time, a further indirect benefit may accrue from psychological control. As employees become aware through the control system of the cost of supplies, they may become more cost-conscious and pay more attention to reducing excess usage and other forms of wastage.

SERVICES

Many hospitality operators view purchases for services (as opposed to tangible products) with far less concern than they should. They consider them as necessary expenditures that little can be done about. Certainly some services (such as insurance and legal fees) are commitments that, once negotiated, have to be paid. Even these expenses can be renegotiated from time to time, however, and many others can be reduced by following certain procedures.

Any reduction gained in these expenditures has the same effect that a reduction in purchase prices has for tangible products: it adds directly to the bottom-line profit. Discretionary service expenditures are particularly important here. For example, consider the cost of hiring a contractor to do grounds maintenance. The contractor employed might wish (because it is in his or her own interest to do so to increase revenue) to visit the premises three times a week. If the operator's evaluation of the situation shows that only two visits a week can keep the grounds in good appearance, however, then a saving on grounds maintenance costs of one third can be immediately made.

Apart from contracted grounds maintenance, other services that are often contracted out by hospitality operations are snow removal, pest control, garbage removal, advertising, vending machines, and janitorial work.

Guidelines

Some guidelines for consideration with reference to service contracts are as follows:

- Prepare specifications in a similar way to those prepared for tangible products. Specifications in some cases may not be easy to prepare, but at the very least they can include what service is to be provided, how frequently it is to be provided, and what testing and/or inspection procedures will be used to evaluate the service.
- In every case obtain three bids for each separate service contract. In many cases service companies are small firms that are anxious for business and are prepared to make pricing concessions to obtain it. Negotiation is therefore possible, even with the lowest bidder. Before accepting the lowest bid, however, visit other properties where that supplier has done work (or at least talk to that property's manager) to obtain some assessment of the quality of the work. If a service supplier does not perform to promised standards, not only is the job not done but also it will likely still have to be fully paid for.
- When negotiating the final contract, ensure that it is subject to review and possible cancellation after a stipulated period of time. Most services can be judged only after the event, and if the service supplier's work is deemed unsatisfactory, then it is important to be able to cancel the contract and move to another supplier.
- In all cases, do not negotiate any contract for longer than one year at a time.

- Make sure that work provided by a service supplier is inspected. Many managers who would not allow products to be received without a delivery dock inspection often do not bother inspecting work provided by a service supplier. How can value for money for a service be evaluated if the results are not inspected?
- Evaluate work done in-house with the possibility of contracting it out on a service basis. More and more small entrepreneurial companies can now provide many of the services performed by employees on the operation's payroll. For example, consider the cost of employees who provide valet parking for guests' cars. Traditionally, hotels and restaurants have hired permanent employees to do this. If the operation is unionized, these employees may have to be paid for a full shift even if they are needed for only a limited period of time each day. In many cities, specialized companies can now provide this service on a contractual basis only when needed (for example, to park the cars of guests arriving for and departing from a banquet). The cost savings may be considerable.

CAPITAL EQUIPMENT

Capital equipment is defined as equipment that has a useful life in excess of one year and that is depreciated over time. *Depreciated* means that part of its original cost is written off as an expense year by year over the equipment's useful life.

The analysis of equipment needs is a far more serious problem than for many food and beverage products because equipment purchases are a high-cost, long-term investment in which a mistaken decision can have expensive long-range repercussions. As Stefanelli (1985, p. 496) states, "If you received a poor batch of tomatoes yesterday, it is relatively easy to rectify this problem. But if you select and procure an inappropriate ice machine, you may have to live with this white elephant for longer than you care to." Generally, capital equipment includes kitchen equipment, housekeeping and maintenance equipment, guest room and public space furnishings, office equipment, and similar items. Capital items also include the initial purchase of kitchen tools such as pots, pans, dish racks, service trays, and serving carts. (Note that as these items are replaced they are not capitalized and depreciated but are usually recorded as an operating expense at the time of purchase.)

Only large chain hospitality operations normally buy sufficient quantities of equipment to have them designed to their own specifications. Most purchasers are limited to selecting from a small number of standard or stock items available from suppliers. Generally, however, this limited number can satisify the basic requirements of even the smallest operation, and they are usually offered with various options to allow some purchasing flexibility.

Selection Criteria

Equipment must be purchased to perform a particular function or functions. The key element in selection is how well it performs those functions. The purchaser must determine what the real needs are before any item of equipment is purchased. In addition, other purchase selection criteria to consider are

- What is the equipment's length of useful life?
- What are potential maintenance problems, downtimes, and costs?
- What options are available?
- How will its purchase affect the use of existing equipment?
- Can two pieces of present equipment (that both need replacing) be replaced by only one new item?
- What warranties and services are included?
- What energy-saving benefits are there?

According to Kotschevar and Terrell (1985, p. 407), the criteria to use in selecting equipment are identified as

- Need: Will the piece of equipment help improve the quality, increase the quantity, or reduce the time for or cost of the job for which it is to be used?
- Cost: Can its cost be justified? Cost includes not only initial purchase price but also installation costs and subsequent repair, maintenance, and other operating costs.
- Performance: Does the equipment fully do the job for which it is intended?
- Satisfaction of need: Will the equipment be able to cope not only with present needs but also with future requirements?
- Safety and sanitation: Is the equipment safe to use and easy to clean? Does it have the approval of licensed sanitation authorities?
- Appearance and design: Where important, do its appearance and design conform to the decor of the establishment? Does its design optimize the space it takes up?
- General utility value: Are mobility, size, quietness of operation, and similar factors acceptable?

Although these criteria were developed for the purchase of food-preparation equipment, they are equally valid for most other types of equipment.

Specifications

The purchaser's main involvement in purchasing equipment is in helping the user draw up purchase specifications and negotiating the actual purchase with a supplier. Sometimes drawing up two sets of alternative purchase specifications is useful, especially if otherwise only one supplier would be suitable. A lack of comparable equipment alternatives limits supplier competition and restricts negotiation possibilities. In other situations, specifying a particular brand of equipment may be better when the purchaser knows that it can do the job or because it is compatible with present equipment, and then a number of suppliers can be found who handle this brand. Sometimes purchasers draw up specifications on an "or equal" basis by specifying a suitable brand but allowing suppliers to bid on other brands if the supplier judges, and can prove, that the equipment will do the job equally well.

With an equipment specification, Kelly (1976, p. 138) suggests giving it "to all potential suppliers, along with the request for their evaluation of it based on their experience selling similar pieces of equipment." He suggests that nothing is wrong with placing this type of onus on potential suppliers and requiring them "to provide some kind of evaluative response to the specification."

The replacement of certain equipment items such as dishwashing machine racks and refrigerator trays can be a problem. Sometimes they have to be purchased from the supplier from whom the original equipment was purchased. Today, however, there is sufficient standardization of equipment that competitive purchasing can be practiced.

Most equipment manufacturers or distributors sell from established, printed price lists that offer various levels of discount for volume purchases. In other cases, they offer special discounts. Purchasers in need of equipment should seek out these opportunities and take advantage of them.

Bidding

After specifications have been prepared and distributed, the second stage in equipment purchasing is the request for sealed bids. Many small operators consider this a process that only large establishments and chain operations should undertake because of the almost ritualistic formality involved. However, as a percentage of total costs, expenditures on equipment by small operators are every bit as significant as they are for large ones. The procedure for bidding generally includes the following steps:

- Along with specifications, send to potential suppliers a written outline of the bidding procedures to be used, including a blank form (for reasons of standardization) on which the bid should be submitted, the date by which the bid must be made, and the date and place where bids will be opened.
- Advise all potential suppliers that the bid is competitive to encourage them to keep their pencils sharp.
- In bid instructions, make clear that the bid must be FOB the place of installation and include all costs for installation. Without this, potential suppliers might quote FOB their warehouse or FOB the establishment's delivery dock, and only later is it discovered that transportation and/or installation costs considerably increase the bid price quoted.
- Advise all potential suppliers to include in their bid their product warranty and

service responsibility during that warranty period. In particular, any supplier who does not clearly state what the warranty period is and what services are included under it should not be considered.

- Advise all potential suppliers that the establishment reserves the right to reject any bid that is not deemed acceptable. This protects the establishment from low-ball bids submitted by an unqualified supplier or one who has previously provided an unsatisfactory experience or whose reputation is poor.
- Normally, once bids are opened and reviewed and any unsatisfactory ones eliminated, the contract is awarded to the lowest bidder.

Buying Used Equipment

An alternative to buying new equipment is to consider the purchase of suitable used equipment. Frequently, slightly used equipment can be purchased at a considerable discount from its original price. This discount possibility is particularly likely for food equipment (because of the high mortality rate of foodservice operations) where the supplier has repossessed the equipment and is anxious to resell it directly or through an auction. In some cases, used equipment that is still in good working condition and with a useful life of several years can be purchased for as little as 25 to 50 percent of its original cost.

Equipment Leasing

Another option to consider is equipment leasing. Many equipment suppliers offer to lease equipment such as beverage dispensers, dishwashing machines, sales control registers, and music machines. The factors to consider in leasing are

- The cost of leasing versus purchasing. For example, even if cash is available to make an outright purchase, would the funds nevertheless be better invested in some other way, such as in short-term high-interest securities, until needed? If an equipment item is purchased rather than leased, the cost of this "lost" interest (opportunity cost) must be considered.
- The depreciation rate of purchased equipment. If equipment is purchased, the establishment will be able to depreciate it. Depreciation is not normally allowed if the equipment is leased because it still belongs to the supplier. However, the operator will be able to deduct the entire cost of the lease payments.
- Obsolescence. With leased equipment that is replaced on the market with a more efficient machine, leasing companies will often replace the old equipment with new equipment. When a machine is owned outright, it may have to be scrapped so that the operation can buy the newer equipment. The cost of discarding the old equipment must be considered.
- The supplier services offered under each option. Are the services equivalent under

each? If the supplier's reliability is in question if the equipment is purchased, then this might influence the decision in favor of leasing.

Equipment Programs

An alternative to either leasing or buying equipment is to enter into an equipment program with a supplier. With an equipment program, the supplier agrees to install a piece of equipment at little or no initial cost. The equipment is then paid for by the supplier collecting a "fee" from the operation. This fee could be a surcharge over the normal cost of products used with the equipment (for example, for each package of paper purchased for use in a photocopying machine or for each pound of coffee purchased for use in a coffee-dispensing machine). A comparison can then be made of the cost of an outright purchase of the machine versus the cost of the fee (surcharge).

Consider, for example, a soft drink–vending machine that a supplier has installed at no charge on condition that soft drinks be purchased from that supplier and that a surcharge of ten cents will be added for each soft drink purchased. If the cost of the equipment were one thousand dollars if purchased outright, then ten thousand soft drinks must be purchased before the leased equipment is "paid for." If one thousand soft drinks were sold per month, then in ten months the equipment would be paid for. However, if the surcharge continues for the life of the equipment and the equipment has a five-year or sixty-month life, then by the time the equipment is replaced it will have been paid for six times over.

Therefore, before any equipment program is agreed to, negotiate that the surcharge will continue only until the equipment is paid for, rather than continuing to pay for the equipment on a product-surcharge basis for the length of its life.

Another question to be answered is who owns the equipment once sufficient surcharges have been collected to pay for it. Does the operator now own it, or does ownership remain with the supplier, with the operator having the right to use it as long as he or she continues to buy the product used in the equipment? Obviously, for the operator ownership of the equipment would be preferable so that any scrap value in it at the end of its useful life can be recovered by the operation. By owning the equipment, the operation also has the right to depreciate it.

Some suppliers install equipment with a small down payment and an agreement that ownership of it is with the operator from the time it is installed and that the surcharges are simply contractual periodic payments that reduce the balance owed to the supplier until the equipment is fully paid for. Even though the operator is still locked into buying products from that supplier for a stipulated period of time, the advantage to the operator is that depreciation can be claimed as an expense from the day the equipment is installed. This arrangement has tax and cash flow advantages.

Note also that equipment programs limit the flexibility of the operator to change products and suppliers during the life of the agreement. Some suppliers actually require the operator to sign a contract that once the equipment is installed the operator must continue purchasing the product from the supplier for a specific period of time that may be far beyond the time when the machine is actually paid for. This contract protects the supplier and, as long as the operator agrees to it, is a factor that must be considered in evaluating the equipment program.

Some other words of caution:

- Be alert to a supplier who wants to have its equipment installed "free" but does not identify the amount of surcharge that will be levied and for what period of time.
- Make sure that any equipment program agreement states that the equipment supplier is fully responsible for equipment repair and maintenance until it is paid for and ownership of it is taken over by the operator.
- Have the contract stipulate the period of time in which service must be provided while the supplier still has ownership of the equipment. Most reputable suppliers will guarantee service within a few hours of any problems. At the very most, the time period should not exceed twenty-four hours.
- With an equipment program, have the company lawyer go over the agreement before signing it.

In summary, where an establishment has the cash to pay for equipment outright, being locked into an equipment program probably has little value.

DISCUSSION QUESTIONS

1. Discuss the role of specifications for the purchase of supplies.
2. Define the term *permanent ware.*
3. Define the term *glaze* with reference to china.
4. Explain why stainless-steel flatware is used by most restaurants today.
5. Explain why many operations purchase cleaning supplies from national suppliers, even though their prices may be higher.
6. List four guidelines for selecting cleaning supplies.
7. List two considerations in selecting cleaning tools.
8. Define the term *disposable ware* as it applies to a restaurant.
9. Give the formula that can be used to calculate the cost per use of a linen item.
10. List six supply items (other than food and beverages) that you think would be important to control in a coffee shop.
11. Give an example of a situation where the usage of the same supply item might differ considerably in each of two departments that uses that item.
12. Why does the text suggest that the control of certain supply items may act as a form of psychological control?

13. List three guidelines to use in contracting for services.
14. Define the terms *capital equipment* and *depreciation*.
15. List four procedures that should be used in the bid process for equipment.
16. Define and briefly discuss what an equipment program is.

PROBLEMS

1. A restaurant is investigating the purchase of new linen tablecloths. Each tablecloth weighs 1.6 lbs, costs 60¢ per pound to launder, and is expected to last for 225 launderings. Initial cost per tablecloth is $19.40. Calculate each tablecloth's cost per use.

2. For each of the following supply items, state what you might use as the standard unit for control purposes:
   a. Water glasses in a coffee shop
   b. Guest account forms in a hotel front office
   c. Side plates in a dining room
   d. Individual soap bars in a hotel's guest rooms
   e. Dishwashing machine detergent in a restaurant's kitchen
   f. Drink stir-sticks in a cocktail bar

3. You have the following information about the usage of a particular item whose standard unit is dollars of sales:

Month	Usage	Sales
January	200	$40,000
February	210	41,000
March	205	41,000
April	315	42,000
May	205	41,000
June	208	53,000
July	199	41,000
August	203	42,000
September	206	43,000
October	204	42,000
November	195	38,000
December	190	37,000

   a. For each month, calculate the standard sales unit (to the nearest dollar) for each one of this item used.
   b. You will note that, in both April and June, the figures seem quite different from the remaining months. Investigation shows that, in April, a case containing one hundred of this item was water damaged and had to be

discarded, and in June, sales included $11,000 from a large function at which none of this item was used. Adjust for these two unusual situations and then calculate the average monthly standard unit for this item to the nearest dollar.

c. For the next month, sales are forecast to be $41,000. Presently thirteen of this item are on hand in the department. How many should be requisitioned from the storeroom to carry the department through next month? A safety margin of ten items should be allowed for.

4. Assume you are the manager of a family-style restaurant open seven days a week that uses permanent ware. The dishwashing machine is an old one and is fully depreciated. To handle the dishwashing, two full-time dishwashers are paid per day. Each one works an eight-hour shift and is paid $4.95 per hour plus 20 percent fringe benefits. You are considering replacing the permanent ware with disposable ware. Disposable ware is estimated to cost the equivalent of 5 percent of monthly sales. Average monthly sales are $90,000. If disposable ware is used, the dishwashers will no longer be required. As the manager, will you replace the permanent ware with disposables? What other information might you want before making the decision?

REFERENCES AND SUGGESTED READINGS

Avery, A. C. 1985. *A Modern Guide to Foodservice Equipment.* Boston: Van Nostrand Reinhold.

Bell, Donald A. 1984. *Food and Beverage Cost Control.* Berkeley, Calif.: McCutchan, pp. 298–310.

Keister, Douglas C. 1977. *Food and Beverage Control.* Englewood Cliffs, N.J.: Prentice-Hall, pp. 351–61.

Kelly, Hugh J. 1976. *Food Service Purchasing: Principles and Practices.* New York: Lebhar-Friedman, pp. 56–8, 119–26, 129–34, 137–44, 213–18.

Khan, Mahmood A. 1987. *Foodservice Operations.* Westport, Conn.: AVI, pp. 111–39.

Kotschevar, Lendal H., and Charles Levinson. 1988. *Quantity Food Purchasing.* New York: Macmillan, pp. 513–40, 543–54.

Kotschevar, Lendal, and Margaret E. Terrell. 1985. *Food Service Planning: Layout and Equipment.* New York: Wiley.

Peddersen, Raymond B. 1981. *Foodservice and Hotel Purchasing.* Boston: CBI, pp. 563–637, 641–51, 671–88.

Rey, Anthony, and Ferdinand Wieland. 1985. *Management of Service in Food and Beverage Operations.* East Lansing, Mich.: Educational Institute of the American Hotel & Motel Association, pp. 73–81.

Scriven, Carl, and James Stevens. 1989. *Food Equipment Facts*. New York: Van Nostrand Reinhold.

Stefanelli, John M. 1985. *Purchasing: Selection and Procurement for the Hospitality Industry*. New York: John Wiley, pp. 455–71, 475–91, 495–523.

Virts, William B. 1987. *Purchasing for Hospitality Operations*. East Lansing, Mich.: The Educational Institute of the American Hotel & Motel Association, pp. 259–69.

Wilkinson, Jule. 1981. *The Complete Book of Cooking Equipment*. Boston: CBI.

20

Computers and Purchasing Cost Control

OBJECTIVES

- Define computer terms such as *time-sharing* and *networking*.
- State the main advantage of a computer system over a manual system.
- Differentiate between a microprocessor and a microcomputer.
- Differentiate between computer hardware and computer software, and list the main hardware items that make up a computer system.
- Discuss computer software languages and the ways in which software can be obtained.
- Differentiate between an integrated software system and an application-oriented software system.
- Discuss various types of application-oriented software such as word processing, a database manager, and a spreadsheet, state what each will do, and define an *integrated work station*.
- Define and differentiate between an ECR and a POS.
- List the ways in which a computer can aid in inventory control.
- Explain bar coding and how it can aid in inventory control, and define the acronym UPC.
- Describe how a recipe- or ingredient-based food cost-control system works.

Even though computers have been used for some applications (for example, payroll accounting) in certain segments of the hospitality industry such as large organizations and chain operations for the same length of time they have been used in other

452

businesses, their use was not common in control aspects of the business. Dittmer and Griffin (1984, p. 69) offer three reasons.

1. The high cost of computer systems, designed primarily for major corporations, could not be justified by most individual hotel and restaurant units.
2. Systems reliable enough for most industries were simply not reliable enough for hotels and restaurants, which could not tolerate the "down time" resulting from system failure.
3. Early programs for hotels and restaurants required a level of operator sophistication that was uncommon among typical industry employees.

However, the introduction of the small, low-cost (but still very powerful) microcomputer, or personal computer, has made computers available to even small independent hospitality entrepreneurs, who account for most hospitality operations. Today's microcomputers are so low in price that an independent computer could be used cost-effectively by a single department within a larger operation, for example, to maintain storeroom inventory records.

TYPES OF COMPUTERS

In general, three broad types of computers can be identified: mainframe computers, minicomputers, and microcomputers.

Mainframe Computers

In the early days computers required specialist operators and dedicated, air-conditioned rooms. The computers were often remote from the departments that needed the information that they could provide. Sometimes the main computer could be accessed by terminals of one type or another in an individual department or in individual operations that were part of a chain. A large, centralized computer of this type is often referred to today as a *mainframe* computer.

Minicomputers

With the introduction of minicomputers, this situation changed. A minicomputer was smaller and cheaper than its mainframe predecessors. A branch of a chain organization, although still perhaps linked to its head office's mainframe, could now afford to have its own minicomputer on its premises. Moreover, a number of users could be connected through terminals to the minicomputer at the same time, an arrangement known as *time-sharing*. When a user accesses the minicomputer, the computer can quickly locate that user's information, receive and process instructions from the user to manipulate or add to that information, and then re-store it until the user next requests it. In order to do this for several users, the computer has to do a lot of housekeeping so that information from different users is not mixed up and to respond to each user in turn if several are using the computer at the same time.

The result is that time-shared computers (either mainframe or minicomputer) run at only about 50 percent efficiency. As the computer gets busier (because more users are accessing it), it begins to slow down. Its response time is also irregular; if the computer does not respond promptly, a user may not know whether the machine is slowed down from heavy use or because the user has entered information that the computer does not understand and cannot process.

A minicomputer may also need a complicated set of instructions and an expensive communication system, as well as extra levels of security, including passwords and protected security levels, to link it with all its users and prevent unauthorized access to confidential information.

Finally, with a large, time-shared computer or a minicomputer with several users, every user is out of business when the computer breaks down unless a backup computer is linked to the first one.

Despite these shortcomings, mainframe and minicomputers are valuable in situations where common information must be shared by several users. This might be the case in purchasing, where product information may be needed by buyers, receivers, storekeepers, and user department heads, such as the chef in the case of food products.

Microcomputers

A more recent innovation is the microcomputer. The heart of a microcomputer is the microprocessor, which is sometimes referred to as a "microcomputer on a chip," but is actually only a processing and controlling subsystem on an electronic chip (a very small part of the actual microcomputer). These computer chips are so small that twenty thousand of them can fit into a regular-size briefcase. When the microprocessor chip was introduced, it dramatically changed the accessibility of computer power and substantially reduced the cost of this power. Now, a complete stand-alone microcomputer or personal computer can cost as little as a few thousand dollars and can easily fit on a manager's desk or on a table beside that desk. No specialist expertise is required to operate these computers. Indeed, knowing how a computer works in order to use it is no more necessary than knowing how a car works in order to drive it.

Although the terms *microprocessor* and *microcomputer* are sometimes used interchangeably, they do not mean the same thing. A microprocessor is what is on the chips that make a microcomputer function. Microcomputers derive their name from the fact that their systems are miniaturized. A microcomputer could therefore be simply described as a small computer, although that term can be misleading because today's microcomputers are as powerful as mainframe computers were twenty years ago.

Microcomputers today are so low in price, so independent, and so versatile that buying an extra machine for a special type of job is often better (and cheaper) than creating a special time-sharing program for several users. Indeed, independent microcomputers can be linked together to access information that users need from time to time (such as the names and telephone numbers of regular suppliers). This linking together of several independent computers is known as "networking."

As the networking capability is further advanced, a hospitality enterprise may someday be able to transmit its needs by its microcomputer to a network of suppliers' computers, for example, for product ordering.

Speed and Accuracy

The main difference between a computerized system and a manual one is the computer's speed; computers are also invariably more accurate! Nevertheless, computerized systems cannot do anything that cannot be done manually. Computers can produce information a lot more rapidly, but they do not relieve management of its major responsibility for decision making once the information is produced.

Computers no longer have to be expensive, take up otherwise valuable space, or require a highly skilled technician to operate them. No longer need they be operated by specialist computer departments, remote from day-to-day operations and decision making and producing voluminous reports long after the information they contain has become obsolete.

The new, low-cost computers may dictate a change in the way that hospitality managers behave on the job. For competitive survival, these managers may have to learn to use computer resources effectively and to harness the wealth of information they can provide.

HARDWARE VERSUS SOFTWARE

The hardware of a computer system is the actual physical equipment that responds to a predetermined set of instructions in a self-directed fashion.

These instructions are developed by programmers. Once a program (or set of instructions) is put into the hardware, the computer can carry out those instructions without any operator intervention. Any intelligence that a computer has must be programmed into it, and any weaknesses in that intelligence are attributable to the program.

Each individual computer may be required to operate with many different programs for different jobs. Each program is copied into the computer when it is needed. When a new program is fed in (loaded), the previous program is replaced. When the machine is turned off, any program currently in the machine is erased from its memory. Because of the temporary nature in the computer of each program, programs are known as *software*. Software is generally stored on tape or on disks; when it is loaded into the machine, it is not removed from the tape or disk but only copied into the computer's electronic memory. Therefore, software storage tapes or disks are the permanent record of the program.

The problem for a hospitality operator in implementing a computer system involves finding good software. Software has to be written (contain instructions) in a program language, or set of codes, that the computer can understand. The computer then converts these instructions into a more efficient (but less intelligible) machine language of its own before it actually carries out the instructions. More than two thousand different computer languages are available to programmers today, and many of these languages may have several dialects of their own.

Sometimes the word *firmware* is used to describe a piece of software that is permanently built into the computer. In other words, firmware is a piece of hardware that behaves like software. It generally comprises some electronic circuits that always load some instructions into the computer as soon as it is turned on. For example, firmware might contain security identification codes that require users to identify themselves properly in order to use the computer at all or in order to use some of its restricted applications.

Hardware Systems

Computer hardware systems often consist of a number of components because even a small microcomputer by itself cannot do much without the aid of some other hardware, or peripheral equipment. The main part of the computer, where all the work or manipulation is performed, is the central processing unit (CPU). To load the instructions, or program, into the CPU another device is required. On microcomputers that operate from programs stored on disks, the input device is a disk drive. On some microcomputers, the disk drive (or drives) may be built right into the CPU. Another input device is required to enable the user to interact with the CPU as work proceeds. This input device is a keyboard, which closely resembles a typewriter keyboard. Again, this keyboard is sometimes built into the CPU rather than existing as a separate hardware device linked to the CPU. Yet another hardware device is the monitor, screen, cathode-ray tube (CRT), or video display unit (VDU), which displays the output of the computer session: prompts to the user from the CPU, data and instructions input from the keyboard by the user, and the end result of the work that is being done. On some microcomputers, this monitor may be an integral part of the CPU. Finally, for most output work the system must be connected to a printer. The printer is invariably a separate piece of equipment attached by cable to the CPU.

Obviously, a high degree of compatibility is necessary between these various pieces of hardware if all the parts are to work together. In addition to compatibility of hardware, the software used must have language compatibility with each of the pieces of hardware.

Software

The question sometimes arises of whether obtaining software specifically written for an individual hospitality operation's needs is better than buying an already-written software package ("canned" software). Arranging to have software specifically written is far more expensive than buying a canned program, and hotels and restaurants as generally small businesses do not normally have the resources necessary to carry out the systems analysis and program design work necessary to develop their own computer software.

Canned programs have usually been widely tested and sold, and as a result most errors (bugs) originally in them have been caught and corrected. In most cases, canned software can be seen in action through demonstrations before a decision to purchase is made. The costs to buy and install it and to train employees to use it can be determined in advance, and any compromises that are necessary between an operation's needs and the software's capabilities can be reached in advance.

A successful, widely used canned software package thus offers proven performance for an economical price. In addition, specialized software packages are now available for the hospitality industry in such areas as food and beverage purchasing, inventory, and cost control.

Obviously, the benefits of using off-the-shelf software have to be considered against the disadvantages. A software package written for broad hospitality and foodservice requirements may not be as convenient or as fast as one that is custom-designed, but the trade-off is that it is much cheaper and relatively bug-free.

INTEGRATED SOFTWARE SYSTEMS

Analysis of the flow of information in a hospitality operation will reveal that some of the same information is used more than once. A food item in inventory might be used in ordering, receiving, storing, issuing, recipes, production, and sales control.

With a computer system, using integrated software is feasible, sensible, and advantageous. In integrated software systems, the objective is to record an item of data only once and thereafter use it in that same form in every possible way to provide information for planning and control purposes. If the item of data had to be entered into the computer each time it was wanted, extra time at the keyboard would be expended and errors could be made that demand additional time and money to correct. If the entry can be made only once, error possibilities are reduced and the process is simplified.

A hospitality operation can be viewed as a system for which a completely integrated package of computer software could control and plan every single operational aspect. However, a completely integrated software package to handle all operational aspects of a system would be extremely costly and complex. It would probably incur higher training costs because of its complexity, and it might also create severe maintenance and data security problems. Further, if one part of the system failed, it would create difficulties in all departments or areas of the business. For these reasons, a small property would find a completely integrated system (of which purchasing might be one part) difficult to justify financially.

APPLICATION-ORIENTED SOFTWARE SYSTEMS

At the other extreme is a software system that is single-application oriented. A computer system that is application oriented (sometimes known as a *dedicated* or *stand-alone* system) is generally designed to handle one specific type of job and allows for much less integration. An example is a food inventory control system that is not integrated with food purchasing and food costing.

Because of their relative simplicity, application-oriented software systems can be evaluated fairly easily to see if they will perform precisely the limited jobs they are intended to carry out. These systems are cheaper than integrated systems to buy and install, and they can be introduced into an operation over time as finances allow. An ideal situation would be to move from a piecemeal, stand-alone set of application systems to an integrated system over time—as long as each part can be made compatible with the others. In this type of in-house network, each computer system is able to operate on a stand-alone basis but can network with all others to allow transmission of certain data back and forth.

Obviously, the narrower an application-oriented system is, the easier it is to develop and the lower its cost. It will also be more efficient (because it controls fewer functions) and may be more reliable. At the same time, the narrower an application system becomes, the less efficient it may be in terms of overall control. If a food purchasing and inventory control system has to be supported by a separate food cost-control system, then two packages of software are required, two different computer hardware systems may be needed, and two sets of user or operator systems have to be learned.

Initially, most microcomputer applications in the hospitality industry were stand-alone applications. As the power and the memory capacity of these machines have improved over the past years, however, the software systems available have become less stand-alone and more integrated. Consequently, microcomputers now offer software capable of doing as much as or more than could be done on minicomputers a few years ago.

The manager's tasks are to decide which applications of the operation should be linked and which should be kept separate and to seek software that is compatible with those objectives.

Three common stand-alone or application-oriented software packages are word processing packages, database managers, and spreadsheets.

Word Processing

The term *word processing* refers to a computer system that is programmed to manipulate words (text, including numbers). Any small computer can be programmed for word processing. Surprisingly, many people do not think that machines used exclusively for word processing are true computers, but a machine that can be programmed to do full-service word processing can be programmed to do other things as well. (Some electronic typewriters with very little memory can do some limited form of word processing but are not true word processors or computers.)

Studies have shown that computers purchased primarily to do word processing do not reduce office labor costs. However, purchasing a low-cost computer to use primarily for word processing is a good way to introduce computers into a business. They can be very useful where a large amount of paperwork is handled, such as in purchasing where a great deal of documentation is required (such as purchase requisitions, purchase orders, and receiving reports).

The main purpose of a word processor is to facilitate text creation and editing, and the ease with which this can be done is a major factor in selecting word processing software.

Database Manager

A database is any collection of records or data, for example, addresses of regular suppliers, a food or beverage inventory listing, or a file of recipes. A database manager is simply a software package that allows quick access to and ready manipulation of the records that are in a particular database. In other words, it is much like a filing system in a regular office. A database manager that offers easy sorting and selection procedures is invaluable.

An integrated software package that includes both word processing and a database manager is often useful. For example, a hotel may want to send out a form letter to all the suppliers it does business with to advise them of a change in purchasing procedures. The computer can be programmed to take each supplier's address in turn, type it on the hotel's letterhead, type in the letter, then move to the next address and letter on a new page, and repeat the procedure until all addresses have been processed. All of this can be done without any operator intervention, once the process has begun.

Spreadsheet

Spreadsheet software basically consists of a large electronic sheet with rows down the side and columns across the top. Most managers have struggled with budgets, using pencils and column pads, and have become frustrated when they wish to see what would happen, for example, if the food cost ratio to sales were altered over a twelve-month annual budget. The number of changes that would have to be made to food cost, gross profit, and net profit in this case would amount to thirty-six changes of numbers, considerable erasing and correcting, and a risk that one or more errors would result. An electronic spreadsheet, once programmed, allows a manager to answer "what if" questions error-free in seconds and prints out the results. Indeed, multiple "what if" changes can be made simultaneously at rapid speed.

Spreadsheets lend themselves to budgeting and also to such matters as forecasting. For example, a sophisticated spreadsheet might have in its memory a record of all the various menu items a restaurant offers, including how many of each are sold (on average) by meal period and by day of the week for each specific month. The spreadsheet could then forecast for the current month, based on past performance, how many portions of each menu item need to be produced by the kitchen for each meal period on each day of the current month and also translate those quantities into total purchase requirements product by product by day, week, month, or other desired period of time.

Integrated Work Stations

As far as planning and control are concerned, the three application software packages just described (word processing packages, database managers, and spreadsheets) are closely related and are major types of software packages for small computers. A computer ought to be able to pass data from its database manager to a spreadsheet and then pass the results to a word processor for addition of text and final printing of a report (including graphics, where these would be valuable).

Indeed, single software packages available for many microcomputers today include all three of these software systems on one disk. These are known as integrated work stations.

ECR AND POS SYSTEMS

For locations where product sales are recorded—particularly in food and beverage areas—two kinds of systems are available: the electronic cash register (ECR) and the point-of-sale (POS) system. Basically, the ECR is a stand-alone electronic register; in contrast, a POS system links several ECRs to a separate, often remote computer, and the POS system's registers are primarily keyboards rather than separate machines. Unfortunately, the terms ECR and POS are often used interchangeably. Technically speaking, however, a POS system is much more sophisticated than a stand-alone ECR, although even an ECR can provide a great deal more information on cost of sales (that is, product costs) than could its predecessors (mechanical sales registers).

Electronic Cash Registers (ECRs)

The ECRs have allowed management to dispense with cashiers in most establishments because the servers can act as their own cashiers and because the machine records (among other things) sales by server so that each knows how much cash to turn in at the end of each shift. These ECRs have automatic pricing (so that pricing errors can be eliminated).

Computerized ECRs can summarize sales not only by server but also by various categories such as appetizers, entrees, and desserts. In chain operations this sales information might be networked to the head office computer for further, more detailed processing.

Some ECRs can be programmed to print out the most popular combinations of appetizer, entree, and dessert that customers choose. This information is useful for menu sales mix planning and purchasing. The ECRs can also have scales attached to them for automatic price calculation of items (such as salads) that are sold by weight.

Some ECRs can also provide inventory control for items that can be quantified easily, such as steaks. In order to be used for complete inventory control, the ECR would have to be programmed to remember the recipe of each dish, and that sort of inventory control might better be left to a separate computer control system. Alternatively, the ECR might be linked to another computer and might send sales information to this computer so that the food cost control work can be done there.

Integrated Point-of-Sale (POS) Systems

Generally a POS system is a series of individual sales terminals linked to a remote CPU located, for example, in the manager's office. Food and beverage POS systems may be used as stand-alone systems, but they are more commonly linked to other POS terminals in other sales locations. They can also be linked to other equipment, such as to a printer in the kitchen that tells the kitchen what has been recorded in the register and needs to be prepared in the kitchen, without requiring the server (who has rung up the item on the register) to walk to the kitchen.

In other words, a POS system has much more power than a single ECR and can produce a broader range of management reports by sales outlet and in total for an entire operation. The system has a larger visual display (CRT) and generally is totally programmable and easily modifiable within the business to accommodate changes in pricing and many other items. It can be linked to a chain operation's head office where data from individual outlets can be analyzed by the mainframe computer, results can be compared from unit to unit, and data can be consolidated by region and for the chain as a whole. In some systems, analysis reports for each individual unit can be sent back to the unit through a process known as *downloading*. Where it is in place, downloading could also be used to provide each unit's computer with new menu-pricing and recipe-costing information. A POS system can also accommodate a large number of peripheral devices (including remote ones) such as printers, and its cost-benefit advantage increases as the size of the business grows larger.

The major disadvantage of a POS system is that if the CPU fails then the entire system fails (because terminals cannot operate independently of the CPU) unless the system is backed up on storage disks or unless the individual terminals can be upgraded to operate in at least a limited way with some memory capability and to produce some reports independent of the CPU.

INVENTORY CONTROL

Computers can be very valuable as a tool in inventory control. As Warfel and Waskey (1979, p. 214) state with regard to the use of computers in food storage,

> It is also now possible for the computer automatically to place orders with approved dealers who submitted the best price for the items and quantities needed. A computer can alert management when prices are not the best ones quoted by approved dealers, and it can let both management and the food buyer know when quantities purchased exceed prescribed limits for storeroom stock.

Computers capable of this depth of sophistication can also

- From purchasing department employee input, prepare purchase orders for suppliers as well as lists of items to be received from each supplier to be sent to receiving employees so that they can compare what is delivered with what should be delivered
- As products are received and product information is recorded in the computer from invoice information, compare this information against purchase orders and specifications for those items
- Issue appropriate credit memoranda for goods short-shipped or returned to suppliers
- Produce food and beverage receiving reports for products delivered and make necessary day-end calculations of storeroom purchases (and keep a perpetual inventory of those items) and direct purchases (so that daily food cost and beverage cost can be calculated)

- Record all issues from the storeroom from information entered from requisitions, use this information to adjust the perpetual inventory of that item, and calculate the total cost of all items issued each day to aid in the calculation of a daily food cost and beverage cost
- Calculate the cost of items requisitioned by any individual department for any period of time
- Compare requisition signatures (using a scanner) with a record of those signatures stored in the computer to ensure they are authentic
- Compare at any time quantity information of actual inventory for any specific item with what the inventory should be, according to invoices and requisitions since the last comparison was made
- Issue monthly dead-stock reports showing items that have not moved in a stipulated period, such as thirty, sixty, or ninety days
- Provide each month a list of all items that were either over- or short-stocked during that period
- List how many units of each item were purchased from any one supplier and note if that purchase was made at the best-quoted price
- List how many of each item was used during each month and compare this with what should have been used according to actual food and/or beverage sales based on standard recipes and portion sizes
- Compute and compare labor hours actually used with what should have been used according to standard work practices (this type of information could be useful in comparing the costs of buying convenience foods or preparing them fully on-site)
- Verify supplier month-end statements against receiving invoices and/or receiving reports, and issue checks in payment of those statements

A sophisticated inventory control computer program can also adjust the volume of storeroom inventory required in accordance with the level of business. Thus, instead of leaving it to management to establish a fixed minimum and maximum level of stock for each storeroom item, the computer can adjust the reorder level and the order quantity to the actual usage or sales (which may change over time or by season) for that item. Each day, the computer then prints out a list of items to be ordered, the quantities needed, and the economic order quantity (if this factor is built into the system). If particular suppliers are under contract to provide specific storeroom items at contracted prices, the actual purchase orders can be prepared for those suppliers.

Bar Codes

One of the advances in inventory control that has been made in recent years that allows computers to handle a great deal more purchasing and inventory control is the use of bar codes on product containers. The bar code is represented by a series of parallel black bars of varying width on a white background. The scanners that read the code can be counter-level models (such as those found at checkout stands in supermarkets) or hand-held wands (which is the type most useful in hospitality industry receiving so that heavy cases do not have to be lifted up to pass over the scanner).

One common bar code is the ten-digit universal product code (UPC) system in which the first five digits identify the manufacturer or processor and the second five digits give information about the product. The product does not have to be in a sealed container such as carton or box. Even crates of fresh produce such as apples and lettuce can be bar coded. The bar code information read and recorded by the computer can include the product's name, package size, and quantity of the item, from which inventory records can be adjusted. For example, part of the bar code can represent specifications for each product. As Warfel and Waskey (1979, p. 218) state, "If the code number calls for a 1.06 specific gravity tomato puree, that is what the product should be."

The UPC has also been a boon to suppliers who may have dozens of different qualities and container sizes of a particular product, each of which can be quickly identified by reading its bar code and matching it with the purchaser's purchase order specification.

Bar coding in a hospitality operation offers the following advantages:

- Fast order processing
- Reduction in purchasing time
- Reduction in specification misunderstandings between purchaser and seller
- More accurate purchasing, ordering, receiving, and inventory records
- Improved food, beverage, and supplies cost control
- Improved supplier delivery schedules and performance
- Simplification of receiving procedures
- Improved inventory and issuing control (as items are issued they can again be passed over the scanner so that perpetual inventory count will be adjusted and proper cost information recorded on requisitions)

FOOD COST CONTROL SYSTEMS

Many hospitality operations control their food purchasing and cost control systems by manual means based on recipe costs for each separate menu item. Unfortunately, because of the constant flux of food costs, a restaurant with an extensive menu would find the task of keeping recipe costs up to date by manual means prohibitively time-consuming and thus hardly worth the effort. Computers can be programmed to do this work by using a database system operating from a file of recipes and their ingredients. As new purchases are made, the inventory (ingredient) quantity and cost information is entered into the computer from the invoices. Terminals can also be equipped with a bar code reader at the receiving area. The reader automatically enters product information (quantity and size) into the computer. If an item does not have the UPC code, the relevant information for it has to be entered into the computer manually. The UPC placed on the container by the manufacturer does not contain price information (because the product's manufacturer is unlikely to know the end-price that the supplier quotes to the hospitality industry purchaser). Thus, price information must be entered into the computer manually from invoices.

As new ingredient information is entered, the computer automatically updates all total recipe costs for any recipes containing these ingredients. A report can be printed showing what recipes are affected and what the new food cost is in dollars and percentages for each recipe; it may even flag the recipe to call to management's attention the need to change the menu selling price.

Food Production Control

Each day before production commences, the chef or other designated person enters into the computer the name of each recipe item and the number of portions to be produced that day. The computer then prints out the standard cost for all of those recipe items individually, and in total, prints out the recipes and the ingredient lists for the required numbers of portions, and prints a requisition listing the ingredients and specifying the quantities required from the storeroom. If more than a required quantity must be requisitioned for a particular day (for example, a No. 10 can of an item, when only half a can is required for production), the computer makes a note of this excess and takes it into account when future requisitions are prepared.

Inventory Control

As requisitions are printed out, the computer also adjusts the storeroom inventory count for period-end stocktaking and provides a value for items requisitioned but not yet used in production (for example, the half No. 10 can mentioned earlier). From time to time, a normal storeroom inventory reconciliation must be carried out, comparing the physical count of items actually in stock with the computer listing of what should be there, according to production usage.

Taking a physical (or actual) inventory is also easier to do with a computer. Programs are available that print an inventory form, complete with current item costs, leaving only the count quantity to be inserted manually. After the count is performed, the figures can be entered into the computer, and a final printout can be made showing extensions (item count times price) for all items and the total inventory value.

If bar-coded products are used, inventory taking is further simplified. A count of those products is not required. A hand-held bar code reader can be passed over and count all containers or products that are coded, and the actual inventory (including pricing and total valuation) is compiled. The computer can also issue a report showing how this actual inventory, either in total or product by product, differs from the computer's records (compiled from invoices and requisitions) of what it should be.

Management Reports

Finally, management reports can be prepared to show such things as planning errors (overproduction of menu items because of poor forecasting). A completely comprehensive and integrated food cost control system would have built into it (through linkage to POS registers) the actual sales histories of various menu items, in combination with other menu items, and would provide the kitchen with daily food production requirements to minimize such things as overproduction planning errors.

Other management reports might show operational errors (wastage because standard recipes were not followed) and costing errors (loss of potential revenue in comparison to actual revenue because selling prices have not kept up with rising food costs). Other possible reports might relate to dead stock (ingredients that have remained unissued from stores for a certain specified period) that is tying up money in inventory and to pricing trends for major purchase items (to assist in forward menu price planning).

DISCUSSION QUESTIONS

1. What is computer time-sharing? What are the problems associated with time-sharing?
2. Differentiate between a microprocessor and a microcomputer.
3. What is computer networking?
4. What is the main advantage of a computerized system over a manual one?
5. Differentiate between computer hardware and computer software.
6. What are the main hardware items that constitute a computer system?
7. What is a software language, and why is using one necessary in order to run a computer?
8. List the two major ways in which one can obtain software, along with the pros and cons of each method.
9. Differentiate between an integrated software system and an application-oriented software system.
10. What is word processing software? Describe a job in the purchasing process that it could perform.
11. What is database manager software? Describe a job in the purchasing process that it could perform.

12. What is spreadsheet software? Describe a job in the purchasing process that it could perform.
13. What is an integrated work station?
14. Differentiate between an ECR and a POS.
15. List six ways in which a computer can aid in inventory control.
16. Explain bar coding, how it can aid in inventory control, and define the acronym UPC.
17. Describe how a computerized recipe- or ingredient-based food cost control system works.

REFERENCES AND SUGGESTED READINGS

Bell, Donald A. 1984. *Food and Beverage Cost Control.* Berkeley, Calif.: McCutchan, pp. 323–34.

Dittmer, Paul R., and Gerald G. Griffin. 1984. *Principles of Food, Beverage & Labor Cost Controls for Hotels and Restaurants.* New York: Van Nostrand Reinhold, pp. 64–73.

Gamble, Paul R. 1984. *Small Computers and Hospitality Management.* London: Hutchinson.

Kasavana, Michael L. 1984. *Computer Systems for Foodservice Operations.* Boston: CBI.

Kasavana, Michael L., and John J. Cahill. 1987. *Managing Computers in the Hospitality Industry.* East Lansing, Mich.: Educational Institute of the American Hotel & Motel Association.

Kotschevar, Lendal H., and Charles Levinson. 1988. *Quantity Food Purchasing.* New York: Macmillan, pp. 556–77.

Powers, Thomas F., and Jo Marie Powers. 1984. *Food Service Operations: Planning and Control.* New York: John Wiley, pp. 44–74.

Schmidgall, Raymond S. 1986. *Hospitality Industry Managerial Accounting.* East Lansing, Mich.: The Educational Institute of the American Hotel & Motel Association, pp. 565–77.

Warfel, M. C., and Frank H. Waskey. 1979. *The Professional Food Buyer.* Berkeley, Calif.: McCutchan.

APPENDIX A

Fish

Bluefish

Characteristics: Fatty, with a flavorful, oily flesh that is blue when raw but turns grey when cooked. Weight range is from one to ten pounds.

Sources: New England to Gulf states.

Availability: Year-round, and abundant and inexpensive from June to October.

Market forms: Dressed, filleted, smoked. Bluefish does not freeze well.

Catfish

Varieties: Fidler and Blue Channel.

Characteristics: Freshwater, with no scales and a firm flesh. It is usually skinned before frying or pan-frying it. Weight range is from one to eight pounds.

Sources: In many U.S. rivers and lakes but also pond-raised commercially.

Availability: Year-round.

Market forms: Whole, dressed, skinless fillets, steaks, stuffed.

Cod

Varieties: Cod, pollock, whiting (silver hake), and haddock are all members of the cod family. Each of these varieties is discussed under its own section.

Characteristics: Usually weighs between three and twenty-five pounds with an age range of six to nine years. Lean fish that is mild-flavored and moist, with a white meat with large flakes. It is the most commonly used fish in the United States.

Sources: Both U.S. coasts, Canada, Denmark, England, Iceland, Japan, Norway, and Scotland.

Availability: Year-round, but main season is March through December.

Market forms: Drawn, dressed, steaks, fillets, frozen breaded raw or cooked sticks and portions. Freezes well.

Comment: The term *scrod* is a size category (2.5 pounds or less) under which cod may be marketed. This fish is good for breading and is the fish most commonly used for fish sticks and other processed items.

Flounder

Varieties: Summer (or fluke), winter (or blackback), American plaice (or dab), yellowtail, Arrowtooth, Pacific sanddab, starry, witch. Sole is also a member of this family, but is discussed under its own section.

Characteristics: Ranges in weight from 0.75 to four pounds, but summer flounder can weigh up to twelve pounds. A flat fish very lean or low in fat. Often confused with sole. Flounder has a white flesh, fine flakes, and mild, sweet flavor.

Sources: Both U.S. coasts, Bering Sea, Canada, Denmark, Iceland, and Scotland.

Availability: Primarily July through December, with limited availability the rest of the year.

Market forms: Drawn, dressed, fillets, frozen breaded raw fillets, or cooked fillets and portions.

Haddock

Varieties: A lean fish and a member of the cod family but not as abundant as cod and thus is higher priced.

Characteristics: Averages three to seven pounds but may be as light as one pound or as large as fifteen pounds. A lean fish with whiter flesh than cod.

Sources: Both U.S. coasts, Canada, Denmark, England, Iceland, Norway, and Scotland.

Availability: Year-round, but prime season is July through December.

Market forms: Drawn, fillets, dressed, frozen breaded raw fillets, or cooked fillets, sticks, and portions.

Comment: The term *scrod* is a size category under which haddock (as well as cod and pollock) may be marketed. Note that finnan haddie is smoked haddock and not a separate type of fish.

Halibut

Characteristics: A flat fish that ranges in weight from five to one hundred pounds. A halibut under ten pounds is sometimes known as a *chicken halibut*. It has a moist, white, mild-flavored flesh. Halibut looks like a giant flounder but has a thicker flesh and more delicate flavor. Usually cut into steaks and fillets.

Sources: North Pacific and Atlantic coasts, Alaska, Japan, and Soviet Union.

Availability: Primarily July through September.

Market forms: Whole, fillets, or steaks.

Mackerel

Varieties: Jack (or Atlantic blue), King, Pacific, and Spanish (the most common variety).

Characteristics: King and Spanish are strong-flavored fish but high in fat. Most mackerel weigh less than one pound, but king can weigh twelve pounds or more. Flesh is fat and firm, with a rich flavor and slightly dark color.

Sources: Jack from U.S. North Atlantic; King from the South Atlantic, Gulf of Mexico, and U.S. Pacific Coast; Pacific from North Pacific; and Spanish from Gulf of Mexico and Mexican Pacific.

Availability: Jack and Pacific from July through October, King and Spanish from December through March.

Market forms: Whole, dressed or headless, skin-on fillets, steaks, smoked, canned.

Perch

Varieties: Ocean perch are sometimes known as *redfish* or *rosefish.* Freshwater varieties are sheepshead and yellow.

Characteristics: Weight ranges from 0.5 to five pounds. Freshwater perch weigh less than 0.75 pounds. Both ocean and freshwater varieties are lean fish. They have a mild-flavored, flaky, white flesh with fine grain and firm texture.

Sources: Great Lakes, both U.S. coasts, Canada, Germany, Iceland, Japan, and Norway.

Availability: Mainly May through December, with limited availability the rest of the year.

Market forms: Whole, drawn, dressed, fillets, butterfly fillets.

Comment: The walleyed pike, despite its name, is a perch and not a pike.

Pike

Varieties: A freshwater fish. Northern pike is the most common one in North Amer-

ica. Other varieties are walleye and sauger.

Characteristics: Firm white flesh similar to perch but with many small bones.

Sources: North American lakes.

Availability: Fresh in season from April to November, otherwise in frozen form.

Market forms: Whole, drawn, fillets, steaks.

Comment: Walleyed pike is not a pike but a perch.

Pollock

Varieties: A lean fish and a member of the cod family but with a darker flesh and more fat. It is thus considered less desirable and therefore lower priced than cod.

Characteristics: Usually ranges in weight from 1.5 to eighteen pounds. They reach the larger sizes at about six years of age when they have a length of twenty to thirty inches.

Sources: U.S. East Coast, Alaska, Canada, Japan, Iceland, Norway, and Scotland.

Availability: Year-round, but main season is July to December.

Market forms: Drawn, dressed, steaks, fillets, frozen breaded raw or cooked sticks and portions.

Comment: The term *scrod* is a size category under which pollock can be marketed.

Red Snapper

Varieties: Mangrove, yellowtail, and vermillion.

Characteristics: The skin of this fish is red. A lean fish with a delicate, firm, sweet, white flesh with large flakes. Weight range is from one to fifteen pounds.

Sources: Gulf of Mexico, Brazil, Ecuador, Mexico, and Taiwan.

Availability: Year-round.

Market forms: Whole, dressed, fillets.

Comment: The only true red snapper, with a pink-to-red-tinged flesh, is the Gulf of Mexico variety. Asian varieties tend to have gray flesh and be less flavorful. Grouper is sometimes substituted for red snapper but is not a true snapper.

Salmon

Varieties: Chinook (or king), chum (or dog or fall), coho (or silver), pink (or humpback), sockeye (or red).

Characteristics: All salmon are fat fish. Chinook has a bright salmon color, chum is light to pinkish red and has the strongest flavor, coho has a reddish orange color, pink has a light pink color, and sockeye has a dark reddish color and strong flavor. A favored fish because of its flavor and meaty texture. Weight range is from four to twenty-five pounds.

Sources: Northwest Pacific. A limited supply is also available from the North Atlantic. Most frozen and canned salmon originates in Alaska; Washington and Oregon provide the fresh varieties.

Availability: August through November.

Market forms: Dressed, steaks, fillets, smoked, canned.

Comment: Some classify salmon as a freshwater fish because it travels up rivers to spawn. A great deal of salmon is also smoked or processed in canned form.

Shad

Varieties: Buck, roe, and white.

Characteristics: A fat, oily fish with a rich flavor and many bones. Weight range is from 1.5 to five pounds.

Sources: Both U.S. coasts.

Availability: Highly seasonal, generally only from February to May.

Market forms: Whole, drawn, fillets, canned, smoked. Shad roe is also available fresh, frozen, or canned.

Sole

Varieties: Dover, lemon, gray, petrale, and rex. Sole is actually a member of the flounder family.

Characteristics: Ranges in weight from 0.75 to four pounds. This is a flat fish. Price varies considerably, depending on variety and availability. A lean fish somewhat longer and narrower than flounder but with a similar but firmer flesh. Popular and therefore quite expensive.

Sources: Atlantic (lemon and gray), other varieties from Pacific, except for Dover sole from the English coast.

Availability: Mainly July to December, with limited availability year-round.

Market forms: Whole, fillets, breaded sticks and portions, stuffed, stuffed and breaded.

Dover sole is usually available only as fillets.

Swordfish

Characteristics: A fat fish with a meaty-textured flesh. Because weight range may be as high as one thousand pounds, available mostly in steak form.

Sources: Atlantic, Pacific, Gulf of Mexico.

Availability: Year-round.

Market forms: Steaks and chunks.

Trout

Varieties: Freshwater varieties are rainbow, brook, river, and lake. Sea trout are sometimes known as weakfish.

Characteristics: Generally weight ranges from half a pound to three pounds for freshwater trout, and from two to ten pounds for sea trout. Freshwater trout are considered fat fish; sea trout are lean fish. A soft, fine-textured flesh with a rich and delicate flavor. Flesh color can range from white to dark pink.

Sources: Idaho (fish farms), Great Lakes (lake trout), Denmark, and Japan. Sea trout are available from the Middle and South Atlantic, with limited availability from the Gulf of Mexico and from Central and South America.

Availability: Year-round.

Market forms: Whole, drawn, fillets, steaks.

Tuna

Varieties: Albacore, bluefin, skipjack, and yellowfin.

Characteristics: Tuna can weigh from a few pounds up to 150 pounds. Mostly firm, light-fleshed meat with good flavor. The major fish sold in canned form.

Sources: From any area with warm waters, such as the coast of western Mexico and the waters of Central and South America.

Availability: Year-round.

Market forms: Fillets, loins, steaks. A great deal of tuna is canned, usually in sixty-ounce sizes for the hospitality industry.

Comment: Canned albacore is labeled white meat, and other varieties are labeled light meat. The bluefin variety is used for raw products in Oriental cuisine.

Turbot

Varieties: Also known as blue halibut, gray halibut, mock halibut, or Greenland halibut.

Characteristics: A large, flat fish that ranges in weight from one to forty pounds. Flesh is lean, white, firm, and delicate.

Sources: Greenland, Iceland, Newfoundland, and Norway.

Availability: July to November.

Market forms: Dressed with head on or in fillets.

Whitefish

Characteristics: A freshwater fish (and a member of the salmon and trout families) with a flaky, white flesh and a slightly sweet flavor. Weight range is from 1.5 to six pounds.

Sources: Great Lakes and Canadian waters.

Availability: Year-round.

Market forms: Whole, drawn, dressed, fillets, smoked.

Whiting (Hake)

Varieties: A member of the cod family. Whiting is the common name for various species of hake.

Characteristics: Usually weight range is from 0.5 to four pounds. Whiting is an inexpensive lean fish, but its flesh is fragile with a mild flavor. It has to be carefully handled.

Sources: New England coast, Argentina, Brazil, Canada, and South Africa.

Availability: Year-round.

Market forms: Whole, drawn, dressed, fillets, smoked, frozen breaded raw or cooked sticks and portions.

APPENDIX B

Shellfish

Clams

Varieties: East Coast varieties are either hard-shell or soft-shell. Hard-shell varieties include littleneck, cherrystone, and chowder and are also sometimes known as *quahogs* (or *quahaugs*). Soft-shell varieties are sometimes known as *longnecks* (because of a long tube that protrudes from their shells) or *steamers* (because of the way they are generally cooked). West Coast varieties are butter, cherrystone, littleneck, pismo, razor, and surf.

Characteristics: Littlenecks are the smallest and most tender clams and can be eaten raw or steamed. Cherrystones are a medium-size and common variety. They are also used raw or steamed. Chowders are tougher and are usually chopped and fried or used in chowders.

Sources: Both U.S. coasts.

Availability: Year-round, unless weather has been a problem.

Quality: Clams in the shell must be alive when received. Shells should be tightly closed or, if open, close quickly when tapped. Dead ones should be discarded. Live and shucked ones should smell fresh. A strong odor indicates spoilage.

Market forms: Sold in the shell by bushel or bag with counts varying by source. Also sold shucked (fresh or frozen) with counts varying from one hundred to seven hundred per gallon, canned (whole or chopped), and frozen breaded (raw or cooked).

Storage: Live clams should be kept in a cold, wet area in the container in which they are delivered. They can be stored for up to a week. Shucked clams should be refrigerated at 30 to 34°F (-1 to 1°C) and also keep for a week. Frozen clams should be stored at 0°F (-18°C) or lower. They should be thawed in the refrigerator before using.

Comments: Only New England soft-shell clams are true clams. All hard-shell clams are also known as *quahogs* when they are large. Quahogs take on a bitter flavor as they mature, which is why large ones are used for clam chowder. The geoduck is a type of clam from Washington State's Puget Sound.

Crabs

Varieties: Blue, Dungeness, king, snow, and stone.

Characteristics: Alaskan king crab (the most expensive variety) weight range is from six to twenty pounds. They are popular in restaurants because the meat can be removed in large pieces. Alaskan snow crab is smaller than king and is often used as a less-expensive substitute. East Coast blue crabs are small, weighing less than half a pound, and yield very little meat. Meat is usually frozen. West Coast Dungeness crabs weigh from 1.5 to four pounds and have a sweet meat. With stone crabs, only the claws are used.

Sources: Blue from mid-Atlantic coast (particularly from Maryland's Chesapeake Bay) round to the Gulf of Mexico, Dungeness from Oregon and Washington, king and snow from Alaska, stone from the Gulf of Mexico.

Availability: During warm months in producing areas. King and snow crab are processed by very few companies.

Quality: Crabs taste best if they are alive when purchased and kept alive until cooked. They should be delivered in damp seaweed and be kept cool.

Market forms: Usually sold by count if alive. Most crabs are purchased cooked in the shell, cooked frozen in the shell, or as parts (legs and claws). Frozen crab is very perishable once it is thawed. Also available canned as well as breaded (raw or cooked).

Storage: Cooked meat should be kept covered and refrigerated at 30 to 34°F (−1 to 1°C). Frozen meat should be stored at 0°F (−18°C) or lower until used.

Comments: Most live crabs are utilized near their growing area. A soft-shell crab is harvested before the new shell of a molting blue crab has hardened. It is usually fried and eaten with the shell.

Langouste (see Spiny Lobsters)

Lobsters

Varieties: True (or American).

Characteristics: North American lobster has two large claws. A lobster with only one claw or a broken or deformed one is known as a cull and is usually sold at a reduced price. Northern lobster is the most popular type because it has a large, flexible tail, two large claws, and four pairs of legs. Shell is dark green or blue-green but turns red when cooked. Meat from tail, claws, and legs is white and sweet with a distinctive flavor. The red roe or eggs and the green liver in the body part of lobster can also be eaten. A one-pound lobster yields only about a quarter-pound of cooked meat.

Sources: Northeast coastline of North America.

Availability: Generally year-round.

Quality: Live lobsters must be alive when delivered (indicated by leg and claw movements and a tightly curled tail that will straighten out when cooked). Lobsters should be kept alive until cooked. If dead when cooked, the meat falls apart. Cooked lobster meat should smell fresh and sweet if unfrozen and also when defrosted if purchased frozen.

Market forms: Sold live by the pound. A jumbo lobster is over 2.5 pounds, large (or select) is 1.5 to 2.5 pounds, a quarter is 1.25 to 1.5 pounds, and a chicken is 0.75 to 1 pound. Lobster is also available as cooked fresh or frozen meat and canned.

Storage: Live lobster should be packed in moist seaweed or paper and be kept in a cool place. Alternatively, it can be kept in a specially manufactured aerated saltwater tank. Cooked meat should be kept covered and refrigerated at 30 to 34°F (−1 to 1°C) and be used within a day or so because of its perishable nature.

Comments: The spiny (spider or rock) lobster is really a type of crayfish without the large claws of the true lobster. See Spiny Lobster.

Because some people like to eat lobster coral (available only in females), being able to differentiate males from females is important. The tiny legs under the tail are soft and flexible in the female and hard in the male.

Mussels

Characteristics: Mussels resemble small dark clams, although shells are not as heavy. Flesh is very soft and yellow.

Sources: Coastal areas, particularly the New England coast.

Availability: Widely available and most plentiful from October to April.

Quality: Mussels are best if purchased live. Shells should be tightly closed, or close quickly if lightly tapped. Discard lightweight ones or any that are heavy because they are full of sand.

Market forms: Available live in the shell (with counts from forty-five to fifty-five to the bushel), canned, or frozen in sauces. Also available shucked and packed in brine.

Storage: Refrigerate at 32 to 35°F (0 to 2°C) and away from a light source. Store them in the containers in which they are delivered. If purchased in sacks, keep the sack moist.

Oysters

Varieties: Atlantic or Eastern varieties are bluepoint, Chincoteague, Long Island, and some others. Pacific varieties are European, Olympia, Westcott Bay, and Japanese.

Characteristics: Rough, irregular shells with a slightly bowl-shaped bottom and flat top shell. Flesh has a high water content and is soft and delicate.

Sources: U.S. Atlantic coast including Gulf of Mexico, U.S. Pacific coast. Also available from many other parts of the world.

Availability: Year-round, but best quality is in fall and winter. Those from colder waters are considered a better quality.

Quality: Live oysters should have tightly closed shells, or shells that quickly close if lightly tapped. Dead oysters should be discarded. Live or shucked oysters should have a mild, sweet smell. Discard those with strong odors indicating spoilage.

Market forms: If sold live, they are in the shell packed in cartons by count. For example, two hundred per carton would represent a medium-size oyster. If shucked, they are sold by the gallon. Shucked Atlantic oysters are available as extra large (160 or fewer per gallon), large or extra selects (161–210 per gallon), medium or selects (211–300 per gallon), standards or small (301–500 per gallon), or very small (more than 500 per gallon). Shucked Pacific oysters are available as large (fewer than 65 per gallon), medium (65–96 per gallon), small (97–144 per gallon), and extra-small (more than 144 per gallon). Also available breaded (raw or cooked), canned, and smoked.

Storage: Store live oysters in a cold, wet area in the container or sack in which they are delivered. Store fresh-shucked oysters in their delivery container at 30 to 34°F (−1 to 1°C). Live and shucked oysters can be kept up to a week. Store frozen oysters at 0°F (−18°C) or colder until used. Thaw only in the refrigerator and never at room temperature.

Comments: Canned oysters are available but are seldom used in foodservice. Oyster farming is now becoming popular and may make oysters available year-round, particularly when regular oyster fishing stops in the warm months of May through August.

Prawns (see Shrimp)
Rock Lobster (see Spiny Lobster)
Scallops

Varieties: Two main varieties are bay and sea. Bay scallops are considered superior to sea varieties.

Characteristics: Bay scallops are small with a delicate flavor and texture. Sea scallops are larger but not as tender or delicate. All scallops are creamy white with a sweet taste.

Sources: U.S. Atlantic Coast and Gulf of Mexico but also from many other parts of the world.

Availability: Year-round in many producing areas. July through December for North America.

Quality: Freshness is indicated by a clean, sweet smell. A strong, fishy smell and/or a brownish color are signs of age or spoilage.

Market forms: Scallops are generally sold fresh and shucked by the gallon or pound. The only part eaten is the muscle that closes the shell. The jumbo is ten to fifteen per pound, and the large is sixteen to twenty-two per pound. Higher count sizes are also available, but the higher the count, the smaller the scallop. Also available as IQF, block frozen, and breaded (raw or cooked).

Storage: Store covered and refrigerated at 30 to 34°F (−1 to 1°C). Do not store on ice; otherwise, they lose flavor and become watery.

Shrimp

Varieties: Brown, pink, and white. Other common varieties are blue, California rock, northern, and red. In most cases, the particular variety used in restaurants is not important.

Characteristics: Shrimp are small crustaceans with the appearance of tiny, clawless lobsters. Normally only the tail is used. Color of shrimp varies only before cooking. After cooking, no color difference is discernible.

Sources: Gulf of Mexico is main U.S. source (usually brown shrimp variety). Also available from many other countries.

Availability: Year-round from some producing countries. July through December for North America.

Quality: White are considered the best variety, then pink, then brown, but note that shrimp quality is more a result of their feeding habits and handling after catch than of variety difference. Frozen shrimp should be solidly frozen when received, and if glazed should be shiny with no signs of freezer burn. If fresh, or when defrosted, all shrimp should smell fresh and sweet. A strong, fishy, or iodine odor indicates age or spoilage.

Market forms: Fresh shrimp are normally readily available only near their source. Mostly they are sold frozen in five-pound blocks. It is one of the few seafood products with international count standards per pound; for example, 16/20 means sixteen to twenty per pound. Sold with shell on (known as *green*), peeled and deveined (PD), peeled, deveined, and cooked (PDC) or breaded and cooked. Generally PD are packed frozen in five-pound boxes in the following sizes: fewer than 15 per pound, 16 to 20, 21 to 25, and so forth. The higher the count, the smaller the shrimp. Large shrimp are more expensive per pound but require less kitchen preparation labor. Yield from a pound of raw shrimp tails in the shell is about half a pound of cooked meat. Also available frozen and breaded (raw or cooked), canned, and butterflied (split in the shell).

Storage: Frozen shrimp should be kept at 0°F (−18°C) or lower. Thaw only in the refrigerator and never at room temperature. Fresh or thawed shrimp must be kept on crushed ice, but peeled shrimp lose flavor if kept on ice unwrapped. Therefore, wrap them before placing on ice, or else cover them and keep in the refrigerator.

Comments: If count is less than fifteen per pound, they are then known as *prawns,* although the use of this terminology varies from region to region. Prawns are also often confused with scampi, a kind of crustacean common in Italy, but not often found in North America.

Spiny Lobster

Varieties: Also known as *rock lobster* or *langouste.*

Characteristics: Spiny lobsters are warm-water relatives of northern-water lobsters but have no claws. Only the tail is used, usually marketed as lobster tails. Flesh is similar to northern lobsters but somewhat drier, coarser, and less flavorful.

Sources: Available from many parts of the world including the Gulf of Mexico and the Bahamian flats (between Florida and the Bahamas).

Availability: Year-round for Gulf of Mexico and Caribbean. November through March for Australia, New Zealand, and South Africa.

Quality: Same as for lobster.

Market forms: Tail sizes vary from two to twelve ounces, depending on source, and are usually sold IQF. Pack sizes vary from ten-pound to twenty-five-pound boxes. Specify the ounce size of tail and count per carton desired.

Storage: Same as for other frozen shellfish.

Comments: Cold-water spiny lobsters from Australia, New Zealand, and South Africa are considered to be better than warm-water lobsters. They are thus generally higher priced.

Crayfish or crawfish are freshwater relatives of lobsters and are popular mostly in southern cuisine. Most tails weigh only a few ounces.

APPENDIX C

Common Fruit

Apples

Varieties: Golden Delicious and Red Delicious are main types of eating apples. Others are McIntosh, Jonathan, Winesap, Newtown Pippin, Rome, and York.

Sources: California, Michigan, New York, Pennsylvania, Virginia, and Washington.

Availability: Year-round because picked apples are stored in a controlled atmosphere with gases to preserve them.

Quality: Mature apples have a fruity aroma, softer texture than unripe fruit, and brown seeds. Skins should be smooth and bruise-free. Old, overripe apples are soft with a mushy texture and often a shriveled skin. Overripe apples are indicated by skin yielding to a slight pressure. Poor-quality apples have blemishes, bruises, decay, and/or a poor texture.

Pack sizes: Loose in cartons or boxes weighing 38 to 42 pounds, or in tray-pack cartons weighing 40 to 45 pounds. Counts may range from 48 (very large) to 216 (very small) per carton.

Storage: Summer varieties (available until fall) do not keep well. Maximum storage time is two months. Fall and winter varieties keep well until the next summer. Maximum storage time is six months. Store at temperature of about 30°F (-1°C). Apples soften quickly at room temperature and thus lose their quality.

Approximate yield: 75%.

Apricots

Varieties: Major varieties are Moorpack (sweet, medium-sized, light amber flesh), Royal (small, sweet, reddish yellow flesh), and Tilton (large, tart, light flesh). Other varieties are Blenheim, King Derby, and Perfection.

Sources: Primarily California.

Availability: April through August with peak months June and July.

Quality: Apricots are a fragile fruit. They need to be firm when picked as a mature fruit. Greenish and/or overly firm fruit are immature. Accept only tree-ripened fruit with a golden yellow color and firm, plump texture. A dull color, soft or mushy flesh, and wrinkled, blemished, cracked, or decayed skin all indicate overripe fruit.

Pack sizes: Lugs or crates weighing twenty-four to twenty-six pounds.

Storage: At temperature of 32 to 36°F (0–2°C). Best eaten within ten days of harvesting.

Approximate yield: 95%.

Avocados

Varieties: Most popular are Booth 7 (round with a bright green skin), Booth 8 (more oblong, with medium green skin), Fuerte (pear shaped with a thin, softish skin), and Hass (round with a medium-thick, leathery skin green at maturity and ready to eat when black). Others are Bacon, Zutano, Rincon, McArthur, Nabal, Anaheim, Reed, Lula, and Waldin.

Sources: Primarily California (Fuerte and Hass) and Florida (Booth 7 and Booth 8).

Availability: Year-round but not always plentiful in summer.

Quality: Avocados continue to ripen when picked. They should be purchased green and without dark, sunken spots, cracks, or bruises. They are ripe when they yield to gentle pressure or if a thin skewer or toothpick penetrates the stem cavity with only slight pressure. They should have a fresh appearance and be heavy for their size.

Pack sizes: California: single-layer flats weighing 12.5 pounds with counts of 9 to 35. Florida: double-layer flats weighing twenty-five pounds with counts of 18 to 96.

Storage: Ripen at room temperature for a few days and then refrigerate at 50°F (10°C) until needed. Ripening time is shortened if placed in a closed paper or plastic bag. Maximum storage time is one month.

Approximate yield: 75%.

Bananas

Varieties: Major variety is Cavendish.

Sources: Costa Rica, Ecuador, Honduras, and Mexico. Bananas are not grown in the United States.

Availability: Year-round.

Quality: Bananas are picked green and then ripen and develop flavor as skins turn yellow. Ripe ones will be plump and smooth and should be without bruises. Avoid overripe fruit.

Pack sizes: Cartons of forty pounds of various sizes (medium size are about three per pound), although 150-count uniform small-size bananas are sometimes available.

Storage: Purchase at ripeness degree desired that allows them to be held at room temperature until needed. Cooling slows the ripening process, but temperatures below 50°F (10°C) may turn skins black. This darkening may not affect the flesh but discourages people from eating them. Maximum storage time is about ten days.

Approximate yield: 70%.

Blackberries

Varieties: Various. A dewberry is a trailing, ground-running type of blackberry. Boysenberry is a type of dewberry grown in California, Oregon, and Texas; berries are big, dark, and red. Loganberries are a type of dewberry grown on the Pacific coast; berries are also big, dark, and red.

Sources: Usually local only.

Availability: For short periods only when mature from June to September.

Quality: Should be firm, plump, ripe colored, and free of hulls. Inspect for mold or spoiled berries. Wet spots on containers may indicate damaged fruit.

Pack sizes: Twelve half-pint baskets on a tray weighing 5.5 to 7.5 pounds.

Storage: Refrigerate at 32°F (0°C) until needed. Blackberries do not keep well. Maximum storage time is about ten days.

Approximate yield: 90 to 95%.

Blueberries

Sources: Michigan, New Jersey, North Carolina, Pacific Northwest, Maine, and Nova Scotia.

Availability: May through September with July the peak month.

Quality: Should be plump, firm, and dry with a dark blue color and silvery sheen. Size should be uniform. Large-size blueberries have a better flavor. Soft, dull, or moldy berries are deteriorated. Maine and Nova Scotia berries are a wild variety that is smaller, firmer, and tarter. They also store better. Wet spots on containers may indicate spoiled fruit.

Pack sizes: In full baskets in twelve-pint flats weighing eleven to twelve pounds. Berry size is based on count in half-pint baskets with counts ranging from 90 or less (large berries) to 190 (small berries).

Storage: Refrigerate in original container at 32°F (0°C). Blueberries do not keep well. Maximum storage time is about ten days.

Approximate yield: 90 to 95%.

Cantaloupe melons (Muskmelons)

Varieties: Many different ones, but Hales Best is the most popular.

Sources: Arizona, California, Texas, and Mexico.

Availability: Mexico early in the season, otherwise May through September from Arizona, California, and Texas.

Quality: Mature melons should have no stem attached but only a shallow dip or smooth scar (known as *full slip*) on the stem end. Full slip, which indicates the fruit was picked ripe, should be specified. If part or all of the stem remains, the melon was picked before it was mature. Rind should be yellow with little or no green. Rind netting should be raised and coarse, and the rind between the netting should be beige or pale yellow. Fruit should be heavy for its size with a good aroma. A mature melon yields to slight pressure at the blossom ends, and seeds may rattle if shaken.

Pack sizes: Half-crates weighing about 40 pounds, two-thirds crates weighing 53 to 55 pounds, and full crates weighing 75 to

85 pounds. Counts range from 12 to 46 depending on container size.

Storage: At 40°F (4°C). Canteloupe held at room temperature two to three days before serving results in a softer and juicier (but not sweeter) flesh. Maximum storage time is about ten days.

Approximate yield: 50 to 55%.

Casaba melons

Sources: Arizona and California.

Availability: June to November.

Quality: The casaba melon is pumpkin shaped, weighs six to eight pounds and has a ridged, furrowed rind. Mature, ripe melons have a golden yellow skin color and white, sweet, juicy flesh. Fruit should be heavy for its size with a rich aroma and slightly soft blossom end.

Pack sizes: Cartons or crates containing four to six melons with a total weight of thirty-two to thirty-four pounds or flat crates with five or six melons weighing about fifty pounds.

Storage: At 40°F (4°C). Maximum storage time is about six weeks.

Approximate yield: 50 to 55%.

Cherries

Varieties: Of the many varieties, main sweet varieties are Bing and Lambert; sour (tart) varieties are Montmorency and English Morello.

Sources: Sweet cherries are primarily from California, Idaho, Oregon, and Washing-ton. Sour cherries are produced primarily in Michigan.

Availability: Domestic: May through August. Imported: September through April.

Quality: Should be fresh, firm, and juicy, with a uniform dark red to almost black color (except that Royal Anne cherries are creamy white with a reddish blush), and no blemishes or bruises. Shriveled or dull skins and fruit softness are indications of spoilage.

Pack sizes: Usually in twenty-pound lugs.

Storage: Must be handled carefully to avoid bruising. Refrigerate at 34°F (1°C) until needed. Maximum storage time for sour varieties is two weeks and for sweet varieties four weeks.

Approximate yield: 80 to 85%.

Coconuts

Sources: Mexico and Central America.

Availability: Year-round with peak months from September through April.

Quality: When shaken, listen for inside milk movement. Coconuts without milk should not be purchased. Also check the three soft spots (known as *eyes*) at one end; if they are wet or moldy, the coconut is spoiled. Also avoid cracked fruit.

Pack sizes: Usually purchased by the dozen, weighing from thirty to thirty-four pounds.

Storage: At 34°F (1°C).

Approximate yield: 50%.

Cranberries

Sources: Massachusetts and Wisconsin primarily; also New Jersey, Oregon, and Washington.

Availability: September through January.

Quality: Maturity indicated by color, but different varieties have different colors at maturity. Should be firm, and baskets should have minimum bush residue (leaves and twigs). Watch for mold or spoiled fruit. Wet spots on containers may indicate spoilage.

Pack sizes: Cartons of twenty-four one-pound baskets and twenty-five-pound gross weight.

Storage: Refrigerate in original container at 32°F (0°C) until needed. Cranberries store better than other berries. Maximum storage time is four months.

Approximate yield: 90 to 95%.

Crenshaw melons

Varieties: Crenshaw is a hybrid variety of muskmelon.

Sources: California and Mexico.

Availability: July through October for California and from Mexico the rest of the year.

Quality: Should have a full slip (see Canteloupe melons). Mature melon skin should be a deep golden yellow with light yellow flecks and orange flesh and should yield slightly to pressure at the blossom end.

Pack sizes: Cartons containing four to eight melons weighing a total of thirty-two to thirty-four pounds or in flat crates weighing thirty-five to fifty pounds.

Storage: At 40°F (4°C). Maximum storage time is about ten days.

Approximate yield: 50 to 55%.

Dates

Varieties: Main commercial variety is the Deglet Noor (Date of Light).

Source: California.

Availability: September to May, with November the peak month.

Quality: When fully ripe, fresh dates are plump with a golden brown luster and smooth skin. Poor-quality dates have variable sizes and colors, deformed fruit, or puffiness and sunburn.

Pack sizes: Pitted and unpitted dates are available in a variety of pack sizes.

Storage: Keep indefinitely if properly stored between 30 and 40°F (-1 to 4°C), although recommended maximum time is six months. The lower the temperature, the longer quality remains. Do not store near onions, fish, or other odorous products because dates absorb those odors.

Yield: Unpitted, 50%; pitted, 100%.

Figs

Varieties: Two main varieties of the many available are Calimyrna (light green when ripe) and Missions (nearly black when ripe), which are also known as *Adriatic*.

Sources: Primarily California and Texas.

Availability: Generally year-round with peak months from June through September.

Quality: Should be plump and soft without spoilage or sour odor.

Pack sizes: One-layer flats weighing five to six pounds or two-layer flats weighing ten to fifteen pounds.

Storage: Rinse and drain, remove stem ends, and store as short a time as possible because they are very perishable as they ferment and turn sour.

Approximate yield: 95% (only 80 to 85% if peeled).

Grapefruit

Varieties: Marsh seedless and Duncan are the most popular. Pink-fleshed varieties are Foster Pinks, Thompson Pinks, and Ruby Reds.

Sources: Florida (usually best quality) and Texas. Arizona and California also produce grapefruit, but it is less flavorful and more pulpy than Florida's.

Availability: Year-round.

Quality: Weight (should be heavy for size) and appearance are the best quality criteria. A heavy fruit is an indication of juiciness. Skins should be smooth and even, but minor skin blemishes do not affect eating quality. A rough skin usually means a thick skin, as does a bulge or "nose" at the stem end. Soft spots indicate spoilage. Quality and ripeness are not reflected by skin color, which can range from yellow to russet or bronze. Avoid puffy, soft fruit and those with pointed ends.

Pack sizes: 7/10-bushel cartons weighing about forty pounds with counts ranging from twenty-seven (large) to sixty-four (small). However, Florida also uses a 4/5-bushel (forty-five-pound) size, and Texas has a 1 2/5 (eighty-pound) size.

Storage: At 50°F (10°C). Maximum storage time is two months.

Approximate yield: 45 to 50% (without membrane).

Grapes

Varieties: Two main domestic types are Eastern (or American) and Western (or European). Eastern types have a loose skin and seeds are difficult to remove from the pulp. Eastern varieties (all containing seeds) are Concord (sweet, blue or black skin), Catawba (large, purplish red skin), and Delaware (small, pink skin). Western varieties have tight skins, and any seeds they have can be easily removed from flesh. Common varieties are Thompson (small, sweet, seedless, green skinned, olive shaped), Emperor (large, sweet, cherry flavor, dark red skin, with seeds), Flame (large, sweet, round shape, bright red skin), and Perlette (seedless, small, green skinned, and the earliest-maturing California variety). Other seedless varieties are Beauty and Ruby. Other seeded varieties are Calmeria, Emperor, Ribier, Tokay, Exotic, Queen, Red Globe, and Christmas Rose.

Sources: Primarily California.

Availability: Domestic from June to January, imported (for example, from Chile) from February to May.

Quality: Grapes do not ripen further or improve in quality when picked, which should be when they are mature. Ripe grapes should be soft to the touch and seeds of seeded varieties should be brown (not green). Bunches should be full and grapes firmly attached to stems and not fall off when shaken. Bunches should be well formed and uniform, with no mold. Watch for rotting at stem ends. Stems should be green and pliable (lengthy storage makes them brown and easy to break). To indicate maturity (and ripeness), red grapes should have no green color, and white grapes no amber or brown color.

Pack sizes: Various, depending on growing area. Generally flats weigh seventeen to twenty pounds, and lugs weigh twenty to twenty-six pounds.

Storage: Eastern types do not keep well and are mainly used for juice and jelly. Western types can be stored for several months under proper conditions. Store at 32°F (0°C) in original container. Grapes are highly perishable at room temperature.

Approximate yield: 90%.

Honeydew melons

Sources: Arizona, California, Texas, Mexico, and Latin America. Best are generally from California.

Availability: June to October for domestic and the rest of the year from Mexico.

Quality: Honeydews (unlike some other melons) ripen after picking. Aroma should be distinct. Mature fruit has a velvety rind that should be creamy white to yellowish and not green. Ripeness can be tested by pressure and aroma. Larger melons usually have the best flavor. Best size is 6.5 to seven

inches in diameter and weighing from five to seven pounds.

Pack sizes: Cartons weighing about thirty pounds.

Storage: May need to be preripened by leaving at a warm temperature for as much as several days; then refrigerate at 40°F (4°C). Maximum storage time is one month.

Approximate yield: 50 to 55%.

Kiwifruit

Sources: This fruit is basically a Chinese gooseberry that is today commercially grown primarily in New Zealand. Also available from California.

Availability: June through October (New Zealand); October through May (California).

Quality: Ripe fruit should be firm but slightly soft to the touch with a furry skin and no bruises or soft spots. Flesh should be soft like a ripe pear.

Pack sizes: One-layer cartons (from New Zealand) weighing five to six pounds. Two-layer flats (from California) weighing eleven to twelve pounds.

Storage: Ripen at room temperature; then refrigerate at 32°F (0°C)

Approximate yield: 80%.

Lemons

Sources: Primarily Arizona and California for fresh lemons. Florida lemons are mostly used in processed foods and beverages.

Availability: Year-round and abundant from May to July.

Quality: Should be well-formed and have bright, waxy, smooth skin. Color can vary, but best color is yellow. A green-tinged lemon indicates one high in acid. Rough or uneven skins indicate a thick skin and therefore less juice. Large, soft-skinned lemons generally lack flavor.

Pack sizes: 7/10-bushel cartons weighing between thirty-seven and forty pounds, with counts ranging from 75 (large) to 235 (small) per carton. Also in small cartons weighing about ten pounds with counts from eighty to eighty-four.

Storage: At 50 to 60°F (10–16°C). Maximum storage time is four months.

Approximate yield: 40 to 45% (juiced).

Limes

Varieties: The two main acid types are Mexican (small with thin green skins when picked, turning yellow when ripe, such as the Key lime variety), and Tahiti (large, seedless, with a light greenish yellow skin, such as the Persian variety).

Sources: California and Mexico.

Availability: Year-round.

Quality: Should have firm, smooth skin. Color may vary; limes may be green or yellow. A dull, dry skin indicates aging and loss of acid flavor. Fruit should be heavy for their size.

Pack sizes: Cartons weighing ten, twenty, and forty pounds. For the more popular twenty-pound carton, counts range from 72 to 126.

Storage: At 50°F (10°C). Maximum storage time is two months.

Approximate yield: 40 to 45% (juiced).

Mandarin oranges

Varieties: Tangerines, Satsumas (a Japanese variety), Tangelo (grapefruit and tangerine hybrid), and Tangor.

Sources: Primarily Florida, but also California and Arizona.

Availability: November through April, with peak months December through February.

Quality: Should have firm, smooth skins and be heavy for their size. May feel puffy.

Pack sizes: Various carton sizes weighing from twenty-five to forty-five pounds, with counts ranging from 56 (large) to 162 (small).

Storage: At 35 to 40°F (3–4°C). Maximum storage time is two months.

Approximate yield: 60 to 65% (sections without membranes).

Melons (see Canteloupe melons, Casaba melons, Crenshaw melons, Honeydew melons, and Watermelons)

Nectarines

Varieties: Various. Some varieties have been crossbred with peaches to increase size and firmness. Stones (pits) may cling to or be free from fruit flesh.

Sources: Primarily California.

Availability: Mid-May through September.

Quality: Must be mature when picked because they do not increase in sweetness after harvesting. Avoid green fruit, which are immature and do not ripen well. A dark red color does not denote ripeness. That is indicated by yellow areas between the red ones, as well as fruit fullness and firmness. Should have no bruises or blemishes.

Pack sizes: Generally in double-layered lugs of twenty pounds with counts ranging from fifty to eighty-four.

Storage: Let ripen at room temperature, and then store in original container at 35°F (2°C).

Approximate yield: 85% (with peels).

Oranges

Varieties: Navel, Hamlin, Temple, Valencia, and Pineapple orange.

Sources: Florida primarily, but also Arizona and California. Fruit from the latter two states have thicker skins than Florida varieties.

Availability: Year-round with peak months from January through May.

Quality: Early-season fruit have higher acidity and thus a tarter taste; later season varieties are sweeter. Spotted (russeted) skins on Florida fruit do not affect quality. Poor-quality oranges have a dull, dry skin and soft, spongy texture. Skins should be firm and smooth and fruit heavy for size. Avoid puffy fruit or those with pointed ends. The heavier an orange is for its size, the juicier it is. If Florida oranges are labeled "color added," they have been coated with an orange dye that does not affect quality.

Pack sizes: Cartons weighing from forty to forty-five pounds, depending on the growing area, with counts ranging from 48 to 180 depending on carton size. A good eating-size count is 88.

Storage: Refrigerate at 35°F (2°C) until needed. Maximum storage time is two months.

Approximate yield: 45 to 50% (fruit without membrane).

Papayas

Sources: Main sources are California, Florida, Hawaii, and Puerto Rico.

Availability: Year-round.

Quality: Should be firm and symmetrical and have no bruises or mold spots. When ripe, they should be slightly soft and mostly yellow, with only a little green. Do not buy dark green fruit, which may not ripen properly.

Pack sizes: Generally cartons weighing about ten pounds.

Storage: After ripening, refrigerate at 32°F (0°C). Maximum storage time is two weeks.

Approximate yield: 65%.

Peaches

Varieties: Many, but for eating purposes the Fay Elberta freestone variety is the best known. Clingstone varieties require too much labor for peeling and are used primarily for processing.

Sources: California, Georgia, West Virginia, Michigan, and Washington.

Availability: California product is available as early as May, and Washington's as late as October. Peak months are July and August.

Quality: Should be plump, well formed, yellow-red, and free of bruises and spots. A red color (blush) on the skin is not a true sign of eating quality. Avoid green fruit, which are immature and will not ripen well. Many growers pick the fruit just before maturity and shower them with ice water (known as *hydrocooling*) to retard ripening. Purchasers should specify precooled products, which will have less spoilage from long shipping. Overripeness is indicated by a deep red-brown skin color, fruit softness, and skin shriveling at the stem end.

Pack sizes: Many different containers weighing from twenty to forty pounds with counts ranging from forty to eighty.

Storage: Shelf life is only two to three weeks after picking. Peaches ripen rapidly at room temperature; therefore, refrigerate when ripe in the original containers at 32°F (0°C) until needed.

Approximate yield: 75%.

Pears

Varieties: Four major varieties are Bartlett or summer pear (bell shaped, thin skin, white, juicy flesh), D'Anjou (short stem-end, yellow-white flesh, spicy sweet flavor), Bosc (dark yellow or cinnamon color, long tapered stem-end, juicy yellow-white flesh), and Comice (greenish yellow skin, round shape, juicy flesh). Other varieties are Nelis, Forelle, and Seckel.

Sources: Primarily California, Oregon, and Washington.

Availability: Bartlett: July through November; D'Anjou: October through May; Bosc and Comice: September through February.

Quality: Pears are picked green but continue to mature. Ripeness is judged by skin color. Bartlett skin color should be clear yellow when mature. D'Anjou skin may be yellow, yellow-green, or green when mature. Avoid those with blemishes or bruises.

Pack sizes: Cartons or boxes weighing about forty-five pounds, with counts ranging from 80 to 180, with 100 a good eating size.

Storage: At room temperature until ripe; then refrigerate at 32°F (0°C). Maximum storage time is three months.

Approximate yield: 75% (peeled and cored).

Pineapples

Sources: Hawaii, Mexico, Central America, Philippines. Hawaiian fruit generally is sweeter and has less acidity.

Availability: Year-round, but peak season is March through June.

Quality: Best-quality indicators are fragrant aroma and appearance with orange-yellow color. Avoid those with soft spots, watery spots, or bruises. Fruit should yield under slight pressure but not be too soft on the flat (butt) end. Outer skin should be dry, golden brown in color, have a slight pine aroma, and show no bruises. Skin "eyes" should be firm, and spiky leaves fresh and green. Size does not equate with quality, but larger fruit is generally sweeter and provides more yield. Hard fruit may require a week to mature.

Pack sizes: Cartons weighing forty pounds with counts varying from eight to sixteen. Also half-cartons weighing twenty pounds with counts ranging from four to seven.

Storage: Store at room temperature away from heat and sunlight until ripe to reduce tartness; then hold at 45°F (7°C) or refrigerate. Maximum storage time is one month.

Approximate yield: 50%.

Plums

Varieties: Two major types are Japanese (medium to large, never blue or purple) and European (smaller than Japanese and always blue or purple). Most European varieties are milder in flavor and firmer in texture than Japanese varieties. Prunes are a variety of plum that are particularly suitable for drying.

Sources: Primarily California.

Availability: May through September.

Quality: Should have good color for the variety and be soft enough to yield with slight pressure and not be hard. Avoid fruit with bruises or blemishes.

Pack sizes: Usually available in twenty-eight-pound lugs with counts ranging from 126 to 225.

Storage: At 34°F (1°C). Maximum storage time is ten days.

Approximate yield: 95% (pitted but not peeled).

Raspberries

Varieties: Wild red varieties are native to northern states. Black varieties are from the South. Various other-colored varieties are also available.

Sources: Generally local only when mature.

Availability: For short periods only from mid-April to November with June and July the peak months.

Quality: Should be firm, plump, free of hulls, and with a fully ripe color. Flesh when ripe should be soft enough to yield to slight pressure. Watch for mold or spoiled fruit, as well as skin breaks or brown discoloration. Wet spots on carton indicate damaged fruit.

Pack sizes: Twelve half-pint baskets on a tray weighing from 5.5 to 7.5 pounds.

Storage: Refrigerate in original container at 32°F (0°C) until used. Raspberries do not keep well. Maximum storage time is ten days.

Approximate yield: 90 to 95%.

Strawberries

Sources: California, Florida, and Mexico.

Availability: Generally year-round, but California peak months are April through June.

Quality: Should be bright, dry, and with no mold. The strawberry's cap should remain attached even with mature fruit. California berries hold for longer periods. Florida berries are smaller and more flavorful. Mexican berries are small, are often badly formed, and contain more seeds. Watch for mold or spoiled fruit. Wet spots on carton may indicate damaged fruit. Size of berry is not an indication of sweetness.

Pack sizes: Full baskets in twelve-pint flats weighing ten to twelve pounds. Also in sixteen-quart crates weighing thirty-two pounds.

Storage: Refrigerate in original container at 32°F (0°C) until needed. Strawberries do not keep well. Maximum storage time is ten days.

Approximate yield: 90 to 95%.

Tangerines (see Mandarin oranges)
Watermelons

Varieties: Charleston and Thurmont Gray are considered the best quality.

Sources: East: Florida, Georgia, North and South Carolina, Virginia, and Maryland. West: Arizona, California, and Texas. Mexico also produces watermelon.

Availability: May through September for domestics, later in the year for Mexican products. Some watermelon is usually available year-round today.

Quality: Mature fruit have a smooth, glossy skin with the underside a whitish yellow color, and seeds will be black or dark brown. Should be free of sunburn or hail marks and not have a hard white core (known as *hollow heart*) running through the fruit. Large sizes have the best yield.

Pack sizes: Usually purchased individually with a stated weight specification (such as twenty-pound size).

Storage: Do not store below 32°F (0°C) or above 50°F (10°C). Maximum storage time is three weeks.

Approximate yield: 50 to 55%.

APPENDIX D

Common Vegetables

Artichokes

Types: Main type is Green Globe. Jerusalem artichoke (sometimes marketed under the name *sunchoke*) is neither an artichoke nor from Jerusalem but a North American tuber of a type of sunflower plant.

Availability: Year-round and abundant in April and May.

Quality: Should be heavy for size. Should have plump globes and good green color with few or no brown blemishes. Browning could mean old age, bruising, or frost damage. Leaves should be compact and tight.

Pack sizes: Cartons weighing twenty to twenty-five pounds, with counts ranging from eighteen to sixty.

Storage: At 40 to 45°F (4–7°C) for short periods only.

Approximate yield: 80% (whole, trimmed).

Asparagus

Availability: February through June.

Quality: Asparagus is highly perishable. It should be picked when mature and then hydrocooled before shipping. Stalks should be straight and dry, with tightly closed tips and stalks that are firm and not withered. The white part should be about an inch long and moist. Total stalk length should be about seven inches. Stalks should have a bright color with no mold, decay, or mushiness.

Pack sizes: Identification is often based on size. The following California terms are used: Colossal (seven stalks per pound), Jumbo (eight stalks), Extra Select (nine stalks), Select (ten stalks), Extra Fancy (eleven stalks), and Fancy (twelve stalks). They are shipped bunched in crates. Each crate contains about a dozen bunches, each weighing about two pounds. Alternatively they may bought loose in crates with a total weight of about thirty pounds.

Storage: Leave packed upright in crates at a temperature of 40 to 45°F (4–7°C) for short periods only.

Approximate yield: 55%.

Beans (Green or Wax)

Types: Two main types of stringless are bush beans and vining (pole beans such as Kentucky Wonder).

Availability: Year-round, with peak period May through October.

Quality: Pods should be long and straight (with few shriveled ends) and have even color without blemishes. When broken in two, they should be crisp and snap apart. When pods ridge and bulge, beans are old and tough.

Pack sizes: Cartons weighing from twenty to thirty pounds.

Storage: At 45 to 50°F (7–10°C) for short periods.

Approximate yield: 90%.

Beans (Lima)

Types: Two main types are small (also known as baby or potato) and large (also known as butter or fordhook). Fava beans are similar to lima beans but rounder, with thicker and larger pods.

Availability: Year-round, with peak period from July to October.

Quality: Should have clean, well-filled, dark green pods that contain plump green or greenish white beans with tender skins. Flabby pods mean poor-quality beans.

Pack sizes: Cartons weighing from twenty-six to thirty-one pounds.

Storage: At 45 to 50°F (7–10°C) for short periods.

Approximate yield: 40%.

Beets

Availability: Year-round with peak period from May to October.

Quality: Should be firm, round, and uniform in size with a smooth skin. Tops, if any, should be fresh and not yellow or deteriorated. Flesh should be a rich deep red. Large, rough beets are often woody inside. Deteriorated beets show black spots, frayed edges, and brown or light pink color.

Pack sizes: Half-crates of thirty-five pounds or ⅘-bushel of thirty-two pounds.

Storage: At 32°F (0°C). Beets deteriorate rapidly under dry conditions.

Approximate yield: 75% without tops; 40 to 45% with tops.

Bibb (Limestone) Lettuce

Types: Similar to Boston lettuce but smaller and more delicate, with the head only a few inches across.

Availability: Locally in season. Year-round from Arizona, California, and Texas.

Quality: Color ranges from dark green outside leaves to creamy yellow ones at center. Heads should be firm and compact (but not hard, indicating overmaturity) and trimmed without an abundance of outer leaves.

Pack sizes: Various.

Storage: At 34°F (1°C) for short periods only.

Approximate yield: 75%.

Boston (Butterhead) Lettuce

Types: Big Boston, White Boston, Bibb, May King.

Availability: Generally year-round.

Quality: Small, round heads with soft, pliable, light yellow inner leaves and green outer leaves.

Pack sizes: Various.

Storage: At 34°F (1°C). This lettuce bruises easily and does not keep well.

Approximate yield: 75%.

Broccoli

Availability: Year-round but may be in short supply in July and August.

Quality: Should be dark green with no yellow (which indicates an old and tough vegetable) with no insect damage. The head may have a purplish sheen and should be tightly bound without leaves and with tightly closed buds. Stems should be tender, firm, and not tough.

Pack sizes: Half-cartons containing fourteen to eighteen bunches, each bunch approximately 1.5 pounds.

Storage: At 32 to 34°F (1°C) for short periods only. Good ventilation is important because of the great amount of heat released by this vegetable as it breathes.

Approximate yield: 65 to 75%.

Brussel Sprouts

Availability: September through March, with peak period November through January.

Quality: Should be firm and compact, with a bright green color. Heads should be tight and uniform in size. Yellowing and/or wilted leaves are a sign of deterioration, as are puffy or soft sprouts.

Pack sizes: Pint containers (twelve per tray), totaling about nine pounds. Also available in loose-pack twenty-five-pound containers.

Storage: At 32 to 34°F (1°C) for short periods only.

Approximate yield: 80%.

Cabbage

Types: Three major types are common green, Savoy (with crimped leaves), and Red. Celery cabbage (also known as *Chinese cabbage)* is mainly used in salads.

Availability: Common green year-round, with peak period from October through May.

Quality: Heads should be tight, heavy for their size, without excess leaves, and show no sign of decay, worm damage, or internal rot. Leaves should have good color and be crisp and finely ribbed.

Pack sizes: Cartons or sacks weighing fifty to sixty pounds (with about fifteen medium-size heads), except for Savoy variety, which is in forty-pound cartons.

Storage: At 34°F (1°C). Cabbage wilts quickly if not refrigerated. Fall and winter cabbage stores best.

Approximate yield: 80%.

Carrots

Availability: Year-round.

Quality: Should be purchased without green tops, which deprive the carrot of moisture. Shape should be well formed, with blunt rather than tapered ends. Texture should be crisp and not woody, which indicates over-maturity (as do root straggles). Large carrots are sometimes woody. Color should be bright and not pale. A green top indicates "sunburn" and has to be removed, reducing yield. Avoid carrots with green shoots or with yellow tops (indicating they are old or have been improperly stored). Excessive forking or cracks reduce yield.

Pack sizes: Various. Could be bulk bags weighing twenty-five to eighty pounds or packed in one-pound packages in a forty-eight pound container.

Storage: May be stored for several months at 34°F (1°C).

Approximate yield: 75 to 80%.

Cauliflower

Cauliflower is the cultivated descendant of common cabbage.

Availability: Year-round, with peak period from October through December.

Quality: Leaves should be fresh green and well trimmed. Head should be white (and not yellow or brownish) with finely grained, tightly closed buds. If the "flowers" in the head have started growing, the cauliflower is of inferior quality. Loose, open flowers mean overmaturity.

Pack sizes: Generally in two-layer cartons containing twelve to sixteen trimmed and wrapped heads weighing eighteen to twenty-four pounds total.

Storage: At 32°F (0°C). Cauliflower should always be stored with the head down to avoid moisture collecting in the base.

Approximate yield: 55%.

Celery

Types: Main type is Pascal (green), which is free of tough strands and has a distinctive flavor. Less common is Golden Hart, which has a bleached-white color but can be stringy.

Availability: Year-round, with peak period November through May.

Quality: Stalks should be tight, trimmed, crisp, and well-formed with unwilted leaves. Stalks should be brittle enough to snap easily. Stalk color should be fresh green. Inside of stalks should be smooth and not rough or puffy. Celery heart should be whitish yellow and free of rot or decay. Avoid hearts that are pithy and hollow (known as *hollow heart*) or have black or brown spots (known as *black heart*). Leaflets should be fresh.

Pack sizes: Various cartons or crates of forty-five to sixty pounds, with counts varying from eighteen to forty-eight bunches. A good count is thirty with sixteen-inch bunches of about 1.75 pounds each.

Storage: At 32°F (0°C).

Approximate yield: 75%.

Celery root (knob celery or celeriac)

This vegetable is cultivated for its root rather than its stem or stalk.

Availability: Year-round.

Quality: Should be firm and heavy for its size. Select small, round roots because large roots are often soft and spongy in the center.

Pack sizes: Generally cartons holding twelve to eighteen bags (each containing two or three hearts) weighing twenty-four to twenty-eight pounds.

Storage: At 32°F (0°C) after trimming roots and tops.

Approximate yield: 75%.

Corn (sweet)

Types: As many as two hundred different types available.

Availability: Year-round. Abundant from May to September, with California and Florida supplying corn in winter.

Quality: Husk should be bright green and moist. Avoid yellow or wilted husks. Kernel rows should be well formed and full, with no space between rows and no worm damage. Best-developed corn has either twelve or fourteen rows of kernels with no missing rows. Kernels should be to the tip of each ear. Cobs with small, soft kernels are immature. Deteriorated corn has underdeveloped ears and depressed and deep yellow kernels. Kernels, when punctured, should be tender and milky.

Pack sizes: Crates of forty to sixty pounds, with counts ranging from fifty-four to sixty-six.

Storage: At 32°F (0°C) for short period. Corn on the cob should be kept for only twenty-four hours because longer storage reduces its sweetness.

Approximate yield: 30% (after husking and cutting from cob).

Cucumber

Types: Three main types are common field-grown (thick and long with small white spines), hothouse, and pickling (small with black or white spines). Common cucumber is also known as *slicing* or *table cucumber.* Another variety is English (or European), which is long, seedless, and light green.

Availability: Year-round, abundant from May to August.

Quality: Should be firm with a bright green color. Slicing cucumbers should be firm, crisp, dark green, and well shaped. A yellow or dull green color indicates overmaturity. Avoid wilted, spongy, shriveled, or decayed cucumbers.

Pack sizes: Various containers from twenty-five to sixty pounds.

Storage: At 45 to 50°F (7–10°C).

Approximate yield: 75% to 95% (depending on peeling).

Eggplant

Availability: Year-round, with peak months July through September.

Quality: Should be shiny, heavy, and plump with a dark purple color and no soft spots or blemishes. Heaviness and firmness of flesh are also good quality indicators. Best size is pear shaped with three- to six-inch diameter.

Pack sizes: Various containers from twenty to thirty pounds.

Storage: 45 to 50°F (7–10°C) for short periods only.

Approximate yield: 90% (75% if peeled).

Endive

Endive is sometimes referred to as *French chicory, Belgian chicory, true endive, Belgian endive, French endive,* or *Witloof chicory.* Terminology varies throughout the country.

Availability: Year-round, with peak period August through October.

Quality: Should have tightly formed, elongated leaves around a solid head and a bleached pale, yellow-green color because it is grown away from direct sunlight. Endive should be four to six inches long with leaves that are crisp, waxy textured, and slightly bitter.

Pack sizes: Generally cartons containing twenty-four heads weighing thirty to thirty-six pounds.

Storage: At 32°F (0°C) for short periods only. Endive storage life is very short but can be prolonged by sprinkling shaved ice around packages.

Approximate yield: 75%.

Escarole lettuce

Escarole is also known as *curly leaf endive* (or *curly leaf chicory*), even though it has nothing to do with true endive.

Availability: Generally year-round.

Quality: Outer leaves should be dark green and curly in a bunched head, with inner leaves yellowish white.

Pack sizes: Generally in cartons containing twenty-four heads and weighing from thirty to thirty-six pounds.

Storage: Surround with crushed ice at 32°F (0°C). Store for short periods only.

Approximate yield: 75%.

Head (Iceberg) Lettuce

Availability: Year-round. This is the most popular of all lettuces.

Quality: Heads should be firm and compact but not hard (indicating overmaturity) and trimmed with no more than six wrapper leaves. The cut end may have some brown color caused by oxidation, but a reddish tinge may indicate lettuce "rust." Leaf color varies from light green to green. Leaf tips should not be discolored (tip burn), which indicates exposure to either cold or heat that can rapidly spoil the lettuce (discoloration of wrapper leaves is not a problem). Avoid "seeders" (a seeder stem running through the lettuce), which reduces yield. In specifications, require vacuum cooling to retard spoilage if a long trip from grower to an East Coast user is involved. Deteriorated heads likely show tan or brownish leaf stem discoloration at the base of the head.

Pack sizes: Various. Weight per case can vary from thirty-five to fifty-five pounds, with counts ranging from eighteen to thirty.

Storage: At 34°F (1°C). This lettuce keeps well as long as it is stored away from fruit.

Approximate yield: 75%.

Kale

Availability: Abundant throughout winter.

Quality: Dark green heads are best. Leaves should be crisp, clean, and without damage from bruising or crushing. Tough, fibrous leaf stems or decayed, yellowed, or badly wilted leaves indicate an overripe vegetable of poor quality.

Pack sizes: Generally sold by the bushel, weighing from twenty to twenty-five pounds.

Storage: At 40°F (4°C) in a moist atmosphere for short periods.

Approximate yield: 70%

Kohlrabi

Availability: Year-round.

Quality: Should be crisp, firm, uniformly light green, and two to three inches in diameter. Avoid those with coarse stems or dry or yellowing leaves.

Pack sizes: Generally sold by the pound or by the bushel.

Storage: At 40°F (4°C) up to two weeks.

Approximate yield: 55%.

Leaf (Garden or Hothouse) Lettuce

Availability: Usually only in season locally.

Quality: This loose-leaf lettuce (that is, leaves branch out loosely from stalks) does not have a tight head. Avoid tip burn, discolored or wilted leaves, and interior decay.

Pack sizes: Varies, but generally in twenty-four-quart baskets weighing about ten pounds.

Storage: At 34°F (1°C) for up to two weeks in plastic bags.

Approximate yield: 75%

Leeks

Availability: September through November.

Quality: Leaves should be fresh green and have two to three inches of white. White part should be crisp, tender, and not fibrous. Avoid those with decaying leaves.

Pack sizes: Crates holding ten one-pound bags.

Storage: At 32°F (0°C) for up to two months.

Approximate yield: 50%.

Lettuce (see Bibb lettuce, Boston lettuce, Escarole lettuce, Head lettuce, Leaf lettuce, and Romaine lettuce)

Mushrooms (cultivated)

Availability: Year-round, with peak months October through April.

Quality: Caps should be firm, white or pale brown, and closed at the stem. Stems should be short. There should be no dark spots, bruises, or mold. Withered mushrooms are a sign of age. Size is no indication of tenderness.

Pack sizes: Cartons holding ten one-pound bags or nine eight-ounce packages or loose in ten-pound containers.

Storage: At 32 to 34°F (0–1°C). Mushrooms oxidize and turn brown quickly at room temperature. Store in brown paper (not plastic) bags.

Approximate yield: 90%.

Okra (Gumbo)

Availability: Year-round, with peak period July through October.

Quality: Uniformly green or white. Pods may be either long and thin or short and chunky but should be tender and full rather than dry or shriveled. Pods that snap easily indicate a good quality. Best pods are two to four inches long. Seeds should be white and soft. Dull, dry-looking pods indicate old age.

Pack sizes: Various containers from eighteen to thirty pounds.

Storage: At 50°F (10°C) for up to two weeks.

Approximate yield: 80%.

Onions (dry)

Types: Three main types are Early (mild, crisp, and large with yellow or white skins and a short shelf life), Main (also known as *late domestic* or *yellow globe,* with yellow, white, or red skin; stores well), and Yellow Sweet Spanish (globe shaped, flavorful, but also with a short shelf life).

Availability: Year-round.

Quality: Onions should be hard, firm, and well shaped, with thin necks. Outer skins should be papery and dry enough for skin crackle over bright, hard bulbs. They should have no mold, fungus, or green shoots. Wet or very soft neck stems can indicate spoilage or immature onions. Avoid those with thick, hollow, or woody neck centers. Size is no indication of quality.

Pack sizes: Usually in fifty-pound fiber-mesh bags.

Storage: In dry conditions at room temperature, but do not store with potatoes, which absorb moisture from them and decay quickly.

Approximate yield: 90%.

Onions, green (Scallions)

Availability: Year-round, with peak months April through June.

Quality: Tops should be fresh, crisp, and green, with little or no bulb formation at white part. Wilted or discolored tops indicate poor quality.

Pack sizes: Eighteen-pound containers holding four dozen bunches or crates weighing from twenty-five to fifty pounds.

Storage: At 32 to 34°F (O–1°C) for up to two weeks.

Approximate yield: 60 to 70%.

Parsnips

Availability: August through May, with peak months October and November.

Quality: Should be firm, smooth, and well shaped, with a light, uniform color and free of root straggles. Select small or medium sizes, as large parsnips are often woody.

Pack sizes: Cartons holding twelve one-pound bags.

Storage: This hardy vegetable stores well at 32° F (0°C) but wilts quickly under dry conditions.

Approximate yield: 70 to 75%.

Peas (green and black-eyed)

Availability: Year-round, with peak months May through August.

Quality: Pods should be fairly large, firm, fresh, and moderately filled out. Pods should snap easily. Yellowish or wilted pods indicate overmaturity and toughness as well as starchy peas. Avoid mildewed, swollen, or highly speckled pods.

Pack sizes: Various containers from thirty to thirty-five pounds.

Storage: At 32°F (0°C) in the pod. Peas lose their sugar content if not stored at this temperature.

Approximate yield: 40% in pods (but seldom purchased this way because of labor cost to remove them from pods).

Peppers (sweet, green or red)

Types: Many types with different colors, shapes, and sizes, but the Bell (California Wonder) is the main sweet type used.

Availability: Year-round, with peak months June through October.

Quality: Should be shiny and bright green or red, with no blemishes or rot. Pale color and soft seeds indicate an immature product. Should be firm and well shaped, with thick walls and no soft spots or shriveling. Sunken, blisterlike spots on the skin indicate that decay is imminent. Pale green dull color or lack of firmness indicates poor quality.

Pack sizes: Containers of twenty-five to thirty pounds, with various counts up to 110, depending on size.

Storage: At 46 to 48°F (7–9°C) for up to two weeks. Do not store below 45°F (7°C).

Approximate yield: 80%.

Potatoes

Types: Many types, but main ones for the hospitality industry are Long White (also known as *White Rose* and ideal for boiling because it does not darken after cooking) and Russet, with the Russet Burbank (from Idaho) the major baking potato that also is good for making French fries.

Availability: Russet is seasonal, California Long Whites year-round.

Quality: Skin should be dry, firm, and smooth and not soft or shriveled. Skins should have no cracks, blemishes, or rotten spots. Eyes should be shallow. They should have no sprouts because they are then high in sugar. Skin should show no green (caused by storage in bright light), which has a bitter taste and can be poisonous in large quantities. If baking potatoes are kept at temperatures that are too low, their starch content turns to sugar. High starch is desirable for bakers, and wet spots or high skin moisture indicates high sugar. Potatoes should be free of cuts, bruises, hollow centers (dark, hollow parts from too-rapid growth), and freeze damage. Potatoes should be uniform in size and appearance. Size is no indication of quality.

Pack sizes: Cartons of fifty pounds with counts ranging from 60 to 120 per carton. Also available in hundred-pound sacks and in ten- or twenty-pound bags.

Storage: Do not refrigerate raw potatoes. Temperatures below 45°F (7°C) convert potato starch to sugar. Sugar can be converted back to starch by storing at 50°F (10°C) for two weeks. Store in a cool, dark area at 55 to 60°F (13–16°C). Potatoes sprout if held at high temperatures. New potatoes do not keep well; purchase only a few days' supply at a time.

Approximate yield: 80%.

Potatoes, sweet (including yams)

Types: Main types are Jersey (dry, less sweet, light yellowish or fawn skin) and Porto Rico (also known as *Mancy Hall* or *yams,* with sweeter flavor and darker color varying from whitish tan to brownish red).

Availability: Year-round, with peak months August through April.

Quality: Skins should be clean, dry, firm, and not shriveled or blemished. Fat, regular shapes (rather than long, tapered ends) are preferable to reduce trim waste. Should have no bruises, cuts, decay, or insect damage. Skin color is no indication of quality. Even though yams are moister and a deeper orange than regular sweet potatoes, they are otherwise not distinguishable for most cooking purposes.

Pack sizes: Normally in bushel containers weighing about fifty pounds.

Storage: At 60 to 65°F (15–18°C) for short periods only. Do not refrigerate.

Approximate yield: 80%.

Radishes

Types: Red button type is the most popular. The long, white, mild-flavored ones are also known as *icicle radishes.*

Availability: Year-round, with peak months from April through July.

Quality: Should be firm, tender, and crisp, with a good shape and color. They should never be soft and spongy. Condition and color of leaves are not quality indicators. Diameter varies from one to four inches for buttons, and length from three to ten inches for icicles. Radishes with cuts or gouges often discolor and decay quickly.

Pack sizes: Various containers from fifteen to twenty-five pounds.

Storage: At 32°F (0°C). If stored with tops on, then store on ice.

Approximate yield: 90%.

Romaine (cos) Lettuce

Types: Self-closing and loose-closing. This is the main lettuce used in Caesar salad.

Availability: Year-round.

Quality: Head should be elongated with loosely packed, long, narrow leaves. Inner leaves should be smaller than outer ones and have a pale yellow-green color. Texture should be crisp. Outer leaves should be dark green. Heads that lack dark green indicate that deterioration has set in. Heads with irregular shapes indicate overgrown central stems. Tip burn or tan or brown leaf margins should be avoided.

Pack sizes: Primarily in cartons containing twenty-four heads and weighing about forty pounds.

Storage: At 34°F (1°C). This variety is less fragile than other lettuces and keeps well.

Approximate yield: 75%.

Rutabagas (see Turnips)

Spinach

Availability: Year-round, with peak months November through June.

Quality: Leaves should be fresh, crisp, and dark green without rot, slime, or bad bruising. Leaf stems should be short. Small, straggly, or overgrown stalky plants are often tough. Avoid wilted ones and those turning yellow.

Pack sizes: Various containers from twenty to twenty-five pounds.

Storage: At 32°F (0°C).

Approximate yield: 50 to 70%.

Squash (including Zucchini)

Types: Summer and winter. Note that these terms are not an indication of availability. Summer squash is on the market all winter, and winter squash is on the market virtually all year.

Availability: Year-round.

Quality: Should be firm, heavy, and crisp, with tender skins and no blemishes. Summer-type skins are soft; winter-type are hard. Summer-type deterioration is indicated by a dull surface and tough rind showing overmaturity. Winter-type deteri-

oration is indicated by water-soaked or moldy spots resulting from freezing or early stages of decay.

Pack sizes: Various containers from twenty-one to forty-two pounds.

Storage: Some varieties of winter squash keep up to six months at 32 to 40°F (0–4°C), but summer squash is perishable and keeps poorly.

Approximate yield: 90% (summer and zucchini); 65 to 85% (winter).

Tomatoes

Types: Tomatoes are actually a fruit but are included as a vegetable here because most people consider them as such. Main broad categories are commercial (often picked green and ripened during shipping), and locally grown, vine-ripened, or hothouse tomatoes that are more flavorful. Also available are cherry tomatoes.

Availability: Usually only seasonally for local ones; otherwise, year-round from California, Texas, and Mexico.

Quality: Purchasers should specify color such as green (no red showing), turning (minimum red color), pink (more than 50 percent red), hard ripe (fully colored but not yet ripe), and full ripe (ready to use). Tomatoes should have a firm skin and be firm but not hard, with little or no green core and no bruises, blemishes, cracks, or discoloration. External appearance should show no scars, cracks, puffiness, or handling damage. High-quality tomatoes are heavy for their size.

Pack sizes: By the box varying from ten to thirty pounds. Tomato size is important.

Tomatoes are packed in layers such as a one-layer ten-pound box or a two-layer twenty-pound box (the most common sizes). A five-by-six packing, that is, thirty per layer, contains a smaller tomato than a five-by-five layer (twenty-five count). Cherry tomatoes are usually packed in twelve-pound flats, and consistent sizing can be a problem.

Storage: At 55°F (13°C) until they have ripe color and then at 40 to 50° F (4–10°C) until used. Tomatoes are sensitive to extreme cold and should be stored in a warmer re-frigerator area (such as near the door). They should be sorted daily for ripeness.

Approximate yield: 90% (skinned).

Turnips (and Rutabagas)

Types: White-fleshed and yellow-fleshed (the more common commercial one).

Availability: Year-round, with peak months October through November.

Quality: Should be firm and heavy, with good color and no blemishes. Turnips more than 2.5 inches in diameter may be woody or spongy.

Pack sizes: Generally bags of either twenty-five or fifty pounds.

Storage: At 32°F (0°C) for up to one week.

Approximate yield: 90%.

Index